Program Authors

Dr. Diane August
Dr. Donald Bear
Dr. Janice A. Dole
Dr. Jana Echevarria
Dr. Douglas Fisher
Dr. David J. Francis
Dr. Vicki Gibson
Dr. Jan Hasbrouck
Margaret Kilgo
Dr. Scott G. Paris
Dr. Timothy Shanahan
Dr. Josefina V. Tinajero

Mc
Graw
Hill
Education

Also Available from McGraw-Hill Education

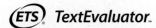 *TextEvaluator.*

Cover and Title Pages: Nathan Love

www.mheonline.com/readingwonders

Send all inquiries to:
McGraw-Hill Education
2 Penn Plaza
New York, NY 10121

ISBN: 978-0-07-680030-8
MHID: 0-07-680030-X

Printed in the United States of America.

2 3 4 5 6 7 8 9 WEB 20 19 18 17 16   B

❝*The students love their books. With this curriculum, we have fantastic informational text and a variety of genres.* **❞**

— Becky Boyle, Campbell Elementary, Lincoln, NE

❝*I feel that my students are lucky to be exposed to Wonders. It makes a world of difference. The online piece has made my job easier and allowed me to become a better teacher.* **❞**

— Todd Kimmel, Horatio B. Hackett School, Philadelphia, PA

❝*Students are able to do more than we thought they could. We have raised the rigor and they want more. The conversations that are happening between my students are more sophisticated.* **❞**

— Heather Griffith, Lakeside Farms Elementary, Lakeside, CA

PROGRAM AUTHORS

Dr. Diane August
American Institutes for Research, Washington, D.C.

Managing Researcher
Education Program

Dr. Donald R. Bear
Iowa State University

Professor, Iowa State University
Author of *Words Their Way, Words Their Way with English Learners, Vocabulary Their Way,* and *Words Their Way with Struggling Readers, 4-12*

Dr. Janice A. Dole
University of Utah

Professor, University of Utah
Director, Utah Center for Reading and Literacy
Content Facilitator, National Assessment of Educational Progress (NAEP)
CCSS Consultant to Literacy Coaches, Salt Lake City School District, Utah

Dr. Jana Echevarria
California State University, Long Beach

Professor Emerita, California State University
Author of *Making Content Comprehensible for English Learners: The SIOP Model*

Dr. Douglas Fisher
San Diego State University

Co-Director, Center for the Advancement of Reading, California State University
Author of *Language Arts Workshop: Purposeful Reading and Writing Instruction, Reading for Information in Elementary School;* coauthor of *Close Reading and Writing from Sources, Rigorous Reading: 5 Access Points for Comprehending Complex Text,* and *Text-Dependent Questions, Grades K-5* with N. Frey

Dr. David J. Francis
University of Houston

Director of the Center for Research on Educational Achievement and Teaching of English Language Learners (CREATE)

Consulting Authors

Kathy R. Bumgardner
National Literacy Consultant

Strategies Unlimited, Inc.
Gastonia, NC

Jay McTighe
Jay McTighe and Associates

Author of *Essential Questions: Opening Doors to Student Understanding, The Understanding by Design Guide to Creating High Quality Units* and *Schooling by Design: Mission, Action, Achievement* with G. Wiggins, and *Differentiated Instruction and Understanding By Design* with C. Tomlinson

Dr. Doris Walker-Dalhouse
Marquette University

Associate Professor, Department of Educational Policy & Leadership
Author of articles on multicultural literature, struggling readers, and reading instruction in urban schools

Dinah Zike
Educational Consultant

Dinah-Might Activities, Inc.
San Antonio, TX

FOLDABLES

Dr. Scott G. Paris
Educational Testing Service,
Vice President, Research Professor,
Nanyang Technological University,
Singapore, 2008–2011

Professor of Education and Psychology,
University of Michigan, 1978–2008

Dr. Timothy Shanahan
University of Illinois at Chicago

Distinguished Professor, Urban Education
Director, UIC Center for Literacy Chair,
Department of Curriculum & Instruction
Member, English Language Arts Work
Team and Writer of the Common Core
State Standards
President, International Reading
Association, 2006

Dr. Josefina V. Tinajero
University of Texas at El Paso

Professor of Bilingual Education &
Special Assistant to the Vice President
of Research

Dr. Vicki Gibson
Educational Consultant Gibson
Hasbrouck and Associates

Author of *Differentiated Instruction:
Grouping for Success, Differentiated
Instruction: Guidelines for Implementation,*
and *Managing Behaviors to Support
Differentiated Instruction*

Dr. Jan Hasbrouck
J.H. Consulting
Gibson Hasbrouck and Associates

Developed Oral Reading Fluency Norms for
Grades 1–8
Author of *The Reading Coach: A How-
to Manual for Success* and *Educators as
Physicians: Using RTI Assessments for
Effective Decision-Making*

Margaret Kilgo
Educational Consultant
Kilgo Consulting, Inc., Austin, TX

Developed Data-Driven Decisions
process for evaluating student
performance by standard
Member of Common Core State
Standards Anchor Standards
Committee for Reading and Writing

National Program Advisors

Mayda Bahamonde-Gunnell, Ed.D
Grand Rapids Public Schools
Rockford, MI

Maria Campanario
Boston Public Schools
Boston, MA

Sharon Giless Aguina
Waukegan Community Unit School District #60
Waukegan, IL

Carolyn Gore, Ph.D.
Caddo Parish School District
Shreveport, LA

Kellie Jones
Department of Bilingual/ESL Services
Brockton, MA

Michelle Martinez
Albuquerque Public Schools Curriculum and
 Instruction
Albuquerque, NM

Jadi Miller
Lincoln Public Schools
Lincoln, NE

Matthew Walsh
Wissahickon School District
Ambler, PA

CONNECTED LITERACY TOOLS

Weekly Concept and Essential Question

The Keys to Unlock the Week

Reading/Writing Workshop

Weekly Opener Video

Academic and domain-specific vocabulary

Teach and Model

With Rich Opportunities for Collaborative Conversations

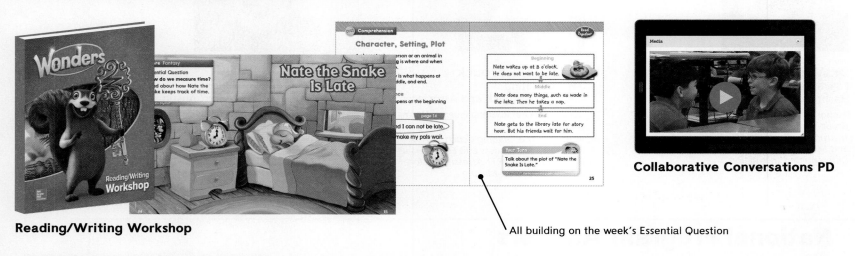

Reading/Writing Workshop

Collaborative Conversations PD

All building on the week's Essential Question

Practice and Apply

Close Reading, Writing to Sources, Grammar, Spelling, and Phonics

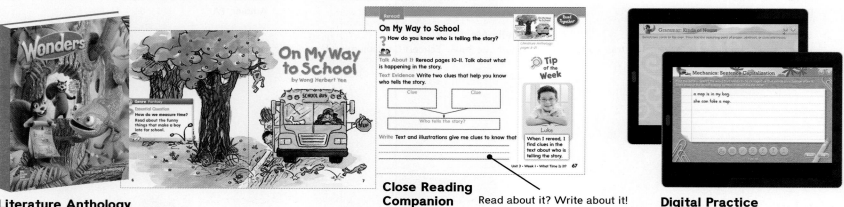

Literature Anthology

Close Reading Companion

Read about it? Write about it!

Digital Practice

Build Knowledge and Skills at Every Level

Differentiate to Accelerate

Move students ahead as soon as they're ready

Also available:
- WonderWorks
- Wonders for English Learners
- Wonders Adaptive Learning

Over 6500 more leveled readers online!

Nonfiction Leveled Readers

Fiction Leveled Readers

Adaptive Learning

Foundational Skills

Build phonemic awareness, phonics, word recognition and fluency

Decodable Readers

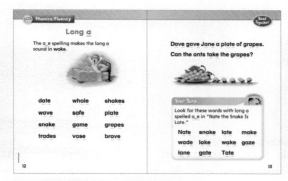

Reading/Writing Workshop

Visual Vocabulary Cards

Retelling Cards

Assess

Specific skills and standards for every student, assignment, and class

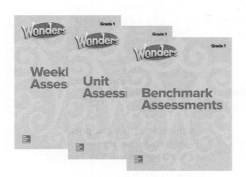

Weekly, Unit, Benchmark Assessments

Specific recommendations for every skill and standard.

Data Dashboard

Proficiency Report

PROGRAM COMPONENTS
Print and Digital

Reading/Writing Workshop

Literature Big Books

Literature Anthology

Close Reading Companion

Interactive Read-Aloud Cards

Teacher Editions

Teaching Poster

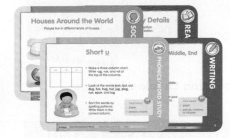

Decodable Readers

Leveled Readers

Leveled Reader Lesson Cards

Classroom Library Trade Books

Your Turn Practice Book

Leveled Workstation Activity Cards

Retelling Cards

Visual Vocabulary Cards

Sound-Spelling Cards

Photo Cards

High-Frequency Word Cards

Weekly Assessment

Unit Assessment

Benchmark Assessment

Additional Digital Resources

For You

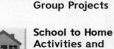

Plan
Customizable Lesson Plans

Assess
Online Assessments Reports and Scoring

Professional Development
Model Lessons and PD Videos

Teach
Classroom Presentation Tools Instructional Lessons

Collaborate
Online Class Conversations Interactive Group Projects

Additional Online Resources
- Leveled Practice
- Grammar Practice
- Phonics/Spelling
- ELL Activities
- Genre Study
- Reader's Theater
- Tier 2 Intervention
- Instructional Routine Handbook

Manage and Assign
Student Grouping and Assignments

School to Home
Activities and Messages

For Your Students

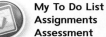

My To Do List
Assignments Assessment

Words to Know
Build Vocabulary

Read
e Books Interactive Texts

Play
Interactive Games

Write
Interactive Writing

School to Home Support
- Activities for Home
- Messages from the Teacher

---

www.connected.mcgraw-hill.com

viii

Figure It Out

Unit Planning

Weekly Lessons

Model Lesson Extended Complex Text

Program Information

(t to b) Les & Dave Jacobs/Cultura/Getty Images; Image Source/Getty Images; SuperStock; Fuse/Getty Images; Huntstock/Getty Images

UNIT OVERVIEW

Week 1	Week 2	Week 3
SEE IT, SORT IT	**UP IN THE SKY**	**GREAT INVENTIONS**

READING

Week 1

ESSENTIAL QUESTION
How can we classify and categorize things?

Build Background

CCSS **Oral Vocabulary**
L.I.5c *classify, distinguish, entire, organize, startled*

CCSS **Word Work**
RF.I.2 Phonemic Awareness: Contrast Sounds, Phoneme Categorization/Blending/Segmentation
RF.I.3 Phonics/Spelling: Words with /är/ *ar*
RF.I.3 Structural Analysis: Irregular Plurals
RF.I.3g High-Frequency Words: *four, none, only, large, put, round*
Vocabulary Words: *trouble, whole*
L.I.4a Context Clues: Multiple Meanings

CCSS **Comprehension**
Strategy: Make/Confirm Predictions
RL.I.2 Skill: Point of View
Genre: Fantasy

CCSS **Fluency**
RF.I.4b Phrasing

Week 2

ESSENTIAL QUESTION
What can you see in the sky?

Build Background

CCSS **Oral Vocabulary**
L.I.5c *certain, observe, remained, thoughtful, vast*

CCSS **Word Work**
RF.I.2 Phonemic Awareness: Rhyme, Phoneme Substitution/Blending/Deletion/Segmentation
RF.I.3 Phonics/Spelling: Words with /ûr/
RF.I.3 Structural Analysis: Inflectional Ending -er
RF.I.3g High-Frequency Words: *another, climb, full, great, poor, through*
L.I.5d Vocabulary Words: *leaped, stretched*
Shades of Meaning/Intensity

CCSS **Comprehension**
Strategy: Make/Confirm Predictions
RL.I.3 Skill: Plot: Cause and Effect
Genre: Fantasy

CCSS **Fluency**
RF.I.4b Intonation

Week 3

ESSENTIAL QUESTION
What inventions do you know about?

Build Background

CCSS **Oral Vocabulary**
L.I.5c *complicated, curious, device, imagine, improve*

CCSS **Word Work**
RF.I.2 Phonemic Awareness: Phoneme Categorization/Substitution/Blending/Addition
RF.I.3 Phonics/Spelling: Words with /ôr/
RF.I.3 Structural Analysis: Abbreviations
RF.I.3g High-Frequency Words: *began, better, guess, learn, right, sure*
L.I.4b Vocabulary Words: *idea, unusual*
Prefixes

CCSS **Comprehension**
RI.I.1 Strategy: Ask/Answer Questions
RI.I.3 Skill: Connections Within Text: Problem and Solution
Genre: Nonfiction/Biography

CCSS **Fluency**
RF.I.4b Phrasing

LANGUAGE ARTS

Week 1

CCSS **Writing**
W.I.5 Write to Sources
Trait: Sentence Fluency

CCSS **Grammar**
RF.I.1 Words That Join
L.I.2 Mechanics: Capitalize Proper Nouns

Week 2

CCSS **Writing**
W.I.5 Write to Sources
Trait: Word Choice

CCSS **Grammar**
RF.I.1 Adjectives
L.I.2 Mechanics: Capitalization and End Punctuation

Week 3

CCSS **Writing**
W.I.5 Write to Sources
Trait: Word Choice

CCSS **Grammar**
RF.I.1 Adjectives That Compare
L.I.2 Mechanics: Capitalize Proper Nouns

Figure It Out

Review and Assess

Week 4	Week 5	Week 6
SOUNDS ALL AROUND	**BUILD IT!**	

Week 4 — SOUNDS ALL AROUND

ESSENTIAL QUESTION
What sounds can you hear? How are they made?

Build Background

CCSS Oral Vocabulary
L.I.5c *distract, nervous, senses, squeaky, volume*

CCSS Word Work
RF.I.2 Phonemic Awareness: Phoneme Substitution/Isolation/Blending/Segmentation
RF.I.3 Phonics/Spelling: Diphthongs *ou, ow*
RF.I.3 Structural Analysis: Inflectional Endings *-er, -est*
RF.I.3g High-Frequency Words: *color, early, instead, nothing, oh, thought*
L.I.4b Vocabulary Words: *scrambled, suddenly*
Suffixes

CCSS Comprehension
RL.I.I Strategy: Ask/Answer Questions
RL.I.3 Skill: Plot: Problem and Solution
Genre: Realistic Fiction

CCSS Fluency
RF.I.4b Expression

Week 5 — BUILD IT!

ESSENTIAL QUESTION
How do things get built?

Build Background

CCSS Oral Vocabulary
L.I.5c *contented, intend, marvelous, project, structure*

CCSS Word Work
RF.I.2 Phonemic Awareness: Phoneme Blending/Segmentation/Categorization
RF.I.3 Phonics/Spelling: Diphthongs *oi, oy*
RF.I.3 Structural Analysis: Final Stable Syllables
RF.I.3g High-Frequency Words: *above, build, fall, knew, money, toward*
L.I.4c Vocabulary Words: *balance, section*
Inflectional Endings

CCSS Comprehension
RI.I.I Strategy: Ask/Answer Questions
RF.I.3 Skill: Connections Within Text: Cause and Effect
Genre: Informational Text

CCSS Fluency
RF.I.4b Intonation and Phrasing

Week 6

CCSS Reader's Theater
RF.I.4 Assign Roles
Fluency: Phrasing, Rate, and Expression

CCSS Reading Digitally
RI.I.5 Take Notes
W.I.6 Access Interactive Elements
Navigate Links

CCSS Research and Inquiry
W.I.7 Retell Information
Unit Projects
Presentation of Ideas

Unit 5 Assessment

Unit Assessment Book
pages 99–124

Fluency Assessment
pages 38–49

Week 4 (Writing/Grammar)

CCSS Writing
W.I.5 Write to Sources
Trait: Sentence Fluency

CCSS Grammar
RF.I.I Other Adjectives
L.I.2 Mechanics: Capitalize/Underline Book Titles

Week 5 (Writing/Grammar)

CCSS Writing
W.I.5 Write to Sources
Trait: Organization

CCSS Grammar
RF.I.I Prepositions/Prepositional Phrases
L.I.2 Mechanics: Abbreviations

Week 6 (Writing)

CCSS Writing
W.I.5 Write to Sources
Publishing Celebrations
Portfolio Choice

UNIT OPENER

Reading/Writing Workshop

Unit 5

Figure It Out

The **Big** Idea

How can we make sense of the world around us?

My Shadow

I have a little shadow that
goes in and out with me,

And what can be the use of
him is more than I can see.

He is very, very like me from
the heels up to the head;

And I see him jump before me,
when I jump into my bed.

—by Robert Louis Stevenson

112   113

READING/WRITING WORKSHOP, *pp. 112–113*

The Big Idea *How can we make sense of the world around us?*

COLLABORATE

Talk About It

Have children read the Big Idea aloud. Ask them what they can see, hear, smell, and feel in the classroom. Children may mention seeing other students, coats, and desks; hearing traffic sounds or birds chirping outside; smelling someone's lunch or an air freshener; or feeling the chair and desk where they are sitting.

Ask: *What do you hear and see every day?* Have children discuss with partners or in groups, then share their ideas with the class. Let children know that they will discuss the Big Idea throughout the unit. Each week they will talk, read, and write about an Essential Question related to the Big Idea.

Read the Poem: "My Shadow"

Read aloud "My Shadow." Ask children questions to explore the theme.

- Who is the shadow?
- How is the shadow like the speaker?
- Why does the shadow jump?

Repetition Explain that poets often repeat words in order to make readers pay attention to those words. Ask: *Which words are repeated in the poem? (very, jump) Why do you think the author repeated those words?*

RESEARCH AND INQUIRY WRITING

Weekly Projects Each week children will produce a project related to the Essential Question. They will then develop one of these projects more fully for the Unit Research Project. Through their research, children will focus their attention on:

- presenting information in different ways.
- describing what they see.
- collecting information from print and online sources.
- working with a partner or group.

Shared Research Board You may wish to develop a Shared Research Board. Children can post ideas and information about the unit theme. Children can post drawings or facts they gather as they do their research. They can also post notes with questions they have as they conduct their research.

> **WEEKLY PROJECTS**
> Children work in pairs or small groups.
> **Week 1** Illustrated Labeled Poster, T44
> **Week 2** Informative Report, T122
> **Week 3** Labeled Diorama, T200
> **Week 4** Labeled Diagram, T278
> **Week 5** Informative Poster, T356
> **WEEK 6**
> Children work in small groups to complete and present one of the following projects
>
> - Graph
> - Constellation
> - Report
> - Play
> - Comparison Chart

Write About the Text Throughout the unit children will respond to writing prompts on a variety of texts. As students practice close reading by reading and rereading a text, they take notes and cite text evidence. After reading, children write briefly about what they recall about the text in order to build writing fluency. Through the scaffolded instruction in writing about text in Shared Writing, the teacher then guides the class to respond to a writing prompt, using sentence frames as needed. In Interactive Writing the children analyze a student model response that includes the weekly writing trait before they respond to a new prompt together. In Independent Writing, children write independently, applying their close reading skills and the trait to their own writing.

WEEKLY WRITING TRAITS
Week 1 Sentence Fluency: Complete Sentences, T28
Week 2 Word Choice: Describing Words, T106
Week 3 Word Choice: Time-Order Words, T184
Week 4 Sentence Fluency: Complete Sentences, T262
Week 5 Organization: Topic, T340

COLLABORATE
Post children's questions and monitor student online discussions. Create a Shared Research Board.

WRITER'S WORKSPACE
Ask children to work through their writing using the online tools for support.

Build Knowledge
See It, Sort It

? Essential Question:
How can we classify and categorize things?

Teach and Model
Close Reading and Writing

Big Book and Little Book

Reading Writing Workshop

A Barn Full of Hats, 120–129
Genre Fantasy **Lexile** 320

Interactive Read Aloud

"Goldilocks,"
Genre Folktale

Practice and Apply
Close Reading and Writing

Literature Anthology

A Lost Button, 140–154
Genre Fantasy **Lexile** 340

Paired Read

"Sort It Out"
Genre Nonfiction **Lexile** 210

Differentiated Texts

APPROACHING
Lexile 170

ON LEVEL
Lexile 360

BEYOND
Lexile 390

ELL
Lexile 260

Leveled Readers

Extended Complex Texts

The Top Job
Genre Fiction
Lexile 880

Owl at Home
Genre Fiction
Lexile 370

Classroom Library

Student Outcomes

Close Reading of Complex Text

- Cite relevant evidence from text
- Acknowledge differences in point of view
- Retell the text

RL.2.6, RL.1.2

Writing

Write to Sources

- Draw evidence from fiction text
- Write opinion text
- Conduct short research on seeing and sorting.

W.1.1, W.1.7

Speaking and Listening

- Engage in collaborative conversation about seeing and sorting
- Retell and discuss *A Barn Full of Hats*
- Present information on seeing and sorting

SL.1.1c, SL.1.2, SL.1.3

Content Knowledge

- Explore how animals adapt to their environment

Language Development

Conventions

- Use Words that Join

Vocabulary Acquisition

- Develop Oral Vocabulary

  | distinguish | classify | organize |
  | entire | startled | |

- Acquire and use academic vocabulary

  | trouble | whole |

- Use sentence clues to understand words

L.1.1g, L.1.4a, L.1.6

Foundational Skills

Phonics/Word Study/Spelling

- *r*-controlled vowel *ar*
- plurals (irregular)
- cart, barn, arm, art, yarn, harm

High-Frequency Words

four   large   none   only   put   round

Fluency

- Phrasing

Decodable Text

- Apply foundational skills in connected text

RF.1.3, RF.1.3g, RF.1.4a, RF.1.4b, RF.1.4c, L.1.1c

Professional Development

- See lessons in action in real classrooms.
- Get expert advice on instructional practices.
- Collaborate with other teachers.
- Access PLC Resources

Go Digital! www.connected.mcgraw-hill.com.

INSTRUCTIONAL PATH

1 ## Talk About Categorizing

Guide children in collaborative conversations.

Discuss the essential question: *How can we classify and categorize things?*

Develop academic language.

Listen to "Goldilocks" to summarize and make and confirm predictions.

2

Read *A Barn Full of Hats*

Apply foundational skills in connected text. Model close reading.

Read

A Barn Full of Hats to learn how to sort things, citing text evidence to answer text-dependent questions.

Reread

A Barn Full of Hats to analyze text, craft, and structure, citing text evidence.

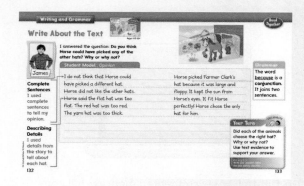

Write About *A Barn Full of Hats*

3

Model writing to a source.

Analyze a short response student model.

Use text evidence from close reading to write to a source.

4 Read and Write About *A Lost Button*

Practice and apply close reading of the anchor text.

Read

A Lost Button **(from *Frog and Toad Are Friends*)** to learn about how to classify buttons.

Reread

A Lost Button **(from *Frog and Toad Are Friends*)** and use text evidence to understand how the author uses text, craft, and structure to develop a deeper understanding of the story.

Integrate

Information about different ways to classify and sort objects.

Write to a Source, citing text evidence to explain who was the better friend, Frog or Toad.

5 Independent Partner Work

Gradual release of support to independent work

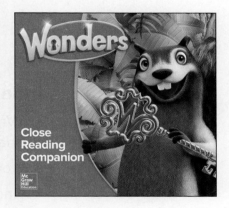

- Text-Dependent Questions
- Scaffolded Partner Work
- Talk with a Partner
- Cite Text Evidence
- Complete a sentence frame.
- Guided Text Annotation

6 Integrate Knowledge and Ideas

Connect Texts

Text to Text Discuss how each of the texts answers the question; How can we classify and categorize things?

Text to Poetry Compare information about sorting in the texts read with the poem "Wild Beasts."

Conduct a Short Research Project

Create a graph that sorts objects.

Write to Sources: Opinion

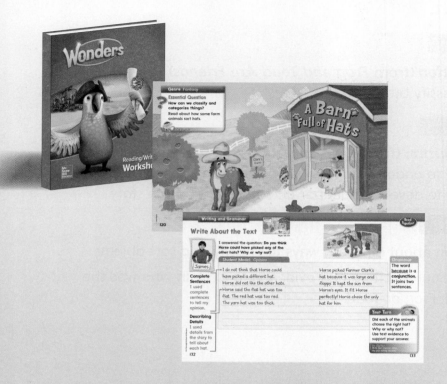

Day 1 and Day 2

Shared Writing

- Write about *A Barn Full of Hats,* p. T18

Interactive Writing

- Analyze a student model, p. T28

- Write about *A Barn Full of Hats,* p. T29

- Find Text Evidence

- Apply Writing Trait: Sentence Fluency: Use Complete Sentences, p. T29

- Apply Grammar Skill: Words That Join, p. T29

Day 3, Day 4 and Day 5

Independent Writing

- Write about *A Lost Button* (from *Frog and Toad Are Friends*), p. T36

- Provide scaffolded instruction to meet student needs, p. T36

- Find Text Evidence, p. T36

- Apply Writing Trait: Sentence Fluency: Use Complete Sentences, p. T36

- Prewrite and Draft, p. T36

- Revise and Edit, p. T42

- Final Draft, p. T43

- Present, Evaluate, and Publish, p. T48

Grammar

Words That Join

- Use words that join to tell about what is happening, pp. T19, T29, T37, T43, T49

- Apply grammar to writing, pp. T19, T36, T42, T49

Mechanics: Capitalize Proper Nouns (places)

- Use capitalization in proper nouns, pp. T37, T43, T49

Online PDFs

Grammar Practice, pp. 101–105

Online Grammar Games

Spelling

Words with /är/ar

- Spell words with /är/ar

Online PDFs

Phonics/Spelling blms
pp. 101–105

Online Spelling Games

SUGGESTED LESSON PLAN

READING		DAY 1	DAY 2
Teach, Model and Apply Wonders Reading/Writing Workshop	Core	**Build Background** See it, Sort It, T8–T9 **Oral Vocabulary** *distinguish, classify,* T8 **Word Work** T12–T15 • Fluency: Phrasing • Phonemic Awareness: Contrast Vowel Sounds • Phonics/Spelling: Introduce /är/ *ar* • High-Frequency Words: *four, large, none, only, put, round* • Vocabulary: *trouble, whole* **Shared Read** *A Barn Full of Hats,* T16–T17	**Oral Language** See It, Sort, T20 **Oral Vocabulary** *organize, entire, distinguish, classify, startled,* T20 **Word Work** T22–T25 • Phonemic Awareness: Phoneme Categorization • Structural Analysis: Irregular Plurals • Vocabulary: *trouble, whole* **Shared Read** *A Barn Full of Hats,* T26–T27 • Genre: Fantasy, T26 • Skill: Point of View, T27
	Options	**Listening Comprehension** "Goldilocks," T10–T11	**Listening Comprehension:** "Goldilocks," T21 **Word Work** T22–T25 • Phonics/Spelling: Review /är/ *ar* • High-Frequency Words

LANGUAGE ARTS			
Writing **Grammar**	Core	**Shared Writing** T18 **Grammar** Words That Join, T19	**Interactive Writing** T28 **Grammar** Words That Join, T29
	Options		

DIFFERENTIATED INSTRUCTION
Use your data dashboard to determine each student's needs. Then select instructional supports options throughout the week.

APPROACHING LEVEL

Leveled Reader
Nuts for Winter, T52–T53
"Sort by Color!," T53
Literature Circles, T53

Phonological Awareness:
Contrast Sounds, T54 (TIER 2)
Phoneme Categorization, T54
Phoneme Blending, T55
Phoneme Segmentation, T55

Phonics
Connect *ar* to /är/, T56 (TIER 2)
Blend Words with /är/ *ar,* T56 (TIER 2)
Build Words with /är/ *ar,* T57
Build Fluency with Phonics, T57

Structural Analysis Review Irregular Plurals, T58

Words to Know Cumulative Review, T59

Comprehension
Read for Fluency, T60 (TIER 2)
Identify Characters, T60
Review Point of View, T61
Self-Selected Reading, T61

ON LEVEL

Leveled Reader
Dog Bones, T62–T63
"Sorting Balls," T63
Literature Circles, T53

Phonics
Build Words with /är/ *ar,* T64

CUSTOMIZE YOUR OWN LESSON PLANS

www.connected.mcgraw-hill.com

WEEK 1

DAY 3	DAY 4	DAY 5
Fluency Phrasing, T31 **Word Work** T32–T35 • Phonemic Awareness: Phoneme Blending • Phonics/Spelling: Blend Words with /är/*ar* • Vocabulary Strategy: Context Clues/Multiple Meanings **Close Reading** *A Lost Button,* from *Frog and Toad Are Friends,* T35A–T35J	**Extend the Concept** T38–T39 • Text Feature: Photographs and Illustrations, T38 • Close Reading: "Sort it Out," T39A–T39B **Word Work** T40–T41 • Phonemic Awareness: Phoneme Categorization • Structural Analysis: Irregular Plurals **Integrate Ideas** • Research and Inquiry, T44–T45	**Word Work** T46–T47 • Phonemic Awareness: Phoneme Blending/ Segmentation • Phonics/Spelling: Blend and Build Words with /är/*ar* • Structural Analysis: Irregular Plurals • High-Frequency Words • Vocabulary: *trouble, whole* **Integrate Ideas** • Text Connections, T50-T51
Oral Language See It, Sort It, T30 **Word Work** T32–T35 • Structural Analysis: Irregular Plurals • High-Frequency Words	**Word Work** T40–T41 • Fluency: Sound-Spellings • Phonics/Spelling: Build Words with /är/ *ar* • High-Frequency Words • Vocabulary: *trouble, whole* **Close Reading** *A Lost Button,* from *Frog and Toad Are Friends,* T35A–T35J	**Word Work** T46–T47 • Fluency: Phrasing **Integrate Ideas** • Research and Inquiry, T50 • Speaking and Listening, T51
Independent Writing T36 **Grammar** Mechanics: Capitalize Proper Nouns (places), T37	**Independent Writing** T42 **Grammar** Mechanics: Capitalize Proper Nouns (Places), T43	**Independent Writing** T48 **Grammar** Words That Join, T49
Grammar Words That Join, T37	**Grammar** Words That Join, T43	**Grammar** Mechanics: Capitalize Proper Nouns (places), T49

	BEYOND LEVEL		ENGLISH LANGUAGE LEARNERS	

Words to Know
Review Words, T64

Leveled Reader
Spark's Toys, T66–T67
"Sorting Fruit," T67
Literature Circles, T67

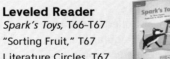

Vocabulary
Antonyms, T68

Comprehension
Review Point of View, T65
Self-Selected Reading, T65

Comprehension
Review Point of View, T69
Self-Selected Reading, T69

 Gifted and Talented

Shared Read
A Barn Full of Hats, T70–T71

Leveled Reader
Dog Bones, T72–T73
"Sorting Balls," T73
Literature Circles, T73

Vocabulary
Preteach Vocabulary, T74
Preteach ELL Vocabulary, T74

Words to Know
Review Words, T75
Reteach High-Frequency Words, T75

Writing/Spelling
Writing Trait: Sentence Fluency, T76
Words with /ä/*ar,* T76

Grammar
Joining Sentences, T77

DIFFERENTIATE TO ACCELERATE

  Scaffold to **A**ccess **C**omplex **T**ext

IF the text complexity of a particular selection is too difficult for children

THEN see the references noted in the chart below for scaffolded instruction to help children Access Complex Text.

Qualitative / Quantitative
Reader and Task
TEXT COMPLEXITY

	Reading/Writing Workshop	Literature Anthology	Leveled Readers	Classroom Library

Quantitative	*A Barn Full of Hats* **Lexile** 320	*A Lost Button* (from *Frog and Toad Are Friends*) **Lexile** 340 "Sort It Out" **Lexile** 210	**Approaching Level** **Lexile** 170 **Beyond Level** **Lexile** 390	**On Level** **Lexile** 360 **ELL** **Lexile** 260	*The Top Job* **Lexile** 880 *Owl at Home* **Lexile** 370
Qualitative	**What Makes the Text Complex?** **Foundational Skills** • Decoding with *r*-controlled vowel *ar*, T12–T13 • Reading words with irregular plurals, T23 • Identifying high-frequency words, T14–T15 *See Scaffolded Instruction in Teacher's Edition, T12–T13, T14–T15, and T23.*	**What Makes the Text Complex?** • **Organization,** T35B, T35E • **Connection of Ideas,** T35B, T35D **ACT** *See Scaffolded Instruction in Teacher's Edition, T35B, T35D, and T35E.*	**What Makes the Text Complex?** **Foundational Skills** • Decoding with *r*-controlled vowel *ar* • Reading words with irregular plurals • Identifying high-frequency words *four large none only put round* *See Level Up lessons online for Leveled Readers.*		**What Makes the Text Complex?** • **Purpose** • **Specific Vocabulary** • **Prior Knowledge** • **Sentence Structure** • **Organization** • **Connection of Ideas** • **Genre** **ACT** *See Scaffolded Instruction in Teacher's Edition, T413–T415.*
Reader and Task	**The** Introduce the Concept lesson on pages T8–T9 will help determine the reader's knowledge and engagement in the weekly concept. See pages T16–T17, T26–T27, T44–T45 and T50–T51 for questions and tasks for this text.	**The** Introduce the Concept lesson on pages T8–T9 will help determine the reader's knowledge and engagement in the weekly concept. See pages T35A–T35J, T39–T39B, T44–T45 and T50–T51 for questions and tasks for this text.	**The** Introduce the Concept lesson on pages T8–T9 will help determine the reader's knowledge and engagement in the weekly concept. See pages T52–T53, T62–T63, T66–T67, T72–T73, T44–T45 and T50–T51 for questions and tasks for this text.		**The** Introduce the Concept lesson on pages T8–T9 will help determine the reader's knowledge and engagement in the weekly concept. See pages T413–T415 for questions and tasks for this text.

Monitor and *Differentiate*

✓ Quick Check

To differentiate instruction, use the Quick Checks to assess students' needs and select the appropriate small group instruction focus.

Comprehension Strategy Make and Confirm Predictions, T11

Comprehension Skill Point of View, T27

Phonics Words with *r*-Controlled Vowel /är/*ar,* T15, T25, T35, T41, T47

High-Frequency Words and Vocabulary T15, T25, T35, T41, T47

If No →

| Approaching Level | Reteach T52–T61 |
| ELL | Develop T70–T77 |

If Yes →

| On Level | Review T62–T65 |
| Beyond Level | Extend T66–T69 |

Using Weekly Data

Check your data Dashboard to verify assessment results and guide grouping decisions.

Level Up with Leveled Readers

IF children can read their leveled text fluently and answer comprehension questions

THEN work with the next level up to accelerate children's reading with more complex text.

Beyond — Spark's Toys — T63

On Level — Dog Bones

Approaching — Nuts for Winter — T53

ELL — Dog Bones — T73

ELL ENGLISH LANGUAGE LEARNERS

Small Group Instruction

Use the ELL small group lessons in the *Wonders* Teacher's Edition to provide focused instruction.

Language Development
Vocabulary preteaching, oral vocabulary preteaching, high-frequency word review and reteach, pp. T74–T75

Close Reading
Interactive Question-Response routines for scaffolded text-dependent questioning for reading and rereading the Shared Read and Leveled Reader, pp. T70–T73

Writing
Focus on the writing trait, grammar, and spelling, pp. T76–T77

Additional ELL Support

Use Wonders for English Learners for ELD instruction that connects to the core.

Language Development
My Language Book for ample opportunities for discussions and scaffolded language support

Close Reading
Guided support for the Shared Read, Big Books, and Interactive Read Alouds. Differentiated texts about the weekly concept

Writing
Guided support in Interactive and Independent Writing and writing to sources

Wonders for ELs Teacher Edition and My Language Book

Materials

Visual Vocabulary Cards

classify	organize
distinguish	startled
entire	

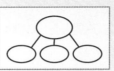

High-Frequency Word Cards

four	only
large	put
none	round

Teaching Poster

Vocabulary Cards

trouble
whole

Reading/Writing Workshop
VOLUME 4

Reading/Writing Workshop Big Book
UNIT 5

Think Aloud Clouds

a b c

Word-Building Cards

Interactive Read-Aloud Cards

Sound-Spelling Cards

Introduce the Concept

Go Digital

See It, Sort It

Video

school

Visual Glossary

Graphic Organizer

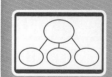

MINILESSON 5 Mins

Build Background

Reading/Writing Workshop Big Book

OBJECTIVES

CCSS Ask questions to clear up any confusion about the topics and texts under discussion. **SL.1.1c**

- Build background knowledge
- Discuss the Essential Question

ACADEMIC LANGUAGE
- *sort, categories*
- Cognate: *categorías*

ESSENTIAL QUESTION

How can we classify and categorize things?

Tell children that this week they will be talking and reading about different ways to sort things.

Oral Vocabulary Words

Tell children that you will share some words that they can use as they sort things. Use the Define/Example/Ask routine to introduce the oral vocabulary words **distinguish** and **classify**.

Visual Vocabulary Cards

Oral Vocabulary Routine

<u>Define:</u> To **distinguish** is to understand the difference between two or more people, animals, or things.

<u>Example:</u> I can distinguish between Mindy and her sister Patty.

<u>Ask:</u> How can you distinguish a butterfly from a bee?

<u>Define:</u> To **classify** is to sort or decide what group something belongs in.

<u>Example:</u> I can classify *run, jump,* and *swim* as action words.

<u>Ask:</u> How would you classify peaches, grapes, and apples?

Discuss the theme of "See It, Sort It" and explain that there are many ways to sort objects. Have children look around at each other's hair. *How can you classify hair by color? How else could we put our hairstyles into groups?*

Reading/Writing Workshop, pp. 114–115

Talk About It: See It, Sort It

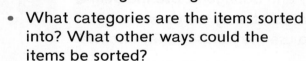

Guide children to discuss what the girl is classifying.

- What is the girl sorting?
- What categories are the items sorted into? What other ways could the items be sorted?

Use Teaching Poster 40 and prompt children to complete the Graphic Organizer.

Children can look at page 115 of their Reading/Writing Workshop and do the Talk About It activity with a partner.

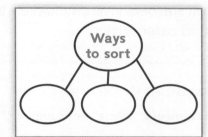

Teaching Poster

Collaborative Conversations

Ask and Answer Questions As children engage in partner, small-group, and whole-group discussions, encourage them to:

- ask questions about ideas they do not understand.
- give others a chance to think after asking a question.
- write down questions they want to ask the teacher or the whole class.

ENGLISH LANGUAGE LEARNERS SCAFFOLD

Beginning

Use Visuals Point to the bins and explain that these are used for recycling trash. Point to the bin in the girl's hand. Ask: *Is this paper? Is it plastic?* Restate children's responses in complete sentences. Name the other items for children.

Intermediate

Describe Ask children to describe what the girl wants to recycle. Have them explain what goes in each of the bins. Elicit more details to support children's answers.

Advanced/High

Discuss Have children describe what goes in each bin. Have them give an example of an item that could be put in each bin. Model correct pronunciation as needed.

→ # Listening Comprehension

MINILESSON
10 Mins

Read the Interactive Read Aloud

OBJECTIVES

CCSS Participate in collaborative conversations with diverse partners about grade 1 topics and texts with peers and adults in small and larger groups. **SL.1.1**

• Develop concept understanding

• Develop reading strategy make and confirm predictions

ACADEMIC LANGUAGE

• *predictions, evidence, illustrations*

• Cognates: *predicciones, evidencia, ilustraciones*

Connect to Concept: See It, Sort It

"Goldilocks"

Tell children that they will now read a story about a little girl and a family of bears.
Ask: *What do you know about Goldilocks?*

Focus on Oral Vocabulary

Review the oral vocabulary words *classify* and *distinguish*. Use the Define/Example/Ask routine to introduce the oral vocabulary words *entire, organize,* and *startled*. Prompt children to use the words as they discuss classifying and categorizing.

Oral Vocabulary Routine

<u>Define:</u> **Entire** means "whole" or "complete."

<u>Example:</u> Kip was so hungry that he ate the entire sandwich. There was nothing left over.

<u>Ask:</u> Can you eat an entire watermelon by yourself?

<u>Define:</u> When you **organize** things, you arrange them a certain way.

Visual Vocabulary Cards

<u>Example:</u> Sal tried to organize the dolls by lining them up from smallest to largest.

<u>Ask:</u> How do we organize our art supplies in the classroom?

<u>Define:</u> You feel **startled** when something suddenly surprises you.

<u>Example:</u> Pam was startled when the door slammed.

<u>Ask:</u> Do loud noises sometimes make you feel startled? How do you react?

Go Digital

"Goldilocks"

I predicted _____ because...

Make and Confirm Predictions

school

Visual Glossary

Retell

Set a Purpose for Reading

- Display the Interactive Read-Aloud Cards.
- Read aloud the title.
- Tell children that you will be reading a story about a girl who sneaks into a house where three bears live. Tell children to read to find out what the girl does in the bears' house.

Strategy: Make and Confirm Predictions

❶ Explain Remind children that as they read or listen to a story, they can make predictions about what will happen next. Then they can use the evidence in the story to check whether their predictions were correct.

Think Aloud To make a prediction, think about the characters and the story events so far. Then use the information to guess what will happen next. Today, as we read "Goldilocks," think about what might happen next. Then check your predictions by reading ahead and seeing what really happens in the text.

❷ Model Read the selection. As you read, use the Think Aloud Cloud to model applying the strategy.

Think Aloud Remember that you can make predictions and then check the text and the illustrations to see if you were correct. Goldilocks sees three bowls of porridge on the table. I know that Goldilocks was naughty enough to go in the bears' house even though nobody was home, so I think she will eat the porridge, too. Let's read on to find out if my prediction is correct.

❸ Guided Practice As you continue to read, pause to elicit predictions from children. *What do you think might happen next? What clues in the story make you think that?* Pause to ask children if their predictions were correct. Guide children in using the evidence in the text and illustrations to confirm their predictions.

Respond to Reading

After reading, prompt children to retell "Goldilocks." Discuss what predictions they made and whether their predictions were correct. Then discuss with children how Goldilocks classified the food, chairs, and beds in the bears' house.

ENGLISH LANGUAGE LEARNERS SCAFFOLD

Beginning

Engage Display Card 4 of "Goldilocks." Point to the bears. *Are these the bears? Is Goldilocks asleep? Let's make a prediction. Will Goldilocks be afraid when she sees the bears?*

Intermediate

Describe Display Card 3 of "Goldilocks." Have children describe the illustration. *Let's make a prediction. How do you think the bears will feel when they see the broken chair?* Allow ample time for children to respond.

Advanced/High

Describe Display Card 4 of "Goldilocks." *What is happening here? What do you think will happen next? Why?* Clarify children's responses as needed by providing vocabulary.

Monitor and *Differentiate*

 Quick Check

Can children apply the strategy make and confirm predictions?

Small Group Instruction

If No → | Approaching | Reteach pp. T52–53
| ELL | Develop pp. T70–73

If Yes → | On Level | Review pp. T62–63
| Beyond Level | Extend pp. T66–67

→ # Word Work

Quick Review

Build Fluency: Sound-Spellings
Display the **Word-Building Cards:** *ar, ey, igh, oa, oe, ee, ea, ai, ay, e_e, u_e, o_e, dge, i_e a_e, ch, tch, wh, ph, th, sh, ng, mp, sk, st, nt, nk, nd, _ ce, _ge.* Have children say the sounds.

MINILESSON 5 Mins

Phonological Awareness

OBJECTIVES

CCSS Isolate and pronounce initial, medial vowel, and final sounds (phonemes) in spoken single-syllable words. **RF.1.2c**

CCSS Decode regularly spelled one-syllable words. **RF.1.3b**

Contrast Vowel Sounds

❶ **Model** Show children how to contrast sounds in words. *Listen carefully as I say two words. Listen:* barn, bone. *I hear different middle sounds in the words. Only one has the /är/ sounds: /b/ /är/ /n/.* Bone *does not have the /är/ sounds.* Repeat with *shack/shark* and *bark/bake.*

❷ **Guided Practice/Practice** Have children practice contrasting sounds. Do the first one with them. *I will say two words. Which word has the /är/ sounds? Say the word.*

arm, aim	pat, part	jay, jar	march, make
art, ate	head, hard	harp, hope	dark, dirt

Go Digital

Phonological Awareness

MINILESSON 5 Mins

Phonics

Introduce /är/*ar*

Sound-Spelling Card

Star

Phonics

❶ **Model** Display the *Star* **Sound-Spelling Card.** Teach /är/ spelled *ar* using *star. This is the* Star *Sound-Spelling Card. The sounds at the end of the word* star *are /är/. Listen: /stär/. When the vowel* a *is followed by an* r *the sound changes. Together* a *and* r *stand for /är/. Say the sounds with me: /är/. I'll say /är/ as I write the letters* a *and* r *several times.*

Handwriting

❷ **Guided Practice/Practice** Have children practice connecting the letters *ar* to the sounds /är/ by writing them. *Now do it with me. Say /är/ as I write the letters* ar. *This time, write the letters* ar *five times as you say the /är/ sounds.*

SKILLS TRACE

/är/*ar*

Introduce Unit 5 Week 1 Day 1

Review Unit 5 Week 1 Days 2, 3, 4, 5

Assess Unit 5 Week 1

Blend Words with /är/ar

1 Model Display the **Word-Building Cards** f, a, r, m. Model how to blend the sounds. *This is the letter* f. *It stands for /f/. These are the letters* a *and* r. *Together they stand for /är/. This is the letter* m. *It stands for /m/. Listen as I blend these sounds together: /fffärmmm/. Say it with me.*

Continue by modeling the words *arm, yard, large,* and *start.*

2 Guided Practice/Practice Display the Day 1 Phonics Practice Activity. Read each word in the first row, blending the sounds; for example: */ärt/. The word is* art. Have children blend each word with you. Prompt children to read the connected text, sounding out the decodable words.

art	dark	barn	car	hard	yarn
harm	sharp	scarf	part	chart	charge
had	hard	match	march	smart	apart
child	party	coat	fried	hockey	night

A dog started to bark in the dark yard.

Can a shark live in a barn on a farm?

Clark will park his car in the backyard.

Also online

Day 1 Phonics Practice Activity

Corrective Feedback

Sound Error Model the sound that children missed, then have them repeat the sound. Say: *My turn.* Tap under the letters and say: *Sounds? /är/. What's the sound?* Return to the beginning of the word. Say: *Let's start over.* Blend the word with children again.

Daily Handwriting

Throughout the week teach uppercase and lowercase letters *Hh* using the Handwriting models.

ON-LEVEL PRACTICE BOOK p. 2ll

The letters **ar** together make the sounds you hear at the end of **car**.

Read the words in the box. Listen for the ar sounds. Write the word that names each picture.

scarf	arm	shark	star

1. star
2. arm
3. shark
4. scarf

Write your own sentence using a word from the box.

5. Sentences will vary but should correctly use a word from the box.

APPROACHING p. 2ll	BEYOND p. 2ll	ELL p. 2ll

 # → Word Work

Quick Review

High-Frequency Words: Read, Spell, and Write to review last week's high-frequency words: *found, hard, near, woman, would, write.*

 ## Spelling

MINILESSON 5 Mins

Words with /är/*ar*

Dictation Use the Spelling Dictation routine for each word to help children transfer their knowledge of sound-spellings to writing.

Pretest After dictation, pronounce each spelling word. Say a sentence for each word and pronounce the word again. Ask children to say each word softly, stretching the sounds, before writing it. After the pretest, display the spelling words and write each word as you say the letter names. Have children check their words.

cart	barn	arm	art	yarn
harm	happy	key	four	none

For Approaching Level and Beyond Level children, refer to the Differentiated Spelling Lists for modified word lists.

High-Frequency Words

MINILESSON 5 Mins

four, large, none, only, put, round

1 Model Display the **High-Frequency Word Cards** *four, large, none, only, put,* and *round.* Use the Read/Spell/Write routine to teach each word.

- **Read** Point to and say the word *four. This is the word* four. *Say it with me:* four. *A horse has four legs.*

- **Spell** *The word* four *is spelled* f-o-u-r. *Spell it with me.*

- **Write** *Let's write the word in the air as we say each letter:* f-o-u-r.

- Repeat to introduce *large, none, only, put,* and *round.*

- As children spell each word with you, point out the irregularities in sound-spellings, such as the /u/ sound spelled *o_e* in the word *none.*

 - Have partners create sentences using each word.

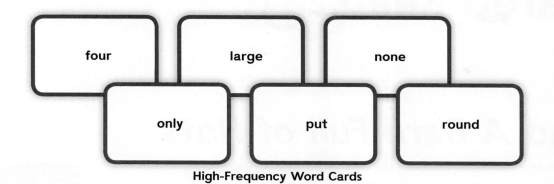

four	large	none
only	put	round

High-Frequency Word Cards

2 **Guided Practice** Have children read the sentences. Prompt them to identify the high-frequency words in connected text and to blend the decodable words.

1. I see **four** fish in the fish tank.
2. I saw a **large** dog in the park.
3. Ted has one left, but Mark has **none**.
4. The card **only** costs five cents.
5. Where did you **put** my book?
6. A penny is **round**.

MINILESSON

5 Mins

Introduce Vocabulary

trouble, whole

1 **Model** Introduce the new words using the routine.

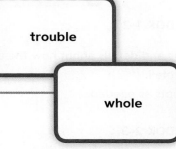

trouble
whole

Vocabulary Cards

Vocabulary Routine

<u>Define:</u> If you have **trouble** doing something, you have problems doing it.

<u>Example:</u> *I had some trouble learning to ride my bike.*

<u>Ask:</u> What do you have trouble doing? What don't you have trouble doing? EXAMPLES

<u>Define:</u> When something is **whole**, it is complete. None of it is missing.

<u>Example:</u> *I ate the whole sandwich. Nothing was left.*

<u>Ask:</u> How is a whole pie different from a piece of pie? EXPLANATION

2 **Review** Use the routine to review last week's vocabulary words.

Monitor and *Differentiate*

✓ **Quick Check**

Can children read and decode words with *r*-controlled vowel *ar*?

Can children recognize and read high-frequency and vocabulary words?

Small Group Instruction

If No → Approaching   Reteach pp. T56–59

           ELL   Develop pp. T70–77

If Yes → On Level   Review pp. T64–65

           Beyond Level Extend pp. T68–69

→ **Shared Read**

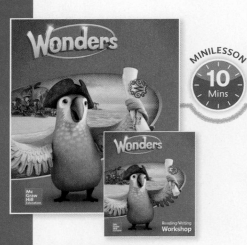

**Reading/Writing
Workshop Big Book
and Reading/Writing
Workshop**

OBJECTIVES

CCSS Decode regularly
spelled one-syllable
words. **RF.1.3b**

CCSS Recognize and read
grade-appropriate
irregularly spelled
words. **RF.1.3g**

**ACADEMIC
LANGUAGE**

• *fantasy, classify,
categorize*

• Cognates: *fantasía,
clasificar, categorizar*

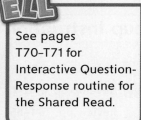

See pages
T70–T71 for
Interactive Question-
Response routine for
the Shared Read.

Read *A Barn Full of Hats*

MINILESSON 10 Mins

Focus on Foundational Skills

Review with children the words and letter-sounds they will see in *A Barn Full of Hats.*

• Have children use pages 116–117 to review high-frequency words *four, large, round, put, none, only* and vocabulary words *trouble* and *whole.*

• Have children use page 118–119 to review that the letters *ar* can stand for the /är/ sound. Guide them to blend the sounds to read the words.

• Display the story words *farmer, horse, wear,* and *eyes.* Spell each word and model reading it. Tell children they will be reading the words in the selection.

Read Guide children in reading *A Barn Full of Hats.* Point out the high-frequency words, vocabulary words, and words in which *ar* stands for the/är/ sounds.

Close Reading Routine

Read DOK 1–2

• Identify key ideas and details about how the animals pick hats.
• Take notes and retell.
• Use (A C T) prompts as needed.

Reread DOK 2–3

• Analyze the text, craft, and structure.
• Use the Reread minilessons.

Integrate DOK 4

• Integrate knowledge and ideas.
• Make text-to-text connections.
• Use the Integrate Lesson.

Genre: Fantasy Tell children that *A Barn Full of Hats* is a fantasy. A fantasy is a made-up story that could not really happen and often has animal characters who talk and act like real people.

A Barn Full of Hats

A Barn Full of Hats

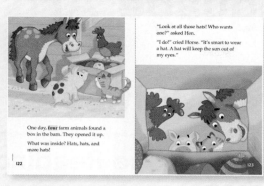

READING/WRITING WORKSHOP, pp. 120–129   **Lexile** 320

Connect to Concept: See It, Sort It

ESSENTIAL QUESTION Explain to children that as they read *A Barn Full of Hats,* they will look for key ideas and details that will help them answer the Essential Question: *How can we classify and categorize things?*

- Pages 122–123: What is in the box? Why does Horse want a hat?
- Pages 124–125: What type of hat does Pig find?
- Pages 126–127: What does Cat do with her hat?
- Pages 128–129: Why does Horse like Farmer Clark's hat?

Focus on Fluency

With partners, have children read *A Barn Full of Hats* to develop fluency. Remind them that they can ask themselves questions to make sure they understand what they are reading. Have them use both text and illustrations to answer their questions.

Retell Have partners use key ideas and details to retell *A Barn Full of Hats.* Invite them to tell which type of hat each animal chose.

Make Connections

Read together Make Connections on page 129. Have partners talk about how to classify and categorize things to wear using this sentence starter:

One category we can use to sort things to wear is . . .

Guide children to connect what they have read to the Essential Question.

→ # Language Arts

**Reading/Writing
Workshop**

Go Digital

MINILESSON 5 Mins

Shared Writing

Write About the Reading/Writing Workshop

Analyze the Prompt Tell children that today the class will work together to write a response to a prompt. Read aloud the prompt. *Why did the animals choose the hats they chose?* Say: *To respond to this prompt, we need to look at the text and illustrations in* A Barn Full of Hats.

Find Text Evidence Explain that first you will reread the text and take notes. Read aloud pages 124–125. Say: *The story and illustrations tell us why the animals chose the hats they chose. For example, on page 124, Hen chooses a flat hat because it makes a good nest. Then, on page 125, Pig chooses a red hat because he thought the color looked fine. These are details that will help us respond to the prompt. Let's write them in our notes.*

Write to a Prompt Reread the prompt to children. *Why did the animals choose the hats they chose?* Say: *First, we will write a topic sentence telling what we are writing about: The animals chose their hats for different reasons.* Write the sentence. Ask: *What did we write in our notes about why Hen chose her hat?* (because it was flat and would make a good nest) *Let's write our next sentence about that: Hen chose a flat hat because it would make a good nest.* Write the sentence. *Now, we will read our notes and use them to tell why Pig, Cat, and Horse chose their hats.* Track the print as you reread the notes.

Guide children to dictate complete sentences for you to record based on their notes. Read the final response as you track the print.

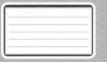

**Graphic
Organizer**

Writing

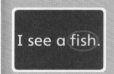

I see a fish.

Grammar

Grammar

5 Mins

Join Sentences with *and, but, or*

1 Explain Tell children that two complete sentences can be joined together with a joining word. Explain that the words *and, but,* and *or* are used to put two sentences together. Display the following sentences:

> You march to the top of the hill. You look for the barn.
>
> You march to the top of the hill and you look for the barn.
>
> Walk by the lake. Do not go in the water.
>
> Walk by the lake but do not go in the water.
>
> Marge might win the prize. Charlie might win the prize.
>
> Marge might win the prize or Charlie might win the prize.

Circle the joining words and explain to children the difference in meaning of *and, but,* and *or.*

2 Guided Practice/Practice Display the sentences below and read them aloud. Have children identify the word used to join the two sentences.

> Who is he and where is he from? (and)
>
> You can take the high path or you can take the low path. (or)
>
> We were going to take a car trip but we ran out of gas. (but)

Talk About It Have partners work together to orally generate sentences with *and, but,* and *or* as they discuss how they sort things in their desks.

Link to Writing Say: *Let's look back at our writing and see if we used any joining words to combine sentences. Did we use them correctly?* Review the Shared Writing for the correct use of the joining words *and, but,* and *or.* If these joining words are not in the Shared Writing, work with children to add them and reread the response together.

ENGLISH LANGUAGE LEARNERS SCAFFOLD

Beginning

Demonstrate Comprehension Point to the Explain sentences. *You can put two sentences together and make one. Can you use the word* and *to join two sentences? Name other words that can join two sentences.* Help children circle the words *and, but,* and *or* in the example sentences.

Intermediate

Explain Ask children to circle the word *and* in the first Explain sentence. *Why is* and *used in this sentence?* Continue with each example sentence, circling *but* and *or.* Repeat correct answers.

Advanced/High

Expand Have children write a pair of related sentences and then help them combine them into a single sentence. Have them explain why they chose *and, but,* or *or* to combine them.

Daily Wrap Up

- Encourage children to discuss the Essential Question using the oral vocabulary words. Ask them to name ways to classify things.

- Prompt children to share what skills they learned. Ask: *How might you use those skills?*

Materials

Reading/Writing Workshop
VOLUME 4

Visual Vocabulary Cards

classify   organize
distinguish   startled
entire

Spelling Word Cards

cart

four

High-Frequency Word Cards

four   only
large   put
none   round

Character	Clue	Point of View

Teaching Poster

trouble

Vocabulary Cards

trouble
whole

a b c

Word-Building Cards

Interactive Read-Aloud Cards

ar
star

Sound-Spelling Cards

→ Build the Concept

Go Digital

school

Visual Glossary

"Goldilocks"

MINILESSON 5 Mins Oral Language

OBJECTIVES

CCSS Ask and answer questions about key details in a text read aloud or information presented orally or through other media. **SL.1.2**

• Discuss the Essential Question
• Build concept understanding

ACADEMIC LANGUAGE

• *events, characters, prediction*
• Cognate: *predicción*

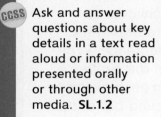
COLLABORATE

ESSENTIAL QUESTION

Remind children that this week you've been talking and reading about how we classify and categorize things. Remind them of how the animals sorted and chose hats and how Goldilocks classified things in the bear's home. Guide children to discuss the Essential Question using information from what they read and discussed on Day 1.

Oral Vocabulary Words

Review the oral vocabulary words. Use the Define/Example/Ask routine to review the oral vocabulary words *classify, distinguish, entire, organize,* and *startled*.

• How could you classify pens and pencils? Apples and grapes?

• How could you distinguish the shape of a ball with your eyes closed?

• Would you rather read an entire book or parts of a few books? Why?

• How do we organize toys and books in the classroom?

• What might you do if you were suddenly startled by a loud noise?

Listening Comprehension

MINILESSON
5 Mins

Reread the Interactive Read Aloud

Strategy: Make and Confirm Predictions

Remind children that as they listen, they can they make predictions about what might happen next in a story and check them by using evidence in the text.

"Goldilocks"

Tell children that you will reread "Goldilocks." Display the Interactive Read-Aloud Cards. Pause as you read to model applying the strategy.

Think Aloud When I read this the first time, I used what I had read about the characters and events to make predictions about what would happen next. Then I read on to see if my predictions were correct. At the beginning of the story, the text said that Goldilocks saw the bowls of porridge on the table and they made her feel hungry. I predicted that she would eat their porridge. I read on and found out that I was right!

Make Connections

COLLABORATE

Discuss partners' responses to "Goldilocks."

- *What did Goldilocks find in the bears' house? What did she like? What did she dislike?*

- *How did Goldilocks classify and categorize the things in the bears' house?*

- *How did the bears feel when they found Goldilocks? Would you feel the same way if it were your house?*

Write About It Have children write an alternate ending to "Goldilocks" in their Writer's Notebooks. Guide children by asking questions such as, *What might have happened if Goldilocks didn't run away when she saw the bears? What might she have said to them? What might the bears have said to her?* Have children write continuously for six minutes.

 → **Word Work**

Quick Review

Build Fluency: Sound-Spellings
Display the **Word-Building Cards:** *ar, ey, igh, oa, oe, ee, ea, ai, ay, e_e, u_e, o_e, dge, i_e, a_e, ch, tch, wh, ph, th, sh, ng, mp, sk, st, nt, nk, nd, _ce, _ge.* Have children say the sounds.

 MINILESSON **5** Mins

Phonemic Awareness

OBJECTIVES

 Isolate and pronounce initial, medial vowel, and final sounds (phonemes) in spoken single-syllable words. **RF.1.2c**

 Decode regularly spelled one-syllable words. **RF.1.3b**

Recognize and use irregular plurals

Phoneme Categorization

1 Model Show children how to categorize phonemes. *Listen as I say three words:* yarn, coat, bark. *Two of the words have the same sounds in the middle. One does not.* Yarn *and* bark *have the /är/ sounds.* Coat *does not.* Coat *does not belong.*

2 Guided Practice/Practice Have children practice identifying the word with different sounds. Do the first one together. *I will say three words. Tell me which word does not belong and why.*

sharp, hard, beach	pain, mark, late	charge, main, cart
scarf, back, hand	store, guard, charm	stork, bird, first

 MINILESSON **5** Mins

Phonics

Review /är/ *ar*

1 Model Display the *Star* **Sound-Spelling Card**. Review the sounds /är/ spelled *ar* using the words *star* and *park*.

2 Guided Practice/Practice Have children practice connecting the letters and sounds. Point to the letters *ar* on the Sound-Spelling Card. *What are these letters? What sounds do they stand for?*

Go Digital 🖐

Phonemic Awareness

Phonics

Structural Analysis

Handwriting

Blend Words with /är/ *ar*

1 Model Display **Word-Building Cards** *m, a, r, k* to form the word *mark*. Model how to generate and blend the sounds to say the word. *This is the letter* m. *It stands for /m/. These are the letters* a *and* r. *Together they stand for /är/. This is the letter* k. *It stands for /k/. Listen as I blend these sounds together: /mmmärk/. Say it with me:* mark. Continue by modeling the words *dark, start,* and *large*.

2 Guided Practice/Practice Repeat the routine with children with *far, arm, hard, bark, chart, scar, charge, march, sharp, barnyard, restart*.

Build Words with /är/ *ar*

1 Model Display the Word-Building Cards *c, a, r, d*. Blend: /k/ /är/ /d/, /kärd/, *card*.

- Replace *c* with *h* and repeat with *hard*.
- Change *d* to *p* and repeat with *harp*.

2 Guided Practice/Practice Continue with *sharp, shark, park, part, cart, chart, charm, harm, farm, far, bar, car, scar, scarf*.

MINILESSON 5 Mins

Structural Analysis

Irregular Plurals

1 Model Write and read aloud *shark, sharks, marsh,* and *marshes*. Circle the *-s* and *-es* endings. Review that we add *-s* or *-es* to many words to make them mean "more than one." Then write and read *man* and *men*. Explain that some words change in other ways to make them mean "more than one." Tell children *men* means "more than one man." Circle the *a* and *e*. Explain that the vowel sound and spelling changed. *One man sat down. Two men stood up.*

Write and read aloud *sheep*. Explain that some words do not change to make them mean "more than one." Tell children that *sheep* can mean "one sheep" or "more than one sheep." Use *sheep* in sentences: *One sheep has black wool. Five sheep have white wool.*

2 Guided Practice/Practice On index cards, write *child, woman, person, deer, foot, children, women, people, deer, feet*. Place the cards in two columns in a pocket chart. Read the words. As you point to and reread each singular noun, have children match it to its plural. Ask children to use the singular and plural noun pairs in sentences.

→ # Word Work

Quick Review

High-Frequency Words: Read, Spell, and Write to review this week's high-frequency words: *four, large, none, only, put, round.*

5 Mins
MINILESSON

Spelling

Word Sort with *-art, -arn, -arm*

① Model Display the **Spelling Word Cards** from the Teacher's Resource Book, one at a time. Have children read each word, listening for *r*-controlled vowel *ar* and the ending sound.

Make cards for *part, darn,* and *charm* to create a three-column chart. Say each word and pronounce the sounds, emphasizing the /är/ sounds plus final consonant sound. Ask children to chorally spell each word.

② Guided Practice/Practice Have children place each Spelling Word Card in the column with the word containing the same *ar* spelling pattern. When completed, have children chorally read the words in each column. Then call out a word. Have a child find the word card and point to it as the class chorally spells the word.

OBJECTIVES

CCSS Recognize and read grade-appropriate irregularly spelled words. **RF.1.3g**

CCSS Use conventional spelling for words with common spelling patterns and for frequently occurring irregular words. **L.1.2d**

ENGLISH LANGUAGE LEARNERS

Provide Clues Practice spelling by helping children generate more words with *ar* vowel patterns. Provide clues: *Think of a word that begins with* f *and rhymes with* harm. Write the word and have children practice reading it. Correct their pronunciation if needed.

ANALYZE ERRORS/ARTICULATION SUPPORT

Use children's pretest errors to analyze spelling problems and provide corrective feedback. Some children might leave out the letter *a* when spelling words with /är/ because they hear the letter name "r" (for example, *crt/cart*).

For these children, provide additional articulation support hearing and feeling /är/. In addition, provide practice contrasting *ar* patterned words with other similar words (for example, *cat/cart, am/arm/, at/art, from/farm, bran/barn, scrap/scarf*). Have children read and sort the words (words with *ar*, words without *ar*).

Go Digital

er	ir	or	ur
her			
girl curb			word

Spelling Word Sort

they	together
how	eat

High-Frequency Word Routine

school

Visual Glossary

High-Frequency Words

four, large, none, only, put, round

1 Guided Practice Say each word and have children Read/Spell/ Write it. Ask them to picture the word and write it the way they see it. Display the high-frequency words for children to self-correct.

- Point out the previously taught soft *g* sound at the end of *large*.

2 Practice Add the high-frequency words *four, large, none, only, put,* and *round* to the cumulative word bank.

- Have partners create sentences using the words.
- Have children look at the words and compare their sounds and spellings to words from previous weeks.
- Suggest that children write about things that are round, things that come in fours, or things that are large.

Cumulative Review Review last week's words using the Read/Spell/ Write routine.

- Repeat the routine, mixing the words and having children say each.

Reinforce Vocabulary

trouble, whole

1 Guided Practice Use the **Vocabulary Cards** to review this week's and last week's vocabulary words. Work together with children to generate a new context sentence for each word.

2 Practice Have children work with a partner to orally complete each sentence stem on the Day 2 Vocabulary Practice Activity using this week's and last week's vocabulary words.

clever	signal	trouble	whole

1. Dad and Bart were spending the ____ night in the woods.
2. Bart got lost. "Now I'm in ____," he said.
3. Bart was a ____ boy. He had a flashlight with him.
4. He used the light as a ____. Dad spotted the light and saved Bart.

Also online

Day 2 Vocabulary Practice Activity

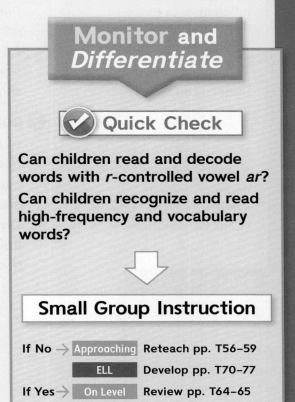

ON-LEVEL PRACTICE BOOK p. 212

Complete each sentence. Use one of the words in the box.

four	none	only	large	put	round

1. The shape of this cake is ____ round ____.

2. I see ____ only ____ one cat here.

3. That shark is ____ large ____!

4. Carl wants an apple, but there are ____ none ____.

5. There are ____ four ____ swings.

6. I can help ____ put ____ the dishes in the sink.

APPROACHING p. 212	BEYOND p. 212	ELL p. 212

Monitor and *Differentiate*

✓ Quick Check

Can children read and decode words with *r*-controlled vowel *ar*?

Can children recognize and read high-frequency and vocabulary words?

⬇

Small Group Instruction

If No → Approaching Reteach pp. T56–59

ELL Develop pp. T70–77

If Yes → On Level Review pp. T64–65

Beyond Level Extend pp. T68–69

Comprehension

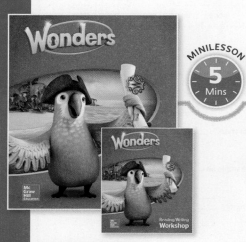

Reading/Writing Workshop Big Book and Reading/Writing Workshop

---

OBJECTIVES

CCSS Acknowledge differences in the points of view of characters, including by speaking in a different voice for each character when reading dialogue aloud. **RL.2.6**

Understand fantasy genre

ACADEMIC LANGUAGE

• *fantasy, point of view*

• Cognate: *fantasía*

MINILESSON 5 Mins

Reread *A Barn Full of Hats*

Genre: Fantasy

1 Model Tell children they will now reread the fantasy selection *A Barn Full of Hats*. Explain that as they read, they will look for information in the text to help them understand the selection.

Review the characteristics of a fantasy. It:

• is a made-up story.

• could not really happen.

• often has animal characters that look and act like real people.

Tell children that like other fiction, fantasies often have dialogue. Remind children that dialogue is what the characters say. Dialogue has quotation marks around it.

Display pages 122–123: *The illustration shows that the story takes place in a barn. The animals are talking to each other, just like people. There is dialogue that shows what Hen and Horse are saying. I know that fiction often has dialogue that shows what the characters say. And I know that hens and horses can't really talk. These details show me that this story is fantasy fiction.*

2 Guided Practice/Practice Display pages 124 and 125 of *A Barn Full of Hats*. Read page 124 aloud. Say: *These animals are doing things that animals cannot really do. That helps me know that the story could not really happen.* Then read page 125 aloud. *These animals are talking to each other. The dialogue tells us what the characters say to each other. We know that fiction often has dialogue. Can animals really talk to each other? No. What does that tell us about this story? Yes, it tells us that it is fantasy fiction.*

Go Digital

A Barn Full of Hats

Genre

Point of View

SKILLS TRACE

POINT OF VIEW

Introduce Unit 4 Week 4

Review Unit 5 Weeks 1, 4; Unit 6 Week 1

Assess Unit 4 Week 4, Unit 5 Week 1

Skill: Point of View

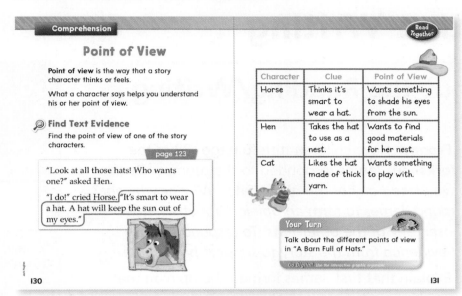

Reading/Writing Workshop, pp. 130–131

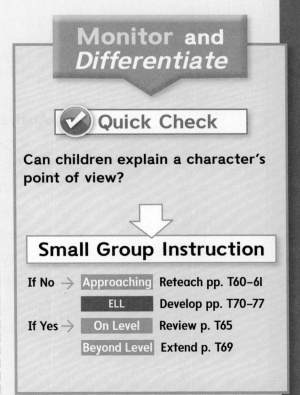
1 Model Tell children that when they read a fantasy, they can use text and illustrations to understand how a character thinks and feels. Have children look at pages 130–131 in their Reading/Writing Workshop. Read together the definition of point of view. *Point of view is the way a story character thinks or feels. What a character says helps you understand his or her point of view.*

2 Guided Practice/Practice Read together the Find Text Evidence section and model finding the point of view of the Horse in *A Barn Full of Hats.* Point out the information added to the graphic organizer. *On page 123, we find out that Horse wants to wear a hat. The dialogue tells us that he wants something to shade his eyes from the sun. That helps us understand how he thinks and feels. This information has been added to the Point of View chart. What clues tell us about other characters' points of view?*

Character	Clue	Point of View

Teaching Poster

Monitor and *Differentiate*

✓ Quick Check

Can children explain a character's point of view?

⬇

Small Group Instruction

If No → **Approaching** Reteach pp. T60–6I

ELL Develop pp. T70–77

If Yes → **On Level** Review p. T65

Beyond Level Extend p. T69

→ # Language Arts

Wonders
Reading/Writing
Workshop

MINILESSON
5 Mins

Interactive Writing

Write About the Reading/Writing Workshop

Analyze the Model Prompt Have children turn to page 132 in the **Reading/Writing Workshop**. James responded to the prompt: *Do you think Horse could have picked any of the other hats? Why or why not?* Say: *The prompt is asking James to form an opinion about whether Horse could have chosen any of the other hats. To respond to this prompt, James used evidence from the story to support his opinion.*

Find Text Evidence Explain that first James formed the opinion that Horse could not have picked a different hat. Then, James looked for text evidence from the story to support his opinion.

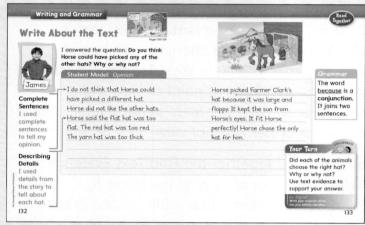

Reading/Writing Workshop

Reading/Writing Workshop

OBJECTIVES

CCSS Write opinion pieces in which they introduce the topic or name the book they are writing about, state an opinion, supply a reason for the opinion, and provide some sense of closure. **W.1.1**

CCSS Use frequently occurring conjunctions (e.g., *and, but, or, so, because*). **L.1.1g**

ACADEMIC LANGUAGE

• describe, details, opinion, conjunctions

• Cognates: *describir, detalles, opinión, conjunción*

Analyze the Student Model Read the model. Discuss the callouts.

• **Complete Sentences** James correctly used complete sentences to tell his opinion. Using complete sentences made his writing understandable. **Trait: Sentence Fluency**

• **Describing Details** James found details from the story to tell about each hat and support his opinion about Horse's hat. **Trait: Ideas**

• **Words That Join** James used the conjunction *because* to join two sentences. **Grammar**

Point out that James used a topic sentence to tell his opinion at the beginning of his writing.

Go Digital

Graphic Organizer

Writing

I see a fish.

Grammar

Your Turn: Write an Opinion Say: *Now we will write to a new prompt.* Have children turn to page 133 of the **Reading/Writing Workshop**. Read the Your Turn prompt together. *Did each of the animals choose the right hat? Why or why not? Use text evidence to support your answer.*

Find Text Evidence Say: *To respond to this prompt, we need to look back at the story and illustrations and take notes. We can use this information to support our opinion about whether each animal chose the right hat.* Track the print as you reread the notes.

Write to a Prompt Say: *Our first sentence should tell our opinion about whether each animal chose the right hat. Did the animals pick the right hats?* Let children vote about whether the animals picked the right hats and then write your first sentence according to the opinion of the majority. *Now we need to give reasons to support our opinion. Let's look at our notes about each animal and the hat each chose.* Tell children you will reread the notes to find details from the story to support your opinion. Track the print as you reread the notes. Then guide children in forming complete sentences as you share the pen in writing them. Say: *Did we tell our opinion in the first sentence and write complete sentences? Did we use details from the story to support our opinion?* Read the final response as you track the print.

For additional practice with the Writing Trait, have children turn to page 222 of the **Your Turn Practice Book**.

MINILESSON
5 Mins

Grammar

Join Sentences with *so* and *because*

1 Explain/Model Remind children that two sentences can be joined together. Explain that a cause and an effect can be joined into one sentence. Write the following sentences:

> Chen is cold. He does not have his coat.
>
> Chen is cold because he does not have his coat.
>
> Barb lives far away. She rides the bus to school.
>
> Barb lives far away so she rides the bus to school.

Guide children to circle the words that join the sentences together. Explain the difference between *so* and *because*.

2 Practice Have children create new sentences using *so* and *because*.

COLLABORATE
Talk About It Act out simple cause-and-effect situations and have partners tell each other what happened using sentences with *so* and *because*.

ENGLISH LANGUAGE LEARNERS

Explain Direct children to the first combined Model sentence. *What two sentences were joined to make this sentence? How did the author join the two sentences?* Repeat for the second Model sentence.

Act Out Write cause-and-effect sentences on sentence strips. Have pairs pick a sentence and act it out for others to guess. Guide children to use the words *so* or *because* in their responses.

Daily Wrap Up

- Discuss the Essential Question and encourage children to use the oral vocabulary words. Ask: *How could we classify and categorize the hats in A Barn Full of Hats?*

- Prompt children to discuss what they learned today by asking: *How will the skills you learned help you become a better reader and writer?*

Materials

Reading/Writing Workshop
VOLUME 4

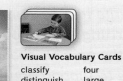 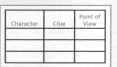
Literature Anthology
VOLUME 4

Visual Vocabulary Cards

classify	four
distinguish	large
entire	none
organize	only
startled	put
trouble	round
whole	

Teaching Poster

Character	Clue	Point of View

Interactive Read-Aloud Cards

a b c
Word-Building Cards

cart
Spelling Word Cards

Sound-Spelling Cards

(→) # Build the Concept

Go Digital

Visual Glossary

A Barn Full of Hats

MINILESSON
5 Mins

Oral Language

OBJECTIVES
Read grade-level text orally with accuracy, appropriate rate, and expression. **RF.1.4b**

Review sequence of events

ACADEMIC LANGUAGE
- *sequence, events, comma, pause*
- Cognates: *secuencia, coma*

ESSENTIAL QUESTION
Remind children that this week you have been talking and reading about how we sort and classify things. Remind them of what Goldilocks found at the bears' house and how the animals chose hats. Guide children to discuss the question using information from what they have read and talked about throughout the week.

Review Oral Vocabulary
Review the oral vocabulary words *classify, distinguish, entire, organize,* and *startled* using the Define/Example/Ask routine. Prompt children to use the words as they discuss sorting and classifying.

Visual Vocabulary Cards

Comprehension/ Fluency

MINILESSON 10 Mins — Plot: Sequence

1 **Explain** Tell children they have been learning about using point of view to help them understand the stories they read. Remind them they have also learned how to look for the sequence of events to help them understand the plot of stories. *As we read, we can think about which events happen first, next, and last. Understanding the sequence of events can help us to better understand the plot.*

Reading/Writing Workshop

2 **Model** Display pages 122 and 123 of *A Barn Full of Hats. I read in the text that some animals find a box. They open the box and see it is full of hats. This is the first event. On the next page, Hen asks who wants a hat, and Horse says he does. This is the next event.*

3 **Guided Practice/Practice** Reread *A Barn Full of Hats.* Use text evidence to identify the sequence of events in the plot.

MINILESSON 5 Mins — Phrasing: Commas

1 **Explain** Tell children that as you read the passage, you will pause slightly when you get to a comma. Explain that a comma separates one idea or piece of information from another. *A comma is also used in dialogue. The comma helps show when the character's words end and the narrator's words start again.* Point out sentences in the passage that have commas.

2 **Model** Read sentences with commas in the Shared Read. *This sentence has a comma, so I pause slightly.* Point out how the pause tells listeners there is a comma in the sentence. Also point out how you pause for other punctuation.

3 **Guided Practice/Practice** Have children reread the passage chorally. Remind them to pause when they get to a comma.

Fluency Practice Children can practice using Practice Book passages.

→ # Word Work

MINILESSON
5 Mins

Phonemic Awareness

OBJECTIVES

CCSS Orally produce single-syllable words by blending sounds (phonemes), including consonant blends. **RF.1.2b**

CCSS Decode regularly spelled one-syllable words. **RF.1.3b**

Recognize and use irregular plurals

Phoneme Blending

① Model Show children how to blend sounds to form words. *I am going to say a word sound by sound. Listen carefully to these sounds: /f/ /är/. Now listen as I blend the sounds: /fffär/,* far. *The word is* far. *Repeat with* farm.

② Guided Practice/Practice Have children practice blending sounds to say a word. Guide practice with the first three. *Let's do some together. I will say a word sound by sound. Then we will blend the sounds to say a word.* Pronounce the /är/ sounds together.

/är/ /t/   /k/ /är/   /sh/ /är/ /p/   /y/ /är/ /d/

/s/ /t/ /är/   /d/ /är/ /t/   /l/ /är/ /j/   /s/ /m/ /är/ /t/

MINILESSON
5 Mins

Phonics

Blend Words with /är/ *ar*

① Model Display **Word-Building Cards** *h, a, r, m.* Model how to blend the sounds. *This is the letter* h. *It stands for /h/. These are the letters* a *and* r. *Together they stand for /är/. This is the letter* m. *It stands for /m/. Let's blend the sounds: /härmmm/. The word is* harm. Continue by modeling the words *scar, charge, shark,* and *start.*

② Guided Practice/Practice Review the words and sentences on the Day 3 Phonics Practice Activity with children. Read each word in the first row, blending the sounds; for example: */l/ /är/ /j/; /lllärj/. The word is* large.

Have children blend each word with you. Prompt children to read the connected text, sounding out the decodable words.

large	farm	barn	sharp	smart
marsh	mark	dark	spark	charge
man	men	foot	feet	sheep
child	children	tooth	teeth	mice
barnyard	postcard	bookmark	charcoal

Mars is a planet far away.

Mark put large jars in his cart at the market.

Also online

Day 3 Phonics Practice Activity

Decodable Reader Have children read "Charm Scarves" (pages 1–4) to practice decoding words in connected text.

MINILESSON 5 Mins

Structural Analysis

Irregular Plurals

1 Model Write and read the words *child* and *children*. Review that *child* means "one child" and *children* means "more than one child." Use the words in sentences: *One child runs to the swings. Many children go down the slide.*

2 Practice/Apply Write: *man, ox, foot, person, fish.* As you point to and read each word, ask children to repeat it and say its plural form. Write the plural forms beside the singular forms. Then have children use the words in sentences to show their meaning.

Corrective Feedback

Corrective Feedback Say: *My turn.* Then lead children in blending the sounds. Say: *Do it with me.* You will respond with children to offer support. Then say: *Your turn. Blend.* Have children chorally blend. Return to the beginning of the word. Say: *Let's start over.*

Word Work

Quick Review

High-Frequency Words: Read, Spell, and Write to review this week's high-frequency words: *four, none, only, large, put, round.*

MINILESSON 5 Mins

Spelling

OBJECTIVES

CCSS Use conventional spelling for words with common spelling patterns and for frequently occurring irregular words. **L.1.2d**

CCSS Use sentence-level context as a clue to the meaning of a word or phrase. **L.1.4a**

-art, -arn, -arm Word Families

1 Model Make index cards for *-art, -arn, -arm* and form three columns in a pocket chart. Blend the sounds with children.

Hold up the *cart* **Spelling Word Card**. Say and spell *cart*. Pronounce each sound clearly: /k/ /är/ /t/. Blend the sounds, emphasizing the /är/ sounds: /kärt/. Place the word below the *-art* card. Repeat this step with the word *art*.

2 Guided Practice/Practice Have children spell each word. Repeat the process with the *-arn* and *-arm* words.

Display *happy, key, four,* and *none* in a separate column. Read and spell the words together. Point out that they do not contain the /är/ sounds.

Conclude by asking children to orally generate additional words that rhyme with each word. Write the additional words on the board.

Go Digital

er	ir	or	ur
her			
girl curb			word

Spelling Word Families

school

Visual Glossary

MINILESSON 5 Mins

High-Frequency Words

PHONICS/SPELLING PRACTICE BOOK p. 103

four, large, none, only, put, round

1 Guided Practice Say each word and have children Read/Spell/Write it. Point out the /ů/ sound spelled *u* in *put*.

Display **Visual Vocabulary Cards** to review this week's words.

Read the spelling words in the box.

cart	barn	arm	art
yarn	harm	four	none

Find the spelling words in the puzzle. Draw a circle around each word.

c	u	x	s	p	j	k	i	e
a	k	i	y	a	g	m	s	w
r	t	b	a	r	b	a	r	n
t	j	r	s	t	v	a	r	m
g	z	f	m	u	y	j	m	e
a	q	o	f	b	a	k	u	i
t	j	u	x	m	r	g	t	v
s	h	r	u	a	n	o	n	e
c	r	s	w	t	c	f	r	p
g	h	a	r	m	b	q	y	f

Visual Vocabulary Cards

2 Practice Repeat the activity with last week's words.

Build Fluency: Word Automaticity

Have children read the following sentences aloud together at the same pace. Repeat several times.

> Mom put four round cookies into the jar.
>
> Once I ate two, only two were left.
>
> Dad ate two. Now there are none left.

Word Bank

Review the current and previous words in the word bank. Discuss with children which words should be removed, or added back, from previous high-frequency word lists.

MINILESSON 5 Mins

Vocabulary

trouble, whole

Review Use the **Visual Vocabulary Cards** to review this week's words using the Define/Example/Ask routine. Have partners generate context sentences for each vocabulary word.

Visual Vocabulary Cards

Strategy: Context Clues/ Multiple Meanings

1 Model Tell children that some words have more than one meaning. Use *A Barn Full of Hats* to model how to figure out which meaning of a word is used.

Think Aloud In *A Barn Full of Hats*, we read the sentence: "'I do!' cried Horse." I know *cried* can have more than one meaning. Someone can cry tears when they feel very sad. *Cried* can also mean "yelled out with excitement." I use the context, or other words, to figure out that in this sentence *cried* means "yelled out with excitement," since Horse is not sad.

2 Guided Practice Help children say sentences for each meaning of *cried*. Then have children look in the story for these words that have more than one meaning: *box, fine, play.* Discuss the meanings used in the story. Then have children say sentences for the other meanings.

3 Practice Have partners find *trouble* in the story and discuss what it means. Then have them use *trouble* in sentences to show other meanings, such as, *I got into trouble because I didn't make my bed.* Repeat for *whole.*

A Lost Button
from Frog and Toad Are Friends
by Arnold Lobel

Genre Fantasy

Essential Question
How can we classify and categorize things?
Read about what happens when Toad loses his button.

Go Digital!

140

141

LITERATURE ANTHOLOGY, pp. 140–141

A Lost Button

CLOSE READING

Lexile 340

Literature Anthology

Close Reading Routine

Read   DOK 1–2

• Identify key ideas and details about how we see and sort things.
• Take notes and retell.
• Use **A C T** prompts as needed.

Reread   DOK 2–3

• Analyze the text, craft, and structure.
• Use *Close Reading Companion,* pp. 133–135.

Integrate   DOK 4

• Integrate knowledge and ideas.
• Make text-to-text connections.
• Use the Integrate Lesson.

Read

ESSENTIAL QUESTION

Read aloud the Essential Question: *How can we classify and categorize things?* Tell children to think about how the characters classify and categorize buttons in the story. Read aloud the title. Ask: *What do you predict this story will be about?*

Story Words Read and spell the words *meadow, house, hurt, worry, lose, square, covered,* and *sewed.* Review word meaning as needed. Explain that children will read these words in the selection.

Note Taking: Graphic Organizer As children read the selection, guide them to fill in **Your Turn Practice Book** page 214.

Toad and Frog
went for a long walk.
They walked across
a **large** meadow.
They walked in the woods.
They walked along the river.
At last they went back home
to Toad's house.
"Oh, drat," said Toad. **1**

"Not **only** do my feet hurt,
but I have lost
one of the buttons on my jacket."

142   143

LITERATURE ANTHOLOGY, pp. 142–143

1 Skill: Point of View

Teacher Think Aloud Point of view is the way a character thinks or feels. What characters say helps us understand their point of view. Toad says, "Oh, drat." That tells me Toad is upset. Let's think about what each character says and how that tells us about its point of view.

2 Strategy: Make and Confirm Predictions

Teacher Think Aloud Before I read a story, I read the title and look at the illustrations to predict what it will be about. The title is *The Lost Button*. The illustrations look like Toad has lost a coat button and finds many buttons. I think he will find his lost button. I will read on to see if my prediction is correct.

A C T Access Complex Text

▶ **What makes this text complex?**

- **Organization** In this story, dialogue is the primary means of telling the story. Children may be unfamiliar with a story that is organized in this way.

- **Connection of Ideas** Many buttons are found and are compared to the button Toad lost. Children must understand that each button is different.

Build Vocabulary page 142
meadow: a field of grass and flowers

"Don't worry," said Frog. **3**
"We will go back
to all the places where we walked.
We will soon find your button."
They walked back to the large meadow.
They began to look for the button
in the tall grass.

144

"Here is your button!" cried Frog.
"That is not my button," said Toad.
"That button is black.
My button was white."
Toad **put** the black button
in his pocket. **4**

145

LITERATURE ANTHOLOGY, pp. 144–145

Read

3 Skill: Point of View

What does Frog say to Toad? What does this tell the reader about Frog's point of view about finding the lost button? Let's add this information to the Point of View chart.

Character	Clue	Point of View
Frog	Frog says not to worry.	Frog is calm and patient.

4 Reread

Teacher Think Aloud After reading page 145, I realize I don't understand if Frog found Toad's button. I will reread to follow what Frog and Toad are saying. Now I understand. Frog thought he found Toad's button, but the button he found is not the same color as Toad's lost button.

5 Strategy: Make and Confirm Predictions

Teacher Think Aloud I stop and think about the prediction I made before reading. I was correct that Toad lost a button. I wonder if my prediction that he will find his button is correct. I could change my prediction, but I still think Toad will find it. I will read to see if my prediction is correct.

A sparrow flew down.
"Excuse me," said the sparrow.
"Did you lose a button? I found one."
"That is not my button," said Toad.
"That button has two holes.
My button had **four** holes."
Toad put the button with two holes
in his pocket. 5

146

They went back to the woods
and looked on the dark paths.
"Here is your button," said Frog.
"That is not my button," cried Toad. 6
"That button is small.
My button was big."
Toad put the small button
in his pocket.

147

LITERATURE ANTHOLOGY, pp. 146–147

6 **Skill: Point of View**

COLLABORATE

Discuss with a partner how Toad feels when he learns the button Frog found is not the right one. Discuss what clues in the text tell how Toad feels.

Reread   *Close Reading Companion,* 133

Author's Craft: Dialogue

Reread page 144. How does the author use dialogue to show that Frog is a good friend to Toad? (When Toad is upset about losing his button, Frog tells his friend not to worry because he will help him look for it, and he did.)

Build Vocabulary page 146
sparrow: a small brown bird

A C T Access Complex Text

▶ **Connection of Ideas**

Children may need help understanding that multiple buttons have been found and that each is being compared to Toad's lost button.

Review the pages you have read and point out each of the three buttons that have been found. Explain that Frog has found two buttons and the sparrow has found one. Review how each button is different from Toad's lost button.

A raccoon came out from behind a tree.
"I heard that you were looking
for a button," he said.
"Here is one that I just found."
"That is not my button!" wailed Toad.
"That button is square.
My button was **round**."
Toad put the square button
in his pocket.

148

Frog and Toad went back to the river.
They looked for the button
in the mud.
"Here is your button," said Frog.
"That is not my button!" shouted Toad. **7**
"That button is thin.
My button was thick."

149

LITERATURE ANTHOLOGY, pp. 148–149

A **C** **T** **A**ccess **C**omplex **T**ext

▶ Organization

Children not familiar with a story told through dialogue
may have trouble following the action.

Have children do a theater reading of pages
142–148, taking the roles of narrator, Toad, Frog,
the sparrow, and the raccoon. Have them identify
who is telling the story (the narrator). Point out
the narrator is not a character, but is outside
telling the action in the story. Discuss how the
dialogue tells how the characters feel, their
problems, and their points of view.

Read

7 **Skill: Point of View**

On page 149, Toad shouts, "That is not my
button!" What does this tell us about Toad's point
of view? (When someone is upset and mad, they
sometimes shout. Toad is upset that everyone finds
buttons, but not one of them is his lost button.)
Let's add this to our chart.

Character	Clue	Point of View
Frog	Frog says not to worry.	Frog is calm and patient.
Toad	Toad shouts.	Toad is upset and mad.

Toad put the thin button
in his pocket. He was very angry.
He jumped up and down
and screamed,
"The **whole** world
is covered with buttons,
and not one of them is mine!"

150

Toad ran home and slammed the door.
There, on the floor,
he saw his white, four-holed,
big, round, thick button. **8**
"Oh," said Toad.
"It was here all the time.
What a lot of **trouble**
I have made for Frog."

151

LITERATURE ANTHOLOGY, pp. 150–151

---

8 Structural Analysis: Syllabication

Remember, when we read longer words, we can look for how many vowels to help us know how many syllables. *Button* has two vowels, and both are short. It is a closed-syllable word.

Build Vocabulary pages 150 and 151
screamed: yelled
slammed: shut with force and noise

Reread   *Close Reading Companion,* 134

Author's Craft: Word Choice

Reread page 149. What do we learn about Toad when the author says Toad shouted? (Toad shouts because he is tired and upset that he can't find his button.)

Illustrator's Craft

Reread page 151. How does the illustration help you understand how Toad is a good friend? (The text says Toad knows he made a lot of trouble for Frog. In the illustration, Toad looks sad. He is feeling sorry for how he treated his friend.)

Toad took all of the buttons
out of his pocket.
He took his sewing box
down from the shelf.
Toad sewed the buttons
all over his jacket.

152

The next day Toad gave
his jacket to Frog.
Frog thought that it was beautiful.
He put it on and jumped for joy.
None of the buttons fell off.
Toad had sewed them on very well.

153

LITERATURE ANTHOLOGY, pp. 152–153

Read

Skill: Point of View

What can we add about Frog at the end of the story? What clues tell how Frog feels? Let's add these details about Frog to our chart. Review the chart and discuss how each character's point of view is different and how a character's point of view can change.

Return to Purposes

Review children's predictions. Ask children if their predictions were correct. Guide them to use evidence in the text to confirm their predictions. Discuss what they learned about classifying buttons by reading the story. Ask if they learned what they wanted to know by reading the story.

Character	Clue	Point of View
Frog	Frog says not to worry.	Frog is calm and patient.
Toad	Toad shouts.	Toad is upset and mad.
Frog	Frog jumped for joy.	Frog is happy to get the jacket.

Meet Arnold Lobel

Arnold Lobel was often sick and missed many days of school when he was young. When he went back to school, he made friends by telling stories and drawing pictures.

Many years later, Lobel's children liked to catch frogs and toads. Lobel loved the animals and wrote about them in his Frog and Toad stories.

Author's Purpose

Arnold Lobel wanted to write about good friends. Write about your friend. Tell how you help each other.

154

LITERATURE ANTHOLOGY, p. 154

Meet the Author/Illustrator

Arnold Lobel

Read aloud page 154 with children. Ask them why they think Arnold Lobel wrote about a frog and a toad. *What got Arnold Lobel started as a writer and illustrator? How did he first learn about frogs and toads?*

Author's Purpose

Have children write about how friends help each other. Use sentence starters: *My friend _____ and I help each other. I _____ my friend. My friend _____ me.*

AUTHOR'S CRAFT

Focus on Repetition

Guide children to see Arnold Lobel uses one sentence over and over to add humor and feelings to the story.

- *What sentence does Toad say on both pages 145 and 147?* (That is not my button.)

- *How is the punctuation different for this repeating sentence on page 148?* (It ends in an exclamation point.)

- *What does this tell about how Toad feels?* (He is getting more excited.)

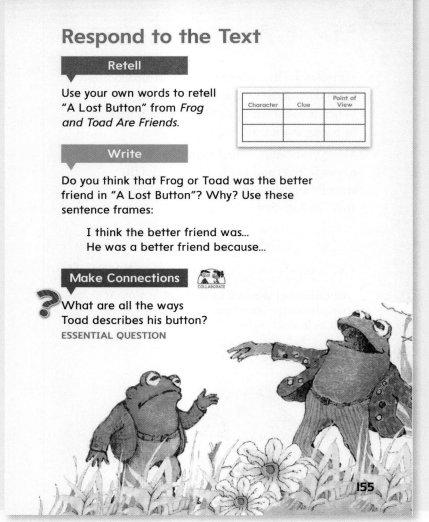

Respond to the Text

Retell

Use your own words to retell "A Lost Button" from *Frog and Toad Are Friends.*

Character	Clue	Point of View

Write

Do you think that Frog or Toad was the better friend in "A Lost Button"? Why? Use these sentence frames:

I think the better friend was...
He was a better friend because...

Make Connections

What are all the ways Toad describes his button?
ESSENTIAL QUESTION

155

LITERATURE ANTHOLOGY, p. 155

Respond to the Text

Read

Retell

Guide children in retelling the selection. Remind them that as they read *A Lost Button,* they paid attention to each character's point of view. Have children use the information they recorded on their Point of View chart to help them retell the story.

Reread

Analyze the Text

After children read and retell the selection, have them reread *A Lost Button* to develop a deeper understanding of the text by answering the questions on pages 133–135 of the *Close Reading Companion*. For students who need support finding text evidence to support their responses, use the scaffolded instruction from the Reread prompts on pages T35D–T35F.

Write About the Text

Review the writing prompt with students. Remind them to use their responses from the *Close Reading Companion* and cite text evidence to support their answers.

For a full lesson on writing a response supported by text evidence, see pages T36–T37.

<u>Answer:</u> Opinions will vary, but children should write complete sentences and support their opinions with details from the text. <u>Evidence:</u> On pages 144–149, Frog helps Toad look for his button. On pages 149–150, Toad yells at Frog because he is frustrated. On page 151, Toad finds his button and feels badly about how he treated Frog. On pages 152–153, Toad makes something for Frog to show he is sorry.

Integrate

Make Connections
COLLABORATE

Essential Question Answers will vary, but remind children to use text evidence from *A Lost Button* to help them tell the ways Toad describes his button.

<u>Answer:</u> Toad describes his button as big, round, thick, and white, with four holes. <u>Evidence:</u> On page 145, Toad says his button is white. On page 146, Toad says his button has four holes. On page 147, Toad describes his button as big. On page 148, Toad says his button is round. On page 149, Toad knows the button Frog finds is not his button because it is thin instead of thick.

ELL

ENGLISH LANGUAGE LEARNERS

Retell Help children by looking at each page of the story and asking a prompt, such as: *What are Frog and Toad doing?* Provide sentence starters to help children retell the selection, such as: *Toad lost a _____. Frog and Toad look for the _____. Toad finds the button _____. Toad _____.*

CONNECT TO CONTENT
SORTING OBJECTS

Remind children they have been learning about how they can classify and categorize objects. Review the story and guide children to name the different ways in which Toad classifies the buttons Frog and the other characters find. Discuss the observable features the characters use to classify the buttons.

STEM

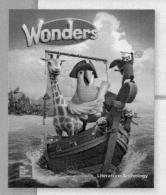

Literature Anthology

OBJECTIVES

CCSS Write opinion pieces in which they introduce the topic or name the book they are writing about, state an opinion, supply a reason for the opinion, and provide some sense of closure. **W.1.1**

CCSS Use frequently occurring conjunctions (e.g., *and, but, or, so, because*). **L.1.1g**

CCSS Produce and expand complete simple and compound declarative, interrogative, imperative, and exclamatory sentences in response to prompt. **L.1.1j**

ACADEMIC LANGUAGE

- *evidence, notes, draft, prewrite, details*
- Cognates: *evidencia, notas, detalles*

MINILESSON 5 Mins

Independent Writing

Write About the Literature Anthology

Analyze the Prompt Have children turn to page 155 in the **Literature Anthology**. Read the prompt: *In A Lost Button, do you think Frog or Toad was the better friend? Why?* Say: *The first part of this prompt is asking for your opinion about which character was the better friend. The second part of the prompt asks you to explain your opinion using evidence from the text.*

Find Text Evidence Say: *To respond to the prompt, we need to find evidence in the text and illustrations. What can we tell about how Frog and Toad treat each other?* Have children take notes as they look for evidence to respond to the prompt. Tell children they can use text evidence to make inferences about which character is a better friend to the other.

Write to the Prompt Guide children as they begin their writing.

- **Prewrite** Have children review their notes and plan their writing. Guide them to think about the evidence they wrote in their notes and the inferences they made as they decide which character was the better friend. Then guide children to organize their ideas and choose details to support their writing.

- **Draft** Have children write a response to the prompt. Remind them to begin their writing with a topic sentence that states their opinion. As children write their drafts, have them focus on the week's skills.

  - **Complete Sentences** Use complete sentences so their writing will make sense to the reader. **Trait: Sentence Fluency**

  - **Describing Details** Use details from the story that support their opinion. **Trait: Ideas**

  - **Words That Join** Use conjunctions to join sentences. **Grammar**

Tell children they will continue to work on their responses on Day 4.

Grammar

5 Mins · MINILESSON

Join Sentences with *and, but, or*

1 Review Have children look at page 133 in the **Reading/Writing Workshop**. Remind them that *and, but, or, so,* and *because* are words that are used to join sentences together. Ask children to identify the conjunction in the model sentence.

Say: *Tell me the joining word in this sentence:* Horse picked Farmer Clark's hat because it was large and floppy. *The word* because *is used to join the two sentences "Horse picked Farmer Clark's hat" and "It was large and floppy."*

2 Guided Practice/Practice Guide children to join two other sentences in James's writing using a conjunction. Have them work with partners to write new sentences and circle the conjunctions.

Talk About It Have partners work together to orally generate new sentences with conjunctions.

Mechanics: Capitalize Proper Nouns

1 Explain Remind children that the names of specific places are proper nouns. Proper nouns begin with capital letters.

2 Guided Practice Prompt children to correct each sentence.

Let's go play in barney park. (Let's go play in Barney Park.)

We got peaches at stone farm. (We got peaches at Stone Farm.)

Daily Wrap Up

- Review the Essential Question and encourage children to discuss using the oral vocabulary words. Ask: *How might you classify and categorize your responses about Frog and Toad?*

- Prompt children to review and discuss the skills they used today.

Materials

Visual Vocabulary Cards

classify	four
distinguish	large
entire	none
organize	only
startled	put
trouble	round
whole	

Literature Anthology
VOLUME 4

Teaching Poster

a b c

Word-Building Cards

cart

Spelling Word Cards

My Name | clouds-- puffy and white
sun | birds-- flying fast

Dinah Zike's **FOLDABLES**

→ # Extend the Concept

CLOSE READING

MINILESSON **5** Mins

Sort It Out

OBJECTIVES

CCSS Use the illustrations and details in a text to describe its key ideas. **RI.1.7**

Review vocabulary

ACADEMIC LANGUAGE

• *photograph, illustration*

• Cognates: *fotografía, ilustración*

ESSENTIAL QUESTION

Remind children that this week they have been learning about how we sort and classify things. Guide children to discuss the question using information from what they have read and discussed. Use the Define/Example/Ask routine to review the oral vocabulary words *classify, distinguish, entire, organize,* and *startled.* Then review last week's oral vocabulary words *advice, career, remarkable, soothe,* and *trust.*

Text Feature: Photographs and Illustrations

1 **Explain** Tell children they can use nonfiction selections to find facts and details. Explain that nonfiction text often has photographs or illustrations that go with the text. We can use photographs and illustrations to learn important facts and details.

2 **Model** Display Teaching Poster 12. Point to the left-hand photograph. *This photograph shows a real classroom. We can use the photograph to find facts and details. I can see there is one teacher with many children. I can see maps on the wall and books on the shelves. This tells me what the children learn in school.*

3 **Guided Practice/Practice** Point to the right-hand photograph. Guide children to identify the details in the photograph. *What are the raccoons doing?* Tell children to look for information in photographs and illustrations as they read informational texts.

Close Reading

Compare Texts

Tell children as they read "Sort It Out," they should think about how the buttons in *The Lost Button* could be sorted. Point out the words *alike, different,* and *sort.*

Go Digital

Visual Glossary

Teaching Poster

"Sort It Out"

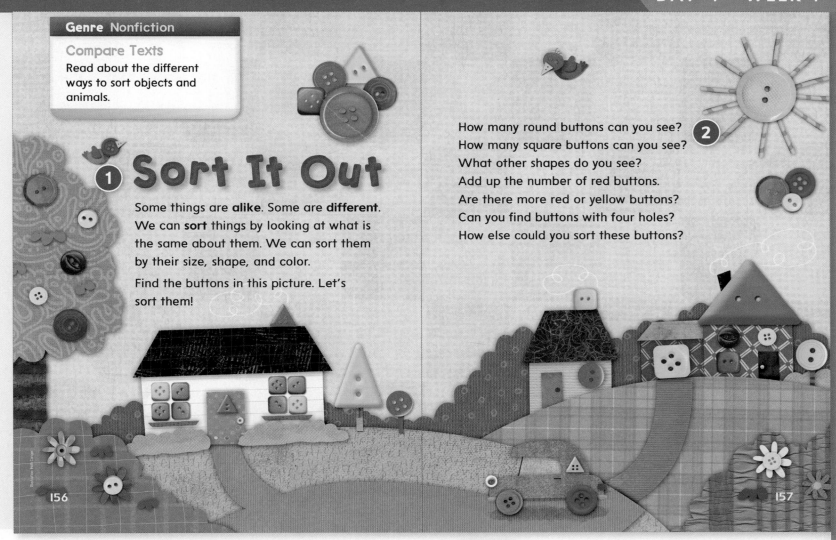

Genre Nonfiction

Compare Texts
Read about the different ways to sort objects and animals.

Sort It Out

Some things are **alike**. Some are **different**. We can **sort** things by looking at what is the same about them. We can sort them by their size, shape, and color.

Find the buttons in this picture. Let's sort them!

How many round buttons can you see?
How many square buttons can you see?
What other shapes do you see?
Add up the number of red buttons.
Are there more red or yellow buttons?
Can you find buttons with four holes?
How else could you sort these buttons?

156
157

LITERATURE ANTHOLOGY, pp. 156–157

Lexile 210

Read

❶ Strategy: Make and Confirm Predictions

Teacher Think Aloud I read the title, "Sort It Out," and I look at the illustrations. I know when we sort things we look at what is the same about them. I see buttons all over the illustration. I think we will sort them. I look at the illustrations on pages 157–161. I wonder what we might sort on these pages. I predict sorting animals and sorting by activities. I will read on to see if my predictions are correct.

❷ Text Feature: Use Illustrations

Teacher Think Aloud I remember that, like photographs, illustrations can give information about nonfiction text. The text says to find the buttons in the picture. I see buttons in the sky, trees, flowers, windows, chimneys, garage, cars, and on the sun. I will use the illustration to answer the questions in the text.

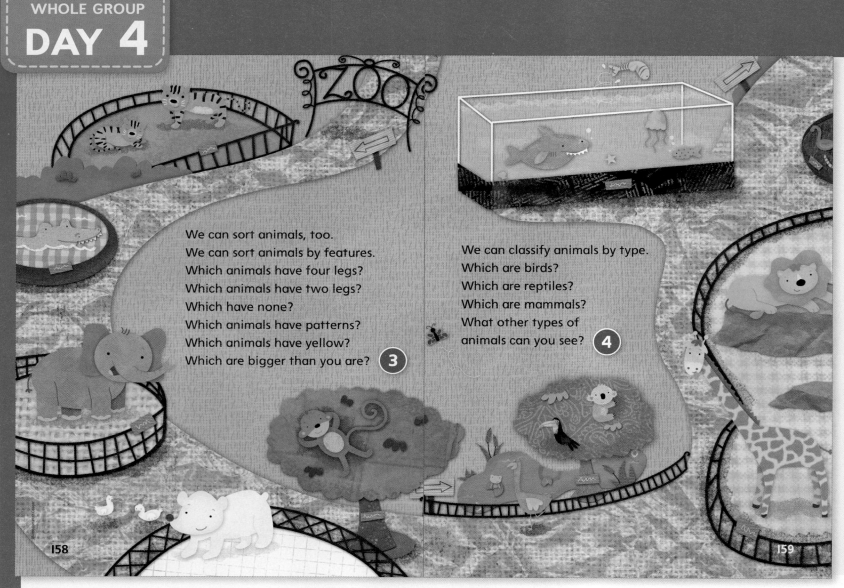

We can sort animals, too.
We can sort animals by features.
Which animals have four legs?
Which animals have two legs?
Which have none?
Which animals have patterns?
Which animals have yellow?
Which are bigger than you are? **3**

We can classify animals by type.
Which are birds?
Which are reptiles?
Which are mammals?
What other types of
animals can you see? **4**

158

159

LITERATURE ANTHOLOGY, pp. 158–159

Read

❸ Text Features: Use Illustrations

Teacher Think Aloud I use the illustration of the zoo to answer the questions in the text. Tigers, alligators, elephants, monkeys, bears, koalas, giraffes, and lions all have four legs.

❹ Text Features: Use Illustrations

Which animals in the illustration are birds? (parrot, flamingo, ducks) Which animals are mammals? (tigers, elephant, monkey, koala, giraffe, lion) What other ways can we sort animals? (Possible responses: animals that live in water, that run, that fly, that swim, that have fur)

❺ Text Features: Use Illustrations

How can we sort things in this scene by the way they move? (things that float, walk, move on wheels, jump, fly) How can we sort the food in the illustration? (Possible response: things we drink and things we eat) What are some other ways you can use the illustration to sort things? (by activities people do in a park, by types of landforms, by ways people travel)

Retell

Guide children to use key details to retell the selection.

There are lots of ways to sort the things in this scene. Think of as many ways as you can.

Sorting is a lot of fun! Let's sort things in this scene. Think about what they have in common.

Which of these things have wheels?
Which eat food?
Which can fly?
Which have stripes?
Which have windows?
Which would you play with?

160

Make Connections

How can we sort objects?
How can we sort animals?
Essential Question

161

LITERATURE ANTHOLOGY, pp. 160–161

Reread

After children retell, have them reread to develop a deeper understanding of the text by annotating and answering the questions on pages 136–138 of the *Close Reading Companion*. For children who need support citing text evidence, use these Reread questions:

- How do the illustrations help you understand the selection?

- Why do you think the author asks questions in "Sort It Out?"

Integrate

Make Connections
COLLABORATE

Essential Question Have children use text evidence from *Sort It Out* to tell how we can sort objects and animals.

CONNECT TO CONTENT
SCIENCE
SORTING OBJECTS

Remind children that this week they have been classifying and categorizing things by their observable features. *What are some things we categorized in this selection? What features did we use to sort them? What categories did we create?*

STEM

→ Word Work

Quick Review

Build Fluency: Sound-Spellings
Display the **Word-Building Cards**: *ar, ey, igh, oa, oe, ee, ea, ai, ay, e_e, u_e, o_e, dge, i_e, a_e, ch, tch, wh, ph, th, sh, ng, mp, sk, st, nt, nk, nd, _ce, _ge.* Have children say the sounds.

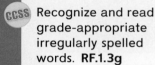

Phonemic Awareness

OBJECTIVES

CCSS Isolate and pronounce initial, medial vowel, and final sounds (phonemes) in spoken single-syllable words. **RF.1.2c**

CCSS Recognize and read grade-appropriate irregularly spelled words. **RF.1.3g**

- Recognize and use irregular plurals
- Use synonyms to expand vocabulary

Phoneme Categorization

❶ **Model** Show children how to categorize phonemes. *Listen:* barn, wait, marsh. Barn *and* marsh *have the* /är/ *sounds.* Wait *does not.* Wait *does not belong.*

❷ **Guided Practice/Practice** Have children practice. Do the first one together. *I will say three words. Tell me which word does not belong and why.*

part, harm, chase   match, harp, cat   horn, mark, force

night, like, dare   cart, feel, charm   boat, sharp, charge

Phonics/Structural Analysis

Build Words with /är/ *ar*

Review *The sounds* /är/ *can be represented by the letters* ar. *We'll use* **Word-Building Cards** *to build words with the* /är/ *sounds.*

Place the letters *t, a, r. Let's blend the sounds together and read the word:* /tär/. *Now let's change the* t *to* f. Blend the sounds and read the word: *far*. Continue with *farm, charm, chart, cart, car, bar, bark, barn, yarn, yard, hard, harp, sharp, shark.*

Decodable Reader   Have children read "Car Parts" (pages 5–8) to practice decoding words in connected text.

Irregular Plurals

Review Remind children that some words do not add *-s* or *-es* to make them mean "more than one." Write and read *woman* and *women*. Underline *a* and *e*. Discuss how *woman* was changed to make it mean "more than one woman." Then use the words in sentences.

Write: *foot, man, child, sheep, children, feet, men.* Have partners sort the words into singular and plural. Then have them use the words in sentences: for example, *I see one short man and three tall men.*

Go Digital

Phonemic Awareness

Phonics

Structural Analysis

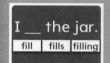

Spelling Word Sort

Visual Glossary

Spelling

Word Sort with *-art, -arn, -arm*

Review Provide pairs of children with copies of the **Spelling Word Cards**. While one partner reads the words one at a time, the other partner should orally segment the word and then write the word. After reading all the words, partners should switch roles.

Have children correct their own papers. Then have them sort the words by ending spelling pattern: *-art, -arn, -arm,* or no *ar* pattern.

High-Frequency Words

four, large, none, only, put, round

Review Display **Visual Vocabulary Cards** for high-frequency words *four, large, none, only, put, round.* Have children Read/Spell/Write each word.

- Point to a word and call on a child to use it in a sentence.
- Review last week's words using the same procedure.

Expand Vocabulary

trouble, whole

Have children use the Visual Vocabulary Cards to review the vocabulary words *trouble* and *whole.*

1 Explain Explain to children that a word part can be added to a word to make a new word. Write *trouble* and *troublemaker* on the board. Explain to children that a troublemaker is someone who makes trouble, or does something wrong.

2 Model Ask children for examples of what a troublemaker might do. Help them come up with sentences using the word.

3 Guided Practice Have partners write sentences using *trouble* and *troublemaker.* Then have them share their sentences with another pair of children.

Monitor and *Differentiate*

✓ Quick Check

Can children read and decode words with *r*-controlled vowel *ar*?

Can children recognize and read high-frequency and vocabulary words?

Small Group Instruction

If No → | Approaching | Reteach pp. T56–59
| ELL | Develop pp. T70–77
If Yes → | On Level | Review pp. T64–65
| Beyond Level | Extend pp. T68–69

→ # Language Arts

Literature Anthology

OBJECTIVES

CCSS With guidance and support from adults, focus on a topic, respond to questions and suggestions from peers, and add details to strengthen writing as needed. **W.1.5**

CCSS Use frequently occurring conjunctions (e.g., *and, but, or, so, because*) **L.1.1g**

CCSS Produce complete sentences when appropriate to task and situation. **SL.1.6**

ACADEMIC LANGUAGE

- *complete sentence, details, revision, errors*
- Cognates: *detalles, revisión, errores*

MINILESSON
5 Mins

Independent Writing

Write About the Literature Anthology

Revise

Reread the prompt about *A Lost Button*: In A Lost Button, *do you think Frog or Toad was the better friend? Why?* Have children read their drafts to see if they responded to the prompt. Then have them check for:

- **Complete Sentences** Did they use complete sentences so their writing makes sense? **Trait: Sentence Fluency**

- **Describing Details** Did they find describing details in the story and use them to support their opinion? **Trait: Ideas**

- **Words That Join** Did they use conjunctions to join sentences? **Grammar**

COLLABORATE **Peer Review** Have children work in pairs to do a peer review and read their partner's draft. Ask partners to check that the response includes a topic sentence that tells their opinion, complete sentences, and describing details. They should take notes about what they liked most about the writing, questions they have for the author, and additional ideas they think the author could include. Have partners discuss these topics. Provide time for them to make revisions.

Proofread/Edit

Have children check for the following:

- Conjunctions are used to join sentences.
- Names are capitalized.
- Singular and plural nouns are used with matching verbs.

COLLABORATE **Peer Edit** Next, have partners exchange their drafts and take turns reviewing them against the checklist. Encourage partners to discuss and fix errors together.

Go Digital

Writing

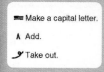

■ Make a capital letter.
Λ Add.
✒ Take out.

Proofreader's Marks

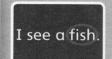

I see a fish.

Grammar

Final Draft

After children edit their writing and finish their peer edits, have them write their final draft. Tell children to write neatly so others can read their writing. Or, work with children to explore a variety of digital tools to produce and publish their writing, including collaborating with peers. Have them include details that help make their writing clear and interesting and add a drawing if needed to make their ideas clear.

Teacher Conference As children work, conference with them to provide guidance. Check to make sure they are writing complete sentences and including describing details to support their opinions.

MINILESSON
5 Mins

Grammar

Join Sentences with *so* and *because*

1 Review Review with children that *so* and *because* are used to join two sentences when there is a cause and effect.

2 Guided Practice Guide children to identify the joining words as you say some sentences.

> We were late for the bus so we had to run.
>
> Carly gave back the jar of jam because it was too tart.

3 Practice Display the following sentences. Have children complete the sentences with *so* or *because*.

> I can't come over and play ____ I have to help my dad. (because)
>
> The joke was funny ____ I laughed. (so)
>
> My dog got very muddy ____ I had to wash her. (so)

COLLABORATE

Talk About It Have partners work together to orally generate questions with *so* and *because*.

Mechanics: Capitalize Proper Nouns

1 Review Remind children that specific place names begin with a capital letter.

2 Practice Display sentences with errors. Read each aloud. Have children work together to fix the sentences.

> Gran lives in des arc, Arkansas. (Gran lives in Des Arc, Arkansas.)
>
> We Hiked in big bend park. (We hiked in Big Bend Park.)

Daily Wrap Up

- Review the Essential Question and encourage children to discuss it using the oral vocabulary words. Ask: *What did you learn to classify this week?*

- Prompt children to discuss the skills they practiced and learned today by asking, *What skills did you use today?*

→ Integrate Ideas

OBJECTIVES

CCSS Participate in shared research and writing projects. **W.1.7**

- Build background knowledge
- Research information using technology

RESEARCH AND INQUIRY

Make a Graph

Tell children that today they will do a research project with a partner to learn more about classifying and categorizing objects. Begin by gathering an assortment of classroom objects, such as books, toys, clothing, maps, school supplies, and art supplies.

STEP 1 **Choose a Topic**

Help children categorize each object according to its function. Have children make a list of the categories. Guide partners to pick which categories they want to include in their graphs.

STEP 2 **Find Resources**

Discuss how to use what children have read and talked about during the week to categorize the objects according to how they are used. Guide them to find examples of graphs in reference books and online. Have children use the Research Process Checklist online.

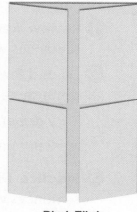

STEP 3 **Keep Track of Ideas**

Have children make a Four-Door Foldable® to record the categories for their graphs.

Dinah Zike's
FOLDABLES

Go Digital

Resources: Research and Inquiry

Collaborative Conversations

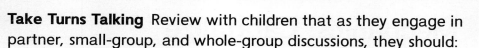

Take Turns Talking Review with children that as they engage in partner, small-group, and whole-group discussions, they should:

- take turns talking and not speak over others.
- raise their hand if they want to speak.
- ask others to share their ideas and opinions.

STEP 4 **Create the Project: Graph**

Explain the characteristics of a graph.

- **Information** A graph can give information about how many there are of something. In this project, the graph will give information about how many objects they categorized and what the categories are.

- **Numbers and Bars** A graph can have numbers along one side and bars along the other side. In this project, each bar will represent a category. The length of the bar will show how many objects are in the category.

- **Labels** A graph can have labels to name what is shown in the graph. In this project, the labels will tell what category each bar represents.

Have children create a graph showing which objects are in each category and how many objects are in each category.

- Guide them to make their bar graph and label it with the names of their categories.

- Prompt children to draw pictures of objects that are in each category.

INFORMATIVE GRAPH

ENGLISH LANGUAGE LEARNERS
SCAFFOLD

Beginning	Intermediate	Advanced/High
Use Sentence Frames Use sentence frames to help children discuss what category their objects fall into. For example: *The ____ is a ____.*	**Discuss** Guide children to focus on the function of their objects. Ask: *What is this? What is it used for?*	**Describe** Prompt children to elaborate on their objects. Ask them to tell what each object is used for and when and why it is used.

Materials

Reading/Writing Workshop
VOLUME 4

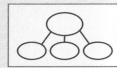

Literature Anthology
VOLUME 4

Visual Vocabulary Cards

four none only

put round large

Teaching Poster

a b c

Word-Building Cards

cart

Spelling Word Cards

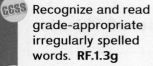

→ Word Work

MINILESSON 5 Mins

Phonemic Awareness

OBJECTIVES

CCSS Decode regularly spelled one-syllable words. **RF.1.3b**

CCSS Recognize and read grade-appropriate irregularly spelled words. **RF.1.3g**

CCSS Use conventional spelling for words with common spelling patterns and for frequently occurring irregular words. **L.1.2d**

Recognize and use irregular plurals

Phoneme Blending

Review Guide children to blend sounds to form words. *Listen as I say a group of sounds. Then blend those sounds to form a word.*

/h/ /är/ /d/   /ch/ /är/ /t/   /s/ /t/ /är/   /s/ /p/ /är/ /k/

Phoneme Segmentation

Review Guide children to segment sounds in words. *Now I am going to say a word. I want you to say each sound in the word.* Tell children that they can say the /är/ sounds together because they are difficult to pronounce separately.

car   yard   bark   charm   marsh   scarf

MINILESSON 5 Mins

Phonics/Structural Analysis

Blend and Build Words with /är/*ar*

Review Have children read and say the words *card, march, dark,* and *smart.* Then have children follow the word-building routine with **Word-Building Cards** to build *mart, cart, chart, art, arm, harm, charm, farm, far, tar, star, scar, car, bar, bark, park, spark, shark, sharp.*

Word Automaticity Help children practice word automaticity. Display decodable words and point to each word as children chorally read it. Test how many words children can read in one minute. Model blending words children miss.

Go Digital

Phonemic Awareness

m a n t p

Phonics

I __ the jar.
fill | fills | filling

Structural Analysis

school

Visual Glossary

Fluency: Word Automaticity

Irregular Plurals

Review Have children explain ways to make words mean "more than one." Have children write the plurals for: *man, child, foot, woman.*

Quick Review

Build Fluency: Sound-Spellings
Display the **Word-Building Cards**: *ar, ey, igh, oa, oe, ee, ea, ai, ay, e_e, u_e, o_e, dge, i_e a_e, ch, tch, wh, ph, th, sh, ng, mp, sk, st, nt, nk, nd, _ce, _ge.*
Have children say the sounds.

Spelling

Word Sort with *-art, -arn, -arm*

Review Have children use the **Spelling Word Cards** to sort the weekly words by vowel and ending sounds.

Assess Assess children on their abilities to spell words in the *-art, -arn,* and *-arm* word families. Say each word and provide a sentence. Then allow them time to write down the words.

High-Frequency Words

four, large, none, only, put, round

Review Display **Visual Vocabulary Cards** for the words. Have children Read/Spell/Write each word and write a sentence with each.

Review Vocabulary

trouble, whole

Review Write the words and ask children to use each in a sentence. Write the sentences and reinforce word meanings as needed.

Monitor and *Differentiate*

 Quick Check

Can children read and decode words with *r*-controlled vowel *ar*?

Can children recognize and read high-frequency and vocabulary words?

Small Group Instruction

If No → | Approaching | Reteach pp. T56–59
| ELL | Develop pp. T70–77
If Yes → | On Level | Review pp. T64–65
| Beyond Level | Extend pp. T68–69

Fluency

Phrasing

Review Review with children that a comma indicates that you should pause slightly while reading. A comma separates one idea or piece of information from another.

Read aloud from the Shared Read and have children echo. Point out how you pause when you get to a comma. Then have partners reread, working on how they read sentences with commas.

Literature Anthology

OBJECTIVES

CCSS With guidance and support from adults, use a variety of digital tools to produce and publish writing, including in collaboration with peers. **W.1.6**

CCSS Follow agreed-upon rules for discussions (e.g., listening to others with care, speaking one at a time about the topics and texts under discussion). **SL.1.1a**

CCSS Describe people, places, things, and events with relevant details, expressing ideas and feelings clearly. **SL.1.4**

ACADEMIC LANGUAGE

- *evaluate, presentation, blog*
- Cognates: *evaluar, presentación,*

MINILESSON
5 Mins

Independent Writing

Write About the Literature Anthology

Prepare

Tell children they will plan what they will say about their finished writing and drawing to the class. Remind children to:

- Think about the describing details from the story they used to support their opinion.
- Think about how they used complete sentences to make their writing understandable.

Present

Have children take turns giving presentations of their responses to the prompt about *A Lost Button*: *In A Lost Button, do you think Frog or Toad was the better friend? Why?* If possible, record their presentations so children can self-evaluate. Tell children to:

- Support their opinions using relevant describing details.
- Speak in complete sentences.
- Listen carefully and quietly to the presenter.

Evaluate

Have children discuss their own presentations and evaluate their performance using the presentation rubric.

Use the teacher's rubric to evaluate children's writing. Have children add their writing to their Writer's Portfolio. Encourage children to look back at previous writing. Then have them discuss what they would like to improve about their writing. Have children share their observations with a partner.

Publish

After children finish presenting their opinions, guide them to use digital tools to publish their writing. Discuss how the class will publish their opinions in a class blog. Suggest that as children read other stories, they write additional opinion pieces to post on the blog.

Go Digital

Writing

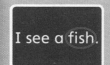

Checklists

I see a fish.

Grammar

Grammar

Joining Sentences

1 Review Remind children that two sentences can be joined using *and, but, or, so,* or *because.* Write the following sentences and have children identify the joining words:

My dog barked because he was happy to see me. (because)

Miss Carlin parked her car and walked into the shop. (and)

Do you like oatmeal or do you like toast? (or)

Dad wanted to make meatloaf but he didn't have any meat. (but)

Art likes to make kids laugh so he acts silly. (so)

2 Practice Ask: *How are* so *and* because *used when joining sentences? What two sentences were joined to make each Review sentence?*

Have children write new sentences using *and, but, or, so,* and *because.*

Mechanics: Capitalize Proper Nouns

1 Review Remind children that the names of specific places are capitalized.

2 Practice Write the following sentences. Read each aloud. Have children fix the sentences.

we rode our sleds on snowflake hill in rome. (We rode our sleds on Snowflake Hill in Rome.)

Stop in tell City before you go to hobart. (Stop in Tell City before you go to Hobart.)

Daily Wrap Up

- Review the Essential Question and encourage children to discuss using the oral vocabulary words.

- Review with children that they can make predictions and think about characters' points of view as they read.

- Review words with *r*-controlled vowel *ar.*

- Use the Visual Vocabulary Cards to review the Words to Know.

- Remind children that a fantasy is a made-up story that could not happen in real life.

Integrate Ideas

Close Reading Routine

Read   DOK 1–2

- Identify key ideas and details about seeing and sorting things.
- Take notes and retell.
- Use prompts as needed.

Reread   DOK 2–3

- Analyze text, craft, and structure.

Integrate   DOK 4

- Integrate knowledge and ideas and make text-to-text connections.
- Use the Integrate Lesson.
- Use *Close Reading Companion*, p. 139.

TEXT CONNECTIONS

Connect to the Essential Question

Write the essential question on the board: *How can we classify and categorize things?* Read the essential question aloud. Tell children that they will think about all of the information they have learned about classifying and categorizing things. Say: *We have read many selections on this topic. We will compare the information from this week's* **Leveled Readers** *and* A Barn Full of Hats, **Reading/Writing Workshop** *pages 120–129.*

Evaluate Text Evidence Guide children to review the selections and their completed graphic organizers. Have children work with partners to compare information from all the week's reads. Children can record notes using a Foldable®. Guide them to record information from the selections that helps them answer the Essential Question.

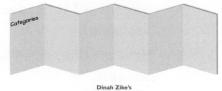

Dinah Zike's
FOLDABLES
Study Organizer

See It, Sort It

OBJECTIVES

CCSS Participate in shared research and writing projects. **W.1.7**

RESEARCH AND INQUIRY

Have children create a checklist and review their graphs:

- Does their graph give information about objects and categories?
- Did they include all the categories they wanted to include? Did they show numbers of objects on their graph?
- Did they draw pictures and label them?
- Do they wish to make any changes or add information to their graph?
- Have they taken notes about what they would like to talk about when presenting their graphs to the class?

Guide partners to practice sharing their graphs with each other. Children should practice speaking and presenting their information clearly.

Guide children to present their work. Prompt children to ask questions to clarify when something is unclear: *What objects are in each category? Did you include numbers to show how many objects there are? Did you label your categories?* Have children use the Presentation Checklist online.

Text to Poetry

Read aloud with children the Integrate activity on page 139 of the *Close Reading Companion*. Have partners share reactions to the poem. Then guide them to discuss how it is similar to the selections they read earlier in the week. Have partners collaborate to complete the Integrate page by following the prompts.

Present Ideas and Synthesize Information

When children finish their discussions, ask for a volunteer from each pair to share the information from their Foldable® and their Integrate pages. After each pair has presented their ideas, ask: *How does thinking about the ways that objects are different help you answer the Essential Question, How can we classify and categorize things?* Lead a class discussion asking students to use the information from their charts to answer the Essential Question.

OBJECTIVES

CCSS Identify basic similarities in and differences between two texts on the same topic (e.g., in illustrations, descriptions, or procedures). **RI.1.9**

SPEAKING AND LISTENING

As children work with partners in their *Close Reading Companion* or on their graphs, make sure they are actively participating in the conversation and, when necessary, remind them to use these speaking and listening strategies:

Speaking Strategies

- Take turns speaking one at a time, try not to speak over others, and raise a hand when they want to speak during group discussions.

- Invite others to share ideas and feedback, and respond to questions and feedback using complete sentences.

- Refer to pictures, graphs, and other visual aids as they describe objects and events in their discussions.

Listening Strategies

- Listen with care and do not interrupt the speaker.

- Listen closely and ask questions about details in others' presentations and in any visuals the presenter uses.

- Feel comfortable about asking questions when they don't understand.

OBJECTIVES

CCSS Follow agreed-upon rules for discussions. **SL.1.1a**

CCSS Ask and answer questions about key details in a text read aloud or information presented orally or through other media. **SL.1.2**

CCSS Describe people, places, things, and events with relevant details, expressing ideas and feelings clearly. **SL.1.4**

→ Approaching Level

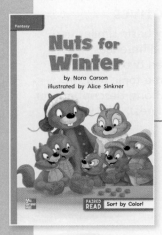

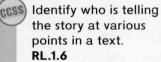

Lexile 170

OBJECTIVES

CCSS Acknowledge differences in the points of view of characters, including by speaking in a different voice for each character when reading dialogue aloud. **RL.2.6**

CCSS Identify who is telling the story at various points in a text. **RL.1.6**

Make and confirm predictions

Leveled Reader:
Nuts for Winter

Before Reading

Preview and Predict

Have children turn to the title page. Read the title and the author's name and have children repeat. Preview the selection's illustrations. Prompt children to predict what the selection might be about.

Review Genre: Fantasy

Have children recall that a fantasy has invented characters, settings, or other elements that could not exist in real life.

ESSENTIAL QUESTION

Remind children of the Essential Question: *How can we classify and categorize things?* Set a purpose for reading: *Let's read about how a squirrel family finds nuts for winter.*

Remind children that as they read a selection, they can ask questions about what they do not understand or what they want to know more about.

During Reading

Guided Comprehension

As children whisper read *Nuts for Winter,* monitor and provide guidance, correcting blending and modeling the key strategies and skills.

Strategy: Make and Confirm Predictions

Remind children that as they read they can make predictions about what might happen next. Model using the strategy. *On page 3, I read that Bobby's family thinks he is too young to hunt for nuts. I predict he will find a lot of nuts.* Continue reading the story to confirm the prediction.

Skill: Point of View

Remind children to pay attention to what the characters say and do. This will help them identify each character's point of view. As you read, ask: *What did Bobby say? What does this tell us about his point of view?* Display a Point of View chart for children to copy.

Go Digital

Nuts for Winter

Graphic Organizer

Retell

Model recording children's answers in the boxes. Have children record the answers in their own charts.

Think Aloud As I read I look for clues to tell me each character's point of view. On page 2, Dad says they must hunt for nuts. This tells me he cares about taking care of his family and being prepared for winter.

Guide children to use the text and illustrations to complete the chart.

After Reading

Respond to Reading

Have children complete the Respond to Reading on page 12.

Retell

Have children take turns retelling the selection, using the **Retelling Cards** as a guide. Help children make a personal connection by saying: *Bobby sorted nuts by size. What are some things you have sorted in school? How did you sort them?*

Model Fluency

Read the sentences, one at a time. Have children chorally repeat. Point out to children how you pause at commas.

Apply Have partners practice reading. Provide feedback as needed.

PAIRED READ ...

"Sort by Color!"

Make Connections: Write About It *Analytical Writing*

Before reading, ask children to note that the genre of this selection is informational text. Then discuss the Compare Texts direction. After reading, ask children to connect the information in "Sort by Color!" with that in *Nuts for Winter*. Provide a sentence frame such as: *Two different ways to sort are _____.*

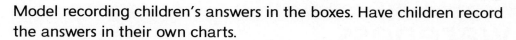

Leveled Reader

Analytical Writing

COMPARE TEXTS

- Have children use text evidence to compare fantasy to informational text.

Lead children in conducting a literature circle using the Thinkmark questions to guide the discussion. You may wish to discuss what children have learned about different ways to sort things from both selections in the Leveled Reader.

Level Up

Level-up lessons available online.

IF children can read *Nuts for Winter*, Approaching Level with fluency and correctly answer the Respond to Reading questions,

THEN tell children that they will read another story about sorting.

- Use page 7 of *Dog Bones* On Level to model using Teaching Poster 35 to list a point of view.

- Have children read the selection, checking their comprehension by using the graphic organizer.

Approaching Level

Phonological Awareness

CONTRAST SOUNDS

OBJECTIVES

 Isolate and pronounce initial, medial vowel, and final sounds (phonemes) in spoken single-syllable words. **RF.1.2c**

Contrast vowel sounds in words

 I Do Explain to children that they will listen for the middle sound in words. *Listen as I say two words:* farm, fame. *Which word has the /är/ sounds in the middle? I hear /är/ in* farm *so I will say* farm, /fff/ /är/ /mmm/. Fame *does not have the /är/ sounds.*

 We Do *Listen as I say two words:* bike, bark. *Which word has the /är/ sounds? That's right,* bark *has the /är/ sounds. Say it with me:* bark, /b/ /är/ /k/.

Repeat this routine with the following words:

shark, shack   deck, dark   star, stay

 You Do *It's your turn. Which word has the /är/ sounds?*

arm, am   poke, park   him, harm

Repeat the contrast sounds routine with additional /är/ words.

PHONEME CATEGORIZATION

OBJECTIVES

 Isolate and pronounce initial, medial vowel, and final sounds (phonemes) in spoken single-syllable words. **RF.1.2c**

Categorize words by phoneme

I Do Explain to children that they will be listening for words with the same sounds in the middle. *Listen as I say three words:* yard, back, dart. *Two words have the same sound in the middle. When I say* yard *and* dart, *I can hear the /är/ sounds.* Back *has the /a/ sound.* Back *does not belong.*

 We Do *Listen as I say three words:* man, sharp, cart. *Which word does not belong? That's right,* man *does not belong.* Sharp *and* cart *have the /är/ sounds.* Man *does not.*

Repeat this routine with the following word sets:

march, far, save   feet, hard, charm   smart, hand, large

 You Do *It's your turn. Which words go together? Which word does not belong?*

scarf, bee, tar   harm, part, road   name, arm, art

Repeat the categorization routine with additional /är/ words.

PHONEME BLENDING

OBJECTIVES

Orally produce single-syllable words by blending sounds (phonemes), including consonant blends. **RF.1.2b**

 I Do Explain to children that they will be blending sounds to form words. *Listen as I say a word sound by sound: /är/ /m/. I'm going to blend the sounds together: /är/ /mmm/, /ärmmm/, arm. I blended the word* arm.

 We Do *Listen as I say the sounds in a word: /f/ /är/. Repeat the sounds: /f/ / är/. Let's blend the sounds together: /fff/ /är/, /fffär /, far. We made one word:* far.

Repeat this routine with the following words:

/k/ /är/　　/s/ /t/ /är/　　/b/ /är /n/　　/s/ /t/ /är/ /t/　　/sh/ /är/ /p/

 You Do *It's your turn. Blend the sounds I say together to form a word.*

/s/ /k/ /är/　　/är/ /ch/　　/ch/ /är/ /m/　　/k/ /är/ /d/

/p/ /är/ /t/　　/h/ /är/ /d/　　/f/ /är/ /m/　　/s/ /m/ /är/ /t/

PHONEME SEGMENTATION

OBJECTIVES

Segment spoken single-syllable words into their complete sequence of individual sounds (phonemes). **RF.1.2d**

 I Do Tell children they will be saying the sounds in words. *Listen as I say a word:* art. *I hear the sounds /är/ and /t/.* Tell children that they can say the /är/ sounds together since they are difficult to pronounce separately.

 We Do *Let's do some together. I am going to say a word: /fffärmmm/. What sounds do you hear? The sounds in* farm *are /f/ /är/ and /m/.*

Repeat this routine with the following words:

bar　　jar　　dark　　yarn　　sharp　　spark　　charge　　barn

 You Do *I'll say a word. Tell me what sounds you hear.*
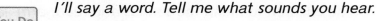

march　　scar　　Mars　　arm　　shark　　smart　　hard　　large

ELL ENGLISH LANGUAGE LEARNERS

For the **children** who need **phonemic awareness, phonics,** and **fluency** practice, use scaffolding methods as necessary to ensure children understand the meaning of the words. Refer to the Language Transfers Handbook for phonics elements that may not transfer in children's native languages.

Approaching Level

Phonics

CONNECT *ar* TO /är/

 TIER **2**

OBJECTIVES

 Know and apply grade level phonics and word analysis skills in decoding words. **RF.1.3**

 I Do Display the **Word-Building Card** *ar*. *These letters are lowercase* a *and* r. *Together they can stand for /är/. I am going to trace the letters* ar *while I say /är/.* Trace the letters *ar* while saying /är/ five times.

 We Do *Now do it with me.* Have children take turns saying /är/ while using their fingers to trace lowercase *ar*. Then have them say /är/ as they use their fingers to trace the letters *ar* five more times.

 You Do Have children connect the letters *ar* to /är/ by saying /är/ as they trace lowercase *ar* on paper five to ten times. Then ask them to write the letters *ar* while saying /är/ five to ten times.

Repeat, connecting the letters *ar* to /är/ through tracing and writing the letters *ar* throughout the week.

BLEND WORDS WITH /är/ *ar*

TIER **2**

OBJECTIVES

Decode regularly spelled one-syllable words. **RF.1.3b**

Blend and decode words with *r*-controlled *ar*

 I Do Display Word-Building Cards *b, ar, n*. *This is the letter* b. *It stands for /b/. Say it with me: /b/. These are the letters* a *and* r. *Together they stand for /är/. Let's say it together: /är/. This is the letter* n. *It stands for /n/. I'll blend the sounds together: /bärnnn/,* barn.

 We Do Guide children to blend the sounds and read: *arm, jar, arch, card, yarn, smart, sharp, chart.*

 You Do Have children use Word-Building Cards to blend and read: *art, car, star, mark, park, start, scarf, charge.*

Repeat, blending additional /är/ words.

You may wish to review Phonics with **ELL** using this section.

BUILD WORDS WITH /är/ *ar*

OBJECTIVES

 Decode regularly spelled one-syllable words. **RF.1.3b**

Build and decode words with *r*-controlled *ar*

 I Do Display Word-Building Cards *ar, m*. These are the letters a, r, *and* m. *The letters* a *and* r *together stand for* /är/. *The letter* m *stands for* /m/. *I will blend* /är/ *and* /mmm/ *together:* /ärmmm/, arm. *The word is* arm.

 We Do *Now let's do one together.* Change the letter *m* in *arm* to *t*. *Let's blend the new word:* /är/ /t/, /ärt/, art.

Place the letter *p* in front of *art*. *Let's blend and read the new word:* /p/ /är/ /t/, /pärt/, part.

 You Do Have children build the words *cart, chart, charm, harm, farm, far, bar, barn, yarn, yard, hard, harp, sharp, shark, spark.*

BLEND WORDS WITH /är/ *ar*

OBJECTIVES

 Decode regularly spelled one-syllable words. **RF.1.3b**

Decode words with *r*-controlled *ar*

I Do Display Word-Building Cards *d, ar, k*. *This is the letter* d. *It stands for* /d/. *These are the letters* a *and* r. *Together they stand for* /är/. *This is the letter* k. *It stands for* /k/. *Listen as I blend all three sounds:* /därk/, dark. *The word is* dark.

 You Do Let's do some together. Blend and read the words *star, yard, spark,* and *large* with children.

 We Do Display the words to the right. Have children blend and read the words.

art	dark	barn	car	hard	bark
harm	scar	chart	part	scarf	yarn
sharp	shape	smart	march	much	apart
child	party	coat	cart	puppy	charge

A dog started to bark in the dark yard.

Does a shark live in a barn on a farm?

Clark will park his car and march home.

Decodable Reader Have children read "Charm Scarves" (pages 1–4) and "Car Parts" (5–8).

BUILD FLUENCY WITH PHONICS

Sound-Spellings Fluency

Display the following Word-Building Cards: *ar, ey, igh, oa, oe, ee, ea, ai, ay, e_e, u_e, o_e, dge, i_e, a_e, ch, tch, wh, ph, th, sh, ng, mp, sk, st, nt, nk, nd, _ce, _ge.* Have children chorally say the sounds. Repeat and vary the pace.

Fluency in Connected Text

Have children review the **Decodable Reader** selections. Identify /är/ *ar* words. Blend words as needed.

Have partners reread the selections for fluency.

→ ## Approaching Level

Structural Analysis

REVIEW IRREGULAR PLURALS

OBJECTIVES

CCSS Demonstrate command of the conventions of standard English grammar and usage when writing or speaking. **L.1.1**

Identify and use irregular plural forms

Remind children that words can change in different ways to make them mean "more than one." Write and read *person* and *people*. Person *is one*. People *means "more than one person."* Write and read *sheep*. *Some words do not change.* Sheep *can mean both "one sheep" and "more than one sheep."* Use the plurals in sentences.

Write and read *foot* and *feet*. *What does* feet *mean? Yes*, feet *means "more than one foot." Let's use* foot *and* feet *in sentences.* Repeat with *woman* and *women*.

Write or make word cards for *man, men, child, children, ox, oxen*. Have partners match the singular nouns to their plurals and use the words in sentences.

Repeat Have partners write sentences for the singular and plural nouns used in the lesson.

RETEACH IRREGULAR PLURALS

OBJECTIVES

CCSS Demonstrate command of the conventions of standard English grammar and usage when writing or speaking. **L.1.1**

Reteach irregular plural forms

Write *foot* and *feet*. *With most nouns, we add -s or -es to tell about more than one: one book, two books.* Point to *foot* and *feet*. *Some words change spellings to show more than one: Wiggle your right foot. Wiggle your two feet.* Repeat for *tooth* and *teeth*.

Have one child stand. *This is one child.* Write and read child. Then have two children stand. *These are two children.* Write and read *children. What does* children *mean? Yes,* "more than one child." Repeat for *person* and *people*.

Write and read these words: *mouse, mice; goose, geese; man, men; woman, women*. Have partners draw pictures for the words. Ask them to label their pictures.

Repeat Have partners say or write sentences about their pictures. Make sure they use the singular and plural nouns correctly.

Words to Know

REVIEW HIGH-FREQUENCY WORDS

OBJECTIVES

 CCSS Recognize and read grade-appropriate irregularly spelled words. **RF.1.3g**

Review *four, large, none, only, put, round*

 I Do Use **High-Frequency Words** to **Read/Spell/Write** each high-frequency word. Use each word orally in a sentence.

 We Do Guide children to Read/Spell/Write each word on their **Response Boards**. Help them generate oral sentences using the words.

 You Do Have partners work together to Read/Spell/Write the words *four, large, none, only, put,* and *round*. Ask them to say sentences for the words.

CUMULATIVE REVIEW

OBJECTIVES

 CCSS Recognize and read grade-appropriate irregularly spelled words. **RF.1.3g**

Review previously taught high-frequency words

 I Do Display the High-Frequency Word Cards from the previous weeks. Use the Read/Spell/Write routine to review each word.

 We Do Guide children as they Read/Spell/Write the words on their Response Boards. Have children complete sentence frames for the words. *I found _____. I know I would laugh if we were _____.*

 You Do Have partners take turns displaying and reading the words. Ask them to use the words in sentences.

Fluency Display the High-Frequency Word Cards. Point to words in random order. Have children chorally read each word. Repeat at a faster pace.

REVIEW VOCABULARY WORDS

OBJECTIVES

 CCSS Identify real-life connections between words and their use (e.g., note places at home that are *cozy*). **L.1.5c**

 I Do Display **Visual Vocabulary Cards** for *trouble* and *whole*. Review each word using the Define/Example/Ask routine.

Invite children to tell what *trouble* means and to point to things that are *whole*. Then work with them to complete these sentence starters: *(1) Dogs can get into trouble when _____. (2) I ate a whole _____.*

 You Do Have partners write two sentences on their own, using each of the words. Provide assistance as needed.

Approaching Level

Comprehension

READ FOR FLUENCY

 TIER 2

OBJECTIVES

 Read grade-level text orally with accuracy, appropriate rate, and expression. **RF.1.4b**

 I Do Read the first page of the Practice Book story aloud. Model using appropriate phrasing for commas in dialogue.

 We Do Read the next page of the story aloud and have children repeat each sentence after you. Point out how you use appropriate phrasing by pausing when you come to commas.

You Do Have children read the rest of the story aloud. Remind them to use appropriate phrasing.

IDENTIFY CHARACTERS

 TIER 2

OBJECTIVES

Describe characters, settings, and major events in a story, using key details. **RL.1.3**

 I Do Remind children that all stories have characters. *When I read a story, I think about the characters in the story. Characters are whom the story is about. I can find details about the characters in the pictures and in the words.*

We Do Read the first page of the Practice Book story aloud. Pause to discuss the characters. *Look at the picture. How many characters do you see? Yes, the story has four characters: Cat, Dog, Pig, Chick. Say the names with me. What did we learn from the words on this page? Yes, it is Cat's birthday.*

 You Do Guide children as they read the rest of the Practice Book story. Prompt them to find details about the characters from the words and pictures.

REVIEW POINT OF VIEW

OBJECTIVES

CCSS Acknowledge differences in the points of view of characters, including by speaking in a different voice for each character when reading dialogue aloud. **RL.2.6**

Remind children that point of view is the way a story character thinks or feels. *The point of view in a story is the way a character thinks or feels. When I read a story, I think about the point of view of each character. I use what the characters say and do to help me figure out their thoughts and feelings.*

Read the first sentence of the Practice Book story together. Pause to discuss Cat's point of view. *We read that today is Cat's birthday. What is her point of view? Let's ask ourselves how she feels. Yes, she is excited about her birthday and wants to have a party to celebrate. That is her point of view.*

Record Cat's point of view on a Point of View chart. Guide children as they continue to read. Have them discuss the other characters' points of view. Have children add this information to their charts.

SELF-SELECTED READING

OBJECTIVES

 With prompting and support, read prose and poetry of appropriate complexity for grade 1. **RL.1.10**

Apply the strategy and skill to read a text

Read Independently

Have children pick a fantasy story for sustained silent reading. Remind them that:

• they should think about what the characters say and do to identify each character's point of view.

• as they read, they should make and confirm predictions about the story.

Read Purposefully

Have children record information about the characters on a Point of View chart. After reading, guide children to participate in a group discussion about the story they read. Guide children to:

• share the information they recorded on their Point of View charts.

• tell whether they agree with or liked the characters' points of view.

• share predictions they made and tell if their predictions were correct.

On Level

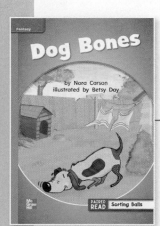

Lexile 360

OBJECTIVES

CCSS Acknowledge differences in the points of view of characters, including by speaking in a different voice for each character when reading dialogue aloud. **RL.2.6**

CCSS Identify who is telling the story at various points in a text. **RL.1.6**

Make and confirm predictions

Leveled Reader:
Dog Bones

Before Reading

Preview and Predict

Have children turn to the title page. Read the title and the author's name and have children repeat. Preview the story's illustrations. Prompt children to predict what the story might be about.

Review Genre: Fantasy

Have children recall that a fantasy has invented characters, settings, or other elements that could not exist in real life.

ESSENTIAL QUESTION

Remind children of the Essential Question: *How can we classify and categorize things?* Set a purpose for reading: *Let's find out how Max categorizes his dog bones.*

Remind children that as they read a selection, they can ask questions about what they do not understand or want to know more about.

During Reading

Guided Comprehension

As children whisper read *Dog Bones*, monitor and provide guidance, correcting blending and modeling the key strategies and skills.

Strategy: Make and Confirm Predictions

Remind children that as they read they can make predictions about what will happen. Then they can read on to see if they are right. Model using the strategy: *On pages 4–5, I see Max wants to know where he buried his bones. I think he will find them. I read page 6. Was my prediction correct?*

Skill: Point of View

Remind children to pay attention to what the characters say and do. This will help them identify each character's point of view. As you read, ask: *What is Max feeling? How do you know?* Display a Point of View chart for children to copy.

Go Digital

Dog Bones

Graphic Organizer

Retell

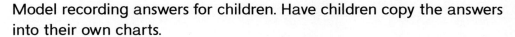

Model recording answers for children. Have children copy the answers into their own charts.

Think Aloud On page 9, I see Max with a big bone strapped to his back. The words "This bone is the biggest," tells me he is feeling excited about the contest.

Guide children to use the text and illustrations to complete the chart.

After Reading

Respond to Reading

Have children complete the Respond to Reading on page 12.

Retell

Have children take turns retelling the selection, using the **Retelling Cards** as a guide. Help children make a connection by asking: *What have you collected? How could you sort the things you collected?*

Model Fluency

Read the sentences, one at a time. Have children chorally repeat. Point out to children how to pause at commas.

Apply Have partners practice reading. Provide feedback as needed.

PAIRED READ ...

"Sorting Balls"

Make Connections:
Write About It ✏ *Analytical Writing*

Before reading, ask children to note that the genre of this selection is informational text. Then discuss the Compare Texts direction. After reading, ask children to make connections between what they learned from *Dog Bones* and the information in "Sorting Balls."

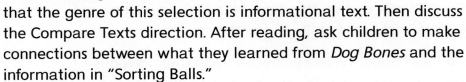

Leveled Reader

✏ *Analytical Writing*

COMPARE TEXTS

• Have children use text evidence to compare fantasy to informational text.

Literature Circles

Lead children in conducting a literature circle using the Thinkmark questions to guide the discussion. You may wish to discuss what children have learned about different ways to sort from the two selections in the Leveled Reader.

Level Up

Level-up lessons available online.

IF children can read *Dog Bones,* On Level with fluency and correctly answer the Respond to Reading questions,

THEN tell children that they will read another story about sorting.

• Use page 3 of *Spark's Toys* Beyond Level to model using Teaching Poster 35 to list a point of view.

• Have children read the selection, checking their comprehension by using the graphic organizer.

On Level

Phonics

BUILD WORDS WITH /är/ar

OBJECTIVE
Decode regularly spelled one-syllable words. **RF.1.3b**

 I Do
Display **Word-Building Cards** *f, ar, m. These are the letters* f, a, r, *and* m. *They stand for the sounds* /f/ /är/ *and* /m/. *I will blend* /f/ /är/ *and* /m/ *together:* /fffärmmm/, farm. *The word is* farm.

 We Do
Now let's do one together. Change the letter *f* to *h*. *Let's blend and read the new word:* /h/ /är/ /mmm/, /härmmm/, harm. *The new word is* harm.

 You Do
Have children build and blend these words: *arm, art, dart, dark, mark, park, part, cart, chart, charm, charge, large.*

Repeat with additional *r*-controlled *ar* words.

Decodable Reader Have children read "Charm Scarves" and "Car Parts" (pages 1–8).

Words to Know

REVIEW WORDS

OBJECTIVE
Recognize and read grade-appropriate irregularly spelled words. **RF.1.3g**

Review high-frequency words *four, large, none, only, put,* and *round*; review vocabulary words *trouble* and *whole*

 I Do
Use the **Read/Spell/Write** routine to review each high-frequency and vocabulary word. Use each word orally in a sentence.

 We Do
Guide children to Read/Spell/Write each word using their **Response Boards**. Then work with the group to create oral sentences for the words.

 You Do
Have partners use the Read/Spell/Write routine on their own using the high-frequency words *four, large, none, only, put,* and *round* and the vocabulary words *trouble* and *whole*. Have partners write sentences about this week's stories. Each sentence must contain at least one high-frequency or vocabulary word.

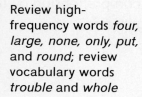

Comprehension

REVIEW POINT OF VIEW

OBJECTIVES

Acknowledge differences in the points of view of characters, including by speaking in a different voice for each character when reading dialogue aloud. **RL.2.6**

I Do Remind children that point of view is the way a character thinks or feels. *When I read a story, I think about each character's point of view. I use what the character says and does to help me understand the character's point of view.*

We Do Read the first two pages of the Practice Book story aloud. Pause to identify the characters and Cat's point of view. *We read the beginning of a story about Cat. What is Cat's point of view?* Point out that Cat is excited and wants to celebrate.

You Do Guide children to read the rest of the Practice Book story. Remind them to think about the point of view of each character. Then invite children to discuss the characters and their points of view.

SELF-SELECTED READING

OBJECTIVES

With prompting and support, read prose and poetry of appropriate complexity for grade 1. **RL.1.10**

Apply the strategy and skill to read a text

Read Independently

Have children pick a fantasy story for sustained silent reading. Remind them to:

- pay attention to the point of view of each character.

- make and confirm predictions about the story.

Read Purposefully

Have children record details on a Point of View chart. After reading, guide partners to:

- share the information they recorded on their Point of View charts.

- tell whether they agree with the characters' points of view.

- share predictions they made and tell if their predictions were correct.

Beyond Level

Lexile 390

OBJECTIVES

CCSS Acknowledge differences in the points of view of characters, including by speaking in a different voice for each character when reading dialogue aloud. **RL.2.6**

CCSS Identify who is telling the story at various points in a text. **RL.1.6**

Make and confirm predictions

Leveled Reader:
Spark's Toys

Before Reading

Preview and Predict

Read the title and author name. Have children preview the title page and the illustrations. Ask: *What do you think this book will be about?*

Review Genre: Fantasy

Have children recall that a fantasy has invented characters, settings, or other elements that could not exist in real life. Prompt children to name key characteristics of a fantasy. Tell them to look for these as they read the Leveled Reader.

ESSENTIAL QUESTION

Remind children of the Essential Question: *How can we classify and categorize things?* Set a purpose for reading: *Let's find out what Spark does with his toys.*

During Reading

Guided Comprehension

Have children whisper read *Spark's Toys*. Have them place self-stick notes next to difficult words. Remind children that when they come to an unfamiliar word, they can look for familiar spellings. They will need to break longer words into smaller chunks and sound out each part.

Monitor children's reading. Stop periodically and ask open-ended questions to facilitate rich discussion, such as *What does the author want you to know about Spark?* Build on children's responses to develop deeper understanding of the text.

Strategy: Make and Confirm Predictions

Remind children that as they read they can make predictions about what will happen next. Then they can read on to see if they are right. Say: *As you read, stop and predict what will happen. Read on to see if you are correct.*

Go Digital

Spark's Toys

Graphic Organizer

Skill: Point of View

Remind children what the characters say and do will help them identify each character's point of view. As you read, ask: *What is Spark feeling? How can you tell?* Display a Point of View chart for children to copy.

Model how to record the information. Have children use the text and illustrations to complete the chart.

Think Aloud As I read I look for clues that show what the character is thinking or saying. On page 7, the words "Ah, this is the life" tell me Spark is happy and doesn't want things to change.

After Reading

Respond to Reading

Have children complete the Respond to Reading on page 12.

Retell

Have children take turns retelling the selection. Help them make a personal connection by writing about their own toys or classroom toys. *Write about different toys you play with. Tell how you could sort them.*

Leveled Reader

PAIRED READ ...

"Sorting Fruit"

Make Connections:
Write About It ✏️ *Analytical Writing*

Before reading "Sorting Fruit," have children preview the title page and prompt them to identify the genre. Discuss the Compare Texts direction. After reading, have children work with a partner to discuss the information they learned in "Sorting Fruit" and the story *Spark's Toys*. Ask children to make connections by comparing and contrasting the ways things are sorted in each selection. Prompt children to discuss what they learned about sorting.

✏️ *Analytical Writing*

COMPARE TEXTS

• Have children use text evidence to compare fantasy to informational text.

Literature Circles

Lead children in conducting a literature circle using the Thinkmark questions to guide the discussion. You may wish to discuss what children have learned about different ways to sort from reading the two selections in the Leveled Reader.

Gifted and Talented

SYNTHESIZE Challenge children to write about different ways they could classify animals. Encourage them to write category headings, then list animals under each category.

EXTEND Have them use facts they learned from the week or do additional research to find out more about how animals are classified.

Beyond Level

Vocabulary

ORAL VOCABULARY: ANTONYMS

OBJECTIVES

 With guidance and support from adults, demonstrate understanding of figurative language, word relationships and nuances in word meanings **L.1.5**

 Review the meaning of the oral vocabulary word *organize*.

Remind children that an antonym means the opposite of another word. If you organize objects, you create organization. If something is out of order, it is in chaos. Being in chaos is the opposite of being organized. *Organization* and *chaos* are antonyms.

 Have children take turns using the words *disorganization* and *chaos* in sentences.

 Have partners explain why they might want to put objects that are in a state of disorganization or chaos into categories.

 Extend Have children plan and act out short plays about trying to organize something that is in a state of disorder. Challenge them to use the antonyms they learned, *disorganization, chaos* and *disorder,* in their skits.

VOCABULARY WORDS: ANTONYMS

OBJECTIVES

 With guidance and support from adults, demonstrate understanding of figurative language, word relationships and nuances in word meanings **L.1.5**

 Review with children the meaning of the vocabulary word *whole.* Write the sentence *I ate the whole sandwich.* Read the sentence aloud, and have children repeat. Discuss what *whole* means in the sentence.

Remind children that an antonym means the opposite of another word. *When you eat a whole sandwich you eat all of it. You eat the complete sandwich, and there is none left. What is the opposite of* whole? *Antonyms for* whole *might be* part or incomplete.

 Have children use the words *part* and *incomplete* in sentences. Ask them to draw or demonstrate the meanings.

 Have partners use *whole* and one of its antonyms in sentences that show the opposite meanings.

Comprehension

REVIEW POINT OF VIEW

OBJECTIVES

 Acknowledge differences in the points of view of characters, including by speaking in a different voice for each character when reading dialogue aloud. **RL.2.6**

 I Do Discuss with children what point of view is in a story. Prompt them to explain that point of view is the way a character thinks or feels.

 We Do Guide children in reading the first page of the Practice Book story aloud. Pause to prompt children to discuss Cat's point of view. *What is Cat's point of view? How do you know?*

 You Do Have children read the rest of the Practice Book story independently. Remind them to think about the points of view of the characters. Then invite children to discuss the points of view.

SELF-SELECTED READING

OBJECTIVES

 With prompting and support, read prose and poetry of appropriate complexity for grade 1. **RL.1.10**

Apply the strategy and skill to read a text

Read Independently

Have children pick a fantasy story for sustained silent reading. Tell them that they should use a Point of View chart to record details about what characters think and feel. Remind them to make and confirm predictions as they read.

Read Purposefully

Have children record details on a Point of View chart. After reading, guide children to:

- share the information they recorded on their Point of View charts with partners.

- record the predictions they made about the story in a reading response journal.

 Independent Study Have children write an alternate ending for the story they read using one of the predictions they made. Encourage them to share their work with the class.

→ English Language Learners

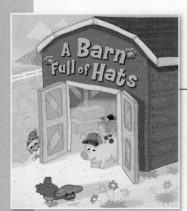

Reading/Writing Workshop

OBJECTIVES

Acknowledge differences in the points of view of characters, including by speaking in a different voice for each character when reading dialogue aloud. **RL.2.6**

Identify who is telling the story at various points in a text. **RL.1.6**

Shared Read
A Barn Full of Hats

Before Reading

Build Background

Read the Essential Question: *How can we classify and categorize things?*

- Explain the meaning of the Essential Question: *We can think of ways that things are alike. Then we can make a group of these things. When we sort and make groups, we think about how things are alike and different.*

- **Model an answer:** *I can sort, or classify, things by size. Some things might be big and some might be small. I can also sort, or classify, by color. I can classify things by shape, too.*

- Ask children a question that ties the Essential Question to their own background knowledge. *Think of different kinds of shirts. What is one way that the shirts are alike? What is one way that you could sort the shirts?* Ask partners to share their answers.

During Reading

Interactive Question-Response

- Ask questions that help children understand the meaning of the text after each paragraph.

- Reinforce the meanings of key vocabulary by providing meanings embedded in the questions.

- Ask children questions that require them to use key vocabulary.

- Reinforce comprehension strategies and skills of the week by modeling.

Go Digital

A Barn Full of Hats

Graphic Organizer

A Barn Full of Hats

Pages 120–121

Point to the title. *Listen as I read the title of this fantasy story.* Point to each word as you read it, and then point to the word *Hats. Say this word with me:* hats. *This word helps me know what the story is going to be about.*

Point to the picture of the farm. *I see lots of animals. Say the names of the animals with me.* Point to each animal as you say its name. *These animals are characters in the story. They talk and act like people. Let's read and find out what the animals are going to do with the hats.*

Pages 122–123

Point to the box. *I see a box. What is inside the box?* (hats) *Listen as I read the words that tell why Horse wants a hat:* "It's smart to wear a hat. A hat will keep the sun out of my eyes." *Why does Horse want a hat?* (to keep the sun out of his eyes) *Now let's read these sentences together.*

Explain and Model High-Frequency Words
Point to the word *four* and have children say it with you. *Let's count and clap four times: one, two, three, four. How many animals are in this story?* (four) *Who are the animals?* (Hen, Horse, Pig, Cat) *There are four animals.*

What is Horse's point of view? How do you know? (He is excited. The words "I do!" show his excitement about finding a hat.)

Pages 124–125

Look at the picture on page 124. *What shape is Hen's hat?* (round) *Draw a round circle in the air.* Demonstrate how to draw a circle in the air. *What color is the hat?* (purple) *What things in our classroom are purple?*

Now let's look at the picture on page 125. What color is this hat? (red) *Who is going to wear this hat?* (Pig)

Explain and Model the Strategy Reread page 125. *We can stop and make predictions as we read. We can use words and pictures to guess what might happen next in the story. Do you think Horse will find a hat to wear?*

Pages 126–127

Let's look at page 127. Now let's read what Cat is saying: "Thick yarn is nice," said Cat. "I will take the whole hat apart, so I can play with the yarn." *Does Horse have a hat yet?* (no) *How do you think Horse is feeling?* (sad) *Show me how your face looks when you feel sad.*

What is Cat's point of view? How do you know? (She is happy. The words "I will take the whole hat apart so I can play with the yarn," tell the reader she is happy to have found a hat.)

Pages 128–129

Let's look at the picture on page 128. What does Farmer Clark's hat look like? (large, floppy; straw)

Explain and Model the Skill *Horse has been unhappy because he doesn't have a hat. Listen to what Horse says about Farmer Clark's hat. Reread Horse's words on page 129. How does Horse feel about that hat?* (The words "Yes, this is the hat for me!" tell me Horse is happy to have found a hat.)

Explain and Model Phonics *I am going to say some words. Raise your hand when you hear a word with the /är/ sounds:* hat, farmer, head, Clark, well, barnyard. *Now say the words with the /är/ sounds after me:* farmer, Clark, barnyard.

What was the farmer's point of view? How do you know? (He was pleased his animals found hats to wear. The farmer laughs, puts his hat on Horse, and says, "It fits well.")

After Reading

Make Connections

- Review the Essential Question.

→ English Language Learners

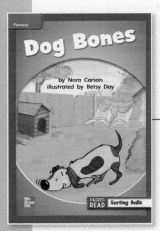

Fantasy

Dog Bones

by Nora Carson
illustrated by Betsy Day

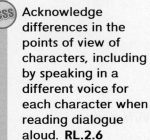

PAIRED READ Sorting Balls

Lexile 260

OBJECTIVES

CCSS Acknowledge differences in the points of view of characters, including by speaking in a different voice for each character when reading dialogue aloud. **RL.2.6**

CCSS Identify who is telling the story at various points in a text. **RL.1.6**

Make and confirm predictions

Leveled Reader:
Dog Bones

Before Reading

Preview

Read the title. Ask: *What is the title? Say it again.* Repeat with the author's name. Preview the illustrations. Have children describe the pictures. Use simple language to tell about each page. Follow with questions, such as: *What does Max find here?*

ESSENTIAL QUESTION

Remind children of the Essential Question: *How can we classify and categorize things?* Say: *Let's read to find out how sorting helps Max.* Encourage children to ask for help when they do not understand a word or phrase.

During Reading

Interactive Question-Response

Pages 2–3 *Look at the poster. Let's read the words together: "Contest! Biggest Bone." What does the poster mean?* (There is a contest. Whoever has the biggest bone will win.) *Let's make a prediction or guess what will happen. Do you think Max will have the biggest bone and win the contest?*

Pages 4– 5 *Max has a problem, doesn't he? Talk with your partner about Max's problem. Tell how he tries to solve the problem.* (He can not remember where he buried his bones. He sniffs and digs.) *Let's read the words together that tell us if Max solved his problem.* (He finds a round ball but he does not find the bones.)

Pages 6–7 *Look at page 6. What did Max find? Point to the picture to help you answer.* (a whole bunch of bones) *Now look at page 7. What is Max doing? Tell your partner about how Max is sorting his bones.*

Pages 8–9 *What did Max find?* (bigger bones) *Do you think his find is big enough to win the contest? Let's read on to see if our prediction was right.*

Pages 10–11 *What did we predict would happen? Let's read the words that tell whether our prediction was correct or not.* (Max and Bob do not win the prize. But Max is happy because he helped his pal!)

Go Digital

Dog Bones

Character	Setting	Point of View

Graphic Organizer

Retell

After Reading

Respond to Reading

Revisit the Essential Question. Ask children to work with partners to fill in the graphic organizer and answer the questions on page 12. Pair children with peers of varying language abilities.

Retell

Model retelling using the **Retelling Card** prompts. Say: *Look at the illustrations. Use details to help you retell the story.* Help children make personal connections by asking: *What are some things we can sort in school? How can we sort them?*

Phrasing Fluency: Commas

Read the pages in the book, one at a time. Help children echo-read the pages expressively and with appropriate phrasing. Remind them to pause when they come to a comma.

Apply Have children practice reading with partners. Pair children with peers of varying language abilities. Provide feedback as needed.

PAIRED READ ...

Leveled Reader

"Sorting Balls"

Make Connections: Write About It *Analytical Writing*

Before reading, tell children to note that this selection is informational text. Then discuss the Compare Texts direction.

After reading, ask children to make connections between the information they learned from "Sorting Balls" and the story *Dog Bones*. Prompt children by providing a sentence frame: *In both stories we read how to sort things by ____.*

Analytical Writing

COMPARE TEXTS

- Have children use text evidence to compare fantasy to informational text.

Literature Circles

Lead children in conducting a literature circle using the Thinkmark questions to guide the discussion. You may wish to discuss what children have learned about sorting from the two selections in the Leveled Reader.

Level Up

Level-up lessons available online.

IF children can read *Dog Bones* ELL Level with fluency and correctly answer the Respond to Reading questions,

THEN tell children that they will read a more detailed version of the story.

- Use page 2 of *Dog Bones* On Level to model using Teaching Poster 35 to list a point of view.

- Have children read the selection, checking their comprehension by using the graphic organizer.

English Language Learners

Vocabulary

PRETEACH ORAL VOCABULARY

 OBJECTIVES
Produce complete sentences when appropriate to task and situation. **SL.1.6**

LANGUAGE OBJECTIVE
Use oral vocabulary words

 Display images from the **Visual Vocabulary Cards** one at a time and follow the routine to preteach the Oral Vocabulary words *distinguish* and *classify*.

 Display the images again and explain how they illustrate or demonstrate the words. Model using sentences to describe the image.

 Display each word again and have partners discuss how the pictures demonstrate the words *distinguish* and *classify*.

Beginning	Intermediate	Advanced/High
Arrange or sort some colored blocks and use the words in sentences about them. Have children repeat.	Have partners sort colored blocks and use the words to describe what they did.	Have partners sort colored blocks and use the words to ask and answer questions about the arrangements.

PRETEACH VOCABULARY

 OBJECTIVES
Identify real-life connections between words and their use (e.g., note places at home that are cozy). **L.1.5c**

LANGUAGE OBJECTIVE
Use vocabulary words

 Display images from the **ELL Visual Vocabulary Cards** one at a time and follow the routine to preteach the vocabulary words *proud* and *contest*. Say each word and have children repeat it. Define each word in English.

 Display the image again and explain how it illustrates or demonstrates the word. Model using sentences to describe the image.

 Display each word again and have children say the word and then spell it. Provide opportunities for children to use the words in speaking and writing. Provide sentence starters.

Beginning	Intermediate	Advanced/High
Say a sentence about an image. Have children repeat the sentence and match it to its picture.	Say sentences about the images, but leave out the words. Have children repeat the sentences and complete them with the correct words.	Ask children to use the words to say sentences about the images.

Words to Know

REVIEW WORDS

OBJECTIVES

Recognize and read grade-appropriate irregularly spelled words. **RF.1.3g**

LANGUAGE OBJECTIVE

Review high-frequency and vocabulary words

I Do Display the **High-Frequency Word** and **Vocabulary Cards** for *four, large, none, only, put, round* and *trouble* and *whole*. Read each word. Use the Read/Spell/Write routine to teach each word. Have children write the words on their **Response Boards**.

We Do Write sentence frames on separate lines. Track the print as children read and complete the sentences: *(1) I have four ____. (2) None of my pals ____. (3) I have only one ____. (4) The large chair ____. (5) Where did you put ____? (6) We found two round ____. (7) We had some trouble making ____. (8) Mel watched the whole ____.*

You Do Display the High-Frequency Word Cards from the previous weeks. Display one card at a time as children chorally read the word. Mix and repeat. Note words children need to review. Repeat with vocabulary words.

Beginning	Intermediate	Advanced/High
Use the words in sentences about pictures in this week's stories and have children repeat.	Say sentences about pictures in this week's stories but leave out the words. Have children repeat and complete the sentences.	Challenge partners to use the words in sentences to tell about the stories they have read this week.

RETEACH HIGH-FREQUENCY WORDS

OBJECTIVES

Recognize and read grade-appropriate irregularly spelled words. **RF.1.3g**

LANGUAGE OBJECTIVE

Reteach high-frequency words

I Do Display each Visual Vocabulary Card and say the word aloud. Define the word in English and, if appropriate, in Spanish. Identify any cognates.

We Do Point to the image again and explain how it illustrates or demonstrates the word. Ask children to repeat the word. Engage children in structured partner-talk about the image as prompted on the back of the card. Ask children to chorally say the word three times.

YouDo Display each visual in random order, hiding the word. Have children identify the word and define it in their own words.

Beginning	Intermediate	Advanced/High
Say a word. Have children find its picture. Use the word in a sentence and have children repeat.	Have children complete sentences frames for the words.	Have children say a sentence but leave out the word. Ask others to tell what word completes the sentence.

English Language Learners
Writing/Spelling

WRITING TRAIT: SENTENCE FLUENCY

OBJECTIVES

 Produce and expand complete simple and compound declarative, interrogative, imperative, and exclamatory sentences in response to prompts. **L.1.1j**

_____

LANGUAGE OBJECTIVE

Use complete sentences

 I Do Explain that writers use complete sentences in their writing. Write and read this sentence: *Animals live on a farm.* Help children tell what makes this a complete sentence. (It has a subject and a verb.)

 We Do Read aloud the first sentence on page 122 of *A Barn Full of Hats.* Ask children who the sentence is about. (four farm animals) Then ask what the animals did. (found a box) Repeat with the first sentence on page 124. (Hen; stuck her head in the box)

 You Do Have children write sentences about animals that live in the sea, on a farm, or in the woods. Remind them to use complete sentences.

Beginning	Intermediate	Advanced/High
Have children complete these sentences to tell about animals: ____ *live on a farm.* ____ *live in the woods.* ____ *live in the sea.*	Have children find pictures of animals in this week's stories. Have them tell where the animal lives: *The ____ lives ____.*	Have children write sentences that tell what animals swim, fly, and run on land.

WORDS WITH /är/ *ar*

OBJECTIVES

 Use conventional spelling for words with common spelling patterns and for frequently occurring irregular words. **L.1.2d**

_____

LANGUAGE OBJECTIVE

Spell words with *r*-controlled *ar*

 I Do Read aloud the first Spelling Word on page T14, *cart*. Segment the word into sounds and attach a spelling to each sound. Point out the /är/ sounds and spelling. Repeat for the remaining words, and have children repeat.

 We Do Say a sentence for *cart*. Then say the /är/ word slowly and ask children to repeat. Have them write the word. Repeat for the remaining words.

 You Do Display the words. Have children work with partners to check their spelling lists. Have children correct misspelled words on their lists.

Beginning	Intermediate	Advanced/High
Help children say the words and copy them with the correct spelling.	After children have corrected their words, have pairs quiz each other.	Challenge children to think of other words that have the /är/ sounds.

Grammar

JOINING SENTENCES

OBJECTIVES

Use frequently occurring conjunctions (e.g., *and, but, or, so, because*). **L.1.1g**

LANGUAGE OBJECTIVE

Use *and, but, or, so,* and *because* to join sentences

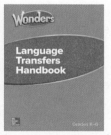

Language Transfers Handbook

TRANSFER SKILLS

Hmong speakers may omit the conjunctive words when combining sentences. In Hmong, more than one main verb can be used without conjunctions: *Î wanted a snack ate a peach.*

 I Do Review that the words *and, but, or, so,* and *because* can be used to join sentences. Write these sentences on the board: *A blue whale swims. A blue jay flies. A blue whale swims, but a blue jay flies.* Read the sentences. Circle *but. I used the word* but *to join two sentences into one longer sentence.*

 We Do Write the sentences on the board. Have children read each long sentence, circle the word that joined two shorter sentences, and read the shorter sentences that the word joined.

Would you like a dog, or would you like a cat?

I was late because I missed the bus.

A car has wheels and skates have blades.

I wanted a snack so I ate a peach.

 You Do Write the following sentence frames on the board. Have partners fill in the blanks with *and, but, or, so,* or *because.*

I like to ride my bike _____ you like to jog.

You can come to my home _____ I can meet you at school.

I can't play today _____ I am helping my mom.

I am cold _____ I will put on a coat.

Today I will go to the market _____ I will go to the park.

As children work, circulate, listen in, and take note of each child's language use and proficiency.

Beginning	Intermediate	Advanced/High
Help children describe a picture from one of this week's stories. Say short sentences and give a joining word. Have children repeat the sentences with the joining word.	Help children describe a picture from one of this week's stories. Say the first part of a sentence and a joining word. Have children complete the sentence.	Ask partners to use conjunctions in sentences about pictures from one of this week's stories.

PROGRESS MONITORING

Unit 5 Week 1 Formal Assessment	Standards Covered	Component for Assessment
Comprehension Point of View	RL.2.6	• *Selection Test* • *Weekly Assessment*
Vocabulary Strategy Context Clues: Multiple Meanings	L.1.4a	• *Selection Test* • *Weekly Assessment*
Phonics *r*-Controlled Vowel *ar*	RF.1.3	*Weekly Assessment*
Structural Analysis Plurals (irregular)	RF.1.3g	*Weekly Assessment*
High-Frequency Words *four, large, none, only, put, round*	RF.1.3g	*Weekly Assessment*
Writing Writing About Text	RL.2.6	*Weekly Assessment*
Unit 5 Week 1 Informal Assessment		
Research/Listening/Collaborating	SL.1.1c, SL.1.2, SL.1.3	• *RWW* • *Teacher's Edition*
Oral Reading Fluency (ORF) **Fluency Goal:** 13-33 words correct per minute (WCPM) **Accuracy Rate Goal:** 95% or higher	RF.1.4a. RF.1.4b, RF.1.4c	*Fluency Assessment*

Using Assessment Results

Weekly Assessment Skills	If . . .	Then . . .
COMPREHENSION	Children answer 0–3 multiple-choice items correctly . . .	. . . assign Lesson 34–36 on Point of View from the *Tier 2 Comprehension Intervention online PDFs*.
VOCABULARY	Children answer 0–2 multiple-choice items correctly . . .	. . . assign Lesson 92 on Using Context Clues: Multiple- Meaning Words from the *Tier 2 Vocabulary Intervention online PDFs*.
PHONICS/ STRUCTURAL ANALYSIS/HFW	Children answer 0–6 multiple-choice items correctly . . .	. . . assign Lesson 87 on *r*-Controlled Vowels /är/ *ar* and Lesson 82 on Irregular Plurals from the *Tier 2 Phonics/Word Study Intervention online PDFs*.
WRITING	Children score less than "2" on the constructed response . . .	. . . reteach necessary skills using Section 13 on Write About Reading from the *Tier 2 Comprehension Intervention online PDFs*.
FLUENCY	Children have a WCPM score of 13 . . .	. . . assign a lesson from Section 1, 9, or 10 of the *Tier 2 Fluency Intervention online PDFs*.
	Children have a WCPM score of 0–12 . . .	. . . assign a lesson from Sections 2–8 of the *Tier 2 Fluency Intervention online PDFs*.

Using Weekly Data

Check your data Dashboard to verify assessment results and guide grouping decisions.

Data-Driven Recommendations

Response to Intervention

Use the children's assessment results to assist you in identifying children who will benefit from focused intervention.

Use the appropriate sections of the *Placement and Diagnostic Assessment* to designate children requiring:

TIER 2 Intervention Online PDFs

TIER 3 WonderWorks Intervention Program

Build Knowledge
Up in the Sky

 **Essential Question:**
What can you see in the sky?

Teach and Model
Close Reading and Writing

Big Book and Little Book

Reading Writing Workshop

A Bird Named Fern, 140–149
Genre Fantasy Lexile 360

Interactive Read Aloud

"Why the Sun and Moon are in the Sky"
Genre Folktale

Practice and Apply
Close Reading and Writing

Literature Anthology

Kitten's First Full Moon, 162–195
Genre Fantasy Lexile 550

Paired Read

"The Moon," 196–201
Genre Nonfiction Lexile 400

Differentiated Texts

APPROACHING
Lexile 280

ON LEVEL
Lexile 310

BEYOND
Lexile 420

ELL
Lexile 310

Leveled Readers

Extended Complex Texts

The Top Job
Genre Fiction
Lexile 880

Owl at Home
Genre Fiction
Lexile 370

Classroom Library

Student Outcomes

Close Reading of Complex Text

- Cite relevant evidence from text
- Describe plot events: Cause and Effect
- Retell the text

RL.1.3, RL.1.2

Writing

Write to Sources

- Draw evidence from fiction
- Write informative text
- Conduct short research on what you can see in the sky

W.1.2, W.1.7

Speaking and Listening

- Engage in collaborative conversation about what you can see in the sky
- Retell and discuss *A Bird Named Fern*
- Present information on what you can see in the sky

SL.1.1c, SL.1.2, SL.1.3

Content Knowledge

- Explore how animals respond to the things around them.

Language Development

Conventions

- Use adjectives in writing

Vocabulary Acquisition

- Develop Oral Vocabulary

observe	vast	thoughtful
certain	remained	

- Acquire and use academic vocabulary

  leaped   stretched

- Use context clues to understand shades of meaning

L.1.4, L.1.6, L.1.5d

Foundational Skills

Phonics/Word Study/Spelling

- r-controlled vowels *er, ir, ur, or*
- inflectional ending *-er*
- her, bird, fur, fern, dirt, work

High-Frequency Words

another climb full great poor through

Fluency

- Intonation

Decodable Text

- Apply foundational skills in connected text

RF.1.3, RF.1.3f, RF.1.3g, RF.1.4a, RF.1.4b, RF.1.4c

Professional Development

- See lessons in action in real classrooms.
- Get expert advice on instructional practices.
- Collaborate with other teachers.
- Access PLC Resources

Go Digital! www.connected.mcgraw-hill.com.

INSTRUCTIONAL PATH

1 Talk About the Sky

Guide children in collaborative conversations.

Discuss the essential question: *What can you see in the sky?*

Develop academic language.

Listen to "Why the Sun and the Moon Are in the Sky" and make and confirm predictions.

2 Read *A Bird Named Fern*

Apply foundational skills in connected text. Model close reading.

Read

A Bird Named Fern to learn how a bird learns about clouds, citing text evidence to answer text-dependent questions.

Reread

A Bird Named Fern to analyze text, craft, and structure, citing text evidence.

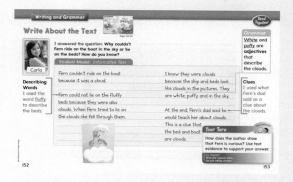

3 Write About *A Bird Named Fern*

Model writing to a source.

Analyze a short response student model.

Use text evidence from close reading to write to a source.

4 Read and Write About *Kitten's First Full Moon*

Practice and apply close reading of the anchor text.

Read

Kitten's First Full Moon to learn about what Kitten sees in the sky.

Reread

Kitten's First Full Moon and use text evidence to understand how the author uses text, craft, and structure to develop a deeper understanding of the story.

Integrate

Information about what you can see in the night sky.

Write to a Source, citing text evidence to explain why Kitten couldn't drink the milk in the sky.

5 Independent Partner Work

Gradual release of support to independent work

- Text-Dependent Questions
- Scaffolded Partner Work
- Talk with a Partner
- Cite Text Evidence
- Complete a sentence frame.
- Guided Text Annotation

6 Integrate Knowledge and Ideas

Connect Texts

Text to Text Discuss how each of the texts answers the question: What can you see in the sky?

Text to Photography Compare information about the sky in the texts read with a photograph.

Conduct a Short Research Project

Create a poster about what can be seen in the sky.

DEVELOPING READERS AND WRITERS

Write to Sources: Informative

Day 1 and Day 2

Shared Writing

- Write about *A Bird Named Fern,* p. T96

Interactive Writing

- Analyze a student model, p. T106

- Write about *A Bird Named Fern,* p. T107

- Find Text Evidence

- Apply Writing Trait: Word Choice: Describing Adjectives, p. T107

- Apply Grammar Skill: Adjectives, p. T107

Day 3, Day 4 and Day 5

Independent Writing

- Write about *Kitten's First Full Moon,* p. T114

- Provide scaffolded instruction to meet student needs, p. T114

- Find Text Evidence, p. T114

- Apply Writing Trait: Word Choice: Describing Adjectives, p. T114

- Prewrite and Draft, p. T114

- Revise and Edit, p. T120

- Final Draft, p. T121

- Present, Evaluate, and Publish, p. T126

Grammar

Adjectives

- Use adjectives to tell about what is happening, pp. T97, T107, T115, T121, T127
- Apply grammar to writing, pp. T97, T114, T120, T127

Mechanics: Capitalization and End Marks

- Use capitalization and end marks, pp. T115, T121, T127

Online PDFs

Grammar Practice, pp. 106–110

Online Grammar Games

Spelling

Words with /ûr/er, ir, ur, or

- Spell words with /ûr/er, ir, ur, or

Online PDFs

Phonics/Spelling blms
pp. 106–110

Online Spelling Games

SUGGESTED LESSON PLAN

READING		DAY 1	DAY 2
Teach, Model and Apply Wonders Reading/Writing Workshop	Core	**Build Background** Up in the Sky, T86–T87 **Oral Vocabulary** *certain, remained, thoughtful,* T86–T88 **Word Work** T90–T93 • Phonemic Awareness: Identify and Generate Rhyme • Phonics/Spelling: Introduce /ûr/er, ir, ur, or • High-Frequency Words: *another, climb, full, great, poor, through* • Vocabulary: *leaped, stretched* **Shared Read** *A Bird Named Fern,* T94–T95	**Oral Language** Up in the Sky, T98 **Oral Vocabulary** *remained, thoughtful, certain, observe, vast* **Word Work** T100–T103 • Phonemic Awareness: Phoneme Substitution • Structural Analysis: Inflectional Ending *-er* • Vocabulary: *leaped, stretched* **Shared Read** *A Bird Named Fern,* T104–T105 • Genre: Fantasy, T104 • Skill: Plot: Cause and Effect, T105
	Options	**Listening Comprehension** "Why the Sun and Moon Are in the Sky," T88–T89	**Listening Comprehension** "Why the Sun and Moon Are in the Sky," T99 **Word Work** T100–T103 • Phonics/Spelling: Review /ûr/ *er, ir, ur, or* • High-Frequency Words

LANGUAGE ARTS			
Writing **Grammar**	Core	**Shared Writing** T96 **Grammar** Adjectives, T97	**Interactive Writing** T106 **Grammar** Adjectives, T107
	Options		

DIFFERENTIATED INSTRUCTION Use your data dashboard to determine each student's needs. Then select instructional supports options throughout the week.

APPROACHING LEVEL

Leveled Reader
Little Blue's Dream, T130–T131
"Hello, Little Dipper!," T131
Literature Circles, T131

Phonological Awareness:
Identify and Generate Rhyme, T132 **TIER 2**
Phoneme Blending, T132
Phoneme Substitution, T133
Phoneme Deletion, T133

Phonics
Connect *er, ir, ur, or* to /ûr/, T134 **TIER 2**
Blend Words with /ûr/ T134 **TIER 2**
Build Words with /ûr/, T135
Build Fluency with Phonics, T135

Structural Analysis Review Inflectional Ending *-er,* T136

Words to Know Review, T137

Comprehension
Read for Fluency, T138 **TIER 2**
Identify Events, T138 **TIER 2**
Review Plot: Cause and Effect, T139
Self-Selected Reading, T139

ON LEVEL

Leveled Reader
Hide and Seek!, T140–141
"Our Sun Is a Star!," T141
Literature Circles, T141

Phonics
Build Words with /ûr/, T142

DAY 3

Fluency Intonation, T109
Word Work T110–T113
- Phonemic Awareness: Phoneme Blending
- Phonics/Spelling: Blend Words with /ûr/ *er, ir, ur, or*
- Vocabulary Strategy: Shades of Meaning/Intensity

Close Reading *Kitten's First Full Moon*, T113A–T113R

DAY 4

Extend the Concept T116–T117
- Text Feature: Captions, T116
- Close Reading: "The Moon," T117–T117B

Word Work T118–T119
- Phonemic Awareness: Phoneme Deletion
- Structural Analysis: Inflectional Ending *-er*

Integrate Ideas
- Research and Inquiry, T122–T123

DAY 5

Word Work T124–T125
- Phonemic Awareness: Phoneme Blending/ Substitution
- Phonics/Spelling: Blend and Build Words with /ûr/ *er, ir, ur, or*
- Structural Analysis: Inflectional Ending *-er*
- High-Frequency Words
- Vocabulary: *leaped, stretched*

Integrate Ideas
- Text Connections, T128–T129

Oral Language Up in the Sky, T108
Word Work T110–T113
- Structural Analysis: Inflectional Ending *-er*
- High-Frequency Words

Word Work T118–T119
- Fluency: Sound-Spellings
- Phonics/Spelling: Build Words with /ûr/ *er, ir, ur, or*
- High-Frequency Words
- Vocabulary: *leaped, stretched*

Close Reading *Kitten's First Full Moon*, T113A–T113R

Word Work T124–T125
- Fluency: Intonation

Integrate Ideas
- Research and Inquiry, T128
- Speaking and Listening, T129

Independent Writing T114
Grammar Mechanics: Capitalization and End Marks, T115

Independent Writing T120
Grammar Mechanics: Capitalization and End Marks, T121

Independent Writing T126
Grammar Adjectives, T127

Grammar Adjectives, T115

Grammar Adjectives, T121

Grammar Mechanics: Capitalization and End Marks, T127

BEYOND LEVEL

Words to Know
Review Words, T142

Leveled Reader
The Foxes Build A Home, T144–T145
"Sunrise and Sunset," T145
Literature Circles, T145

Vocabulary
Suffixes, T146

Comprehension
Review Plot: Cause and Effect, T143
Self-Selected Reading, T143

Comprehension
Review Plot: Cause and Effect, T147
Self-Selected Reading, T147

Gifted and Talented

ENGLISH LANGUAGE LEARNERS

Shared Read
A Bird Name Fern, T148–T149

Leveled Reader
Hide and Seek!, T150–T151
"Our Sun Is a Star!," T151
Literature Circles, T151

Vocabulary
Preteach Oral Vocabulary, T152
Preteach ELL Vocabulary, T152

Words to Know
Review Words, T153
Reteach High-Frequency Words, T153

Writing/Spelling
Writing Trait: Word Choice, T154
Words with /ûr/ *er, ir, ur, or*, T154

Grammar
Adjectives, T155

DIFFERENTIATE TO ACCELERATE

  Scaffold to Access Complex Text

IF the text complexity of a particular selection is too difficult for children

THEN see the references noted in the chart below for scaffolded instruction to help children Access Complex Text.

Qualitative   Quantitative

Reader and Task

TEXT COMPLEXITY

	Reading/Writing Workshop	Literature Anthology	Leveled Readers	Classroom Library

Quantitative

Reading/Writing Workshop

A Bird Named Fern
Lexile 360

Literature Anthology

Kitten's First Full Moon
Lexile 550

"The Moon"
Lexile 400

Leveled Readers

Approaching Level
Lexile 280

On Level
Lexile 310

Beyond Level
Lexile 420

ELL
Lexile 310

Classroom Library

The Top Job
Lexile 880

Owl at Home
Lexile 370

Qualitative

What Makes the Text Complex?

Foundational Skills
- Decoding with *r*-controlled vowels *er, ir, ur, or,* T90–T91
- Reading words with inflectional ending *-er,* T101
- Identifying high-frequency words, T92–T93

See Scaffolded Instruction in Teacher's Edition, T90–T91, T92–T93, and T101.

What Makes the Text Complex?

- **Connection of Ideas,** T113B, T113C, T113J, T113N
- **Sentence Structure,** T113B, T113E, T113G, T113I, T113O

A C T *See Scaffolded Instruction in Teacher's Edition T113B, T113C, T113E, T113G, T113I, T113J, T113N, and T113O.*

What Makes the Text Complex?

Foundational Skills
- Decoding with *r*-controlled vowels *er, ir, ur, or*
- Reading words with inflectional ending *-er*
- Identifying high-frequency words
  another climb full great poor through

See Level Up lessons online for Leveled Readers.

What Makes the Text Complex?

- **Purpose**
- **Specific Vocabulary**
- **Prior Knowledge**
- **Sentence Structure**
- **Organization**
- **Connection of Ideas**
- **Genre**

A C T *See Scaffolded Instruction in Teacher's Edition, T413–T415.*

Reader and Task

The Introduce the Concept lesson on pages T86–T87 will help determine the reader's knowledge and engagement in the weekly concept. See pages T94–T95, T104–T105, T122–T123 and T128–T129 for questions and tasks for this text.

The Introduce the Concept lesson on pages T86–T87 will help determine the reader's knowledge and engagement in the weekly concept. See pages T113A–T113R, T117–T117B, T122–T123 and T128–T129 for questions and tasks for this text.

The Introduce the Concept lesson on pages T86–T87 will help determine the reader's knowledge and engagement in the weekly concept. See pages T130–T131, T140–T141, T144–T145, T150–T151, T122–T123 and T128–T129 for questions and tasks for this text.

The Introduce the Concept lesson on pages T86–T87 will help determine the reader's knowledge and engagement in the weekly concept. See pages T413–T415 for questions and tasks for this text.

Go Digital! www.connected.mcgraw-hill.com

Monitor and *Differentiate*

✓ Quick Check

To differentiate instruction, use the Quick Checks to assess students' needs and select the appropriate small group instruction focus.

Comprehension Strategy Make and Confirm Predictions, T89

Comprehension Skill Plot: Cause and Effect, T105

Phonics Words with /ûr/, T93, T103, T113, T119, T125

High-Frequency Words and Vocabulary T93, T103, T113, T119, T125

If No →

| Approaching Level | Reteach T130–T139 |
| ELL | Develop T148–T155 |

If Yes →

| On Level | Review T140–T143 |
| Beyond Level | Extend T144–T147 |

Using Weekly Data

Check your data Dashboard to verify assessment results and guide grouping decisions.

Level Up with Leveled Readers

IF → children can read their leveled text fluently and answer comprehension questions

THEN → work with the next level up to accelerate children's reading with more complex text.

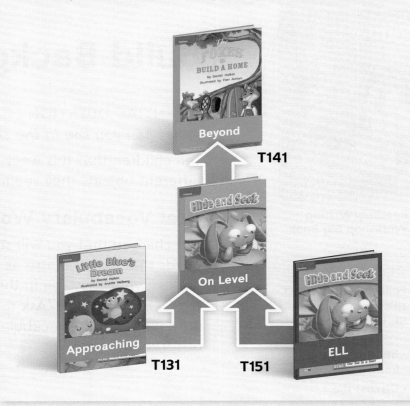

Beyond **T141**

On Level

Approaching **T131**   **T151** ELL

ELL ENGLISH LANGUAGE LEARNERS

Small Group Instruction

Use the ELL small group lessons in the *Wonders* Teacher's Edition to provide focused instruction.

Language Development
Vocabulary preteaching, oral vocabulary preteaching, high-frequency word review and reteach, pp. T152–T153

Close Reading
Interactive Question-Response routines for scaffolded text-dependent questioning for reading and rereading the Shared Read and Leveled Reader, pp. T148–T151

Writing
Focus on the writing trait, grammar, and spelling, pp. T154–T155

Additional ELL Support

Use Wonders for English Learners for ELD instruction that connects to the core.

Language Development
My Language Book for ample opportunities for discussions and scaffolded language support

Close Reading
Guided support for the Shared Read, Big Books, and Interactive Read Alouds. Differentiated texts about the weekly concept

Writing
Guided support in Interactive and Independent Writing and writing to sources

Wonders for ELs Teacher Edition and My Language Book

Materials

Reading/Writing Workshop VOLUME 4

Reading/Writing Workshop Big Book UNIT 5

Visual Vocabulary Cards

certain   observe
remained   vast
thoughtful

Think Aloud Clouds

High-Frequency Word Cards

another   great
climb   poor
full   through

leaped

Vocabulary Cards
leaped
stretched

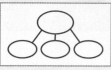

Interactive Read-Aloud Cards

Teaching Poster

a b c

Word-Building Cards

er ir ur

shirt

Sound-Spelling Cards

Reading/Writing Workshop Big Book

OBJECTIVES

CCSS Follow agreed-upon rules for discussions. **SL.1.1a**

- Build background knowledge
- Discuss the Essential Question

ACADEMIC LANGUAGE
- *observe, objects*
- Cognates: *observar, objetos*

→ # Introduce the Concept

Go Digital

Build Background
5 Mins MINILESSON

ESSENTIAL QUESTION

What can you see in the sky?

Tell children that this week they will be talking and reading about different objects they see in the sky, from birds to the stars.

Oral Vocabulary Words

Tell children that you will share some words that they can use as they discuss what they see in the sky. Use the Define/Example/Ask routine to introduce the oral vocabulary words **observe** and **vast**.

Visual Vocabulary Cards

Oral Vocabulary Routine

<u>Define:</u> To **observe** is to watch carefully.

<u>Example:</u> I can observe what the birds do in the birdbath.

<u>Ask:</u> What have you sat and observed?

<u>Define:</u> When something is **vast**, it is very large.

<u>Example:</u> We sailed on the vast ocean.

<u>Ask:</u> What is something that you think is vast?

Discuss the theme of "Up in the Sky." Explain that the sky above us is not empty and that we see many things in the sky. *What might you observe in the sky at night? What have you observed in the sky during the day?*

Up in the Sky

Video

Photos

SCHOOL

Visual Glossary

Graphic Organizer

READING/WRITING WORKSHOP, *pp. 134–135*

Talk About It: Up in the Sky

Guide children to discuss what the girl sees in the sky.

- What is the girl looking at?

- What is she using? How will it change what she can see?

Use Teaching Poster 40 and prompt children to complete the Word Web. Talk about all of the stars that the girl might see through the telescope.

Children can look at page 134 of their Reading/Writing Workshop and do the Talk About It activity with a partner.

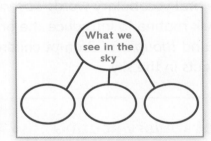

Teaching Poster

Collaborative Conversations

Listen Carefully As children engage in partner, small-group, and whole-group discussions, encourage them to:

- always look at the speaker.

- respect others by not interrupting them.

- repeat others' ideas to check understanding.

ENGLISH LANGUAGE LEARNERS SCAFFOLD

Beginning

Use Visuals Tell children about the objects in the sky. *The girl sees stars in the sky. Do you like looking at stars?* Restate children's responses in complete sentences.

Intermediate

Describe Ask children to describe what they see in the sky. Elicit more details to support children's answers.

Advanced/High

Discuss Have children elaborate on what they see in the sky. Have them compare what the child sees to their own observations of objects in the sky. Elicit more details to support children's answers.

→ # Listening Comprehension

Read the Interactive Read Aloud

OBJECTIVES

CCSS Participate in collaborative conversations with diverse partners about *grade 1 topics and texts* with peers and adults in small and larger groups. **SL.1.1**

- Develop concept understanding
- Develop reading strategy: make and confirm predictions

ACADEMIC LANGUAGE
- *prediction, confirm, characters, events*
- Cognates: *predicción, confirmar*

Connect to Concept: Up In the Sky

Tell children that they will now read a story about how the sun and the moon came to be in the sky. Tell children that folktales are very old stories that people shared to explain why things are the way they are.

"Why the Sun and Moon Are in the Sky"

Focus on Oral Vocabulary

Review the oral vocabulary words *observe* and *vast*. Use the Define/Example/Ask routine to introduce the oral vocabulary words *certain*, *remained*, and *thoughtful*. Prompt children to use the words as they discuss objects in the sky.

Oral Vocabulary Routine

<u>Define:</u> If you are **certain** about something, you are sure it is true.

<u>Example:</u> Juan is certain that he will have fun at the fair.

<u>Ask:</u> What are you certain will happen later today?

<u>Define:</u> **Remained** means "stayed the same" or "stayed in place."

<u>Example:</u> The kite got stuck in the tree, and it remained there until the wind blew it down.

Visual Vocabulary Cards

<u>Ask:</u> What has remained in the classroom for a long time?

<u>Define:</u> A person who is **thoughtful** is kind and thinks about how others feel.

<u>Example:</u> Kayla was thoughtful when she baked her grandmother bread.

<u>Ask:</u> What thoughtful things could you do for a friend who was sick in bed?

Go Digital

"Why the Sun and Moon Are in the Sky"

Make and Confirm Predictions

SCHOOL
Visual Glossary

Retell

Set a Purpose for Reading

- Display the Interactive Read-Aloud Cards.
- Read aloud the title and the information about where the story comes from.
- Tell children that you will be reading a story about three friends, the Sun, the Moon, and the Sea. Say: *In this story, the Sun, Moon, and Sea are characters who can move and talk.* Tell children to read to find out what Sun, Moon, and Sea do and say.

Strategy: Make and Confirm Predictions

1 Explain Remind children that as they read or listen to a story, they can make predictions about what will happen next. Then they can confirm their predictions by reading on and seeing if their prediction was correct. This will help them to better connect to the story.

Think Aloud Making predictions and checking to see if they were correct is a good way to better understand a story. Today, as we read "Why the Sun and Moon Are in the Sky," use what you have heard about the characters and events so far to make a guess about what will happen next. Then continue listening to confirm your prediction.

2 Model Read the selection. As you read, use the Think Aloud Cloud to model the strategy.

Think Aloud Remember that you can make predictions about what will happen next and check them as you read. In the text I read that the Sun and the Moon invite the Sea to come visit. I know they are all are good friends, so I predict that the Sea will accept their invitation. Now I will keep reading to see if my guess was correct.

3 Guided Practice As you continue to read, pause to elicit predictions from children. *What do you think might happen next? What clues in the story make you think that?* Pause to ask children if their predictions were correct. Guide children in using the evidence in the text and illustrations to confirm their predictions.

Respond to Reading

After reading, prompt children to retell "Why the Sun and Moon Are in the Sky." Discuss what predictions they made and how they confirmed their predictions.

ENGLISH LANGUAGE LEARNERS SCAFFOLD

Beginning

Engage Display Card 2 of "Why the Sun and Moon Are in the Sky." Point to the house. *Is this a house? Are the Sun and the Moon building the house? Let's make a prediction. Will the Sea visit the house?*

Intermediate

Describe Display Card 2 of "Why the Sun and Moon Are in the Sky." Have children describe the illustration. *Let's make a prediction. Do you think the Sea will fit inside this new house?* Elicit more details to support children's answers.

Advanced/High

Describe Display Card 2 of "Why the Sun and Moon Are in the Sky." *Why are the Sun and the Moon building a house? Do you think the house will be big enough for the Sea and all her children? Why or why not?*

Monitor and *Differentiate*

 Quick Check

Can children apply the strategy make and confirm predictions?

⬇

Small Group Instruction

If No →	Approaching	Reteach pp. T130–131
	ELL	Develop pp. T148–151
If Yes →	On Level	Review pp. T140–141
	Beyond Level	Extend pp. T144–145

→ Word Work

Phonological Awareness

MINILESSON 5 Mins

OBJECTIVES

CCSS Decode regularly spelled one-syllable words. **RF.1.3b**

Recognize and generate rhyming words

Identify and Generate Rhyme

1 Model Show children how to identify and generate rhyming words. *I am going to say two words. Listen:* shirt, hurt. Shirt *and* hurt *rhyme because they both end in the same sounds: /ûrt/. Listen: /sh/ /ûrt/,* shirt; */h/ /ûrt/,* hurt. *What other words rhyme with* shirt *and* hurt? *To figure that out, I need to think of words that end in /ûrt/. I know one:* dirt, */d/ /ûrt/. The word* dirt *ends in /ûrt/, so it rhymes with* shirt *and* hurt.

2 Guided Practice/Practice Have children practice identifying and generating rhymes. Do the first two examples with children. *I will say a group of words. Tell me which two words in the group rhyme. Then think of other words that rhyme with the rhyming pair.*

turn, torn, earn	make, far, scar	heard, chirp, third
rain, plane, pay	roar, cart, core	goal, oat, goat

Phonics

MINILESSON 10 Mins

Introduce /ûr/ *er, ir, ur, or*

Sound-Spelling Card

1 Model Display the *Shirt* Sound-Spelling Card. Teach /ûr/ spelled *er, ir, ur,* and *or* using *her, shirt, fur,* and *worm*. *This is the* Shirt *Sound-Spelling Card. The sounds in the middle of* shirt *are /ûr/. Listen: /shûrt/,* shirt. *The /ûr/ sounds can be spelled with the letters* ir *as in* shirt, er *as in* her, ur *as in* fur, *and* or *as in* worm. *Say the sounds with me: /ûr/. I'll say /ûr/ as I write the different spellings several times.*

2 Guided Practice/Practice Have children practice connecting the letters *er, ir, ur,* and *or* to the sounds /ûr/ by writing them. *Now do it with me. Say /ûr/ as I write the letters* er, ir, ur, *and* or. *This time, write the spellings five times each as you say the /ûr/ sounds.*

SKILLS TRACE

/ûr/er, ir, ur, or

Introduce Unit 5 Week 2 Day 1

Review Unit 5 Week 2 Days 2, 3, 4, 5

Assess Unit 5 Week 2

Blend Words with /ûr/ *er, ir, ur, or*

1 Model Display **Word-Building Cards** *g, i, r, l.* Model how to blend the sounds. *This is the letter* g. *It stands for /g/. These are the letters* i *and* r. *Together they stand for /ûr/. This is the letter* l. *It stands for /l/. Listen as I blend these sounds together: /gûrlll/. Say it with me:* girl.

Continue by modeling the words *germ, curb,* and *world.*

2 Guided Practice/Practice Display the Day 1 Phonics Practice Activity. Read each word in the first row, blending the sounds; for example: */hûr/. The word is* her. Have children blend each word with you. Prompt children to read the connected text, sounding out the decodable words.

her	bird	curl	first	worm	dirt
word	verb	turn	jerk	nurse	curve
bun	burn	clock	clerk	shirt	skirt
large	lucky	flight	better	return	surprise

The girls at work were thirsty.

A big bird lurks on top of the church.

Fern will hurry back to change her skirt.

> Also online

Day 1 Phonics Practice Activity

Corrective Feedback

Sound Error Model the sound that children missed, then have them repeat the sound. Say: *My turn.* Tap under the letter and say: *Sound? /ûr/. What's the sound?* Return to the beginning of the word. Say: *Let's start over.* Blend the word with children again.

Daily Handwriting

Throughout the week teach uppercase and lowercase letters *Kk* using the Handwriting models.

ON-LEVEL PRACTICE BOOK p. 223

The end sound you hear in **fur** can be spelled **er** as in **her, ir** as in **dirt, ur** as in **turn,** and **or** as in **word.**

A. Read the words. Listen for the sound at the end of fur. Circle the word that names the picture.

1. wide (worm) 2. bed (bird)

3. (shirt) show 4. sun (surf)

B. Use a word from the box to complete each sentence.

| her | nurse | skirt | work |

5. There is a ___nurse___ at my school.

6. ___Her___ hat is green.

7. I have a pretty blue ___skirt___

| APPROACHING p. 223 | BEYOND p. 223 | ELL p. 223 |

Word Work

Quick Review

High-Frequency Words: Read, Spell, and Write to review last week's high-frequency words: *four, large, none, only, put, round.*

Go Digital

MINILESSON 5 Mins Spelling

OBJECTIVES

CCSS Recognize and read grade-appropriate irregularly spelled words. **RF.1.3g**

CCSS Use conventional spelling for words with common spelling patterns and for frequently occurring irregular words. **L.1.2d**

Words with *er, ir, ur, or*

Dictation Use the Spelling Dictation routine for each word to help children transfer their knowledge of sound-spellings to writing.

Pretest After dictation, pronounce each spelling word. Say a sentence for each word and pronounce the word again. Ask children to say each word softly, stretching the sounds, before writing it. After the pretest, display the spelling words and write each word as you say the letter names. Have children check their words.

her	bird	fur	fern	dirt
work	barn	arm	climb	through

For Approaching Level and Beyond Level children, refer to the Differentiated Spelling Lists for modified word lists.

Spelling Word Routine

they	together
how	eat

High-Frequency Word Routine

MINILESSON 5 Mins High-Frequency Words

school

Visual Glossary

another, climb, full, great, poor, through

① Model Display **High-Frequency Word Cards** *another, climb, full, great, poor, through.* Use the Read/Spell/Write routine to teach each word.

- **Read** Point to and say the word *another. This is the word* another. *Say it with me:* another. *I need another pencil.*

- **Spell** *The word another is spelled* a-n-o-t-h-e-r. *Spell it with me.*

- **Write** *Let's write the word in the air as we say each letter:* a-n-o-t-h-e-r.

- Repeat to introduce *climb, full, great, poor,* and *through.*

- As children spell each word with you, point out the irregularities in sound-spellings, such as the silent letter *b* at the end of *climb.*

- Have partners create sentences using each word.

ENGLISH LANGUAGE LEARNERS

Pantomime Review the meaning of these words by using pictures, pantomime, or gestures when possible. Have children repeat or act out the word.

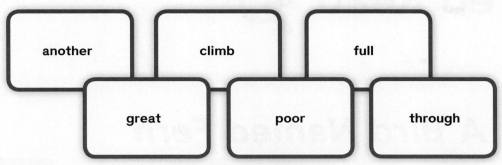

High-Frequency Word Cards

❶ Guided Practice Have children read the sentences. Prompt them to identify the high-frequency words in connected text and to blend the decodable words.

1. The cat will **climb another** tree.
2. The glass is not **full**!
3. The **poor** dog needs more water.
4. This park is **great,** so let's walk **through** it.

MINILESSON

5 Mins

Introduce Vocabulary

leaped, stretched

❷ Model Introduce the new words using the routine.

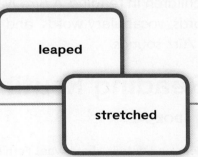

Vocabulary Cards

Vocabulary Routine

<u>Define:</u> If you **leaped**, you made a big jump.

<u>Example:</u> *The dog leaped in the air to catch the ball.*

<u>Ask:</u> What is the difference between *leaped* and *hopped*? COMPARE AND CONTRAST

<u>Define:</u> When someone has **stretched**, they have extended a body part.

<u>Example:</u> *The girl stretched her arms and legs before playing basketball.*

<u>Ask:</u> Why is it a good idea to stretch before you play sports? IDEA

❷ Review Use the routine to review last week's vocabulary words.

Monitor and *Differentiate*

✓ Quick Check

Can children read and decode words with *r*-controlled vowels *er, ir, ur, or*?

Can children recognize and read high-frequency and vocabulary words?

Small Group Instruction

If No →	Approaching	Reteach pp. T134–137
	ELL	Develop pp. T148–155
If Yes →	On Level	Review pp. T142–143
	Beyond Level	Extend pp. T146–147

Shared Read

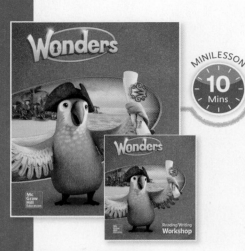
OBJECTIVES

 Decode regularly spelled one-syllable words. **RF.1.3b**

 Recognize and read grade-appropriate irregularly spelled words. **RF.1.3g**

ACADEMIC LANGUAGE
• *fantasy, fiction*
• Cognates: *fantasía, ficción*

Read *A Bird Named Fern*

Focus on Foundational Skills

Review with children the words and letter-sounds they will see in *A Bird Named Fern*.

• Have children use pages 136–137 to review high-frequency words *full, great, climb, through, another, poor,* and vocabulary words *leaped* and *stretched*.

• Have children use pages 138–139 to review that the letters *er, ir, or,* and *ur* can stand for the /ûr/ sounds. Guide them to blend the sounds to read the words.

• Display the story words *always, cloud, questions, saw,* and *something*. Spell each word and model reading it. Tell children they will be reading the words in the selection.

Read Guide children in reading *A Bird Named Fern*. Point out the high-frequency words, vocabulary words, and words in which *er, ir, ur,* and *or* stand for the /ûr/ sounds.

Close Reading Routine

Read **DOK 1–2**

• Identify key ideas and details about what Fern sees in the sky.
• Take notes and retell.
• Use **A C T** prompts as needed.

Reread **DOK 2–3**

• Analyze the text, craft, and structure.
• Use the Reread minilessons.

Integrate **DOK 4**

• Integrate knowledge and ideas
• Make text-to-text connections.
• Use the Integrate Lesson.

Genre: Fantasy Tell children that *A Bird Named Fern* is a fantasy. A fantasy is a made-up story that could not happen in real life and often has animal characters that talk and act like people.

A Bird Named Fern

READING/WRITING WORKSHOP, pp. 140–149 **Lexile** 360

Connect to Concept: Up In the Sky

ESSENTIAL QUESTION Explain to children that as they read *A Bird Named Fern,* they will look for key ideas and details that will help them answer the Essential Question: *What can you see in the sky?*

- Pages 142–143: What does Fern think she sees in the sky?
- Pages 144–145: What does the boat look like now?
- Pages 146–147: What happens when Fern tries to rest on the beds?
- Pages 148–149: What does Fern learn when she gets home?

Focus on Fluency

 With partners, have children read *A Bird Named Fern* to develop fluency. Remind them that they can ask themselves questions to make sure they understand what they are reading.

Retell Have partners use key ideas and details to retell *A Bird Named Fern*. Invite them to tell what Fern learned about the sky.

Make Connections

 Read together Make Connections on page 149. Have partners talk about what the clouds looked like to Fern using this sentence starter:

> *First, Fern thought the cloud looked like. . .*

Guide children to connect what they have read to the Essential Question.

SHARED READ **T95**

→ # Language Arts

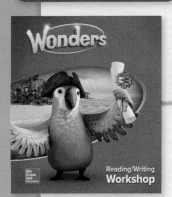

Reading/Writing Workshop

OBJECTIVES

CCSS Write informative/explanatory texts in which they name a topic, supply some facts about the topic, and provide some sense of closure. **W.1.2**

CCSS Use frequently occurring adjectives. **L.1.1f**

ACADEMIC LANGUAGE

• *describe, text, illustrations, adjective*

• Cognates: *describir, texto, ilustraciónes, adjetivo*

MINILESSON **5** Mins

Shared Writing

Write About the Reading/Writing Workshop

Analyze the Prompt Tell children you will work together to write a response to a prompt. Read aloud the question. *What did Fern do in* A Bird Named Fern? Say: *To respond to this prompt, we need to look at the text and illustrations in the story.*

Find Text Evidence Explain that you will reread the text and take notes to respond to the prompt. Read aloud pages 142–144. Say: *On page 143, Fern thinks she sees a boat in the sky and wants to find out more about it.* Point to the illustration of Fern looking at the clouds. Say: *On page 144, Fern flies off to find out more about the boat.* Point to the illustration of Fern leaving the nest on page 145. Say: *These are details that will help us respond to the prompt. Let's write them in our notes.*

Write to a Prompt Reread the prompt to children. *What did Fern do in* A Bird Named Fern? Say: *We can use our notes to tell what Fern did in order: First, Fern thought she saw a big, white boat in the sky.* Write the sentence. *Let's check our notes to find out what Fern did next and write our second sentence: Next, she left the nest to find out more about the boat.* Write the sentence. *Now, we will read our notes and use them to tell what else Fern did in order.* Track the print as you reread the notes.

Guide children to dictate complete sentences for you to record based on their notes. Read the final response as you track the print.

Go Digital

Graphic Organizer

Writing

I see a fish.

Grammar

Grammar

Adjectives

1 Model Tell children that an adjective is a word that describes a noun. Explain that adjectives tell number, color, size, or shape. They also tell how things look, sound, feel, smell, or taste. Display the following sentences:

A big crow floated in the sky.

I feel the hot sun on my face.

Explain that *big* and *hot* are adjectives. Point out that *big* describes size and *hot* tells how something feels.

2 Guided Practice/Practice Display the sentences below and read them aloud. Have partners work together to identify the adjectives.

Did you see the girl in the red skirt? (red)

I see six birds on the tree. (six)

I ate a sweet peach at lunch. (sweet)

Talk About It Have partners work together to orally generate sentences that tell about the size and shape of objects on their desks.

Link to Writing Say: *Let's look back at our writing and see if we used adjectives to describe nouns. Did we use them correctly?* Review the Shared Writing for the correct use of adjectives. Point out that you used the adjectives *big* and *white* to describe the noun *boat*.

ENGLISH LANGUAGE LEARNERS SCAFFOLD

Beginning

Demonstrate Comprehension Ask children to point to the adjectives in the Model sentences. *Use your hands to show me the size of a big crow. Is* crow *an adjective? Is* big *an adjective? Show me what it feels like to have hot sun on your face. Is* hot *an adjective?*

Intermediate

Explain Ask children to circle the adjective in the first Model sentence. *How do you know* big *is an adjective?* Continue with the second sentence. Repeat correct answers to the class.

Advanced/High

Expand Remove the adjectives in the Practice sentences and have children provide new adjectives to complete the sentences. Model correct pronunciation as needed.

Daily Wrap Up

- Encourage children to discuss the Essential Question using the oral vocabulary words. Ask: *What can you see in the sky today?*

- Prompt children to share what skills they learned. Ask: *How will these skills help you read and write?*

Materials

Reading/Writing Workshop VOLUME 4

Visual Vocabulary Cards
certain   thoughtful
observe   vast
remained

Word-Building Cards

another

High-Frequency Word Cards
another
climb
full
great
poor
through

Teaching Poster

leaped

Vocabulary Cards
leaped
stretched

Interactive Read-Aloud Cards

her

Spelling Word Cards

shirt

Sound-Spelling Cards

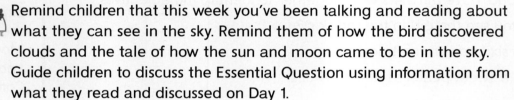

→ Build the Concept

Go Digital

Oral Language

MINILESSON 5 Mins

OBJECTIVES

CCSS Ask and answer questions about key details in a text read aloud or information presented orally or through other media. **SL.1.2**

- Discuss the Essential Question
- Build concept understanding

ACADEMIC LANGUAGE
- events, characters, prediction
- Cognate: *predicción*

ESSENTIAL QUESTION

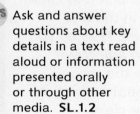

Remind children that this week you've been talking and reading about what they can see in the sky. Remind them of how the bird discovered clouds and the tale of how the sun and moon came to be in the sky. Guide children to discuss the Essential Question using information from what they read and discussed on Day 1.

Oral Vocabulary Words

Review the oral vocabulary words. Use the Define/Example/Ask routine to review the oral vocabulary words *certain*, *observe*, *remained*, *thoughtful*, and *vast*. Guide children to use the words as they answer these questions.

- How can you be certain of how long something is?
- How can a telescope help you observe the stars at night?
- Do you want to grow up or remain small? Why?
- What might be a thoughtful gift for a friend who is sick?
- Which is more vast: a swimming pool or the ocean?

Visual Glossary

"Why the Sun and Moon Are in the Sky"

Listening Comprehension

Reread the Interactive Read Aloud

Strategy: Make and Confirm Predictions

Remind children that as they listen, they can make predictions about what might happen next in a story and check them by continuing to listen. This can help them understand the story.

Tell children that you will reread "Why the Sun and Moon Are in the Sky." Display the Interactive Read-Aloud Cards. Pause as you read to apply the strategy.

"Why the Sun and Moon Are in the Sky"

Think Aloud When I read this story the first time, I used what I had read about the characters and events to make predictions about what would happen next. Then I read on to see if my predictions were correct. When I read that Sea was filling Sun and Moon's house with water, I thought about the story's title and about how vast the sea is. I predicted Sun and Moon's home would be filled with Sea's water and they would have to go up into the sky. I read on and found that I was right!

Make Connections

Discuss partners' responses to "Why the Sun and Moon Are in the Sky."

- *How did you feel when Sun and Moon had to stand on their table to avoid the water? Did you think Sea would stop coming in?*

- *Why do you think Sea kept coming?*

- *What might have happened if Sea stopped coming into their home?*

Write About It Have children write in their Writer's Notebooks about what might have happened if Sea stopped coming into Sun and Moon's home. Guide children by asking questions, such as: *Do you think Sun and Moon would still have gone up to the sky? What other reasons might have caused them to leave their home for the sky?* Have children write continuously for six minutes.

 # Word Work

Quick Review

Build Fluency: Sound-Spellings
Display the **Word-Building Cards:** *er, ir, ur, or, ar, ey, igh, oa, oe, ee, ea, ai, ay, e_e, u_e, o_e, dge, i_e, a_e, ch, tch, wh, ph, th, sh, ng, mp, sk, st, nt.* Have children say the sounds.

Phonemic Awareness

OBJECTIVES

CCSS Decode regularly spelled one-syllable words. **RF.1.3b**

CCSS Read words with inflectional endings. **RF.1.3f**

Substitute phonemes in words

Phoneme Substitution

1 Model Show children how to change sounds in words to make new words. *Listen carefully as I say a word:* bird, /bûrd/. *I will change the /b/ sound to /h/, and make a new word. The new word is* herd, /hûrd/.

2 Guided Practice/Practice *Let's do some together. The word is* turn. *Say it with me:* /tûrnnn/. *We will change the first sound /t/ to /b/. Let's say the new word together:* burn. *Now listen as I say some words. I want you to change the first sound in each word to the sound I give you to make a new word.* Do the first one with children.

dirt, /h/ (hurt)	dried, /f/ (fried)	jumpy, /b/ (bumpy)
burst, /th/ (thirst)	term, /w/ (worm)	my, /sh/ (shy)
cart, /h/ (heart)	nurse, /p/ (purse)	rail, /m/ (mail)

Phonics

Review /ûr/*er, ir, ur, or*

1 Model Display the *Shirt* **Sound-Spelling Card**. Review the sounds /ûr/ using the words *term, firm, surf,* and *work*.

2 Guided Practice/Practice Have children practice connecting the letters and sounds. Point to the Sound-Spelling Card. *What letters are these? What sounds do they stand for?*

Go Digital

Phonemic Awareness

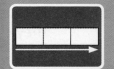

Phonics

Structural Analysis

Handwriting

Blend Words with /ûr/ *er, ir, ur, or*

1 Model Display **Word-Building Cards** t, h, i, r, s, t to form the word *thirst*. Model how to generate and blend the sounds to say the word. *These are the letters* t *and* h. *Together they stand for /th/. These are the letters* i *and* r. *Together they stand for /ûr/. This is the letter* s. *It stands for /s/. This is the letter* t. *It stands for /t/. Listen as I blend these sounds together: /thûrst/. Say it with me:* thirst.

Continue by modeling the words *chirp, fern, burn, worm.*

2 Guided Practice/Practice Repeat the routine with children with *sir, worse, skirt, hurl, birth, girl, word, turn, stir, church.*

Build Words with /ûr/ *er, ir, ur, or*

1 Model Display the Word-Building Cards g, e, r, m. Blend: /j/ /ûr/ /m/, /jûrmmm/, *germ.*

- Change *g* to *t* and repeat with *term.*
- Change *t* to *p* and repeat with *perm.*

2 Guided Practice/Practice Continue with *perk, jerk, clerk, curl, hurl, hurt, shirt, skirt, skit, sit, bit, bid, bird, third, word.*

ENGLISH LANGUAGE LEARNERS

Build Vocabulary Review the meanings of example words that can be explained or demonstrated in a concrete way. For example, ask children to point to a *girl* or a *word*. Model the action for *turn* saying, "I can turn the doorknob." Provide sentence starters such as "When I am thirsty, I ___" for children to complete. Correct grammar and pronunciation as needed.

MINILESSON 5 Mins

Structural Analysis

Inflectional Ending *-er*

1 Model Tell children that the ending *-er* can be added to some words to make new words. Explain that adding *-er* to a verb, or action word, changes the verb to a noun, or naming word. Write and read aloud *teach* and *teacher*. Underline the *-er*. Explain that a teacher is a person who teaches. Have children use both words in a sentence.

2 Guided Practice/Practice Write the following words and read them with children: *work, learn, farm, fight, read.* Have children add *-er* to each word and explain what the new word means. Then have them use each word in a sentence.

→ # Word Work

Quick Review
High-Frequency Words: Read/Spell and Write to review this week's high-frequency words: *another, climb, full, great, poor, through.*

MINILESSON 5 Mins

Spelling

OBJECTIVES

CCSS Recognize and read grade-appropriate irregularly spelled words. **RF.1.3g**

CCSS Use conventional spelling for words with common spelling patterns and for frequently occurring irregular words. **L.1.2d**

Word Sort with *er, ir, ur, or*

1 Model Display the **Spelling Word Cards** from the Teacher's Resource Book, one at a time. Have children read the words and listen for the /ûr/ sounds.

Use cards for *verb, girl, turn,* and *worm* to make a four-column chart. Note the spelling of /ûr/ as you say the words. Ask children to chorally spell the words.

2 Guided Practice/Practice Have children place each Spelling Word Card in the column with words containing the same spelling of /ûr/. When done, have children chorally read the words. Call out a word. Have a child find the word card and point to it as the class spells the word.

ANALYZE ERRORS/ARTICULATION SUPPORT

Use children's pretest errors to analyze spelling problems and provide corrective feedback. For example, the words *her, bird, fur,* and *work* all have the same vowel + -r sounds, but they are spelled in different ways.

Write the spelling words on the board for children to read and have them circle the /ûr/ spelling in each word. Create additional /ûr/ sorts (with the spelling words and others) to allow children to analyze and learn the common /ûr/ spelling patterns.

ELL

ENGLISH LANGUAGE LEARNERS

Provide Clues Practice spelling by helping children generate more words with *er, ir, ur,* and *or* patterns. Provide clues: *Think of a word that begins with* f *and rhymes with* thirst. Write the word and have children practice reading it. Correct their pronunciation as needed.

MINILESSON 5 Mins

High-Frequency Words

another, climb, full, great, poor, through

1 Guided Practice Say each word and have children Read/Spell/Write it. Ask children to picture each word in their minds and write it the way they see it. Display the words for children to self-correct.

- Point out irregularities in sound-spellings, such as the long *a* sound spelled *ea* in *great.*

2 Practice Add the high-frequency words *another, climb, full, great, poor,* and *through* to the cumulative word bank.

- Have children work with a partner to create sentences using the words.
- Have children look at the words and compare their sounds and spellings to words from previous weeks.
- Suggest that they write about what they see in the sky.

Cumulative Review Review last week's words using the Read/Spell/Write routine.

- Repeat the above routine, mixing the words and having children chorally say each one.

MINILESSON 5 Mins
Reinforce Vocabulary

leaped, stretched

1 Guided Practice Use the **Vocabulary Cards** to review this week's and last week's vocabulary words. Work together with children to generate a new context sentence for each word.

2 Practice Have children work with a partner to orally complete each sentence stem on the Day 2 Vocabulary Practice Activity using this week's and last week's vocabulary words.

| trouble | whole | leaped | stretched |

1. He ate the _____ pie.
2. The cat _____ up on top of the box.
3. Jim _____ out his arm to reach the top shelf.
4. Beth had no _____ taking care of the good dog.

Also online

Day 2 Vocabulary Practice Activity

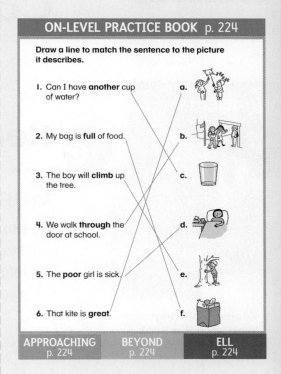

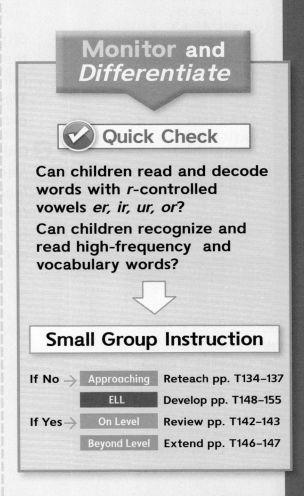

Monitor and *Differentiate*

✓ Quick Check

Can children read and decode words with *r*-controlled vowels *er, ir, ur, or*?

Can children recognize and read high-frequency and vocabulary words?

⬇

Small Group Instruction

If No →	Approaching	Reteach pp. T134–137
	ELL	Develop pp. T148–155
If Yes →	On Level	Review pp. T142–143
	Beyond Level	Extend pp. T146–147

Comprehension

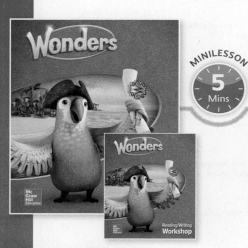

Reading/Writing Workshop Big Book and Reading/Writing Workshop

OBJECTIVES

CCSS Describe characters, settings, and major events in a story, using key details. **RL.1.3**

Understand fantasy genre

ACADEMIC LANGUAGE
• *cause, effect*
• Cognates: *causa, efecto*

SKILLS TRACE

PLOT

Introduce Unit 3 Week 1

Review Unit 3 Weeks 2, 3; Unit 4 Weeks 1, 4; Unit 5 Weeks 1, 2, 3; Unit 6 Weeks 3, 4

Assess Unit 3 Weeks 1, 2, 3; Unit 4 Week 1; Unit 5 Weeks 2, 4; Unit 6 Week 3

MINILESSON **5 Mins**

Reread *A Bird Named Fern*

Genre: Fantasy

1 Model Tell children they will now reread the fantasy story *A Bird Named Fern*. Explain that as they read, they will look for information in the text to help them understand the selection.

Review the characteristics of fantasy. It:

• is a made-up story.

• could not really happen.

• often has animal characters that look and act like real people.

Explain that a fantasy is a made-up story. Often the characters are animals that talk and act like real people. Tell children that, like other fiction stories, fantasies have a beginning, a middle, and an end.

Display pages 142–143: *The illustration shows that the setting of the story is a forest. The characters are a family of birds. The birds talk. This information helps me know that the story is a fantasy. This is the beginning of the story. The author introduces the main character and tells me that she wants to know about everything.*

2 Guided Practice/Practice Display pages 146 and 147 of *A Bird Named Fern. This is the middle of the story. In the beginning, we learned that Fern wants to explore everything. Now, in the middle, the text explains that Fern thought the cloud was a pillow. She wanted to rest on it, but she fell through the cloud! Could these events happen in real life? Why or why not?*

Go Digital

A Bird Named Fern

Genre

Cause and Effect

Skill: Plot/Cause and Effect

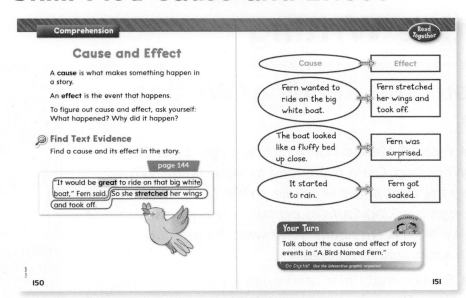

Reading/Writing Workshop, pp. 150–151

1 Model Tell children that when they read a fantasy, they need to think about what happens and why these events happen. This information will help them understand the plot. Have children look at pages 150–151 in their Reading/Writing Workshop. Read together the definition of cause and effect. *A cause is what makes something happen in a story. An effect is the event that happens.*

2 Guided Practice/Practice Read together the Find Text Evidence section and model finding a cause and effect in *A Bird Named Fern*. Point out the information added to the graphic organizer. *On page 144, we read that Fern wanted to ride on the big white boat. This is the cause, what makes something happen in the story. Then Fern stretched her wings and took off. This is the effect, the event that happens. This information has been added to the Cause and Effect chart. Can you find other causes and effects in the story?*

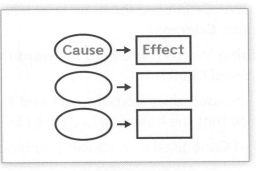

Teaching Poster

Monitor and *Differentiate*

✓ Quick Check

Can children identify cause and effect in a fantasy selection?

Small Group Instruction

If No → **Approaching** Reteach pp. T138–139

ELL Develop pp. T148–155

If Yes → **On Level** Review p. T143

Beyond Level Extend p. T147

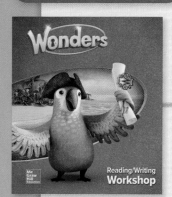

Wonders

Reading/Writing Workshop

Reading/Writing Workshop

OBJECTIVES

CCSS Write informative/ explanatory texts in which they name a topic, supply some facts about the topic, and provide some sense of closure. **W.1.2**

CCSS Use frequently occurring adjectives. **L.1.1f**

ACADEMIC LANGUAGE

- *inference, evidence, notes*
- Cognates: *inferencia, evidencia, notas*

MINILESSON 5 Mins

Interactive Writing

Write About the Reading/Writing Workshop

Analyze the Model Prompt Have children turn to page 152 in the **Reading/Writing Workshop**. Carla responded to the prompt: *Why couldn't Fern ride on the boat in the sky or lie on the beds? How do you know?* Say: *The prompt is asking Carla to explain why Fern couldn't ride on the boat in the sky or lie on the beds. To answer this prompt, Carla found text evidence and made inferences.*

Find Text Evidence Explain that Carla used evidence in the text and illustrations to take notes. Then, she used her notes to make inferences about why Fern couldn't ride the boat or lie on the beds.

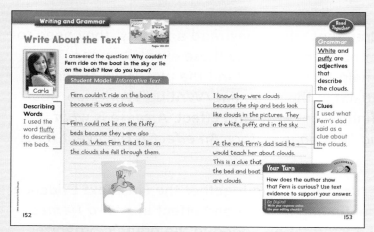

Reading/Writing Workshop

Analyze the Student Model Read the model. Discuss the callouts.

- **Adjectives** Carla used the adjectives *white* and *puffy* to describe the clouds. **Grammar**
- **Describing Words** Carla used the word *fluffy* to describe the bed. **Trait: Word Choice**
- **Clues** She used clues from the text and illustrations to make an inference that the boat and beds are clouds. **Trait: Ideas**

Point out that Carla used a concluding sentence to end her writing.

Go Digital

Graphic Organizer

Writing

I see a fish.

Grammar

Your Turn: Write About the Text Say: *Now we will write to a new prompt.* Have children turn to page 153 of the **Reading/Writing Workshop**. Read the Your Turn prompt. *How does the author show that Fern is curious? Use text evidence to support your answer.*

Find Text Evidence Say: *To respond to this prompt, we need to look back at the story and illustrations and take notes. The author does not state that Fern is curious. However, we can look for clues in the text and illustrations that show she is curious. What clue does the author give us on page 142?* (The author describes Fern as "always full of questions.") Remind children that they will need to make inferences to respond to the prompt.

Write to a Prompt Say: *Let's use some of the words from the prompt to write our first sentence together: The author gives clues in the story and illustrations that show Fern is curious.* Tell children you will reread the notes to help them complete the response. Track the print as you reread the notes. Then guide children in forming complete sentences as you share the pen in writing them. Say: *Did we use clues from the text to make inferences? Did we use adjectives and describing words correctly?* Read the final response as you track the print.

For additional practice with the Writing Trait, have children turn to page 234 of the **Your Turn Practice Book**.

Grammar

5 Mins

Adjectives

1 Review Remind children that an adjective tells number, color, size, shape, and how things look, sound, feel, smell, or taste. *Words like red, big, round, soft, and sour are adjectives. These words describe things.* Write the following sentences:

> I took off my wet socks and put them in the tan basket.
>
> Can you climb to the top of the high cliff?

Guide children to circle the adjectives in each sentence.

2 Guided Practice Write sample sentences. Have children work in pairs to identify and circle each adjective.

> Curtis got three stars on his math homework. (three)
>
> Can you put the blue sheets on the bed? (blue)

3 Practice Once children have identified the adjectives, have them each pick one sentence to illustrate. Then have partners exchange pictures and read the sentence that matches.

 Talk About It Have partners pick a common classroom object and describe it using as many adjectives as possible.

Daily Wrap Up

- Discuss the Essential Question and encourage children to use the oral vocabulary words. Ask: *What are your favorite things to see in the sky?*

- Prompt children to discuss what they learned today by asking: *How will the skills you learned help you become a better reader and writer?*

Materials

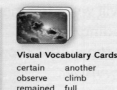

Reading/Writing Workshop
VOLUME 4

Literature Anthology
VOLUME 4

Visual Vocabulary Cards

certain	another
observe	climb
remained	full
thoughtful	great
vast	poor
leaped	through
stretched	

Teaching Poster

Cause → Effect

Word-Building Cards

a b c

Spelling Word Cards

her

→ # Build the Concept

Go Digital

MINILESSON
5 Mins

Oral Language

ESSENTIAL QUESTION

Remind children that this week you've been talking and reading about what they can see in the sky. Remind them of how the bird discovered clouds and how the sun and moon came to be in the sky. Guide children to discuss the question using information from what they have read and talked about throughout the week.

Review Oral Vocabulary

Review the oral vocabulary words *certain, observe, remained, thoughtful,* and *vast* using the Define/Example/Ask routine. Prompt children to use the words as they discuss what we can see in the sky.

Visual Glossary

school

A Bird Named Fern

Visual Vocabulary Cards

Comprehension/ Fluency

ENGLISH LANGUAGE LEARNERS

Retell Guide children to retell by using a question prompt on each page. *What does Fern see in the sky?* Provide sentence starters for children to complete orally. *Fern sees a _____ in the sky.*

Plot: Sequence

MINILESSON 10 Mins

1. **Explain** Tell children they have been learning about using cause and effect to understand stories they read. Remind them they have also learned how to look for the sequence of events. *As we read, we can think about which events happen first, next, and last. Understanding the sequence of events can help us to better understand the plot of the story.*

Reading/Writing Workshop

2. **Model** Display page 143 of *A Bird Named Fern.* Say: *I read in the text that Fern sees something in the sky. She wonders what it is. This is the first event. On the next page, Fern decides she would like to ride the thing in the sky, so she spreads her wings and takes off. This is the second event.*

3. **Guided Practice/Practice** Reread the story with children. Use text evidence to identify the sequence of events in the plot.

Intonation: Exclamations

MINILESSON 5 Mins

1. **Explain** Tell children that as you read, you will read sentences with exclamation points slightly louder and with enthusiasm. Explain that exclamation marks show strong feeling and indicate the sentence should be read with excitement.

2. **Model** Model reading exclamations in the Shared Read. *This sentence has an exclamation mark. I will read it louder and with more enthusiasm than the other sentences.* Point out how your voice shows stronger emotion when you read exclamations marks. Also point out how you pause for punctuation.

3. **Guided Practice/Practice** Have children reread the passage chorally. Remind them to read sentences ending with an exclamation mark louder and with enthusiasm.

Fluency Practice Children can practice using Practice Book passages.

 → # Word Work

Quick Review

Build Fluency: Sound-Spellings
Display the **Word-Building Cards**: *er, ir, ur, or, ar, ey, igh, oa, oe, ee, ea, ai, ay, e_e, u_e, o_e, dge, i_e, a_e, ch, tch, wh, ph, th, sh, ng, mp, sk, st, nt.* Have children say the sounds.

OBJECTIVES

CCSS Orally produce single-syllable words by blending sounds (phonemes), including consonant blends. **RF.1.2b**

CCSS Decode regularly spelled one-syllable words. **RF.1.3b**

CCSS Read words with inflectional endings. **RF.1.3f**

 MINILESSON 5 Mins

Phonemic Awareness

Phoneme Blending

❶ **Model** Show children how to blend sounds to make words. *Listen as I say the sounds in a word: /g/ /ûr/ /l/. Now I will blend the sounds together and say the word: /gûrlll/,* girl. *Let's say the word together:* girl.

❷ **Guided Practice/Practice** Have children practice blending sounds to make words. Do the first two examples together. *I am going to say some words, sound by sound. Blend the sounds together to say the word.*

/w/ /ûr/ /d/ /b/ /ûr/ /th/ /t/ /ûr/ /n/   /n/ /ûr/ /s/ /f/ /ûr/ /m/
/w/ /ûr/ /k/ /b/ /ûr/ /n/ /th/ /ûr/ /d/ /p/ /ûr/ /s/ /s/ /w/ /ûr/ /v/

MINILESSON 5 Mins

Phonics

Blend Words with /ûr/ *er, ir, ur, or*

❶ **Model** Display the **Word-Building Cards** *h, u, r, t.* Model how to blend the sounds. *This is the letter* h. *It stands for /h/. These are the letters* u *and* r. *Together they stand for /ûr/. This is the letter* t. *It stands for /t/. Let's blend the sounds: /hûrt/. The word is* hurt.

Continue by modeling the words *fern, shirt, worth,* and *burst.*

❷ **Guided Practice/Practice** Review the words and sentences on the Day 3 Phonics Practice Activity with children. Read each word in the first row, blending the sounds; for example: */s/ /ûr/ /f/; /sssûrfff/. The word is* surf.

- Have children blend each word with you. Prompt children to read the connected text, sounding out the decodable words.

Go Digital

Phonemic Awareness

Phonics

Structural Analysis

Handwriting

surf	her	first	work	never
girl	nurse	verb	herself	turned
worker	surfer	teacher	starter	fighter
painter	helper	farmer	renter	player
sharp	barge	birdbath	silly	valley

The bird is in a hurry to catch the worm.

Those workers never have to work on Thursday.

Also online

Day 3 Phonics Practice Activity

Decodable Reader Have children read "Sir Worm and Bird Girl" (pages 9–12) and "Ginger and the Stars" (17–20).

MINILESSON
5 Mins

Structural Analysis

Inflectional Ending *-er*

1 Model Say the words *work* and *worker*. Ask children to listen closely to hear what is different. Point out the *-er* at the end of *worker*.

- Write the words *work* and *worker*. Underline the letters *-er*. Tell children that the letters *-er* at the end of *a word make the word* mean "someone who does something." A *worker* is a person who works. Repeat with *learn* and *learner*.

2 Practice/Apply Help children blend the words *jump, jumper; surf, surfer; paint, painter; help, helper;* and *farm, farmer*. Then have them use both words in each pair in one sentence.

Corrective Feedback

Corrective Feedback Say: *My turn.* Model blending. Then lead children in blending. Say: *Do it with me.* Then say: *Your turn. Blend.* Have children chorally blend. Return to the beginning of the word. Say: *Let's start over.*

→ # Word Work

OBJECTIVES

CCSS Recognize and read grade-appropriate irregularly spelled words. **RF.1.3g**

CCSS Use conventional spelling for words with common spelling patterns and for frequently occurring irregular words. **L.1.2d**

 MINILESSON **5 Mins**

Spelling

Word Sort with *er, ir, ur, or*

1 Model Make index cards for *er, ir, ur, or,* and form four columns in a pocket chart. Blend the sounds with children.

Hold up the *her* **Spelling Word Card**. Say and spell it. Pronounce each sound clearly: /h/ /ûr/. Blend the sounds, emphasizing the /ûr/ sounds: /hûr/. Repeat with *fern*. Place both words below the *er* card.

2 Guided Practice/Practice Have children spell each word. Repeat the process with the *ir, ur,* and *or* words.

Display the words *barn, arm, climb,* and *through* in a separate column. Read and spell the words together with children. Point out that these spelling words do not contain the /ûr/ sounds.

Conclude by asking children to orally generate additional words that rhyme with each word. Write the additional words on the board.

Go Digital

er	ir	or	ur
her			
girl curb			word

Spelling Word Sort

school

Visual Glossary

MINILESSON **5 Mins**

High-Frequency Words

another, climb, full, great, poor, through

1 Guided Practice Say each word and have children Read/Spell/Write it. Display the **Visual Vocabulary Cards** to review this week's words.

Visual Vocabulary Cards

2 Practice Repeat the activity with last week's words.

PHONICS/SPELLING PRACTICE BOOK p. 108

her	bird	fur	fern
dirt	work	climb	through

Add the word parts together to make a spelling word. Write the spelling word on the line.

1. b + ird =   bird

2. h + er =   her

3. w + ork =   work

4. cl + imb =   climb

5. f + ur =   fur

6. f + ern =   fern

7. d + irt =   dirt

8. thr + ough =   through

Build Fluency: Word Automaticity

Have children read the following sentences aloud together at the same pace. Repeat several times.

> Can we go through the park another time?
>
> The poor puppy cannot climb out of the box.
>
> That was a great meal, but I am too full now!

Word Bank

Review the current and previous words in the word bank. Discuss with children which words should be removed, or added back, from previous high-frequency word lists.

MINILESSON

5 Mins

Vocabulary

leaped, stretched

Review Use the **Visual Vocabulary Cards** to review this week's words using the Define/Example/Ask routine. Have partners generate context sentences for each vocabulary word.

Visual Vocabulary Cards

Strategy: Shades of Meaning/Intensity

❶ **Model** Remind children that similar words and phrases can have small differences in meaning. Use *A Bird Named Fern* to model how to pick out the differences between similar words.

Think Aloud In *A Bird Named Fern,* the word *great* is in this sentence: "It would be great to ride on that big white boat." *Great* is similar in meaning to the word *good,* but *great* means more than good; it means "wonderful" or "extra special." *Great* has more intensity than *good.*

❷ **Guided Practice** Guide children to explain the meaning of the word *soaked* from *A Bird Named Fern:* "Poor Fern was soaked when she got home." Ask children to picture how Fern would look if the sentence said "Poor Fern was damp when she got home." Have children describe how Fern looks when the sentence says she was *soaked.*

❸ **Practice** Use *hopped* and *jumped* to demonstrate shades of meaning for *leaped.* Use extended to demonstrate a shade of meaning for *stretched.*

Monitor and *Differentiate*

✓ **Quick Check**

Can children read and decode words with *r*-controlled vowels *er, ir, ur, or*?

Can children recognize and read high-frequency and vocabulary words?

Small Group Instruction

If No →	Approaching	Reteach pp. T134–137
	ELL	Develop pp. T148–155
If Yes →	On Level	Review pp. T142–143
	Beyond Level	Extend pp. T146–147

Genre Fantasy

Essential Question

What can you see in the sky?
Read about a kitten who thinks the moon is a bowl of milk.

Go Digital!

(162) (163)

LITERATURE ANTHOLOGY, pp. 162–163

Wonders
Literature Anthology

Literature Anthology

Kitten's First Full Moon

CLOSE READING

Lexile 550

Close Reading Routine

Read   DOK 1–2

- Identify key ideas and details about what Kitten sees in the sky.
- Take notes and retell.
- Use **A C T** prompts as needed.

Reread   DOK 2–3

- Analyze the text, craft, and structure.
- Use *Close Reading Companion*, pp. 140–142.

Integrate   DOK 4

- Integrate knowledge and ideas.
- Make text-to-text connections.
- Use the Integrate Lesson.

Read

ESSENTIAL QUESTION

Read aloud the Essential Question: *What can you see in the sky?* Tell children that as they read, they should think about what things they can see in the sky at night. Ask: *What do you predict Kitten will do in this story?*

Story Words Read, spell, and define the words *moon, tongue, wiggled, ear, tumbled, scared,* and *thought.* Review word meaning as needed. Explain that children will read these words in the selection.

Note Taking: Graphic Organizer As children read the selection, guide them to fill in **Your Turn Practice Book** page 226.

It was Kitten's first full moon.
When she saw it, she thought,
There's a little bowl of milk in the sky.
And she wanted it. **1**

164

165

LITERATURE ANTHOLOGY, pp. 164–165

1 **Skill: Cause and Effect**

Events in the plot happen for a reason, or cause. The effect is what happens because of the cause. On page 164, we read that Kitten thinks the full moon is a bowl of milk. Why does she want it? (She thinks it is a bowl of milk.) Let's add these details to our Cause and Effect chart.

Reread *Close Reading Companion,* 140

Author's Craft

What clues help you know why Kitten thought the moon was a bowl of milk? (*It was Kitten's first full moon,* so she'd never seen one before. Also, the moon looks round and white like a bowl of milk.)

A C T Access Complex Text

▶ **What makes this text complex?**

- **Connection of Ideas** The plot of the story is based on Kitten's mistaking the full moon for a bowl of milk. Reinforce that Kitten thinks the moon is really a bowl of milk.

- **Sentence Structure** Uncommon punctuation such as the dash and the use of the conjunction *and* instead of serial commas may impede children's understanding of some sentences and of the plot.

So she closed her eyes
and **stretched** her neck **2**
and opened her mouth and licked.

166

But Kitten only ended up
with a bug on her tongue.
Poor Kitten! **3**

167

LITERATURE ANTHOLOGY, pp. 166–167

Read

2 Word Parts: Inflectional Endings

Remember, to figure out the meaning of a word with an ending, we can use parts of the word we already know. In *stretched,* I see the word *stretch.* I also see the ending *-ed,* which I know means the stretch happened in the past. What other words on this page do you see with the *-ed* ending? (licked)

3 Strategy: Make and Confirm Predictions

Teacher Think Aloud I read Kitten tries to get the milk by licking it. That does not work. I predict that Kitten will try other ways to get the bowl of milk. I will read on to find out what Kitten does.

Build Vocabulary page 166
closed: shut

A C T **A**ccess **C**omplex **T**ext

▶ **Connections of Ideas**

Help children connect the ideas at the beginning of the story and on these pages.

• Guide children to retell the beginning of the story. *What did Kitten think when she first saw the full moon? What did she want to do?*

• Help them identify how these events are caused by Kitten thinking the moon is a milk bowl. Guide them to see that the cause of the bug on her tongue is her trying to lick the moon.

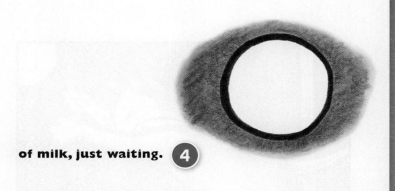

Still, there was the little bowl

of milk, just waiting. **4**

168

169

LITERATURE ANTHOLOGY, pp. 168–169

4 Visualize

Teacher Think Aloud On these pages, I read about what Kitten sees and thinks. She still sees the full moon. She still thinks it is a bowl of milk. Let's stop and create a picture in our minds of what we read. I see Kitten sitting on the porch. There is a round white moon and a few stars high up in the sky. Kitten licks her lips. What do you see in your picture?

Student Think Aloud I see Kitten looking up at the moon. Her eyes are open wide. Her head is tipped as she thinks about how to get the bowl of milk up in the sky.

Reread

Author's Craft: Point of View

Reread pages 168–169. Why does the author call the moon a little bowl of milk here? (That is what Kitten thinks. The author wants us to know that she still thinks the moon is a bowl of milk.)

Author's Craft: Word Choice

Why did the author write that the bowl of milk was *just waiting*? (The author chose words that tell us what Kitten thinks and feels. The words tell us that Kitten thinks the moon is waiting for her to come and drink it. They also give us a hint that Kitten is going to try to get the bowl of milk.)

So she pulled herself together
and wiggled her bottom
and sprang from the top step of the porch. **5**

170

But Kitten only tumbled—
bumping her nose and banging her ear
and pinching her tail.
Poor Kitten!

171

LITERATURE ANTHOLOGY, pp. 170–171

Read

❺ Strategy: Make and Confirm Predictions

Teacher Think Aloud I predicted that Kitten would keep trying to get the bowl of milk. I can use the words and illustration on this page to confirm my prediction. I was right. What do you predict will happen when Kitten leaps from the steps?

Student Think Aloud I predict that Kitten will fall onto the ground.

Build Vocabulary pages 170 and 171
wiggled: made small movements side to side
sprang: jumped suddenly
tumbled: fell down

A C T **A**ccess **C**omplex **T**ext

▶ Sentence Structure

Remind children that we usually use commas when we tell about three or more actions. Explain that sometimes authors use *and* instead of commas.

- Read page 170, and point to each *and*. Have children look for the three things Kitten does.

- Read page 171, but do not point to each *and*. Have children look for three things that happen when Kitten tumbles.

Still, there was the little bowl

of milk, just waiting.

172

173

LITERATURE ANTHOLOGY, pp. 172–173

Reread   *Close Reading Companion,* 141

Author's Craft: Repetition

Reread pages 170–173. Why does the author repeat the words "little bowl of milk"? (The author repeats "little bowl of milk" because that is what Kitten still thinks the moon is. Her point of view has not changed.)

SCIENCE CONNECT TO CONTENT
OBSERVE THE SKY

Remind children that this week they have been learning about what they see in the sky. Point out that the setting of this story is nighttime. The moon is full. Ask, *What does the moon look like when it is full? Does it always look big and round like this?* Explain that on another day the moon would not be full and would not look like a bowl of milk. *What else might Kitten see in the sky?* Ask pairs of children to choose one of the objects children name and discuss what Kitten might mistake it for.

STEM

So she chased it— **6**
down the sidewalk,
   through the garden,
      past the field,
         and by the pond.
7 But Kitten never seemed to get
closer.
Poor Kitten!

LITERATURE ANTHOLOGY, pp. 174–175

A C T Access Complex Text

▶ Sentence Structure

Point out the punctuation and format.

- Point out the dash at the end of the first line. Explain that writers use a dash to mark a pause within a sentence. Here the pause provides a break between telling that Kitten chased the bowl of milk (the moon) and *where* she chased it.

- Show how the text is printed to show Kitten's movement from garden to field to pond.

- Reread the sentence, emphasizing the pauses.

Read

6 Skill: Cause and Effect

Lots of things have happened to Kitten. When we started, we read that Kitten thinks the moon is a bowl of milk. The effect of this is that she wants it. Now what has happened? The moon is still there, waiting. What does this cause Kitten to do? Let's add that to our chart.

7 Structural Analysis: Syllabication

As we read, we come across longer words. How many vowels are in the word *kitten*? What kinds of syllables are they? Asking questions like these helps us read words such as *kitten, sidewalk,* and *garden*.

Build Vocabulary page 174
chased: ran after

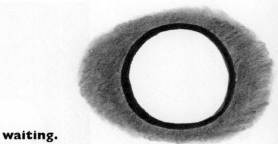

Still, there was the little bowl

of milk, just waiting.

176

177

LITERATURE ANTHOLOGY, pp. 176–177

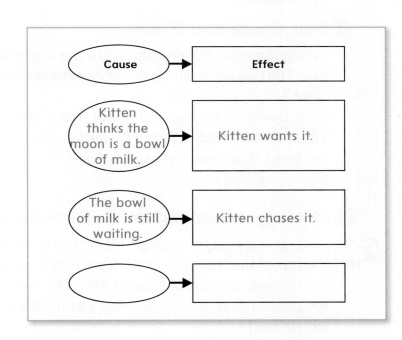

Cause	Effect
Kitten thinks the moon is a bowl of milk.	Kitten wants it.
The bowl of milk is still waiting.	Kitten chases it.

Reread

Author's Craft: Illustrations

Reread pages 176–177. How does the illustration help you know what Kitten is thinking about? (The illustration shows Kitten looking at the moon and ready to pounce. She looks like she will try again to get to the bowl of milk in the sky.)

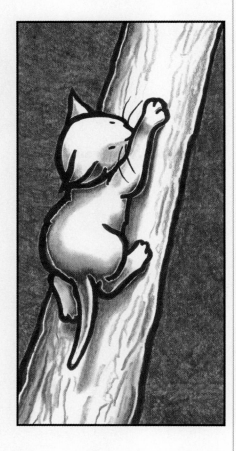

So she ran
to the tallest tree
she could find,
and she **climbed**
and climbed
and climbed
to the very top.

178

But Kitten
still couldn't reach
the bowl of milk,
and now she was
scared. **8**
Poor Kitten!
What could she do?

179

LITERATURE ANTHOLOGY, pp. 178–179

A C T Access Complex Text

▶ Sentence Structure

Remind children that a sentence that tells about several things usually has commas and one *and* to separate them, but sometimes authors use *and* several times instead of commas.

- Read aloud the sentence on page 178, emphasizing Kitten's actions.

- Point to each *and* as you reread the sentence. Have children count, then name the things Kitten does. (four things: ran, climbed, climbed, climbed)

Build Vocabulary page 179
scared: afraid

Read

8 Skill: Cause and Effect

On these pages, Kitten climbed to the top of a tree. That was the effect. What caused her to climb? (She was trying to reach the bowl of milk.) Now, being at the very top of the tree is a cause. What is the effect of kitten's being at the top of the tree? How does it make her feel? (Being at the top of the tree makes Kitten scared.)

9 Strategy: Make and Confirm Predictions

 Look at the picture on page 181. Kitten is sitting in the top of the tree. She looks down and sees what she thinks is anotherM bowl of milk. This one is in the pond. Tell your partner what you think Kitten will do next.

Then, in the pond, Kitten saw
another bowl of milk.
And it was bigger.
What a night!

180

9   181

LITERATURE ANTHOLOGY, pp. 180–181

Reread   *Close Reading Companion,* 142

Author's Craft: Illustrations

Reread pages 180–181. How does the illustration help you understand what is happening in the story? (The text says Kitten saw another bowl of milk in the pond that is bigger than the one in the sky. The picture shows the moon in the sky and its reflection in the pond. The reflection is big. Kitten sees the reflection and thinks it is a bigger bowl of milk.)

A C T Access Complex Text

▶ Connection of Ideas

Prompt children to make connections between the ideas in the story so far and on these pages.

• Have children recall what Kitten sees, what she thinks, and what she wants.

• Have children take turns telling one thing Kitten has done so far in order.

• Focus on these pages. *What does Kitten see?* (the reflection of the full moon) *What does Kitten think she sees?* (a bigger bowl of milk)

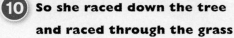 **So she raced down the tree
and raced through the grass**

**and raced to the edge of the pond.
She leaped with all her might—**

182

183

LITERATURE ANTHOLOGY, pp. 182–183

Read

⑩ Skill: Cause and Effect

The author begins these pages with the word *So:
So she raced down the tree* . . . The word *So* here
signals a connection to what happened before.
What happened before is the cause. What was
the cause that we just read about? (Kitten saw
what she thought was a bigger bowl of milk.)
What do we learn here that is the effect? (Kitten
is running down the tree and to the pond to get
the bigger bowl of milk.)

Build Vocabulary page 182
raced: moved quickly
might: strength

⑪ Strategy: Make and Confirm Predictions

Did you predict when Kitten saw what she thought
was a bowl of milk in the pond that she would try
to get it? Then you were right! Now, she has raced
to the pond and leaped. What do you think will
happen?

⑫ Genre: Fantasy

Could this story really happen? We know real cats
like milk, and real cats run and can climb trees.
But the main character, Kitten, is an animal that
thinks like a person. Real kittens do not think like
people, so Kitten could not really exist. This tells us
it is a fantasy story.

Poor Kitten!

She was wet and sad and tired

and hungry. (13)

(14)

184   185

LITERATURE ANTHOLOGY, pp. 184–185

(13) **Strategy: Make and Confirm Predictions**

Turn to a partner and discuss your prediction. Was it correct? Share the prediction you made and use details from the words and picture to tell whether it was correct. Make a prediction about what you think will happen next.

(14) **Skill: Cause and Effect**

Poor Kitten! What happened to make her wet and sad and tired and hungry? Let's add this cause to our chart.

Build Vocabulary page 184
hungry: needing to eat

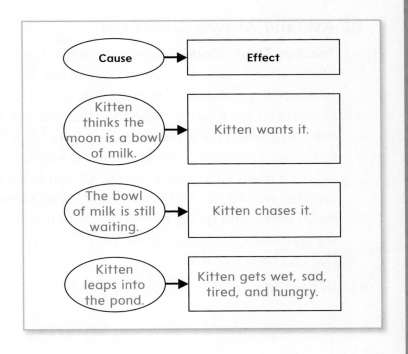

Cause	→	Effect
Kitten thinks the moon is a bowl of milk.	→	Kitten wants it.
The bowl of milk is still waiting.	→	Kitten chases it.
Kitten leaps into the pond.	→	Kitten gets wet, sad, tired, and hungry.

So she went
back home—

186

187

LITERATURE ANTHOLOGY, pp. 186–187

Read

ⓕ Ask and Answer Questions

Teacher Think Aloud Sometimes, when I wonder about what I read, I ask myself questions. Then I answer the questions. On page 186, I read that Kitten goes back home. I see that she gets out of the pond and returns the way she came. I see the full moon in the night sky above her. I wonder: Is Kitten really going back home? Or will she try another way to get it? On page 187, I see Kitten reach home and go up on the porch. I answered my questions. And now I know that Kitten really does go back home.

ⓖ Maintain Skill: Sequence

A lot has happened to Kitten. She chased the moon, climbed a tree, saw another bowl of milk in the pond, and raced toward it. Then what did she do? (She jumped into the pond.) Now what is she doing? (She's going home.) Let's use the pictures to tell the order of what she does. (First, climbs out of the pond; next, goes through a field; then, walks along the sidewalk; and finally, climbs the steps to the porch)

and there was

a great big

bowl of milk

on the porch, ⑰

188

189

LITERATURE ANTHOLOGY, pp. 188–189

---

⑰ **Strategy: Make and Confirm Predictions**

COLLABORATE Discuss the prediction you made before with a partner. Was it correct? Share the prediction you made and discuss how details from the words and picture tell you whether it was correct.

Reread

Author's Craft: Point of View

Reread pages 188 to 189. What words does the author use to help us understand Kitten's point of view? (The words "great big bowl of milk" help me understand that Kitten is excited to have finally found a bowl of milk after trying to catch one all night.)

A C T Access Complex Text

▶ **Connection of Ideas**

Prompt children to connect story ideas.

- Have children recall what Kitten wants at the beginning. (the bowl of milk she thinks is in the night sky)

- Ask where the full moon is throughout the story. (up in the sky) What does Kitten think it is? (a bowl of milk waiting for her)

- Guide children to identify what is actually waiting for her. (a bowl of milk at home)

just waiting for her.

190

191

LITERATURE ANTHOLOGY, pp. 190–191

Read

18 Strategy: Reread Text

If we don't understand part of a story, we can reread. The phrase on this page is the end of a sentence. The sentence starts on page 186, with "So." That means it comes after another idea. Let's reread from page 184. Now we understand Kitten, tired and hungry, found a bowl of milk on the porch!

A C T Access Complex Text

▶ Sentence Structure

Guide children in understanding the text and the unusual sentence structure.

- Point out that the words on this page are the end of a long sentence. Turn back to page 186 and read the entire sentence with children.

- Point out that the sentence has a dash and a comma. Reread the sentence aloud, emphasizing the pause at the dash and at the comma.

Lucky Kitten!

192

193

LITERATURE ANTHOLOGY, pp. 192–193

Skill: Cause and Effect

Complete the chart with children. *What happens at the end? Why did Kitten go home? What happened because she went home? Let's add this last cause and effect to our chart.*

Return to Purposes

Review children's predictions and ask them if their predictions were correct. Guide them to use text evidence to confirm whether their predictions were accurate. Discuss what children learned about what they can see in the night sky.

Build Vocabulary page 193
lucky: have good things happen

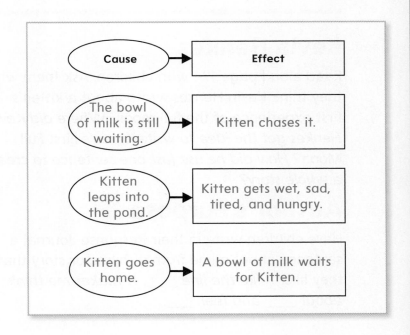

Cause	Effect
The bowl of milk is still waiting.	Kitten chases it.
Kitten leaps into the pond.	Kitten gets wet, sad, tired, and hungry.
Kitten goes home.	A bowl of milk waits for Kitten.

Read Together

Meet Kevin Henkes

Kevin Henkes got the idea for *Kitten's First Full Moon* from a story he had begun to write many years before. Although he never finished this story, there was a line that read, "The cat thought the moon was a bowl of milk." He couldn't get this line out of his head, and slowly over the years the story of *Kitten's First Full Moon* formed.

Author's Purpose

Kevin Henkes got his story idea from a line he liked. Can you think of a line from a rhyme or story that you like? Draw and write about it.

Respond to the Text

Retell

Use your own words to retell *Kitten's First Full Moon*. The information on your Cause and Effect chart can help.

Cause → Effect

Write

Why couldn't Kitten drink the milk in the sky? How do you know? Use these sentence frames:

Kitten couldn't drink the milk because...
Kitten thought...

Make Connections

How is the moon like a bowl of milk? What else could the moon look like?
ESSENTIAL QUESTION

LITERATURE ANTHOLOGY, pp. 194–195

Meet the Author

Kevin Henkes

Read aloud page 194 with children. Ask them why they think Kevin Henkes wrote about a kitten's first experience of the full moon. *Where did Kevin Henkes get the idea to write* Kitten's First Full Moon? *How did he use just one sentence to create a whole story?*

Author's Purpose

Have children write in their Response Journal a sentence about a line from a rhyme or story that they like. *I like the line ____. It makes me think about ____ and feel ____.*

AUTHOR/ILLUSTRATOR'S CRAFT

Focus On Characters in Illustrations

Explain authors and illustrators often use pictures to help readers understand a story.

- Kevin Henkes uses pictures to help readers understand what Kitten thinks and feels.

- On page 165, Kitten looks curious. Her ears point up because she is alert and interested as she looks at the moon.

- Have children find other story illustrations that help readers understand what Kitten thinks and feels, such as her expression of surprise on page 167.

Respond to the Text

Retell

Guide children in retelling the selection. Remind them that as they read *Kitten's First Full Moon*, they made and confirmed predictions about the events, and thought about causes and effects. Have children use the information they recorded on their Cause and Effect chart to help them retell the story.

Analyze the Text

When children read and retell the selection, have them reread *Kitten's First Full Moon* to develop a deeper understanding of the text by answering the questions on pages 140–142 of the *Close Reading Companion*. For students who need support finding text evidence to support their responses, use the scaffolded instruction from the Reread prompts on pages T113B–T113N.

Write About the Text

Review the writing prompt with students. Remind them to use their responses from the *Close Reading Companion* and cite text evidence to support their answers.

For a full lesson on writing a response supported by text evidence, see pages T114–T115.

<u>Answer:</u> Kitten could not drink the milk in the sky because it was actually the moon. <u>Evidence:</u> On page 163, the title of the story shows that Kitten has never seen a full moon before. On pages 170–171, the author shows that Kitten is determined to reach the milk in the sky, but she can't because the bowl of milk isn't really there. On page 181, Kitten still doesn't understand that the bowl of milk is the full moon.

Make Connections
COLLABORATE

Essential Question <u>Answer:</u> The moon is round and looks white like a full bowl of milk. The moon could also look like a ball. <u>Evidence:</u> On page 165, we see a picture of the full moon in the sky. It looks round and white. It looks like a bowl of milk or a large, white ball.

 CONNECT TO CONTENT
OBSERVE THE SKY

Have children share what they have seen in the night sky. Provide vocabulary if needed to help children describe what they have seen. Ask what children see regularly, and only sometimes, in the night sky. Point out that some objects are often visible, but the moon, planets, and many stars are not always visible, and are not scattered evenly throughout the sky. Encourage children to share infrequent phenomena they have seen, such as shooting stars, meteors, or a comet.

STEM

Literature Anthology

OBJECTIVES

CCSS Write informative/ explanatory texts in which they name a topic, supply some facts about the topic, and provide some sense of closure. **W.1.2**

CCSS Use frequently occurring adjectives. **L.1.1f**

Use capitalization and end punctuation in sentences

ACADEMIC LANGUAGE
• details, respond, prewrite, draft
• Cognates: *detalles, responder*

MINILESSON
5 Mins

Independent Writing

Write About the Literature Anthology

Analyze the Prompt Have children turn to page 195 in the **Literature Anthology**. Read the prompt: *Why couldn't Kitten drink the milk in the sky? How do you know?* Point out that the prompt has two parts. First, the prompt is asking you to tell why Kitten couldn't drink the milk in the sky and then it is asking you to explain your answer. The next step is finding text evidence and making inferences.

Find Text Evidence Say: *To respond to the prompt, we need to find evidence in the text and illustrations. We can use clues to help us figure out why Kitten couldn't drink the milk she thought she saw in the sky. What happens to Kitten when she first tries to drink the milk?* (She catches a bug on her tongue.) *What happens when Kitten tries to get closer to the bowl of milk?* (She chases it, but she can never get closer to it.) Have children take notes as they look for evidence to respond to the prompt. Remind children that they will have to make an inference to answer the prompt.

Write to the Prompt Guide children as they begin their writing.

• **Prewrite** Have children review their notes and plan their writing. Guide them to decide how they want to answer the question and what details from the text and illustrations to choose to support their answer.

• **Draft** Have children write a response to the prompt. Remind them to begin their writing with a topic sentence that tells what they will be writing about. As children write their drafts, have them focus on the week's skills.

  • **Adjectives** Use adjectives to describe nouns in their writing. **Grammar**

  • **Describing Words** Use describing words to explain what happens when Kitten tries to drink the milk in the sky. **Trait: Word Choice**

  • **Clues** Use clues from the text and illustrations to explain why Kitten can't drink the milk in the sky. **Trait: Ideas**

Tell children they will continue to work on their responses on Day 4.

Go
Digital

Present the Lesson

Graphic Organizer

Writing

I see a fish.

Grammar

Grammar

Adjectives

1 **Review** Have children look at page 153 in the **Reading/Writing Workshop.** Remind them that adjectives describe size, shape, number, and color, and how things look, sound, feel, smell, and taste. Have children identify the adjectives in the model sentence.

Ask: *Which words in this sentence are adjectives?* (white, puffy) *What noun do these words describe?* (the clouds)

2 **Guided Practice/Practice** Guide children to identify another adjective in Carla's writing. Remind them that an adjective is a word that describes a noun. Have children tell what noun the other adjective describes.

Talk About It Have partners work together to orally generate sentences with adjectives. Challenge them to include two or more adjectives in each sentence.

Mechanics: Capitalization and End Marks

1 **Explain** Remind children that the word *I*, proper nouns, and every sentence begin with a capital letter. Review that sentences must end with a punctuation mark: exclamation mark, question mark, or period. Review the three types of sentences.

2 **Guided Practice** Prompt children to correct each sentence.

four birds are in the Little birdbath? (Four birds are in the little birdbath.)

do bert and carly live on skylark farm (Do Bert and Carly live on Skylark Farm?)

help, i dropped my purse in the mud? (Help, I dropped my purse in the mud!)

ENGLISH LANGUAGE LEARNERS SCAFFOLD

Beginning

Demonstrate Comprehension Provide sentence frames for partners as they write their responses. *Kitten couldn't drink the milk in the sky because _____.* Elicit more details to support the response.

Intermediate

Explain Help children think of adjectives to describe nouns in their responses. Have children circle the nouns they write and add an adjective for each. Clarify children's responses as need.

Advanced/High

Expand As children complete their responses, ask: *What adjectives did you use? How do your adjectives help the reader? Which words did you capitalize? Why?* Repeat correct answers to the class.

Daily Wrap Up

- Review the Essential Question and encourage children to discuss using the oral vocabulary words. Ask: *What can you observe in the night sky?*

- Prompt children to review and discuss the skills they used today.

Materials

Visual Vocabulary Cards

certain   another
observe   climb
remained   full
thoughtful   great
vast   poor
leaped   through
stretched

Teaching Poster

Spelling Word Cards

Literature Anthology
VOLUME 4

a **b** **c**

Word-Building Cards

Dinah Zike's
FOLDABLES

My Name   clouds—puffy and white

san   birds—flying fast

→ # Extend the Concept 🔍 *CLOSE READING*

MINILESSON
5 Mins

The Moon

OBJECTIVES

CCSS Know and use various text features (captions) to locate key facts or information in a text. **RI.2.5**

Review vocabulary

ACADEMIC LANGUAGE

- *caption, fact, detail, description, information*
- Cognate: *detalle, descripción, información*

ESSENTIAL QUESTION

Remind children that this week they have been learning about what they can see in the sky. Guide children to discuss the question using information from what they have read and talked about. Use the Define/Example/Ask routine to review the oral vocabulary words *certain, observe, remained, thoughtful,* and *vast.* Then review last week's oral vocabulary words *classify, distinguish, entire, organize,* and *startled.*

Text Feature: Captions

❶ **Explain** Tell children they can use informational selections to find facts and details. Explain that informational text often has photographs and captions, short descriptions giving information about the photograph.

❷ **Model** Display Teaching Poster 18. Read the caption: *"Tall buildings are called skyscrapers."* The caption gives information about the photograph. The caption tells us what the tall buildings in the photograph are called. This is not information we can get from the photograph alone.

❸ **Guided Practice/Practice** Read together the caption: *"These workers use tools to fix the road."* Guide children to discuss the information in the caption. *What does the caption tell us? What information is in the caption but not in the photograph?* Tell children to look for captions as they read informational text.

Close Reading
Compare Texts

Tell children that as they read they should think about how the moon looks the same and different in *Kitten's First Full Moon* and "The Moon." Point out the words *Earth, telescopes,* and *astronauts.*

Go Digital

school

Visual Glossary

Teaching Poster

THE MOON

"The Moon"

Genre Nonfiction

Compare Texts
Read about something you see in the night sky.

THE MOON

The moon looks much smaller than it really is because it is so far away. **1**

Think of what you see in the night sky. You see stars and the moon.

The moon is the neighbor closest to **Earth** in space. But it is very far away. The moon is about 250,000 miles from Earth!

On some nights the moon looks bright and round. But it does not make its own light. Light from the sun shines on the moon. The light bounces back to Earth. We only see the lighted part of the moon that faces Earth. **2**

196

197

LITERATURE ANTHOLOGY, pp. 196–197

Lexile 400

Read

❶ Text Features: Captions

Teacher Think Aloud When I read selections with photographs, I read the captions with the photographs. The captions give information about the photographs. The caption on page 197 explains the size of the moon as we see it in the sky.

❷ Strategy: Make and Confirm Predictions

Teacher Think Aloud On these pages, I read about where the moon is and what it looks like. I wonder what else this text is about. I will make a prediction about what I will learn while reading this text. I predict I will learn what the moon is made of. I will keep reading to find out whether my prediction is correct.

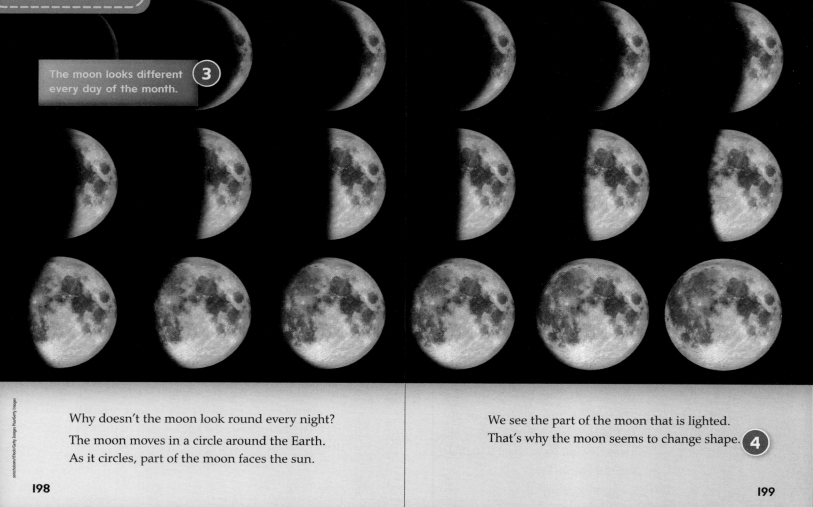

The moon looks different every day of the month. (3)

Why doesn't the moon look round every night?

The moon moves in a circle around the Earth. As it circles, part of the moon faces the sun.

198

We see the part of the moon that is lighted.

That's why the moon seems to change shape. (4)

199

LITERATURE ANTHOLOGY, pp. 198–199

Read

❸ Text Features: Captions

What information does the caption tell that the main text does not? (that the moon looks different every day) What information do the main text and the caption tell that help you understand the different moons in the photograph? (The photograph is showing the way the moon looks at different times.)

❹ Reread

Teacher Think Aloud I am not sure I understand what I read on this page. What does the author mean about the part of the moon that is lighted? I will reread the text on both of these pages. Now I understand: The part of the moon that is facing the sun is the part that is lighted by the sun. That is the part we see.

Retell

Guide children to use key details to retell the selection.

We can see the moon better with a telescope.

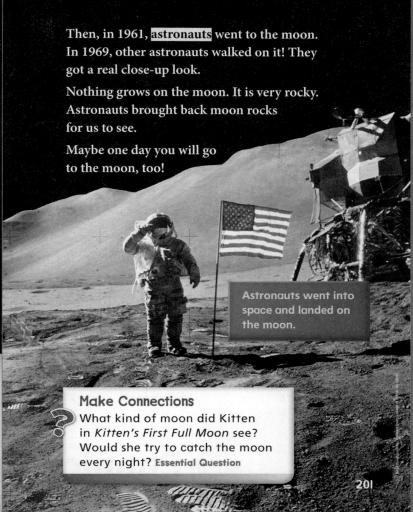

Then, in 1961, **astronauts** went to the moon. In 1969, other astronauts walked on it! They got a real close-up look.

Nothing grows on the moon. It is very rocky. Astronauts brought back moon rocks for us to see.

Maybe one day you will go to the moon, too!

Astronauts went into space and landed on the moon.

People once thought the moon was made of cheese. They saw the face of a man in the moon.

Then **telescopes** helped us see the moon better. The telescopes showed hills and flat places. They showed craters, or big holes, too.

200

Make Connections
What kind of moon did Kitten in *Kitten's First Full Moon* see? Would she try to catch the moon every night? **Essential Question**

201

LITERATURE ANTHOLOGY, pp. 200–201

 CONNECT TO CONTENT
OBSERVE THE SKY

Discuss with children their observations of the moon. *Do you notice the changing shapes of the moon? What colors have you noticed the moon being? What else have you noticed about the moon?* Explain that sometimes the moon appears large and close; other times it looks small and far away. We cannot see details about the moon very well with our eyes alone. With tools like telescopes, people can look more closely at the moon and other far-away objects in the sky.

STEM

Reread

 After children retell, have them reread to develop a deeper understanding of the text by annotating and answering the questions on pages 143–145 of the *Close Reading Companion*. For children who need support citing text evidence, use these Reread questions:

• Why is "Moon" a good title for this text?

• Why do you think the author tells what people thought about the moon?

Integrate

Make Connections

Essential Question Have children use text evidence to tell what kind of moon Kitten saw.

Word Work

Phonemic Awareness

5 Mins — MINILESSON

Phoneme Deletion

1 Model Show children how to delete a sound in a word. *Listen carefully as I say a word:* turn. *The word* turn *has these sounds:* /t/ /ûr/ /n/. *I'll take away the first sound* /t/ *to make a new word:* /ûr/ /n/, earn. *The new word is* earn.

2 Guided Practice/Practice Do the first one with children. *Listen as I say a word. I want you to delete, or take away, the first sound in the word to make a new word.*

twirl   part   train   spark   fright   farm

Phonics/Structural Analysis

10 Mins — MINILESSON

Build Words with /ûr/*er, ir, ur, or*

Review *The /ûr/ sounds can be represented by the letters* er, ir, ur, *and* or. *We'll use* **Word-Building Cards** *to build words with the /ûr/ sounds.*

Place the letters t, u, r, n. *Let's blend the sounds together and read the word:* /tûrnnn/, turn. *Now change the* t *to* b. *Blend the sounds and read the word:* /bûrnnn/, burn. *Continue with* burst, bust, bud, bid, bird, third, thirst, first, fern, herd, verb.

Decodable Reader Have children read "Birds in the Sky" (pages 13–16) and "Bats Under the Dark Sky" (21–24).

Inflectional Ending *-er*

Review Write *herd* and *herder* and read them. Remind children that the *-er* ending means "someone who." Point out that a herder is someone who herds animals. Write: *teach, play, lead, read.* Have children work in pairs to construct words with the *-er* ending. Then have them write a sentence with each word.

OBJECTIVES

CCSS Decode regularly spelled one-syllable words. **RF.1.3b**

CCSS Read words with inflectional endings. **RF.1.3f**

CCSS Use conventional spelling for words with common spelling patterns and for frequently occurring irregular words. **L.1.2d**

Go Digital

Phonemic Awareness

Phonics

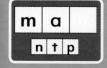
Structural Analysis

Spelling Word Sort

Visual Glossary

Spelling

Word Sort with *er, ir, ur, or*

Review Provide partners with copies of the **Spelling Word Cards**. While one partner reads the words one at a time, the other orally segments the word and then writes it. After reading all the words, partners switch roles and repeat.

Have children self-correct their papers. Then have partners sort the words by spelling pattern: *er, ir, ur, or,* or no /ûr/ spelling pattern.

High-Frequency Words

another, climb, full, great, poor, through

Review Display **Visual Vocabulary Cards** for high-frequency words *another, climb, full, great, poor,* and *through.* Have children Read/ Spell/Write each word.

- Point to a word and call on a child to use it in a sentence.
- Review last week's words using the same procedure.

Expand Vocabulary

leaped, stretched

Use the Visual Vocabulary Cards to review *leaped* and *stretched.*

1 **Explain** Explain to children that words have different forms. Help children generate different forms of this week's words by adding, changing, or removing inflectional endings *-ed, -ing,* and *-s* or *-es.* Review the meaning of each ending.

2 **Model** Use a four-column chart to model how to add endings to the word *leap.* Write the vocabulary word *leap* in the first column. Then write *leaped, leaping,* and *leaps* in the next three columns. Read aloud the words with children.

Point out how the different endings change the meaning of *leap.* Discuss each form of the word and its meaning. Have children share aloud sentences using *leap, leaped, leaping,* and *leaps.*

3 **Guided Practice** Have partners fill in a chart for *stretch.* Then have children share sentences using different forms of the word.

Monitor and *Differentiate*

✔ Quick Check

Can children read and decode words with *r*-controlled vowels *er, ir, ur, or*?

Can children recognize and read high-frequency and vocabulary words?

Small Group Instruction

If No →  Approaching Reteach pp. T134–137

ELL Develop pp. T148–155

If Yes → On Level Review pp. T142–143

Beyond Level Extend pp. T146–147

Language Arts

OBJECTIVES

CCSS With guidance and support from adults, focus on a topic, respond to questions and suggestions from peers, and add details to strengthen writing as needed. **W.1.5**

CCSS Use frequently occurring adjectives. **L.1.1f**

CCSS Build on others' talk in conversations by responding to the comments of others through multiple exchanges. **SL.1.1b**

ACADEMIC LANGUAGE

• prewrite, revise, edit, capitalization, end marks

• Cognates: revisar, editar

MINILESSON

5 Mins

Independent Writing

Write About the Literature Anthology

Revise

Reread the prompt about the story *Kitten's First Full Moon: Why couldn't Kitten drink the milk in the sky? How do you know?* Have children read their drafts to see if they responded to the prompt. Then have them check for:

• **Adjectives** Did they use adjectives to describe nouns in their writing? **Grammar**

• **Describing Words** Did they use describing words to respond to the prompt? **Trait: Word Choice**

• **Clues** Did they use clues to make inferences about why Kitten couldn't drink the milk in the sky? **Trait: Ideas**

Peer Review Have children work in pairs to do a peer review and read their partner's draft. Ask partners to check that the response includes adjectives, clues, and describing words. They should take notes about what they liked most about the writing, questions they have for the author, and additional ideas they think the author could include. Have partners discuss these topics by responding to each other's comments. Provide time for them to make revisions.

Proofread/Edit

Have children check for the following:

• Adjectives are used correctly.

• Sentences begin with capitals and end with punctuation.

• All sentences are complete.

Peer Edit Next, have partners exchange their drafts and take turns reviewing them against the checklist. Encourage partners to discuss and fix errors together.

Go Digital

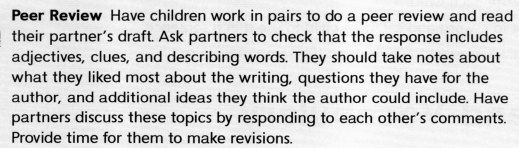

Writing

▬ Make a capital letter.

∧ Add.

✐ Take out.

Proofreader's Marks

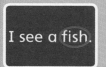

I see a fish.

Grammar

Final Draft

After children edit their writing and finish their peer edits, have them write their final draft. Tell children to write neatly so others can read their writing. Or, work with children to explore a variety of digital tools to produce and publish their writing, including collaborating with peers. Have them include details that help make their writing clear and interesting and add a drawing if needed to make their ideas clear.

Teacher Conference As children work, conference with them to provide guidance. Check to make sure they are including describing words and inferences based on clues from the story.

Grammar

Adjectives

❶ **Review** Review with children that adjectives describe size, shape, number, and color. Remind them that adjectives also tell how things look, sound, feel, smell, and taste.

❷ **Guided Practice** Guide children to identify the adjectives as you say some sentences.

The chirping bird sits in the little nest. (chirping, little)

Miss Cox teaches in the yellow classroom. (yellow)

❸ **Practice** Display the following sentences. Have children identify each adjective and the noun it describes.

The funny kitten chases yarn. (funny—kitten)

The big bowl is filled with plums. (big—bowl)

Talk About It Have partners orally generate sentences with each adjective from the Practice exercise.

Mechanics: Capitalization and End Marks

❶ **Review** Remind children that the word *I*, proper nouns, and every sentence begin with a capital letter. Review that every sentence has ending punctuation: an exclamation mark, question mark, or period.

❷ **Practice** Display a sentence with errors. Have children work together to fix the sentence.

patty and marge write postcards from play World (Patty and Marge write postcards from Play World.)

Daily Wrap Up

- Review the Essential Question and encourage children to discuss it using the oral vocabulary words. Ask: *What did you read about the sky this week?*

- Prompt children to discuss the skills they practiced and learned today by asking, *How will you use these skills again?*

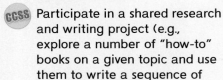
 # → Integrate Ideas

OBJECTIVES

CCSS Participate in a shared research and writing project (e.g., explore a number of "how-to" books on a given topic and use them to write a sequence of instructions). **W.1.7**

CCSS Give, restate, and follow simple two-step directions. **SL.1.2a**

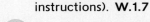

- Build background knowledge
- Research information using technology

ACADEMIC LANGUAGE

- *poster, sky, objects, describe*
- Cognates: *objeto, describir*

 ## RESEARCH AND INQUIRY

Make a Poster

Tell children that today they will do a research project with a partner to learn more about what they see in the sky. Review the steps in the research process.

STEP 1 Choose a Topic

Guide partners to choose a time of day to observe the sky, day or night.

STEP 2 Find Resources

Have children observe the sky and take note of what they see. Guide children to use the selections, reference materials, and online sources to find out about things they may see in the sky. Have them use the Research Process Checklist online.

STEP 3 Keep Track of Ideas

Have children make a Four-Tab Foldable® to record ideas.

Dinah Zike's
FOLDABLES

Go Digital

Resources:
Research and
Inquiry

Collaborative Conversations

Listen Carefully As children engage in partner, small-group, and whole-group discussions, remind them to:

- always look at the speaker.
- respect others by not interrupting them.
- repeat others' ideas to check understanding.

STEP 4 **Create the Project: Poster**

Explain the characteristics of a poster.

- Information A poster can give information. In this project, the poster will give information about what you can see in the sky.
- Image A poster can have images that illustrate the information.
- Text A poster can have text. Your poster will have text that describes what you see in the sky.

Have children create a poster showing what they see in the sky.

- Before children get started, you may wish to have partners give and restate the directions.
- Then guide them to make a drawing of the sky and the objects in it. They can also cut out pictures from magazines or newspapers.
- Prompt children to write sentences describing the things they see.

STEM

The Daytime Sky

The clouds are white. A bird flies fast

INFORMATIVE POSTER

ENGLISH LANGUAGE LEARNERS
ELL SCAFFOLD

Beginning	Intermediate	Advanced/High
Use Sentence Frames Use sentence frames to help children discuss what they see in the sky. For example: *I see a ____. It is ____.*	**Discuss** Guide children to focus on the most important details about the sky. Ask: *What objects do you see? What color are they? Are the objects moving?*	**Describe** Prompt children to list words that describe the sky and the objects in it. Encourage them to think about how their choice of words could make their posters more interesting.

Materials

Reading/Writing Workshop
VOLUME 4

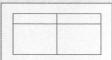

Literature Anthology
VOLUME 4

Visual Vocabulary Cards

another
climb
full
great
poor
through

Teaching Poster

Word-Building Cards

a b c

her

Spelling Word Cards

→ Word Work

Go Digital

MINILESSON 5 Mins
Phonemic Awareness

Phonemic Awareness

Phoneme Blending

OBJECTIVES

CCSS Orally produce single-syllable words by blending sounds (phonemes), including consonant blends. **RF.1.2b**

CCSS Decode regularly spelled one-syllable words. **RF.1.3b**

CCSS Read words with inflectional endings. **RF.1.3f**

CCSS Recognize and read grade-appropriate irregularly spelled words. **RF.1.3g**

Review Guide children to blend phonemes to form words. *Listen as I say a group of sounds. Then blend those sounds to form a word.*

/f/ /ûr/ /n/   /b/ /ûr/ /d/   /th/ /ûr/ /d/   /s/ /w/ /ûr/ /v/   /p/ /ûr/ /s/

Phoneme Substitution

Phonics

Review Have children practice substituting the /ûr/ sounds in words to form new words. *Listen for the /ûr/ sounds in the words I say. Replace the /ûr/ sounds with the sound or sounds I say to make a new word.*

fur, /är/ (far)   burn, /är/ (barn)   herd, /e/ (head)

term, /ā/ (tame)   shirt, /ôr/ (short)   stir, /ā/ (stay)

MINILESSON 10 Mins
Phonics/Structural Analysis

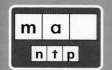
I __ the jar.
fill   fills   filling
Structural Analysis

Blend and Build with /ûr/ *er, ir, ur, or*

Review Have children read and say the words *her, girl, burn,* and *word.* Then have children follow the word building routine with **Word-Building Cards** to build *worm, word, worth, world, worse, worst.* Then start over with *dirt, shirt, skirt, first, firm, term, herd.*

Word Automaticity Help children practice word automaticity. Display decodable words and point to each word as children chorally read it. Test how many words children can read in one minute. Model blending words children miss.

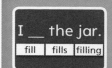
school
Visual Glossary

Fluency: Word Automaticity

Inflectional Ending -er

Review Have children explain how the inflectional ending -er changes the meaning of a word. Then have children practice writing and saying words with -er, such as *worker*, *teacher*, and *farmer*.

Spelling

Word Sort with *er, ir, ur, or*

Review Have children use the **Spelling Word Cards** to sort the weekly words by vowel sounds.

Assess Assess children on their abilities to spell words with /ûr/ spelled *er, ir, ur, or*. Say each word and provide a sentence. Then allow them time to write the words.

High-Frequency Words

another, climb, full, great, poor, through

Review Display the **Visual Vocabulary Cards**. Have children Read/Spell/Write each word and write a sentence with each word.

Review Vocabulary

leaped, stretched

Review Write *leaped* and *stretched*. Point to each word and ask children to use the word in a sentence. Write the sentences and reinforce word meanings as necessary.

Fluency

Intonation

Review Review with children that exclamation marks show strong feeling and indicate that the sentence should be read louder and with excitement in the voice. Read aloud a few pages of the Shared Read. Have children echo each sentence. Point out how you read a sentence ending with an exclamation mark louder and with enthusiasm. Then have partners reread the selection, working on how they read exclamations.

Quick Review

Build Fluency: Sound-Spellings
Display the **Word-Building Cards:** *er, ir, ur, or, ar, ey, igh, oa, oe, ee, ea, ai, ay, e_e, u_e, o_e, dge, i_e, a_e, ch, tch, wh, ph, th, sh, ng, mp, sk, st, nt.* Have children say the sounds; vary the pace.

Monitor and *Differentiate*

✓ Quick Check

Can children read and decode words with *r*-controlled vowels *er, ir, ur, or*?

Can children recognize and read high-frequency and vocabulary words?

Small Group Instruction

If No → **Approaching** Reteach pp. T134–137

ELL Develop pp. T148–155

If Yes → **On Level** Review pp. T142–143

Beyond Level Extend pp. T146–147

Literature Anthology

OBJECTIVES

CCSS With guidance and support from adults, use a variety of digital tools to produce and publish writing, including in collaboration with peers. **W.1.6**

CCSS Describe people, places, things, and events with relevant details, expressing ideas and feelings clearly. **SL.1.4**

CCSS Produce complete sentences when appropriate to task and situation. **SL.1.6**

ACADEMIC LANGUAGE

• *evaluate, presentation*
• Cognates: *evaluar, presentación*

MINILESSON 5 Mins
Independent Writing

Write About the Literature Anthology

Prepare

Tell children they will plan what they will say to the class about their finished writing and drawing. Remind children to:

• Think about the describing words they used to respond to the prompt.

• Think about how they used clues to make an inference about why Kitten couldn't drink the milk in the sky.

Present

Have children take turns giving presentations of their responses to the prompt about the story *Kitten's First Full Moon: Why couldn't Kitten drink the milk in the sky? How do you know?* If possible, record their presentations so children can self-evaluate. Tell children to:

• Describe what happened in the story using relevant details and expressing ideas and feelings clearly.

• Speak in complete sentences.

• Explain any drawing they may have made as they share their words.

Evaluate

Have children discuss their own presentations and evaluate their performance using the presentation rubric.

Use the teacher's rubric to evaluate children's writing. Have children add their writing to their Writer's Portfolio. Encourage children to look back at previous writing. Then have them discuss with a partner what they liked best about their writing.

Publish

After children finish presenting their stories, explain that the class will make a bulletin board that explains why Kitten can't drink the milk in the sky. Let children decide how to arrange on the bulletin board their responses and any drawings they made. Guide children to use digital tools to publish their writing.

Go Digital

Writing

Checklists

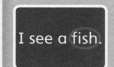

Grammar

MINILESSON 5 Mins

Grammar

Adjectives

1 Review Review with children that adjectives describe size, shape, number, and color. Remind them that adjectives also tell how things look, sound, feel, smell, and taste. Write the following sentences and have children identify the adjectives:

Lin saw two worms in the big garden. (two, big)

The bright sun shone on the hot car. (bright, hot)

Would you like the pink scarf? (pink)

I do not like that sweet drink. (sweet)

2 Practice Ask: *What word does an adjective describe? What senses do adjectives tell about?*

Write color, shape, and size adjectives on cards. Have partners pick two cards and write rhyming couplets that use the two adjectives. Allow pairs to read their rhymes to the group.

Mechanics: Capitalization and End Marks

1 Review Remind children that the word *I*, proper nouns, and every sentence begin with a capital letter. Review that every sentence has ending punctuation.

2 Practice Write the following sentences. Read each aloud. Have children fix the sentences.

curtis and i are in Miss mark's class
(Curtis and I are in Miss Mark's class.)

can you meet Me by the Flagpole on church road!
(Can you meet me by the flagpole on Church Road?)

mom, dad, and Gran moved here from chad? (Mom, Dad, and Gran moved here from Chad.)

Daily Wrap Up

- Review the Essential Question and encourage children to discuss using the oral vocabulary words.

- Review with children that to figure out a cause and effect in a story, they should ask: *What happened? Why did it happen?*

- Review that the letters *er, ir, ur,* and *or* can make the /ûr/ sounds.

- Use the Visual Vocabulary Cards to review the Words to Know.

- Remind children a fantasy is a made-up story that could not really happen.

→ Integrate Ideas

Close Reading Routine

Read — DOK 1–2

- Identify key ideas and details about objects in the sky.
- Take notes and retell.
- Use **ACT** prompts as needed.

Reread — DOK 2–3

- Analyze text, craft, and structure.

Integrate — DOK 4

- Integrate knowledge and ideas and make text-to-text connections.
- Use the Integrate Lesson.
- Use *Close Reading Companion*, p. 146.

TEXT CONNECTIONS

Connect to the Essential Question

Write the essential question on the board: *What can you see in the sky?* Read the essential question aloud. Tell children they will think about all the stories they have read and what they have learned about objects in the sky. Say: *We have read many selections on this topic. We will compare the information from this week's* **Leveled Readers** *and* A Bird Named Fern, **Reading/Writing Workshop** *pages 140–149.*

Evaluate Text Evidence Guide children to review the selections and their completed graphic organizers. Have children work with partners to compare information from all the week's reads. Children can record notes using a Foldable®. Guide them to record information from the selections that helps them answer the Essential Question.

Dinah Zike's
FOLDABLES
Study Organizer

Up In The Sky

OBJECTIVES

CCSS Participate in shared research and writing projects. **W.1.7**

Go Digital

Collaborate

RESEARCH AND INQUIRY

Have children create a checklist and review their posters:

- Does their poster show the objects they wanted to include? Is there anything they want to add to the poster?
- Does the poster give information about objects people can see in the sky?
- Did they add drawings or cut-out pictures to show the objects in the sky?
- Does their text describe the objects? Did they use complete sentences?
- Have they thought about how they will describe their poster when presenting it to the class?

Guide partners to practice sharing their posters with each other. Children should practice speaking and presenting their information clearly.

Guide children to present their work. Prompt children to ask questions to clarify when something is unclear: *What things did you see in the day or night? How are the things different in the day and night?* Have children use the Presentation Checklist online.

Text to Photography

Read aloud with children the Integrate activity on page 146 of the *Close Reading Companion*. Have partners share reactions to the photograph. Then guide them to discuss how it is similar to the selections they read earlier in the week. Have partners collaborate to complete the Integrate page by following the prompts.

Present Ideas and Synthesize Information

When children finish their discussions, ask for a volunteer from each pair to share the information from their Foldable® and their Integrate pages. After each pair presents their ideas, ask: *How does learning about what different characters and people see in the sky help you answer the Essential Question: What can you see in the sky?* Lead a class discussion asking students to use the information from their charts to answer the Essential Question.

OBJECTIVES

CCSS Identify basic similarities in and differences between two texts on the same topic (e.g., in illustrations, descriptions, or procedures). **RI.1.9**

SPEAKING AND LISTENING

As children work with partners in their *Close Reading Companion* or on their poster, make sure they are actively participating in the conversation and, when necessary, remind them to use these speaking and listening strategies:

Speaking Strategies

- Take turns talking and respond to questions asked of them.
- Ask others' opinions and ask questions when they are unsure of the speaker's meaning.
- Discuss drawings or pictures and refer to them as they explain their thoughts and ideas.

Listening Strategies

- Look at the person speaking and pay attention to drawings or visuals.
- Wait until the speaker is finished before talking.
- Listen carefully and repeat others' ideas to confirm understanding.

OBJECTIVES

CCSS Build on others' talk in conversations by responding to the comments of others through multiple exchanges. **SL.1.1b**

CCSS Ask and answer questions about what a speaker says in order to gather additional information or clarify something that is not understood. **SL.1.3**

CCSS Add drawings or other visual displays to descriptions when appropriate to clarify ideas, thoughts, and feelings. **SL.1.5**

→ Approaching Level

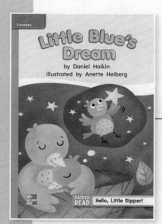

Lexile 280

Little Blue's Dream

OBJECTIVES

(CCSS) Describe characters, settings, and major events in a story, using key details. **RL.1.3**

- Make and confirm predictions
- Recognize cause and effect

Leveled Reader:
Little Blue's Dream

Before Reading

Preview and Predict

Have children turn to the title page. Read the title and the author's name and have children repeat. Preview the selection's illustrations. Prompt children to predict what the selection might be about.

Review Genre: Fantasy

Have children recall that a fantasy has invented characters, settings, or other elements that could not exist in real life.

ESSENTIAL QUESTION

Remind children of the Essential Question: *What can you see in the sky?* Set a purpose for reading: *Let's read to find out what Little Blue's dream is.*

Remind children that as they read a selection, they can ask questions about what they do not understand or want to know more about.

Graphic Organizer

During Reading

Guided Comprehension

As children whisper read *Little Blue's Dream,* monitor and provide guidance, correcting blending and modeling the key strategies and skills.

Strategy: Make and Confirm Predictions

Remind children that as they read they can make predictions about what will happen. Then they can read on to see if they are right. Model using the strategy. *On page 5, I read that Little Blue wants to fly to the stars. I predict she will try to reach the stars.* Read page 6. *My prediction was right. Little Blue started to climb the tree.*

Skill: Plot/Cause and Effect

Remind children that a cause is an event that makes something happen. An effect is what happens. As you read, ask: *What caused Little Blue to climb the tree?* Display a Cause and Effect chart for children to copy.

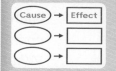

Retell

Model recording children's answers in the boxes. Have children record the answers in their own charts.

Think Aloud On page 6, I read Little Blue climbs the tree. That is an effect. Why does she do this? To try to reach the stars! That is the cause. I will write that cause and effect in my chart.

Guide children to use the text and illustrations to complete the chart.

After Reading

Respond to Reading

Have children complete the Respond to Reading on page 12.

Retell

Have children take turns retelling the selection, using the **Retelling Cards** as a guide. Help children make a personal connection by saying: *Do you like looking at the stars in the sky? Why or why not?*

Model Fluency

Read the sentences, one at a time. Have children chorally repeat. Point out to children how your voice sounds when you read exclamations.

Apply Have partners practice reading. Provide feedback as needed.

PAIRED READ ...

"Hello, Little Dipper!"

Make Connections: Write About It *Analytical Writing*

Before reading, ask children to note that the genre of this selection is informational text. Then discuss the Compare Texts direction. After reading, ask children to make connections between the information they learned from "Hello, Little Dipper!" and *Little Blue's Dream*.

Leveled Reader

> **FOCUS ON SCIENCE**
>
> Children can extend their knowledge of what we see in the sky by completing the science activity on page 16.
> **STEM**

Literature Circles

Lead children in conducting a literature circle using the Thinkmark questions to guide the discussion. You may wish to discuss what children have learned about stars from the two selections in the Leveled Reader.

Level Up

Level-up lessons available online.

IF children can read *Little Blue's Dream*, Approaching Level with fluency and correctly answer the Respond to Reading questions,

THEN tell children that they will read another story about things in the sky.

- Use page 5 of *Hide and Seek!* On Level to model using Teaching Poster 32 to list a cause and an effect.

- Have children read the selection, checking their comprehension by using the graphic organizer.

APPROACHING LEVEL **T131**

→ Approaching Level

Phonemic Awareness

IDENTIFY AND GENERATE RHYME

 TIER 2

OBJECTIVES

Isolate and pronounce initial, medial vowel, and final sounds (phonemes) in spoken single-syllable words. **RF.1.2c**

Recognize and generate rhyming words

 I Do Explain that children will be listening for words that rhyme. *Listen as I say two words:* firm, worm. *The words* firm *and* worm *rhyme because they both end in /ûrm/. Listen: /f/ /ûrm/,* firm; */w/ /ûrm/,* worm. *Rhyming words end in the same sounds.*

Another word that ends with /ûrm/ is germ, */j/ /ûrm/. Germ rhymes with* firm *and* worm *because it ends in /ûrm/:* firm, worm, germ.

 We Do *Listen to these word pairs. If the words rhyme, clap and then tell why they rhyme. If they do not, remain silent.* Do the first two word pairs together.

first, thirst   turning, burning   word, worse   furry, hurry

Say the rhyming pairs and work together to name another word that rhymes.

 You Do *It's your turn. I'm going to say the words. If they rhyme, clap and then tell why they rhyme. Then name another word that rhymes. If not, remain silent.*

curb, herb   shirt, dirt   bird, bark   curly, early   jelly, belly

PHONEME BLENDING

 TIER 2

OBJECTIVES

Orally produce single-syllable words by blending sounds (phonemes) including consonant blends. **RF.1.2b**

 I Do Explain to children that they will blend sounds to make words. *Listen as I say the sounds in a word: /t/ /ûr/ /n/. Now I will blend the sounds together and say the word: /tûrn/,* turn. *Let's say the word together:* turn.

 We Do *Let's do some together. Listen as I say the sounds in a word: /b/ /ûr/ /d/. Now let's blend the sounds together to say the word: /bûrd/,* bird.

Repeat this routine with the following words:

/sh/ /ûr /t/   /w/ /ûr/ /d/   /b/ /ûr/ /n/   /f/ /ûr/ /m/

 You Do *It's your turn. I am going to say some words, sound by sound. Blend the sounds together to say the word.*

/f/ /l/ /ûr/ /t/   /g/ /ûr/ /l/   /w/ /ûr/ /m/   /ch/ /ûr/ /p/

PHONEME SUBSTITUTION

OBJECTIVES

 Isolate and pronounce initial, medial vowel, and final sounds (phonemes) in spoken single-syllable words. **RF.1.2c**

Substitute phonemes in words

 I Do *Listen carefully as I say a word: /f/ /ûr/, fur. I will change the /f/ to /h/ and make a new word: /h/ /ûr/, her. The new word is* her.

 We Do *Let's do some together. We'll start with* her. *Say it with me: /h/ /ûr/, her. We will change the first sound /h/ to /w/. Let's say the new word together: /w/ /ûr/, were. Let's do some more together.*

Repeat this routine with the following words:

car, far   burn, fern   dirt, hurt   turn, stern

 You Do *It's your turn. Say the following word with me:* work. *Now change the /k/ to /th/. What is the new word?* (worth)

Repeat this routine with the following words:

girl, whirl   furry, hurry   bird, word   first, thirst

PHONEME DELETION

OBJECTIVES

 Isolate and pronounce initial, medial vowel, and final sounds (phonemes) in spoken single-syllable words. **RF.1.2c**

Delete initial phonemes to form new words

 I Do Explain that children will be taking away sounds to form a new word. *Listen carefully as I say a word:* park. *The word* park *has these sounds: /p/ /är/ /k/; I'll take away the first sound /p/, and make a new word:* arc.

 We Do *Let's do some together. Listen as I say a word:* band, /b/ /a/ /n/ /d/. *Now I'll say the word without the first sound and make a new word:* and.

Repeat this routine with the following words:

broom   star   glitter   clamp   howl   grate

 You Do *It's your turn. Listen carefully. Then say the word without the first sound.*

clash   twirl   prod   brush   burn   goat

 ENGLISH LANGUAGE LEARNERS

For the **children** who need **phonemic awareness, phonics,** and **fluency** practice, use scaffolding methods as necessary to ensure children understand the meaning of the words. Refer to the Language Transfers Handbook for phonics elements that may not transfer in children's native languages.

Approaching Level

Phonics

CONNECT *er, ir, ur, or* TO /ûr/

 TIER 2

OBJECTIVES

 Decode regularly spelled one-syllable words. **RF.1.3b**

I Do Display the **Word-Building Card** *er. These are the letters lowercase* e *and lowercase* r. *I am going to trace the letters* e, r *while I say* /ûr/. Trace the letters *e, r* while saying /ûr/ five times. Repeat with Word-Building Cards *ir, ur,* and *or.*

We Do *Now do it with me.* Have children trace the lowercase *e, r* with their finger while saying /ûr/ with you five times. Repeat with Word-Building Cards *ir, ur,* and *or.*

You Do Have children connect the letters *er* to the sound /ûr/ by tracing lowercase *er* with their finger, while saying /ûr/. Once children have traced on paper five to ten times, they should then write the letters *er* while saying /ûr/ five to ten times. Repeat with Word-Building Cards *ir, ur,* and *or.*

Repeat, connecting the letters *er, ir, ur, or* to /ûr/ through tracing and writing the letters *er, ir, ur, or* throughout the week.

BLEND WORDS WITH /ûr/ *er, ir, ur, or*

 TIER 2

OBJECTIVES

 Decode regularly spelled one-syllable words. **RF.1.3b**

I Do Display Word-Building Cards *f, ir, m. This is the letter* f. *It stands for* /f/. *Say it with me:* /f/. *These are the letters* i *and* r. *They stand for* /ûr /. *Let's say the sounds together:* /ûr/. *This is the letter* m. *It stands for* /m/. *Let's blend the sounds together:* /fûrm/, firm.

We Do Guide children to blend the sounds and read: *work, birth, curl, term, bird, nurse, squirt.*

You Do Have children blend and decode: *her, worm, churn, hurt, shirt, worst, fur, stern, whirl, stir, germ.*

Repeat, blending additional /ûr/ words spelled *er, ir, ur, or.*

You may wish to review Phonics with **ELL** using this section.

BUILD WORDS WITH /ûr/ *er, ir, ur, or*

OBJECTIVES

CCSS Decode regularly spelled one-syllable words. **RF.1.3b**

 I Do Display **Word-Building Cards** *s, ir*. *These are the letters* s, i, r. *They stand for /s/ and /ûr/. I will blend /s/ and /ûr/ together: /sûr/,* sir. *The word is* sir.

 We Do *Let's build a new word together.* Make the word fir. *I am going to change the letter* s *in* sir *to the letter* f. *Let's blend and read the new word: /fûr/,* fir.

 You Do Have children continue building and blending the words: *fur, surf, turf, turn, churn, burn, burst, first, worst, work, worm.*

Repeat, building additional words with /ûr/ spelled *er, ir, ur, or.*

BLEND WORDS WITH /ûr/ *er, ir, ur, or*

OBJECTIVES

CCSS Decode regularly spelled one-syllable words. **RF.1.3b**

 I Do Display Word-Building Cards *d, ir, t.* *This is the letter* d. *It stands for /d/. These are the letters* i, r. *They stand for /ûr /. This is the letter* t. *It stands for /t/. Listen as I blend the sounds: /dûrt/,* dirt. *The word is* dirt.

 We Do *Let's blend some words together.* Blend and read the words *word, first, hurt,* and *term* with children.

 You Do Display the words to the right. Have children blend and read the words.

her	urn	curb	fir	worm	surf
world	verb	stern	curl	sir	whirl
bird	skirt	lurk	turf	term	barn
start	easy	chain	leave	grove	coax

The girls at work were thirsty.

A bird lurks on top of the church.

She will hurry back to change her shirt and skirt.

Decodable Reader Have children read "Sir Worm and the Bird Girl," "Bird in the Sky," "Ginger and the Stars," and "Bats Under the Dark Sky" (pages 9–24).

BUILD FLUENCY WITH PHONICS

Sound-Spellings Fluency

Display the following Word-Building Cards: *er, ir, ur, or, ar, ey, igh, oa, oe, ee, ea, ai, ay, e_e, u_e, o_e, dge, i_e, a_e, ch, tch, wh, ph, th, sh, ng, mp, sk, st, nt.* Have children chorally say the sounds. Repeat and vary the pace.

Fluency in Connected Text

Have children review the **Decodable Reader** selections. Identify words with the sound /ûr/ spelled *er, ir, or, ur.* Blend words as needed.

Have partners reread the selections for fluency.

→ Approaching Level

Structural Analysis

REVIEW INFLECTIONAL ENDING -er

OBJECTIVES

Read words with inflectional endings.
RF.1.3f

 I Do

Write *surfer.* Read the word: */sûrf/ /ûr /.* I *look at the word* surfer *and I see a word I know,* surf. *The* -er *ending turns a verb into a noun. It tells me that it is someone who does something. I'm going to use* surf *and* surfer *in sentences:* Jan likes to surf at the beach. She has been a surfer for a long time.

 We Do

Write and say *worker.* If *we look at* worker, *is there a word we know? Yes,* work. *We know that* -er *means someone or something that does an action, so* worker *means "one who works." Let's use* work *and* worker *in sentences.*

 You Do

Have children work with partners. Give them several words with -er endings. Children can work together to determine the root word and a sentence that uses each form of the word correctly.

Repeat Have children create additional sentences using words with -er.

RETEACH INFLECTIONAL ENDING -er

OBJECTIVES

Read words with inflectional endings.
RF.1.3f

 I Do

Explain to children that the ending -er can be added to some words. Write *work* and *worker. This is the word* worker. *Underline the letters* er *in* worker. *The* -er *ending can change some words from a word that tells about an action to a word that names a person or thing. A* worker *is a person who works.*

 We Do

Write *farm* and *teach. Let's add* -er. *We get the words* farmer *and* teacher. Have the group come up with sentences for *farmer* and *teacher.*

Repeat the routine adding the ending -er to each of the following.

chirp   paint   farm   read   help

 You Do

Have children add -er to action words. Guide children to repeat the words as needed. *Now it's your turn. Add* -er *to each word, then say each word and use it in a sentence.*

walk   send   help   heal   lead

Repeat Have children add inflectional -er onto the ends of verbs.

Words to Know

REVIEW HIGH-FREQUENCY WORDS

OBJECTIVES

 Recognize and read grade-appropriate irregularly spelled words. **RF.1.3g**

 Use the **High-Frequency Word Cards** to **Read/Spell/Write** each high-frequency word. Use each word orally in a sentence.

 Guide children to Read/Spell/Write each word on their **Response Boards**. Work together to generate oral sentences using the words.

 Have children work with a partner to do the Read/Spell/Write routine on their own using the words *another, climb, full, great, poor, through.*

CUMULATIVE REVIEW

OBJECTIVES

 Recognize and read grade-appropriate irregularly spelled words. **RF.1.3g**

Review previously taught high-frequency words

 Display the High-Frequency Word Cards from the previous weeks. Review each word using the Read/Spell/Write routine.

 Have children write the words on their Response Boards. Complete sentences for each word, such as *I can not find my ____.* or *We need more ____.*

 Show each card and have children chorally read. Mix and repeat.

Fluency Display the High-Frequency Word Cards. Point to the words in random order. Have children chorally read. Repeat at a faster pace.

REVIEW VOCABULARY WORDS

OBJECTIVES

 Determine or clarify the meaning of unknown and multiple-meaning words and phrases based on grade 1 reading and content, choosing flexibly from an array of strategies. **L.1.4**

 Display the **Visual Vocabulary Cards** for *leaped* and *stretched*. Review each word using the Define/Example/Ask routine.

 Invite children to act out each word. Then work with them to complete these sentence starters: *(1) Meg leaped over ____. (2) I stretched to get the ____.*

 Have partners write two sentences on their own, using each of the words. Provide assistance as needed.

→ **Approaching Level**

Comprehension

READD FOR FLUENCY

 TIER 2

 OBJECTIVES

CCSS Read grade-level text orally with accuracy, appropriate rate, and expression. **RF.1.4b**

I Do Read the first page of the Practice Book selection. Model using appropriate intonation, stressing how to sound when reading the exclamation.

We Do Read the rest of the Practice Book selection and have children echo read each sentence. Point out how your voice changes when you read an exclamation. Demonstrate by reading, *"There's a wishing star!"* with and without proper intonation. Reread and have children echo read.

You Do Have children work with a partner and take turns rereading the passage aloud. Remind them to use proper intonation when reading exclamations. Provide feedback as needed.

IDENTIFY EVENTS

 TIER 2

 OBJECTIVES

CCSS Describe characters, settings, and major events in a story, using key details. **RL.1.3**

Identify important events in a fantasy

I Do Remind children that key details and the illustrations can help readers understand the events in a story. *Events are what happens in a story, including what the characters say and do.*

We Do Read the first page of the Practice Book story aloud. Model identifying and describing the major event. *Bethy Bunny looks up at the sky and sees a star. What does she decide to do? Yes, she wishes for a sunhat. This is the first event in the story.*

You Do Guide children to read the rest of the Practice Book story. Prompt them to identify important events that happen in the last part of the story. Remind them to use the illustration to help. *What did Bethy do? What did Freddy Frog do?*

REVIEW PLOT: CAUSE AND EFFECT

OBJECTIVES

 Describe characters, settings, and major events in a story, using key details. **RL.1.3**

I Do Remind children that the plot in a fantasy story includes the characters, what they do, where they go, and what happens. The events are the important things that happen. A plot has a beginning, a middle, and an end. *The events are the important things that happen. Sometimes one event causes another event to happen. The cause is why it happened. What happens is the effect.*

We Do Read the Practice Book story together. Pause to point out the characters, what they do, and what causes events to happen. *We read that Bethy makes a wish. What caused her to make a wish? What happens in the end? What causes the ending?*

You Do Have partners reread the story together. Have them work together as you guide them to complete a Cause and Effect chart.

SELF-SELECTED READING

OBJECTIVES

 With prompting and support, read prose and poetry of appropriate complexity for grade 1. **RL.1.10**

Apply the strategy and skill to read a text

Read Independently

Have children pick a fantasy for sustained silent reading. Remind them to:

- predict what might happen as they read the story.

- identify the causes and order of the events that make up the plot.

- note the parts of the text that show that it is a fantasy.

Read Purposefully

Have children record the important events on a Cause and Effect chart. After reading, guide children to participate in a group discussion about the story they read. Guide children to:

- share their charts.

- tell how they could tell that the selection was a fantasy and whether they liked it.

- share what predictions they made and whether they were correct.

→ On Level

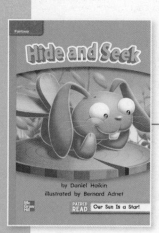

Lexile 310

OBJECTIVES

Describe characters, settings, and major events in a story, using key details. **RL.1.3**

- Make and confirm predictions
- Recognize cause and effect

Leveled Reader:
Hide and Seek!

Before Reading

Preview and Predict

Have children turn to the title page. Read the title and the author's name and have children repeat. Preview the selection's illustrations. Prompt children to predict what the selection might be about.

Review Genre: Fantasy

Have children recall that a fantasy has invented characters, settings, or other elements that could not exist in real life.

ESSENTIAL QUESTION

Remind children of the Essential Question: *What can you see in the sky?* Set a purpose for reading: *Let's read to find out what Harry sees in the sky.*

Remind children that as they read a selection, they can ask questions about what they do not understand or want to know more about.

During Reading

Guided Comprehension

As children whisper read *Hide and Seek!,* monitor and provide guidance, correcting blending and modeling the key strategies and skills.

Strategy: Make and Confirm Predictions

Remind children that as they read they can make predictions about what will happen next. Then they can read on to see if they are right. Model using the strategy. *On page 4, Harry tells Flutter to hide. I think Flutter will hide behind Harry*. Read page 5. *Was my prediction correct? How can you tell?*

Skill: Plot/Cause and Effect

Remind children that a cause is an event that makes something happen. An effect is what happens. As you read, say: *Harry climbed a hill. What caused him to do that?* Display a Cause and Effect chart for children to copy.

Go Digital

Hide and Seek!

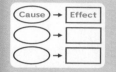

Graphic Organizer

Retell

Model recording answers for children. Have children copy the answers into their own charts.

Think Aloud On page 8, I read that Harry climbed a hill. Why did he do that? He was searching for Flutter! That is the cause. I will write that cause and effect in my chart.

Prompt children to fill in the rest of the chart as they read.

After Reading

Respond to Reading

Have children complete the Respond to Reading on page 12.

Retell

Have children take turns retelling the selection, using the **Retelling Cards** as a guide. Help children make a connection by asking: *Have you seen caterpillars or butterflies? Where did you see them? What did they do?*

Model Fluency

Read the sentences one at a time. Have children chorally repeat. Point out to children how your voice sounds when you read exclamations.

Apply Have partners practice reading. Provide feedback as needed.

PAIRED READ ...

"Our Sun Is a Star!"

Make Connections: Write About It *Analytical Writing*

Before reading, ask children to note that the genre of this selection is informational text. Then read the Compare Texts direction together. After reading the selection, ask children to make connections between the information they learned from "Our Sun Is a Star!" and *Hide and Seek*. What did you learn about the sun?

Leveled Reader

FOCUS ON SCIENCE

Children can extend their knowledge of what we see in the sky by completing the science activity on page 16.
STEM

Literature Circles

Lead children in conducting a literature circle using the Thinkmark questions to guide the discussion. You may wish to discuss what children have learned about the sun in the two selections in the Leveled Reader.

Level Up

Level-up lessons available online.

IF children can read *Hide and Seek!*, On Level with fluency and correctly answer the Respond to Reading questions,

THEN tell children that they will read another story about things in the sky.

• Use page 2 of *The Foxes Build a Home* Beyond Level to model using Teaching Poster 32 to list a cause and an effect from the selection.

• Have children read the selection, checking their comprehension by using the graphic organizer.

On Level

Phonics

BUILD WORDS WITH /ûr/*er, ir, ur, or*

OBJECTIVES

 Decode regularly spelled one-syllable words. **RF.1.3b**

 I Do Display **Word-Building Cards** *t, ur, n. These are the letters* t, ur, n. *They stand for /t/ /ûr/ /n/. I will blend /t/ /ûr/ /n/ together: /tûrn/,* turn. *The word is* turn.

 We Do *Now let's do one together.* Make the word *turn* using Word-Building Cards. Replace the *t* with the letter *b. Let's blend: /b/ /ûr/ /n/, /bûrn/,* burn. *We have a new word,* burn.

Change the letter *n* to *st. I am going to change the letter* n *to* st. *Let's blend and read the new word /b/ /ûr/ /st/, /bûrst/,* burst. *The new word is* burst.

 You Do Have children build and blend the words: *fir, firm, first, thirst, third, bird, birch, birth.*

Repeat with additional words with /ûr/*er, ir, or, ur.*

Decodable Reader Have children read "Sir Worm and Bird Girl," "Birds in the Sky," Ginger and the Stars," and "Bats Under the Dark Sky," (pages 9–24).

Words to Know

REVIEW WORDS

OBJECTIVES

 Recognize and read grade-appropriate irregularly spelled words. **RF.1.3g**

Review high-frequency and vocabulary words: *another, climb, full, great, poor, through, leaped,* and *stretched.*

 I Do Use the Read/Spell/Write routine to teach each high-frequency and vocabulary word. Use each word orally in a sentence.

 We Do Guide children to Read/Spell/Write each word using their **Response Boards**. Then work with the group to generate oral sentences using the words.

 You Do Have partners work together using the Read/Spell/Write routine with the high-frequency words *another, climb, full, great, poor, through* and the vocabulary words *leaped* and *stretched.* Have partners write sentences about this week's stories. Each sentence must contain at least one high frequency word or vocabulary word.

Comprehension

REVIEW SKILL: PLOT: CAUSE AND EFFECT

OBJECTIVES

CCSS Describe characters, settings, and major events in a story, using key details. **RL.1.3**

Identify cause and effect

 I Do Remind children that a plot has a beginning, a middle, and an end. The plot includes the characters, what they say and do, where they go, and what happens. *When we read a story, we look for the important events. We pay attention to what causes each event and what the effects are.*

 We Do Read the first page of the Practice Book selection aloud. Pause to point out who the character is, what she is doing, and why. *We read about Bethy Bunny. What does she do in the beginning of the story? What could be an effect of her making a wish?*

 You Do Guide children to read the rest of the Practice Book selection. Have them use a Cause and Effect chart to record the important events. Discuss the completed charts as a group.

SELF-SELECTED READING

OBJECTIVES

CCSS With prompting and support, read prose and poetry of appropriate complexity for grade 1. **RL.1.10**

Apply the strategy and skill to read a text

Read Independently

Have children pick a fantasy story for sustained silent reading. Remind them to:

- make predictions about what will happen in the story as they read.

- identify the causes and effects of the important events that make up the plot.

Read Purposefully

Have children record the important events on a Cause and Effect chart. After completing the chart, guide partners to:

- share and compare their charts.

- tell what predictions they made and if they were correct.

- identify the parts of the selection that let them know it was a fantasy and talk about the parts they liked best.

Beyond Level

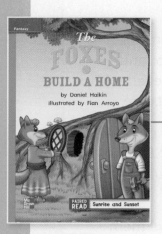

Lexile 420

OBJECTIVES

CCSS Describe characters, settings, and major events in a story, using key details. **RL.1.3**

- Make and confirm predictions
- Recognize cause and effect

Leveled Reader:
The Foxes Build a Home

The Foxes Build a Home

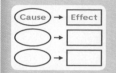

Graphic Organizer

Before Reading

Preview and Predict

Read the title and author name. Have children preview the title page and the illustrations. Ask: *What do you think this book will be about?*

Review Genre: Fantasy

Have children recall that a fantasy has invented characters, settings, or other elements that could not exist in real life. Prompt children to name key characteristics of a fantasy. Tell them to look for these as they read the Leveled Reader.

ESSENTIAL QUESTION

Remind children of the Essential Question: *What can you see in the sky?* Set a purpose for reading: *Let's find out how the sun affects the Fox family.*

During Reading

Guided Comprehension

Have children whisper read *The Foxes Build a Home*. Have them place self-stick notes next to difficult words. Remind children that when they come to an unfamiliar word, they can look for familiar spellings. They will need to break longer words into smaller chunks and sound out each part.

Monitor children's reading. Stop periodically and ask open-ended questions to facilitate rich discussion, such as, *What does the author want you to know about the sun?* Build on children's responses to develop deeper understanding of the text.

Strategy: Make and Confirm Predictions

Remind children that as they read they can make predictions about what will happen next. Then they read on to see if they are right. Say: *Remember, as you read, stop and predict what will happen. Read on to see if you are correct.*

Skill: Plot/Cause and Effect

Remind children that a cause is an event that makes something happen. An effect is what happens. As you read, ask: *Why can't the little foxes help build the home?* Display a Cause and Effect chart for children to copy. Model how to record the information.

Think Aloud On page 2, I read that Papa Fox tells Paddy and Paws to build a pretend home. This was because they were not old enough to help Mama and Papa Fox. I will write that cause and effect in my chart.

Have children fill in their charts as they read.

After Reading

Respond to Reading

Have children complete the Respond to Reading on page 12.

Retell

Have children take turns retelling the selection. Help children make a personal connection by writing about something they had to stop doing because the sun went down. *Tell how you felt and if you finished the next day.*

Leveled Reader

PAIRED READ ...

"Sunrise and Sunset"

Make Connections:
Write About It *Analytical Writing*

Before reading "Sunrise and Sunset," have children preview the title page and prompt them to identify the genre. Read the Compare Texts direction together. After reading the selection, have partners discuss information in "Sunrise and Sunset" and *The Foxes Build a Home.* Have them connect texts by comparing and contrasting the sun in each selection. Prompt children to discuss what they learned about the sun from both selections.

 FOCUS ON SCIENCE

Children can extend their knowledge about what we see in the sky by completing the science activity on page 16.

STEM

 **Literature Circles**

Lead children in conducting a literature circle using the Thinkmark questions to guide the discussion. You may wish to discuss what children have learned about the sun in the two selections in the Leveled Reader.

Gifted and Talented

SYNTHESIZE Challenge children to write about what else they see in the sky when the sun is out and when it is not out. Encourage them to classify their information into two categories: Day Sky and Night Sky.

EXTEND Have them use facts they learned from the week or do additional research to find out more about the things in the sky.

Beyond Level

Vocabulary

ORAL VOCABULARY: SUFFIXES

OBJECTIVES

Use frequently occurring affixes as a clue to the meaning of a word. **L.1.4b**

 Review the meaning of the oral vocabulary word *vast*. Say the sentence: *The sky is dark and vast.* Explain that a suffix is a word part that is added to the end of a base word that changes the meaning.

Vast means "huge" or "large." I can add the suffix -ness *to* vast: *vastness. The vastness of the sky is beautiful. The suffix* -ness *changes a describing word into a noun.*

 Review the meaning of the oral vocabulary word *thoughtful. We can add the suffix* -ness *to the word* thoughtful, *too, to change it into a noun. My sister is thoughtful and helps me. Her thoughtfulness makes me feel _____.* Have children complete the sentence.

 Have partners make up oral sentences with the words *vast, vastness, thoughtful,* and *thoughtfulness.*

 Extend Have partners think of other describing words they can add the suffix *-ness* to. Provide guidance as needed. Challenge them to say sentences using the words they came up with.

VOCABULARY WORDS: SUFFIXES

OBJECTIVES

Use frequently occurring affixes as a clue to the meaning of a word. **L.1.4b**

 Review the meaning of the word *stretched*. Tell children they can take off the *-ed* and add a suffix to *stretch* to change its meaning. *The suffix* -y *changes an action word into a describing word. Let's add the suffix* -y *to the word* stretch. *We formed* stretchy. *I can stretch a rubber band. It is stretchy. Adding the suffix* -y *changes the word* stretch *to a word that describes something that is able to stretch.*

 Have children take turns using the word *stretchy* in a sentence; for example: *This material is stretchy.*

 Have children work with a partner to come up with two sentences, one using *stretch* and one using *stretchy.*

Comprehension

REVIEW SKILL: PLOT: CAUSE AND EFFECT

OBJECTIVES

Describe characters, settings, and major events in a story, using key details. **RL.1.3**

Identify causes and effects in a story

 I Do Discuss with children how they can understand the plot of a fantasy story. *To understand the story I need to identify the events and which events cause other events to happen. Causes make things happen. Effects are what happens.*

 We Do Guide children in reading the first page of the Practice Book selection aloud. Prompt them to discuss the characters, the important event in the beginning of the story, and what caused the event. *Who is the character in this story so far? What is the important event in the beginning of the plot? Why did this event happen?*

You Do Have children read the rest of the Practice Book selection independently. Remind them to use the characters' words and the illustrations to determine the important events and their causes and effects.

SELF-SELECTED READING

OBJECTIVES

With prompting and support, read prose and poetry of appropriate complexity for grade 1. **RL.1.10**

Apply the strategy and skill to read a text

Read Independently

Have children pick a fantasy story for sustained silent reading. Tell them to predict what will happen next as they read and confirm their predictions as they continue to read. Encourage children to focus on the events that happen and what causes them to happen.

Read Purposefully

Have children record events on a Cause and Effect chart. After reading, guide children to:

* share their charts with a partner and discuss the important events in the story they read.

* record information about the story in a reading response journal.

 Independent Study Have children write a letter to a character in the story they read. They should tell the character what they liked about the story, and about any predictions they made while reading.

→ English Language Learners

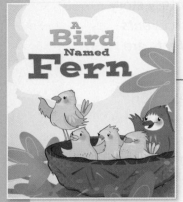

Reading/Writing Workshop

OBJECTIVES

Describe characters, settings, and major events in a story, using key details. **RL.1.3**

Shared Read

A Bird Named Fern

Go Digital

A Bird Named Fern

Before Reading

Build Background

Read the Essential Question: *What can you see in the sky?*

- Explain the meaning of the Essential Question: *I see some things in the sky at night. I see different things during the day.*

- **Model an answer:** *At night I see stars and the moon. During the day I see the sun and clouds. Some clouds are white. Sometimes the clouds are dark gray. That means it might rain or snow!*

- Ask children a question that ties the Essential Question to their own background knowledge. *What do you see in the sky during the day?* Ask partners to share their answers.

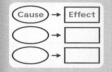

Graphic Organizer

During Reading

Interactive Question-Response

- Ask questions that help children understand the meaning of the text after each paragraph.

- Reinforce the meanings of key vocabulary by providing meanings embedded in the questions.

- Ask children questions that require them to use key vocabulary.

- Reinforce the comprehension strategies and skills of the week by modeling.

A Bird Named Fern

Pages 140–141

Point to the title. *Listen as I read the title of the fantasy story.* Point to each word as you read it. *What is the title?* (A Bird Named Fern)

The characters in this story are birds. One of the birds is named Fern. Point to Fern. *Say her name with me*: Fern. *What is Fern looking at?* (clouds) *Let's read and find out what happens to Fern.*

Pages 142–143

Point to Fern. *I see Fern. Listen as I read about Fern: "Little Fern was always full of questions! She wanted to know about everything in the world." What do we know about Fern?* (She has lots of questions.)

Now let's look at the cloud on page 143. Point to the boat-shaped cloud. *What does this cloud look like?* (a boat) *Fern wants to find out about this cloud. Let's find out what happens next.*

Explain and Model the Strategy Reread page 143. *We can use the words and the pictures to guess what will happen next. What do you think Fern will do? Why do you think so?*

Pages 144–145

Read page 144 together. *Let's reread the sentence that tells what Fern did. Then you can read it after me: "So she stretched her wings and took off." Let's act out what Fern did.* Demonstrate how to flap your arms and fly.

Now let's look at the picture on page 145. Uh-oh! Now the cloud looks different. What does it look like? (a pillow) *When do you use a pillow?* (when you want to sleep or rest)

Explain and Model High-Frequency Words Point to the word *climb* and have children say it with you. *Show me how you would climb.* Model how to role-play climbing.

Talk to your partner about your predictions for the rest of the story.

Pages 146–147

Let's look at the picture on page 146. What happened to Fern? (She fell through the cloud.) *Clouds are not solid, like a real pillow.*

Now let's look at page 147. Point to another cloud that looks like a pillow. Let's read what happens: "I see another bed," said Fern. "I will try to land on that one." *What do you think will happen next? Let's make a prediction.* (Fern will fall through the cloud.) Read the next line, then ask: *Was your prediction right?*

How do you think Fern felt when she fell through the cloud? (afraid; confused)

Pages 148–149

Explain and Model the Skill *An effect is something that happens. A cause is why it happened. Look at the picture on page 148. Fern flew home to her Mom and Dad. What caused her to do this?* (She wanted them to explain why she fell through the clouds.) *That's right, Fern flying home is an effect of her falling through the clouds.*

Listen as I read the last sentence on this page: Poor Fern was soaked by the time she got home. *Look at the picture. Fern is soaked, or very wet. What caused her to get soaked?* (She flew home in the rain.) *Do you think she will jump on a cloud again?*

Explain and Model Phonics Reread the sixth sentence on page 148. *Listen carefully as I read. Which words have the /ûr/ sounds?* (Fern, her) *Now let's say the words together:* Fern, her.

After Reading

Make Connections

- Review the Essential Question.

→ English Language Learners

Lexile 310

OBJECTIVES

 Describe characters, settings, and major events in a story, using key details. **RL.1.3**

Leveled Reader:
Hide and Seek!

Go Digital

Hide and Seek!

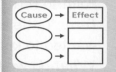

Graphic Organizer

Retell

Before Reading

Preview

Read the title. Ask: *What is the title? Say it again*. Repeat with the author's name. Preview the illustrations. Have children describe the pictures. Use simple language to tell about each page. Follow with questions, such as, *Who is this character? What is this character doing?*

ESSENTIAL QUESTION

Remind children of the Essential Question: *What can you see in the sky?* Say: *Let's read to find out about Harry, his friend Flutter, and the sun.* Encourage children to ask for help when they do not understand a word or phrase.

During Reading

Interactive Question-Response

Pages 2–3 *Look at the illustration on page 2. These are the characters in this story. Who is Flutter? Who is Harry? Tell your partner what Flutter wants to do.* (fly to the sun)

Pages 4–5 *Look at the illustration. Why is Flutter hiding behind Harry?* (to hide from the bird that might eat him) *What game does Harry like to play?* (hide-and-seek) *Talk to your partner about how to play hide-and-seek.*

Pages 6–7 *Who does Harry think is hiding ?* (Flutter) *Who is doing the seeking?* (Harry)

Pages 8–9 *Harry is looking for Flutter. He climbs a big hill and finds the sun. A butterfly flies past. What do you think will happen next? Will Harry find Flutter?* (Responses will vary.)

Pages 10–11 *What did you predict? Were you right? The butterfly is Flutter! Caterpillars make a cocoon. While they're inside, they become butterflies. What is the effect of Flutter becoming a butterfly?* (He can fly!)

After Reading

Respond to Reading

Revisit the Essential Question. Ask children to work with partners to fill in the graphic organizer and answer the questions on page 12. Pair children with peers of varying language abilities.

Retell

Model retelling using the **Retelling Card** prompts. Say: *Look at the illustrations. Use details to help you retell the selection.* Help children make personal connections by asking: *Have you ever seen a caterpillar or butterfly? Where? What did they look like?*

Intonation Fluency: Exclamations

Read the pages in the book, one at a time. Help children echo-read the pages expressively and with appropriate phrasing. Remind them sound excited when they read exclamations.

Apply Have children practice reading with partners. Pair children with peers of varying language abilities. Provide feedback as needed.

PAIRED READ ...

Leveled Reader

"Our Sun Is a Star!"

Make Connections:
Write About It *Analytical Writing*

Before reading, tell children to note that this selection is informational text. Then read the Compare Texts direction.

After reading the selection, ask children to make connections between the information they learned from "Our Sun Is a Star!" and *Hide and Seek!*. Prompt children by providing a sentence frame: *The sun gives us ____. The sun is ____.*

 FOCUS ON SCIENCE

Children can extend their knowledge of things we see in the sky by completing the science activity on page 16. **STEM**

Literature Circles

Lead children in conducting a literature circle using the Thinkmark questions to guide the discussion. You may wish to discuss what children have learned about the sun from the two selections in the Leveled Reader.

Level Up

Level-up lessons available online.

IF children can read *Hide and Seek!* **ELL Level** with fluency and correctly answer the Respond to Reading questions,

THEN tell children that they will read a more detailed version of the story.

• **USE** page 3 of *Hide and Seek!* **On Level** to model using Teaching Poster 32 to list a cause and an effect in the selection.

• **HAVE** children read the selection, checking their comprehension by using the graphic organizer.

English Language Learners
Vocabulary

PRETEACH ORAL VOCABULARY

OBJECTIVES
Produce complete sentences when appropriate to task and situation. **SL.1.6**

LANGUAGE OBJECTIVE
Use oral vocabulary words

 I Do Display images from the **Visual Vocabulary Cards** one at a time to preteach the oral vocabulary words *vast* and *observe*.

 We Do Display the images again and explain how they illustrate or demonstrate the words. Model using sentences to describe the image.

 You Do Display each word again. Have partners talk about how the picture demonstrates the word *vast*.

Beginning	Intermediate	Advanced/High
Have children use gestures to demonstrate each word while saying the word.	Help children use the words *vast* and *observe* in complete sentences to tell about the images on the cards.	Have children tell about something they've seen that is vast or something they observe.

PRETEACH VOCABULARY

OBJECTIVES
Produce complete sentences when appropriate to task and situation. **SL.1.6**

LANGUAGE OBJECTIVE
Use vocabulary words

 I Do Display images from the **ELL Visual Vocabulary Cards** one at a time to preteach the vocabulary words *become* and *playing* and follow the routine. Say the word and have children repeat it. Define the word in English.

 We Do Display the image again and explain how it illustrates or demonstrates the word. Model using sentences to describe the image.

 You Do Display the word again and have children say the word, then spell it. Provide opportunities for children to use the words in speaking and writing. Provide sentence starters.

Beginning	Intermediate	Advanced/High
Help children find examples of or act out each word.	Spell the word and have children identify the word you spelled, then spell it for you.	Have children use their own words to tell what each word means.

Words to Know

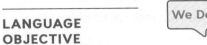

REVIEW WORDS

OBJECTIVES

 CCSS Recognize and read grade-appropriate irregularly spelled words. **RF.1.3g**

LANGUAGE OBJECTIVE

Use high-frequency words *another, climb, full, great, poor,* and *through,* and vocabulary words *leaped* and *stretched*

 I Do Display the **High-Frequency Word Cards** for *another, climb, full, great, poor, through,* and **Vocabulary Cards** for *leaped* and *stretched*. Read each word. Use the **Read/Spell/Write** routine to teach each word. Have children write the words on their **Response Boards**.

 We Do Write sentence frames on separate lines. Track the print as you guide children to read and complete the sentences: *(1) It is time for another ____. (2) When can we climb up ____? (3) This pail is full of ____. (4) That is a great ____! (5) The poor plant has no ____. (6) The boy ran through the ____. (7) What leaped out of ____? (8) Jack stretched his arms to ____.*

You Do Display the High-Frequency Word Cards from the previous weeks. Display one card at a time as children chorally read the word. Mix and repeat. Note words children need to review. Repeat with vocabulary words.

Beginning	Intermediate	Advanced/High
Have children echo read each word. Encourage them to act out words such as *climb, through, leaped,* and *stretched*.	Have children complete sentences with correct word choices, then repeat the sentence. For example, *May I have ____ (another, through) drink?*	Have children write complete sentences for each word.

RETEACH HIGH-FREQUENCY WORDS

OBJECTIVES

 CCSS Recognize and read grade-appropriate irregularly spelled words. **RF.1.3g**

LANGUAGE OBJECTIVE

Use high-frequency words

 I Do Display each Visual Vocabulary Card and say the word aloud. Define the word in English, then in Spanish if appropriate, identifying any cognates.

 We Do Point to the image and explain how it illustrates the word. Have children repeat the word. Engage children in structured partner-talk about the image as prompted on the back of the card. Ask children to chorally say the word three times.

 You Do Display each visual card in random order, hiding the word. Have children identify and define the word in their own words.

Beginning	Intermediate	Advanced/High
Have children echo read each word while looking at its Visual Vocabulary card.	Have partners come up with oral sentences for each word.	Challenge children to write a sentence for each word.

English Language Learners
Writing/Spelling

WRITING TRAIT: WORD CHOICE

OBJECTIVES

 Use frequently occurring adjectives. **L.1.1f**

LANGUAGE OBJECTIVE

Use interesting words

 I Do   Explain that writers use adjectives to describe how things look, sound, smell, taste, and feel. Adjectives also describe size, shape, number, and color.

Write and read: *I see the sky. I see the bright blue sky.* Help children compare the sentences and point out how the adjectives describe what the sky looks like.

 We Do   Read the first sentence on page 143 of *A Bird Named Fern.* Ask children to name the words that describe or tell about the boat. *Yes, the words* big *and* white *help readers picture exactly what the boat looks like.* Repeat the exercise with the last sentence on page 144, focusing on the word *fluffy*.

 You Do   Have children write a sentence about the sky. Remind them to include interesting words to describe the sky.

Beginning	Intermediate	Advanced/High
Brainstorm words to describe the sky and have children complete the sentence: *The sky is ____.*	Have children answer with complete sentences: *What does the night sky look like? What do you see in it?*	Have children say more than one sentence to describe the sky.

WORDS WITH /ûr/er, ir, ur, or

OBJECTIVES

 Use conventional spelling for words with common spelling patterns and for frequently occurring irregular words. **L.1.2d**

LANGUAGE OBJECTIVE

Spell words with long /ûr/ spelled er, ir, or, ur

 I Do   Read aloud the Spelling Words on page T92. Segment *her* into sounds and attach a spelling to each sound. Point out the /ûr/ sound-spelling. Read aloud, segment, and spell the remaining words and have children repeat.

 We Do   Say a sentence for *her*. Then, say *her* slowly and ask children to repeat. Have them write the word. Repeat the process for the remaining words.

 You Do   Display the words. Have children work with a partner to check their spelling lists. Have children correct misspelled words on their list.

Beginning	Intermediate	Advanced/High
Help children copy the words with correct spelling and say the word.	After children have corrected their words, have pairs quiz each other.	Challenge children to think of rhyming words for two of the spelling words.

Grammar

ADJECTIVES

OBJECTIVES

Use frequently occurring adjectives. **L.1.1f**

Language Transfers Handbook

TRANSFER SKILLS
Cantonese and Korean speakers consistently place adjectives after nouns rather than before. For example: *I see the sun hot.* Provide additional practice by writing pairs of adjectives and nouns on individual index cards. Have children arrange each pair in the correct order and read them aloud.

Adjectives: dark, bright, hot

Nouns: sky, sun, stars

 I Do Review that adjectives tell number, color, size, shape, and how things look, sound, feel, smell, or taste.

Write the following sentence on the board. *The black cat leaped.* Underline the adjective *black.* Say: *The adjective in this sentence tells what color the cat is. It is a black cat.*

 We Do Write the sentence frames on the board. Have children echo read the sentence and guide them to underline the adjective in each. Have them say: *The adjective is _____.*

The bright stars shine. (bright)

The hot sun is in the sky. (hot)

I see three stars. (three)

 You Do Write the following sentences on the board.

I like looking at the _____ moon.

I see _____ birds in the sky.

Pair children and have them complete each sentence frame by providing adjectives based on this week's readings. Circulate, listen in, and take note of each child's language use and proficiency.

Beginning	Intermediate	Advanced/High
Display pictures from *A Bird Named Fern* and point to objects. Say sentences with adjectives to describe the objects. Have children repeat the sentences.	Have children choose a picture from *A Bird Named Fern* and describe something in the picture. Encourage them to use complete sentences.	Have children use at least two adjectives in sentences about pictures from *A Bird Named Fern*.

PROGRESS MONITORING

Unit 5 Week 2 Formal Assessment	Standards Covered	Component for Assessment
Comprehension Plot: Cause and Effect	RL.1.3	• *Selection Test* • *Weekly Assessment*
Vocabulary Strategy Shades of Meaning/Intensity	L.1.5d	• *Selection Test* • *Weekly Assessment*
Phonics *r*-Controlled Vowels *er, ir, ur, or*	RF.1.3	*Weekly Assessment*
Structural Analysis Inflectional Ending *-er*	RF.1.3f	*Weekly Assessment*
High-Frequency Words *another, climb, full, great, poor, through*	RF.1.3g	*Weekly Assessment*
Writing Writing About Text	RL.1.3	*Weekly Assessment*
Unit 5 Week 2 Informal Assessment		
Research/Listening/Collaborating	SL.1.1c, SL.1.2, SL.1.3	• *RWW* • *Teacher's Edition*
Oral Reading Fluency (ORF) **Fluency Goal:** 13-33 words correct per minute (WCPM) **Accuracy Rate Goal:** 95% or higher	RF.1.4a. RF.1.4b, RF.1.4c	*Fluency Assessment*

Using Assessment Results

Weekly Assessment Skills	If . . .	Then . . .
COMPREHENSION	Children answer 0–3 multiple-choice items correctly . . .	. . . assign Lessons 28-30 on Identify Plot Events and Lessons 43-45 on Cause and Effect (fiction) from the ***Tier 2 Comprehension Intervention online PDFs***.
VOCABULARY	Children answer 0–2 multiple-choice items correctly . . .	. . . assign Lesson 118 on Shades of Meaning: Verbs and Lesson 119 on Shades of Meaning: Adjectives from the ***Tier 2 Vocabulary Intervention online PDFs***.
PHONICS/ STRUCTURAL ANALYSIS/HFW	Children answer 0–6 multiple-choice items correctly . . .	. . . assign Lesson 88 on *r*-Controlled Vowels /ûr/ (*ir, ur, er, or*) and Lesson 83 on Inflectional Ending *-er, -est* from the ***Tier 2 Phonics/Word Study Intervention online PDFs***.
WRITING	Children score less than "2" on the constructed response . . .	. . . reteach necessary skills using Section 13 on Write About Reading from the ***Tier 2 Comprehension Intervention online PDFs***.
FLUENCY	Children have a WCPM score of 13 . . .	. . . assign a lesson from Section 1, 9, or 10 of the ***Tier 2 Fluency Intervention online PDFs***.
	Children have a WCPM score of 0–12 . . .	. . . assign a lesson from Sections 2–8 of the ***Tier 2 Fluency Intervention online PDFs.***

Using Weekly Data

Check your data Dashboard to verify assessment results and guide grouping decisions.

Data-Driven Recommendations

Response to Intervention

Use the children's assessment results to assist you in identifying children who will benefit from focused intervention.

Use the appropriate sections of the ***Placement and Diagnostic Assessment*** to designate children requiring:

TIER 2 **Intervention Online PDFs**

TIER 3 **WonderWorks Intervention Program**

Build Knowledge
Great Inventions

 Essential Question:
What inventions do you know about?

Teach and Model
Close Reading and Writing

Big Book and Little Book

Reading Writing Workshop

The Story of a Robot Inventor, 160–169
Genre Biography **Lexile** 420

Interactive Read Aloud

"Great Inventions,"
Genre Nonfiction

Practice and Apply
Close Reading and Writing

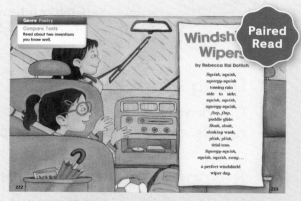

Literature Anthology   *Thomas Edison, Inventor,* 202–219
Genre Biography **Lexile** 510

Paired Read

"Windshield Wipers" and "Scissors": 222–225
Genre Poetry **Lexile: NP**

Differentiated Texts

APPROACHING
Lexile 410

ON LEVEL
Lexile 500

BEYOND
Lexile 660

ELL
Lexile 430

Leveled Readers

Extended Complex Texts

Snowflake Bentley
Genre Nonfiction
Lexile 830

*A Weed Is a Flower:
The Life of George
Washington Carver*
Genre Nonfiction **Lexile** 690

Classroom Library

Student Outcomes

Close Reading of Complex Text

- Cite relevant evidence from text
- Describe connections within text: problem and solution
- Retell the text

RI.1.3, RI.1.2

Writing

Write to Sources

- Draw evidence from biography
- Write informative text
- Conduct short research on great inventions

W.1.2, W.1.7

Speaking and Listening

- Engage in collaborative conversation about great inventions
- Retell and discuss *The Story of a Robot Inventor*
- Present information on great inventions

SL.1.1c, SL.1.2, SL.1.3

Content Knowledge

- Explore how inventors of the past are similar to and different from today's inventors

Language Development

Conventions

- Use Adjectives that Compare *-er* and *-est*

Vocabulary Acquisition

- Develop oral vocabulary

curious	improve	complicated
imagine	device	

- Acquire and use academic vocabulary

idea	unusual

- Use context clues to understand prefixes

L.1.4b, L.1.6, L.2.4b

Foundational Skills

Phonics/Word Study/Spelling

- *r*-controlled vowels *or, ore, oar*
- abbreviations
- born, corn, core, more, roar, soar

High-Frequency Words

began, better, guess, learn, right, sure

Fluency

- Appropriate Phrasing

Decodable Text

- Apply foundational skills in connected text

RF.1.3, L.1.2, RF.1.3g, RF.1.4a, RF.1.4b, RF.1.4c

Professional Development

- See lessons in action in real classrooms.
- Get expert advice on instructional practices.
- Collaborate with other teachers.
- Access PLC Resources

Go Digital! www.connected.mcgraw-hill.com.

INSTRUCTIONAL PATH

1 Talk About Great Inventions

Guide children in collaborative conversations.

Discuss the essential question: *What inventions do you know about?*

Develop academic language.

Listen to "The Great Inventions" to learn information about inventions that changed the world.

2 Read About An Inventor

Apply foundational skills in connected text. Model close reading.

Read

The Story of a Robot Inventor to learn about a man who invents robots, citing text evidence to answer text-dependent questions.

Reread

The Story of a Robot Inventor to analyze text, craft, and structure, citing text evidence.

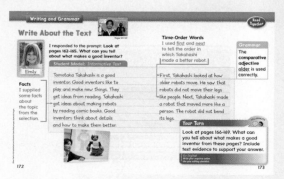

3 Write About Inventions

Model writing to a source.

Analyze a short response student model.

Use text evidence from close reading to write to a source.

4 Read and Write About Inventions

Practice and apply close reading of the anchor text.

Read

Thomas Edison, Inventor to learn about the life of one of America's best inventors.

Reread

Thomas Edison, Inventor and use text evidence to understand how the author presents information about Thomas Edison.

Integrate

Information about different types of inventions used in everyday life.

Write to a Source, citing text evidence to explain what made Thomas Edison a good inventor.

5 Independent Partner Work

Gradual release of support to independent work

- Text-Dependent Questions
- Scaffolded Partner Work
- Talk with a Partner
- Cite Text Evidence
- Complete a sentence frame.
- Guided Text Annotation

6 Integrate Knowledge and Ideas

Connect Texts

Text to Text Discuss how each of the texts answers the question: What inventions do you know about?

Text to Photography Compare information about inventions in the texts read with the photograph.

Conduct a Short Research Project

Create a collage about inventions.

DEVELOPING READERS AND WRITERS

Write to Sources: Informative

Day 1 and Day 2

Shared Writing

- Write about *The Story of a Robot Inventor*, p. T174

Interactive Writing

- Analyze a student model, p. T184
- Write about *The Story of a Robot Inventor*, p. T185
- Find Text Evidence
- Apply Writing Trait: Word Choice: Time-Order Words, p. T185
- Apply Grammar Skill: Adjectives That Compare (-*er* and -*est*), p. T185

Day 3, Day 4 and Day 5

Independent Writing

- Write about *Thomas Edison, Inventor*, p. T192
- Provide scaffolded instruction to meet student needs, p. T192
- Find Text Evidence, p. T192
- Apply Writing Trait: Word Choice: Time-Order Words, p. T192
- Prewrite and Draft, p. T192
- Revise and Edit, p. T198
- Final Draft, p. T199
- Present, Evaluate, and Publish, p. T204

Grammar

Adjectives That Compare

- Use adjectives that compare to tell about what is happening, pp. T175, T185, T193, T199, T205

- Apply grammar to writing, pp. T175, T192, T198, T205

Mechanics: Capitalize Days, Months, and Holidays

- Use capitalization in days, months, and holidays, pp. T193, T199, T205

Online PDFs

Grammar Practice, pp. 111–115

Online Grammar Games

Spelling

Words with /ôr/ or, ore, oar

- Spell words with /ôr/ or, ore, oar

Online PDFs

Phonics/Spelling blms
pp. 111–115

Online Spelling Games

SUGGESTED LESSON PLAN

READING		DAY 1	DAY 2
Teach, Model and Apply Wonders Reading/Writing Workshop	Core	**Building Background** Great Inventions, T164–T165 **Oral Vocabulary** *curious, improve*, T164 **Word Work** T168–T171 • Phonemic Awareness: Phoneme Categorization • Phonics/Spelling: Introduce /ôr/ *or, ore, oar,* • High-Frequency Words: *began, better, guess, learn, right, sure* • Vocabulary: *idea, unusual* **Shared Read** *The Story of a Robot Inventor,* T172–T173	**Oral Language** Great Inventions, T176 **Oral Vocabulary** *complicated, curious, device, imagine, improve*, T176 **Word Work** T178–T181 • Phonemic Awareness: Phoneme Substitution • Structural Analysis: Abbreviations • Vocabulary: *idea, unusual* **Shared Read** *The Story of a Robot Inventor,* T182–T183 • Genre: Informational Text/Biography, T182 • Skill: Connections Within Text: Problem and Solution, T183
	Options	**Listening Comprehension** "Great Inventions," T166–T167	**Listening Comprehension** "Great Inventions," T177 **Word Work** T178–T181 • Phonics/Spelling: Review /ôr/ *or, ore, oar* • High-Frequency Words

LANGUAGE ARTS

		DAY 1	DAY 2
Writing **Grammar**	Core	**Shared Writing** T174 **Grammar** Adjectives That Compare, T175	**Interactive Writing** T184 **Grammar** Adjectives That Compare, T185
	Options		

DIFFERENTIATED INSTRUCTION
Use your data dashboard to determine each student's needs. Then select instructional supports options throughout the week.

APPROACHING LEVEL

Leveled Reader
The Wright Brothers, T208–T209
"Fly Away Butterfly," T209
Literature Circles, T209

Phonological Awareness
Phoneme Categorization, T210 ^{TIER 2}
Phoneme Segmentation, T210
Phoneme Addition, T211
Phoneme Substitution, T211

Phonics
Connect /ôr/ to *or, ore, oar,* T212 ^{TIER 2}
Blend Words with /ôr/ *or, ore, oar,* T212 ^{TIER 2}
Build Words with /ôr/ *or, ore, oar,* T213
Build Fluency with Phonics, T213

Structural Analysis Review Abbreviations, T214

High-Frequency Words Review, T215

Comprehension
Read for Fluency, T216 ^{TIER 2}
Identify Key Details, T216 ^{TIER 2}
Review Connections Within Text: Problem and Solution, T217
Self-Selected Reading, T217

ON LEVEL

Leveled Reader
The Wright Brothers, T218–T219
"Fly Away, Butterfly," T219
Literature Circles, T219

Phonics
Build Words with /ôr/ *or, ore, oar,* T220

DAY 3	DAY 4	DAY 5
Fluency Phrasing, T187 **Word Work** T188–T191 • Phonemic Awareness: Phoneme Blending • Phonics/Spelling: Blend Words with /ôr/ *or, ore, oar* • Vocabulary Strategy: Prefixes **Close Reading** *Thomas Edison, Inventor,* T191A–T191L	**Extend the Concept** T194–T195 • Literary Element: Alliteration, T195 • Close Reading: "Windshield Wipers" and "Scissors," T195A–T197B **Word Work** T196–T197 • Phonemic Awareness: Phoneme Addition • Structural Analysis: Abbreviations **Integrate Ideas** • Research and Inquiry, T200–T201	**Word Work** T202–T203 • Phonemic Awareness: Phoneme Blending/ Segmentation • Phonics/Spelling: Blend and Build Words with /ôr/ *or, ore, oar* • Structural Analysis: Abbreviations • High-Frequency Words • Vocabulary: *idea, unusual* **Integrate Ideas** • Text Connections, T206–T207
Oral Language Great Inventions, T186 **Word Work** T188–T191 • Structural Analysis: Abbreviations • High-Frequency Words	**Word Work** T196–T197 • Fluency: Sound-Spellings • Phonics/Spelling: Build Words with /ôr/ *or, ore, oar* • High-Frequency Words • Vocabulary: *idea, unusual* **Close Reading** *Thomas Edison, Inventor,* T191A–T191L	**Word Work** T202–T203 • Fluency: Phrasing **Integrate Ideas** • Research and Inquiry, T206 • Speaking and Listening, T207
Independent Writing T192 **Grammar** Mechanics: Capitalize Days, Months, and Holidays, T193	**Independent Writing** T198 **Grammar** Mechanics: Capitalize Days, Months, and Holidays, T199	**Independent Writing** T204 **Grammar** Adjectives That Compare, T205
Grammar Adjectives That Compare, T193	**Grammar** Adjectives That Compare, T199	**Grammar** Mechanics: Capitalize Days, Months, and Holidays, T205

	BEYOND LEVEL	ENGLISH LANGUAGE LEARNERS	
Words to Know Review Words, T220	**Leveled Reader** *The Wright Brothers,* T222–T223 "Fly Away, Butterfly," T223 Literature Circles, T223 **Vocabulary** Context Clues, T224	**Shared Read** *The Story of a Robot Inventor,* T226–T227 **Leveled Reader** *The Wright Brothers,* T228–T29 "Fly Away, Butterfly," T229 Literature Circles, T229 **Vocabulary** Preteach Oral Vocabulary, T230 Preteach ELL Vocabulary, T230	**Words to Know** Review Words, T231 Reteach High-Frequency Words, T231 **Writing/Spelling** Writing Trait: Word Choice, T232 Words with /ôr/ *or, ore, oar,* T323 **Grammar** Adjectives that Compare (*-er* and *-est*), T233
Comprehension Review Connections Within Text: Problem and Solution, T221 Self-Selected Reading, T221	**Comprehension** Review Connections Within Text: Problem and Solution, T225 Self-Selected Reading, T225 *Gifted and Talented*		

DIFFERENTIATE TO ACCELERATE

  Scaffold to **A**ccess **C**omplex **T**ext

IF → the text complexity of a particular selection is too difficult for children

THEN → see the references noted in the chart below for scaffolded instruction to help children Access Complex Text.

Qualitative | Quantitative
Reader and Task
TEXT COMPLEXITY

	Reading/Writing Workshop	**Literature Anthology**	**Leveled Readers**	**Classroom Library**

Quantitative	*The Story of a Robot Inventor* **Lexile** 420	*Thomas Edison, Inventor* **Lexile** 510 "Windshield Wipers" and "Scissors" **Lexile** NP	**Approaching Level** **Lexile** 410 **Beyond Level** **Lexile** 660	**On Level** **Lexile** 500 **ELL** **Lexile** 430	*Snowflake Bentley* **Lexile** 830 *The Big Dipper* **Lexile** 460
Qualitative	**What Makes the Text Complex?** **Foundational Skills** • Decoding with *r*-controlled vowels *or, ore, oar,* T168–T169 • Reading abbreviations, T179 • Identifying high-frequency words, T170–T171 *See Scaffolded Instruction in Teacher's Edition, T168–T169, T170–T171, and T179.*	**What Makes the Text Complex?** • Genre, T191B, T191E • Organization, T191B, T191C **A C T** *See Scaffolded Instruction in Teacher's Edition, T191B, T191C, and T191E.*	**What Makes the Text Complex?** **Foundational Skills** • Decoding with *r*-controlled vowels *or, ore, oar* • Reading abbreviations • Identifying high-frequency words *began better guess learn right sure* *See Level Up lessons online for Leveled Readers.*		**What Makes the Text Complex?** • Purpose • Specific Vocabulary • Prior Knowledge • Sentence Structure • Organization • Connection of Ideas • Genre **A C T** *See Scaffolded Instruction in Teacher's Edition, T413–T415.*
Reader and Task	**The** Introduce the Concept lesson on pages T164–T165 will help determine the reader's knowledge and engagement in the weekly concept. See pages T172–T173, T182–T183, T200–T201 and T206 –T207 for questions and tasks for this text.	**The** Introduce the Concept lesson on pages T164–T165 will help determine the reader's knowledge and engagement in the weekly concept. See pages T191A–T191L, T195A–T195B, T200–T201 and T206–T207 for questions and tasks for this text.	**The** Introduce the Concept lesson on pages T164–T165 will help determine the reader's knowledge and engagement in the weekly concept. See pages T208–T209, T218–T219, T222–T223, T228–T229, T200–T201 and T206–T207 for questions and tasks for this text.		**The** Introduce the Concept lesson on pages T164–T165 will help determine the reader's knowledge and engagement in the weekly concept. See pages T413–T415 for questions and tasks for this text.

Monitor and *Differentiate*

✓ Quick Check

To differentiate instruction, use the Quick Checks to assess students' needs and select the appropriate small group instruction focus.

Comprehension Strategy Ask and Answer Questions, T167

Comprehension Skill Connections Within Text: Problem and Solution, T183

Phonics /ôr/*or, ore, oar,* T171, T181, T191, T197, T203

High-Frequency Words and Vocabulary T171, T181, T191, T197, T203

If No →
| Approaching Level | Reteach T208–T217 |
| ELL | Develop T226–T233 |

If Yes →
| On Level | Review T218–T221 |
| Beyond Level | Extend T222–T225 |

Using Weekly Data

Check your data Dashboard to verify assessment results and guide grouping decisions.

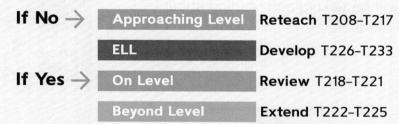

Level Up with Leveled Readers

 IF children can read their leveled text fluently and answer comprehension questions

THEN work with the next level up to accelerate children's reading with more complex text.

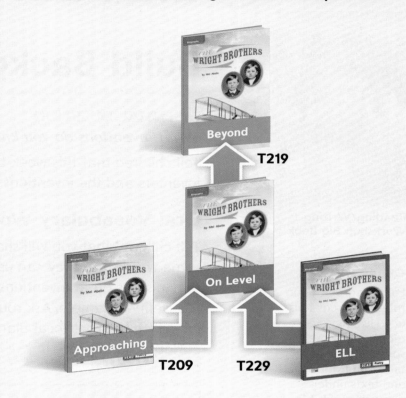

Beyond — **T219**

On Level — **T229**

Approaching — **T209**

ELL

ELL ENGLISH LANGUAGE LEARNERS

Small Group Instruction

Use the ELL small group lessons in the *Wonders* Teacher's Edition to provide focused instruction.

Language Development
Vocabulary preteaching, oral vocabulary preteaching, high-frequency word review and reteach, pp. T230–T231

Close Reading
Interactive Question-Response routines for scaffolded text-dependent questioning for reading and rereading the Shared Read and Leveled Reader, pp. T226–T229

Writing
Focus on the writing trait, grammar, and spelling, pp. T232–T233

Additional ELL Support

Use Wonders for English Learners for ELD instruction that connects to the core.

Language Development
My Language Book for ample opportunities for discussions and scaffolded language support

Close Reading
Guided support for the Shared Read, Big Books, and Interactive Read Alouds. Differentiated texts about the weekly concept

Writing
Guided support in Interactive and Independent Writing and writing to sources

Wonders for ELs Teacher Edition and My Language Book

Materials

Reading/Writing Workshop
VOLUME 4

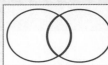

Reading/Writing Workshop Big Book
UNIT 5

Visual Vocabulary Cards

curious   improve
complicated   imagine
device

Vocabulary Cards
idea   unusual

High-Frequency Word Cards

began   learn
better   right
guess   sure

| a | b | c |

Word-Building Cards

Teaching Poster

Think Aloud Clouds

Interactive Read-Aloud Cards

Sound-Spelling Cards

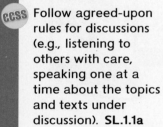

Reading/Writing Workshop Big Book

OBJECTIVES

CCSS Follow agreed-upon rules for discussions (e.g., listening to others with care, speaking one at a time about the topics and texts under discussion). **SL.1.1a**

- Build background knowledge
- Discuss the Essential Question

ACADEMIC LANGUAGE
- *change, compare*
- Cognate: *comparar*

→ Introduce the Concept

MINILESSON
5 Mins

Build Background

ESSENTIAL QUESTION

What inventions do you know about?

Tell children that this week they will be talking and reading about inventors and the inventions they made.

Oral Vocabulary Words

Tell children that you will share some words that they can use as they discuss great inventions. Use the Define/Example/Ask routine to introduce the oral vocabulary words **curious** and **improve**.

Visual Vocabulary Cards

Oral Vocabulary Routine

Define: If you are **curious** about something, you are interested in it and want to know more about it.

Example: I was curious about whales so I read a book about them.

Ask: What might a curious cat do when it sees a toy on the floor?

Define: To **improve** is to make something better.

Example: I added an extra pocket to my backpack to improve it.

Ask: What do you think would improve our classroom?

Discuss the theme of "Great Inventions" and explain that there are many inventions we use every day. *What are some inventions you are curious about? How might an inventor try to improve the world? What invention have you used today?*

Go Digital

Great Inventions

Video

Photos

Visual Glossary

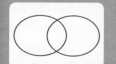

Graphic Organizer

READING/WRITING WORKSHOP, pp. 154–155

Talk About It: Great Inventions

Guide children to discuss the invention in the photograph.

- What are the children looking at?
- How is it different from televisions today? How is it similar?

Use Teaching Poster 39 and prompt children to complete the chart.

Children can look at page 154 of their Reading/Writing Workshop and do the Talk About It activity with a partner.

First Television | Both | Today's Television

Teaching Poster

Collaborative Conversations

Be Open to All Ideas As children engage in partner, small-group, and whole-group discussions, remind them:

- that everyone's ideas are important and should be heard.
- not to be afraid to ask a question if something is unclear.
- to respect the opinions of others.

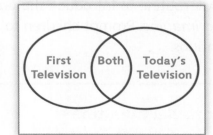

ENGLISH LANGUAGE LEARNERS SCAFFOLD

Beginning

Use Visuals Tell children that the invention in the picture is a television. *Do you watch shows on a television? What do you watch? Is the television in the picture different from the one you use?* Allow children ample time to respond.

Intermediate

Describe Ask children to describe what this invention does. *What do you use a television for?* Model correct pronunciation as needed.

Advanced/High

Discuss Have children talk about what life might have been like before the invention of the television. *Is the television an important invention? Why or why not?* Clarify children's responses as needed by providing vocabulary.

→ # Listening Comprehension

Read the Interactive Read Aloud

MINILESSON
10 Mins

OBJECTIVES

CCSS Participate in collaborative conversations with diverse partners about *grade 1 topics and texts* with peers and adults in small and larger groups. **SL.1.1**

- Develop concept understanding
- Develop reading strategy: ask and answer questions

ACADEMIC LANGUAGE

- *information, nonfiction, text, illustrations*
- Cognates: *información, no ficción, texto, ilustraciones*

Connect to Concept: Great Inventions

Tell children that they will now read about some inventions that have changed the world. Ask: *What might life be like without cars? Without telephones?*

"Great Inventions"

Focus on Oral Vocabulary

Review the oral vocabulary words *curious* and *improve*. Use the Define/Example/Ask routine to introduce the oral vocabulary words *complicated, device,* and *imagine*. Prompt children to use the words as they discuss great inventions.

"Great Inventions"

Ask and Answer Questions

Oral Vocabulary Routine

<u>Define:</u> If something is **complicated**, it has many parts and is difficult to understand.

<u>Example:</u> Sara tried to fix the broken clock, but it was too complicated.

<u>Ask:</u> Which toy is more complicated: a ball or a remote-controlled car?

<u>Define:</u> A **device** is an object made to do a certain job, such as a can opener.

Visual Vocabulary Cards

<u>Example:</u> Dad has a device that measures how much air is in the tires on the car.

<u>Ask:</u> What devices could you use in the kitchen?

<u>Define:</u> When you **imagine** something, you think of something that isn't real or that hasn't happened.

<u>Example:</u> Nina likes to imagine she is a princess living in a castle.

<u>Ask:</u> Imagine riding on a flying carpet. What would that be like?

Visual Glossary

Retell

Set a Purpose for Reading

- Display the Interactive Read-Aloud Cards.
- Read aloud the title.
- Tell children that you will be reading an informational selection about some important inventions. Tell children to read to find out how these inventions help us in our daily lives.

Strategy: Ask and Answer Questions

1 Explain Remind children that as they read or listen to a text, they can ask themselves questions about the text. This can help them read more actively and understand the information.

Think Aloud One way to better understand a text is to ask questions about information in the text and then look for the answers as you read. Today, as we read "Great Inventions," I will ask myself questions about the text. Then I will look for answers in the text and illustrations.

2 Model Read the selection. As you read, use the Think Aloud Cloud to model applying the strategy.

Think Aloud Remember that you can ask questions as you read and then look for the answers in the text and illustrations. The text says that the telephone let people call from their homes and their jobs, but that they needed to call from other places, too. I ask myself how inventors solved this problem. When I read on, I learn that inventors made cell phones that could call from anywhere. As I continue reading, I will look for the answers to more of my questions.

3 Guided Practice As you continue to read, pause to elicit questions and answers from children. *What questions do you have about this section?* Pause to help children find the answers. Guide children in using the evidence in the text and illustrations to answer their questions.

Respond to Reading

After reading, prompt children to retell "Great Inventions." Discuss what questions they asked and where they found the answers. Talk about the inventions in the selection and what childen learned about them.

ENGLISH LANGUAGE LEARNERS SCAFFOLD

Beginning

Engage Display Card 2 of "Great Inventions." *You can look at the illustrations to answer some questions. Have lights changed over the years?*

Intermediate

Describe Display Card 2 of "Great Inventions." Point to the gas light. *We do not use gas lights anymore. I wonder why we stopped using them. Did they cause problems? Let's look for the answer in the text.* Repeat correct answers slowly and clearly to the class.

Advanced/High

Describe Display Card 2 of "Great Inventions." *The text says gas lights cost less and gave more light than candles and oil. I wonder why we stopped using them. Can you find the answer in the text?*

Monitor and *Differentiate*

 Quick Check

Can children apply the strategy ask and answer questions?

Small Group Instruction

If No → | Approaching | Reteach pp. T208–209
         | ELL | Develop pp. T226–229

If Yes → | On Level | Review pp. T218–219
          | Beyond Level | Extend pp. T222–223

→ # Word Work

Quick Review
Build Fluency: Sound-Spellings
Display the **Word-Building Cards**: *or, ore, oar, ar, er, ir, ur, ey, igh, oa, oe, ee, ea, ai, ay, e_e, u_e, o_e, dge, i_e, a_e, ch, tch, wh, ph, th, sh, ng, mp, sk.* Have children say the sounds.

ⓜ Phonemic Awareness

MINILESSON 5 Mins

OBJECTIVES

CCSS Decode regularly spelled one-syllable words. **RF.1.3b**

Categorize words by phoneme

Phoneme Categorization

① **Model** Show children how to categorize phonemes. *Listen as I say three words:* more, treat, shore. *The words* more *and* shore *have the same ending sounds, /ôr/. Listen: /m/ /ôr/, /sh/ /ôr/. The word* treat *does not end in /ôr/. It does not belong.*

② **Guided Practice/Practice** Say the words. Have children identify the word that does not end with the same sounds. Guide practice with the first example.

cart, stack, heart   paid, trade, lend   poor, rake, store

mold, coat, boat   dust, list, trust   fair, bear, burn

ⓟ Phonics

MINILESSON 10 Mins

Sound-Spelling Card

Introduce /ôr/ *or, ore, oar*

① **Model** Display the *Corn* **Sound-Spelling Card**. Teach /ôr/ spelled *or, ore,* and *oar* using *corn, more,* and *roar. This is the* Corn *Sound-Spelling Card. The sounds are /ôr/. Say the sounds with me: /ôr/. These sounds are in the middle of the word* corn. *The /ôr/ sounds can be spelled with the letters* or *as in* corn, ore *as in* more, *and* oar *as in* roar. *I'll say /ôr/ as I write the different spellings for the sounds several times.*

② **Guided Practice/Practice** Have children practice connecting the different spellings to the /ôr/ sounds by writing them. *Now do it with me. Say /ôr/ as I write the letters* o, r. *This time, write the letters* or *five times as you say the /ôr/ sounds.* Continue with the letters *ore* and *oar.*

SKILLS TRACE

/ôr/or, ore, oar

Introduce Unit 5 Week 3 Day 1

Review Unit 5 Week 3 Days 2, 3, 4, 5

Assess Unit 5 Week 3

Go Digital

Phonemic Awareness

Phonics

Handwriting

Blend Words with /ôr/ *or, ore, oar*

1 Model Display **Word-Building Cards** *s, o, r, t.* Model how to blend the sounds. *This is the letter* s. *It stands for /s/. These are the letters* or. *Together they stand for /ôr/. This is the letter* t. *It stands for /t/. Listen as I blend these sounds together: /sssôrt/. Say it with me:* sort.

Continue by modeling the words *north, shore,* and *soar.*

2 Guided Practice/Practice Display the Day 1 Phonics Practice Activity. Read each word in the first row, blending the sounds; for example: /ôr/. *The word is* or. Have children blend each word with you. Prompt children to read the connected text, sounding out the decodable words.

or	for	born	more	store	short
torn	torch	roar	worn	form	board
form	farm	tar	tore	pork	park
verb	third	turn	dark	teacher	artist

The boat's oar was lost in the storm.

Norm likes to play sports.

Can you eat corn with a fork?

Also online

Day 1 Phonics Practice Activity

Corrective Feedback

Sound Error Model the sound that children missed, then have them repeat the sound. Say: *My turn.* Tap under the letter and say: *Sounds? /ôr/ What's the sound?* Return to the beginning of the word. Say: *Let's start over.* Blend the word with children again.

 Daily Handwriting

Throughout the week teach uppercase and lowercase letters *Rr* using the Handwriting models.

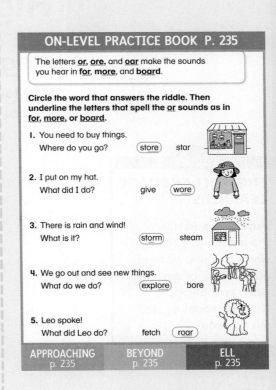

ON-LEVEL PRACTICE BOOK P. 235

The letters **or**, **ore**, and **oar** make the sounds you hear in **for**, **more**, and **board**.

Circle the word that answers the riddle. Then underline the letters that spell the **or** sounds as in **for, more,** or **board.**

1. You need to buy things.
   Where do you go? (store) star

2. I put on my hat.
   What did I do? give (wore)

3. There is rain and wind!
   What is it? (storm) steam

4. We go out and see new things.
   What do we do? (explore) bore

5. Leo spoke!
   What did Leo do? fetch (roar)

| APPROACHING p. 235 | BEYOND p. 235 | ELL p. 235 |

→ # Word Work

> ### Quick Review
>
> **High-Frequency Words:** Read, Spell, and Write to review last week's high-frequency words: *another, climb, full, great, poor, through.*

OBJECTIVES

CCSS Recognize and read grade-appropriate irregularly spelled words. **RF.1.3g**

CCSS Use conventional spelling for words with common spelling patterns and for frequently occurring irregular words. **L.1.2d**

MINILESSON 5 Mins

Spelling

Words with *or, ore, oar*

Dictation Use the Spelling Dictation routine for each word to help children transfer their knowledge of sound-spellings to writing.

Pretest Pronounce each spelling word. Say a sentence for each word and pronounce the word again. Ask children to say each word, stretching the sounds, before writing it. After the pretest, display the spelling words and write each word as you say the letter names. Have children check their words.

born	corn	core	more	roar
soar	her	dirt	learn	sure

For Approaching Level and Beyond Level children, refer to the Differentiated Spelling Lists for modified word lists.

MINILESSON 10 Mins

High-Frequency Words

began, better, guess, learn, right, sure

① Model Display the **High-Frequency Word Cards** *began, better, guess, learn, right,* and *sure.* Use the Read/Spell/Write routine.

- **Read** Point to and say the word *began. This is the word* began. *Say it with me:* began. *I began doing my homework as soon as I got home from school.*
- **Spell** *The word* began *is spelled* b-e-g-a-n. *Spell it with me.*
- **Write** *Let's write the word in the air as we say each letter:* b-e-g-a-n.
- Follow the same steps to introduce *better, guess, learn, right,* and *sure.*
- As children spell each word with you, point out irregularities in sound-spellings, such as the /sh/ sound spelled *s* in *sure.*

 • Have partners create sentences using each word.

Go Digital

Spelling Word Routine

they	together
how	eat

High-Frequency Word Routine

school

Visual Glossary

ELL

ENGLISH LANGUAGE LEARNERS

Pantomime Review the meaning of these words by using pictures, pantomime, or gestures when possible. Have children repeat or act out the word.

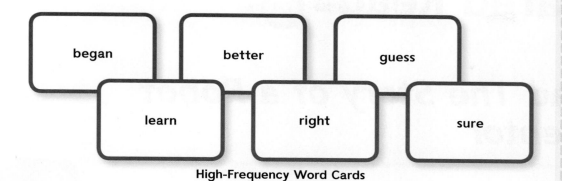

High-Frequency Word Cards

2 **Guided Practice/Practice** Have children read the following sentences. Prompt them to identify the high-frequency words in connected text and to blend the decodable words.

1. It **began** to snow last night.
2. I hope you feel **better**.
3. Can you **guess** how old he is?
4. She will **learn** to ride a bike.
5. This is the **right** way to hold a fork.
6. He is **sure** he will be on time.

MINILESSON
5 Mins

Introduce Vocabulary

idea, unusual

1 **Model** Introduce the new words using the routine.

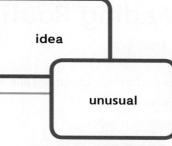

idea

unusual

Vocabulary Cards

Vocabulary Routine

<u>Define:</u> An **idea** is a picture or thought you get in your mind.

<u>Example:</u> *I have an idea of what to give him for a birthday present.*

<u>Ask:</u> What is an idea you have for a fun school field trip? EXAMPLE

<u>Define:</u> If something is **unusual**, it is not common.

<u>Example:</u> *I've never seen food that color. It is unusual.*

<u>Ask:</u> What unusual things have you seen? PRIOR KNOWLEDGE

2 **Review** Use the routine to review last week's vocabulary words.

Monitor *and* Differentiate

✓ **Quick Check**

Can children read and decode words with *r*-controlled vowels *or, ore, oar*?

Can children recognize and read high-frequency and vocabulary words?

⬇

Small Group Instruction

If No → | Approaching | Reteach pp. T212–215
| ELL | Develop pp. T226–233

If Yes → | On Level | Review pp. T220–221
| Beyond Level | Extend pp. T224–225

→ **Shared Read**

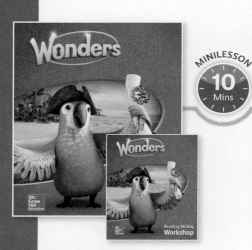

Reading/Writing Workshop Big Book and Reading/Writing Workshop

OBJECTIVES

CCSS Decode regularly spelled one-syllable words. **RF.1.3b**

CCSS Recognize and read grade-appropriate irregularly spelled words. **RF.1.3g**

ACADEMIC LANGUAGE

• nonfiction, biography, robot, inventor, inventions

• Cognates: *no ficción, biografía, robot, inventor/a, invenciones*

ENGLISH LANGUAGE LEARNERS

See pages T226–T227 for Interactive Question-Response routine for the Shared Read.

Read *The Story of a Robot Inventor*

MINILESSON **10** Mins

Focus on Foundational Skills

Review with children the words and letter-sounds they will see in *The Story of a Robot Inventor*.

• Have children use pages 156–157 to review the high-frequency words *began, learn, right, better, guess, sure,* and the vocabulary words *idea* and *unusual*.

• Have children use pages 158–159 to review that the letters *or, ore,* and *oar* can stand for the /ôr/ sounds. Guide them to blend the sounds to read the words.

• Display the story words *company, Hawaii, hours, person, solve, their, waterproof,* and *Tomotaka Takahashi*. Spell each word and model reading it. Tell children they will be reading the words in the selection.

Read Guide children in reading *The Story of a Robot Inventor*. Point out the high-frequency words, vocabulary words, and words in which *or, ore,* and *oar* stand for the /ôr/ sounds.

Close Reading Routine

Read   DOK 1–2

• Identify key ideas and details about Takahashi's robots.
• Take notes and retell.
• Use **A C T** prompts as needed.

Reread   DOK 2–3

• Analyze the text, craft, and structure.
• Use the Reread minilessons.

Integrate   DOK 4

• Integrate knowledge and ideas.
• Make text-to-text connections.
• Use the Integrate lesson.

Genre: Informational Text/Biography Tell children that *The Story of a Robot Inventor* is a biography. Explain that a biography tells about a real person's life and is written by another person. A biography gives facts about the person and is often organized in time-order sequence.

Go Digital

The Story of a Robot Inventor

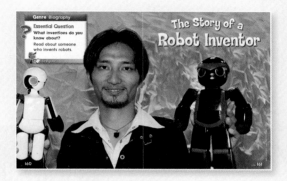
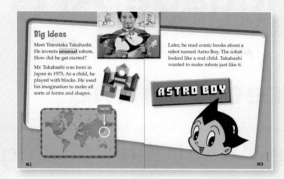

READING/WRITING WORKSHOP, pp. 160–169   **Lexile** 280

Connect to Concept: Great Inventions

ESSENTIAL QUESTION Explain to children that as they read *The Story of a Robot Inventor* they will look for key ideas and details that will help them answer the Essential Question: *What inventions do you know about?*

- Pages 162–163: What activities did Tomotaka Takahashi do as a child?
- Pages 164–165: How did the robot Takahashi made walk?
- Pages 166–167: What can some of Takahashi's robots do?
- Pages 168–169: How did Takahashi solve problems for the contest?

Focus on Fluency

With partners, have children read *The Story of a Robot Inventor* to develop fluency. Remind them that they can ask themselves questions to make sure they understand what they are reading. Have them use both text and photographs to answer their questions.

Retell Have partners use key ideas and details to retell *The Story of a Robot Inventor.* Invite them to tell which robot they find most interesting.

Make Connections

Read together Make Connections on page 169. Have partners talk about the kind of robot they would like to invent using this sentence starter:

> *I would like to invent a robot that can. . .*

Guide children to connect what they have read to the Essential Question.

Reading/Writing Workshop

OBJECTIVES

CCSS Write informative/ explanatory texts in which they name a topic, supply facts about the topic, and provide some sense of closure. **W.1.2**

CCSS Use frequently occurring adjectives. **L.1.1f**

ACADEMIC LANGUAGE

• describe, examples, adjectives, compare
• Cognates: *describir, ejemplos, adjetivos, comparar*

MINILESSON **5** Mins

Shared Writing

Write About the Reading/Writing Workshop

Analyze the Prompt Tell children you will work together to write a response to a question. Read the prompt aloud. *What does Tomotaka Takahashi do? Describe some examples of his work.* Say: *To answer this question, we need to look at the text and photographs in* The Story of a Robot Inventor.

Find Text Evidence Explain that you will reread the text and take notes to help respond to the prompt. Read aloud the first paragraph on page 162. Say: *The text tells me that Tomotaka Takahashi invents unusual robots. I am going to look for text evidence that tells how the robots are unusual.* Read aloud pages 166–167. Say: *The text tells me Takahashi's robots do unusual things. I read that he made robots that can climb a cliff with a rope, ride a bike, and swim. The photographs show a robot riding a bike and a robot swimming. These examples help me understand Takahashi's work. Let's write them in our notes and look for more examples of what Takahashi does.*

Write to a Prompt Reread the prompt to children. *What does Tomotaka Takahashi do? Describe some examples of his work.* Say: *The text tells us he invents unusual robots. Let's write that as our topic sentence because it tells what we are writing about: Tomotaka Takahashi invents unusual robots.* Write the sentence. *The prompt also asks us to describe some examples of his work. Let's look at our notes to find examples. In our notes, we wrote about a robot that can climb. Let's write this note as a sentence: Some of his robots can climb up a cliff on a rope.* Write the sentence. *As I reread the notes, think about other examples we can add to our writing.* Track the print as you reread the notes.

Guide children to dictate complete sentences for you to record. Read the final response as you track the print.

Go Digital

Graphic Organizer

Writing

I see a fish.

Grammar

Grammar

5 Mins

Adjectives That Compare

❶ Explain/Model Explain that we add *-er* to most adjectives to compare two people, places, or things. We add *-est* to most adjectives to compare three or more people, places, or things. Display the following sentences:

Curt is a fast runner.

Sheena is a faster runner than Curt.

Jen is the fastest runner of all!

Explain that *faster* and *fastest* are adjectives that compare. Circle the *-er* and *-est* endings and point out that *faster* is comparing two people and *fastest* is comparing three people.

❷ Guided Practice/Practice Display the sentences below and read them aloud. Have children identify the adjectives that compare.

The first row of corn is long. (long)

The next row of corn is longer. (longer)

The last row of corn is the longest. (longest)

COLLABORATE

Talk About It Have partners work together to use classroom objects and the words *short, shorter, shortest,* and *tall, taller, tallest* to compare.

Link to Writing Say: *Let's look back at our writing and see if we used adjectives that compare two or more things. Did we end the adjectives with* -er *or* -est*?* Review the Shared Writing for comparative adjectives ending in *-er* or *-est*. If there are no comparative adjectives, work with children to add them and reread the response together.

ELL

ENGLISH LANGUAGE LEARNERS SCAFFOLD

Beginning

Demonstrate Comprehension Read each Model sentence and ask children to point to the adjective. *Who is the fastest runner? Did Jen run faster or slower than Sheena?*

Intermediate

Explain Ask children to circle the adjectives in the Model sentences. *Why was* -er *added to* fast*? Why was* -est *added to* fast*?* Clarify children's responses as needed.

Advanced/High

Expand Have children tell what letters are added to adjectives that compare two things. Have them tell what letters are added to adjectives that compare three or more things. Have children compare how fast a snail and a cat can go. Then compare a snail, cat, and horse.

Daily Wrap Up

- Encourage children to discuss the Essential Question using the oral vocabulary words. *What inventions did you read about today?*

- Prompt children to share how the skills they learned will help them become better readers and writers.

Materials

Reading/Writing Workshop
VOLUME 4

Teaching Poster

Vocabulary Cards
idea   unusual

High-Frequency Word Cards
began   learn
better   right
guess   sure

Word-Building Cards

Interactive Read-Aloud Cards

Spelling Word Cards

Sound-Spelling Cards

→ # Build the Concept

MINILESSON
5 Mins

Oral Language

Go Digital

OBJECTIVES

CCSS

Ask and answer questions about key details in a text read aloud or information presented orally or through other media. **SL.1.2**

• Discuss the Essential Question
• Build concept understanding

ACADEMIC LANGUAGE

• *information, text, illustrations*
• Cognates: *información, texto, ilustraciones*

ESSENTIAL QUESTION

Remind children that this week you've been talking and reading about inventions. Remind them of Takahashi's robots and other inventions they've learned about, such as the car, light bulb, telephone, and computer. Guide children to discuss the Essential Question using information from what they read and discussed on Day 1.

Oral Vocabulary Words

Review the oral vocabulary words. Use the Define/Example/Ask routine to review the oral vocabulary words *complicated, curious, device, imagine,* and *improve.*

• Which is more complicated, a bicycle or a car?
• What can you do if you are curious about how airplanes fly?
• Can you think of a device we use to clip papers together?
• Imagine you can fly. What would you do?
• What could you do to improve the playground?

Visual Glossary

"Great Inventions"

Listening Comprehension

Reread the Interactive Read Aloud

MINILESSON
5 Mins

Strategy: Ask and Answer Questions

Remind children that as they listen, they can ask themselves questions about the text. This can help them understand the information.

Tell children you will reread "Great Inventions." Display the Interactive Read-Aloud Cards. Pause as you read to model applying the strategy.

"Great Inventions"

Think Aloud When I read this selection the first time, I asked questions as I read and then looked for the answers in the text and illustrations. When I read the text about how people communicated in the past by letters and telegrams, I asked myself which inventions people use today to communicate. Then I read on to learn about how the telephone and the cell phone were invented to make communication easier.

Make Connections

COLLABORATE

Discuss partners' responses to "Great Inventions."

- *Which invention do you use the most? The least?*
- *What other inventions can you name?*
- *What would life be like without these inventions?*

Analytical Writing

Write About It Have children write in their Writer's Notebooks about an invention they would like to create. Guide children by asking questions, such as *What could you invent to make your life easier? What do you wish you could do differently?* Have children write continuously for six minutes.

 # Word Work

Quick Review

Build Fluency: Sound-Spellings
Display the **Word-Building Cards:** *or, ore, oar, ar, er, ir, ur, ey, igh, oa, oe, ee, ea, ai, ay, e_e, u_e, o_e, dge, i_e, a_e, ch, tch, wh, ph, th, sh, ng, mp, sk.* Have children say the sounds. Repeat, and vary the pace.

 MINILESSON 5 Mins

Phonemic Awareness

OBJECTIVES

CCSS Orally produce single-syllable words by blending sounds (phonemes), including consonant blends. **RF.1.2b**

CCSS Decode regularly spelled one-syllable words. **RF.1.3b**

Recognize common abbreviations

Phoneme Substitution

1 **Model** Show children how to substitute phonemes. *Listen to the sounds in the word* stem: */s/ /t/ /e/ /m/. Stem has the /e/ sound in the middle. Listen as I change the /e/ sound to /ôr/: /s/ /t/ /ôr/ /m/. The word is* storm.

2 **Guided Practice/Practice** Have children practice substituting phonemes. Guide practice with the first one. *I'll say a word. Change one sound to /ôr/ to make a new word.*

pet/port	tin/torn	can/corn	hen/horn
card/cord	park/pork	bare/bore	care/core

MINILESSON 5 Mins

Phonics

Review /ôr/*or, ore, oar*

1 **Model** Display the *Corn* **Sound-Spelling Card.** Review the /ôr/ sounds spelled *or, ore,* and *oar* using the words *torn, wore,* and *board.*

2 **Guided Practice/Practice** Have children practice connecting the letters and sounds. Point to the Sound-Spelling Card. *What are these letters? What sounds do they stand for?*

Go Digital

Phonemic Awareness

Phonics

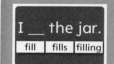
Structural Analysis

Handwriting

Blend Words with /ôr/ *or, ore, oar*

❶ Model Display **Word-Building Cards** *c, o, r, e* to form the word *core*. Model how to generate and blend the sounds to say the word. *This is the letter* c. *It stands for /k/. These are the letters* o, r, e. *Together they stand for /ôr/. Listen as I blend these sounds together: /kôr/. Say it with me:* core.

Continue by modeling the words *porch*, *shore*, and *board*.

❷ Guided Practice/Practice Repeat the routine with children with *oar, fork, form, wore, born, short, more, sort, north, score, torch, roar, soar*.

Build Words with /ôr/ *or, ore, oar*

❶ Model Display the Word-Building Cards *f, o, r, k*. Blend: /f/ /ôr/ /k/, /fffôrk/, fork.

- Replace *f* with *c* and repeat with *cork*.
- Replace *c* with *st* and repeat with *stork*.

❷ Guided Practice/Practice Continue with *store, shore, snore, chore, core, more, bore, sore, soar, roar*.

ENGLISH LANGUAGE LEARNERS

Build Vocabulary Review the meanings of example words that can be explained or demonstrated in a concrete way. For example, ask children to point to the *board* and to name something they *wore* today. Model the meaning of *oar* saying, *"An oar is used to travel through water."* Provide sentence starters, such as: *"I want more ____"* for children to complete. Correct grammar and pronunciation as needed.

⏱ MINILESSON 5 Mins

Structural Analysis

Abbreviations

❶ Model Write and read aloud these sentences: *Mister Ford is my teacher. Mr. Ford is my teacher.* Underline *Mister* and *Mr.* Point out that the sentences sound the same when you read them aloud, but the first word in each sentence looks different. Explain that *Mr.* is an abbreviation. *An abbreviation is a short way of writing a word.* Point out that most abbreviations have a period at the end. Repeat for *Doctor/Dr.*, *Missus/Mrs.*, *Street/St.*, *Avenue/Ave.*, and *Road/Rd.*

❷ Guided Practice/Practice Write these titles and place names on the board: *Mr., Mrs., Dr., St., Ave.* Have children read the abbreviations and then use each abbreviation in a sentence.

→ # Word Work

Quick Review
High-Frequency Words: Read, Spell, and Write to review this week's high-frequency words: *began, better, guess, learn, right, sure.*

OBJECTIVES

CCSS Recognize and read grade-appropriate irregularly spelled words. **RF.1.3g**

CCSS Use conventional spelling for words with common spelling patterns and for frequently occurring irregular words. **L.1.2d**

MINILESSON 5 Mins
Spelling

Word Sort with *or, ore, oar*

1 Model Display the **Spelling Word Cards** from the Teacher's Resource Book. Have children read each word, listening for the /ôr/ sounds.

Use cards for *torn, chore,* and *boar* to create a three-column chart. Say each word and pronounce the sounds. Ask children to spell each word, focusing on the /ôr/ spelling.

2 Guided Practice/Practice Have children place each Spelling Word Card in the column with the same /ôr/ spelling. When completed, have children read the words. Then call out a word. Have a child find the word card and point to it as the class spells the word.

ANALYZE ERRORS/ARTICULATION SUPPORT

Use children's pretest errors to analyze spelling problems and provide corrective feedback. For example, some children might confuse words with *r*-blends and *r*-controlled vowel spellings.

Contrast words with *r*-blends and *r*-controlled vowels, such as *from/form, crowed/cord, croak/cork* to allow children to compare where the *r* sound falls in each word. Say each word pair. Have children repeat. Exaggerate the /ôr/ sounds in the second word in each pair. Then have children write the word.

ENGLISH LANGUAGE LEARNERS

Provide Clues Practice spelling by helping children generate more words with /ôr/ spelling patterns. Say: *Think of a word that begins with* st *and rhymes with* more. Write the word and have children practice reading it. Correct their pronunciation, if needed.

MINILESSON 5 Mins
High-Frequency Words

began, better, guess, learn, right, sure

1 Guided Practice Say each word and have children Read/Spell/Write it. Ask children to close their eyes, picture the word in their minds, and write it the way they see it. Display the high-frequency words for children to self-correct.

- Point out irregularities in sound-spellings, such as the /e/ sound spelled *ue* in *guess.*

Go Digital

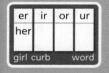

Spelling Word Sort

High-Frequency Word Routine

school

Visual Glossary

---

2 Practice Add the High-Frequency words *began, better, guess, learn, right,* and *sure* to the cumulative word bank.

- Have children work with a partner to create sentences using the words.
- Have children look at the words and compare their sounds and spellings to words from previous weeks.
- Suggest that they write about inventions or inventors.

Cumulative Review Review last week's words using the Read/Spell/Write routine.

- Repeat the above routine, mixing the words and having children chorally say each one.

MINILESSON 5 Mins Reinforce Vocabulary

idea, unusual

1 Guided Practice Use the **Vocabulary Cards** to review this week's and last week's vocabulary words. Work together with children to generate a new context sentence for each word.

2 Practice Have children work with a partner to orally complete each sentence stem on the Day 2 Vocabulary Practice Activity using this week's and last week's vocabulary words.

---

idea	unusual	leaped	stretched

1. It's not _____ to go swimming on a hot day.
2. The cat _____ out of the tree and ran away.
3. I have an _____ for a story I want to write.
4. I _____ the rubber band until it snapped.

Also online

Day 2 Vocabulary Practice Activity

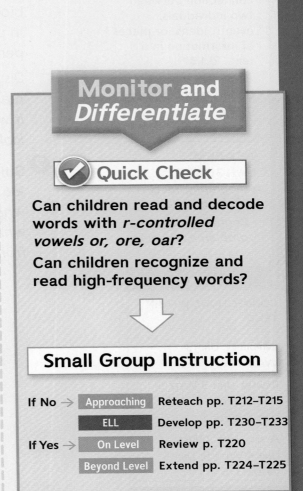

Monitor and *Differentiate*

✓ **Quick Check**

Can children read and decode words with *r-controlled vowels or, ore, oar*?

Can children recognize and read high-frequency words?

⬇

Small Group Instruction

If No → Approaching Reteach pp. T212–T215
        ELL Develop pp. T230–T233
If Yes → On Level Review p. T220
        Beyond Level Extend pp. T224–T225

Comprehension

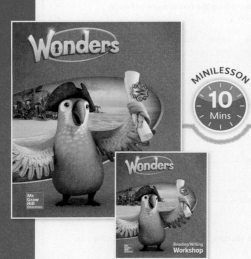

Reading/Writing Workshop Big Book and Reading/Writing Workshop

OBJECTIVES

CCSS Describe the connection between two individuals, events, ideas, or pieces of information in a text. RI.1.3

Understand biography genre

ACADEMIC LANGUAGE
• biography, facts, problem, solution
• Cognates: biografía, problema, solución

Reread *The Story of a Robot Inventor*

MINILESSON **10** Mins

Genre: Informational Text/Biography

1 Model Tell children they will now reread the biography *The Story of a Robot Inventor*. Explain that as they read, they will look for information in the text to help them understand the selection.

Review the characteristics of a biography. It:

• tells about a real person.

• is written by someone else.

• is often organized in time-order sequence.

• often uses photographs or illustrations to give information.

Biographies tell about real people. Point out that photographs in biographies often give information and facts. Often photographs in a biography give information about the person and what the person did.

Display pages 164–165: *I read that Mr. Takahashi invents robots. I read that he wanted to make a robot that didn't bend its legs when it walked. The photograph helps me understand what the new robot looked like and how it worked.*

2 Guided Practice/Practice Display pages 166 and 167. Read page 166 aloud. Say: *The text gives me facts and information about what Mr. Takahashi did. The photographs help me understand what the robots look like and what they do. What can you learn from these photographs?*

Go Digital

The Story of a Robot Inventor

Genre

Problem and Solution

SKILLS TRACE

CONNECTIONS WITHIN TEXT

INTRODUCE UNIT 3 WEEK 4

REVIEW UNIT 3 WEEK 5; UNIT 4 WEEKS 2, 3, 5; UNIT 5 WEEK 3

ASSESS UNIT 3 WEEKS 4, 5; UNIT 4 WEEK 5; UNIT 5 WEEKS 3, 5

Skill: Connections Within Text/ Problem and Solution

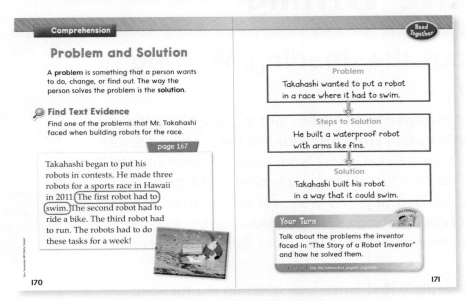

Comprehension

Problem and Solution

A **problem** is something that a person wants to do, change, or find out. The way the person solves the problem is the **solution**.

Find Text Evidence

Find one of the problems that Mr. Takahashi faced when building robots for the race.

page 167

Takahashi began to put his robots in contests. He made three robots for a sports race in Hawaii in 2011. The first robot had to swim. The second robot had to ride a bike. The third robot had to run. The robots had to do these tasks for a week!

Problem
Takahashi wanted to put a robot in a race where it had to swim.

↓

Steps to Solution
He built a waterproof robot with arms like fins.

↓

Solution
Takahashi built his robot in a way that it could swim.

Your Turn

Talk about the problems the inventor faced in "The Story of a Robot Inventor" and how he solved them.

170 171

Reading/Writing Workshop, pp. 170–171

1 Model Tell children that biographies often tell about problems and explain how people find solutions to these problems. Have children look at pages 170–171 in their Reading/Writing Workshop. Read together the definition of problem and solution. *A problem is something that a person wants to do, change, or find out. The way the person solves the problem is the solution.*

2 Guided Practice/Practice Read together the Find Text Evidence section and model finding a problem in *The Story of a Robot Inventor*. Point out the information that was added to the graphic organizer. *On page 167, we see that Mr. Takahashi wants to build a robot that can swim in a race. This is his problem. We can use the text to find the steps he took to solve the problem and the solution he came up with. This information has been added to the Problem and Solution chart. Can you think of any other problems and solutions that Mr. Takahashi faced that we read about in this selection?*

Problem

↓

Steps to Solution

↓

Solution

Teaching Poster

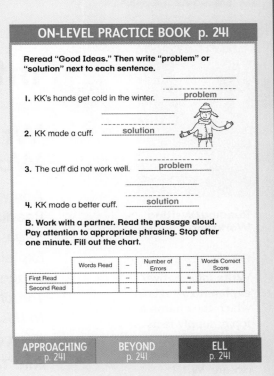
Monitor and *Differentiate*

✓ Quick Check

Can children identify problems and solutions in a biography?

⬇

Small Group Instruction

If No →	Approaching	Reteach pp. T216–217
	ELL	Develop pp. T226–233
If Yes →	On Level	Review p. T221
	Beyond Level	Extend p. T225

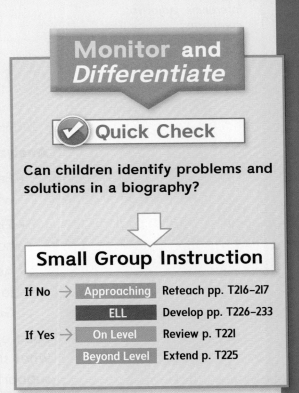
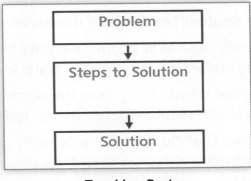

Wonders

Reading/Writing Workshop

Reading/Writing Workshop

OBJECTIVES

CCSS Write informative/ explanatory texts in which they name a topic, supply facts about the topic, and provide some sense of closure. **W.1.2**

CCSS Use frequently occurring adjectives. **L.1.1f**

ACADEMIC LANGUAGE

• *evidence, inference, support, adjectives, compare*

• Cognates: *evidencia, inferencia, adjetivos, comparar*

MINILESSON

5 Mins

Interactive Writing

Write About the Reading/Writing Workshop

Analyze the Model Prompt Have children turn to page 172 in the **Reading/Writing Workshop.** Emily responded to the prompt: *Look at pages 162-165. What can you tell about what makes a good inventor?* Explain to students that the first step in responding to the prompt is to understand what it is asking. Say: *The prompt is asking about things Tomotaka Takahashi does that make him a good inventor. To respond to this prompt, Emily found text evidence about Takahashi and made inferences.*

Find Text Evidence Explain that Emily took notes on the text and photographs. She used her notes about Takahashi to make inferences about what makes a good inventor.

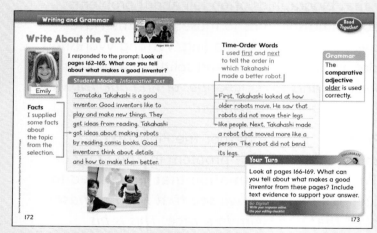

Reading/Writing Workshop

Analyze the Student Model Read the model. Discuss the callouts.

• **Facts** Emily used facts about Takahashi from the text to explain what makes him a good inventor. **Trait: Ideas**

• **Time-Order Words** Emily used the words *first* and *next* to explain how Takahashi made his robot better. **Trait: Word Choice**

• **Adjectives That Compare** She correctly added the ending *-er* to the adjective *old* when describing what robots used to be like. **Grammar**

Point out that Emily began her response with a topic sentence that tells what she is writing about. Then she used facts from the selection to support her ideas.

Go Digital

Graphic Organizer

Writing

I see a fish.

Grammar

Your Turn: Write About the Text Say: Now we will write to a new prompt. Have children turn to page 173 of the **Reading/Writing Workshop.** Read the Your Turn prompt together. *Look at pages 166–169. What can you tell about what makes a good inventor from these pages? Include text evidence to support your answer.*

Find Text Evidence Say: *To answer this question, we need to find evidence in the text and take notes about what makes Takahashi a good inventor.* Remind children that they will have to make inferences about what about makes a good inventor based on the things Takahashi does.

Write to a Prompt Say: *Let's start our writing with a topic sentence that tells what we are writing about: Good inventors like Tomotako Takahashi make many different kinds of inventions.* Write the sentence. *Now we will use evidence from our notes to write about how Takahashi made different kinds of robots.* Tell children you will reread the notes to help them recall facts about Takahashi's robots. Track the print as you reread the notes. Then guide children in forming complete sentences as you share the pen with them. Say: *Let's reread what we wrote. Did we include facts from the selection to explain what makes a good inventor? Have we used time-order words to show the order in which things happened?* Read the final response as you track the print.

For additional practice with the writing traits, have children turn to page 246 of the **Your Turn Practice Book.**

Grammar

5 Mins

MINILESSON

Adjectives That Compare

1 Review Remind children that *-er* can be added to most adjectives to compare two nouns and *-est* can be added to most adjectives to compare three or more nouns. Write the following sentences:

> The bird is high in the sky.
>
> The jet is higher than the bird. (higher, 2)
>
> The spaceship is the highest one of all. (highest, 3 or more)

Guide children to identify which compares two things and which compares more than two things.

2 Guided Practice/Practice Display the sentences below. Have children identify the adjectives and tell if they are comparing two things or three or more things.

> Fall is colder than summer. (colder, 2)
>
> Winter is the coldest of all. (coldest, 3 or more)

Talk About It Have partners work together to orally create their own sentences comparing temperatures.

Daily Wrap Up

- Discuss the Essential Question and encourage children to use the oral vocabulary words. Prompt them with questions, such as: *What inventions did we use today? How did they help us?*

- Prompt children to discuss what they learned today by asking: *What reading skills did you use today?*

Materials

Reading/Writing Workshop
VOLUME 4

Literature Anthology
VOLUME 4

Visual Vocabulary Cards

complicated   began
curious   better
device   guess
imagine   learn
improve   right
idea   sure
unusual

Problem
Steps to Solution
Solution

Teaching Poster

Response Board

born

Spelling Word Cards

a	b	c

Word-Building Cards

→ Build the Concept

MINILESSON 5 Mins

Oral Language

OBJECTIVES

CCSS Describe the connection between two individuals, events, ideas, or pieces of information in a text. **RI.1.3**

CCSS Read grade-level text orally with accuracy, appropriate rate, and expression. **RF.1.4b**

Review sequence

ACADEMIC LANGUAGE

- sequence, events, pause, comma, period
- Cognates: secuencia, coma

ESSENTIAL QUESTION

Remind children that this week you've been talking and reading about inventions. Remind them of Takahashi's robots and the other great inventions they read about. Guide children to discuss the Essential Question using information from what they have read and talked about throughout the week.

Review Oral Vocabulary

Review the oral vocabulary words *complicated, curious, device, imagine,* and *improve* using the Define/Example/Ask routine. Prompt children to use the words as they discuss inventions.

Visual Vocabulary Cards

Comprehension/ Fluency

Connections Within Text: Sequence Review

MINILESSON 10 Mins

1 **Explain** Tell children they have been learning about problems and solutions in stories. Remind them they have also learned how to identify the sequence of events. *As we read, we can think about what events happen first, next, and last.*

2 **Model** Display pages 162 and 163 of *The Story of a Robot Inventor. I read in the text Mr. Takahashi was born in Japan in 1975. This is the first event. Then I read he read comic books about a robot named Astro Boy. This happened next.*

Reading/Writing Workshop

3 **Guided Practice/Practice** Reread the biography. Use text evidence to identify the sequence of events.

Appropriate Phrasing

MINILESSON 5 Mins

1 **Explain** Tell children as you read, you will pause slightly or stop briefly when you come to certain punctuation marks. Explain commas indicate you should pause slightly while reading. A period indicates you should stop briefly.

2 **Model** Read aloud a section of the Shared Read with commas and periods. *This sentence has a comma, so I will pause slightly at the comma. This sentence ends with a period. I will stop briefly when I reach the period. Pausing or stopping for commas and periods helps you know when one idea ends and a new one starts.* Point out how you pause for other punctuation.

3 **Guided Practice/Practice** Have children reread the passage chorally. Remind them to pause slightly for commas and to stop briefly for periods.

Fluency Practice Children can practice using Practice Book passages.

 → **Word Work**

Quick Review

Build Fluency: Sound-Spellings
Display the **Word-Building Cards:** *or, ore, oar, ar, er, ir, ur, ey, igh, oa, oe, ee, ea, ai, ay, e_e, u_e, o_e, dge, i_e, a_e, ch, tch, wh, ph, th, sh, ng, mp, sk.* Have children say the sounds.

MINILESSON 5 Mins

Phonemic Awareness

OBJECTIVES

CCSS Orally produce single-syllable words by blending sounds (phonemes), including consonant blends. **RF.1.2b**

CCSS Decode regularly spelled one-syllable words. **RF.1.3b**

Recognize common abbreviations

Phoneme Blending

1 Model Place markers on the **Response Board** to represent sounds. Show children how to orally blend phonemes. *I'm going to put one marker in each box as I say each sound. Then I will blend the sounds to form a word. Place a marker for each sound as you say:* /s/ /ôr/ /t/. Tell children that one marker may be used for the /ôr/ sounds. *This word has the sounds:* /s/ /ôr/ /t/. *Listen as I blend these sounds:* /sssôrt/, sort. *The word is* sort.

2 Guided Practice/Practice *Let's do some together. Using your own boards, place a marker for each sound you hear. I will say one sound at a time. Then we will blend the sounds to say a word.* Do the first three with children.

/f/ /ôr/   /m/ /ôr/   /p/ /ôr/ /ch/   /r/ /ôr/

/sh/ /ôr/ /t/   /s/ /n/ /ôr/   /n/ /ôr/ /th/   /s/ /p/ /ôr/ /t/

MINILESSON 5 Mins

Phonics

Blend Words with /ôr/ *or, ore, oar*

1 Model Display **Word-Building Cards** *s, p, o, r, t.* Model how to blend the sounds. *This is the letter* s. *It stands for* /s/. *This is the letter* p. *It stands for* /p/. *These are the letters* o, r. *Together they stand for* /ôr/. *This is the letter* t. *It stands for* /t/. *Let's blend the sounds:* /sssport/. *The word is* sport. Continue by modeling the words *score, stork,* and *roar.*

2 Guided Practice/Practice Review the words and sentences on the Day 3 Phonics Practice Activity with children. Read each word in the first row, blending the sounds; for example, /s/ /t/ /ôr/ /m/; /ssstôrmmm/. *The word is* storm.

Have children blend each word with you. Prompt children to read the connected text, sounding out the decodable words.

Go Digital

Phonemic Awareness

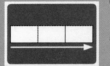

Phonics

Structural Analysis

Handwriting

storm	born	for	more	sore
porch	north	soar	chores	short
forty	support	snowstorm		before
Mr.	Mrs.	St.	Dr.	Ave.
form	firm	board	bird	barn

Does a big cat roar or snore?

Mr. Thorn will report the game's score for us.

Also online

Day 3 Phonics Practice Activity

Decodable Reader Have children read "Born to Learn" (pages 25–28) and "A Board That Can Soar" (33–36).

MINILESSON 5 Mins

Structural Analysis

Abbreviations

1 **Model** Write and read aloud these words: *Sunday, Sun.* Explain that *Sun.* is an abbreviation for *Sunday*. Remind children that an abbreviation is a short way of writing a word and that most abbreviations end with a period. Repeat for the remaining days of the week and months of the year.

2 **Practice/Apply** Write these abbreviations: *Mon., Wed., Fri., Dec., Jan.,* and *Sept.* Ask children to tell where they have seen these abbreviations written and what they stand for. Have children read the abbreviations and then use each one in a sentence.

Corrective Feedback

Corrective Feedback Say: *My turn.* Model blending. Then lead children in blending the sounds. Say: *Do it with me.* Then say: *Your turn. Blend.* Have children chorally blend. Return to the beginning of the word.

→ # Word Work

MINILESSON 5 Mins

Spelling

OBJECTIVES

CCSS Recognize and read grade-appropriate irregularly spelled words. **RF.1.3g**

CCSS Determine the meaning of a new word formed when a known prefix is added to a known word (e.g., happy/unhappy, tell/retell). **L.2.4b**

Recognize and read high-frequency and vocabulary words

-or, -ore, -oar Word Families

1 **Model** Make index cards for *or, ore,* and *oar* and form three columns in a pocket chart. Say or blend the sounds with children.

Hold up the *born* **Spelling Word Card**. Say and spell it. Pronounce each sound clearly: /b/ /ôr/ /n/. Blend the sounds, emphasizing the vowel sound: /bôrn/. Repeat this step with *corn*. Place both words below the *or* card.

2 **Guided Practice/Practice** Have children spell each word. Repeat the process with the *ore* and *oar* words.

Display the words *her, dirt, learn,* and *sure* in a separate column. Read and spell the words together with children. Point out that these spelling words do not contain the /ôr/ sounds spelled *or, ore,* or *oar.*

Conclude by asking children to orally generate additional words that rhyme with each word. Write the additional words on the board.

Go Digital

er	ir	or	ur
her			
girl	curb		word

Spelling Word Families

school

Visual Glossary

MINILESSON 5 Mins

High-Frequency Words

PHONICS/SPELLING PRACTICE BOOK p. 113

A. Read the words in the box. Say each word. Then complete each word to make a spelling word.

born	corn	core	more
roar	soar	learn	sure

1. m o r e   5. b o r n
2. c o r e   6. r o a r
3. s u r e   7. c o r n
4. s o a r   8. l earn

B. Write your own sentence. Use one or two words from the box. Check that your sentence begins with a capital letter.

Check capitalization.

Responses will vary.

began, better, guess, learn, right, sure

1 **Guided Practice** Say each word and have children Read/Spell/Write it.

Display **Visual Vocabulary Cards** to review this week's words.

Visual Vocabulary Cards

2 **Practice** Repeat the activity with last week's words.

Build Fluency: Word Automaticity

Have children read the following sentences aloud together at the same pace. Repeat several times.

He felt better when the show began.

We can learn the right way to do it.

Are you sure, or did you guess?

Word Bank

Review the current and previous words in the word bank. Discuss with children which words should be removed, or added back, from previous high-frequency word lists.

MINILESSON
5 Mins

Vocabulary

idea, unusual

Review Use the **Visual Vocabulary Cards** to review this week's words using the Define/Example/Ask routine. Have partners generate context sentences for each vocabulary word.

Strategy: Prefixes

Visual Vocabulary Cards

❶ **Model** Tell children that a prefix is a group of letters added to the beginning of a word to make a new word. *A prefix changes the meaning of a word.* Use *The Story of a Robot Inventor* to model how to identify a prefix and use it to figure out the meaning of a word.

Think Aloud On the first page of *The Story of a Robot Inventor,* we read: *He invents unusual robots.* The word *unusual* has two parts: the base word *usual* and the prefix *un-.* I know *usual* means "common" or "ordinary." Something that is usual is something you might see every day. I also know the prefix *un-* means "not" or "the opposite of." The word *unusual* must mean "not usual." I can use the meaning of a prefix to help me figure out the meaning of a new word when I read.

❷ **Guided Practice** Work with children to add *un-* to other story words, including *real, wanted, changed,* and *like.* Help them determine the meaning of each new word formed and use it in a sentence.

❸ **Practice** Have children create sentences with *unsure, unusual, unsafe.*

Monitor and *Differentiate*

✓ **Quick Check**

Can children read and decode words with *r*-controlled vowels *or, ore, oar*?

Can children recognize and read high-frequency and vocabulary words?

Small Group Instruction

If No → | Approaching | Reteach pp. T212–215
| ELL | Develop pp. T226–233
If Yes → | On Level | Review pp. T220–221
| Beyond Level | Extend pp. T224–225

Thomas Edison, Inventor
by David A. Adler
illustrated by Sarah Snow

Genre Biography

Essential Question

What inventions do you know about?

Read about inventor, Thomas Edison.

Go Digital!

202   203

LITERATURE ANTHOLOGY, pp. 202–203

Wonders

Literature Anthology

Literature Anthology

Thomas Edison, Inventor

CLOSE READING

Lexile 510

Close Reading Routine

Read   DOK 1–2

- Identify key ideas and details about great inventions.
- Take notes and retell.
- Use **A C T** prompts as needed.

Reread   DOK 2–3

- Analyze the text, craft, and structure.
- Use *Close Reading Companion*, pp. 147–149.

Integrate   DOK 4

- Integrate knowledge and ideas.
- Make text-to-text connections.
- Use the Integrate lesson.

Read

ESSENTIAL QUESTION

Read aloud the Essential Question: *What inventions do you know about?* Tell children that as they read they should think about inventions in the selection they have used. Tell children to predict an invention they might read about.

Story Words Read and spell the words *inventor, questions, young, experiments, goose, worm, world, chemicals, poison,* and *future.* Review word meanings as needed.

Note Taking: Graphic Organizer As children read the selection, guide them to fill in **Your Turn Practice Book** page 238.

Chapter 1

Young Tom Edison asked lots of questions. When someone told him, "I don't know," Tom had one more question. He asked, "Why don't you know?" He did lots of experiments to find out.

Tom watched a goose sit on some eggs. He saw the eggs hatch. He wanted to know what would happen if he sat on eggs.

So, Tom made a nest. Then, he put goose and chicken eggs in the nest. Next, he sat on the eggs and found out. Splat! ❶

204

205

LITERATURE ANTHOLOGY, pp. 204–205

❶ Skill: Problem and Solution

Let's think about the problems and solutions the author tells about. What problem does Tom have? He wants to know what will happen if he sits on an egg. What steps does he take to solve it and what is his solution? Let's add these details to the chart.

> **Problem**
> Tom wonders what will happen if he sits on eggs.
>
> ↓
>
> **Steps to Solution**
> He makes a nest and puts eggs in it. He sits on the eggs.
>
> ↓
>
> **Solution**
> He learns that the eggs break.

A C T Access Complex Text

▶ What makes this text complex?

Genre Children may misconstrue the text as fiction because it is presented like a story.

Organization While the overall organization of the text is chronological, the author describes events from Edison's childhood before mentioning his birth date.

Build Vocabulary page 205
hatch: to come out of a shell

Young Tom also knew that birds ate worms and birds could fly. What if people ate worms? Tom **guessed** that they would fly, too. **2**

So, he gave a girl a cup of chopped worms and water. The girl drank it and got sick. And she didn't fly. **3**

206

Tom Edison, the boy who asked all those questions and did those **unusual** experiments, became the man whose inventions changed the world.

207

LITERATURE ANTHOLOGY, pp. 206–207

Read

❷ Maintain Skill: Sequence

COLLABORATE

The author presents the details of Tom's life in the order they happened. Turn to a partner and discuss what Tom does when he wonders if people could fly if they ate worms. What does he do first? What happens next?

❸ Make and Confirm Predictions

Remember, you can use what you learn from the text and the illustrations to make predictions about what might happen next. The text tells us young Tom did lots of experiments to answer questions he asked himself. What do you think Tom will do when he grows up? Let's read on to find out.

A C T Access Complex Text

▶ Organization

While the overall organization of the text is chronological, the author describes events from Edison's childhood before mentioning his birth date.

Make sure children grasp the overall organization, and understand that with the exception of the information about his birth date, the events in Edison's life are presented in the order in which they occurred

Tom Edison was born in 1847 in Milan, Ohio. He was the seventh and youngest child of Sam and Nancy Edison.

Sam had a lumber mill. Nancy had been a teacher. When Tom had trouble in school, his mother became his teacher at home. **4**

208

209

LITERATURE ANTHOLOGY, pp. 208–209

4 **Strategy: Ask and Answer Questions**

Remember that as you read, you can ask questions about the text and illustrations. Then you can continue reading to find the answers. This helps you focus your reading and better understand what you are reading. Turn to a partner and discuss what you want to learn about Tom's life and how you can find the answers.

COLLABORATE

Build Vocabulary page 208
lumber mill: a place where trees are cut into boards

Reread   *Close Reading Companion,* 147

Author's Craft

Reread pages 206–207. Why does the author include stories about Thomas Edison when he was a boy? (The author shows that young Tom was not afraid to ask questions and try experiments, even if they didn't work.)

Author's Craft: Organization

Reread pages 208–209. Why does the author tell us stories about Tom before we learn facts about when he was born and what his life was like? (The author decided it would be interesting for us to first read some funny stories about Tom.)

Chapter 2

Young Tom did many of his experiments in the cellar of his home. He had lots of jars of chemicals. He wanted to keep people from messing with them. To fix the problem, he had an **idea**. He wrote "poison" on each jar. He thought that would keep others away. He was **right**! **5**

There were often smoke, strange smells, and loud noises in the Edison home. It all came from the cellar and from young Tom's experiments.

210

211

LITERATURE ANTHOLOGY, pp. 210–211

Read

5 Skill: Problem and Solution

Tom worries that people will mess with his jars of chemicals. How does he solve the problem? Let's fill in the details in the chart.

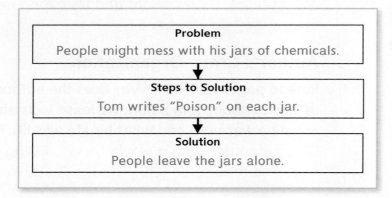

Problem
People might mess with his jars of chemicals.

↓

Steps to Solution
Tom writes "Poison" on each jar.

↓

Solution
People leave the jars alone.

A C T **A**ccess **C**omplex **T**ext

▶ **Genre**

This selection is a biography and presents facts about the life of a historical figure.

- Point out that although the selection is told like a story and has illustrations, the information is all true.

- Remind children that Thomas Edison was a real person and the events presented in the text really happened. Guide them to identify key events in his life.

Build Vocabulary page 210
cellar: basement or room below ground

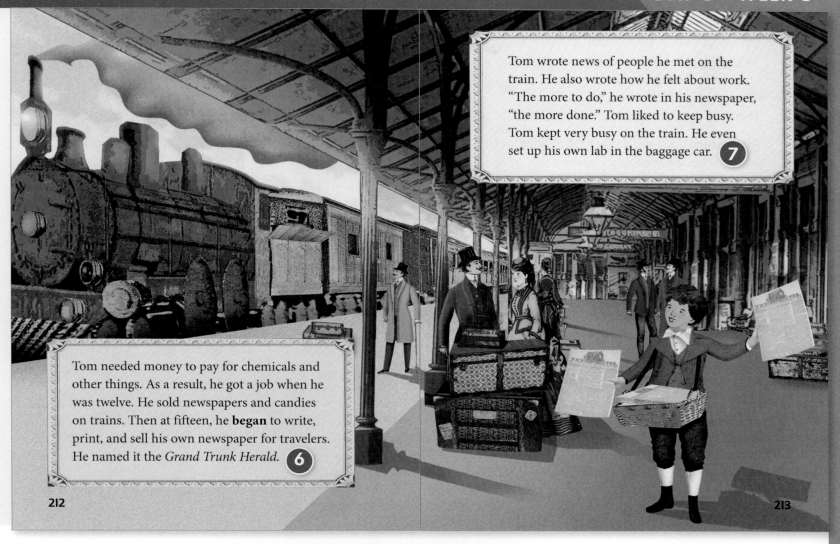

Tom needed money to pay for chemicals and other things. As a result, he got a job when he was twelve. He sold newspapers and candies on trains. Then at fifteen, he **began** to write, print, and sell his own newspaper for travelers. He named it the *Grand Trunk Herald*. **6**

212

Tom wrote news of people he met on the train. He also wrote how he felt about work. "The more to do," he wrote in his newspaper, "the more done." Tom liked to keep busy. Tom kept very busy on the train. He even set up his own lab in the baggage car. **7**

213

LITERATURE ANTHOLOGY, pp. 212–213

6 Strategy: Ask and Answer Questions

Teacher Think Aloud I read that when Tom was 12, he got a job to earn money to buy chemicals and other things. I wonder what job a 12-year-old boy could do? As I keep reading, I learn that his job was selling newspapers and candies on trains. That's the answer to my question.

7 Genre: Biography

This biography has information about a real person. It also has illustrations that provide details and information.

Build Vocabulary page 213
baggage car: a train car for suitcases

Reread　*Close Reading Companion,* 148

Author's/Illustrator's Craft

How do the text and illustrations help you know that Thomas Edison was a hard worker? (I read that Tom had a job at age 12 and started a newspaper at 15. The illustrations show Tom doing experiments and working at a train station.)

Author's Craft: Word Choice

Reread page 211. How does the author help you visualize what Thomas Edison's experiments were like? (The author uses words such as *smoke, strange smells,* and *loud noises.* I can picture the smoke and imagine the sounds and smells. The words help me understand that Tom tried many things when he did experiments.)

As Tom got older, he kept doing great things. There were no telephones at the time. Instead, messages were sent through telegraph wires. They were sent in a code of dots and dashes.

Tom **learned** the code. He got a job sending and reading telegraph messages. He found new ways to use the telegraph. Those were some of his first inventions.

214

Chapter 3

When Tom grew up, he became an inventor. He invented all kinds of things that helped people.

At that time, burning gas lights lit homes and streets. Sometimes smoke from the lights filled a room. Sometimes fire from the lights burned a home down. **8**

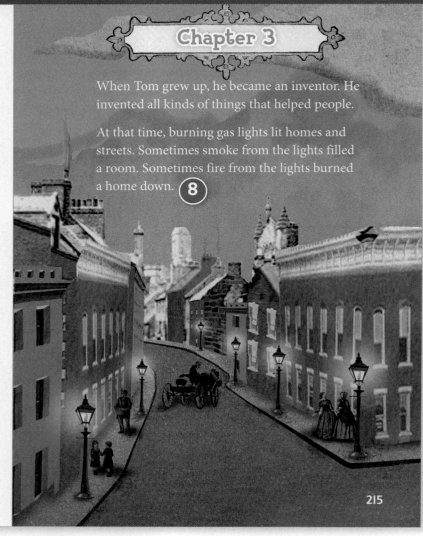

215

LITERATURE ANTHOLOGY, pp. 214–215

Read

8 Skill: Problem and Solution

Teacher Think Aloud On this page, I read that homes and streets were lit by gas lights. The author says smoke from the gas lights sometimes filled rooms, and the fire from the gas lights sometimes made homes burn down. This sounds like a serious problem. I'll write it in our Problem and Solution chart. I wonder if Tom finds a solution to the problem. I'll keep reading to find out.

Build Vocabulary page 214
messages: short notes or letters
code: a way of writing without letters

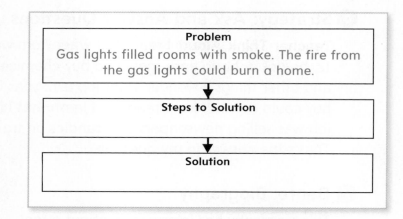

Problem
Gas lights filled rooms with smoke. The fire from the gas lights could burn a home.

Steps to Solution

Solution

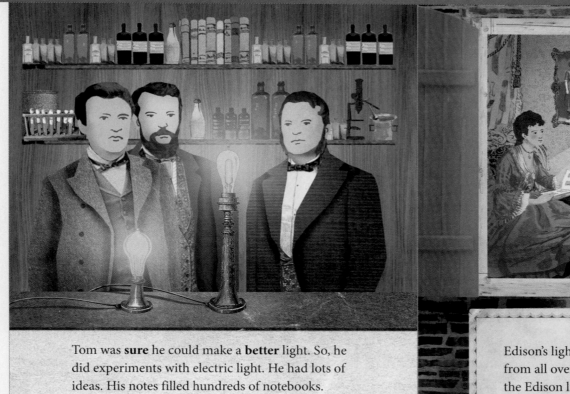

Tom was **sure** he could make a **better** light. So, he did experiments with electric light. He had lots of ideas. His notes filled hundreds of notebooks.

After more than a year of work, Tom did it. He made a light that was safe to use.

"The electric light is the light of the future," Tom said. "And it will be my light." **9**

216

Edison's lights were big news. People came from all over to see them. Once they saw the Edison lights, they wanted them in their homes. Tom's lights brightened the world.

Tom Edison spent his whole life making great things. The things he made helped people everywhere.

217

LITERATURE ANTHOLOGY, pp. 216–217

9 Skill: Problem and Solution

We read that gas lights could cause problems. What steps did Tom take to solve the problems? What was the solution? Let's add these details to our chart.

Problem
Gas lights filled rooms with smoke. The fire from the gas lights could burn a home.

↓

Steps to Solution
Tom did experiments with electric light.

↓

Solution
Tom made a safe electric light.

Build Vocabulary page 217
brightened: brought light to

Reread   *Close Reading Companion,* 149

Author's Craft: Events

Reread pages 214–215. How does the author show you that Tom kept trying new things? (The author tells me that Tom learned the code of telegraphs and got a job reading and sending messages. Then, Tom found new ways to use the telegraph. This tells me Tom kept trying new things.)

Author's Craft: Organization

Why do you think the author decided to end Chapter Two and start Chapter Three? (Chapter Two tells about when Tom was a boy. Chapter Three tells what happened when he was a grownup. The author wants to show how things Tom did as a boy helped him be a great inventor.)

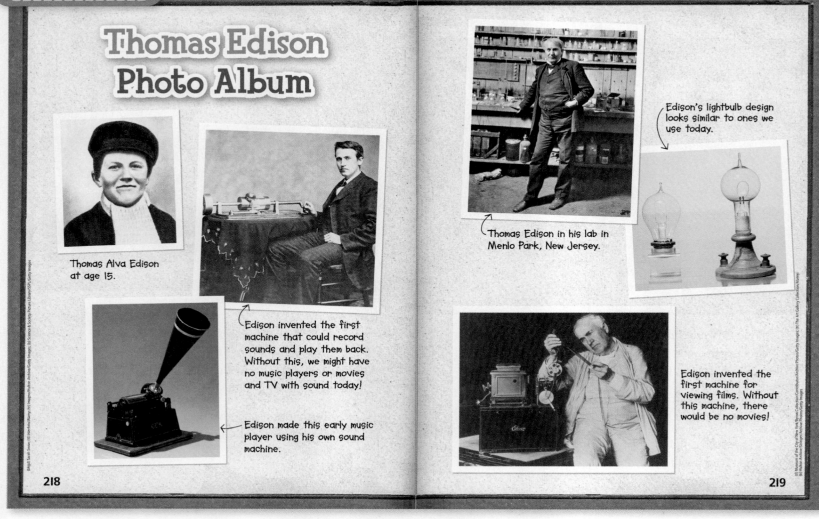

LITERATURE ANTHOLOGY, pp. 218–219

Skill: Problem and Solution

Review with children the problems and solutions you recorded. *What problems did Thomas Edison have? How did he solve those problems? Let's review the details we added to our Problem and Solution charts.*

Return to Purposes

Review children's predictions. Guide them to use the evidence in the text to confirm whether their predictions were accurate. Discuss what children learned about Tom Edison and familiar inventions by reading the selection.

Problem
Gas lights filled rooms with smoke. The fire from the gas lights could burn a home.

↓

Steps to Solution
Tom did experiments with electric light.

↓

Solution
Tom made a safe electric light.

LITERATURE ANTHOLOGY, p. 220

Meet the Author

David A. Adler

Read aloud page 220 with children. Ask them why David A. Adler might admire Tom Edison. *Why do you think he wanted to write about Tom Edison and his inventions?*

Author's Purpose

Have children write in their Response Journals about what they could do to find out about something that makes them curious. *I am curious about ____. I could ____.*

ILLUSTRATOR'S CRAFT

Focus on Collage

Tell children that the illustrator of *Thomas Edison, Inventor* is Sarah Snow. She created the collages on the computer by cutting and pasting different images. Tell children that the illustrations are collages.

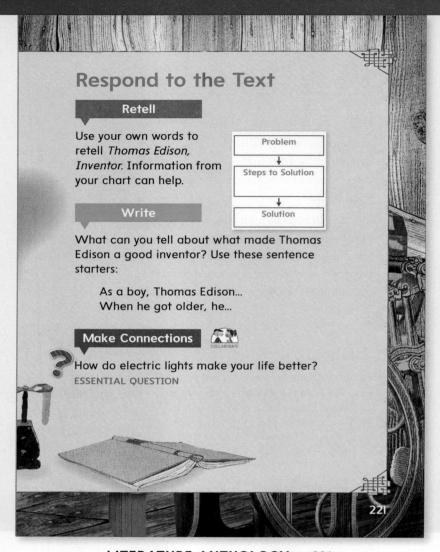

Respond to the Text

Retell

Use your own words to retell *Thomas Edison, Inventor.* Information from your chart can help.

Problem
↓
Steps to Solution
↓
Solution

Write

What can you tell about what made Thomas Edison a good inventor? Use these sentence starters:

As a boy, Thomas Edison...
When he got older, he...

Make Connections

? How do electric lights make your life better?
ESSENTIAL QUESTION

221

LITERATURE ANTHOLOGY, p. 221

Respond to the Text

Read

Retell

Guide children in retelling the selection. Remind them that as they read *Thomas Edison, Inventor,* they paid attention to problems and solutions and asked and answered questions about the text. Have children use the information they recorded on their Problem and Solution charts to help them retell the selection.

Reread

Analyze the Text

After children read and retell the selection, have them reread to develop a deeper understanding of the text by answering the questions on pages 147–149 of the *Close Reading Companion.* For children who need support finding text evidence to support their responses, use the scaffolded instruction from the Reread prompts on pages T191D–T191H.

Write About the Text

Review the writing prompt with children. Remind them to use their responses from the *Close Reading Companion* and to cite text evidence to support their answers.

For a full lesson on writing a response supported by text evidence, see pages T192–T193.

<u>Answer:</u> Thomas Edison was curious and asked a lot of questions when he was a boy. He did experiments to find answers to his questions. To see what would happen if he sat on eggs, Tom first made a nest. Then he put eggs in it. Next he sat on them. He found out that the eggs would break. Sometimes his experiments didn't work, but he kept doing them. He stayed busy and worked hard. He looked for new ways of doing things. <u>Evidence:</u> On page 204, the text says that Tom asked a lot of questions and did experiments to find answers. On page 205, I read about and saw one of Tom's experiments with a nest and eggs. On pages 212–213, I read about how Tom got a job at age 12. He stayed busy even as a kid, making newspapers and setting up a lab on the train. On page 214, I read about how Tom looked for new ways to use a telegraph machine. As an adult, he invented electric lights, which made the world safer and brighter.

Integrate

Make Connections
COLLABORATE

Essential Question: Answers will vary, but remind children to use text evidence from *Thomas Edison, Inventor* to tell what indoor lighting was like before the invention of electric lights and to think about how electric lights make life better today.

<u>Answer:</u> Electric lights make it easy for me to do things after dark, like read a book in bed or play a game. <u>Evidence:</u> On pages 215–216, I read about how gas lights were dangerous. They made rooms smoky and sometimes started fires. You probably couldn't use them to read a book in bed.

SOCIAL STUDIES

CONNECT TO CONTENT
INFLUENCE OF INDIVIDUALS

Remind children they have been reading and learning about inventions and the people who made them. Review the inventions shown on pages 218–219. Guide children to think about how the inventions Thomas Edison made led to devices they use today. *If Thomas Edison had not invented a film machine, we might not have movies or videos today.* Talk about the lasting influence of some of the inventors you read about this week.

Literature Anthology

OBJECTIVES

CCSS Write informative/explanatory texts in which they name a topic, supply facts about the topic, and provide some sense of closure. **W.1.2**

CCSS Use frequently occurring adjectives. **L.1.1f**

ACADEMIC LANGUAGE

- *evidence, adjectives, compare, proper noun*
- Cognates: *evidencia, adjetivos, comparar*

MINILESSON 5 Mins Independent Writing

Write About the Literature Anthology

Analylyze the Prompt Have children turn to page 221 in the **Literature Anthology**. Read the prompt: *Look at Chapters 1–2. What can you tell about what made Thomas Edison a good inventor? Include text evidence to support your answer.* Say: *To respond to this prompt, we need to find evidence about what Tom was like and make inferences about how that helped him be a good inventor.*

Find Text Evidence Say: *To respond to the prompt, we need to find evidence in the text and the illustrations.* Explain to children that they can use the evidence about things Thomas Edison did as a boy to make inferences about how this helped him be a good inventor. Say: *Look at pages 204–205. What information does the first page give about Tom?* (He asked a lot of questions when he was young. He did experiments to find things out.) *On page 205, why does the author tell about Tom sitting on eggs?* (to show that Tom would do experiments to find out what would happen) *What can we tell about a person who asks a lot of questions and does experiments?* (The person is curious and likes to find answers.) Have children take notes as they look for evidence to respond to the prompt.

Write to the Prompt: Guide children as they begin their writing.

- **Prewrite** Have children review their notes and plan their writing. Guide them to decide what details about Tom they can use to support their ideas about what made him a good inventor.

- **Draft** Remind children to start with a topic sentence. Point out that they can use some words from the prompt in their first sentence. As children write their drafts, have them focus on the week's skills.

  - **Facts** Include facts about Thomas Edison from the selection to support their ideas. **Trait: Ideas**

  - **Adjectives That Compare** Use the correct comparative form of adjectives ending in *-er* or *-est*. **Grammar**

  - **Time-Order Words** Use time-order words when relating a sequence of events. **Trait: Word Choice**

Tell children they will continue to work on their responses on Day 4.

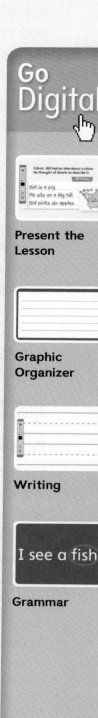

Go Digital

Present the Lesson

Graphic Organizer

Writing

I see a fish.

Grammar

Grammar

Adjectives That Compare

1 **Review** Have children look at page 173 in the **Reading/Writing Workshop**. Remind them to add -*er* to most adjectives to compare two nouns and add -*est* to compare more than two. Have children identify the adjective in the model sentence.

Say: *Name the adjective in this sentence:* First, Takahashi looked at how older robots move. (older) Write a new sentence: *The newest robots move like people.* Have children identify the adjective. (newest)

2 **Guided Practice/Practice** Guide children to find adjectives that compare in the following sentences. Have children work with partners to identify what is being compared in each case.

> The greatest robot ever made will do my chores.
>
> Jake's robot is taller than my robot.

Talk About It Have partners work together to explain how Emily used an adjective to compare.

Mechanics: Capitalize Days, Months, and Holidays

1 **Explain** Have children say the days of the week. Explain that the days of the week are proper nouns. Then have children say the months of the year. Explain that the months of the year are also proper nouns. Remind children that proper nouns begin with a capital letter.

2 **Guided Practice** Prompt children to identify days of the week and months of the year in each sentence and then correct the sentences.

> We had a bad storm on friday, july 12. (Friday, July)
>
> Gran visited from sunday to thursday. (Sunday, Thursday)
>
> Spring starts in march and ends in june. (March, June)

ELL

ENGLISH LANGUAGE LEARNERS SCAFFOLD

Beginning

Demonstrate Comprehension Provide sentence frames for partners to write their responses: *Thomas Edison was a good inventor because ____. He also ____.* Elicit more details to support children's answers.

Intermediate

Explain Guide children to talk about word choice. *Why do you use time-order words? What time-order word do you use at the beginning of a response? What words do you use in the middle? What do you use at the end?* Provide sentence frames, then have children complete and read them.

Advanced/High

Expand After children complete their responses, ask: *What time-order words did you use? Did you use adjectives that compare? Which words did you capitalize?* Repeat correct answers slowly and clearly to the class.

Daily Wrap Up

- Encourage children to discuss the Essential Question using the oral vocabulary words. *What inventions did you read about today?*

- Prompt children to review and discuss the skills they used today.

Materials

Literature Anthology
VOLUME 4

Visual Vocabulary Cards

complicated	began
curious	better
device	guess
imagine	learn
improve	right
idea	sure
unusual	

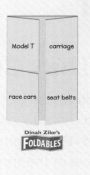

Teaching Poster

 Word-Building Cards

 **Spelling Word Cards**

 Dinah Zike's **FOLDABLES**

→ # Extend the Concept CLOSE READING

MINILESSON **5** Mins

Windshield Wipers and *Scissors*

OBJECTIVES

CCSS Identify words or phrases in stories or poems that suggest feelings or appeal to the senses. **RL.1.4**

Review vocabulary

ACADEMIC LANGUAGE

• alliteration
• Cognate: *aliteración*

ESSENTIAL QUESTION

Remind children that this week they have been learning about inventions and inventors. Guide children to discuss the question using information from what they have read and discussed. Use the **Visual Vocabulary Cards** and the Define/Example/Ask routine to review the oral vocabulary words *complicated, curious, device, imagine,* and *improve.*

Guide children to use each word as they talk about what they have read and learned about inventions. Prompt children by asking questions.

• Is a computer a machine that is simple or complicated?

• What subjects are you curious to learn more about?

• What device do people use to clean their teeth?

• Imagine you are twenty feet tall. What would that be like?

• If you improve, do you get better or worse?

Review last week's oral vocabulary words *certain, observe, remained, thoughtful, vast.*

Go Digital

Visual Glossary

Teaching Poster

"Windshield Wipers"

Literary Element: Alliteration

1 Explain Remind children that they have been reading informational text to learn facts and details about inventions. Tell them that they can also read poetry about inventions. Explain that poems often use alliteration, or words that start with the same sound. This can make the poem more appealing to read or listen to. Alliteration can also add to the meaning of the poem.

2 Model Display Teaching Poster 25. Read the entire poem aloud, and then repeat the third line. *This line of the poem includes alliteration. The words* rumbles, rattles, roars *all begin with the /r/ sound.*

3 Guided Practice/Practice Read together the last line of the poem. Guide children to identify the use of alliteration. *What sound does the word* soaring *begin with? What other words in the line begin with the /s/ sound?* Tell children to listen for alliteration as they read poetry.

ENGLISH LANGUAGE LEARNERS SCAFFOLD

Beginning

Use Sentence Frames Use sentence frames to help children discuss alliteration. *I hear the /r/ sound in the words ____, ____, and ____.*

Intermediate

Describe Guide children to discuss alliteration. *Which words have the same beginning sound? Can you think of other words with the same sound? Let's use those words to make a sentence with alliteration.*

Advanced/High

Discuss Prompt children to add to the poem by writing another line that includes alliteration.

Genre Poetry

Compare Texts
Read about two inventions you know well.

Windshield Wipers
by Rebecca Kai Dotlich

*Squish, squish,
squeegy-squish*
tossing rain
side to side; ❶
*squish, squish,
squeegy-squish,
flap, flap,*
puddle glide.
*Slosh, slosh,
sloshing* wash,
plish, plish, ❷
tidal toss.
*Squeegy-squish,
squish, squish, sway...*

a perfect windshield
wiper day.

222   223

LITERATURE ANTHOLOGY, pp. 222–223

Literature Anthology

Windshield Wipers and *Scissors*   CLOSE READING

Compare Texts

After children read and reread the poems, encourage them to think about the Essential Question. Review with children that in *Thomas Edison, Inventor,* they read about inventions we use in our daily life.

Read

❶ Literary Element: Alliteration

Teacher Think Aloud In the poem, I hear the words *squeegy, squish,* and *side.* These words all begin with the /s/ sound. This is an example of alliteration, or several words close together that begin with the same sound.

❷ Strategy: Ask and Answer Questions

Teacher Think Aloud I ask myself what is making the sounds in the poem. As I read, I look for the answer to my question. The last lines give the answer. The windshield wiper is making the sounds.

❸ Literary Element: Alliteration

Let's listen to the first lines of the poem on pages 224–225. *X slides open, squeezes shut—snip, snip, snip, carve, cut.* Which words begin with the /s/ sound? (slides, squeezes, snip) What other words begin with the same sound? (carve, cut)

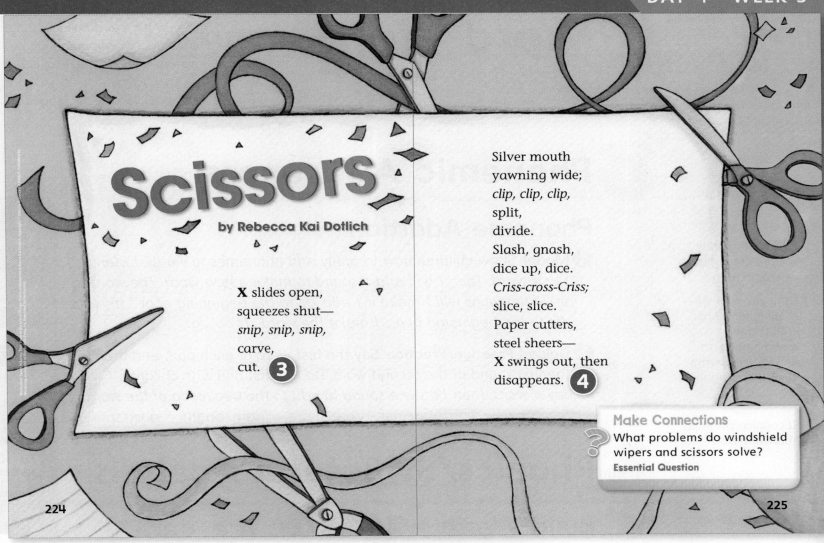

Scissors
by Rebecca Kai Dotlich

X slides open,
squeezes shut—
snip, snip, snip,
carve,
cut. **3**

Silver mouth
yawning wide;
clip, clip, clip,
split,
divide.
Slash, gnash,
dice up, dice.
Criss-cross-Criss;
slice, slice.
Paper cutters,
steel sheers—
X swings out, then
disappears. **4**

Make Connections
What problems do windshield
wipers and scissors solve?
Essential Question

224   225

LITERATURE ANTHOLOGY, pp. 224–225

❹ Literary Element: Alliteration

Now I will read some lines from the end of the poem. *Criss-cross-criss; slice, slice. Paper cutters, steel sheers—X swings out, then disappears.* What sound do the words *criss* and *cross* begin with? (/kr/) Which words begin with the /s/ sound? (slice, steel, swings) Alliteration adds meaning to this poem, too. Why do you thing the author used words that start with the /k/ sound to write about cutting through paper? (the sharp sound reminds the reader of scissors slicing through paper)

Retell

Guide children to retell the poems.

Reread

After children retell the poems, have them reread to develop a deeper understanding of the texts by answering questions on pages 150–152 of the *Close Reading Companion.* For children who need support citing text evidence, use these Reread questions:

• Why does the author repeat the words "squish, squish, squeegy-squish" in "Windshield Wipers"?

• How are the poems' titles helpful?

Integrate

Make Connections

Essential Question Have children use text evidence to tell what problems scissors and wipers solve.

→ # Word Work

Quick Review

Build Fluency: Sound-Spellings
Display the **Word-Building Cards:** *or, ore, oar, ar, er, ir, ur, ey, igh, oa, oe, ee, ea, ai, ay, e_e, u_e, o_e, dge, i_e, a_e, ch, tch, wh, ph, th, sh, ng, mp, sk.* Have children say the sounds.

MINILESSON 5 Mins

Phonemic Awareness

OBJECTIVES

CCSS Decode regularly spelled one-syllable words. **RF.1.3b**

CCSS Use conventional spelling for words with common spelling patterns and for frequently occurring irregular words. **L.1.2d**

Recognize common abbreviations

Phoneme Addition

1 Model Show children how to orally add phonemes to words. *Listen as I say a word. Then I will add a sound to make a new word. The word is:* or. *What word will I make if I add /f/ to the beginning of* or*? If I add /f/ to the beginning of* or*, I make the word /fffôr/,* for.

2 Guided Practice/Practice Say the first word of each pair, and then say the first sound of the second word. Do the first one with children. *I will say a word, then I'll say a sound to add to the beginning of the word. Say the new word.* oar/roar   ore/more   right/bright   port/sport

MINILESSON 5 Mins

Phonics/Structural Analysis

Build Words with /ôr/ *or, ore, oar*

Review *The /ôr/ sounds can be represented by the letters* or, ore, *or* oar. *We'll use* **Word-Building Cards** *to build with /ôr/.*

Place the letters b, o, a, r. *Let's blend the sounds together and read the word: /bôr/,* boar. *Now let's change the* b *to* r. *Blend the sounds and read the word: /rrrôr/,* roar . *Continue with* soar, oar, or, for, fork, fort, short, shore, snore, score, store. *Discuss the words* oar *and* or, *which sound alike but are spelled differently and have different meanings.*

Decodable Reader Have children read "Sports Stars" (pages 29–32) and "Hard Chores" (37–40).

Abbreviations

Review Write the words *Mrs., Tues., Aug.,* and *Rd.* on the board and read them with children. Remind children that an abbreviation is a short way of writing a word and most abbreviations end with a period.

Write the following words: *Doctor, December, Wednesday, Street, Dr., Dec., Wed., St.* Have children work in pairs to match abbreviations to full names. Then have them write sentences with abbreviations.

Go Digital

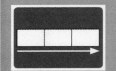
Phonemic Awareness

Phonics

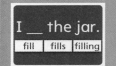
Structural Analysis

Spelling Word Sort

school
Visual Glossary

Spelling

Words with *or, ore, oar*

Review Provide pairs of children with copies of the **Spelling Word Cards**. While one partner reads the words one at a time, the other partner should orally segment the word and then write the word. After reading all the words, partners should switch roles.

Have children correct their own papers. Then have them sort the words by vowel spelling pattern: *or, ore, oar,* or no /ôr/ pattern.

High-Frequency Words

began, better, guess, learn, right, sure

Review Display **Visual Vocabulary Cards** for high-frequency words *began, better, guess, learn, right, sure.* Have children Read/Spell/Write each word.

- Point to a word and call on a child to use it in a sentence.
- Review last week's words using the same procedure.

Expand Vocabulary

idea, unusual

Use the Visual Vocabulary Cards to review *idea* and *unusual.*

1 Explain Explain to children that words have different forms. Help children generate different forms of this week's words by adding the inflectional ending -*s* to *idea* and by removing the prefix *un-* from *unusual.* Review the meanings of the plural ending -*s* and the prefix *un-*.

2 Model Write the word *unusual* on the board. Model how to remove the prefix *un-* from the word. Then write *usual.* Discuss each form of the word and its meaning. Have children share aloud sentences using *unusual* and *usual.*

3 Guided Practice Have children work in pairs to pluralize *idea.* Then have children share sentences using the different word forms.

Monitor and *Differentiate*

✓ Quick Check

Can children read and decode words with *r*-controlled vowels *or, ore, oar?*

Can children recognize and read high-frequency and vocabulary words?

Small Group Instruction

If No → **Approaching** Reteach pp. T212–215

       ELL Develop pp. T226–233

If Yes → **On Level** Review pp. T220–221

      Beyond Level Extend pp. T224–225

Literature Anthology

OBJECTIVES

CCSS With guidance and support from adults, focus on a topic, respond to questions and suggestions from peers, and add details to strengthen writing as needed. **W.1.5**

CCSS Use frequently occurring adjectives. **L.1.1f**

CCSS Ask questions to clear up any confusion about the topics and texts under discussion. **SL.1.1c**

___

ACADEMIC LANGUAGE

• revise, facts, adjectives, proper noun
• Cognates: revisar, adjetivos

MINILESSON 5 Mins

Independent Writing

Write About the Literature Anthology

Revise

Reread the prompt about the selection *Thomas Edison, Inventor. Look at Chapters 1–2. What can you tell about what made Thomas Edison a good inventor? Include text evidence to support your answer.* Have children read their drafts to see if they responded to the prompt. Then have them check for:

- **Facts** Does their response include facts about what Thomas Edison did that made him a good inventor? **Trait: Ideas**

- **Adjectives That Compare** Did they use the correct form of adjectives ending in *-er* or *-est* when comparing? **Grammar**

- **Time-Order Words** Did they use time-order words to show a sequence of events? **Trait: Word Choice**

 Peer Review Have children work in pairs to do a peer review and read their partner's draft. Ask partners to check that the response includes facts, time-order words, and adjectives that compare. They should take notes about what they liked most about the writing, questions they have for the author about anything that confused them, and additional ideas they think the author could include. Have partners discuss these topics. Provide time for them to make revisions.

Proofread/Edit

Have children check for the following:

- Adjectives that compare are used correctly.

- Proper nouns are capitalized.

- Past-tense verbs are used correctly.

 Peer Edit Next, have partners exchange their drafts and take turns reviewing them against the checklist. Encourage partners to discuss and fix errors together.

Go Digital

Writing

≡ Make a capital letter.
∧ Add.
✄ Take out.

Proofreader's Marks

I see a fish.

Grammar

Final Draft

After children edit their writing and finish their peer edits, have them write their final draft. Tell children to write neatly so others can read their writing. Or, work with children to explore a variety of digital tools to produce and publish their writing, including collaborating with peers. Have them include details that help make their writing clear and interesting and add a drawing to make their ideas clear.

Teacher Conference As children work, conference with them to provide guidance. Make sure children used facts from the selection to support their answer and that they used time-order words to show the order of events.

Grammar

Adjectives That Compare

1 Review Remind children that most adjectives that compare two nouns end in -er and most adjectives that compare three or more nouns end in -est.

2 Practice Display the following sentences. Have children change each adjective to one that compares.

> The big couch is (soft) _____ than the little couch. (softer)
>
> Of the three kids, Cord is the (short) _____. (shortest)
>
> The truck is (long) _____ than the car. (longer)
>
> The sky is (dark) _____ at night than it is in the morning. (darker)

Talk About It Have partners work together to orally generate sentences with *softer, shortest, longer* and *darker*.

Mechanics: Capitalize Days, Months, and Holidays

1 Explain Explain to children that the names of holidays are proper nouns. Remind them that proper nouns begin with capital letters.

2 Practice Display the sentences. Read each aloud. Have children identify the holiday in each sentence. Then have children fix each sentence.

> We fly a flag on flag day. (We fly a flag on Flag Day.)
>
> Martin luther king day is on a Monday. (Martin Luther King Day is on a Monday.)

Daily Wrap Up

- Have children discuss the Essential Question using the oral vocabulary words. Ask: *What inventions do you use everyday?*

- Prompt children to discuss the skills they practiced and learned today by asking, *What skills did you use today?*

OBJECTIVES

 CCSS Participate in shared research and writing projects (e.g., explore a number of "how-to" books on a given topic and use them to write a sequence of instructions). **W.1.7**

- Build background knowledge
- Research information using technology

ACADEMIC LANGUAGE

- *collage, materials, invention*
- Cognates: *collage, materiales, invenciones*

RESEARCH AND INQUIRY

Make a Collage

Review the steps in the research process. Tell children that today they will do a research project with a partner to learn more about an invention.

STEP 1 ## Choose a Topic

Name common inventions, such as the telephone or computer. Prompt children to suggest other inventions. Guide partners to choose an invention to research.

STEP 2 ## Find Resources

Discuss how to use the selections, reference materials, and online resources to find information on their chosen inventions. Have partners research the invention's history and other facts about it. Have them use the Research Process Checklist online.

STEP 3 ## Keep Track of Ideas

Have children make a Four-Tab Foldable® to record ideas and facts from sources. Model recording the names of the sources.

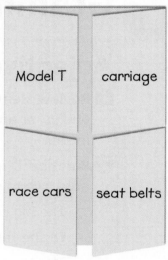

| Model T | carriage |
| race cars | seat belts |

Dinah Zike's
FOLDABLES

Go Digital

Resources
Research and
Inquiry

Collaborative Conversations

Be Open to All Ideas As children engage in partner, small-group, and whole-group discussions, remind them:

- that everyone's ideas are important and should be heard.
- not to be afraid to ask a question if something is unclear.
- to respect the opinions of others.

STEP 4 **Create the Project: Collage**

Explain the characteristics of a collage.

- Title A collage can have a title. In this project, the title of the collage will be the name of an invention, such as *Telephone* or *Toothbrush*.

- Mixed Materials Collages can be made from many different materials. They can have images or words cut from magazines, newspapers, or packaging; scraps of yarn or fabric and other craft materials; or small items, such as tiny plastic toys.

- Images A collage can have images. For this project, your collage will have images related to an invention. The images can be drawings or photographs that show its history and how it affects our lives.

Have children create a collage about their chosen invention.

- Prompt children to write the name of the invention as the title.

- Have children write sentences about how their invention makes life easier.

STEM

ILLUSTRATED COLLAGE

Materials

Reading/Writing Workshop
VOLUME 4

Literature Anthology
VOLUME 4

Visual Vocabulary Cards
began
better
guess
learn
right
sure
idea
unusual

Inventions	How They Help

Teaching Poster

born

Spelling Word Cards

a b c
Word-Building Cards

Word Work

MINILESSON 5 Mins

Phonemic Awareness

Phoneme Blending

Review Guide children to blend phonemes. *Listen as I say a group of sounds. Then blend those sounds to form a word.*

/m/ /ôr/   /sh/ /ôr/   /s/ /n/ /ôr/   /p/ /ôr/ /ch/

Phoneme Segmentation

Review Guide children to segment words into phonemes. *Now I am going to say a word. I want you to say each sound in the word.* Tell children they can say the /ôr/ sounds together.

for   roar   sort   born   sport   chore

MINILESSON 5 Mins

Phonics/Structural Analysis

Blend and Build Words with /ôr/ *or, ore, oar*

Review Have children read and say the words *for, store,* and *soar.* Then have them follow the word-building routine to build *more, score, shore, store, torn, horn, sworn, born, boar.*

Word Automaticity Help children practice word automaticity. Display decodable words and point to each word as children chorally read it. Test how many words children can read in one minute. Model blending words children miss.

Abbreviations

Review Have children explain abbreviations. Then have them write abbreviations, such as *Mr., Mrs., Dr., St., Rd., Sat., Thurs., Feb.,* and *Dec.* Have partners think of new sentences using each abbreviation.

Go Digital

Phonemic Awareness

m a
n t p
Phonics

I __ the jar.
fill | fills | filling
Structural Analysis

school
Visual Glossary

Fluency: Word Automaticity

Spelling

Word Sort with *or, ore, oar*

Review Have children use the **Spelling Word Cards** to sort the weekly words by vowel patterns.

Assess Assess children on spelling with /ôr/ spelled *or, ore,* and *oar*. Provide a sentence for each word. Allow time to write the words. As a challenge, provide an additional word for each sound-spelling.

High-Frequency Words

began, better, guess, learn, right, sure

Review Display **Visual Vocabulary Cards** for the words. Have children Read/Spell/Write and write a sentence with each word.

Review Vocabulary

idea, unusual

Review Write *idea* and *unusual*. Have children use each in a sentence. Write the sentences and reinforce word meanings as necessary. Repeat the activity with last week's words or other previously taught words children need to review.

Fluency

Appropriate Phrasing

Review Remind children that commas indicate you should pause slightly while reading. A period indicates you should stop briefly.

Read aloud a few pages of the Shared Read. Have children echo each sentence. Point out how you pause or stop briefly at every comma or period. Emphasize that this helps listeners know when one idea ends and a new one starts. Then have partners reread the selection, working on how they read sentences with commas and periods.

Quick Review

Build Fluency: Sound-Spellings
Display the **Word-Building Cards:** *or, ore, oar, ar, er, ir, ur, ey, igh, oa, oe, ee, ea, ai, ay, e_e, u_e, o_e, dge, i_e, a_e, ch, tch, wh, ph, th, sh, ng, mp, sk.* Have children say the sounds.

Monitor and *Differentiate*

 Quick Check

Can children read and decode words with *r*-controlled vowels *or, ore, oar*?

Can children recognize and read high-frequency and vocabulary words?

Small Group Instruction

If No → Approaching Reteach pp. T212–215

ELL Develop pp. T226–233

If Yes → On Level Review pp. T220–221

Beyond Level Extend pp. T224–225

WORD WORK **T203**

→ # Language Arts

Literature Anthology

OBJECTIVES

CCSS With guidance and support from adults, use a variety of digital tools to produce and publish writing, including in collaboration with peers. **W.1.6**

CCSS Describe people, places, things, and events with relevant details, expressing ideas and feelings clearly. **SL.1.4**

CCSS Add drawings or other visual displays to descriptions when appropriate to clarify ideas, thoughts, and feelings. **SL.1.5**

ACADEMIC LANGUAGE

• *present, evaluate, publish, capitalize*
• Cognates: *presentar, evaluar*

MINILESSON
5 Mins

Independent Writing

Write About the Literature Anthology

Prepare

Tell children they will plan what they will say about their finished writing and drawing to the class. Remind children to:

• Think about how the facts they used from the selection support their answer.

• Think about how they used time-order words to show the order in which events happened.

Present

Have children take turns giving presentations of their responses to the prompt about *Thomas Edison, Inventor: Look at Chapters 1–2. What can you tell about what made Thomas Edison a good inventor? Include text evidence to support your answer.* If possible, record their presentations so children can self-evaluate. Tell children to:

• Explain their drawings to help clarify their ideas.

• Express their ideas clearly.

• Use relevant details to describe what made Thomas Edison a good inventor.

Evaluate

Have children discuss their own presentations and evaluate their performance using the presentation rubric.

Use the teacher's rubric to evaluate children's writing. Have children add their writing to their Writer's Portfolio. Encourage children to look back at previous writing. Guide children to discuss what they learned about Thomas Edison and his inventions by writing their response to the prompt. Have children share their observations with a partner.

Publish

After children finish presenting their writing, discuss how the class will compile and publish their responses in a book. Guide children to use digital tools to create the book. Suggest that children brainstorm and then vote on a book title. Allow children to make decisions regarding the organization of the class book.

Go Digital

Writing

Checklists

I see a fish.

Grammar

Grammar

Adjectives That Compare

1 Review Have children describe when adjectives with *-er* and adjectives with *-est* are used. Write the following sentences and have children identify the adjectives that compare.

I am the tallest kid on the baseball team. (tallest)

The blue car is smaller than the gray one. (smaller)

This was the wettest day in June. (wettest)

2 Practice Display the incorrect sentences. Have children correct them.

The dog is loudest than the TV show. (The dog is louder than the TV show.)

Plums are sweet than green beans. (Plums are sweeter than green beans.)

Miss Beck is old than Miss York. Coach North is the older of the three. (Miss Beck is older than Miss York. Coach North is the oldest of the three.)

Mechanics: Capitalize Days, Months, and Holidays

1 Review Remind children that all days, months, and holidays are capitalized.

2 Practice Write the following sentences. Read each aloud. Have children fix the sentences.

The ship came into the seaport on monday, may 6. (The ship came into the seaport on Monday, May 6.)

New year's day Is january 1. (New Year's Day is January 1.)

We will pick you up at the Airport on labor day, monday, september 5. (We will pick you up at the airport on Labor Day, Monday, September 5.)

Daily Wrap Up

- Review the Essential Question and encourage children to discuss using the oral vocabulary words.

- Review that asking questions as they read and making connections between problems and solutions in selections can help children better understand what they read.

- Review words with /ôr/ spelled *or*, *oar*, and *ore*.

- Use Visual Vocabulary Cards to review the Words to Know.

- Remind children that a biography is an informational text about a person that is written by another person.

DAY 5

→ Integrate Ideas

Close Reading Routine

 Read   DOK 1–2

- Identify key ideas and details about great inventions.
- Take notes and retell.
- Use prompts as needed.

Reread   DOK 2–3

- Analyze text, craft, and structure.

Integrate   DOK 4

- Integrate knowledge and ideas and make text-to-text connections.
- Use the Integrate Lesson.
- Use *Close Reading Companion*, p. 153.

TEXT CONNECTIONS

Connect to the Essential Question

Write the essential question on the board: *What inventions do you know about?* Read the essential question aloud. Tell children that they will think about all of the selections they have read and what they have learned about inventions. Say: *We have read many selections on this topic. We will compare the information from this week's* **Leveled Readers** *and* The Story of a Robot Inventor, **Reading/Writing Workshop** *pages 160–169.*

Evaluate Text Evidence Guide children to review the selections and their completed graphic organizers. Have children work with partners to compare information from all the week's reads. Children can record notes using a Foldable®. Guide them to record information from the selections that helps them answer the Essential Question.

Dinah Zike's
FOLDABLES
Study Organizer

Great Inventions

RESEARCH AND INQUIRY

OBJECTIVES

CCSS Participate in shared research and writing projects. **W.1.7**

Go Digital

Collaborate

Have children create a checklist and review their collages:

- Does their collage focus on a single invention and give information about how the invention affects us?

- Did they include a title? Does the title tell what the collage is about?

- Did they include images and materials to explain the invention? Did they write text to explain the invention's significance?

- Have they taken notes about what they will say when they present their collage to the class?

Guide partners to practice sharing their collages with each other. Children should practice speaking and presenting their information clearly.

Guide students to share their work. Prompt children to ask questions to clarify when something is unclear: *Why did you include this picture or item in your collage? How does the invention affect our lives?* Have children use the Presentation Checklist online.

OBJECTIVES

CCSS Identify basic similarities in and differences between two texts on the same topic (e.g., in illustrations, descriptions, or procedures). **RI.1.9**

Text to Photography

Read aloud with children the Integrate activity on page 153 of the *Close Reading Companion*. Have partners share reactions to the photograph. Then guide them to discuss how it is similar to the selections they read earlier in the week. Have partners collaborate to complete the Integrate page by following the prompts.

Present Ideas and Synthesize Information

When children finish their discussions, ask for a volunteer from each pair to share the information from their Foldable® and their Integrate pages. After each pair has presented their ideas, ask: *How does learning about different inventors and inventions help you answer the Essential Question, What inventions do you know about?* Lead a class discussion asking students to use the information from their charts to answer the Essential Question.

SPEAKING AND LISTENING

OBJECTIVES

CCSS Ask questions to clear up any confusion about the topics and texts under discussion. **SL.1.1c**

CCSS Add drawings or other visual displays to descriptions when appropriate to clarify ideas, thoughts, and feelings. **SL.1.5**

CCSS Produce complete sentences when appropriate to task and situation. **SL.1.6**

As children work with partners in their *Close Reading Companion* or on their collages, make sure that they are actively participating in the conversation and, when necessary, remind them to use these speaking and listening strategies:

Speaking Strategies

- Speak in a clear voice so that others can hear them and to speak in complete sentences when making presentations.

- Remember to explain pictures and other visual aids so listeners understand their ideas.

Listening Strategies

- Make eye contact with the speaker, to nod to show that they understand, and to wait until the speaker stops before asking questions.

- Think about what is unclear to them and what questions they have for the speaker.

- Pay attention to what the speaker says as well as to any pictures or media that the speaker is discussing.

→ Approaching Level

Leveled Reader:
The Wright Brothers

Lexile 410

OBJECTIVES

Describe the connection between two individuals, events, ideas, or pieces of information in a text. **RI.1.3**

Recognize problem and solution in a text

The Wright Brothers

Graphic Organizer

Retell

Before Reading

Preview and Predict

Have children turn to the title page. Read the title and the author's name and have children repeat. Preview the selection's photographs. Prompt children to predict what the selection might be about.

Review Genre: Informational Text/Biography

Have children recall that a biography is the true story of a person's life written by another person.

ESSENTIAL QUESTION

Remind children of the Essential Question: *What inventions do you know about?* Set a purpose for reading: *Let's read to find out what the Wright Brothers invented.*

Remind children that as they read a selection, they can ask questions about what they do not understand or what they want to know more about.

During Reading

Guided Comprehension

As children whisper read *The Wright Brothers,* monitor and provide guidance, correcting blending and modeling the key strategies and skills.

Strategy: Ask and Answer Questions

Remind children that as they read, they can ask themselves questions and then use the words to find the answers. Model using the strategy on page 8. *The words say that they were sure they could make a flying machine. How will they make it? I'll read on for the answer.*

Skill: Connections Within Text/Problem and Solution

Remind children that what characters want to do, change, or find out is the problem. The way the problem is solved is the solution. Say: *The Wright brothers wanted to make a plane. What do they do to solve this problem?* Display a Problem and Solution chart for children to copy.

Model recording children's answers in the boxes. Have children record the answers in their own charts.

Think Aloud On page 8, I read that the Wright Brothers wanted to make a plane. I'll write that in the Problem box. Then I can read on to find the steps they followed in order to solve their problem.

Guide children to use the details to determine the steps and solution.

After Reading

Respond to Reading

Have children complete the Respond to Reading on page 12.

Retell

Have children take turns retelling the selection, using the **Retelling Cards** as a guide. Help them make a personal connection: *Describe airplanes you have seen. Have you ever flown in an airplane? Tell about your experience.*

Model Fluency

Read each sentence. Have children chorally repeat. Point out how you pause when you come to a comma or a period.

Apply Have partners practice reading. Provide feedback as needed.

PAIRED READ ...

Leveled Reader

"Fly Away, Butterfly"

Make Connections:
Write About It *Analytical Writing*

Before reading, ask children to note the genre of this text is poetry. Then discuss the Compare Texts direction. After reading, ask children to make connections between the information they learned from *The Wright Brothers* and "Fly Away, Butterfly" Provide sentence frames such as: *Butterflies and airplanes are alike because ____. They are different because ____.*

FOCUS ON SCIENCE

Children can extend their knowledge of things that fly by completing the science activity on page 16. **STEM**

Literature Circles

Lead children in conducting a literature circle using the Thinkmark questions to guide the discussion. You may wish to discuss what children have learned about flying from both selections in the Leveled Reader.

Level Up

Level-up lessons available online.

IF children can read *The Wright Brothers* Approaching Level with fluency and correctly answer the Respond to Reading questions,

THEN tell children that they will read a more detailed version of the selection.

• Use page 8 of *The Wright Brothers* On Level to model using Teaching Poster 36 to list the selection problem.

• Have children read the selection, checking their comprehension by using the graphic organizer.

Approaching Level

Phonemic Awareness

PHONEME CATEGORIZATION

TIER **2**

OBJECTIVES

 Isolate and pronounce initial, medial vowel, and final sounds (phonemes) in spoken single-syllable words. **RF.1.2c**

Categorize words by phoneme

I Do Explain to children that they will listen for words that end with the same sound. *Listen as I say three words. Two words will end with the same sound and one will end with a different sound:* core, walk, door. Core *and* door *end with* /ôr/. Walk *does not.* Walk *does not belong.*

We Do *Listen as I say three words:* force, penny, puppy. *Two words end with the same sound:* penny *and* puppy *end with* /ē/. Force *does not end with the* /ē/ *sound. That word does not belong in this group.*

Continue the activity with these groups of words:

forth, path, card   horn, sneeze, breeze   chore, hip, more

You Do *Are you ready? Which words go together? Which word does not belong?*

bird, board, nurse   talk, chalk, born   more, help, snore

Repeat the categorization routine with additional /ôr/ words.

PHONEME SEGMENTATION

TIER **2**

OBJECTIVES

 Segment spoken single-syllable words into their complete sequence of individual sounds (phonemes). **RF.1.2d**

I Do Explain that children will be segmenting words into sounds. *Listen as I say a word:* cord. *I hear these sounds in* cord: /k/ /ôr/ /d/.

We Do *Listen as I say another word:* porch. *Let's say the sounds:* /p/ /ôr/ /ch/, porch. Tell children that they can say the /ôr/ sounds together since they are difficult to pronounce separately.

Repeat the routine with these words: *forth, roar, core, storm, fork, soar.*

You Do *Are you ready? I'll say a word. Tell me what sounds you hear.*

shore   fort   worn   corn   term   tore

PHONEME ADDITION

OBJECTIVES

 Isolate and pronounce initial, medial vowel, and final sounds (phonemes) in spoken single-syllable words. **RF.1.2c**

Add phonemes to words

 Listen carefully as I say a word: core. *The word* core *has the sounds /k/ /ôr/. I'm going to add /s/ to the beginning of* core: */sss/ /kôr/,* score. *Say it with me:* score.

 Let's do one together. Listen as I say: or. *Say the word with me: /ôr/. Now let's add /b/ to the beginning: /b/ /ôr/. Let's say the new word together:* bore.

Repeat with these words:

/s/ take   /s/ mile   /f/ or   /m/ ask   /s/ tore

 Repeat the word that I say. Then add a beginning sound to make a new word.

/s/ corn   /b/ ride   /r/ oar   /p/ art   /w/ ink   /s/ core

Repeat the addition routine with additional word pairs.

PHONEME SUBSTITUTION

OBJECTIVES

 Isolate and pronounce initial, medial vowel, and final sounds (phonemes) in spoken single-syllable words. **RF.1.2c**

Substitute phonemes in words

 Listen as I say a word: face. *I'm going to change the vowel sound from /ā/ to /u/. Here is the new word: /fff/ /uuu/ /sss/, /fuuus/,* fuss.

 Let's try it together. Listen as I say: port. *Let's change the vowel sound from /ôr/ to /âr: /pârt/,* part. *The new word is* part.

Repeat with these words:

phone, fine   form, farm   stick, steak   parch, porch

 Now it's your turn to make new words. Change the vowel sound and make a new word.

choke, cheek   core, care   scare, score   stark, stork

ELL ENGLISH LANGUAGE LEARNERS

For the **children** who need **phonemic awareness**, **phonics**, and **fluency** practice, use scaffolding methods as necessary to ensure children understand the meaning of the words. Refer to the Language Transfer Handbook for phonics elements that may not transfer in children's native languages.

→ Approaching Level

Phonics

CONNECT /ôr/ TO *or, ore, oar*

TIER 2

OBJECTIVES

 Know and apply grade-level phonics and word analysis skills in decoding words. **RF.1.3**

 I Do Display the **Word-Building Card** *or*. *These are the letters* o, r. *Together they make one sound: /ôr/. I'm going to trace these letters while I say /ôr/.* Trace the letters *or* while saying /ôr/ several times. Continue with *ore* and *oar*.

 We Do *Now do it with me.* Have children trace *or* with their fingers while saying /ôr/. Trace the letters and say /ôr/ five times with children. Repeat with *ore* and *oar*.

You Do Have children connect the letters *or* to /ôr/ by tracing *or* on their palms while saying /ôr/. Then have children write the letters on their **Response Boards** as they say the sounds. Repeat with *ore* and *oar*.

Repeat, connecting *or, ore* and *oar* and the /or/ sounds throughout the week.

BLEND WORDS WITH /ôr/*or, ore, oar*

TIER 2

OBJECTIVES

 Decode regularly spelled one-syllable words. **RF.1.3b**

I Do Display Word-Building Cards *c, ore*. *This is the letter* c. *It stands for /k/. These are the letters* o, r, e. *In many words they stand for the sounds /ôr/. Say it with me: /ôr/. The* e *at the end of the word is silent. Now I'll blend the sounds: /kôr/. The word is* core. Continue with fork *and* roar.

 We Do Guide children to blend the sounds and read: *porch, more, tore, soar, fort.*

 You Do Ask children to use World-Building Cards to blend and read: *torch, horn, worn, corn, cork, fork, fort, sort, sore, soar.*

 Repeat, blending additional words with /ôr/.

You may wish to review Phonics with **ELL** using this section.

BUILD WORDS WITH /ôr/ *or, ore, oar*

OBJECTIVES

 CCSS
Decode regularly spelled one-syllable words. **RF.1.3b**

 I Do
Display Word-Building Card *oar*. *These are the letters* o, a, r. *They stand for one sound: /ôr/. These letters also make a word:* oar.

 We Do
Now let's build a word together. Point to the card for *oar* and read it together. Add the letter *s*. *I am going to add the letter* s. *Let's blend and read the new word: /sss/ /ôr/, /sssôr/,* soar.

 You Do
Have children build and blend the words *tore, store, more, bore, boar, board.*

Repeat, building additional words with *r*-controlled vowels *or, ore, oar.*

BLEND WORDS WITH /ôr/ *or, ore, oar*

OBJECTIVES

CCSS
Decode regularly spelled one-syllable words. **RF.1.3b**

 I Do
Display the Word-Building Cards *b, ore. This is the letter* b. *It stands for the /b/ sound. These are the letters* ore. *Together they stand for /ôr/. Listen as I blend the sounds in this word: /bôr/,* bore. *The word is* bore.

 We Do
Let's try some together. Blend and read: *chore, score, snore, store, wore* with children.

 You Do
Display the words to the right. Help children blend and read the words.

form	cord	cork	pork	Norm
chore	more	shore	sore	store
oar	board	roar	soar	boar
harm	thorn	gray	herd	quirk

Norm got more corn at the store.

The oar is on the shore.

What sort of sport is listed on the board?

Decodable Reader Have children read "Born to Learn," "Sport Stars," "A Board That Can Soar," and "Hard Choices" (pages 25–40).

BUILD FLUENCY WITH PHONICS

Sound-Spellings Fluency

Display the following Word-Building Cards: *or, ore, oar, ar, er, ir, ur, ey, igh, oa, oe, ee, ea, ai, ay, e_e, u_e, o_e, dge, i_e, a_e, ch, tch, wh, ph, th, sh, ng, mp, sk.* Have children chorally say the sounds. Repeat and vary the pace.

Fluency in Connected Text

Have children review the **Decodable Reader** selections. Identify words with *r*-controlled vowels and blend words as needed.

Have partners reread the selections for fluency.

→ Approaching Level

Structural Analysis

REVIEW ABBREVIATIONS

OBJECTIVES

 Know and apply grade-level phonics and word analysis skills in decoding words. **RF.1.3**

Recognize and use abbreviations

 I Do Write the word *street* and read it together. *An abbreviation is a short way to write a longer word.* Write *St*. *This is the abbreviation for* street. *Remember, with abbreviations we don't use all the letters. For street, I use uppercase* S, *lowercase* t, *and a period to show it's an abbreviation.*

 We Do Write *Mister* and read it together. *Let's write the abbreviation for* Mister. *We take away the middle letters, write an uppercase first letter, and add a period. Let's write the abbreviation:* Mr.

Repeat for *Doctor* and *Missus* and their abbreviations.

 You Do Have partners write sentences using the abbreviations St., Mr., Dr., and Mrs.

RETEACH ABBREVIATIONS

OBJECTIVES

 Know and apply grade-level phonics and word analysis skills in decoding words. **RF.1.3**

Recognize and use abbreviations

 I Do Write *Friday* and *Fri*. *An abbreviation is a short way to write a word. Here is the word* Friday *and here is the abbreviation for* Friday. *I take away day and added a period:* Fri. *When I read an abbreviation, I read the whole word, Friday.*

 We Do List and read *Sunday, Street,* and *Road. Read these words with me:* Sunday, Street, Road. *Then list the abbreviations* Rd., St., Sun. *Guide children in matching the abbreviation to the word it stands for. Then given examples of sentences using each of the words.*

 You Do Have partners work together to use the abbreviations *Fri., Sun., St., Rd.* in sentences.

Words to Know

REVIEW HIGH-FREQUENCY WORDS

OBJECTIVES

 Recognize and read grade-appropriate irregularly spelled words. **RF.1.3g**

Review *began, better, guess, learn , right, sure*

 I Do Use **High-Frequency Word Cards** to **Read/Spell/Write** each high-frequency word. Use each word orally in a sentence.

 We Do Help children to Read/Spell/Write each word on their **Response Boards**. Help them create oral sentences that include the words.

You Do Have partners do the Read/Spell/Write routine using the words *began, better, guess, learn, right, sure.*

CUMULATIVE REVIEW

OBJECTIVES

 Recognize and read grade-appropriate irregularly spelled words. **RF.1.3g**

Review previously taught high-frequency words

 I Do Display the High-Frequency Word Cards from the previous weeks. Review each word using the Read/Spell/Write routine.

 We Do Have children write each word on their Response Boards. Complete sentences for each word, such as: *Would you like another ____? Let's eat lunch before ____.*

Show each card and have children read each word together. Ask volunteers to use the words in sentences.

You Do **Fluency** Display the High-Frequency Word Cards. Point to the words in random order. Have children chorally read each word. Then repeat at a faster pace.

REVIEW VOCABULARY WORDS

OBJECTIVES

 Identify real-life connections between words and their use (e.g., note places at home that are *cozy*). **L.1.5c**

 I Do Display the **Visual Vocabulary Cards** for *idea* and *unusual*. Review each word using the Define/Example/Ask routine.

 We Do Invite children to find pictures in books or magazines that represent each word. Then work with them to complete these sentence starters: **(1)** *What is your idea about ____?* **(2)** *The unusual bike had a ____.*

 You Do Have partners write two sentences on their own, using each of the words. Provide assistance as needed.

Approaching Level

Comprehension

READ FOR FLUENCY

OBJECTIVES

CCSS Read grade-level text orally with accuracy, appropriate rate, and expression. **RF.1.4b**

 I Do Read the first page of the Practice Book selection. Model phrasing as you read, pausing slightly at the comma and longer for periods.

 We Do Read the next page of the Practice Book selection. Have children read each sentence after you. Point out how to pause slightly for commas and longer when you see a period or other end-of-sentence punctuation. Talk about how the sentence makes more sense when you pause.

 You Do Have partners alternate reading each sentence of the selection aloud. Remind them to use phrasing, and to pause for commas and end punctuation.

IDENTIFY KEY DETAILS

OBJECTIVES

CCSS Describe the connection between two individuals, events, ideas, or pieces of information in a text. **RI.1.3**

Identify key details

 I Do Remind children that they have been reading informational selections about inventors. Point out that they can find key details in the text and the illustrations.

 We Do Read the first sentences of the Practice Book selection aloud. *I can use the text and the illustration to understand more about KK's invention. The words tell what the cuff is. The illustration gives key details. Look at the illustration. How would you describe the cuff?*

 You Do Help children read the rest of the selection. Remind them to look for key details as they read.

REVIEW CONNECTIONS WITHIN TEXT: PROBLEM AND SOLUTION

OBJECTIVES

 Describe the connection between two individuals, events, ideas, or pieces of information in a text. **RI.1.3**

Identify problems and solutions in informational text

 I Do Remind children that they have been reading informational selections about inventors. As children read, they can make connections between the ideas in the text. *I can identify a problem and how it is solved and ask myself why certain events happened. Making connections helps me understand and remember what I read.*

 We Do Read the first two pages of the Practice Book selection aloud. *What was KK's problem? Let's continue reading to see how she solved her problem.*

 You Do Guide children to read the rest of the Practice Book selection. Pause and talk about KK's problem and the steps to the solution of the problem. Help children record their ideas on a Problem and Solution chart.

SELF-SELECTED READING

OBJECTIVES

 With prompting and support, read informational texts appropriately complex for grade 1. **RI.1.10**

Apply the strategy and skill to read a text

Read Independently

Have children choose an informational selection for sustained silent reading. Remind them to:

- identify the problem and the steps to the problem's solution.

- look for key details to help them.

- make connections as they read.

Read Purposefully

Guide children to record the problem and steps to the solution on a Problem and Solution chart. Then have children participate in a group discussion about the selection they read. Encourage them to:

- discuss the information that they recorded on the chart.

- tell which details helped them make connections as they read.

→ On Level

Lexile 500

OBJECTIVES

CCSS Describe the connection between two individuals, events, ideas, or pieces of information in a text. **RI.1.3**

Recognize problem and solution in a text

Leveled Reader:
The Wright Brothers

Before Reading

Preview and Predict

Have children turn to the title page. Read the title and the author's name and have children repeat. Preview the selection's photographs. Prompt children to predict what the selection might be about.

Review Genre: Nonfiction/Biography

Have children recall that a biography is the true story of a person's life written by another person.

ESSENTIAL QUESTION

Remind children of the Essential Question: *What inventions do you know about?* Set a purpose for reading: *Let's read to find out what the Wright Brothers invented.*

Remind children that as they read a selection, they can ask questions about what they do not understand or what they want to know more about.

During Reading

Guided Comprehension

As children whisper read *The Wright Brothers,* monitor and provide guidance, correcting blending and modeling the key strategies and skills.

Strategy: Ask and Answer Questions

Remind children that as they read, they can ask themselves questions and then look for answers in the text. This will help them clarify and understand the information they read. Model using the strategy on page 8. *The words say that they were sure they could make a flying machine. How will they make it? Let's read on to find out.*

Skill: Connections Within Text/Problem and Solution

Remind children that what characters want to do, change, or find out is the problem. The way the problem is solved is the solution. As you read, ask: *What did the Wright Brothers want to do?* Display a Problem and Solution chart for children to copy.

The Wright Brothers

Graphic Organizer

Retell

Model recording answers for children. Have children copy the answers into their own charts.

Think Aloud On page 8 I read that the Wright Brothers wanted to make a plane. I'll write that in the Problem box. Then I can read on to find the steps they took to solve that problem.

As they read, prompt children to fill in the chart.

After Reading

Respond to Reading

Have children complete the Respond to Reading on page 12.

Retell

Have children take turns retelling the selection, using the **Retelling Cards** as a guide. Help children make a connection by asking: *What kind of airplanes have you seen? Have you ever flown in an airplane? What was it like? What did you like most about it?*

Model Fluency

Read the sentences one at a time. Have children chorally repeat. Point out to children how to pause when you come to a comma or a period.

Apply Have partners practice reading. Provide feedback as needed.

PAIRED READ …

"Fly Away, Butterfly"

Make Connections:
Write About It *Analytical Writing*

Before reading, ask children to note that
the genre of this text is poetry. Then read the Compare Texts direction together. After reading the poem, ask children to make connections between the information they learned from "Fly Away, Butterfly" and *The Wright Brothers. How are butterflies and airplanes alike? How are they different?*

Leveled Reader

FOCUS ON SCIENCE

Children can extend their knowledge of things that fly by completing the science activity on page 16. **STEM**

Literature Circles

Lead children in conducting a literature circle using the Thinkmark questions to guide the discussion. You may wish to discuss what children have learned about flying in both selections in the Leveled Reader.

Level Up

Level-up lessons available online.

IF children can read *The Wright Brothers* On Level with fluency and correctly answer the Respond to Reading questions,

THEN tell children that they will read a more detailed version of the selection.

• Use page 8 of *The Wright Brothers* Beyond Level to model using Teaching Poster 36 to list the selection problem.

• Have children read the selection, checking their comprehension by using the graphic organizer.

On Level

Phonics

BUILD WORDS WITH /ôr/ *or, ore, oar*

OBJECTIVES

Know and apply grade-level phonics and word analysis skills in decoding words. **RF.1.3**

Build and decode words with /ôr/ *or, ore, oar*

 I Do

Display **Word-Building Cards** *p, or, k.* These are the letters p, o, r, k. *They stand for /p/ /ôr/ /k/. I'll blend /p/ /ôr/ /k/ together: /pôrk/,* pork. *The word is* pork. Remind children as needed that *or, ore,* and *oar* can all stand for the /ôr/ sound.

 We Do

Let's try blending a word together. Add *s* to the beginning of *pork* and change the *k* to *t. Let's blend: /spôrt/,* sport. *We made the word* sport.

Remove the *s* from the beginning of sport. *Let's blend and read the new word: /p/ /ôr/ /t/, /pôrt/,* port.

 You Do

Have children build and blend these words: *fork, cork, core, score, shore, short, horn, born, boar, roar.*

Decodable Reader Have children read "Born to Learn," "Sports Stars," "A Board That Can Soar," and "Hard Chores," (pages 25–40).

Words to Know

REVIEW WORDS

OBJECTIVES

Recognize and read grade-appropriate irregularly spelled words. **RF.1.3g**

Review high-frequency words: *began, better, guess, learn, right, sure* and vocabulary words *idea* and *unusual*

 I Do

Use the **Read/Spell/Write** routine to review the high-frequency words *began, better, guess, learn, right, sure* and the vocabulary words *idea* and *unusual.* Use each word orally in a sentence.

 We Do

Guide children to Read/Spell/Write each word using their **Response Boards**. Then work with them to create oral sentences using the words.

 You Do

Have partners work together to do the Read/Spell/Write routine on their own using the high-frequency words *began, better, guess, learn, right, sure* and the vocabulary words *idea* and *unusual.* Have partners write sentences about this week's selections. Each sentence must contain at least one high-frequency or vocabulary word.

Comprehension

REVIEW CONNECTIONS WITHIN TEXT: PROBLEM AND SOLUTION

OBJECTIVES

Describe the connection between two individuals, events, ideas, or pieces of information in a text. **RI.1.3**

Identify problems and solutions in informational text

Remind children that as they read, they can make connections to help them understand what they read. *I can identify a problem and how it is solved and think about the order of events. These connections help me understand what I am reading.*

Read the first two pages of the Practice Book selection aloud. *What was KK's problem? What did she do to solve her problem?*

Guide children to read the rest of the selection. Have them take time to think about KK's problem and the steps to the solution. Help them record their ideas on a Problem and Solution chart. Encourage them to use key details to help.

SELF-SELECTED READING

OBJECTIVES

With prompting and support, read informational text appropriately complex for grade 1. **RI.1.10**

Apply the strategy and skill to read a text

Read Independently

Have children choose an informational selection for sustained silent reading. Remind them to:

- identify the problem, the steps taken to solve it, and the solution.

- ask questions about things they don't understand or want to know more about as they read.

Read Purposefully

Have children record the information on a Problem and Solution chart. After they read, encourage children to take part in a group discussion about the selection they read. Guide children to:

- share information that they recorded on their chart.

- tell what interesting facts they learned reading the selections.

→ Beyond Level

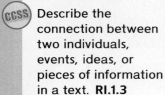

Lexile 660

 OBJECTIVES

CCSS Describe the connection between two individuals, events, ideas, or pieces of information in a text. **RI.1.3**

CCSS Know and use various text features (e.g., headings, tables of contents, glossaries, electronic menus, icons) to locate facts or information in a text. **RI.1.5**

Recognize problem and solution in a text

Leveled Reader:
The Wright Brothers

Before Reading

Preview and Predict

Read the title and author name. Have children preview the title page and the photographs. Ask: *What do you think this selection is about?*

Review Genre: Informational Text/Biography

Have children recall that a biography is the story of a person's life written by another person. Prompt children to name key characteristics of a biography. Tell them to look for these as they read the Leveled Reader. Point out that informational texts, such as biographies, often have glossaries and indexes to help define or locate information.

ESSENTIAL QUESTION

Remind children of the Essential Question: *What inventions do you know about?* Set a purpose for reading: *Let's read to find out about the Wright Brothers' invention.*

During Reading

Guided Comprehension

Have children whisper read *The Wright Brothers.* Have them place self-stick notes next to difficult words. Remind children that when they come to an unfamiliar word, they can look for familiar spellings. Point out that the glossary on page 15 can help them define and sound out some of the challenging words in the selection.

Monitor children's reading. Stop periodically and ask open-ended questions to facilitate rich discussion, such as *What does the author want you to know about the Wright brothers?* Build on children's responses to develop deeper understanding of the text.

Strategy: Ask and Answer Questions

Remind children that asking and answering questions about a selection can help them understand the information they read. Say: *Look for the answers to your questions in the text, photos, and captions.*

Go Digital

The Wright Brothers

Graphic Organizer

Skill: Connections Within Text/Problem and Solution

Remind children that what characters want to do, change, or find out is the problem. The way the problem is solved is the solution. As you read, ask: *What problems are the Wright Brothers trying to solve?* Display a Problem and Solution chart for children to copy. Model how to record the information.

Think Aloud On page 8 I read the Wright Brothers wanted to build a plane. I'll write that in the Problem box. Then I can read on to find the steps they took to solve the problem.

Have children fill in their charts as they continue reading.

After Reading

Respond to Reading

Complete the Respond to Reading on page 11 after reading.

Retell

Have children take turns retelling the selection. Help children make a personal connection by writing about an invention they use everyday. *Tell how the invention helps make your life easier.*

Leveled Reader

PAIRED READ ...

"Fly Away, Butterfly"

Make Connections: Write About It *Analytical Writing*

Before reading, "Fly Away, Butterfly," have children preview the title page and prompt them to identify the genre. Read the Compare Texts direction together. After reading the poem, have children work with a partner to discuss the information they learned in "Fly Away, Butterfly" and *The Wright Brothers.* Ask children to make connections by comparing and contrasting each selection. Prompt children to discuss what they learned about flying from both selections.

FOCUS ON SCIENCE

Children can extend their knowledge about things that fly by completing the science activity on page 16. **STEM**

Literature Circles

Lead children in conducting a literature circle using the Thinkmark questions to guide the discussion. You may wish to discuss what children have learned about flying in both selections in the Leveled Reader.

Gifted and Talented

SYNTHESIZE Challenge children to write about what life might be like if the Wright brothers had not invented the airplane. Encourage them to tell about other modes of transportation that might be used instead.

EXTEND Have children use facts they learned from the week or do additional research to find out more about transportation inventions.

Beyond Level

Vocabulary

ORAL VOCABULARY: CONTEXT CLUES

OBJECTIVES

 Use sentence-level context as a clue to the meaning of a word or phrase. **L.1.4a**

 I Do Discuss different ways that children can find the meaning of unfamiliar words. *One way to find the meaning of a word is to use context clues. I can look for words in the sentence that I already know and think about what they mean.*

 We Do Say this sentence: *The kitten was curious and explored its new home.*

Let's find the meaning of the word curious. *Let's think about words that we already know.* Guide children to use the words *new* and *explore* as clues to determining the meaning of the word *curious*.

 You Do Ask partners to create an oral sentence using the word *curious* that includes clues to the word's meaning.

 Gifted and Talented **Extend** Have partners make up a silly oral story about a curious animal. Tell them to include what the animal is curious about and what happens to it. Encourage them to draw a picture of their curious animal.

VOCABULARY WORDS: CONTEXT CLUES

OBJECTIVES

 Use sentence-level context as a clue to the meaning of a word or phrase. **L.1.4a**

I Do Remind children that sometimes they need to figure out the meaning of a word by using context. *If I don't know the meaning of a word, I can see how the word is used in the sentence and what other words in the sentence I know. That information may give me a clue about the word's meaning.*

 We Do Write and read these sentences: *"It was an unusual day. I woke up late and forgot to make my lunch. My friends also left for school early. These things never happen to me!"* Let's figure out the meaning of the word *unusual.* Guide children in identifying the last sentence as a context clue.

 You Do **Extend** Have partners write three sentences. One sentence should use the word *unusual*. The other two should provide context clues for the word.

Comprehension

REVIEW CONNECTIONS WITHIN TEXT: PROBLEM AND SOLUTION

OBJECTIVES

 CCSS Describe the connection between two individuals, events, ideas, or pieces of information in a text. **RI.1.3**

Identify problems and solutions in informational text

 I Do Discuss how children can make connections within a text by asking themselves questions, such as: *What is happening? What is the problem in the story?* They can also look for key details to help them make connections.

 We Do Ask children to read the first two pages of the Practice Book selection aloud. *What is KK's problem? How might KK solve the problem?*

 You Do Have children read the rest of the Practice Book selection independently. Have them fill in a Problem and Solution chart as they read. Remind them to use key details to help.

SELF-SELECTED READING

OBJECTIVES

 CCSS With prompting and support, read informational texts appropriately complex for grade 1. **RI.1.10**

Apply the strategy and skill to read a text

Read Independently

Have children choose an informational selection for sustained silent reading. Tell them that they should use a Problem and Solution chart to note a problem and how it was solved. They should look for details about the problem and its solution in the text and illustrations.

Read Purposefully

Have children fill in a Problem and Solution chart as they read. After reading, guide children to:

- share the information they recorded on the chart with a partner and discuss connections that they made.

- record information about the story in a reading response journal.

 Independent Study Have children write a paragraph about another way the problem in the selection they read could have been solved. Encourage them to share their paragraphs in small groups.

→ English Language Learners

Reading/Writing Workshop

OBJECTIVES

(CCSS) Describe the connection between two individuals, events, ideas, or pieces of information in a text. **RI.1.3**

Shared Read
The Story of a Robot Inventor

Go Digital

The Story of a Robot Inventor

Graphic Organizer

Before Reading

Build Background

Read the Essential Question: *What inventions do you know about?*

- Explain the meaning of the Essential Question: *An invention is something that someone creates. Sometimes people create an invention to fix a problem or change the world. Sometimes an invention makes something else better.*

- **Model an answer:** *This morning I used inventions. I used a microwave to heat up my breakfast. I used my computer to send an e-mail. Microwaves and computers are inventions.*

- Ask children a question that ties the Essential Question to their own background knowledge. *Think of things you used this morning to get ready for school. What things did someone invent?* Ask partners to share their answers.

During Reading

Interactive Question-Response

- Ask questions that help children understand the meaning of the text after each paragraph.

- Reinforce the meanings of key vocabulary by providing meanings embedded in the questions.

- Ask children questions that require them to use key vocabulary.

- Reinforce the comprehension strategies and skills of the week by modeling.

The Story of a Robot Inventor

Pages 160–161

Point to the title. *Listen as I read the title of this biography.* Point to each word as you read it. *Say the title with me.* Point to the word *Robot.* *A robot is a machine that looks a little like a person. Some robots can do jobs that people do.*

Point to the photo of Tomotaka Takahashi. *This man's name is Tomotaka Takahashi. He invents, or creates, robots. This biography will tell us about Mr. Takahashi's life and what he does.*

Pages 162–163

Point to the chapter title. *This chapter title is* Big Ideas. *Read the title with me. When Mr. Takahashi was young, he played with blocks.* Point to the last sentence. *Listen as I read this sentence:* "He used his imagination to make all sorts of forms and shapes." *That means he built things with blocks that he thought of in his mind.* Point to your head.

Read page 163. *Mr. Takahashi liked to read comic books about robots. What does the robot on page 164 look like?* (a boy) *Takahashi wanted to make a robot like this.*

What big ideas did Mr. Takahashi have as a boy? (He wanted to make a robot that looked real.)

Pages 164–165

Explain and Model the Skill *A problem can be something that needs to be fixed or changed. Mr. Takahashi learned more about robots by taking classes. What problem did he have with the robots he was studying?* (The robots bent their legs. People do not walk that way.) *Mr. Takahashi thought this was a problem. He wanted to make a robot that moves like a person.*

Explain and Model High-Frequency Words
Point to the word *learn* and have children say it with you. *What are some things that you would like to learn about?*

Pages 166–167

Point to the chapter title. *Let's read the chapter title together: "Making Better Robots." What do you think this chapter will be about? Listen as I read what Mr. Takahashi's robots could do:* "A short robot climbed up a cliff with a rope. A bigger robot lifted a car with its arms. Another robot rode a bike for 24 hours." *Point to the robot in the photo that is riding a bike.*

Let's look at page 167. What is this robot doing?

Explain and Model the Strategy *Reread the first sentence on page 167. We can stop and ask ourselves questions as we read: What will the robots do in the contests? Then we can read on to find the answers. We can also look for answers in the photographs.*

What steps do you think Mr. Takahashi took to get his robots ready for the contest?

Pages 168–169

Let's read the first sentence on page 168 together: "For the race, there were many problems to solve." One robot had to swim in water. Mr. Takahashi changed the arms to look like fins. What animal has fins? (a fish) *Fins helped the robot swim faster.*

Explain and Model Phonics *Reread page 169. Listen carefully. Raise your hand when you hear a word with the /ôr/ sounds.* (soar, more) *Now let's say the words together:* soar, more.

What do you think Mr. Takahashi will invent next?

After Reading

Make Connections
• Review the Essential Question.

→ English Language Learners

Lexile 430

OBJECTIVES

 Describe the connection between two individuals, events, ideas, or pieces of information in a text. **RI.1.3**

Leveled Reader:
The Wright Brothers

Before Reading

Preview

Read the title. Ask: *What is the title? Say it again.* Repeat with the author's name. Preview the photographs. Have children describe the photos. Use simple language to tell about each page. Follow with questions, such as: *What are the Wright Brothers doing in this photo?*

ESSENTIAL QUESTION

Remind children of the Essential Question: *What inventions do you know about?* Say: *Let's read to find out what the Wright Brothers invented.* Encourage children to ask for help when they do not understand a word or phrase.

During Reading

Interactive Question-Response

Pages 2–3 *Remember that a biography is the story of a person's life written by another person. Talk with a partner about what you know so far about the Wright Brothers and what you would like to find out.* (They flew the first airplane. They grew up in many places and loved to learn. Sample answer: Did they invent the airplane?)

Pages 4–5 *What happened to Wilbur?* (He got hurt playing hockey.) *The photo on page 4 shows where he lived when he was hurt. What does the photo on page 5 show? Let's read the caption to find out.*

Pages 6–7 *Look at the photographs on page 6. What were bicycles like before Wilbur and Orville made their bike?* (wheels were different sizes) *Now let's read page 7. Why did the Wrights save their money?* (to learn about flight)

Pages 8–9 *Look at the pictures on page 8-9. Let's read these pages together and list the steps the brothers took to solve their problem.*

Pages 10–11 *Look at the pictures on pages 10-11. Talk to your partner about why you think there is a statue for the Wright brothers on the beach.*

Go Digital

The Wright Brothers

Graphic Organizer

Retell

After Reading

Respond to Reading

Revisit the Essential Question. Ask children to work with partners to fill in the graphic organizer and answer the questions on page 12. Pair children with peers of varying language abilities.

Retell

Model retelling using the **Retelling Card** prompts. Say: *Look at the illustrations. Use details to help you retell the selection.* Help children make personal connections by asking: *Have you ever flown in an airplane? If yes, tell what it was like? If no, would you like to? Why or why not?*

Phrasing Fluency: Commas, Period

Read the pages in the book, one at a time. Help children echo-read the pages expressively and with appropriate phrasing. Remind them to pause when they come to a comma or period.

Apply Have children practice reading with partners. Pair children with peers of varying language abilities. Provide feedback as needed.

PAIRED READ ...

"Fly Away, Butterfly"

Make Connections: Write About It *Analytical Writing*

Before reading, tell children to note that this text is poetry. Then read the Compare Texts direction together.

After reading the poem, ask children to make connections between the information they learned from "Fly Away, Butterfly" and *The Wright Brothers*. Prompt children by providing a sentence frame: *An airplane is like a butterfly because ____.*

Leveled Reader

FOCUS ON SCIENCE

Children can extend their knowledge of things that fly by completing the science activity on page 16. **STEM**

Literature Circles

Lead children in conducting a literature circle using the Thinkmark questions to guide the discussion. You may wish to discuss what children have learned about flying from the two selections in the Leveled Reader.

Level Up

Level-up lessons available online.

IF children can read *The Wright Brothers* ELL Level with fluency and correctly answer the Respond to Reading questions,

THEN tell children that they will read a more detailed version of the selection.

• Use page 8 of *The Wright Brothers* On Level to model using Teaching Poster 36 to list the story problem.

• Have children read the selection, checking their comprehension by using the graphic organizer.

English Language Learners
Vocabulary

PRETEACH ORAL VOCABULARY

OBJECTIVES

Produce complete sentences when appropriate to task and situation. **SL.1.6**

LANGUAGE OBJECTIVE

Use oral vocabulary words

 I Do Display the images from the **Visual Vocabulary Cards** to preteach the oral vocabulary words *curious* and *improve*.

 We Do Display the images again and talk about how they illustrate or demonstrate the words. Model using sentences to describe the image.

You Do Display each word again and have partners discuss how the picture demonstrates each word. Ask children to chorally say the words several times.

Beginning	Intermediate	Advanced/High
Ask: *What is something unusual you see?* Emphasize the vocabulary word and point to the Visual Vocabulary Card.	Have children find a picture in a classroom book that relates to each word. Help them use the word to describe the picture.	Challenge children to use both words in a sentence. Help them to read and write the sentences.

PRETEACH VOCABULARY

OBJECTIVES

Identify real-life connections between words and their use (e.g., note places at home that are *cozy*). **SL.1.6**

LANGUAGE OBJECTIVE

Use vocabulary words

 I Do Display images from the **ELL Visual Vocabulary Cards** one at a time to preteach the vocabulary words *flight* and *tested* and follow the routine. Say the word and have children repeat it. Define the word in English.

 We Do Display the image again and explain how it illustrates the word. Ask children what they see in the picture. Model using sentences to discuss the image.

 You Do Display the word again. Have children say and spell the word. Provide opportunities for children to use the words in speaking and writing. Provide sentence starters.

Beginning	Intermediate	Advanced/High
Ask children to repeat each word. Say a sentence for them to repeat.	Have children complete sentence starters using the words.	Have partners write their own sentence for each word.

Words to Know

REVIEW WORDS

OBJECTIVES

Recognize and read grade-appropriate irregularly spelled words. **RF.1.3g**

_____

LANGUAGE OBJECTIVE

Use high-frequency and vocabulary words

 I Do Display the **High-Frequency Word** and **Vocabulary Cards** for _began, better, guess, learn, right, sure,_ and _idea_ and _unusual._ Read each word. Use the Read/Spell/Write routine to teach each word. Help children write each word on their **Response Boards**.

 We Do Write sentence frames. Track the print as children read and complete the sentences: **(1)** _The game began at ____._ **(2)** _Do you like rice better than ____?_ **(3)** _Mom made a guess about ____._ **(4)** _What did you learn about ____?_ **(5)** _The person to my right is ____._ **(6)** _Are you sure about the ____?_ **(7)** _He had a good idea for making ____._ **(8)** _Look at that unusual ____!_

 You Do Display the High-Frequency Word Cards from the previous weeks. Display one card at a time as children chorally read the word. Mix and repeat. Note words children need to review. Repeat with vocabulary words.

Beginning	Intermediate	Advanced/High
Display the cards and read each word together. Use each word in a sentence and have children point to the card.	List the words. Have partners use Word-Building Cards to form and read the words.	Give clues and have children name the word. _This word has five letters. It begins with the /b/ sound._

RETEACH HIGH-FREQUENCY WORDS

OBJECTIVES

Recognize and read grade-appropriate irregularly spelled words. **RF.1.3g**

_____

LANGUAGE OBJECTIVE

Use high-frequency words

 I Do Display each Visual Vocabulary Card and say the word aloud. Define the word in English and, if appropriate, in Spanish. Identify any cognates.

 We Do Point to the image again and explain how it illustrates or demonstrates the word. Ask children to repeat the word. Guide children in structured partner-talk about the image as prompted on the back of the card. Ask children to chorally say the word several times.

 You Do Display each visual in random order, hiding the word. Have children identify the word and explain it in their own words.

Beginning	Intermediate	Advanced/High
Display the High-Frequency Word Cards and read the words. Then hold up a Visual Vocabulary Card and have children find the matching card.	List the words and read them together. Ask questions to reinforce the meaning of each word.	Have partners take turns using the words in oral sentences.

English Language Learners
Writing/Spelling

WRITING TRAIT: WORD CHOICE

OBJECTIVES

 Write narratives in which they recount two or more appropriately sequenced events, include some details regarding what happened, use temporal words to signal event order, and provide some sense of closure. **W.1.3**

LANGUAGE OBJECTIVE

Use time-order words

I Do Explain that writers use special words to show when events happen and the order in which they happen. Write and read: *Meg and Dad made the cart. Next they painted it. After the paint dried, Meg took a ride.* Point out time-order words *Next* and *After*. Have children identify the order of events.

We Do Read the first sentence on page 163 of *The Story of a Robot Inventor*. Ask children which word helps show when events happen. *(Later)* Explain that writers use time-order words to help readers understand what they wrote. Repeat the exercise on page 164. (In 1999; *began; then*)

You Do Have children write two sentences about something they built or made with someone. Remind them to include time-order words.

Beginning	Intermediate	Advanced/High
Have children tell what they made. Repeat back using time-order words. Have them repeat the sentences.	Provide sentence frames for children to complete: *First we ____. Then we ____.* Have them read the completed sentences.	Have children write their own sentences. Challenge them to write more than two sentences.

WORDS WITH /ôr/or, ore, oar

OBJECTIVES

 Use conventional spelling for words with common spelling patterns and for frequently occurring irregular words. **L.1.2d**

LANGUAGE OBJECTIVE

Spell words with *r*-controlled vowels *or, ore, oar*

I Do Read aloud the Spelling Words on page T170. Write *born* and point out the *or* spelling pattern. Explain that these letters stand for the /ôr/ sounds. Segment and read the word. Continue with the rest of the words.

We Do Say a sentence for *born*. Then say the word *born* slowly and ask children to repeat. Have them write the word. Repeat the process for the remaining words.

You Do Display the words. Have partners check their spelling lists. Help children correct any misspelled words.

Beginning	Intermediate	Advanced/High
Help children write each word and say it with you.	Have partners use words to ask and answer questions.	Ask children to sort words by the spellings for /ôr/: *or, ore, oar.* Have them use the words in sentences.

Grammar

ADJECTIVES THAT COMPARE

OBJECTIVES

Use frequently occurring adjectives. **L.1.1f**

LANGUAGE OBJECTIVE
Use correct form of comparison adjectives

Language Transfers Handbook

TRANSFER SKILLS
Hmong, Korean, Spanish, or Khmer speakers may avoid comparison adjectives. For example, they may say: The dog is more big than the cat. Provide support for these children by substituting and modeling the correct adjective: *More big means bigger. The dog is bigger than the cat.*

 I Do

Remind children that some adjectives help us tell how two or more people, places, or things are alike or different. Write the sentences on the board: *The dog jumps a high fence. Then he jumps a higher fence.* Underline the words *high* and *higher*.

The word high *tells how high one fence was. I added* -er *to the word* high *to make* higher. *This word compares the two fences. One fence was higher than another fence.* Sketch the two fences and point to the one that is higher. Then draw an even higher fence. *This fence is the highest. The ending* -est *tells us that. We use* -est *to compare more than two things.*

 We Do

Write these sentences and work together to read them. Underline the comparison adjective.

The water here is deep.

The pond water is deeper. (deeper)

The sea has the deepest water. (deepest)

Say: *The adjectives compare how deep water is in three places. Which place has the water that is the deepest? Which ending did we add to* deep *to compare?*

 You Do

Write these words on the board:

dark   darker   darkest

Have partners use each word in a sentence. Talk about the comparisons. Listen as you circulate and help children who need guidance.

Beginning	Intermediate	Advanced/High
Help children use comparison adjectives to describe pictures in this week's stories. Provide sentence frames to help.	Display pictures from the week's stories and ask children to explain what they see. Help them use comparison adjectives.	Display a story from the week and guide children to retell the story. Encourage them to use comparison adjectives.

PROGRESS MONITORING

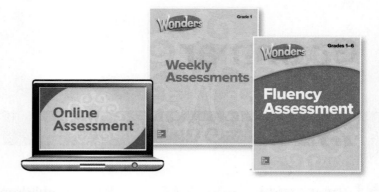

Unit 5 Week 3 Formal Assessment	Standards Covered	Component for Assessment
Comprehension Connections Within Text: Problem and Solution	RI.1.3	• *Selection Test* • *Weekly Assessment*
Vocabulary Strategy Prefixes	L.2.4b	• *Selection Test* • *Weekly Assessment*
Phonics *r*-Controlled Vowels *or, ore, oar*	RF.1.3	*Weekly Assessment*
Structural Analysis Abbreviations	RF.1.3	*Weekly Assessment*
High-Frequency Words *began, better, guess, learn, right, sure*	RF.1.3g	*Weekly Assessment*
Writing Writing About Text	RI.1.3	*Weekly Assessment*
Unit 5 Week 3 Informal Assessment		
Research/Listening/Collaborating	SL.1.1c, SL.1.2, SL.1.3	• *RWW* • *Teacher's Edition*
Oral Reading Fluency (ORF) **Fluency Goal:** 13-33 words correct per minute (WCPM) **Accuracy Rate Goal:** 95% or higher	RF.1.4a. RF.1.4b, RF.1.4c	*Fluency Assessment*

Using Assessment Results

Weekly Assessment Skills	If . . .	Then . . .
COMPREHENSION	Children answer 0–3 multiple-choice items correctly . . .	. . . assign Lessons 79-81 on Problem and Solution and Lessons 88-90 on Text Connections from the *Tier 2 Comprehension Intervention online PDFs*.
VOCABULARY	Children answer 0–2 multiple-choice items correctly . . .	. . . assign Lesson 100 on Prefixes *un-, dis-* from the *Tier 2 Vocabulary Intervention online PDFs*.
PHONICS/ STRUCTURAL ANALYSIS/HFW	Children answer 0–6 multiple-choice items correctly . . .	. . . assign Lesson 89 on *r*-Controlled Vowels /ôr/ *or*, Lesson 90 on *r*-Controlled Vowels /ôr/ *ore, oar*, and Lesson 85 on Abbreviations from the *Tier 2 Phonics/Word Study Intervention online PDFs*.
WRITING	Children score less than "2" on the constructed response . . .	. . . reteach necessary skills using Section 13 on Write About Reading from the *Tier 2 Comprehension Intervention online PDFs*.
	Children have a WCPM score of 13 . . .	. . . assign a lesson from Section 1, 9, or 10 of the *Tier 2 Fluency Intervention online PDFs*.
	Children have a WCPM score of 0–12 . . .	. . . assign a lesson from Sections 2–8 of the *Tier 2 Fluency Intervention online PDFs*.

Using Weekly Data

Check your data Dashboard to verify assessment results and guide grouping decisions.

Response to Intervention

Data-Driven Recommendations

Use the children's assessment results to assist you in identifying children who will benefit from focused intervention.

Use the appropriate sections of the *Placement and Diagnostic Assessment* to designate children requiring:

TIER 2 Intervention Online PDFs

TIER 3 WonderWorks Intervention Program

Build Knowledge
Sounds All Around

 Essential Question:
What sounds can you hear? How are they made?

Teach and Model
Close Reading and Writing

Big Book and Little Book

Reading Writing Workshop

Now, What's That Sound?, 180–189
Genre Realistic Fiction **Lexile** 240

Interactive Read Aloud

"The Squeaky Bed,"
Genre: Folktale

Practice and Apply
Close Reading and Writing

Literature Anthology *Whistle for Willie,* 226–255
Genre Fiction **Lexile** 520

Paired Read

"Shake! Strike! Strum!," 256–259
Genre Nonfiction Text **Lexile** 290

Differentiated Texts

APPROACHING
Lexile 180

ON LEVEL
Lexile 390

BEYOND
Lexile 420

ELL
Lexile 170

Leveled Readers

Extended Complex Texts

The Top Job
Genre Fiction
Lexile 880

Owl at Home
Genre Fiction
Lexile 370

Classroom Library

Student Outcomes

Close Reading of Complex Text

- Cite relevant evidence from text
- Describe plot events: problem and solution
- Retell the text

RL.1.3, RL.1.2

Writing

Write to Sources

- Draw evidence from fiction text
- Write narrative text
- Conduct short research about what sounds can be heard

W.1.3, W.1.7

Speaking and Listening

- Engage in collaborative conversation the sounds around us
- Retell and discuss *Whistle for Willie*
- Present information on what sounds can be heard

SL.1.1c, SL.1.2, SL.1.3

Content Knowledge

- Explore the sounds around us

Language Development

Conventions

- Use *a, an, this,* and *that*

Vocabulary Acquisition

- Develop oral Vocabulary

  | volume | senses | squeaky |
  | nervous | distract | |

- Acquire and use academic vocabulary

  suddenly   scrambled

- Use context clues to understand suffixes

L.1.1h, L.1.4b, L.1.6

Foundational Skills

Phonics/Word Study/Spelling

- diphthongs *ou, ow*
- comparative inflectional endings *-er, -est*
- cow, town, mouse, how, out, mouth

High-Frequency Words

color   early   instead   nothing   oh   thought

Fluency

- Expression

Decodable Text

- Apply foundational skills in connected text

RF.1.3, RF.1.3f, RF.1.3g, RF.1.4a, RF.1.4b, RF.1.4c

Professional Development

- See lessons in action in real classrooms.
- Get expert advice on instructional practices.
- Collaborate with other teachers.
- Access PLC Resources

Go Digital! www.connected.mcgraw-hill.com.

INSTRUCTIONAL PATH

1 ## Talk About Sounds All Around

Guide children in collaborative conversations.

Discuss the essential question: *What sounds can you hear? How are they made?*

Develop academic language.

Listen to "The Squeaky Bed" to ask and answer questions about the story.

2 ## Read *Now What's That Sound?*

Apply foundational skills in connected text. Model close reading.

Read

Now, What's That Sound? to learn about the sounds you hear, and where they come from, citing text evidence to answer text-dependent questions.

Reread

Now, What's That Sound? to analyze text, craft, and structure, citing text evidence.

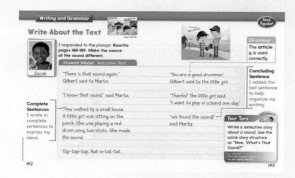

3 ## Write About *Now What's That Sound?*

Model writing to a source.

Analyze a short response student model.

Use text evidence from close reading to write to a source.

4 Read and Write About *Whistle for Willie*

Practice and apply close reading of the anchor text.

Read

Whistle for Willie to learn about the sounds we can create.

Reread

Whistle for Willie and use text evidence to understand how the author uses text, craft, and structure to develop a deeper understanding of the story.

Integrate

Information about sounds you can create.

Write to a Source, citing text evidence to write a new story about a time Willie learned to play an instrument or sing a song.

5 Independent Partner Work

Gradual release of support to independent work

- Text-Dependent Questions
- Scaffolded Partner Work
- Talk with a Partner
- Cite Text Evidence
- Complete a sentence frame.
- Guided Text Annotation

6 Integrate Knowledge and Ideas

Connect Texts

Text to Text Discuss how each of the texts answers the question: What sounds can you hear? How are they made?

Text to Songs Compare information about sounds in the texts read with the sounds in the song "I Have a Car."

Conduct a Short Research Project

Create a sound effects chart.

DEVELOPING READERS AND WRITERS

Write to Sources: Narrative

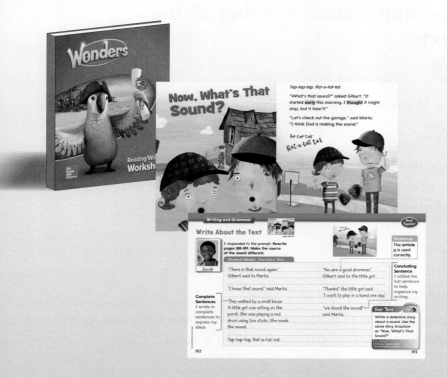

Day 1 and Day 2

Shared Writing

- Write a new page with sound words for the middle of the story, p. T252

Interactive Writing

- Analyze a student model, p. T262

- Write a new detective story about a sound, p. T263

- Find Text Evidence

- Apply Writing Trait: Sentence Fluency: Use Complete Sentences, p. T263

- Apply Grammar Skill: Using *a*, *an*, *this*, and *that*, p. T263

Day 3, Day 4 and Day 5

Independent Writing

- Write a new story about Peter from *Whistle for Willie*, p. T270

- Provide scaffolded instruction to meet student needs, p. T270

- Find Text Evidence, p. T270

- Apply Writing Trait: Sentence Fluency: Use Complete Sentences, p. T270

- Prewrite and Draft, p. T270

- Revise and Edit, p. T276

- Final Draft, p. T277

- Present, Evaluate, and Publish, p. T282

Grammar

Other Adjectives

- Use other adjectives to tell about what is happening, pp. T253, T263, T271, T277, T283

- Apply grammar to writing, pp. T253, T270, T276, T283

Mechanics: Capitalize/Underline Book Titles

- Use capitalization and underlines with book titles, pp. T271, T277, T283

Online PDFs

Grammar Practice, pp. 116–120

Online Grammar Games

Spelling

Words with Diphthongs *ou, ow*

- Spell words with Diphthongs *oi, oy*

Online PDFs

Phonics/Spelling blms
pp. 116–120

Online Spelling Games

SUGGESTED LESSON PLAN

READING		DAY 1	DAY 2
Teach, Model and Apply	**Core**	**Build Background** Sounds All Around, T242–T243	**Oral Language** Sounds All Around, T254
		Oral Vocabulary *volume, senses,* T242	**Oral Vocabulary** *distract, nervous, senses, squeaky, volume,* T254
		Word Work T246–T249	**Word Work** T256–T259
		• Fluency: Sound-Spellings	• Phonemic Awareness: Phoneme Isolation
		• Phonemic Awareness: Phoneme Substitution	• Structural Analysis: Inflectional Endings *-er, -est*
		• Phonics/Spelling: Introduce Diphthongs *ou, ow*	• Vocabulary: *scrambled, suddenly*
		• High-Frequency Words: *color, early, instead, nothing, oh, thought*	**Shared Read** *Now, What's That Sound?* T260–T261
		• Vocabulary: *scrambled, suddenly*	• Genre: Realistic Fiction, T260
		Shared Read *Now, What's That Sound?* T250–T251	• Skill: Plot: Problem and Solution, T261
	Options	**Listening Comprehension** "The Squeaky Bed," T244–T245	**Listening Comprehension** "The Squeaky Bed," T255
			Word Work T256–T259
			• Phonics/Spelling: Review Diphthongs *ou, ow*
			• High-Frequency Words

LANGUAGE ARTS			
Writing **Grammar**	**Core**	**Shared Writing** T252	**Interactive Writing** T262
		Grammar Using *A* and *An,* T253	**Grammar** Using *This* and *That,* T263
	Options		

DIFFERENTIATED INSTRUCTION Use your data dashboard to determine each student's needs. Then select instructional supports options throughout the week.

APPROACHING LEVEL

Leveled Reader
Thump, Jangle, Crash, T286–T287
"How to Make Maracas," T287
Literature Circles, T287

Phonological Awareness:
Phoneme Isolation, T288 [TIER 2]
Phoneme Blending, T288
Phoneme Substitution, T289

Phonics
Connect *ou, ow* to /ou/, T290 [TIER 2]
Blend Words with /ou/ *ou, ow,* T290 [TIER 2]
Build Fluency with Phonics, T291

Structural Analysis
Review Inflectional Endings, T292

Words to Know Review, T293

Comprehension
Read for Fluency, T294 [TIER 2]
Identify Events, T294 [TIER 2]
Review Connection Within Text: Problem and Solution, T295
Self-Selected Reading, T295

ON LEVEL

Leveled Reader
Down on the Farm, T296–T297
"How To Make a Rain Stick," T297
Literature Circles, T297

Phonics
Build Words with /ou/ *ou, ow,* T298

DAY 3	DAY 4	DAY 5
Fluency Expression, T265 **Word Work** T266–T269 • Phonemic Awareness: Phoneme Blending • Phonics/Spelling: Blend with Diphthongs *ou, ow* • Vocabulary Strategy: Suffixes **Close Reading** *Whistle for Willie,* T269A–T269P	**Extend the Concept** T272–T273 • Text Feature: Directions, T273 • Close Reading: "Shake! Strike! Strum!" T273A–T273B **Word Work** T274–T275 • Phonemic Awareness: Phoneme Isolation • Structural Analysis: Infectional Endings *-er, -est* **Integrate Ideas** • Research and Inquiry, T278–T279	**Word Work** T280–T281 • Phonemic Awareness: Phoneme Blending/ Sustitution • Phonics/Spelling: Blend and Build with /ou/*ou, ow* • Structural Analysis: Inflectional Endings *-er, -est* • High-Frequency Words • Vocabulary: *scrambled, suddenly* **Integrate Ideas** • Text Connections, T284–T285
Oral Language Sounds All Around, T264 **Word Work** T266-T269 • Structural Analysis: Inflectional Endings *-er, -est* • High-Frequency Words	**Word Work** T274–T275 • Fluency: Sound-Spellings • Phonics/Spelling: Build Words with Diphthongs *ou, ow* • High-Frequency Words • Vocabulary: *scrambled, suddenly* **Close Reading:** *Whistle for Willie,* T269A–T269P	**Word Work** T280–T281 • Fluency: Expression **Integrate Ideas** • Research and Inquiry, T284 • Speaking and Listening, T285
Independent Writing T270 **Grammar** Mechanics: Capitalize/Underline Book Titles, T271	**Independent Writing** T276 **Grammar** Mechanics: Capitalize/Underline Book Titles, T277	**Independent Writing** T282 **Grammar** Mechanics: Capitalize/Underline Book Titles, T283
Grammar Using *A, An, This,* and *That,* T271	**Grammar** Using *A, An, This,* and *That,* T277	**Grammar** Using *A, An, This,* and *That,* T283

BEYOND LEVEL

Words to Know
Review Words, T298

Comprehension
Review Connections Within Text: Problem and Solution, T299
Self-Selected Reading, T299

Leveled Reader
Going on a Bird Walk, T300–T301
"How to Make a Wind Chime," T301
Literature Circles, T301

Vocabulary
Multiple Meaning Words, T302

Comprehension
Review Problem and Solution, T303
Self-Selected Reading, T303

Gifted and Talented

ENGLISH LANGUAGE LEARNERS

Shared Read
Now, What's That Sound? T304–T305

Leveled Reader
Down on the Farm, T306–T307
"How to Make a Rain Stick," T307
Literature Circles, T307

Vocabulary
Preteach Oral Vocabulary, T308
Preteach ELL Vocabulary, T308

Words to Know
Review Words, T309
Reteach High-Frequency Words, T309

Writing/Spelling
Writing Trait: Sentence Fluency, T310
Words with /ou/*ou, ow,* T310

Grammar
Using *A, An, This,* and *That,* T311

DIFFERENTIATE TO ACCELERATE

  Scaffold to **A**ccess **C**omplex **T**ext

IF	the text complexity of a particular selection is too difficult for children
THEN	see the references noted in the chart below for scaffolded instruction to help children Access Complex Text.

TEXT COMPLEXITY
Qualitative / Quantitative
Reader and Task

Reading/Writing Workshop	Literature Anthology	Leveled Readers	Classroom Library

Quantitative

Now, What's That Sound? **Lexile** 240	*Whistle for Willie* **Lexile** 520 *"Shake! Strike! Strum!"* **Lexile** 290	**Approaching Level** **Lexile** 180 **Beyond Level** **Lexile** 420 **On Level** **Lexile** 390 **ELL** **Lexile** 170	*The Top Job* **Lexile** 880 *Owl at Home* **Lexile** 370

Qualitative

What Makes the Text Complex?	**What Makes the Text Complex?**	**What Makes the Text Complex?**	**What Makes the Text Complex?**
Foundational Skills • Decoding with diphthongs *ou, ow*, T246–T247 • Reading words with inflectional endings *-er, -est*, T257 • Identifying high-frequency words, T248–T249 *See Scaffolded Instruction in Teacher's Edition, T246–T247, T248–T249, and T257.*	• **Sentence Structure,** T269B, T269C • **Organization,** T269B, T269E, T269I **ACT** *See Scaffolded Instruction in Teacher's Edition, T269B, T269C, T269E, and T269I.*	**Foundational Skills** • Decoding with diphthongs *ou, ow* • Reading words with inflectional endings *-er, -est* • Identifying high-frequency words *color early instead nothing oh thought* *See Level Up lessons online for Leveled Readers.*	• **Purpose** • **Specific Vocabulary** • **Prior Knowledge** • **Sentence Structure** • **Organization** • **Connection of Ideas** • **Genre** **ACT** *See Scaffolded Instruction in Teacher's Edition, T413–T415.*

Reader and Task

The Introduce the Concept lesson on pages T242–T243 will help determine the reader's knowledge and engagement in the weekly concept. See pages T250–T251, T260–T261, T278–T279 and T284–T285 for questions and tasks for this text.	**The** Introduce the Concept lesson on pages T242–T243 will help determine the reader's knowledge and engagement in the weekly concept. See pages T269A–T269P, T273A–T273B, T278–T279 and T284–T285 for questions and tasks for this text.	**The** Introduce the Concept lesson on pages T242–T243 will help determine the reader's knowledge and engagement in the weekly concept. See pages T286–T287, T296–T297, T300–T301, T306–T307, T278–T279 and T284–T285 for questions and tasks for this text.	**The** Introduce the Concept lesson on pages T242–T243 will help determine the reader's knowledge and engagement in the weekly concept. See pages T413–T415 for questions and tasks for this text.

Go Digital! www.connected.mcgraw-hill.com

Monitor and *Differentiate*

✓ Quick Check

To differentiate instruction, use the Quick Checks to assess students' needs and select the appropriate small group instruction focus.

Comprehension Strategy Ask and Answer Questions, T245

Comprehension Skill Plot: Problem and Solution, T261

Phonics /ou/ *ou, ow,* T249, T259, T269, T275, T281

High-Frequency Words and Vocabulary T249, T259, T269, T275, T281

If No →

| Approaching Level | Reteach T286–T295 |
| ELL | Develop T304–T311 |

If Yes →

| On Level | Review T296–T299 |
| Beyond Level | Extend T300–T303 |

Using Weekly Data

Check your data Dashboard to verify assessment results and guide grouping decisions.

Level Up with Leveled Readers

IF children can read their leveled text fluently and answer comprehension questions

THEN work with the next level up to accelerate children's reading with more complex text.

Going on a Bird Walk — Beyond — T297

Down on the Farm — *by Amy Helfer, illustrated by Cory Pillo* — On Level

Thump, Jangle, Crash — *by Amy Helfer, illustrated by Michelle Dorenkamp* — Approaching — T287

Down on the Farm — *by Amy Helfer, illustrated by Cory Pillo* — ELL — T307

ELL ENGLISH LANGUAGE LEARNERS

Small Group Instruction

Use the ELL small group lessons in the *Wonders* Teacher's Edition to provide focused instruction.

Language Development
Vocabulary preteaching, oral vocabulary preteaching, high-frequency word review and reteach, pp. T308–T309

Close Reading
Interactive Question-Response routines for scaffolded text-dependent questioning for reading and rereading the Shared Read and Leveled Reader, pp. T304–T307

Writing
Focus on the writing trait, grammar, and spelling, pp. T310–T311

Additional ELL Support

Use Wonders for English Learners for ELD instruction that connects to the core.

Language Development
My Language Book for ample opportunities for discussions and scaffolded language support

Close Reading
Guided support for the Shared Read, Big Books, and Interactive Read Alouds. Differentiated texts about the weekly concept

Writing
Guided support in Interactive and Independent Writing and writing to sources

Wonders for ELs Teacher Edition and My Language Book

Materials

Reading/Writing Workshop
VOLUME 4

Reading/Writing Workshop Big Book
UNIT 5

Visual Vocabulary Cards
distract
nervous
senses
squeaky
volume

color

High-Frequency Word Cards
color
early
instead
nothing
oh
thought

suddenly

Vocabulary Cards
suddenly
scrambled

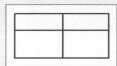

Teaching Poster

ow
ou
cow

Sound-Spelling Cards

Interactive Read-Aloud Cards

Think Aloud Clouds

a b c

Word-Building Cards

→ # Introduce the Concept

Go Digital

Reading/Writing Workshop Big Book

OBJECTIVES

CCSS Ask questions to clear up any confusion about the topics and texts under discussion. **SL.1.1c**

• Build background knowledge
• Discuss the Essential Question

ACADEMIC LANGUAGE

• *instrument, list, describe*
• Cognates: *instrumento, lista, describir*

Sounds All Around

Video

school

Visual Glossary

Graphic Organizer

MINILESSON 5 Mins
Build Background

ESSENTIAL QUESTION

What sounds can you hear? How are they made?

Tell children that this week they will be talking and reading about different sounds around them and how they are made.

Oral Vocabulary Words

Tell children that you will share some words that they can use as they discuss sound. Use the Define/Example/Ask routine to introduce the oral vocabulary words **volume** and **senses**.

Visual Vocabulary Cards

Oral Vocabulary Routine

<u>Define:</u> The **volume** is the level of sound—whether loud or soft.

<u>Example:</u> Turn down the volume on the TV when I am on the phone.

<u>Ask:</u> Do you like to listen to music with the volume up or down?

<u>Define:</u> The **senses** give us information about the world around us.

<u>Example:</u> The five senses are seeing, hearing, feeling, tasting, and smelling.

<u>Ask:</u> Which of your senses do you use when you listen to a story your teacher reads?

Discuss the theme of "Sounds All Around" and explain that we are surrounded by sounds. Have children name sounds they hear right now. *Which sound would you like the volume turned down on? Which sound would you like the volume turned up? How are you using your senses right now? What are they telling you?*

READING/WRITING WORKSHOP, pp. 174–175

Talk About It: Sounds All Around

 Guide children to discuss how the children in the picture make sounds.

- What kinds of sounds are the children making?

- What in the picture is making sound?

Use Teaching Poster 42 and prompt children to complete the chart by sharing ideas about instruments and the sounds they make.

Children can look at page 175 of their Reading/Writing Workshop and do the Talk About It activity with a partner.

Instrument	Sound It Makes

Teaching Poster

Collaborative Conversations

Ask and Answer Questions As children engage in partner, small group, and whole group discussions, encourage them to:

- ask questions about ideas they do not understand.

- give others a chance to think after asking a question.

- write down questions they want to ask the teacher or the whole class.

ENGLISH LANGUAGE LEARNERS SCAFFOLD

Beginning

Use Visuals Tell children about the instruments. Ask: *Does a [drum] make sound? Can it make a loud sound? Can it make a soft sound? Show me how you would play a [drum]. Can you make a sound like a [drum]?* Correct the meaning of children's responses as needed.

Intermediate

Describe Ask children to describe the objects in the picture that make sound. Have them identify those they have heard or played. Elicit more details to support children's answers.

Advanced/High

Discuss Have children share their own experiences hearing or playing musical instruments. Model correct pronunciation as needed.

→ # Listening Comprehension

"The Squeaky Bed"

Read the Interactive Read Aloud

MINILESSON
10 Mins

OBJECTIVES

CCSS Participate in collaborative conversations with diverse partners about *grade 1 topics and texts* with peers and adults in small and larger groups. **SL.1.1**

• Develop concept understanding

• Develop reading strategy ask and answer questions

ACADEMIC LANGUAGE

• questions, events, text, illustration, squeaks

• Cognates: *texto, ilustración*

Connect to Concept: Sounds All Around

Tell children that they will now read a story about a bed that squeaks. Ask: *Can you make a sound like a squeaky bed?*

Focus on Oral Vocabulary

Review the oral vocabulary words *senses* and *volume*. Use the Define/Example/Ask routine to introduce the oral vocabulary words *distract, nervous,* and *squeaky*. Prompt children to use the words as they discuss sounds.

> ### Oral Vocabulary Routine
>
> **Define:** If something **distracts** you, it takes your attention away from what you were focused on.
>
> **Example:** The sound of his brother playing can distract Jon from his homework.
>
> **Ask:** What can distract you when you are working?
>
> **Define:** If you feel nervous, you feel worried.
>
> **Example:** Fran was **nervous** about jumping off the diving board for the first time.
>
> **Ask:** What makes you nervous?
>
> **Define:** A **squeaky** sound is a high-pitched sound.
>
> **Example:** The rusty gate made a squeaky sound when it opened.
>
> **Ask:** Would you want to hear squeaky sounds when you were trying to sleep? Why or why not?

Visual Vocabulary Cards

Go Digital

"The Squeaky Bed"

I wonder...

Ask and Answer Questions

school

Visual Glossary

Retell

Set a Purpose for Reading

- Display the Interactive Read-Aloud Cards.
- Read aloud the title and the information about the story's origin.
- Tell children that you will be reading a story about a girl whose squeaky bed scares her. Tell children to read to find out how her family solves the problem.

Strategy: Ask and Answer Questions

1 Explain Remind children that as they read or listen to a story, they can ask themselves questions about the text. This can help them understand the story.

Think Aloud One way to better understand a text is to ask questions about the story events and then look for the answers as you read. Today, as we read "The Squeaky Bed," I will ask myself questions about the story. Then I will look for answers in the text and illustrations.

2 Model Read the selection. As you read, use the Think Aloud Cloud to model the strategy.

Think Aloud Remember that you can ask questions as you read and then look for the answers in the text and illustrations. The text says that Marta curls up in her new bed. I ask myself if she will be able to sleep. When I read on, I learn that the bed squeaks, which makes Marta cry. As I continue reading, I will look for the answers to more of my questions.

3 Guided Practice As you continue to read, pause to elicit questions and answers from children. *What questions can you ask about the story?* Pause to help children find the answers. Guide children in using the evidence in the text and illustrations to ask and answer questions.

Respond to Reading

After reading, prompt children to retell "The Squeaky Bed." Talk about the sounds in the story. Discuss what questions they asked and where they found the answers.

ENGLISH LANGUAGE LEARNERS SCAFFOLD

Beginning

Engage Display Card 1 of "The Squeaky Bed." *You can look at the illustrations to answer some questions. Who is in the girl's family? I see a mother, a father, a dog, and a cat. The picture helped me answer my question.*

Intermediate

Describe Display Card 2 of "The Squeaky Bed." Point to the girl in the illustration. *I wonder why Marta is crying. Is she sad? Let's look for the answer in the text.*

Advanced/High

Describe Display Card 2 of "The Squeaky Bed." Have children describe the illustration. *Why do you think Marta is crying? Can you find the answer in the text?* Clarify children's responses as needed by providing vocabulary.

Monitor and *Differentiate*

 Quick Check

Can children apply the strategy ask and answer questions?

Small Group Instruction

If No →	Approaching	Reteach pp. T286–287
	ELL	Develop pp. T304–311
If Yes →	On Level	Review pp. T296–297
	Beyond Level	Extend pp. T300–301

→ # Word Work

MINILESSON 5 Mins

Phonemic Awareness

OBJECTIVES

CCSS Decode regularly spelled one-syllable words. **RF.1.3b**

Substitute phonemes in words

Phoneme Substitution

1 Model Show children how to orally substitute vowel sounds. *I am going to say a word:* lid, /l/ /i/ /d/. *Now I will change the vowel sound to make a new word. I will change the /i/ sound to /ou/. The new word is /l/ /ou/ /d/,* loud.

2 Guided Practice/Practice Have children practice substituting vowel sounds. *I will say a word. Then I want you to change the vowel sound to /ou/. What's the new word?*

hay/how	coach/couch	den/down	skit/scout
gain/gown	pride/proud	send/sound	math/mouth

MINILESSON 10 Mins

Phonics

Introduce Diphthongs *ou, ow* Sound-Spelling Card

1 Model Display the *Cow* **Sound-Spelling Card**. Teach /ou/ spelled *ow* and *ou* using *cow* and *out*. *This is the* Cow *Sound-Spelling Card. The sound is /ou/. This is the sound at the end of the word* cow. *Listen: /k/ /ou/,* cow. *The /ou/ sound can be spelled with the letters* ow *as in* cow *or* ou *as in* out. *Say the sound with me: /ou/. I'll say /ou/ as I write the letters* ou *and* ow *several times.*

2 Guided Practice/Practice Have children practice connecting the letters *ow* and *ou* to the sound /ou/ by writing them. *Now do it with me. Say /ou/ as I write the letters* ow *and* ou. *This time, write the letters* ow *and* ou *five times each as you say the /ou/ sound.*

SKILLS TRACE

DIPHTHONGS *ou, ow*

Introduce Unit 5 Week 4 Day 1

Review Unit 5 Week 4 Days 2, 3, 4, 5

Assess Unit 5 Week 4

Blend with Diphthongs *ou, ow*

1 Model Display **Word-Building Cards** *s, o, u, n, d.* Model how to blend the sounds. *This is the letter* s. *It stands for /s/. These are the letters* o *and* u. *Together they stand for /ou/. This is the letter* n. *It stands for /n/. This is the letter* d. *It stands for /d/. Listen as I blend these sounds together: /sssounnnd/. Say it with me:* sound.

Continue by modeling the words *now, clown,* and *foul.*

2 Guided Practice/Practice Display the Day 1 Phonics Practice Activity. Read each word in the first row, blending the sounds; for example: */hou/. The word is* how. Have children blend each word with you. Prompt children to read the connected text, sounding out the decodable words.

how	down	out	found	house	bounce
crown	frown	wow	south	mouse	count
shut	shout	pot	pout	find	found
fork	store	girl	burn	part	germs

How loud is the sound of the crowd?

Did the clown frown when he fell down?

Now we found a mouse in the house!

Also online

Day 1 Phonics Practice Activity

Corrective Feedback

Sound Error Model the sound that children missed, then have them repeat the sound. Say: *My turn.* Tap under the letter and say: *Sound? /ou/ What's the sound?* Return to the beginning of the word. Say: *Let's start over.* Blend the word with children again.

 **Daily Handwriting**

Throughout the week teach uppercase and lowercase letters *Xx* using the Handwriting models.

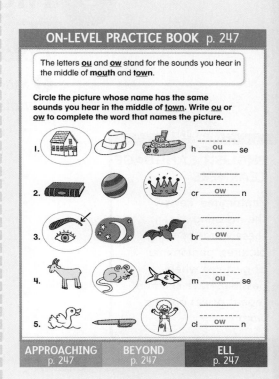

ON-LEVEL PRACTICE BOOK p. 247

The letters **ou** and **ow** stand for the sounds you hear in the middle of **mouth** and **town**.

Circle the picture whose name has the same sounds you hear in the middle of **town**. Write **ou** or **ow** to complete the word that names the picture.

1. h___ou___se
2. cr___ow___n
3. br___ow___
4. m___ou___se
5. cl___ow___n

APPROACHING p. 247	BEYOND p. 247	ELL p. 247

→ # Word Work

Quick Review

High-Frequency Words: Read, Spell, and Write to review last week's high-frequency words: *began, better, guess, learn, right, sure.*

OBJECTIVES

CCSS Recognize and read grade-appropriate irregularly spelled words. **RF.1.3g**

CCSS Use conventional spelling for words with common spelling patterns and for frequently occurring irregular words. **L.1.2d**

MINILESSON 5 Mins

Spelling

Words with *ou, ow*

Dictation Use the Spelling Dictation routine for each word to help children transfer their knowledge of sound-spellings to writing.

Pretest After dictation, pronounce each spelling word. Say a sentence for each word and pronounce the word again. Ask children to say each word softly, stretching the sounds, before writing it. After the pretest, display the spelling words and write each word as you say the letter names. Have children check their words.

cow	town	mouse	how	out
mouth	born	roar	nothing	early

For Approaching Level and Beyond Level children, refer to the Differentiated Spelling Lists for modified word lists.

MINILESSON 5 Mins

High-Frequency Words

color, early, instead, nothing, oh, thought

① Model Display the **High-Frequency Word Cards** *color, early, instead, nothing, oh,* and *thought.* Use the Read/Spell/Write routine.

- **Read** Point to and say the word *color. This is the word* color. *Say it with me:* color. *The color of my shirt is blue.*

- **Spell** *The word* color *is spelled* c-o-l-o-r. *Spell it with me.*

- **Write** *Let's write the word* color *in the air as we say each letter:* c-o-l-o-r.

- Follow the same steps to introduce *early, instead, nothing, oh,* and *thought.*

- As children spell each word with you, point out the irregularities in sound-spellings, such as the /u/ sound spelled *o* in *color* and *nothing.*

 - Have partners create sentences using each word.

ENGLISH LANGUAGE LEARNERS

Pantomime Review the meaning of these words by using pictures, pantomime, or gestures when possible. Have children repeat or act out the word.

Go Digital

Spelling Word Routine

they	together
how	eat

High-Frequency Word Routine

school

Visual Glossary

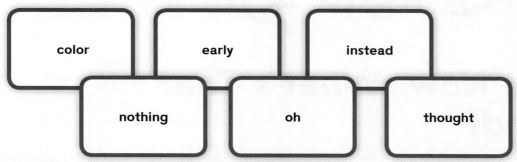

High-Frequency Word Cards

color

early

instead

nothing

oh

thought

② Guided Practice Have children read the sentences. Prompt them to identify the high-frequency words in connected text and to blend the decodable words.

1. The **color** I like best is red.

2. She woke up **early**.

3. What do you want to do **instead**?

4. There is **nothing** to do while we wait.

5. **Oh**, I did not see you!

6. He **thought** we should eat lunch now.

MINILESSON

5 Mins

Introduce Vocabulary

scrambled, suddenly

① Model Introduce the new words using the routine.

scrambled

suddenly

Vocabulary Cards

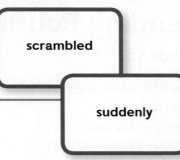

Vocabulary Routine

<u>Define:</u> **Scrambled** means "climbed" or "walked quickly."

<u>Example:</u> *The people scrambled to get in line.*

<u>Ask:</u> Why might you scramble to get in line? EXPLANATION

<u>Define:</u> If something happens **suddenly**, it happens quickly, without notice.

<u>Example:</u> *The sky suddenly got dark.*

<u>Ask:</u> Name a word that is the opposite of *suddenly*. ANTONYMS

② Review Use the routine to review last week's vocabulary words.

Monitor and *Differentiate*

 Quick Check

Can children read and decode words with diphthongs *ou, ow?*

Can children recognize and read high-frequency and vocabulary words?

Small Group Instruction

If No → | Approaching | Reteach pp. T290–293

| ELL | Develop pp. T304–311

If Yes → | On Level | Review pp. T298–299

| Beyond Level | Extend pp. T302–303

→ **Shared Read**

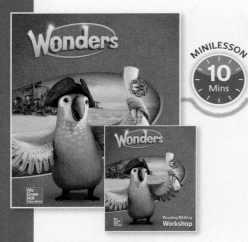

Reading/Writing Workshop Big Book and Reading/Writing Workshop

---

OBJECTIVES

 Decode regularly spelled one-syllable words. **RF.1.3b**

 Recognize and read grade-appropriate irregularly spelled words. **RF.1.3g**

ACADEMIC LANGUAGE

- *fiction, realistic, sound*
- Cognates: *ficción, realista, sonido*

ENGLISH LANGUAGE LEARNERS

See pages T304–T305 for Interactive Question-Response routine for the Shared Read.

Read *Now, What's That Sound?*

Focus on Foundational Skills

Review the words and letter-sounds in *Now, What's That Sound?*

- Have children use pages 176–177 to review high-frequency words *early, thought, instead, oh, color, nothing,* and vocabulary words *suddenly* and *scrambled.*

- Have children use pages 178–179 to review that the letters *ou* and *ow* can stand for the /ou/ sound. Guide them to blend the sounds to read the words.

- Display the words *ball, broom, else, garage, saw,* and *there.* Spell each word and model reading it. Tell children they will be reading the words in the selection.

Read Guide children in reading *Now, What's That Sound?* Point out the high-frequency words, vocabulary words, and words in which *ou* and *ow* stand for the /ou/ sound.

Close Reading Routine

Read   DOK 1–2

- Identify key ideas and details about the sounds in the story.
- Take notes and retell.
- Use **ACT** prompts as needed.

Reread   DOK 2–3

- Analyze the text, craft, and structure.
- Use the Reread minilessons.

Integrate   DOK 4

- Integrate knowledge and ideas.
- Make text-to-text connections.
- Use the Integrate lesson.

Genre: Realistic Fiction Tell children that *Now, What's That Sound?* is realistic fiction. Realistic fiction is a made-up story with characters, settings, and events that could happen in real life. It has a beginning, a middle, and an end.

Now, What's That Sound?

READING/WRITING WORKSHOP, pp. 180–189 **Lexile** 240

Connect to Concept: Sounds All Around

ESSENTIAL QUESTION Explain to children that as they read *Now, What's That Sound?* they will look for key ideas and details that will help them answer the Essential Question: *What sounds can you hear? How are they made?*

- Pages 182–183: Who does Marta think is making the sound?
- Pages 184–185: What is Grandpa doing to make a sound?
- Pages 186–187: Who do Gilbert and Marta find next?
- Pages 188–189: What is making the sound they hear?

Focus on Fluency

With partners, have children read *Now, What's That Sound?* to develop fluency. Remind them that they can ask themselves questions to make sure they understand what they are reading.

Retell Have partners use key ideas and details to retell *Now, What's That Sound?* Invite them to make the sounds from the story.

Make Connections

Read together Make Connections on page 189. Have partners talk about how sounds around them are made using this sentence starter:

> *The sound _____ is made by . . .*

Guide children to connect what they have read to the Essential Question.

Reading/Writing Workshop

OBJECTIVES

CCSS Write narratives in which they recount two or more appropriately sequenced events, include some details regarding what happened, use temporal words to signal event order, and provide some sense of closure. **W.1.3**

CCSS Use determiners (e.g., articles, demonstratives). **L.1.1h**

ACADEMIC LANGUAGE
- article, notes, respond, sound words
- Cognates: *artículo, notas, responder*

MINILESSON

5 Mins

Shared Writing

Write About the Reading/Writing Workshop

Analyze the Prompt Tell children you will work together to write a response to a prompt. Read aloud the prompt: *Add another page to the middle of* Now, What's That Sound? *Be sure to include sound words.* Say: *To respond to this prompt, we need to look at the text and illustrations in* Now, What's That Sound? *so we can add a new page to the story.*

Find Text Evidence Explain that you will reread the text and take notes to help respond to the prompt. Read aloud pages 182–183. Say: *I read that Gilbert and Marta want to find out what is making a sound. On page 183, I see them peeking inside the garage to see if Dad makes the sound. Dad is sawing. He is making a different sound. I see the sound words* zing, zing, zing *in the text and illustration. In my notes, I'll write what the children see and what sounds they hear.*

Write to a Prompt Reread the prompt to children. *Add another page to the middle of* Now, What's That Sound? *Be sure to include sound words.* Say: *We are going to add a page to the story. Let's look at our notes to make sure our new page will fit with the characters and plot.* Point out that on each page, the children tell who they will find. Then they tell the sound they hear. Invite children to suggest another sound Gilbert and Marta might hear and tell who makes the new sound. Use their suggestion to craft the beginning of the story, such as: *Thump-thump-thump. "What's that sound? Let's find [character]. Maybe she is making the sound," said Marta.* Track the print as you reread the notes.

Guide children to dictate complete sentences for you to record. Read the final response as you track the print.

Go Digital

Graphic Organizer

Writing

I see a fish.

Grammar

Grammar

5 Mins

Using *A* and *An*

1 Explain Tell children that the words *a* and *an* are special adjectives called articles. Display the following sentences:

> A hound sniffs the ground.
>
> An ape grabbed my cap!

Explain that we use *a* before a word that begins with a consonant sound (*a hound*). We use *an* before a word that begins with a vowel sound (*an ape*).

2 Guided Practice/Practice Display the sentences below and read them aloud. Have children identify the articles.

> A clown did funny tricks. (a)
>
> My pencil is only an inch long. (an)
>
> I see an oak tree. (an)
>
> Our class keeps a pet mouse in a cage. (a; a)

COLLABORATE

Talk About It Have partners work together to identify the nouns that go with each article. Have them explain why *a* or *an* was used with each.

Link to Writing Say: *Let's look back at our writing and see if we used the words* a *and* an *correctly*. Review the Shared Writing for the articles *a* and *an*. Have children find each article, identify the word that follows, and tell why *a* or *an* should be used.

ENGLISH LANGUAGE LEARNERS SCAFFOLD

Beginning

Demonstrate Comprehension In the Explain section, read the first sentence. Say: *Point to the article. Does* a *come before a word that begins with a consonant sound?* Read the second sentence. *Point to the article. Does* an *come before a word that begins with a consonant or vowel sound?*

Intermediate

Explain Ask children to circle the word *a* in the first Explain sentence. *Why is the article* a *used in this sentence?* Ask children to circle the word *an* in the second Explain sentence. *Why is the article* an *in this sentence?*

Advanced/High

Expand Write nouns *nest, eel, queen, ice cube, crown.* Which nouns would have the article *a* and which would have *an? Why?* Repeat answers clearly to the class.

Daily Wrap Up

- Encourage children to discuss the Essential Question using the oral vocabulary words. Ask: *What sounds do you hear right now?*

- Prompt children to share how the skills they learned will help them become better readers and writers.

Materials

Reading/Writing Workshop
VOLUME 4

Visual Vocabulary Cards
distract
nervous
senses
squeaky
volume

High-Frequency Word Cards
color
early
instead
nothing
oh
thought

Vocabulary Cards
suddenly
scrambled

Teaching Poster

Sound-Spelling Cards

Spelling Word Cards

Word-Building Cards

Interactive Read-Aloud Cards

→ # Build the Concept

MINILESSON
5 Mins

Oral Language

OBJECTIVES

CCSS Ask and answer questions about key details in a text read aloud or information presented orally or through other media. **SL.1.2**

• Discuss the Essential Question

• Build concept understanding

ACADEMIC LANGUAGE

• *information, text, illustrations*

• Cognate: *información, texto, ilustraciones*

ESSENTIAL QUESTION

Remind children that this week you've been talking and reading about sounds and how they are made. Remind them of the sounds Gilbert heard and the sounds caused by the squeaky bed. Guide children to discuss the Essential Question using information from what they read and discussed on Day 1.

Oral Vocabulary Words

Review the oral vocabulary words. Use the Define/Example/Ask routine to review the oral vocabulary words *distract, nervous, senses, squeaky,* and *volume*.

• Does loud music distract you when you are trying to read? Why?

• What sounds make you nervous?

• Which of your senses are you using when you listen to a bird sing?

• Which might be squeaky: a rusty bicycle, or a new car?

• How do you make the volume louder or softer on a radio?

Go Digital

Visual Glossary

"The Squeaky Bed"

Listening Comprehension

Read the Interactive Read Aloud

MINILESSON
5 Mins

Strategy: Ask and Answer Questions

Remind children that as they listen, they can ask themselves questions about the text. This can help them understand the information.

Tell children that you will reread "The Squeaky Bed." Display the Interactive Read-Aloud Cards. Pause as you read to model applying the strategy.

"The Squeaky Bed"

Think Aloud When I first read the story, I asked questions as I read and then looked for the answers in the text and illustrations. The text said that the squeaky bed scared Marta, so her mama and papa let the cat sleep with her to make her feel better. I asked: *Will Marta feel better with the cat?* I read on and learned that Marta was scared of the squeaky bed, even with the cat.

Make Connections

Discuss partners' responses to "The Squeaky Bed."

- Why do you think Marta was afraid of the squeaky bed?
- Have you ever heard noises that made you feel scared?

Write About It Have children write in their Writer's Notebooks about noises that might have made Marta laugh instead of being scared. Guide children by asking questions such as, *What are some silly noises that might be amusing to Marta? What things might make silly noises?* Have children write continuously for six minutes.

→ # Word Work

MINILESSON 5 Mins **Phonemic Awareness**

Phoneme Isolation

OBJECTIVES

CCSS Isolate and pronounce initial, medial vowel, and final sounds (phonemes) in spoken single-syllable words. **RF.1.2c**

CCSS Decode regularly spelled one-syllable words. **RF.1.3b**

CCSS Read words with inflectional endings. **RF.1.3f**

1 Model Show children how to isolate a phoneme in a word. *Listen carefully as I say a word:* out. *What sound do you hear at the beginning of the word? /ou/ The word* out *has the /ou/ sound at the beginning.* Repeat for the medial /ou/ in *gown* and the final /ou/ in *cow.*

2 Guided Practice/Practice Have children practice isolating initial, medial, and final phonemes. *Listen carefully as I say a word. Tell me the sound you hear at the beginning, in the middle, or at the end of the word.*

(beginning)	ouch	aim	eat	out
(middle)	crowd	meat	south	late
(end)	now	how	hi	go

MINILESSON 5 Mins **Phonics**

Review Diphthongs *ou, ow*

1 Model Display the *Cow* Sound-Spelling Card. Review the sound /ou/ spelled *ou* and *ow* using the words *sound* and *now.*

2 Guided Practice/Practice Have children practice connecting the letters and sounds. Point to the Sound-Spelling Card. *What are these letters? What sound do they stand for?*

Go
Digital

Phonemic
Awareness

Phonics

Structural
Analysis

Handwriting

Blend with Diphthongs *ou, ow*

1 Model Display **Word-Building Cards** *p, o, u, n, d* to form the word *pound*. Model how to generate and blend the sounds to say the word. *This is the letter* p. *It stands for /p/. These are the letters* ou. *Together they stand for /ou/. This is the letter* n. *It stands for /n/. This is the letter* d. *It stands for /d/. Let's blend all four sounds together: /pounnnd/. The word is* pound.

Continue by modeling the words *howl, gown,* and *count.*

2 Guided Practice/Practice Repeat the routine with children with the words *cow, how, out, owl, shout, ground, blouse, down, brown, mouth, now, scout, crowd.*

Build with Diphthongs *ou, ow*

1 Model Display the Word-Building Cards *c, o, u, c, h.* Blend: /k/ /ou/ /ch/, /kouch/, *couch.*

- Replace *c* with *sl* and repeat with *slouch.*
- Replace *sl* with *p* and repeat with *pouch.*

2 Guided Practice/Practice Continue with *pound, round, sound, ground, mound, mouth, mount, count, couch, cow, now, how, wow, plow, brow, brown, crown, down.*

ENGLISH LANGUAGE LEARNERS

Build Vocabulary Review the meanings of example words that can be explained or demonstrated in a concrete way. For example, ask children to point to their *mouth* and something that is *brown*. Model the meaning of *down* and *ground,* saying, *"I can bend down and touch the ground,"* and have children repeat. Provide sentence starters, such as, *Now can I _____?* for children to complete. Correct grammar and pronunciation as needed.

MINILESSON 5 Mins

Structural Analysis

Inflectional Endings *-er, -est*

1 Model Write and read aloud *loud, louder, loudest.* Underline *-er* and *-est.* Tell children that we add *-er* and *-est* to adjectives, or describing words, to compare things. For example, *His music is loud. Her music is louder. My music is the loudest of all. We add* -er *to compare two things; we add* -est *to compare three or more things.* Point out that adding *-er* or *-est* adds a syllable to the word.

Repeat with *cute, cuter, cutest; dry, drier, driest;* and *big, bigger, biggest.* Remind children of the rules they learned for dropping final *e,* changing *y* to *i,* and doubling final consonants before adding an ending.

2 Guided Practice/Practice Write the following words on the board: *proud, sharp, kind, high, nice, funny, sad.* Have children add *-er* and *-est* to each word and then use each word in a sentence.

→ # Word Work

Quick Review
High-Frequency Words:
Read, Spell, and Write to review this week's high-frequency words: *color, early, instead, nothing, oh, thought.*

MINILESSON 5 Mins Spelling

OBJECTIVES

CCSS Recognize and read grade-appropriate irregularly spelled words. **RF.1.3g**

CCSS Use conventional spelling for words with common spelling patterns and for frequently occurring irregular words. **L.1.2d**

- Spell words with diphthongs *ou, ow*
- Recognize and read high-frequency and vocabulary words

ENGLISH LANGUAGE LEARNERS

Provide Clues Practice spelling by helping children generate more words with /ou/ spelling patterns. Provide clues: *Think of a word that begins with* h *and rhymes with* mouse. Write the word and have children practice reading it. Correct their pronunciation, if needed.

Word Sort with *ou, ow*

1 **Model** Display the **Spelling Word Cards** from the Teacher's Resource Book. Have children read each word, listening for the vowel sound.

Use cards for *ou* and *ow* to create a two-column chart. Say each word and note the spelling of /ou/. Ask children to chorally spell each word.

2 **Guided Practice/Practice** Have children place each Spelling Word Card in the column for the correct spelling. When completed, have children read the words in each column. Then call out a word. Have a child find the word card and point to it as the class spells the word.

ANALYZE ERRORS/ARTICULATION SUPPORT

Use children's pretest errors to analyze spelling problems and provide corrective feedback. Some children will leave out the *e* at the end of *mouse* or struggle over which /ou/ spelling to use.

Remind children that the *ou* spelling for /ou/ never appears at the end of a word or syllable. A word like *cow* or *how* could never be spelled with *ou* since the /ou/ sound comes at the end of the word. Word sorts will help children become familiar with common /ou/ patterns such as *-ouse, -ow, -own, -outh,* and *-oud.*

MINILESSON 5 Mins High-Frequency Words

color, early, instead, nothing, oh, thought

1 **Guided Practice** Say each word and have children Read/Spell/Write it. Ask children to picture the word in their minds and write it the way they see it. Display the high-frequency words for children to self-correct.

- Point out the /ûr/ sounds spelled *ear* in *early.*

Go Digital

Spelling Word Sort

High-Frequency Word Routine

Visual Glossary

2 Practice Add the high-frequency words *color, early, instead, nothing, oh,* and *thought* to the cumulative word bank.

- Have children work with a partner to create sentences using the words.

- Have children look at the words and compare their sounds and spellings to words from previous weeks.

- Suggest that they write about sounds and how they are made.

Cumulative Review Review last week's words using the Read/Spell/Write routine.

- Repeat the above routine, mixing the words and having children chorally say each one.

MINILESSON
5 Mins

Reinforce Vocabulary

scrambled, suddenly

1 Guided Practice Use the **Vocabulary Cards** to review this week's and last week's vocabulary words. Work together with children to generate a new context sentence for each word.

2 Practice Have children work with a partner to orally complete each sentence stem on the Day 2 Vocabulary Practice Activity using this week's and last week's vocabulary words.

| idea | unusual | scrambled | suddenly |

1. Whose ____ is it to go bike riding?
2. The baby was playing and ____ he started to cry.
3. The squirrel ____ up the tree.
4. It is ____ for him to be awake so early.

Also online

Day 2 Vocabulary Practice Activity

Monitor and *Differentiate*

✓ Quick Check

Can children read and decode words with diphthongs *ou, ow*?

Can children recognize and read high-frequency and vocabulary words?

Small Group Instruction

If No → Approaching Reteach pp. T290–293

ELL Develop pp. T304–311

If Yes → On Level Review pp. T298–299

Beyond Level Extend pp. T302–303

Comprehension

Reading/Writing Workshop Big Book and Reading/Writing Workshop

---

OBJECTIVES

CCSS Describe characters, settings, and major events in a story, using key details. **RL.1.3**

Understand realistic fiction genre

ACADEMIC LANGUAGE

• *realistic fiction*

• Cognate: *ficción realista*

SKILLS TRACE

PLOT

Introduce Unit 3 Week I

Review Unit 3 Weeks 2, 3; Unit 4 Weeks 1, 4; Unit 5 Weeks 1, 2, 4; Unit 6 Weeks 3, 4

Assess Unit 3 Weeks 1, 2, 3; Unit 4 Week 1; Unit 5 Weeks 2, 4; Unit 6 Week 3

Reread *Now, What's That Sound?*

MINILESSON
10 Mins

Genre: Realistic Fiction

❶ Model Tell children they will now reread the realistic fiction story *Now, What's That Sound?* Explain that as they read, they will look for information in the text to help them understand the story.

Review the characteristics of realistic fiction. It:

• is a made-up story about characters and events.

• has characters, setting, and events that could happen in real life.

• has a beginning, a middle, and an end.

Tell children that realistic fiction stories have a setting, characters, and a plot. In realistic fiction, the characters talk and act like real people. The plot is organized into a beginning, a middle, and an end.

Display pages 182–183 and read page 182 aloud. *The characters in the story talk and act like real people. This information helps me know that the story is realistic fiction. This is the beginning of the story. The author introduces the main characters, Gilbert and Marta. The author also sets up the plot, which is that the characters want to know what is making a strange sound.*

❷ Guided Practice/Practice Display pages 184–185 of *Now, What's That Sound?* Read the pages aloud. Say: *This story could happen in real life. The children are trying to solve a problem. What part of the story is this? Yes, it is the middle. What events happen in the middle of the story? Yes, the characters are trying to find out what is making the strange sound.*

Go Digital

Now, What's That Sound?

Genre

Problem and Solution

Skill: Plot/Problem and Solution

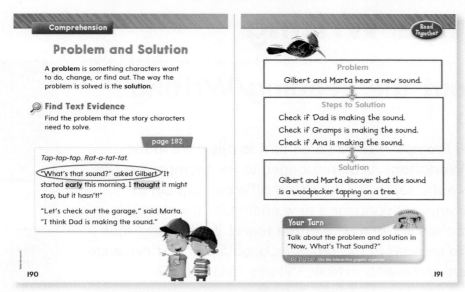

Reading/Writing Workshop, pp. 190–191

ON-LEVEL PRACTICE BOOK p. 253

A. Reread "Dad's Game." Then write "problem," "step to a solution," or "solution" below each sentence.

1. Howie and Dad have a long ride home.

_____
_____
problem

2. Dad says, "We can play a game."

_____
step to a solution

3. "We are back at our brown house," said Dad.

_____
solution

B. Work with a partner. Read the passage aloud. Pay attention to expression. Stop after one minute. Fill out the chart.

	Words Read	–	Number of Errors	=	Words Correct Score
First Read		–		=	
Second Read		–		=	

APPROACHING p. 253	BEYOND p. 253	ELL p. 253

1 Model Tell children that characters in realistic fiction stories usually have a problem that they want to solve. Have children look at pages 190–191 in their Reading/Writing Workshop. Read together the definitions of problem and solution. *A problem is something that the characters want to do, change, or find out. The way the problem is solved in the solution.*

2 Guided Practice/Practice Read together the Find Text Evidence section and model finding a problem in *Now, What's That Sound?* Point out the information added to the graphic organizer. *On page 182, we find out that Gilbert and Marta hear a sound and they don't know what it is. Finding out what is making the noise is the problem. What the characters do to try and discover what is making the noise are the steps to a solution. Discovering the source of the noise is the solution. This information has been added to the Problem and Solution chart.*

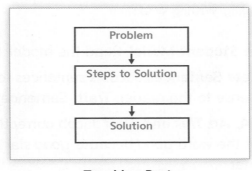

Teaching Poster

Monitor and *Differentiate*

✓ **Quick Check**

Can children identify a problem and a solution in a realistic fiction selection?

Small Group Instruction

If No → **Approaching** Reteach pp. T294–295
ELL Develop pp. T304–311
If Yes → **On Level** Review p. T299
Beyond Level Extend p. T303

Wonders
Reading/Writing Workshop

Reading/Writing Workshop

OBJECTIVES

CCSS Write narratives in which they recount two or more appropriately sequenced events, include some details regarding what happened, use temporal words to signal event order, and provide some sense of closure. **W.1.3**

CCSS Use determiners (e.g., articles, demonstratives). **L.1.1h**

ACADEMIC LANGUAGE

• *adjectives, evidence, inference, complete sentences*
• Cognates: *adjetivos, evidencia, inferencia*

MINILESSON
5 Mins

Interactive Writing

Write About the Reading/Writing Workshop

Analyze the Model Prompt Have children turn to page 192 in the **Reading/Writing Workshop**. Jacob responded to the prompt: *Rewrite pages 188–189. Make the source of the sound different.* Explain to children that the prompt is asking for a new ending for the story. Say: *The prompt says to change the source of the sound, or the thing that makes the sound. To respond to this prompt, Jacob found text evidence about the characters and events in* Now, What's That Sound?

Find Text Evidence Explain that Jacob took notes on the text. He used his notes to make inferences about something else that could make the sound the characters hear and then wrote a new ending for the story.

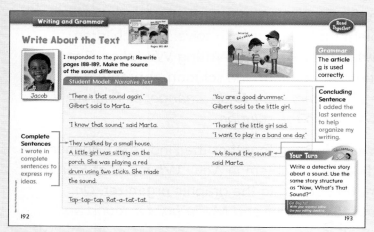

Reading/Writing Workshop

Analyze the Student Model Read the model. Discuss the callouts.

• **Complete Sentences** Jacob's sentences tell complete ideas. They make sense to the reader. **Trait: Sentence Fluency**

• **Using *A, An, This* and *That*** Jacob correctly used the article *a* in front of the word *good* because *good* starts with a consonant sound. **Grammar**

• **Concluding Sentence** Jacob wrote a final sentence that ends the story and tells that the characters solved the problem. **Trait: Organization**

Point out that in his story Jacob told a sequence of events that made sense.

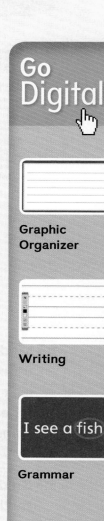

Go Digital

Graphic Organizer

Writing

I see a fish.

Grammar

Your Turn: Write a Story Say: *Now we will write to a new prompt.* Have children turn to page 193 of the **Reading/Writing Workshop.** Read the Your Turn prompt together. *Write a detective story about a sound. Use the same story structure as* Now, What's That Sound?

Find Text Evidence Say: *To respond to this prompt, we need to find evidence and take notes about the story structure, or how the events take place. Then we'll use this information to help us write a new detective story about figuring out a sound.*

Write to a Prompt Say: *Let's start our new story the same way Now,* What's That Sound? *starts. How does that story start?* (with the sound the characters hear) Invite children to plan the new story by naming a sound, describing the characters who hear the sound, and identifying different things that might make the sound. Track the print as you reread the notes to help children identify the story structure of *Now, What's That Sound?* Guide children to use their ideas to form complete sentences as you share the pen with them. Say: *Let's reread our new story. Do our sentences tell a complete idea? Did we put our events in an order that makes sense? Did we write a concluding sentence to tell how our story ends?* Read the final response as you track the print.

For additional practice with the writing traits, have children turn to page 258 of the **Your Turn Practice Book.**

MINILESSON 5 Mins

Grammar

Using *This* and *That*

❶ **Explain** Tell children that the words *this* and *that* are also special adjectives. *This* is used when talking about a thing or person that is close by. *That* is used when talking about a thing or person that is far away. Write the following sentences:

> This tea is too hot to drink.
>
> That owl flew into the park.

Have children identify what is close-by (the tea) and what is far away (the owl).

❷ **Guided Practice/Practice** Display the sentences below and read them aloud. Have children identify the special adjectives.

> That ballpark is too far to walk to.
>
> "This crown is mine," said the queen.

COLLABORATE

Talk About It Have partners work together to identify the nouns that go with *this* or *that* in the Practice sentences. Have them explain why *this* or *that* was used with each.

ENGLISH LANGUAGE LEARNERS

Explain Direct children to the Explain sentences. *Why did the writer use* this *in the first sentence? Is the owl in the second sentence near or far? How do you know?*

Respond Hold up a pencil. Say: *Is this a pencil?* Hand it to a child and have him/her respond, "Yes, *this* is a pencil." Have pairs ask and respond as they hold various familiar classroom objects. Then point to a book on a shelf and ask, *Is that a book?* Have children respond, "Yes, *that* is a book." Have pairs ask and respond using faraway classroom objects.

Daily Wrap Up

- Discuss the Essential Question and encourage children to use the oral vocabulary words. Play music at different volumes and each time ask: *How would you describe this sound?*

- Prompt children to discuss what they learned today by asking: *How will the skills you learned help you be a better reader and writer?*

Materials

Reading/Writing Workshop
VOLUME 4

Literature Anthology
VOLUME 4

 Visual Vocabulary Cards

distract
nervous
senses
squeaky
volume
suddenly
scrambled

color
early
instead
nothing
oh
thought

  Teaching Poster

Problem
↓
Steps to Solution
↓
Solution

Response Board

cow

Spelling-Word Cards

a b c

Word-Building Cards

→ # Build the Concept

MINILESSON 5 Mins

Oral Language

OBJECTIVES

CCSS Read grade-level text orally with accuracy, appropriate rate, and expression. **RF.1.4b**

Review characters' point of view

ACADEMIC LANGUAGE

• *point of view, patterns, repeated, phrase, emphasis*
• Cognates: *patrones, frase, énfasis*

ESSENTIAL QUESTION

Remind children that this week you have been talking and reading about sounds and how they are made. Remind them of how Gilbert and his sister investigated the sounds they heard and all the noises in "The Squeaky Bed." Guide children to discuss the question using information from what they have read and talked about throughout the week.

Review Oral Vocabulary

Display **Visual Vocabulary Cards** for *distract, nervous, senses, squeaky,* and *volume*. Review the oral vocabulary words using the Define/Example/Ask routine. Prompt children to use the words as they discuss the sounds we hear.

Visual Vocabulary Cards

Comprehension/ Fluency

ENGLISH LANGUAGE LEARNERS

Retell Guide children to retell by using a question prompt on each page. *What do the children hear now? What is making the sound?* Provide sentence starters for children to complete orally. *The sound is made by ____.*

Point of View

MINILESSON 10 Mins

❶ **Explain** Tell children they have been learning about using Problem and Solution to understand stories they read. Remind them that they have also learned how to identify point of view. *As we read, we can use the text and illustrations to understand how the characters think and feel about the story events. Understanding a character's point of view can help us to better understand the character's actions.*

Reading/Writing Workshop

❷ **Model** Display page 182 of *Now, What's That Sound? I see in the illustration that the children have stopped playing, and Gilbert is listening to something. I read in the text that he asks what that sound is. This helps us understand his point of view: He is curious about the sound.*

❸ **Guided Practice/Practice** Reread *Now, What's That Sound?* with children. Use text evidence to identify the point of view of Gilbert and of Marta at different points in the story.

Expression: Read Patterns

MINILESSON 5 Mins

❶ **Explain** Tell children some texts contain patterns, or repeated words and phrases. Sometimes they are used for emphasis, and sometimes they are used to make the text fun to read and listen to. Explain that as you read the passage, you will read patterns with emphasis to show they are repeated. Point out the repeated phrase: *"Tap-tap-tap. Rat-a-tat-tat."*

❷ **Model** Model reading the repeated phrase "this is not the sound" on page 183. *Gilbert says this three times in the story. I will emphasize it each time I read it.*

❸ **Guided Practice/Practice** Have children reread the passage. Remind them to emphasize repeated patterns.

Fluency Practice Children can practice using Practice Book passages.

→ # Word Work

OBJECTIVES

CCSS Orally produce single-syllable words by blending sounds (phonemes), including consonant blends. **RF.1.2b**

CCSS Decode regularly spelled one-syllable words. **RF.1.3b**

CCSS Read words with inflectional endings. **RF.1.3f**

MINILESSON 5 Mins

Phonemic Awareness

Phoneme Blending

1 Model Place markers in the **Response Board** to represent sounds. Show children how to orally blend phonemes. *I'm going to put one marker in each box as I say each sound. Then I will blend the sounds to form a word.* Place a marker for each sound as you say: /l/ /ou/ /d/. *This word has three sounds:* /l/ /ou/ /d/. *Listen as I blend these sounds to form a word:* /llloud/, loud. *The word is* loud.

2 Guided Practice/Practice *Let's do some together. Using your own boards, place a marker for each sound you hear. I will say one sound at a time. Then we will blend the sounds to say a word.* Do the first three with children.

/ou/ /t/	/s/ /ou/ /th/	/m/ /ou/ /s/	/h/ /ou/
/d/ /ou/ /n/	/b/ /r/ /ou/ /n/	/k/ /l/ /ou/ /d/	/ou/ /l/

MINILESSON 5 Mins

Phonics

Blend with Diphthongs *ou, ow*

1 Model Display **Word-Building Cards** *g, r, o, w, l.* Model how to blend the sounds. *This is the letter* g. *It stands for* /g/. *This is the letter* r. *It stands for* /r/. *These are the letters* ow. *Together they stand for* /ou/. *This is the letter* l. *It stands for* /l/. *Let's blend the sounds:* /grrroulll/. *Say it with me:* growl. *Continue by modeling* shout, blouse, *and* fowl.

2 Guided Practice/Practice Review the words and sentences on the Day 3 Phonics Practice Activity with children. Read each word in the first row, blending the sounds; for example: */d/ /ou/ /n/, /doun/.* The word is down.

Have children blend each word with you. Prompt children to read the connected text, sounding out the decodable words.

Go Digital

Phonemic Awareness

Phonics

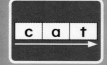

I ___ the jar.
| fill | fills | filling |

Structural Analysis

Handwriting

down	out	how	found	house
crown	wow	out	frown	sound
louder		loudest	rounder	roundest
prouder		proudest	shorter	shortest
playground	doghouse		power	towel

Just now the crowd got very loud.

We found our lost cow in the next town!

Also online

Day 3 Phonics Practice Activity

Decodable Reader Have children read "Up or Down Sounds" (pages 41–44) to practice decoding words in connected text.

MINILESSON
5 Mins

Structural Analysis

Inflectional Endings *-er, -est*

1 Model Write the words *proud, prouder,* and *proudest.* Underline the letters *-er* at the end of *prouder* and *-est* at the end of *proudest.* Remind children that the ending *-er* of an adjective, or describing word, is used to compare two things; *-est* is used to compare three or more things. Repeat with *wide, hot,* and *shy.* Remind children of the rules they learned for dropping final *e,* doubling final consonants, and changing *y* to *i* before adding an ending.

2 Practice/Apply Help children blend the words *sharp, sharper, sharpest; slow, slower, slowest; safe, safer, safest;* and *mad, madder, maddest.* Point out that adding the letters *-er* or *-est* at the end of a word adds a syllable.

Corrective Feedback

Corrective Feedback Say: *My turn.* Model blending the word. Then lead children in blending the sounds. Say: *Do it with me.* You will respond with children to offer support. Then say: *Your turn. Blend.* Have children chorally blend. Return to the beginning of the word.

Word Work

MINILESSON 5 Mins

Spelling

OBJECTIVES

CCSS Use conventional spelling for words with common spelling patterns and for frequently occurring irregular words. **L.1.2d**

CCSS Use frequently occurring affixes as a clue to the meaning of a word. **L.1.4b**

Recognize and read high-frequency and vocabulary words

Word Sort with *ou, ow*

1 Model Make index cards for *ou* and *ow* and form two columns in a pocket chart. Say or blend the sounds with children.

Hold up the *cow* **Spelling Word Card**. Say and spell it. Pronounce each sound clearly: /k/ /ou/. Blend the sounds, emphasizing the vowel sound. Repeat this step with *town* and *how*. Place the words below the *ow* card.

2 Guided Practice/Practice Have children spell each word. Repeat the process with the *ou* words.

Display the words *born, roar, nothing,* and *early* in a separate column. Read and spell the words together with children. Point out that these spelling words do not contain the diphthongs *ou* or *ow*.

Conclude by asking children to orally generate additional words that rhyme with each word. Write the additional words on the board.

MINILESSON 5 Mins

High-Frequency Words

PHONICS/SPELLING PRACTICE BOOK p. 118

color, early, instead, nothing, oh, thought

1 Guided Practice Say each word and have children Read/Spell/Write it.

Display **Visual Vocabulary Cards** to review this week's high-frequency words.

Visual Vocabulary Cards

2 Practice Repeat the activity with last week's words.

Go Digital

er	ir	or	ur
her			
girl curb			word

Spelling Word Sort

school

Visual Glossary

Name _____

cow	town	mouse	how
out	mouth	nothing	early

Look at the spelling words in the box. Write the spelling words that match each spelling pattern.

ow		ou	
I.	cow	4.	mouse
2.	town	5.	out
3.	how	6.	mouth

Order of words in 1–3 and 4–6 may vary.

Write the spelling word that ends with ly.

7. _____ early

Write the spelling word that ends with ing.

8. _____ nothing

Build Fluency: Word Automaticity

Have children read the following sentences aloud together at the same pace. Repeat several times.

> Pick a **color instead** of red.
>
> We did **nothing early** in the day.
>
> **Oh**, I **thought** that game was fun!

Word Bank

Review the current and previous words in the word bank. Discuss with children which words should be removed, or added back, from previous high-frequency word lists.

MINILESSON *5 Mins*

Vocabulary Strategy

scrambled, suddenly

Review Use the **Visual Vocabulary Cards** to review this week's words using the Define/Example/Ask routine. Have partners generate context sentences for each vocabulary word.

Visual Vocabulary Cards

Strategy: Suffixes

❶ Model Tell children that a suffix is a word part that can be added to the end of a word to make a new word. The suffix *-or* means "a person who." The suffix *-less* means "without." The suffix *-ful* means "full of." The suffix *-ly* means "in a way that is."

Think Aloud In *Now, What's That Sound?* on page 187 we read: "This is hopeless!" If I'm not sure what *hopeless* means, I can look at its parts. *Hopeless* has the suffix *-less*. I know that the suffix *-less* means "without." So the word *hopeless* means "without hope."

❷ Guided Practice Read on page 184: *They quickly ran to the back of the house to find Gramps.* Help children figure out the meaning of *quickly*. If needed, remind children that the suffix *-ly* means "in a way that is."

❸ Practice Have children use the strategy to figure out the meaning of more words: *helpful, inventor, kindly, colorless.* If needed, remind children the meanings of different suffixes.

Monitor and *Differentiate*

✓ **Quick Check**

Can children read and decode words with diphthongs *ou, ow*?

Can children recognize and read high-frequency and vocabulary words?

⬇

Small Group Instruction

If No →  Approaching Reteach pp. T290–293

ELL Develop pp. T304–311

If Yes → On Level Review pp. T298–299

Beyond Level Extend pp. T302–303

Whistle
for
Willie

by Ezra Jack Keats

226   227

LITERATURE ANTHOLOGY, pp. 226–227

**Literature
Anthology**

Whistle for Willie   CLOSE READING

Lexile 520

Close Reading Routine

Read   DOK 1–2

• Identify key ideas and details about
  the sounds in the story.
• Take notes and retell.
• Use **A C T** prompts as needed.

Reread   DOK 2–3

• Analyze the text, craft, and structure.
• Use *Close Reading Companion*, p. 154–156.

Integrate   DOK 4

• Integrate knowledge and ideas.
• Make text-to-text connections.
• Use the Integrate lesson.

Read

ESSENTIAL QUESTION

Read aloud the Essential Question: *What sounds
can you hear? How are they made?* Tell children
that as they read they should think about sounds
in the story and how they are made. Ask: *What do
you predict this story will be about?*

Story Words Read and spell the words *whistle,
straight, drew, blew, mirror, practice, father,
and mother.* Explain that children will read these
words in the selection.

Note Taking: Graphic Organizer As children read
the selection, guide them to fill in the graphic
organizer on **Your Turn Practice Book** page 250.

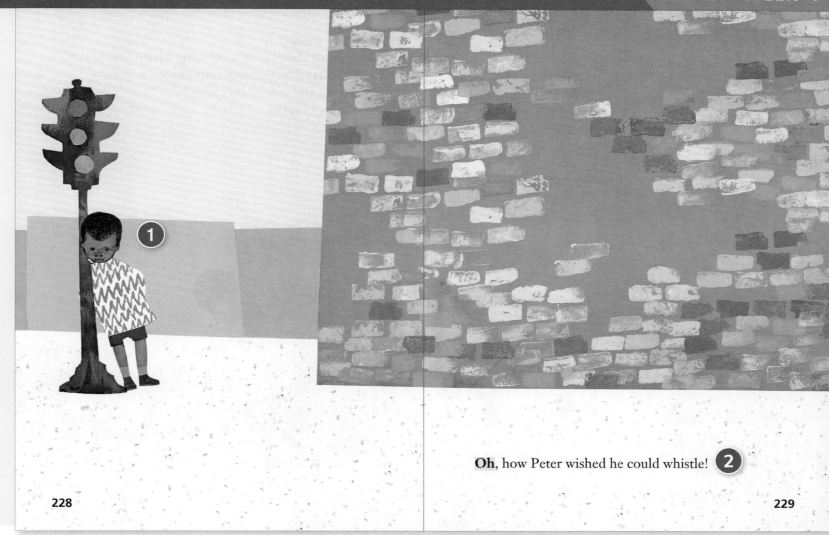

228

Oh, how Peter wished he could whistle! ②

229

LITERATURE ANTHOLOGY, pp. 228–229

❶ **Strategy: Ask and Answer Questions**

Teacher Think Aloud On page 228, I see a boy leaning against a street light. He looks sad. I ask myself "Who is this boy and why is he sad?" Then I read that Peter wishes he could whistle. I ask myself if the boy is Peter. Is he sad because he can't whistle? I will look for answers to these questions on the next pages.

❷ **Skill: Problem and Solution**

Many stories tell about a problem the main character faces and the steps the character takes to solve the problem. What do you think Peter's problem might be? (He can't whistle.)

A C T Access Complex Text

▶ **What makes this text complex?**

• **Sentence Structure** This selection includes dashes and ellipses. Students may need help understanding what these punctuation marks mean.

• **Organization** The selection follows a little boy as he plays and goes about his day. Some of the events may seem random or illogical. Children may need help understanding the sequence of events.

He saw a boy playing with his dog. Whenever the boy whistled, the dog ran straight to him. **3**

Peter tried and tried to whistle, but he couldn't. So **instead** he began to turn himself around—
around and around he whirled …
faster and faster….

230

231

LITERATURE ANTHOLOGY, pp. 230–231

---

3 Skill: Problem and Solution

We talked before about what we thought Peter's problem might be—that he can't whistle. Does the text on page 231 confirm our guess? Why or why not? Let's write about Peter's problem in the first box of our Problem and Solution chart.

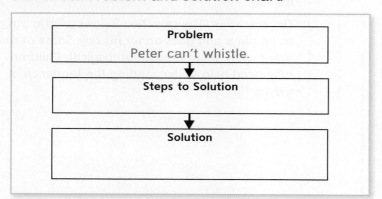

Problem
Peter can't whistle.

↓

Steps to Solution

↓

Solution

A C T Access Complex Text

▶ Sentence Structure

Ask children if they notice any unfamiliar punctuation marks on page 231.

- Help children recognize the dash and ellipses.
- Read the text aloud, emphasizing the effects of the dash and the ellipses.
- Explain that the author uses the dash and the ellipses to help the reader experience Peter's action. These marks show the reader how Peter feels as he is spinning and whirling.

When he stopped
everything turned
down …
and up …

and up …
and down …
and around
and around.

232

233

LITERATURE ANTHOLOGY, pp. 232–233

Reread   *Close Reading Companion,* 154

Author/Illustrator's Craft

Reread pages 230–231. How do the illustrations help you know how Peter feels after he whirls around? (The lights appear to be falling from the traffic light. The street looks diagonal. Peter is bending forward and backward as if he is swaying.)

Reread

Author's Craft: Repetition

Reread pages 232–233. Why do you think the author repeats the words *down* and *up* and switches the order of the words. (to help the reader understand that Peter feels like things are turning upside down)

Peter saw his dog, Willie, coming. Quick as a wink, he hid in an empty carton lying on the sidewalk. **4**

"Wouldn't it be funny if I whistled?" Peter **thought**. "Willie would stop and look all around to see who it was."

Peter tried again to whistle—but still he couldn't. So Willie just walked on. **5**

234

235

LITERATURE ANTHOLOGY, pp. 234–235

Read

4 Strategy: Ask and Answer Questions

Teacher Think Aloud On page 234, Peter sees a box and decides to hide inside it. As I read, I ask myself "Why would he do that?"

Student Think Aloud I think Peter is being silly and playing hide and seek with his dog.

5 Maintain Skill: Point of View

Peter says it would be funny if he whistled and Willie looked around to see where the noise came from. Why do you think Peter says that? (He really wishes he could whistle for Willie.)

Build Vocabulary page 234
carton: a box or container

A C T Access Complex Text

▶ **Organization**

Help children understand the connections between events that are not always obvious.

- Point out that the story follows the course of Peter's afternoon as he plays on his own.

- Help children follow the sequence of the story by listing Peter's activities so far. Ask what Peter did first, second, and next.

- Make sure children understand that Peter is now at home and he is still trying to whistle.

Peter got out of the carton
and started home.
On the way he took some
colored chalks out of his pocket
and drew a long, long line
right up to his door. **6**

236

He stood there and tried to whistle again. **7**
He blew till his cheeks were tired.
But **nothing** happened.

237

LITERATURE ANTHOLOGY, pp. 236–237

6 **Skill: Problem and Solution**

What is Peter's problem in this story? (He can't
whistle.) Do you think he has taken any steps to
change or solve his problem? (He has tried to
whistle, but he hasn't been able to do it.)

7 **Make and Confirm Predictions**

What is Peter trying to do on page 237? (He's
trying to whistle.) How is it working out for him?
(He keeps trying and blowing, but nothing
happens except that his cheeks get tired.)

Turn to a partner and make a prediction about
what will happen. As we read, look for words that
tell if your prediction is correct.

Reread — *Close Reading Companion,* 155

Story Structure

Reread pages 234–237. How does the author
help you know that Peter won't give up trying to
whistle? (The author tells what happens when
Peter tries to whistle. Every time he tries to
whistle, he can't. He takes a break for a while,
but then he tries again. This tells me that Peter
won't give up.)

He went into his house and put on his father's old hat to make himself feel more grown up. He looked into the mirror to practice whistling. Still no whistle! **8**

238

239

LITERATURE ANTHOLOGY, pp. 238–239

Read

8 **Skill: Problem and Solution**

Teacher Think Aloud We said that Peter's problem is that he cannot whistle. On pages 231, 235, 237, and 239, Peter tries to whistle, but he can't. He keeps trying and practicing though. I think this is a step he's taking to solve his problem. Let's write this in the Steps to Solution box in our Problem and Solution chart.

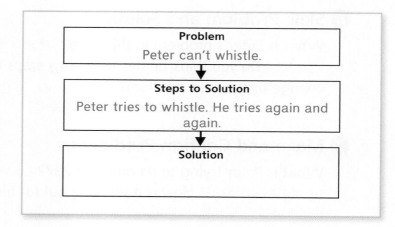

Problem
Peter can't whistle.

Steps to Solution
Peter tries to whistle. He tries again and again.

Solution

When his mother saw what he was doing, Peter pretended that he was his father.

He said, "I've come home **early** today, dear. Is Peter here?" 9

240

His mother answered, "Why no, he's outside with Willie."

"Well, I'll go out and look for them," said Peter.

241

LITERATURE ANTHOLOGY, pp. 240–241

9 Genre: Realistic Fiction

Fiction stories sometimes have dialogue. Dialogue tells us what the characters say. On these pages, the author uses dialogue to tell us what each character says. What does Peter say? (Peter pretends to be his father and says that he is home early.) Is this something that could happen in real life? (Yes.)

Build Vocabulary page 240
pretended: acted

Reread

Point of View

Reread pages 239-241. Why do you think Peter puts on his father's hat and pretends to be his father? What clues help you know? (The text tells me that Peter puts on the hat to feel more grown up. I think Peter thinks he could whistle if he was a grown-up. He feels better when he pretends to be his father.)

First he walked along a crack in the sidewalk. Then he tried to run away from his shadow. **10**

LITERATURE ANTHOLOGY, pp. 242–243

A C T Access Complex Text

▶ Organization

Children might find it difficult to see the connections between events.

- Point out that on the previous page, Peter said he would go outside. Now he is outside and he is playing.

- Review the events and help children understand the connections among them.

Read

10 Make and Confirm Predictions

COLLABORATE

Turn to a partner and talk about what you think Peter will do next. Remember to use the words and illustrations to help you make your predictions. As we read, look for evidence to help you confirm if your prediction was correct.

He jumped off his shadow, but when he landed they were together again. **11**

He came to the corner where the carton was, and who should he see but Willie! **12**

244

245

LITERATURE ANTHOLOGY, pp. 244–245

11 Visualize

Remember, picturing characters and events in your mind can help you understand what you read. Close your eyes and picture how Peter plays with his shadow. On page 243, he was trying to run away from it. Now he's trying to jump off it. Use the words in the story to visualize Peter landing on his shadow.

12 Make and Confirm Predictions

Was your prediction about what Peter would do next correct? How can you tell? Now Peter sees Willie again. What do you think he's going to do next? Remember, making predictions about what you read helps you think about the details in the story and understand them better.

13 Peter **scrambled** under the carton.
He blew and blew and blew.
Suddenly----out came a real whistle! 14

Willie stopped and looked around to see
who it was.

246

247

LITERATURE ANTHOLOGY, pp. 246–247

Read

13 Suffixes

COLLABORATE Remember, when you come to a word with an
ending and you don't know what it means, you
can use what you already know to figure out the
meaning. Sometimes you can pick out a word part
you recognize by removing the ending. Turn to a
partner and talk about the word *suddenly*. Ask:
*What is the main word? What is the ending?
What does the word mean?*

14 Make and Confirm Predictions

What did you predict Peter was going to do? Did
you guess that Peter was going to hide in the box
and whistle?

15 Skill: Problem and Solution

Let's review what we know about the plot. What
was Peter's problem? (He could not whistle.)
What steps did he take to solve his problem? (He
tried and tried to whistle.) Do you think Peter
solved his problem? (Yes. He kept trying until he
finally whistled.) Let's write that in the Solution
box of our Problem and Solution chart.

"It's me," Peter shouted, and stood up. ⑮
Willie raced straight to him.

248

249

LITERATURE ANTHOLOGY, pp. 248–249

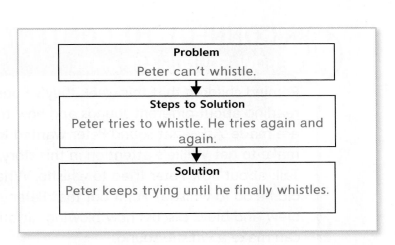

| **Problem** |
| Peter can't whistle. |

↓

| **Steps to Solution** |
| Peter tries to whistle. He tries again and again. |

↓

| **Solution** |
| Peter keeps trying until he finally whistles. |

Reread   *Close Reading Companion,* 156

Author's Craft: Point of View

Reread pages 246–248. How does the author help you know how Peter feels when he whistles? (The author uses the word *suddenly* and an exclamation point to show that Peter is surprised and excited. I know Peter is happy.)

Peter ran home to show his father and mother
what he could do. They loved Peter's whistling.
So did Willie.

250

251

LITERATURE ANTHOLOGY, pp. 250–251

Read

⑯ Visualize

On pages 250–251, Peter is showing his mother
and father what he can do. We see Peter whistling
and his mother clapping. We also see Willie
standing on his hind legs. Close your eyes and
try to make a picture of this scene. What might
Peter's whistle sound like? What is Willie doing?
Can you see his parents smiling?

Build Vocabulary page 252
grocery store: food store

CONNECT TO CONTENT
HOW SOUNDS ARE MADE

Remind children that this week they've been
reading about different sounds and how they
are made. Ask what sound Peter wanted to
make to get Willie's attention in this story.
Talk about how Peter tried to whistle. What
did he do to whistle? Point out that Peter
blew and blew. Discuss how blowing air out
can make a whistle sound.

STEM

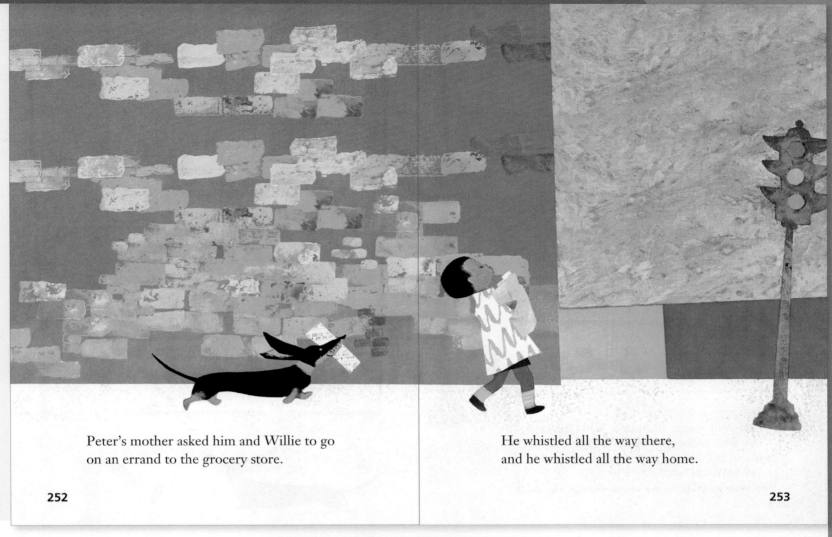

Peter's mother asked him and Willie to go on an errand to the grocery store.

252

He whistled all the way there, and he whistled all the way home.

253

LITERATURE ANTHOLOGY, pp. 252–253

Skill: Problem and Solution

Review the plot of the story and the details children added to the Problem and Solution chart.

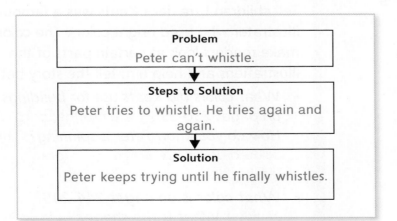

> **Problem**
> Peter can't whistle.
>
> ↓
>
> **Steps to Solution**
> Peter tries to whistle. He tries again and again.
>
> ↓
>
> **Solution**
> Peter keeps trying until he finally whistles.

Reread

Author/Illustrator's Craft

Reread pages 250–253. How do the characters feel about Peter's new skill? How do you know? (I know Peter is proud because he runs home to show his family. In the illustration, I see Peter whistling. His parents are clapping and Willie is sitting up. Everyone looks happy. The text also says Peter whistles all the way to the store and back. He is happy that he can finally whistle.)

Return to Purposes

Review children's predictions. Ask if their predictions were correct. Guide them to use text evidence to confirm if their predictions were accurate.

Meet Ezra Jack Keats

Ezra Jack Keats sold his first painting when he was eight years old! When he grew up, he created many books for children. He used cut-out paper and a special type of paste to make the bright pictures. He won many awards for his work, but he was most pleased by letters from children who had read his books.

Author's Purpose
Ezra Jack Keats wanted to write about a boy who wished he could whistle. Write about something you wish you could do. Tell why you want to do it.

254

Respond to the Text

Retell

Use your own words to retell *Whistle for Willie.*

Problem
↓
Steps to Solution
↓
Solution

Write

Write a new story about a time Peter learned to play a musical instrument or to sing a special song. Use these sentence starters:

Peter wanted to...
Peter tried...

Make Connections

? What other sounds could Peter use to get Willie's attention?
ESSENTIAL QUESTION

255

LITERATURE ANTHOLOGY, pp. 254–255

Meet the Author/Illustrator

Ezra Jack Keats

Read aloud page 254 with children. Ask them what pleased Ezra Jack Keats most about creating children's books. Guide children to flip back and find the part of the story they would share in a letter to Ezra Jack Keats.

Author's Purpose

Children's authors often write about children's experiences, such as learning to whistle. Have children write about something they wish they could do. Check that they tell why they want to do it.

ILLUSTRATOR'S CRAFT

Focus on Color in Graphics

Tell children Ezra Jack Keats was a famous illustrator who used bright colors. The colors make readers look at certain parts of the illustrations and help him tell the story better.

- *What colors did Keats use for buildings on pages 230–231?* (red, orange, purple) *How do you know Peter is spinning?* (The colored boxes are drawn in different directions.)

- *What color is on pages 244–245?* (yellow) *What is the shape?* (a building)

Respond to the Text

Read

Retell

Guide children in retelling the selection. Remind them that as they read *Whistle for Willie*, they paid attention to the character's problem and how he tried to solve it. They also asked and answered questions about the text. Have children use the information they recorded on their Problem and Solution chart to help them retell the selection.

Reread

Analyze the Text

After children read and retell the selection, have them reread *Whistle for Willie* to develop a deeper understanding of the text by answering the questions on pages 154–156 of the *Close Reading Companion*. For children who need support finding text evidence to support their responses, use the scaffolded instruction from the Reread prompts on pages T269D–T269N.

Write About the Text

Review the writing prompt with children. Remind them to use their responses from the *Close Reading Companion* and to cite text evidence to support their answers.

For a full lesson on writing a response supported by text evidence, see pages T270–T271.

<u>Answer:</u> Children's narratives will vary, but should focus on the character Peter learning to play an instrument or to sing a special song and describe how Peter eventually succeeded. <u>Evidence:</u> On pages 228–229, Peter seems unhappy and really wishes he could whistle. The text describes how Peter tries over and over again to whistle. On page 246, Peter is finally able to whistle. On pages 250–253, Peter is pleased that he has learned how to whistle.

Integrate

Make Connections
COLLABORATE

Essential Question: <u>Answer:</u> Peter could clap his hands, snap his fingers, or slap his leg to get Willie's attention. <u>Evidence:</u> On page 230, a boy whistles and his dog comes. When Peter finally whistles on page 246, Willie runs to him.

Language Arts

MINILESSON
5 Mins

Independent Writing

Write About the Literature Anthology

Analyze the Prompt Have children turn to page 255 in the **Literature Anthology**. Read the prompt: *Use what you know about Peter to write a new story about a time he learned to play a musical instrument or to sing a special song.* Say: *The story we read was about how Peter learns to whistle. The prompt is asking us to write a new story about a time Peter learns to play an instrument or to sing a song.* Explain that the next step will be to find text evidence and make inferences.

Find Text Evidence Say: *To respond to the prompt, we need to find evidence in the text and illustrations about what Peter is like and how he learns to whistle.* Explain to children that they can use the evidence from *Whistle for Willie* to help them write a new story about Peter. Say: *Look at pages 234–235. How does the author help us understand what Peter is like?* (The illustration shows Peter hiding inside a box. The text says Peter thinks it would be funny if he whistled and Willie couldn't see him. These clues show that Peter is playful and silly. Even though Peter couldn't whistle, he kept trying.) Have children take notes as they look for evidence to respond to the prompt.

Write to the Prompt Guide children as they begin their writing.

- **Prewrite** Have children review their notes and decide whether to have Peter learn to play an instrument or to sing a song. Guide them to decide what events to include and how best to sequence those events.

- **Draft** Remind children they are writing a new story about Peter learning to do something. Point out that their first sentence can be similar to the first sentence in *Whistle for Willie*. As children write their drafts, have them focus on the week's skills.

  - **Complete Sentences** Write complete sentences that express complete ideas and make sense. **Trait: Sentence Fluency**

  - **Using *A, An, This,* and *That*** Correctly use the articles *a* and *an* and the adjectives *this* and *that*. **Grammar**

  - **Concluding Sentence** Write a final sentence that wraps up the story and tells how Peter solved the problem. **Trait: Organization**

Tell children they will continue to work on their responses on Day 4.

Go Digital

Present the Lesson

Graphic Organizer

Writing

I see a fish.

Grammar

Grammar

Using *A, An, This, That*

1 Review Have children look at page 193 in the **Reading/Writing Workshop**. Remind them that *a* is used before words that start with a consonant sound and *an* is used before words that start with a vowel sound. Review that *this* is used for a noun that is close by and *that* is used for a noun that is far away.

Say: *Name the article in this sentence:* You are a good drummer. A *is used because* good *begins with a consonant sound. Name the adjective in this sentence:* I hear that sound again. That *is used to tell about something that is far away.*

2 Guided Practice/Practice Guide children to find *a* and *that* in Jacob's writing. Have partners circle the words and write new sentences with *a, an, this,* and *that*.

Talk About It Have partners work together to explain why Jacob used the article *a* and the adjective *that*.

Mechanics: Capitalize/Underline Book Titles

1 Explain Explain that we capitalize the first word and all important words in a book title. We don't capitalize little words like *the, a, an, of, and,* and *in*. When we write the title of a book, we underline all the words.

2 Guided Practice Prompt children to correct each sentence.

The cat in the hat is a funny book. (<u>The Cat in the Hat</u> is a funny book.)

I just read the Big snow. (I just read <u>The Big Snow</u>.)

Miss Brown gave me if I were an ant and come out and play, little Mouse to read. (Miss Brown gave me <u>If I Were an Ant</u> and <u>Come Out and Play, Little Mouse</u> to read.)

ENGLISH LANGUAGE LEARNERS SCAFFOLD

Beginning

Demonstrate Comprehension Provide sentence frames for partners as they prepare to write their stories: *Peter will learn to _____. He will _____ because he is _____.* Correct the meaning of children's responses as needed.

Intermediate

Explain Provide questions to help students respond to the prompt. Ask: *Will Peter play an instrument or sing a song? What will the problem be? How will Peter solve the problem?*

Advanced/High

Expand After children complete their stories, ask: *Did you use complete sentences? What adjectives did you use to describe Peter? Does your concluding sentence show how Peter solved a problem?*

Daily Wrap Up

- Encourage children to discuss the Essential Question using the oral vocabulary words. Ask: *What loud sounds have you heard today?*

- Prompt children to review and discuss the skills they used today.

Materials

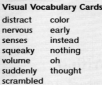   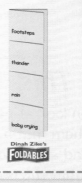

Visual Vocabulary Cards

distract	color
nervous	early
senses	instead
squeaky	nothing
volume	oh
suddenly	thought
scrambled	

Teaching Poster

Literature Anthology
VOLUME 4

a b c

Word-Building Cards

cow

Spelling Word Cards

Dinah Zike's
FOLDABLES

→ Extend the Concept CLOSE READING

🕐 MINILESSON 5 Mins

Shake! Strike! Strum!

OBJECTIVES

CCSS Use the illustrations and details in a text to describe its key ideas. **RI.1.7**

Review vocabulary

ACADEMIC LANGUAGE
directions

ESSENTIAL QUESTION

Remind children that this week they have been learning about sounds and how they are made. Guide children to discuss the question using information from what they have read and discussed. Use the Visual Vocabulary Cards and the Define/Example/Ask routine to review the oral vocabulary words *distract, nervous, senses, squeaky,* and *volume*.

Guide children to use each word as they talk about what they have read and learned about sounds. Prompt children by asking questions.

- What can distract you when you are trying to sleep?
- How do you act when you feel nervous?
- How do we use our senses when we eat food?
- What animals make a squeaky sound?
- What do you sound like when you speak at a low volume? At a loud volume?

Review last week's oral vocabulary words *complicated, curious, device, imagine,* and *improve*.

Go Digital

school

Visual Glossary

Teaching Poster

"Shake! Strike! Strum!"

Text Feature: Directions

1 **Explain** Remind children that they have been reading fiction about sounds and how they are made. Tell children they can also use informational selections to find facts and details about sounds. Explain that informational text sometimes gives directions, a list of steps that tell you how to do something.

2 **Model** Display Teaching Poster 15. *This set of directions tells you how to plant seeds. The child in the photographs is following these directions.* Read the first two steps in the directions. *The first thing you must do is pack dirt in a pot. The second step is to poke holes in the dirt. You can use your fingers to do this, like the child in the photograph.*

3 **Guided Practice/Practice** Read together the remaining steps. Guide children to discuss steps 3, 4, and 5. *What should you do after you poke holes in the dirt? What do you do last?* Tell children to look for directions as they read informational text selections.

ENGLISH LANGUAGE LEARNERS SCAFFOLD

Beginning

Use Sentence Frames Use sentence frames to help children identify the steps. *First, you pack dirt in a ____. Next, you poke holes in the ____.*

Intermediate

Discuss Guide children to focus on the steps in the directions. Have them retell the steps to a partner.

Advanced/High

Discuss Prompt children to discuss how to perform a simple process, such as making a sandwich. Have children give a partner directions on performing the process discussed.

Shake! Strike! Strum!

Shake, strike, strum! **Instruments** can be a lot of fun. Instruments make different kinds of sounds. Strike a drum. Rum-pum-pum. Strum a guitar. Plink, pling. Blow on a horn. Toot, toot. Shake it up!

Some sounds are nice to hear. Others are not. But all sounds have two things in common: pitch and volume.

Pitch is how high or low a sound is. When you whistle for a dog, you make a high-pitched sound.

Volume is how loud or soft a sound is. When you whisper in class, you make a low-volume sound.

① ②

256   257

LITERATURE ANTHOLOGY, pp. 256–257

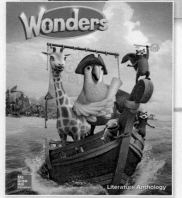

Literature Anthology

Shake! Strike! Strum!   Lexile 290

Compare Texts

As you read and reread "Shake! Strike! Strum!," encourage children to think about how making noise in this selection is like Peter learning to whistle in *Whistle for Willie*. Point out the words *instruments, pitch,* and *volume.*

Read

❶ Strategy: Ask and Answer Questions

Teacher Think Aloud On page 256, I read the word *instruments*. I ask myself what *instruments* are. I read examples of instruments and the sounds they make. Now I understand.

❷ Skill: Key Details

What two things do all sounds have in common? (pitch and volume) What do pitch and volume tell about a sound? (Pitch tells how high or low a sound is; volume tells how loud a sound is.)

❸ Text Features: Directions

Look at the directions. How are the steps organized in the "What to Do" section? (in a numbered list)

Retell

Guide children to use key details to retell the selection.

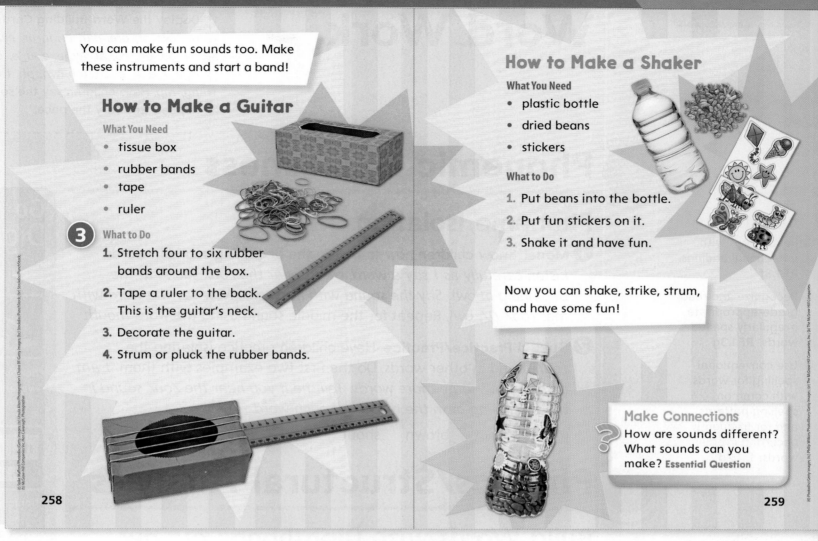

You can make fun sounds too. Make these instruments and start a band!

How to Make a Guitar

What You Need

- tissue box
- rubber bands
- tape
- ruler

3 **What to Do**

1. Stretch four to six rubber bands around the box.
2. Tape a ruler to the back. This is the guitar's neck.
3. Decorate the guitar.
4. Strum or pluck the rubber bands.

258

How to Make a Shaker

What You Need

- plastic bottle
- dried beans
- stickers

What to Do

1. Put beans into the bottle.
2. Put fun stickers on it.
3. Shake it and have fun.

Now you can shake, strike, strum, and have some fun!

Make Connections

? How are sounds different? What sounds can you make? **Essential Question**

259

LITERATURE ANTHOLOGY, pp. 258–259

Reread

After children retell, have them reread to develop a deeper understanding of the text by answering questions on pages 157–159 of the *Close Reading Companion*.

For children who need support citing text evidence, use these Reread questions:

- Why is "Shake! Strike! Strum!" a good title for this selection?
- How is the author's purpose different on pages 256–257 and pages 258–259?
- On page 256, why does the author include words like *rum-pum-pum* and *plink, pling*?
- How do the headings on pages 258–259 help organize the information?

Integrate

Make Connections

COLLABORATE

Essential Question Have children use text evidence to tell how sounds are different and to describe what sounds they can make.

SCIENCE
CONNECT TO CONTENT
HOW SOUNDS ARE MADE

Ask children to think about how the instruments on pages 258–259 make sounds. Would the guitar make high-pitched sounds or low-pitched sounds? Would those sounds be loud or soft? What about the shaker? How does it make sounds?

STEM

→ # Word Work

Quick Review

Build Fluency: Sound-Spellings
Display the **Word-Building Cards:**
*ou, ow, ar, ore, oar, er, ir, ur, ey, igh,
oa, oe, ee, ea, ai, ay, e_e, u_e, o_e,
dge, i_e, a_e, ch, tch, wh, ph, th, sh,
ng, mp.* Have children say the sounds.
Repeat, and vary the pace.

MINILESSON 5 Mins

Phonemic Awareness

OBJECTIVES

CCSS Read words with inflectional endings. **RF.1.3f**

CCSS Recognize and read grade-appropriate irregularly spelled words. **RF.1.3g**

CCSS Use conventional spelling for words with common spelling patterns and for frequently occurring irregular words. **L.1.2d**

Phoneme Isolation

1 Model Show children how to isolate the beginning sound in words. *Listen carefully as I say a word:* owl. *I hear the /ou/ sound at the beginning of* owl. *Say the sound with me: /ou/. Now say the word with me: /ou/ /l/,* owl. *Repeat for the middle sound using the word* mouth.

2 Guided Practice/Practice Have children practice isolating the /ou/ sound in other words. Do the first two examples with them. *I am going to say some more words. Tell me if you hear the /ou/ sound in the beginning or in the middle of each word.*

mouse   out   brown   shout   ouch   ground   owl

MINILESSON 10 Mins

Phonics/Structural Analysis

Build Words with Diphthongs *ou, ow*

Review *The /ou/ sound can be represented by the letters* ou *or* ow. *We'll use* **Word-Building Cards** *to build words with /ou/.*

Place the letters *d, o, w, n. Let's blend the sounds together and read the word: /dounnn/,* down. *Now change the* d *to* t. *Blend the sounds and read the word.*

Continue with *frown, clown, crown, crowd, plow, brow, now, how, house, blouse, spouse, mouse, mouth, mound, found, sound.*

Decodable Reader | Have children read "Sounds Around Us" (pages 45–48).

Inflectional Endings *-er, -est*

Review Write *tall, taller, and tallest* on the board and read them with children. Remind children that the *-er* ending is used to compare two things; the *-est* ending is used to compare more than two things.

Write: *clean, soft, slow, late, dry.* Have children work in pairs to construct comparing words ending with *-er* or *-est*. Then have them write sentences with each word.

Go Digital

Phonemic Awareness

m a
n t p

Phonics

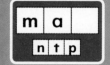

I __ the jar.
fill | fills | filling

Structural Analysis

er | ir | or | ur
her
girl curb   word

Spelling Word Sort

school

Visual Glossary

Spelling

Words Sort with *ou, ow*

Review Provide partners with copies of the **Spelling Word Cards**. While one partner reads the words one at a time, the other partner should orally segment the word and then write the word. After reading all the words, partners should switch roles.

Have children correct their own papers. Then have them sort the words by diphthong spelling pattern: *ou, ow,* or no /*ou*/ pattern.

High-Frequency Words

color, early, instead, nothing, oh, thought

Review Display **Visual Vocabulary Cards** for this week's words. Have children Read/Spell/Write each word.

- Point to a word and call on a child to use it in a sentence.
- Review last week's words using the same procedure.

Expand Vocabulary

scrambled, suddenly

Use the Visual Vocabulary Cards to review *scrambled* and *suddenly*.

❶ **Explain** Explain to children that words have different forms. Help children generate different forms of *scrambled* by changing or removing inflectional endings *-ed, -ing,* and *-s/-es*. Review the meaning of each ending. Then work with children to remove the suffix *-ly* from *suddenly* to make the word *sudden*.

❷ **Model** Draw a four-column chart on the board. Write *scrambled* in the first column. Model how to remove the ending *-ed*. Write *scramble, scrambles,* and *scrambling* in the next three columns. Read the words. Point out how the different endings change the meaning. Have children use the different forms of *scramble*.

❸ **Guided Practice** Have children work in pairs to create sentences for *suddenly* and *sudden*. Then challenge children to generate synonyms for *suddenly* and *scrambled*.

Monitor and *Differentiate*

✓ Quick Check

Can children read and decode words with diphthongs *ou, ow*?

Can children recognize and read high-frequency and vocabulary words?

Small Group Instruction

If No → **Approaching** Reteach pp. T290–293

ELL Develop pp. T304–311

If Yes → **On Level** Review pp. T298–299

Beyond Level Extend pp. T302–303

WORD WORK **T275**

→ # Language Arts

Literature Anthology

OBJECTIVES

CCSS With guidance and support from adults, focus on a topic, respond to questions and suggestions from peers, and add details to strengthen writing as needed. **W.1.5**

CCSS Use determiners (e.g., articles, demonstratives). **L.1.1h**

CCSS Add drawings or other visual displays to descriptions when appropriate to clarify ideas, thoughts, and feelings. **SL.1.5**

Underline book titles

ACADEMIC LANGUAGE

• *adjectives, noun, revise, edit, title*

• Cognates: *adjetivos, revisar, editar, título*

MINILESSON 5 Mins

Independent Writing

Write About the Literature Anthology

Revise

Reread the prompt about the story *Whistle for Willie: Use what you know about Peter to write a new story about a time he learned to play a musical instrument or sing a special song*. Have children read their drafts to see if they responded to the prompt. Then have them check for:

- **Complete Sentences** Do their sentences each express a complete idea? **Trait: Sentence Fluency**

- **Using *A, An, This,* and *That*** Did they correctly use the articles *a* and *an* and the adjectives *this* and *that*? **Grammar**

- **Concluding Sentence** Did they include a final sentence that wraps up the plot of their story? **Trait: Organization**

Peer Review Have children work in pairs to do a peer review and read their partner's draft. Ask partners to check that the response includes complete sentences, correct articles and adjectives, and a concluding sentence. They should take notes about what they liked most about the writing, questions they have for the author about ideas that are not clear, and additional ideas they think the author could include. Have partners use complete sentences when discussing these topics and expressing their ideas. Provide time for them to make revisions.

Proofread/Edit

Have children check for the following:

- Articles are correctly used to describe nouns.

- Names of people are capitalized.

- All sentences are complete and begin with a capital letter.

Peer Edit Next, have partners exchange their drafts and take turns reviewing them against the checklist. Encourage partners to discuss and fix errors together.

Go Digital

Writing

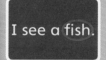

■ Make a capital letter.
⋀ Add.
ℐ Take out.

Proofreader's Marks

I see a fish.

Grammar

Final Draft

After children edit their writing and finish their peer edits, have them write their final draft. Tell children to write neatly so others can read their writing. Or, work with children to explore a variety of digital tools to produce and publish their writing, including collaborating with peers. Have them include details that help make their writing clear and interesting and add a drawing of the characters or events in their story.

Teacher Conference As children work, conference with them to provide guidance. Make sure children's stories use complete sentences and include a concluding sentence.

MINILESSON
5 Mins

Grammar

Using *A, An, This, That*

❶ **Review** Remind children that *a* is used before words that start with a consonant sound and *an* is used before words that start with a vowel sound. Review that *this* is used for a noun that is close and *that* is used for a noun that is far away.

❷ **Practice** Display the following sentences. Have children complete the sentences with *a* or *an*.

> I live in ____ old house. (an)
>
> I take ____ book with me to read. (a)

Have children complete the sentences with *this* or *that*.

> The truck is close. It plows ____ side of the road first. (this)
>
> Why is ____ blouse on the ground by the doghouse? (that)

COLLABORATE

Talk About It Have partners work together to orally generate sentences with *a, an, this,* and *that*.

Mechanics: Capitalize/Underline Book Titles

❶ **Review** Remind children that the important words in book titles are capitalized. Review that book titles are underlined.

❷ **Practice** Display sentences with errors. Read each aloud. Have children work together to fix the sentences.

> Did you read up we go? (Did you read <u>Up We Go</u>?)
>
> little cloud is a fun book. (<u>Little Cloud</u> is a fun book.)

Daily Wrap Up

- Have children discuss the Essential Question using the oral vocabulary words. Ask: *What things make sounds in our classroom?*

- Prompt children to discuss the skills they practiced and learned today by asking, *What skills did you use today?*

OBJECTIVES

 CCSS Participate in shared research and writing projects. **W.1.7**

- Build background knowledge
- Research information using technology

ACADEMIC LANGUAGE

radio play, sound effect, script, character

 SCIENCE

RESEARCH AND INQUIRY

Sound Effects Chart

 COLLABORATE Tell children they will do a research project with a partner to learn more about sounds. Tell students about radio plays, a popular form of entertainment before TV. Explain that they included sound effects to make the play seem more real. Tell children they will research how sound effects for radio plays were made.

STEP 1 ### Choose a Topic

Discuss sound effects and what may be used to make them. Guide partners to choose what sound effects they would like to research.

STEP 2 ### Find Resources

Discuss how to use reference materials and online resources to find out about different sounds and how sound effects can be created. Have children use the Research Process Checklist online.

STEP 3 ### Keep Track of Ideas

Have children make a Four-Tab Foldable® to record ideas and facts from sources. Model recording the names of the sources.

footsteps

thunder

rain

baby crying

Dinah Zike's
FOLDABLES®

 **Go Digital**

Resources Research and Inquiry

Collaborative Conversations

Ask and Answer Questions As children engage in partner, small group, and whole group discussions, remind them to:

- ask questions about ideas they do not understand.
- give others a chance to think after asking a question.
- write down questions they want to ask the teacher or the whole class.

STEP 4 **Create the Project: Sound Effects Chart**

Explain the characteristics of a chart.

- **Information** The purpose of a chart is to give information. In this project, the chart will list sound effects and how they are made.

- **Headings** Headings tell the subject of each column in the chart.

- **Text** A chart has text that gives examples under each heading.

Have children create a two-column sound effects chart.

- Guide children to use the headings: **Sound Effects** and **How They Are Made**.

- Have children complete the chart with three examples based on their research.

- Prompt children to write a sample page of a radio script that includes one or two sound effects from their chart.

 STEM

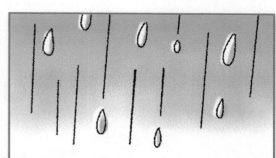

Jon: Oh no, it's raining!
(sound of raindrops)

Amy: Let's go inside so we
don't get wet.
(sound of footsteps)

ILLUSTRATED SOUND EFFECTS CHART

ENGLISH LANGUAGE LEARNERS

ELL SCAFFOLD

Beginning	Intermediate	Advanced/High
Use Sentence Frames Use sentence frames to help children discuss their radio play. For example: *Our play is about ____. It has ____ characters.*	**Discuss** Guide children to focus on the sound effects for their radio play. Ask: *What sound effects will your play have? How will you make those sounds?*	**Describe** Prompt children to explain how the sound effects enhance their radio play. Ask how the sound effects might affect the listeners.

Materials

Reading/Writing Workshop
VOLUME 4

Literature Anthology
VOLUME 4

Visual Vocabulary Cards
color
early
instead
nothing
of
thought

Teaching Poster

cow

Spelling Word Cards

→ # Word Work

MINILESSON
5 Mins

Phonemic Awareness

OBJECTIVES

CCSS Orally produce single-syllable words by blending sounds (phonemes), including consonant blends. **RF.1.2b**

CCSS Decode regularly spelled one-syllable words. **RF.1.3b**

CCSS Read words with inflectional endings. **RF.1.3f**

Phoneme Blending

Review Guide children to blend phonemes to form words. *Listen as I say a group of sounds. Then blend those sounds to form a word.*

/ou/ /t/　　　/s/ /ou/ /th/　　　/t/ /ou/ /n/　　　/f/ /ou/ /n/ /d/

Phoneme Substitution

Review Guide children to substitute vowel sounds in words. *I will say a word. I want you to change the vowel sound and say the new word.*

lid/loud　　shut/shout　　ten/town　　find/found

MINILESSON
10 Mins

Phonics/Structural Analysis

Blend and Build with /ou/ou, ow

Review Have children read and say the words *shout, south,* and *wow.* Then have children follow the word-building routine to build *loud, cloud, clout, pout, shout, out, ouch, couch, pouch, slouch, crouch, crown, clown, down, gown, frown.*

Word Automaticity Help children practice word automaticity. Display decodable words and point to each word as children chorally read it. Test how many words children can read in one minute. Model blending words children miss.

Inflectional Endings -er, -est

Review Have children explain when the *-er* and *-est* endings are used. Then have children practice reading words with *-er* or *-est,* such as *fast, faster, fastest; dark, darker, darkest;* and *safe, safer, safest.*

Go Digital

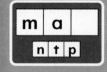

Phonemic Awareness

m a
n t p

Phonics

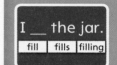

I __ the jar.
fill | fills | filling

Structural Analysis

school

Visual Glossary

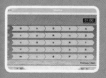

Fluency: Word Automaticity

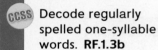

Spelling

Word Sort with *ou, ow*

Review Have children use the **Spelling Word Cards** to sort the weekly words by vowel diphthong spellings.

Assess Assess children on their ability to spell words with /ou/ spelled *ou* and *ow*. Say each word and provide a sentence. Allow time to write the words. To challenge children, provide an additional word with each vowel diphthong spelling.

High-Frequency Words

color, early, instead, nothing, oh, thought

Review Display **Visual Vocabulary Cards** for this week's words. Have children Read/Spell/Write and write a sentence with each word.

Review Vocabulary

scrambled, suddenly

Review Write *scrambled* and *suddenly*. Ask children to use each word in a sentence. Write the sentences and reinforce word meanings as necessary. Repeat the activity with last week's words or other previously taught words that children need to review.

Fluency

Expression

Review Review that some stories contain repeated words and phrases used for emphasis. *Sometimes repeated words and phrases are separated by ellipses. An ellipsis indicates a pause should be taken.*

Read aloud a few pages of the Shared Read. Have children echo each sentence. Point out how you read the repeated text patterns. Then have partners reread the selection, working on how they read repeated text.

Quick Review

Build Fluency: Sound-Spellings
Display the **Word-Building Cards:** *ou, ow, ar, ore, oar, er, ir, ur, ey, igh, oa, oe, ee, ea, ai, ay, e_e, u_e, o_e, dge, i_e, a_e, ch, tch, wh, ph, th, sh, ng, mp.* Have children say the sounds. Repeat, and vary the pace.

Monitor and *Differentiate*

✓ Quick Check

Can children read and decode words with diphthongs *ou, ow*?

Can children recognize and read high-frequency and vocabulary words?

Small Group Instruction

If No → **Approaching** Reteach pp. T290–293

       ELL Develop pp. T304–311

If Yes→ **On Level** Review pp. T209–299

       Beyond Level Extend pp. T302–303

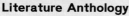

Literature Anthology

OBJECTIVES

CCSS With guidance and support from adults, use a variety of digital tools to produce and publish writing, including in collaboration with peers. **W.1.6**

CCSS Follow agreed-upon rules for discussions (e.g., listening to others with care, speaking one at a time about the topics and texts under discussion). **SL.1.1a**

CCSS Ask and answer questions about key details in a text read aloud or information presented orally or through other media. **SL.1.2**

Underline book titles

ACADEMIC LANGUAGE

• evaluate, presentation, underline, capitalize
• Cognates: *evaluar, presentación*

MINILESSON
5 Mins

Independent Writing

Write About the Literature Anthology

Prepare

Tell children they will plan what they will say about their finished writing and drawing to the class. Remind children to:

• Think about how their sentences express complete ideas.

• Think about how their concluding sentence wraps up the action in the story.

Present

Have children take turns giving presentations of their responses to the prompt about *Whistle for Willie*: *Use what you know about Peter to write a new story about a time he learned to play a musical instrument or sing a special song*. If possible, record their presentations so children can self-evaluate. Tell children to:

• Explain drawings they made that help clarify characters or events in their stories.

• Listen carefully and quietly while the presenter speaks.

• Answer questions about their own presentations.

Evaluate

Have children discuss their own presentations and evaluate their performance using the presentation rubric.

Use the teacher's rubric to evaluate children's writing. Have children add their writing to their Writer's Portfolio. Encourage them to look back at previous writing. Guide children to discuss what they liked best about their story and what they learned about writing stories. Have them share their observations with a partner.

Publish

After children finish presenting their stories, discuss how each child will make his or her own book. Have children give their stories titles. Have them illustrate covers for their stories and add their names as authors. Attach the covers to children's stories and display the individual books in the classroom library or on a bulletin board. Guide children to use digital tools to publish their writing.

Go Digital

Writing

Checklists

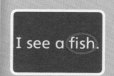

I see a fish.

Grammar

MINILESSON 5 Mins

Grammar

Using *A, An, This, That*

1 Review Have children describe when the adjectives *a, an, this,* and *that* are used. Write the following sentences and have children identify the adjectives:

> This mix needs a cup of water. Could you hand me that cup? (this, a, that)

2 Practice Ask: *What does* this *tell you about where the mix is? What does* that *tell you about where the cup is? Why did the writer use* a *instead of* an?

Have children work in pairs to write sentences using *a, an, this,* and *that.*

Mechanics: Capitalize/Underline Book Titles

1 Review Remind children that the important words in book titles are capitalized and book titles are underlined.

2 Practice Write the following sentences. Read each aloud. Have children fix the sentences.

> I read The rain came down. (I read <u>The Rain Came Down.</u>

> The art in one More sheep is funny! (The art in <u>One More Sheep</u> is funny!)

> Have you looked at the kid's cookbook? (Have you looked at <u>The Kid's Cookbook</u>?)

Daily Wrap Up

- Review the Essential Question and encourage children to discuss using the oral vocabulary words.

- Review with children that a problem is something characters want to do, change, or find out. The way the problem is solved is the solution.

- Review words with diphthongs *ou* and *ow,* such as *found* and *down.*

- Use the Visual Vocabulary Cards to review the Words to Know.

- Remind children that an opinion tells how they feel about something and the reasons they feel that way.

→ Integrate Ideas

Close Reading Routine

Read   DOK 1–2

- Identify key ideas and details about sounds.
- Take notes and retell.
- Use prompts as needed.

Reread   DOK 2–3

- Analyze text, craft, and structure.

Integrate   DOK 4

- Integrate knowledge and ideas and make text-to-text connections.
- Use the Integrate Lesson.
- Use *Close Reading Companion*, p. 160.

TEXT CONNECTIONS

Connect to the Essential Question

Write the essential question on the board: *What sounds can you hear? How are they made?* Read the essential question aloud. Tell children that they will think about all of the selections they have read and what they have learned about how different sounds are made. Say: *We have read many selections on this topic. We will compare the information from this week's* **Leveled Readers** *and* Now, What's That Sound?, **Reading/Writing Workshop** *pages 180–189.*

Evaluate Text Evidence Guide children to review the selections and their completed graphic organizers. Have children work with partners to compare information from all the week's reads. Children can record notes using a Foldable®. Guide them to record information from the selections that helps them answer the Essential Question.

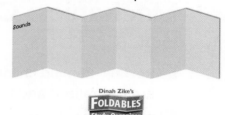

Dinah Zike's
FOLDABLES
Study Organizer

Sounds All Around

RESEARCH AND INQUIRY

Have children create a checklist and review their sound effects chart:

- Does their chart give information about sounds and how they are made?
- Did they use headings, columns, and rows to organize the information? Do the headings tell what's in each column?
- Did they write sentences to explain how each sound is made?
- Have they taken notes about how they will explain their sound effects chart to the class?

Guide partners to practice sharing their charts with each other. Children should practice speaking and presenting their information clearly.

Guide children to share their work. Prompt children to ask questions to clarify when something is unclear: *What sounds did you include in your chart? Did you tell how each sound is made? What did you learn that you didn't know before?* Have children use the Presentation Checklist online.

OBJECTIVES

CCSS Participate in shared research and writing projects. **W.1.7**

Go Digital

Collaborate

OBJECTIVES

CCSS Identify basic similarities in and differences between two texts on the same topic (e.g., in illustrations, descriptions, or procedures). **RI.1.9**

Text to Music

Read aloud with children the Integrate activity on page 160 of the *Close Reading Companion*. Have partners share reactions to the song. Then guide them to discuss how it is similar to the selections they read earlier in the week. Have partners collaborate to complete the Integrate page by following the prompts.

Present Ideas and Synthesize Information

When children finish their discussions, ask for a volunteer from each pair to share the information from their Foldable® and their Integrate pages. After each pair has presented their ideas, ask: *How does learning about sounds and where they come from help you answer the Essential Question, What sounds can you hear? How are they made?* Lead a class discussion asking students to use the information from their charts to answer the Essential Question.

SPEAKING AND LISTENING

As children are working with partners in their *Close Reading Companion* or on their sound effects charts, make sure that they are actively participating in the conversation and, when necessary, remind them to use these speaking and listening strategies:

Speaking Strategies

- Take turns speaking and to focus their comments on the topic being discussed.
- Ask questions about information they don't understand and give others appropriate time to respond to their questions.
- Use gestures and point to visuals to communicate details about the topic.

Listening Strategies

- Listen quietly and remember not to interrupt the speaker.
- Listen to the details others use and try to connect what a speaker says with their own experiences and what they know.
- Take notes and write down questions they have for the speaker.

OBJECTIVES

CCSS Follow agreed-upon rules for discussions. **SL.1.1a**

CCSS Ask and answer questions about what a speaker says in order to gather additional information or clarify something that is not understood. **SL.1.3**

CCSS Describe people, places, things, and events with relevant details, expressing ideas and feelings clearly. **SL.1.4**

→ Approaching Level

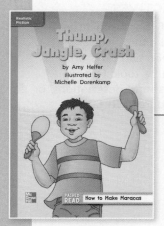

Lexile 180

OBJECTIVES

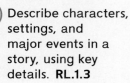 Describe characters, settings, and major events in a story, using key details. **RL.1.3**

Make connections within text by identifying problems and solutions

Leveled Reader:
Thump, Jangle, Crash

Go Digital

Thump, Jangle, Crash

Graphic Organizer

Retell

Before Reading

Preview and Predict

Have children turn to the title page. Read the title and the author's name and have children repeat. Preview the selection's illustrations. Prompt children to predict what the selection might be about.

Review Genre: Realistic Fiction

Have children recall that realistic fiction is a made-up story that could happen in real life.

ESSENTIAL QUESTION

Remind children of the Essential Question: *What sounds can you hear? How are they made?* Set a purpose for reading: *Let's read to find out what things make the sounds* thump, jangle, *and* crash.

Remind children that as they read a selection, they can ask questions about what they do not understand or what they want to know more about.

During Reading

Guided Comprehension

As children whisper read *Thump, Jangle, Crash,* monitor and provide guidance, correcting blending and modeling the key strategies and skills.

Strategy: Ask and Answer Questions

Remind children that as they read, they can stop and ask themselves questions. *After asking questions, read on to find the answers.* Model using the strategy: *On page 2, the words say Marco went into the band room. Will he be in the band? I'll read the next page. Yes, he can join the band.*

Skill: Plot: Problem and Solution

Remind children that the problem is what characters want to do, change, or find out. The solution is the way the problem is solved. As you read, ask: *What is Marco's problem?* Display a Problem and Solution chart for children to copy.

Model recording children's answers in the boxes. Have children record the answers in their own charts.

Think Aloud On page 3, I read Marco didn't know what instrument he wanted to play. I'll write that in the Problem box. Then I can read on to find out how he solves this problem and chooses an instrument.

Guide children to use the details to determine the steps and solution.

After Reading

Respond to Reading

Have children complete the Respond to Reading on page 12.

Retell

Have children take turns retelling the selection, using the **Retelling Cards** as a guide. Help them make a connection: *Which of the instruments Marco tried do we have at school? Which ones have you tried? Which is your favorite?*

Model Fluency

Chorally read the story with children. Model reading with expression as needed.

Apply Have partners practice reading. Provide feedback as needed.

PAIRED READ ...

"How to Make Maracas"

Make Connections:
Write About It *Analytical Writing*

Leveled Reader

Before reading, ask children to note the genre of this text is informational. Then discuss the Compare Texts direction. After reading, ask children to make connections between the information they learned from "How to Make Maracas" and *Thump, Jangle, Crash.* Prompt children as needed by asking: *How did reading about how maracas are made help you understand Marco's decision about which instrument to play?*

FOCUS ON SCIENCE

Children can extend their knowledge of sounds by completing the science activity on page 16. **STEM**

Literature Circles

Lead children in conducting a literature circle using the Thinkmark questions to guide the discussion. You may wish to discuss what children have learned about different sounds from both selections in the Leveled Reader.

Level Up

Level-up lessons available online.

IF children can read *Thump, Jangle, Crash* Approaching Level with fluency and correctly answer the Respond to Reading questions,

THEN tell children that they will read another story about different sounds.

• Use pages 5–6 of *Down on the Farm* On Level to model using Teaching Poster 36 to list a story problem.

• Have children read the selection, checking their comprehension by using the graphic organizer.

Approaching Level

Phonemic Awareness

PHONEME ISOLATION

 TIER 2

OBJECTIVES

Isolate and pronounce initial, medial vowel, and final sounds (phonemes) in spoken single-syllable words. **RF.1.2c**

I Do Explain that children will listen for the first sound in a word. *Listen carefully as I say a word:* out. *I hear /ou/ at the beginning of the word* out. *Say the sound and the word with me: /ou/,* out.

 We Do *Let's do some together. Listen as I say a word:* ouch. *What is the first sound in* ouch? *That's right, the first sound is /ou/.*

Repeat the routine with these words:

| out | board | vase | oat | mouth | town | quick | short |

 You Do *Are you ready? I'll say a word. You say the first sound.*

| night | owl | chart | eel | mouse | no | shout |

PHONEME BLENDING

TIER 2

OBJECTIVES

 Orally produce single-syllable words by blending sounds (phonemes), including consonant blends. **RF.1.2b**

 I Do Explain that children will be blending sounds to say words. *I'm going to say a word sound by sound. Then I'll put the sounds together to say a word: /ou/ /ch/, /ouch/,* ouch. *I blended two sounds to say the word* ouch.

 We Do *Let's blend words together. Listen to these sounds: /m/ /är/ /k/. Let's blend the sounds together: /mmmärk/,* mark. *The word is* mark.

Repeat the routine with these words:

/ch/ /ou/   /n/ /o/ /t/   /k/ /ou/   /m/ /ou/ /th/   /sk/ /ou/ /t/

 You Do *Now it's your turn. Listen carefully. I'll say the sounds of a word. You blend the sounds together to say the word.*

/n/ /ou/   /ch/ /e/ /k/   /s/ /ou/ /n/ /d/   /ou/ /l/   /h/ /ou/ /s/

PHONEME ISOLATION

OBJECTIVES

Isolate and pronounce initial, medial vowel, and final sounds (phonemes) in spoken single-syllable words. **RF.1.2c**

 Explain to children that they will listen for the sound in the middle of a word. *Listen as I say a word: /k/ /ou/ /ch/,* couch. *I hear the /ou/ sound in the middle of the word* couch.

 Let's try it together. Listen as I say the word: count. *What sound do you hear in the middle of the word? Yes, we hear /ou/ in the middle of the word* count.

Continue the activity with these words:

might	scout	quake	found	proud

 It's your turn. I'll say a word. You say the sound that you hear in the middle of the word.

down	shut	round	made	mouth

PHONEME SUBSTITUTION

OBJECTIVES

Isolate and pronounce initial, medial vowel, and final sounds (phonemes) in spoken single-syllable words. **RF.1.2c**

Substitute the medial phoneme in words

 Listen as I say a word: lid. *I hear the /i/ vowel sound in the middle of* lid. *I'm going to change that vowel sound from /i/ to /ou/. Here is the new word: /l/ /ou/ /d/,* loud. *I made a new word,* loud.

 Do it with me. Listen to this word: grind. *Say the word with me:* grind. *Now change the vowel sound /ī/ to /ou/: /ground/,* ground. *The new word is* ground.

Repeat with these words:

card, cord	shut, shout	dine, down	signed, sound

 Let's make some more words. Change the middle sound and make a new word.

cheap, chap	gain, gown	couch, catch	file, foul

ENGLISH LANGUAGE LEARNERS

For the **children** who need **phonemic awareness**, **phonics**, and **fluency** practice, use scaffolding methods as necessary to ensure children understand the meaning of the words. Refer to the Language Transfers Handbook for phonics elements that may not transfer in children's native languages.

→ Approaching Level

Phonics

CONNECT *ou, ow* TO /ou/

 TIER 2

OBJECTIVES

 Know and apply grade-level phonics and word analysis skills in decoding words. **RF.1.3**

 I Do Display the **Word-Building Card** o*u. These are the letters* o, u. *I'm going to trace these letters while I say* /ou/. Trace the letters *ou* while saying /ou/ several times. Repeat with *ow*.

 We Do *Let's do it together.* Have children trace lowercase *ou* on the Word-Building Card with their finger while saying /ou/. Trace the letters *ou* five times and say /ou/ with children. Repeat with *ow*.

You Do Have children connect the letters *ou* and the sound by tracing *ou* in the air while saying /ou/. Then have children write the letters on paper as they say the sound. Repeat with *ow*.

Repeat, connecting *ou* and *ow* and the vowel sound /ou/ throughout the week.

BLEND WORDS WITH /ou/*ou, ow*

 TIER 2

OBJECTIVES

 Decode regularly spelled one-syllable words. **RF.1.3b**

Decode words with diphthongs *ou, ow*

 I Do Display Word-Building Cards *l, ou, d. This is the letter* l. *It stands for the* /l/ *sound. These are the letters* ou. *Together they often stand for the* /ou/ *sound. Say it with me:* /ou/. *This is the letter* d. *It stands for the* /d/ *sound. I'll blend the sounds together:* /loud/. *The word is* loud. Repeat with *down*.

 We Do Guide children to blend sounds and read: *proud, found, bow, plow*. Assist children as necessary.

You Do Ask children to blend the sounds and decode: *cow, how, now, plow, brow, bow*.

You may wish to review Phonics with **ELL** using this section.

BUILD WORDS WITH /ou/ *ou, ow*

OBJECTIVES

(CCSS) Decode regularly spelled one-syllable words. **RF.1.3b**

Build and decode words with diphthongs *ou, ow*

 I Do Display Word-Building Cards *s, ou, n, d. These are the letters* s, o, u, n, d. *They stand for /s/ /ou/ /n/ /d/. I'll blend these sounds to make a word: /sound/,* sound. *The word is* sound.

 We Do *Now let's do one together.* Point to the cards forming *sound* and read it together. *I am going to change the letter* s *to* r. *Change the letter* s *to* r. *Let's blend and read the new word: /round/,* round.

 You Do Have children blend the words: *hound, mount, count, cow, crowd, crown.*

Repeat, building additional words with diphthongs *ou* and *ow.*

BLEND WORDS WITH /ou/ *ou, ow*

OBJECTIVES

(CCSS) Decode regularly spelled one-syllable words. **RF.1.3b**

Build and decode words with diphthongs *ou, ow*

 I Do Display Word-Building Cards *c, r, ow, d. These are the letters* c, r. *They stand for the sounds /kr/. These are the letters* o, w. *Together they stand for the sound /ou/. This is the letter* d. *It stands for the /d/ sound. Listen as I blend the sounds in this word: /kroud/,* crowd. *The word is* crowd.

 We Do *Let's try some together.* Blend and read the words *wow, brow, pout, south,* and *trout* together.

 You Do Display the words to the right. Help children blend and read the words.

Decodable Reader Have children read "Up or Down Sounds" (pages 41–44) and "Sounds Around Us" (45–48).

cloud	loud	house	round	found
mouth	out	scout	shout	spout
chow	how	now	sow	bounce
score	chart	mice	shine	third

I found the house in town.

Now put down the brown card.

The scout will shout to the crowd.

BUILD FLUENCY WITH PHONICS

Sound-Spellings Fluency

Display the following Word-Building Cards: *ou, ow, ar, ore, oar, er, ir, ur, ey, igh, oa, oe, ee, ea, ai, ay, e_e, u_e, o_e, dge, i_e, a_e, ch, tch, wh, ph, th, sh, ng, mp.* Have children chorally say the sounds. Repeat and vary the pace.

Fluency in Connected Text

Have children review the **Decodable Reader** selections. Identify words with diphthongs *ou* and *ow.* Blend words as needed.

Have partners reread the selections for fluency.

Approaching Level

Structural Analysis

REVIEW INFLECTIONAL ENDINGS *-er, -est*

OBJECTIVES

CCSS Know and apply grade-level phonics and word analysis skills in decoding words. **RF.1.3**

Understand comparative endings *-er, -est*

 I Do Write and read the word *shorter. I look at the word* shorter *and I see a word I know,* short. *The -*er *ending tells me this word is comparing two things. I am shorter than my brother.* Repeat with *shortest.*

 We Do Write and read *hotter. If we look at* hotter, *is there a word we know? Yes,* hot. *The ending -*er *tells us two hot things are being compared: Today is hotter than yesterday was.* Write *hottest. What word and ending do you see in* hottest? *Yes! The word* hot *and the ending -*est. *Let's make up a sentence that tells about the hottest day.*

Point out that when the endings *-er* and *-est* are added to words that end with a vowel and consonant, we double the consonant before adding the ending.

 You Do Write *dark* and *light*. Help partners add the inflectional endings *-er* and *-est*. Have them use the words in sentences.

RETEACH INFLECTIONAL ENDINGS *-er, -est*

OBJECTIVES

CCSS Know and apply grade-level phonics and word analysis skills in decoding words. **RF.1.3**

Understand comparative endings *-er, -est*

 I Do Write and read the word *loud.* Say: *We use the word* loud *to tell about sound. The bell is loud. Sometimes we want to compare two things. We can add -*er *to* loud *to compare how loud two things are: The school bell is louder than the doorbell.* Write louder *on the board and underline -*er. Repeat with *loudest.*

 We Do *Write and read the adjective:* big. *Explain that if a word ends with a vowel and a consonant, we double the consonant before adding the ending. Add* bigger *and* biggest *to the board. Read the words with children. Draw three boxes on the board. Have children use the words in sentences to compare them.*

Repeat with *cold, wet,* and *hard.*

 You Do Have children add *-er* and *-est* to adjectives. *Add -*er *and -*est *to each word. Say each word and use it in a sentence.*

dark   flat   mad

Words to Know

REVIEW HIGH-FREQUENCY WORDS

OBJECTIVES

 Recognize and read grade-appropriate irregularly spelled words. **RF.1.3g**

Review *color, early, instead, nothing, oh, thought*

 I Do Use **High-Frequency Word Cards** to **Read/Spell/Write** each high-frequency word. Use each word orally in a sentence.

 We Do Help children to Read/Spell/Write each word on their **Response Boards**. Help them create oral sentences that include the words.

 You Do Have partners do the Read/Spell/Write routine using the words *color, early, instead, nothing, oh, thought.*

CUMULATIVE REVIEW

OBJECTIVES

 Recognize and read grade-appropriate irregularly spelled words. **RF.1.3g**

Review previously taught high-frequency words

 I Do Display the High-Frequency Word Cards from the previous weeks. Review each word using the Read/Spell/Write routine.

 We Do Have children write each word on their Response Boards. Complete sentences for each word, such as: *Do you want to climb? Put the book on the _____.*

 You Do Show each card and have children read each word together. Ask volunteers to use the words in sentences.

Fluency Display the High-Frequency Word Cards. Point to the words in random order. Have children chorally read each word. Then repeat at a faster pace.

REVIEW VOCABULARY WORDS

OBJECTIVES

 Identify real-life connections between words and their use (e.g., note places at home that are *cozy*). **L.1.5c**

 I Do Display the **Visual Vocabulary Cards** for *scrambled* and *suddenly*. Review each word using the Define/Example/Ask routine.

 We Do Invite children to act out or demonstrate each word. Then work with them to complete the sentence starters: **(1)** *The bug scrambled to ____.* **(2)** *Suddenly, the mouse ____.*

 You Do Have partners write two sentences on their own, using each of the words. Provide assistance as needed.

→ Approaching Level

Comprehension

READ FOR FLUENCY

OBJECTIVES
Read grade-level text orally with accuracy, appropriate rate, and expression. **RF.1.4b**

I Do Read the first page of the Practice Book selection. Model reading with expression. Talk about how your voice changes when you read dialogue. *I change my voice when I read the character's words. I want my voice to sound like one of the characters.*

We Do Read the next page of the Practice Book selection, modeling reading with expression. Then reread with children as they choral read the paragraph.

You Do Continue reading the selection, choral reading the story with children. Note if they are reading with expression and fluency.

IDENTIFY EVENTS

OBJECTIVES
Describe characters, settings, and major events in a story, using key details. **RL.1.3**

Identify story events

I Do Remind children that they have been reading realistic fiction. *An event is what takes place in a story. An event tells where the characters go and what they do. The events explain what happens during the story.*

We Do Read the first two pages of the Practice Book selection aloud. Then guide children to explain the events in the story. *We read about Howie and Dad. Where are they? Yes, they are on a bus. What does Dad suggest doing? That's right, he suggests playing a game. Riding the bus and playing a game are events in the story.*

You Do Help children reread the rest of the selection. Remind them to think about what the characters are doing and why. Help them to retell the events in the story.

REVIEW PLOT: PROBLEM AND SOLUTION

OBJECTIVES

CCSS Describe characters, settings, and major events in a story, using key details. **RL.1.3**

Identify problems and solutions in realistic fiction

 I Do Remind children that they have been reading realistic fiction. *The plot is the sequence of events in the story. In many stories, the plot is about a problem and how the characters solve the problem.*

 We Do Read the first two pages of the Practice Book selection together. Ask children to identify the characters and the first event. Then ask: *What is Howie's problem?*

 You Do Have partners read the rest of the selection together. Tell them to discuss Howie's problem and how the problem was solved. Help children record their ideas on a Problem and Solution chart.

SELF-SELECTED READING

OBJECTIVES

 CCSS With prompting and support, read prose and poetry of appropriate complexity for grade 1. **RL.1.10**

Apply the strategy and skill to read a text

Read Independently

Have children choose a realistic fiction selection for sustained silent reading. Remind them to:

- identify the characters and setting in the story.

- identify the key events in the story.

- think about the problem and how it was solved.

Read Purposefully

Guide children to record plot details on a Problem and Solution chart. Then have children participate in a group discussion about the selection they read. Encourage them to:

- discuss the information that they recorded on the chart.

- tell how the events in the story led to the solution of the problem.

On Level

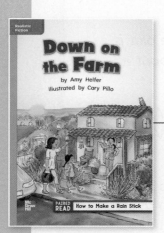

Lexile 390

OBJECTIVES

CCSS Describe characters, settings, and major events in a story, using key details. **RL.1.3**

Make connections within text by identifying problems and solutions

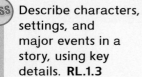

Leveled Reader:
Down on the Farm

Before Reading

Preview and Predict

Have children turn to the title page. Read the title and the author's name and have children repeat. Preview the selection's illustrations. Prompt children to predict what the selection might be about.

Review Genre: Realistic Fiction

Have children recall that realistic fiction is a made-up story that could happen in real life.

ESSENTIAL QUESTION

Remind children of the Essential Question: *What sounds can you hear? How are they made?* Set a purpose for reading: *Let's read to find out what strange sound Jacy hears.* Remind children that as they read a selection, they can ask questions about what they do not understand or what they want to know more about.

During Reading

Guided Comprehension

As children whisper read *Down on the Farm,* monitor and provide guidance. Help children sort farm words and city words into categories.

Strategy: Ask and Answer Questions

Remind children that as they read, they can ask questions and then read on to find the answers. Model using the strategy on pages 5–6. *Jacy wonders where the sounds are coming from. What sounds does Jacy hear? Let's read on and look at the picture on page 6.*

Skill: Plot: Problem and Solution

Remind children that the problem is what characters want to do, change, or find out. What they do to solve the problem is the solution. As you read, ask: *What problem does Jacy have?* Display a Problem and Solution chart for children to copy.

Go Digital

Down on the Farm

Graphic Organizer

Retell

Model recording answers for children. Have children copy the answers into their own charts.

Think Aloud On page 5, I read Jacy was confused. She didn't know where the farm was. I'll write that in the Problem box. Then I can read on to find out how she solves the problem and discovers the farm.

Prompt children to fill in the chart as they read.

After Reading

Respond to Reading

Have children complete the Respond to Reading on page 12.

Retell

Have children take turns retelling the selection, using the **Retelling Cards** as a guide. Help children make a connection: *What animal sounds have you heard? Where did you hear them?*

Model Fluency

Read the selection chorally with children. Model reading with expression.

Apply Have partners practice reading. Provide feedback as needed.

PAIRED READ ...

"How to Make a Rain Stick"

Leveled Reader

Make Connections: Write About It · *Analytical Writing*

Before reading, ask children to note that the genre of this selection is informational text. Then discuss the Compare Texts direction. After reading, ask children to make connections between the information they learned from "How to Make a Rain Stick" and *Down on the Farm. How are the sounds in both stories alike? How are they different?*

Literature Circles

Lead children in conducting a literature circle using the Thinkmark questions to guide the discussion. You may wish to discuss what children have learned about different sounds in both selections in the Leveled Reader.

Level Up

Level-up lessons available online.

IF children can read *Down on the Farm* On Level with fluency and correctly answer the Respond to Reading questions,

THEN tell children that they will read another story about different sounds.

• Use page 6 of *Going on a Bird Walk* Beyond Level to model using Teaching Poster 36 to list the story problem.

• Have children read the selection, checking their comprehension by using the graphic organizer.

FOCUS ON SCIENCE

Children can extend their knowledge of sounds by completing the science activity on page 16. **STEM**

On Level

Phonics

BUILD WORDS WITH /ou/ *ou, ow*

OBJECTIVES

 Know and apply grade-level phonics and word analysis skills in decoding words. **RF.1.3**

Build and decode words with diphthongs *ou, ow*

 I Do   Display **Word-Building Cards** *ou, c, h. These are the letters* o, u, c, h, *They stand for /ou/ /ch/. I will blend /ou/ and /ch/ together:* ouch. *The word is* ouch. Repeat with the word *cow*.

 We Do   *Let's blend a word together.* Make the word *down* using Word-Building Cards. *Let's blend: /d/ /ou/ /n/, /doun/,* down. *We blended the word* down.

Replace the letter *d* with the letters *f* and *r*. *I am going to change the letter* d *in* down *to the letters* f *and* r. *Let's blend and read the new word: /fr/ /ou/ /n/, /froun/,* frown. *The new word is* frown.

 You Do   Have children build and blend these words: *cow, how, now, sow, gown, gout, pout, spout.*

Decodable Reader Have children read "Up or Down Sounds" and "Sounds Around Us," (pages 41–48).

Words to Know

REVIEW WORDS

OBJECTIVES

 Recognize and read grade-appropriate irregularly spelled words. **RF.1.3g**

Review high-frequency words *color, early, instead, nothing, oh, thought* and vocabulary words *scrambled* and *suddenly*

 I Do   Use the **Read/Spell/Write** routine to review the high-frequency words *color, early, instead, nothing, oh, thought* and the vocabulary words *scrambled* and *suddenly*. Use each word orally in a sentence.

 We Do   Guide children to Read/Spell/Write each word using their **Response Boards**. Then work with them to generate oral sentences using the words.

 You Do   Have partners work together to do the Read/Spell/Write routine on their own using the high-frequency words c*olor, early, instead, nothing, oh,* and *thought* and the vocabulary words *scrambled* and *suddenly*. Have partners write sentences about this week's selections. Each sentence must contain at least one high-frequency or vocabulary word.

Comprehension

REVIEW PLOT: PROBLEM AND SOLUTION

OBJECTIVES

 Describe characters, settings, and major events in a story, using key details. **RL.1.3**

 Remind children that they have been reading realistic fiction. *The plot is the sequence of events in the story. The plot usually is about a problem the characters have and how they solve it.*

 Read the first two pages of the Practice Book selection aloud. *What was Howie's problem? What was Dad's idea to solve the problem?*

 Guide children to read the rest of the selection. Have them take time to think about the problem and the solution. Help them record their ideas on a Problem and Solution chart. Encourage them to use key events to help.

SELF-SELECTED READING

OBJECTIVES

With prompting and support, read prose and poetry of appropriate complexity for grade 1. **RL.1.10**

Apply the strategy and skill to read a text

Read Independently

Have children choose a realistic fiction selection for sustained silent reading. Remind them to:

- identify the problem, the steps to solve it, and the solution.

- ask questions while they are reading about anything they don't understand or anything they want to know more about.

Read Purposefully

Have children record details about the plot on a Problem and Solution chart. After they read, encourage children to take part in a group discussion about the selection that they read. Guide children to:

- share information that they recorded on their chart.

- tell what questions they had as they were reading.

Beyond Level

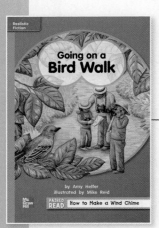

Lexile 420

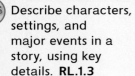

OBJECTIVES

Describe characters, settings, and major events in a story, using key details. **RL.1.3**

Make connections within text by identifying problems and solutions

Leveled Reader:
Going on a Bird Walk

Before Reading

Preview and Predict

Read the title and author name. Have children preview the title page and the illustrations. Ask: *What sounds do you think you will learn about?*

Review Genre: Realistic Fiction

Have children recall that realistic fiction is a made-up story that could happen in real life. Prompt children to name key characteristics of realistic fiction. Tell them to look for these as they read the Leveled Reader.

ESSENTIAL QUESTION

Remind children of the Essential Question: *What sounds can you hear? How are they made?* Set a purpose for reading: *Let's find out what Dee learns about the sounds birds make.*

During Reading

Guided Comprehension

Have children whisper read *Going on a Bird Walk*. Have them place self-stick notes next to difficult words. Remind children that when they come to an unfamiliar word, they can look for familiar spellings. They will need to break longer words into smaller chunks and sound out each part.

Monitor children's reading. Stop periodically and ask open-ended questions to facilitate rich discussion, such as, *What sound does Dee hear now?* Build on children's responses to develop deeper understanding of the text.

Strategy: Ask and Answer Questions

Remind children that asking and answering questions about a selection can help them understand and clarify the information they read. Say: *Look for the answers to your questions in the text and illustrations.*

Go Digital

Going on a Bird Walk

Graphic Organizer

Skill: Plot: Problem and Solution

Remind children a problem is what characters want to do, change, or find out. The way they solve the problem is the solution. As you read, ask: *What problem does Dee have with the bird call?* Display a Problem and Solution chart for children to copy. Model how to record the information.

Think Aloud On page 6, I read that the bird call hurt Dee's ears when she tried it. She doesn't know how to work the bird call. I'll write that in the Problem box. Then I can read on to see how she solves the problem.

Have children fill in their charts as they continue reading.

After Reading

Respond to Reading

Complete the Respond to Reading on page 12 after reading.

Retell

Have children take turns retelling the selection. Help children make a personal connection by writing about birds they have heard.

PAIRED READ ...

Leveled Reader

"How to Make a Wind Chime"

Make Connections: Write About It **Analytical Writing**

Before reading, "How to Make a Wind Chime," have children preview the title page and prompt them to identify the genre. Read the Compare Texts direction together. After reading the selection, have children work with a partner to discuss the information they learned in "How to Make a Wind Chime" and *Going on a Bird Walk*. Ask children to make connections by comparing and contrasting the selections. Prompt children to discuss what they learned about sounds from both selections.

FOCUS ON SCIENCE

Children can extend their knowledge about sounds by completing the science activity on page 16. **STEM**

Literature Circles

Lead children in conducting a literature circle using the Thinkmark questions to guide the discussion. You may wish to discuss what children have learned about sounds from the two selections in the Leveled Reader.

Gifted and Talented

SYNTHESIZE Challenge children to write about one of their favorite sounds. Encourage them to tell if the sounds come from nature or are from things made by people.

EXTEND Have them use information they learned from the week or do additional research to find out more about sounds.

Beyond Level

Vocabulary

ORAL VOCABULARY: MULTIPLE-MEANING WORDS

OBJECTIVES

Use sentence-level context as a clue to the meaning of a word or phrase. **L.1.4a**

I Do Explain that a multiple-meaning word is a word that has several different meanings. Review the meaning of the word *volume* that they learned. *Volume can mean "how loud something is." It can also mean "the amount of space of something." A large box has more volume than a small one. Volume is also another name for a large book.*

We Do *Listen to this sentence:* The small child sat on several thick volumes instead of in a high chair. *What do you think* volume *means in that sentence? Yes, it means "books."*

You Do Have partners make up oral sentences for the all three meanings of the word *volume*.

Gifted and Talented
Extend Have children draw pictures showing the different meanings of the word *volume*. Challenge partners to link all three pictures together in an oral story.

VOCABULARY: MULTIPLE-MEANING WORDS

OBJECTIVES

Use sentence-level context as a clue to the meaning of a word or phrase. **L.1.4a**

I Do Remind children that many words have more than one meaning. Review the meaning of the vocabulary word *scramble* with children. *The word* scramble *can mean "to climb or crawl quickly." I watched the kitten scramble up the post.* Scramble *can also mean "to mix together."*

We Do Write this sentence on the board and have children read it: *Dad stood at the stove and scrambled eggs in a pan.* Say: *What do you think* scrambled *means in that sentence? Yes, it means "mixed together."*

You Do Have partners write sentences for both meanings of the word *scrambled*.

Comprehension

REVIEW PLOT: PROBLEM AND SOLUTION

OBJECTIVES

 Describe characters, settings, and major events in a story, using key details. **RL.1.3**

 I Do Discuss how setting, characters, and events in a story work together to form the plot of the story. *When you read realistic fiction, think about the problem that the characters face. Think about what the characters want to do or change. Look for events that will lead to the solution of the problem.*

We Do Ask children to read the first two pages of the Practice Book selection aloud. *What is Howie's problem? How does Dad help solve the problem?*

You Do Have children read the rest of the Practice Book selection independently. Encourage them to look for the steps that lead to the problem's solution.

SELF-SELECTED READING

OBJECTIVES

 With prompting and support, read prose and poetry of appropriate complexity for grade 1. **RL.1.10**

Apply the strategy and skill to read text

Read Independently

Have children choose a realistic fiction selection for sustained silent reading. Tell them to use a Problem and Solution chart to record the steps that lead to the resolution of the problem.

Read Purposefully

Have children record details about the plot on a Problem and Solution chart. After reading, guide children to:

- share the information they recorded on the chart with a partner.

- record information about the story in a reading response journal.

 Independent Study Have children write a short summary that could go in a newspaper advertisement telling what happened in the story they read.

→ English Language Learners

Reading/Writing Workshop

OBJECTIVES

Describe characters, settings, and major events in a story, using key details. **RL.1.3**

Shared Read

Now, What's That Sound?

Before Reading

Build Background

Read the Essential Question: *What sounds can you hear? How are they made?*

- Explain the meaning of the Essential Question: *A sound is something that we can hear. People make sounds when they talk or laugh. Animals make sounds, too, like barking. Things can make sounds, like ticking.*

- **Model an answer:** *If I listen carefully, I hear many sounds in our classroom. I hear children talking. I hear chairs moving. I hear paper rustling.*

- Ask children a question that ties the Essential Question to their own background knowledge. *What do you hear when you are outside?* Ask partners to share their answers.

During Reading

Interactive Question-Response

- Ask questions that help children understand the meaning of the text after each paragraph.

- Reinforce the meanings of key vocabulary by providing meanings embedded in the questions.

- Ask children questions that require them to use key vocabulary.

- Reinforce the comprehension strategies and skills of the week by modeling.

Go Digital

Now, What's That Sound?

Graphic Organizer

Now, What's That Sound?

Pages 180–181

Point to the title. *Listen as I read the title.* Point to each word as you read it. *What is the title?* Point to the word *sound*. *A sound is something that we hear.*

Point to the people in the illustration. *These are the characters in the story. Who do you think they are?* (Mom, Dad, children, Grandfather) *Where does the story take place?* (at the family's house) *The title of the story tells us what it will be about. Let's read and find out about the sounds.*

Pages 182–183

Explain and Model the Skill Point to the first line on page 182. *These words tell a sound:* "Tap-tap-tap. Rat-a-tat-tat." *Now say these words with me. Gilbert and Marta have a problem, don't they? They heard a sound they don't know. Let's see how they try to solve the problem and find out what is making that sound.*

Let's look at the picture on page 183. Where is Dad? (in the garage) *What is he using to cut wood?* (a saw) Point to the third line. *These words tell the sound that the saw makes:* Zing, zing, zing. *Say the words with me. Now let's read what Gilbert says:* "This is not the sound," said Gilbert. "This sound is smoother."

 What steps do you think Gilbert and Marta will take to solve their problem?

Pages 184–185

Look at the picture on pages 184-185. Where is Gramps? (on the deck) *What is he doing?* (sweeping) *Do you think the broom will make a rat-a-tat-tat sound? Let's read on to find out.*

Read page 185. Point to the second line. *These words tell what the broom sounds like:* Swish, swish, swish. *Let's say these words together. Is this the sound Marta and Gilbert were looking for?* (no)

Pages 186–187

Now the children find Ana. What is Ana doing? (bouncing a basketball) *Show me how you would bounce a ball.*

Let's slowly read the words that tell the sound of the ball: Bam... bam... bam. *That is not the rat-a-tat-tat sound, is it? Gilbert thinks this sound is slower.*

Explain and Model the Strategy Read page 187. *We can stop and ask ourselves questions as we read: What is making the rat-a-tat-tat sound? Then we can read on to find the answer to the question.*

 Ask another question about the story.

Explain and Model Phonics *Listen as I say some words. When you hear a word with the /ou/ sound, repeat the word:* ball, bouncing, bam, sound.

Pages 188–189

Let's read the first line on page 188: Tap-tap-tap. Rat-a-tat-tat. *That is the sound the children want to find, isn't it? Look at the picture. What does Marta see?* (a woodpecker) *Is the bird making the sound?* (yes) *They solved the problem! How do you think Gilbert feels?* (excited) *How do you know?* (He says, "Oh, wow! It's a bird!")

Now let's look at page 189. Listen as I read what Gilbert says: "It's a woodpecker pecking for bugs," said Gilbert. *Why do you think the woodpecker wants bugs?* (to eat them) *Let's read the woodpecker sound together again:* "Tap-tap-tap! Rat-a-tat-tat!"

Explain and Model High-Frequency Words Point to the word *color* and have children say it with you. *What do you see that is the color red?*

 What other sounds do birds make?

After Reading

Make Connections

• Review the Essential Question.

English Language Learners

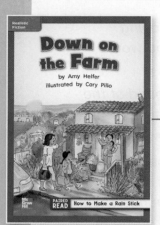

Lexile 170

Leveled Reader:
Down on the Farm

Before Reading

Preview

Read the title. Ask: *What is the title? Say it again.* Repeat with the author's name. Preview the illustrations. Have children describe the pictures. Use simple language to tell about each page. Follow with questions, such as, *Where is Jacy? What does she see? What does she hear?*

ESSENTIAL QUESTION

Review the Essential Question: *What sounds can you hear? How are they made? Let's read to find out about a strange sound on the farm.* Encourage children to ask for help when they do not understand a word or phrase.

During Reading

Interactive Question-Response

Pages 2–3 *Jacy hears lots of sounds in the city. Look at the sound words in the illustration. Let's act out the sounds. Talk with a partner about what things in the city might make these sounds.* (cars, trucks, buses)

Pages 4–5 *Jacy has a problem. Let's read the words that tell about it: "I was confused. Where is the farm?" Let's read on to find the answer or the solution.*

Pages 6–7 *Before we read, let's look at the illustration. Talk with your partner about the picture. Does it solve Jacy's problem?* (Yes, Jacy sees the farm out back. She hears the sounds of the animals and sees the crops.)

Pages 8–9 *Mom and Stella are harvesting vegetables. That means they're picking them. Jacy hears the mystery sound again and asks, "What is that?" Talk with your partner about what you think the sound might be.*

Pages 10–11 *Point to the illustrations. Was your prediction about the mystery sound correct? Let's read the labels together:* goats, milking. *Talk with a partner about the different sounds Jacy heard in the city and on the farm.* (In the city, Jacy heard people and transportation; on the farm she heard animals and rain. It was also quiet at times on the farm.)

Go Digital

Down on the Farm

Graphic Organizer

Retell

After Reading

Respond to Reading

Revisit the Essential Question. Ask children to work with partners to fill in the graphic organizer and answer the questions on page 12. Pair children with peers of varying language abilities.

Retell

Model retelling using the **Retelling Card** prompts. Say: *Look at the illustrations. Use details to help you retell the story.* Help children make personal connections by asking, *What animal sounds do you hear every day? What are the sounds? What animals made them?*

Expression Fluency: Reading Patterns

Read the pages in the book, one at a time. Help children echo read the pages expressively and with appropriate phrasing. Remind them to use proper expression when reading patterns.

Apply Have children practice reading with partners. Pair children with peers of varying language abilities. Provide feedback as needed.

PAIRED READ ...

"How to Make a Rain Stick"

Make Connections: Write About It *Analytical Writing*

Before reading, tell children to note that this text is nonfiction. Then read the Compare Texts direction together.

After reading the selection, ask children to make connections between the information they learned from "How to Make a Rain Stick" and *Down on the Farm*. Prompt children by asking, *What sounds might Jacy hear in the city and on the farm?*

Leveled Reader

FOCUS ON SCIENCE

Children can extend their knowledge of sounds by completing the science activity on page 16. **STEM**

Literature Circles

Lead children in conducting a literature circle using the Thinkmark questions to guide the discussion. You may wish to discuss what children have learned about sounds from the two selections in the Leveled Reader.

Level Up

Level-up lessons available online.

IF children can read *Down on the Farm* **ELL Level** with fluency and correctly answer the Respond to Reading questions,

THEN tell children that they will read a more detailed version of the story.

• Use pages 2–3 of *Down on the Farm* **On Level** to model using Teaching Poster 36 to list the story problem.

• Have children read the selection, checking their comprehension by using the graphic organizer.

English Language Learners
Vocabulary

PRETEACH ORAL VOCABULARY

 OBJECTIVES
Produce complete sentences when appropriate to task and situation. **SL.1.6**

LANGUAGE OBJECTIVE
Use oral vocabulary words

 I Do Display the images from the **Visual Vocabulary Cards** to preteach the oral vocabulary words *volume* and *senses*.

 We Do Display each image again and ask children how it illustrates or demonstrates the word. Model using sentences to describe the image.

You Do Display each word again and have partners discuss how the picture demonstrates the word.

Beginning	Intermediate	Advanced/High
Use the words in several oral sentences about the images for children to repeat.	Have children find a picture in a magazine that relates to each word. Help them think of a sentence that connects to the picture and the word.	Ask partners to draw a picture to show one of the words. Have them say a sentence about their picture.

PRETEACH VOCABULARY

 OBJECTIVES
Identify real-life connections between words and their uses (e.g., note places at home that are *cozy*). **L.1.5c**

LANGUAGE OBJECTIVE
Use vocabulary words

 I Do Display images from the **ELL Visual Vocabulary Cards** one at a time to preteach the vocabulary words *confused* and *mystery* and follow the routine. Say the word and have children repeat it. Define the word in English.

 We Do Display the image again and ask children how it illustrates the word. Model using sentences to describe the image.

 You Do Display the word again. Have children say and spell the word. Provide opportunities for children to use the words in speaking and writing. Provide sentence starters.

Beginning	Intermediate	Advanced/High
Guide children to write and say each word. Provide help as needed for them to orally complete the sentence starters.	Have children independently complete the sentence starters. Ask them to read their completed sentences aloud.	Have children create their own sentences for each word. Ask them to share their sentences with a partner.

Words to Know

REVIEW WORDS

OBJECTIVES

Recognize and read grade-appropriate irregularly spelled words. **RF.1.3g**

LANGUAGE OBJECTIVE

Use high-frequency and vocabulary words

 I Do
Display the **High-Frequency Word** and **Vocabulary Cards** for *color, early, instead, nothing, oh, thought,* and *scrambled* and *suddenly*. Read each word. Use the **Read/Spell/Write routine** to teach each word. Help children write each word on their **Response Boards**.

 We Do
Write sentence frames. Track the print as children read and complete the sentences: (1) *What color is the _____?* (2) *Come early to the _____.* (3) *Color it brown instead of _____.* (4) *There is nothing in the _____.* (5) *Oh, I see the _____.* (6) *I thought about the _____.* (7) *Ben scrambles up the hill to the _____.* (8) *I slept well until suddenly _____.*

 You Do
Display the High-Frequency Word Cards from the previous weeks. Display one card at a time as children chorally read the word. Mix and repeat. Note words children need to review. Repeat with vocabulary words.

Beginning	Intermediate	Advanced/High
Display the cards. Have children read chorally. Use each word in a sentence. Have children point to the card.	List the words. Make another list with the words missing some letters. Children write the missing letters and say the words.	List and read the words with children. Give clues for each word: *This word means "before the regular time."* Children say the word and point to it.

RETEACH HIGH-FREQUENCY WORDS

OBJECTIVES

Recognize and read grade-appropriate irregularly spelled words. **RF.1.3g**

LANGUAGE OBJECTIVE

Use high-frequency words

 I Do
Display each Visual Vocabulary Card and say each word aloud. Define the word in English and, if appropriate, in Spanish. Identify any cognates.

 We Do
Point to the image again and explain how it illustrates or demonstrates the word. Ask children to repeat the word. Guide children in structured partner-talk about the image as prompted on the back of the card. Ask children to chorally say the word several times.

 You Do
Display each visual in random order, hiding the word. Have children identify the word and explain it in their own words.

Beginning	Intermediate	Advanced/High
Help children match each High-Frequency Word Card with the Visual Vocabulary Card.	Display a Visual Vocabulary Card. Ask partners to use the word in a question, then answer, using the word.	Challenge children to use two or more words in one sentence.

English Language Learners
Writing/Spelling

WRITING TRAIT: SENTENCE FLUENCY

OBJECTIVES

CCSS Write informative/ explanatory texts in which they name a topic, supply some facts about the topic, and provide some sense of closure. **W.1.2**

LANGUAGE OBJECTIVE

Use complete sentences

 I Do Explain that writers usually use complete sentences. *A sentence is a group of words that tells a complete thought.* Write and read: *The gray animal. I see a gray animal.* The first group of words is not a complete thought because it has no verb. The second has a verb and noun, so it's a complete thought.

 We Do Have children retell the story *Now, What's That Sound?* Then reread the first sentence on page 183. *How do you know that the words are a complete sentence? Who is the sentence about? What is Dad doing?*

 You Do Have partners talk about why the groups of words below are not complete thoughts. Write or dictate words to complete each sentence.

The girls saw ____.   The dog ____.   ____ went to town.

Beginning	Intermediate	Advanced/High
Help children complete the sentences by providing choices: *Did the dog run or jump? What can the dog do?*	Ask questions to help children complete the sentences: *Who is the sentence about? What might the girls have seen?*	Ask partners to read their sentences and explain why it tells a complete thought.

WORDS WITH /ou/ *ou, ow*

OBJECTIVES

CCSS Use conventional spelling for words with common spelling patterns and for frequently occurring irregular words. **L.1.2d**

LANGUAGE OBJECTIVE

Spell words with diphthongs *ou, ow*

 I Do Read aloud the Spelling Words on page T248. Write *cow* and point out the /ou/*ow* spelling pattern. Segment and read the word and have children repeat. Continue with the rest of the words.

 We Do Say a sentence for *cow*. Then say *cow* slowly and ask children to repeat. Have them write the word. Repeat the process for the remaining words.

 You Do Display the words. Have partners check their spelling lists. Help children correct any misspelled words.

Beginning	Intermediate	Advanced/High
Help children write each word and say it with you.	Have partners quiz one another.	Have children write sentences for rhyming words.

Grammar

USING A, AN, THIS, AND THAT

OBJECTIVES

 Use determiners (e.g., articles, demonstratives). **L.1.1h**

LANGUAGE OBJECTIVE

Use correct form of adjectives

Language Transfers Handbook

TRANSFER SKILLS

Cantonese or Korean speakers may place adjectives after nouns. Continue to model and emphasize adjective placement during daily activities.

 I Do

Review that the words *a, an, this,* and *that* help us tell which one. Write the following sentences on the board: *A boy sat on a bench. This man will help us.* Underline *A, a,* and *This.* Say: *The word* a *tells about a general boy; a boy we don't know. The word* this *tells about a specific man.*

We use a before words that start with a consonant. We use an before words that start with a vowel. We use this to refer to something close to us. We use that to tell about something farther away. Model using *a, an, this,* and *that* in sentences about classroom objects.

 We Do

Write these sentences on the board and read them together.

An owl is big.

This cat is little.

Ask volunteers to circle the words *an* and *this.* Discuss why each word is used in the sentence.

 You Do

Write these sentences on the board.

_____ fish is brown.

_____ ape is strong.

Ask partners to complete each sentence using *a, an, this,* or *that.* Listen and note each child's proficiency with language.

Beginning	Intermediate	Advanced/High
Use *a, an, this,* and *that* to name objects in a picture from one of this week's selections. Have children repeat the words.	Have partners use *a, an, this,* and *that* in sentences about an illustration from one of this week's selections.	Have partners ask each other questions about the illustrations in a selection. Have them use *a, an, this,* and *that* in the questions and answers.

PROGRESS MONITORING

Unit 5 Week 4 Formal Assessment	Standards Covered	Component for Assessment
Comprehension Plot: Problem and Solution	RL.1.3	• *Selection Test* • *Weekly Assessment*
Vocabulary Strategy Suffixes	L.1.4b	• *Selection Test* • *Weekly Assessment*
Phonics Diphthongs *ou, ow*	RF.1.3	*Weekly Assessment*
Structural Analysis Comparative Inflectional Endings *-er, -est*	RF.1.3f	*Weekly Assessment*
High-Frequency Words *color, early, instead, nothing, oh, thought*	RF.1.3g	*Weekly Assessment*
Writing Writing About Text	RL.1.3	*Weekly Assessment*
Unit 5 Week 4 **Informal Assessment**		
Research/Listening/Collaborating	SL.1.1c, SL.1.2, SL.1.3	• *RWW* • *Teacher's Edition*
Oral Reading Fluency (ORF) **Fluency Goal:** 13-33 words correct per minute (WCPM) **Accuracy Rate Goal:** 95% or higher	RF.1.4a. RF.1.4b, RF.1.4c	*Fluency Assessment*

Using Assessment Results

Weekly Assessment Skills	If . . .	Then . . .
COMPREHENSION	Children answer 0–3 multiple-choice items correctly . . .	. . . assign Lessons 28-30 on Identify Plot Events and Lessons 40-42 on Problem and Solution (fiction) from the *Tier 2 Comprehension Intervention online PDFs*.
VOCABULARY	Children answer 0–2 multiple-choice items correctly . . .	. . . assign Lesson 105 on Suffixes *-ful, -less, -ly, -y* from the *Tier 2 Vocabulary Intervention online PDFs*.
PHONICS/ STRUCTURAL ANALYSIS/HFW	Children answer 0–6 multiple-choice items correctly . . .	. . . assign Lesson 93 on Diphthong */ou/ou, ow* and Lesson 83 on Inflectional Endings *-er, -est* from the *Tier 2 Phonics/Word Study Intervention online PDFs*.
WRITING	Children score less than "2" on the constructed response . . .	. . . reteach necessary skills using Section 13 on Write About Reading from the *Tier 2 Comprehension Intervention online PDFs*.
FLUENCY	Children have a WCPM score of 13 . . .	. . . assign a lesson from Section 1, 9, or 10 of the *Tier 2 Fluency Intervention online PDFs*.
	Children have a WCPM score of 0–12 . . .	. . . assign a lesson from Sections 2–8 of the *Tier 2 Fluency Intervention online PDFs*.

Using Weekly Data

Check your data Dashboard to verify assessment results and guide grouping decisions.

Data-Driven Recommendations

Response to Intervention

Use the children's assessment results to assist you in identifying children who will benefit from focused intervention.

Use the appropriate sections of the *Placement and Diagnostic Assessment* to designate children requiring:

TIER 2 Intervention Online PDFs

TIER 3 WonderWorks Intervention Program

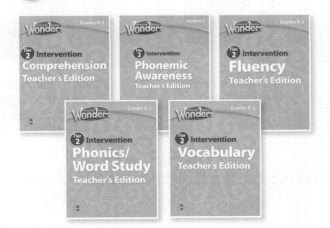

Build Knowledge
Build It!

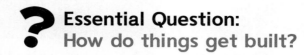

? Essential Question:
How do things get built?

Teach and Model
Close Reading and Writing

Big Book and Little Book

Reading Writing Workshop

The Joy of a Ship, 200–209
Genre Nonfiction Lexile 560

Interactive Read Aloud

"The Sheep, the Pig, and the Goose Who Set Up House,"
Genre Folktale

Practice and Apply
Close Reading and Writing

Literature Anthology

Building Bridges, 260–267
Genre Nonfiction Lexile 550

Paired Read

"Small Joy", 268–269
Genre Nonfiction Lexile 490

Differentiated Texts

APPROACHING
Lexile 430

ON LEVEL
Lexile 440

BEYOND
Lexile 620

ELL
Lexile 390

Leveled Readers

Extended Complex Texts

Snowflake Bentley
Genre Nonfiction
Lexile 830

A Weed Is a Flower: The Life of George Washington Carver
Genre Nonfiction
Lexile 690

Classroom Library

Student Outcomes

Close Reading of Complex Text

- Cite relevant evidence from text
- Describe connections within text: cause and effect
- Retell the text

RI.1.3, RI.1.2

Writing

Write to Sources

- Draw evidence from nonfiction
- Write opinion text
- Conduct short research on how things get built

W.1.1, W.1.7

Speaking and Listening

- Engage in collaborative conversation about building
- Retell and discuss *The Joy of a Ship*
- Present information on how things get built

SL.1.1c, SL.1.2, SL.1.3

Content Knowledge

- Explore engineering solutions to everyday problems

Language Development

Conventions

- Use Prepositions/Prepositional Phrases

Vocabulary Acquisition

- Develop oral vocabulary

structure	project	contented
intend	marvelous	

- Acquire and use academic vocabulary

balance	section

- Use context clues to understand inflectional endings

L.1.1i, L.1.4c, L.1.6

Foundational Skills

Phonics/Word Study/Spelling

- diphthongs *oi, oy*
- final stable syllables
- spoil, coin, join joy, toy, boy

High-Frequency Words

above   build   fall   knew   money   toward

Fluency

- Intonation, Appropriate Phrasing

Decodable Text

- Apply foundational skills in connected text

RF.1.3, RF.1.3d, RF.1.3e, RF.1.3g, RF.1.4a, RF.1.4b, RF.1.4c

Professional Development

- See lessons in action in real classrooms.
- Get expert advice on instructional practices.
- Collaborate with other teachers.
- Access PLC Resources

Go Digital! www.connected.mcgraw-hill.com.

INSTRUCTIONAL PATH

 1 Talk About How Things are Built

Guide children in collaborative conversations.

Discuss the essential question: *How do things get built?*

Develop academic language.

Listen to "The Sheep, the Pig, and the Goose Who Set Up House" to ask and answer questions about the story.

2

Read *The Joy of a Ship*

Apply foundational skills in connected text. Model close reading.

Read

The Joy of a Ship to learn how a ship is built, citing text evidence to answer text-dependent questions.

Reread

The Joy of a Ship to analyze text, craft, and structure, citing text evidence.

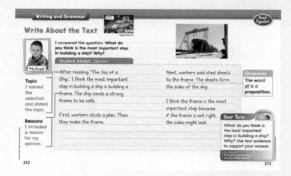

Write About Building a Ship

 3

Model writing to a source.

Analyze a short response student model.

Use text evidence from close reading to write to a source.

4 Read and Write About Building Structures

Practice and apply close reading of the anchor text.

Read

Building Bridges to learn about how bridges are built.

Reread

Building Bridges and use text evidence to understand how the author presents information on different types of bridges.

Integrate

Information about building structures.

Write to a Source, citing text evidence to explain which bridge you think is most interesting.

5 Independent Partner Work

Gradual release of support to independent work

- Text-Dependent Questions
- Scaffolded Partner Work
- Talk with a Partner
- Cite Text Evidence
- Complete a sentence frame.
- Guided Text Annotation

6 Integrate Knowledge and Ideas

Connect Texts

Text to Text Discuss how each of the texts answers the question: How do things get built?

Text to Photography Compare information about structures in the texts read with the photograph.

Conduct a Short Research Project

Make a model of a bridge.

Write to Sources: Opinion

Day 1 and Day 2

Shared Writing

- Write about *The Joy of a Ship,* p. T330

Interactive Writing

- Analyze a student model, p. T340
- Write about *The Joy of a Ship,* p. T341
- Find Text Evidence
- Apply Writing Trait: Organization: Topic, p. T341
- Apply Grammar Skill: Prepositions/Prepositional Phrases, p. T341

Day 3, Day 4 and Day 5

Independent Writing

- Write about *Building Bridges,* p. T348
- Provide scaffolded instruction to meet student needs, p. T348
- Find Text Evidence, p. T348
- Apply Writing Trait: Organization: Topic, p. T348
- Prewrite and Draft, p.T348
- Revise and Edit, p. T354
- Final Draft, p. T355
- Present, Evaluate, and Publish, p. T360

Grammar

Prepositions/Prepositional Phrases

* Use prepositional phrases to tell about what is happening, pp. T331, T341, T349, T355, T361

* Apply grammar to writing, pp. T331, T348, T354, T361

Mechanics: Name Titles (capitals and periods with *Mr., Mrs., Ms., Dr.*)

* Use capitals and periods in name titles (*Mr., Mrs., Ms., Dr.*), pp. T349, T355, T361

Online PDFs

Grammar Practice, pp. 121–125

Online Grammar Games

Spelling

Words with Diphthongs *oi, oy*

* Spell words with diphthongs *oi, oy*

Online PDFs

Phonics/Spelling blms
pp. 121–125

Online Spelling Games

SUGGESTED LESSON PLAN

	READING		DAY 1	DAY 2
Whole Group	**Teach, Model and Apply** Wonders Reading/Writing Workshop	**Core**	**Oral Language** Build It!, T320–T321 **Oral Vocabulary** *project, structure*, T320 **Word Work** T324–T327 • Fluency: Sound-Spellings • Phonemic Awareness: Phoneme Blending • Phonics/Spelling: Introduce Diphthongs *oi, oy* • High-Frequency Words: *above, build, fall, knew, money, toward* • Vocabulary: *balance, section* **Shared Read** *The Joy of a Ship*, T328–T329	**Oral Language** Build It!, T332 **Oral Vocabulary** *marvelous, project, structure, contented, intend*, T332 **Word Work** T334–T337 • Phonemic Awareness: Phoneme Segmentation • Structural Analysis: Final Stable Syllables • Vocabulary: *balance, section* **Shared Read** *The Joy of a Ship*, T338–T339 • Genre: Informational Text/Nonfiction, T338 • Skill: Connections Within Text: Cause and Effect T339
		Options	**Listening Comprehension** "The Sheep and the Pig Who Set Up House," T322–T323	**Listening Comprehension** "The Sheep and the Pig Who Set Up House," T333 **Word Work** T334–T337 • Phonics/Spelling: Review Diphthongs *oi, oy* • High-Frequency Words

LANGUAGE ARTS

			DAY 1	DAY 2
Whole Group	**Writing** **Grammar**	**Core**	**Shared Writing** T330 **Grammar** Prepositions and Prepositional Phrases, T331	**Interactive Writing** T340 **Grammar** Prepositions and Prepositional Phrases, T331
		Options		

DIFFERENTIATED INSTRUCTION Use your data dashboard to determine each student's needs. Then select instructional supports options throughout the week.

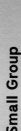

Small Group

APPROACHING LEVEL

Leveled Reader
What Is a Yurt?, T364–T365
"Treehouses," T365
Literature Circles, T365

Phonological Awareness:
Phoneme Categorization, T366 **TIER 2**
Phoneme Blending, T366
Phoneme Segmentation, T367

Phonics
Connect *oy, oi*, to /oi/ T368 **TIER 2**
Blend Words with Diphthongs *oi, oy* T368 **TIER 2**
Build Words with Diphthongs *oi, oy*, T369
Build Fluency with Phonics, T369

Structural Analysis
Review Final Stable Syllables, T370

Words to Know
Review, T371

Comprehension
Read for Fluency, T372
Identify Key Details, T372 **TIER 2**
Review Connections Within Text: Cause and Effect, T373
Self-Selected Reading, T373

ON LEVEL

Leveled Reader
What Is a Yurt?, T374–T375
"Treehouses," T375
Literature Circles, T375

Phonics
Build Words with Diphthongs *oi, oy*, T376

DAY 3	DAY 4	DAY 5
Fluency Intonation and Phrasing, T343 **Word Work** T344–T347 • Phonemic Awareness: Phoneme Categorization • Phonics/Spelling: Blend Words with Diphthongs *oi, oy* • Vocabulary Strategy: Inflectional Endings **Close Read** *Building Bridges,* T347A–T347F	**Extend the Concept** T350–T351 • Text Feature: Captions, T350 **Oral Language** Build It!, T350 • Close Read "Small Joy," T351 **Word Work** T352–T353 • Phonemic Awareness: Phoneme Blending • Structural Analysis: Final Stable Syllables **Integrate Ideas** • Research and Inquiry, T356–T357	**Word Work** T358–T359 • Phonemic Awareness: Phoneme Blending/Segmentation • Phonics/Spelling: Blend and Build Words with Diphthongs *oi, oy* • Structural Analysis: Final Stable Syllables • High-Frequency Words • Vocabulary: *balance, section* **Integrate Ideas** • Text Connections, T362–T363
Oral Language Build It!, T342 **Word Work** T344–T347 • Structural Analysis: Final Stable Syllables • High-Frequency Words	**Word Work** T352–T353 • Fluency: Sound-spellings • Phonics/Spelling: Build Words with Diphthongs *oi, oy* • High-Frequency Words • Vocabulary: *balance, section* **Close Read** *Building Bridges,* T347A–T347F	**Word Work** T358–T359 • Fluency: Intonation and Phrasing **Integrate Ideas** • Research and Inquiry, T362 • Speaking and Listening, T363
Independent Writing T348 **Grammar** Mechanics: Abbreviations, T349	**Independent Writing** T354 **Grammar** Prepositions and Prepositional Phrases, T355	**Independent Writing** T360 **Grammar** Prepositions and Prepositional Phrases, T361
Grammar Prepositions and Prepositional Phrases, T349	**Grammar** Mechanics: Abbreviations, T355	**Grammar** Mechanics: Abbreviations, T361

BEYOND LEVEL

Words to Know
Review Words, T376

Comprehension
Review Connections Within Text: Cause and Effect, T377
Self-Selected Reading, T377

Leveled Reader
What Is a Yurt?, T378–T379
"Treehouses," T379
Literature Circles, T379

Vocabulary
Synonyms, T380

Comprehension
Review Connections Within Text: Cause and Effect, T381
Self-Selected Reading, T381

Gifted and Talented

ENGLISH LANGUAGE LEARNERS

Shared Read
The Joy of a Ship, T382–T383
Leveled Reader
What Is a Yurt?, T384–T385
"Treehouses," T385
Literature Circles, T385

Vocabulary
Preteach Oral Vocabulary, T386
Preteach ELL Vocabulary, T386

Words to Know
Review Words, T387
Reteach Words, T387

Writing/Spelling
Writing Trait: Organization, T388
Words with Diphthongs *oi, oy,* T388

Grammar
Prepositions and Prepositional Phrases, T389

DIFFERENTIATE TO ACCELERATE

 A C T Scaffold to **A**ccess **C**omplex **T**ext

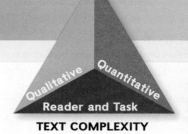

IF the text complexity of a particular selection is too difficult for children

THEN see the references noted in the chart below for scaffolded instruction to help children Access Complex Text.

Qualitative *Quantitative*
Reader and Task
TEXT COMPLEXITY

	Reading/Writing Workshop	Literature Anthology	Leveled Readers		Classroom Library
Quantitative	 Time for Kids: *The Joy of a Ship* **Lexile** 560	 Time for Kids: *Building Bridges* **Lexile** 550 "Small Joy" **Lexile** 490	 **Approaching Level** **Lexile** 430 **Beyond Level** **Lexile** 620	**On Level** **Lexile** 440 **ELL** **Lexile** 390	 *Snowflake Bentley* **Lexile** 830 *A Weed Is a Flower* **Lexile** 690
Qualitative	**What Makes the Text Complex?** **Foundational Skills** • Decoding with diphthongs *oi*, *oy*, T324–T325 • Reading words with final stable syllables, T335 • Identifying high-frequency words, T326–T327 *See Scaffolded Instruction in Teacher's Edition, T324–T325, T326–T327, and T335.*	**What Makes the Text Complex?** • **Genre**, T347B • **Specific Vocabulary**, T347B • **Prior Knowledge**, T347D **A C T** *See Scaffolded Instruction in Teacher's Edition, T347B and T347D.*	**What Makes the Text Complex?** **Foundational Skills** • Decoding with diphthongs *oi*, *oy* • Reading words with final stable syllables • Identifying high-frequency words *above build fall knew money toward* *See Level Up lessons online for Leveled Readers.*		**What Makes the Text Complex?** • **Purpose** • **Specific Vocabulary** • **Prior Knowledge** • **Sentence Structure** • **Organization** • **Connection of Ideas** • **Genre** **A C T** *See Scaffolded Instruction in Teacher's Edition, T413–T415.*
Reader and Task	**The** Introduce the Concept lesson on pages T320–T321 will help determine the reader's knowledge and engagement in the weekly concept. See pages T328–T329, T338–T339, T356–T357 and T362–T363 for questions and tasks for this text.	**The** Introduce the Concept lesson on pages T320–T321 will help determine the reader's knowledge and engagement in the weekly concept. See pages T347A–T347F, T351, T356–T357 and T362–T363 for questions and tasks for this text.	**The** Introduce the Concept lesson on pages T320–T321 will help determine the reader's knowledge and engagement in the weekly concept. See pages T364–T365, T374–T375, T378–T379, T384–T385, T356–T357 and T362–T363 for questions and tasks for this text.		**The** Introduce the Concept lesson on pages T320–T321 will help determine the reader's knowledge and engagement in the weekly concept. See pages T413–T415 for questions and tasks for this text.

Go Digital! www.connected.mcgraw-hill.com

Monitor and *Differentiate*

 **Quick Check**

To differentiate instruction, use the Quick Checks to assess students' needs and select the appropriate small group instruction focus.

Comprehension Strategy Ask and Answer Questions, T323

Comprehension Skill Plot: Cause and Effect, T339

Phonics Diphthongs *oi, oy*, T327, T337, T347, T353, T359

High-Frequency Words and Vocabulary T327, T337, T347, T353, T359

If No →

| Approaching Level | Reteach T364–T373 |
| ELL | Develop T382–T389 |

If Yes →

| On Level | Review T374–T377 |
| Beyond Level | Extend T378–T381 |

Using Weekly Data

Check your data Dashboard to verify assessment results and guide grouping decisions.

Level Up with Leveled Readers

IF children can read their leveled text fluently and answer comprehension questions

THEN work with the next level up to accelerate children's reading with more complex text.

Beyond
T375

On Level

Approaching   T365   T385   ELL

Small Group Instruction

Use the ELL small group lessons in the *Wonders* Teacher's Edition to provide focused instruction.

Language Development
Vocabulary preteaching, oral vocabulary preteaching, high-frequency word review and reteach, pp. T386–T387

Close Reading
Interactive Question-Response routines for scaffolded text-dependent questioning for reading and rereading the Shared Read and Leveled Reader, pp. T382–T385

Writing
Focus on the writing trait, grammar, and spelling, pp. T388–T389

Additional ELL Support

Use Wonders for English Learners for ELD instruction that connects to the core.

Language Development
My Language Book for ample opportunities for discussions and scaffolded language support

Close Reading
Guided support for the Shared Read, Big Books, and Interactive Read Alouds. Differentiated texts about the weekly concept

Writing
Guided support in Interactive and Independent Writing and writing to sources

Wonders for ELs Teacher Edition and My Language Book

Materials

Reading/Writing Workshop
VOLUME 4

Reading/Writing Workshop Big Book
UNIT 5

Visual Vocabulary Cards
contented
intend
marvelous
project
structure

High-Frequency Word Cards
above
build
fall
knew
money
toward

above

Vocabulary Cards
balance
section

balance

Teaching Poster

Word-Building Cards
a b c

Think Aloud Clouds
I wonder...

Interactive Read-Aloud Cards

Sound-Spelling Cards

oi
_oy
boy

Reading/Writing Workshop Big Book

OBJECTIVES

CCSS Follow agreed-upon rules for discussions (e.g., listening to others with care, speaking one at a time about the topics and texts under discussion). **SL.1.1a**

- Build background knowledge
- Discuss the Essential Question

ACADEMIC LANGUAGE

- *building, built, tools, materials*
- Cognate: *materiales*

→ Introduce the Concept

Go Digital

Build It!

Video

Photos

school
Visual Glossary

Retell
Graphic Organizer

MINILESSON 5 Mins

Build Background

ESSENTIAL QUESTION

How do things get built?

Tell children that this week they will be talking and reading about different structures and how they are built.

Oral Vocabulary Words

Tell children that you will share some words that they can use as they discuss buildings. Use the Define/Example/Ask routine to introduce the oral vocabulary words **project** and **structure**.

Visual Vocabulary Cards

Oral Vocabulary Routine

Define: A **project** is something you work on, such as writing a report or drawing a picture.

Example: When we finish our art projects, we will display them so everyone can see them.

Ask: What kind of projects have you worked on at school?

Define: A **structure** is something that has been built, such as a house or a bridge.

Example: Jasper likes to build different kinds of structures with his blocks.

Ask: What kinds of structures are in our town?

Discuss the theme of "Build It!" Have children tell about buildings and other structures they know or like. *What makes it special? What is it made of? How do you know what the structure is made of?*

READING/WRITING WORKSHOP, pp. 194–195

Talk About It: Build It!

Guide children to discuss the construction worker and the building.

- What is the man doing?

- What kind of structure do you think he is making? How do you know?

- What tools and materials is he using?

Use Teaching Poster 41 and prompt children to complete the chart by providing words and phrases to describe the work the man is doing in the photograph.

Have children look at page 195 of their Reading/Writing Workshop and do the Talk About It activity with a partner.

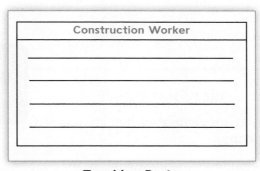

Teaching Poster

Collaborative Conversations

Listen Carefully As children engage in partner, small-group, and whole-group discussions, encourage them to:

- always look at the speaker.

- respect others by not interrupting them.

- repeat others' ideas to check understanding.

→ # Listening Comprehension

MINILESSON
10 Mins

Read the Interactive Read Aloud

Connect to Concept: Build It!

Tell children that they will now read a story about some animals who build a house. Ask: *If you could build a house, what would it be like?*

Focus on Oral Vocabulary

Review the oral vocabulary words *project* and *structure*. Use the Define/Example/Ask routine to introduce the oral vocabulary words *contented, intend,* and *marvelous*. Prompt children to use the words as they discuss buildings.

"The Sheep and the Pig Who Set Up House"

Oral Vocabulary Routine

Define: If you are **contented**, you are pleased or happy.

Example: Josh felt contented after he won the prize.

Ask: What makes you feel contented?

Define: If you **intend** to do something, you are planning to do something.

Example: I intend to play basketball after school today.

Ask: What do you intend to do after school?

Define: If something is **marvelous**, it is wonderful or excellent.

Example: The fruit salad tastes marvelous.

Ask: What foods do you think are marvelous?

Visual Vocabulary Cards

Go Digital

"The Sheep and the Pig Who Set Up House"

I wonder...

Ask and Answer Questions

school

Visual Glossary

Retell

Set a Purpose for Reading

- Display the Interactive Read-Aloud Cards.
- Read aloud the title and the information about the story's origin.
- Tell children that you will be reading a story about some animals that build their own home. Tell children to listen to find out why they build their own home and how they make it.

Strategy: Ask and Answer Questions

❶ Explain Remind children that as they read or listen to a story, they can ask themselves questions about the text. This can help them understand the story.

Think Aloud One way to better understand a text is to ask questions about the story events and then look for the answers as you read. Today, as we read "The Sheep and the Pig Who Set Up House," I will ask myself questions about the story. Then I will look for answers in the text and illustrations.

❷ Model Read the selection. As you read, use the Think Aloud Cloud to model applying the strategy.

Think Aloud Remember that you can ask yourself questions as you read and then look for the answers in the text and illustrations. The text says that the sheep came up with a plan. I wonder what his plan is. When I read on, I learn that he breaks down the door and runs away. As I continue reading, I will look for the answers to more of my questions.

❸ Guided Practice As you continue to read, pause to elicit questions and answers from children. *What questions do you have about the story?* Pause to help children find the answers. Guide children in using the evidence in the text and illustrations to find the answers to their questions.

Respond to Reading

After reading, prompt children to retell "The Sheep and the Pig Who Set Up House." Discuss what questions they asked and where they found the answers. Then have them discuss how the animals built their house. *What did they make the house out of? What did each of the animals do?*

ENGLISH LANGUAGE LEARNERS SCAFFOLD

Beginning

Engage Display Card 1. *You can look at the illustrations to answer some questions. Does the story take place on a farm? Look at the farmer's wife. Is she nice?*

Intermediate

Describe Display Card 1. Point to the sheep in the illustration. *I wonder why the sheep looks surprised. What surprised him? Let's look for the answer in the text.* Restate children's responses.

Advanced/High

Describe Display Card 1. Have children describe the illustration. *Why do you think the sheep looks shocked? Can you find the answer in the text?* Model correct pronunciation as needed.

Monitor and *Differentiate*

✓ Quick Check

Can children apply the strategy ask and answer questions?

Small Group Instruction

If No → | Approaching | Reteach pp. T364–365
| ELL | Develop pp. T382–385

If Yes → | On Level | Review pp. T374–375
| Beyond Level | Extend pp. T378–379

Word Work

Quick Review

Build Fluency: Sound-Spellings
Display the **Word-Building Cards:** *oi, oy, ar, ore, oar, er, ir, ur, ey, igh, oa, oe, ee, ea, ai, ay, e_e, u_e, o_e, dge, i_e, a_e, ch, tch, wh, ph, th, sh, ng, mp.* Have children say the sounds.

Phonemic Awareness

Phoneme Blending

OBJECTIVES

CCSS Orally produce single-syllable words by blending sounds (phonemes), including consonant blends. **RF.1.2b**

CCSS Decode regularly spelled one-syllable words. **RF.1.3b**

❶ **Model** Show children how to orally blend phonemes. *Listen as I say three sounds: /b/ /oi/ /l/. Now I will blend the sounds together and say the word: /boilll/. Let's say the word together:* boil.

❷ **Guided Practice/Practice** Have children practice blending phonemes. *I am going to say some words, sound by sound. Blend the sounds together to say the word.* Do the first two with children.

/j/ /oi/   /v/ /oi/ /s/   /oi/ /l/

/k/ /oi/ /n/   /p/ /oi/ /n/ /t/   /n/ /oi/ /z/

Phonics

Introduce Diphthongs *oi, oy*

Sound-Spelling Card

❶ **Model** Display the *Boy* **Sound-Spelling Card.** Teach /oi/ spelled *oi* and *oy* using *coin* and *boy*. *This is the* Boy *Sound-Spelling Card. The sound is /oi/. This sound is at the end of the word* boy. *Listen: /b/ /oi/,* boy. *The /oi/ sound can be spelled with the letters* oy *as in* boy *or* oi *as in* coin. *Say the sound with me: /oi/. I'll say /oi/ as I write the letters* oi *and* oy *several times.*

❷ **Guided Practice/Practice** Have children practice connecting the letters *oi* and *oy* to the sound /oi/ by writing them. *Now do it with me. Say /oi/ as I write the letters* oi *and* oy. *This time, write the letters* oi *and* oy *five times each as you say the /oi/ sound.*

SKILLS TRACE

DIPHTHONGS *oi, oy*

Introduce Unit 5 Week 5 Day 1

Review Unit 5 Week 5 Days 2, 3, 4, 5

Assess Unit 5 Week 5

Go Digital

Phonemic Awareness

Boy

Phonics

Handwriting

Blend Words with Diphthongs *oi, oy*

1 Model Display **Word-Building Cards** *s, o, i, l*. Model how to blend the sounds. *This is the letter* s. *It stands for /s/. These are the letters* oi. *Together they stand for /oi/. This is the letter* l. *It stands for /l/. Listen as I blend these sounds together: /sssoilll/. Say it with me:* soil. Continue by modeling the words *join, boy, toy*.

2 Guided Practice/Practice Display the Day 1 Phonics Practice Activity. Read each word in the first row, blending the sounds; for example: */joi/. The word is* joy. Have children blend each word with you. Prompt children to read the connected text, sounding out the decodable words.

joy	join	oil	boil	point	moist
joins	joints	joyful	coin	toy	hoist
boil	broil	soil	spoil	oink	ink
loud	found	store	cow	bird	park

Roy found a coin in the soil.

The boy lost his voice from shouting.

That toy makes so much noise!

Also online

Day 1 Phonics Practice Activity

Corrective Feedback

Sound Error Model the sound that children missed, then have them repeat the sound. Say: *My turn.* Tap under the letters and say: *Sound? /oi/ What's the sound?* Return to the beginning of the word. Say: *Let's start over.* Blend the word with children again.

Daily Handwriting

Throughout the week review correct writing position.

ENGLISH LANGUAGE LEARNERS

Phonemic Awareness: Minimal Contrasts Focus on articulation. Say /oi/ and note your mouth position. Use the Sound-Spelling Cards. Repeat for /or/. Have children say both sounds, noticing the differences. Continue with: *toy/tore, moist/more, coin/core*.

Phonics: Variations in Language In Hmong there is no direct sound transfer for /oi/. In Cantonese and Vietnamese, there is only an approximate transfer for /oi/. Emphasize /oi/ and show correct mouth position. Practice with Approaching Level phonics lessons.

ON-LEVEL PRACTICE BOOK p. 259

Phonics: Diphthongs *oi, oy*

Name _____

The letters **oi** and **oy** can stand for the sound you hear in the middle of **noise** and at the end of **joy**.

Use the words in the box to complete each sentence. Write the word on the line.

enjoys	boil	Roy	toy	point	coin

1. My name is ___Roy___

2. This ___coin___ is a dime.

3. She ___enjoys___ painting.

4. This is the baby's ___toy___

5. The water will ___boil___

6. That ___point___ is sharp!

APPROACHING p. 259	BEYOND p. 259	ELL p. 259

$\rightarrow$ # Word Work

Quick Review

High-Frequency Words: Read, Spell, and Write to review last week's high-frequency words: *color, early, instead, nothing, oh, thought.*

MINILESSON 5 Mins

Spelling

OBJECTIVES

CCSS Recognize and read grade-appropriate irregularly spelled words. **RF.1.3g**

CCSS Use conventional spelling for words with common spelling patterns and for frequently occurring irregular words. **L.1.2d**

Words with *oi, oy*

Dictation Use the Spelling Dictation routine to help children transfer their knowledge of sound-spellings to writing.

Pretest After dictation, pronounce each spelling word. Say a sentence for each word and pronounce the word again. Ask children to say each word softly, stretching the sounds, before writing it. After the pretest, display the spelling words and write each word as you say the letter names. Have children check their words.

spoil	coin	join	joy	toy
boy	town	mouse	build	fall

For Approaching Level and Beyond Level children, refer to the Differentiated Spelling Lists for modified word lists.

Go Digital

Spelling Word Routine

High-Frequency Word Routine

Visual Glossary

MINILESSON 5 Mins

High-Frequency Words

above, build, fall, knew, money, toward

1 Model Display the **High-Frequency Word Cards** *above, build, fall, knew, money,* and *toward.* Use the Read/Spell/Write routine to teach each word.

- **Read** Point to and say the word *above. This is the word* above. *Say it with me:* above. *She swims with her head above water.*

- **Spell** *The word* above *is spelled* a-b-o-v-e. *Spell it with me.*

- **Write** *Let's write the word* above *in the air as we say each letter:* a-b-o-v-e.

- Follow the same steps to introduce *build, fall, knew, money, toward.*

- As children spell each word with you, point out unfamiliar sound-spellings, such as the /i/ sound spelled *ui* in *build.*

Have partners create sentences using each word.

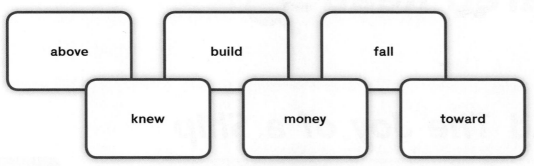

High-Frequency Word Cards

2 **Guided Practice** Have children read the sentences. Prompt them to identify the high-frequency words and to blend the decodable words.

1. How does rain **fall** from the sky **above**?
2. He **knew** how to **build** a town out of blocks.
3. How much **money** does it cost?
4. The dog ran **toward** the yard.

MINILESSON

5 Mins

Introduce Vocabulary

balance, section

1 **Model** Introduce the new words using the routine.

balance

section

Vocabulary Cards

Vocabulary Routine

<u>Define:</u> If something can **balance**, it can stay in a place without falling.

<u>Example:</u> *I can balance a coin on my fingertip.*

<u>Ask:</u> What happens if you don't have good balance? EXAMPLES

<u>Define:</u> A **section** is a small part of something bigger.

<u>Example:</u> *The book bag has a section for pens and pencils.*

<u>Ask:</u> Name a word that means something similar to *section*. SYNONYM

2 **Review** Use the routine to review last week's vocabulary words.

Monitor and *Differentiate*

✓ **Quick Check**

Can children read and decode words with diphthongs *oi, oy*?

Can children recognize and read high-frequency and vocabulary words?

Small Group Instruction

If No → Approaching Reteach pp. T368–371

ELL Develop pp. T382–389

If Yes → On Level Review pp. T376–377

Beyond Level Extend pp. T380–381

→ **Shared Read**

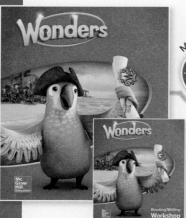

Reading/Writing Workshop Big Book and Reading/Writing Workshop

---

OBJECTIVES

 Decode regularly spelled one-syllable words. **RF.1.3b**

 Recognize and read grade-appropriate irregularly spelled words. **RF.1.3g**

ACADEMIC LANGUAGE
• *nonfiction, ship*
• Cognate: *no ficción*

ENGLISH LANGUAGE LEARNERS

See pages T382–T383 for Interactive Question-Response routine for the Shared Read.

MINILESSON
10 Mins

Read *The Joy of a Ship*

Focus on Foundational Skills

Review the words and letter-sounds in *The Joy of a Ship.*

• Have children use pages 196–197 to review high-frequency words *above, build, fall, knew, money, and toward,* and vocabulary words *balance* and *section.*

• Have children use pages 198–199 to review that the letters *oi* and *oy* can stand for the /oi/ sound. Guide them to blend the sounds to read the words.

• Display the story words *metal, tools, gloves,* and *their.* Spell each word and model reading it. Tell children they will be reading the words in the selection.

Read Guide children in reading *The Joy of a Ship.* Point out the high-frequency words, vocabulary words, and words in which *oy* and *oi* stand for the /oi/ sound.

Close Reading Routine

Read   DOK 1–2

• Identify key ideas and details about how ships are built.
• Take notes and retell.
• Use Ⓐ Ⓒ Ⓣ prompts as needed.

Reread   DOK 2–3

• Analyze the text, craft, and structure.
• Use the Reread minilessons.

Integrate   DOK 4

• Integrate knowledge and ideas.
• Make text-to-text connections.
• Use the Integrate Lesson.

Genre: Informational Text/Nonfiction Tell children that *The Joy of a Ship* is an informational text. An informational text tells about real people, places, things, or events; gives facts and information about a topic; and often uses text and photographs to give information.

Go Digital

The Joy of a Ship

The Joy of a Ship

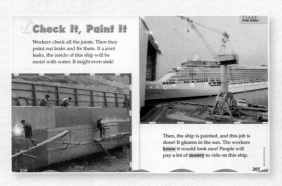

READING/WRITING WORKSHOP, pp. 200–209   **Lexile** 560

Connect to Concept: Build It!

ESSENTIAL QUESTION Explain to children that as they read *The Joy of a Ship,* they will look for key ideas and details that will help them answer the Essential Question: *How do things get built?*

- Pages 202–203: What is the first step in building a ship?
- Pages 204–205: What happens when steel gets cold?
- Pages 206–207: What could happen if a joint on a ship leaks?
- Pages 208–209: What happens when a ship takes its first trip?

Focus on Fluency

With partners, have children read *The Joy of a Ship* to develop fluency. Remind them that they can ask themselves questions to make sure they understand what they are reading. Have them use both text and photographs to answer their questions.

Retell Have partners use key ideas and details to retell *The Joy of a Ship.* Invite them to tell what they learned about how ships are built.

Make Connections

Read together Make Connections on page 209. Have partners talk about what steps in ship building are risky using this sentence starter:

> *Ship building can be risky when . . .*

Guide children to connect what they have read to the Essential Question.

Reading/Writing Workshop

OBJECTIVES

CCSS Write informative/ explanatory texts in which they name a topic, supply some facts about the topic, and provide some sense of closure. **W.1.2**

CCSS Use frequently occurring prepositions (e.g., *during, beyond, toward*). **L.1.1i**

ACADEMIC LANGUAGE

• *text, steps, order, preposition*
• Cognates: *texto, orden, preposición*

MINILESSON
5 Mins

Shared Writing

Write About the Reading/Writing Workshop

Analyze the Prompt Tell children that today the class will work together to write a response to a question. Read aloud the prompt. *What steps does it take to build a ship?* Say: *To respond to this prompt, we need to look at the text and photographs in* The Joy of a Ship.

Find Text Evidence Explain that you will reread the text and take notes to respond to the prompt. Read aloud pages 202–203. Say: *The text and the photographs tell me the steps it takes to build a ship. For example, on page 203, I read that the first step is to build a frame. Then big parts are lifted into place by a crane.* Point to the photograph of the crane. Say: *These are details that will help us answer the question. Let's write them in our notes.*

Write to a Prompt Reread the prompt to children. *What steps does it take to build a ship?* Say: *Let's write the steps in order. The first step to build a ship is building a frame.* Write the sentence. *Let's look back at our notes to find out what the next step is.* (A crane lifts big parts into place.) *Let's write that as a sentence: Next, a crane lifts big parts of the ship into place. As we reread our notes, think about which notes tell us the steps it takes to build a ship.* Track the print as you reread the notes.

Guide children to dictate complete sentences for you to record. Read the final response as you track the print.

Go Digital

Graphic Organizer

Writing

I see a fish.

Grammar

Grammar

5 Mins MINILESSON

Prepositions and Prepositional Phrases

1 Model Explain that a preposition connects a noun or pronoun to another part of a sentence. A prepositional phrase begins with a preposition and ends with a noun or pronoun. Display the following sentence:

The brown mole is <u>in</u> the ground.

Explain: *The word* in *connects the words* the brown mole *and the phrase that tells where the mole is*—the ground.

2 Guided Practice/Practice Display the sentences below and read them aloud. Prompt children to chorally reread them with you.

Have children work with a partner to identify the preposition in each sentence.

The storm is heading toward our town. (toward)

The dark clouds are above our heads. (above)

We should go in the house. (in)

We want to be dry during the storm. (during)

I see the sun beyond the clouds. (beyond)

Talk About It Have partners work together to orally generate sentences with prepositions.

Link to Writing Say: *Let's look back at our writing and see if we used any prepositions to tell the steps it takes to build a ship. Did we use them correctly?* Review the Shared Writing for the correct use of prepositions. Point out that you used the prepositions *of* and *into*.

ELL

ENGLISH LANGUAGE LEARNERS SCAFFOLD

Beginning

Demonstrate Comprehension Display the first Practice sentence. Read it aloud. Underline *our town* and *ask: Does* toward *connect* our town *to the sentence?* Continue the procedure for the rest of the Practice sentences.

Intermediate

Explain Display the Practice sentences. For each sentence ask: *What word connects the noun at the end to the rest of the sentence?* Clarify responses by providing vocabulary.

Advanced/High

Expand Display the Practice sentences. *Ask: How did you decide which word is a preposition? What is the prepositional phrase in each sentence?* Elicit more details to support children's answers.

Daily Wrap Up

• Encourage children to discuss the Essential Question using the oral vocabulary words. Ask: *What are different steps in building a ship?*

• Prompt children to share how they have used the skills they learned.

Materials

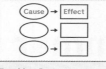

Reading/Writing Workshop
VOLUME 4

Reading/Writing Workshop Big Book
UNIT 5

Visual Vocabulary Cards
contented
intend
marvelous
project
structure

High-Frequency Word Cards
above
build
fall
knew
money
toward

Vocabulary Cards
balance
section

Teaching Poster

Spelling Word Cards

a b c
Word-Building Cards

Interactive Read-Aloud Cards

Sound-Spelling Cards

 Build the Concept

MINILESSON 5 Mins · Oral Language

ESSENTIAL QUESTION

Remind children that this week you've been talking and reading about buildings and how they are built. Remind them of how the ship was built and the house the animals built. Guide children to discuss the Essential Question using information from what they read and discussed on Day 1.

Oral Vocabulary Words

Review the oral vocabulary words. Use the Define/Example/Ask routine to review the oral vocabulary words *contented, intend, marvelous, project,* and *structure*.

- Do you feel contented after eating a delicious meal? Why?
- What do you intend to do next Saturday?
- Have you seen any marvelous movies? What made them marvelous?
- What projects have you worked on at home?
- Which of these is a structure: a house or a flower?

OBJECTIVES

 Ask and answer questions about key details in a text read aloud or information presented orally or through other media. **SL.1.2**

Identify real-life connections between words and their use (e.g., note places at home that are *cozy*). **L.1.5c**

- Discuss the Essential Question
- Build concept understanding

ACADEMIC LANGUAGE

- *ask, answer, question, information, illustration*
- Cognates: *información, ilustración*

Listening Comprehension

Reread the Interactive Read Aloud

Strategy: Ask and Answer Questions

Remind children that as they listen, they can ask themselves questions about the story events and characters. Then they can look for the answers in the text and illustrations.

Tell children that you will reread "The Sheep and the Pig Who Set Up House." Display the Interactive Read-Aloud Cards.

"The Sheep and the Pig Who Set Up House"

Think Aloud When I read, I can ask myself questions about the story and look for the answers in the text and illustrations. I read in the text that the sheep was quite contented with his life until one day when everything changed. I ask myself what changed in his life. As I keep reading, I see that he learns that the people were planning to eat him. As I continue reading, I will look for the answers to more of my questions.

Make Connections

Discuss partners' responses to "The Sheep and the Pig Who Set Up House."

- *How did you feel when the sheep found out the farmers were going to eat him?*
- *What might have happened if the animals were not prepared for the wolf?*
- *Do you think the animals found a good solution to their problems? Why?*

Write About It Have children imagine they are the sheep and write a postcard to the farmer's wife in their Writer's Notebooks. Guide children by asking questions, such as, *How do you think the sheep feels about the farmer's wife? If the sheep could speak to her, what do you think he would say?* Have children write continuously for six minutes.

→ # Word Work

Quick Review

Build Fluency: Sound-Spellings
Display the **Word-Building Cards:** *oi, oy, ar, ore, oar, er, ir, ur, ey, igh, oa, oe, ee, ea, ai, ay, e_e, u_e, o_e, dge, i_e, a_e, ch, tch, wh, ph, th, sh, ng, mp.*
Have children say the sounds.

MINILESSON 5 Mins

Phonemic Awareness

Phoneme Segmentation

OBJECTIVES

CCSS Segment spoken single-syllable words into their complete sequence of individual sounds (phonemes). **RF.1.2d**

CCSS Decode regularly spelled one-syllable words. **RF.1.3b**

CCSS Decode two-syllable words following basic patterns by breaking the words into syllables. **RF.1.3e**

① **Model** Use the **Response Board** to model how to segment a word into phonemes. *Listen carefully as I say a word:* coin. *How many sounds are in the word* coin? *I will place a marker in a box for each sound I hear:* /k/ /oi/ /n/. *I will place three markers because I hear three sounds in the word* coin.

② **Guided Practice/Practice** Have children practice segmenting words into phonemes. Do the first two together. *Listen carefully as I say some words. Place one marker in a box for each sound you hear. Then tell me how many sounds are in each word.*

oil	join	spoil	joy
noise	point	voice	broil

MINILESSON 5 Mins

Phonics

Review Diphthongs *oi, oy*

① **Model** Display the *Boy* **Sound-Spelling Card**. Review the sound /oi/ spelled *oi* and *oy* using the words *boil* and *toy*.

② **Guided Practice/Practice** Have children practice connecting the letters and sounds. Point to the Sound-Spelling Card. *What are these letters? What sound do they stand for?*

Go Digital

Phonemic Awareness

Phonics

Structural Analysis

Handwriting

Blend Words with Diphthongs *oi, oy*

1 **Model** Display **Word-Building Cards** *j, oi, n* to form the word *join*. Model how to generate and blend the sounds to say the word. *This is the letter* j. *It stands for /j/. These are the letters* oi. *Together they stand for /oi/. This is the letter* n. *It stands for /n/. Let's blend: /joinnn/. Say it with me:* join. Continue with *voice, point,* and *boy*.

2 **Guided Practice/Practice** Repeat the routine with children with *boil, foil, oink, joy, toy, oil, soy, spoil, broil, moist, enjoy, cowboy*.

Build Words with Diphthongs *oi, oy*

1 **Model** Display the Word-Building Cards *f, oi, l*. Blend: /f/ /oi/ /l/, /fffoilll/, *foil*.

- Replace *f* with *s* and repeat with *soil*.
- Add *p* after *s* and repeat with *spoil*.

2 **Guided Practice/Practice** Continue with *oil, boil, boy, toy, Roy, joy, enjoy*.

Structural Analysis

MINILESSON
5 Mins

Final Stable Syllables

1 **Model** Write and read aloud *table* and *simple*. Say each word, clapping for each syllable. Have children repeat. Draw a line between the syllables: *ta/ble, sim/ple*. Explain that when we see *le* at the end of a word and there is a consonant before the letters, they make the sound /əl/. The consonant plus *le* are all in the same final syllable. This is called a final stable syllable. Help children pronounce the syllables *ble* (/bəl/) and *ple* (/pəl/).

2 **Guided Practice/Practice** Write the following words: *candle, apple, title, puddle, marble*. Help children divide each word into syllables, and blend the syllables to read the words. Then have children use each word in a sentence.

→ # Word Work

Quick Review

High-Frequency Words: Read, Spell, and Write to review this week's high-frequency words: *above, build, fall, knew, money, toward.*

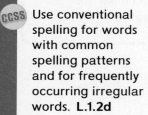

Spelling
MINILESSON 5 Mins

OBJECTIVES

CCSS Recognize and read grade-appropriate irregularly spelled words. **RF.1.3g**

CCSS Use conventional spelling for words with common spelling patterns and for frequently occurring irregular words. **L.1.2d**

Word Sort with *oi, oy*

1 Model Display the **Spelling Word Cards** from the Teacher's Resource Book, one at a time. Have children read each word, listening for the /oi/ sound.

Use cards for *Roy* and *soil* to create a two-column chart. Say each word and pronounce the sounds. Have children spell each word, noticing the /oi/ spelling.

2 Guided Practice/Practice Have children place each Spelling Word Card in the correct column. When completed, have children read the words. Then call out a word. Have a child find the word card and point to it as the class spells the word.

ANALYZE ERRORS/ARTICULATION SUPPORT

Use children's pretest errors to analyze spelling problems and provide corrective feedback. For example, some children may have difficulty determining which /oi/ spelling to use.

Tell children that the *oi* spelling for /oi/ never appears at the end of a word. So, *toy* could never be spelled with *oi* since the /oi/ sound is at end of the word. Create additional /oi/ word sorts to allow children to analyze and learn the common spelling patterns and words associated with them.

ENGLISH LANGUAGE LEARNERS

Provide Clues Practice spelling by helping children generate more words with /oi/ patterns. Provide clues: *Think of a word that begins with* f *and rhymes with* soil. Write the word and have children practice reading it. Correct their pronunciation, if needed.

MINILESSON 5 Mins

High-Frequency Words

above, build, fall, knew, money, toward

1 Guided Practice Say each word and have children Read/Spell/Write it. Ask children to close their eyes, picture the word in their minds, and write it the way they see it. Display the high-frequency words for children to self-correct.

- Point out unfamiliar sound-spellings, such as the silent *k* in *knew*.

Go Digital

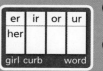

Spelling Word Sort

High-Frequency Word Routine

school

Visual Glossary

2 **Practice** Add the high-frequency words *above, build, fall, knew, money,* and *toward* to the cumulative word bank.

- Have children work with a partner to create sentences using the words.

- Have children look at the words and compare their sounds and spellings to words from previous weeks.

- Suggest that they write about building things.

Cumulative Review Review last week's words using the Read/Spell/ Write routine.

- Repeat the above routine, mixing the words and having children chorally say each one.

MINILESSON 5 Mins

Reinforce Vocabulary

balance, section

1 **Guided Practice** Use the **Vocabulary Cards** to review this week's and last week's vocabulary words. Work together with children to generate a new context sentence for each word.

2 **Practice** Have children work with a partner to orally complete each sentence frame on the Day 2 Vocabulary Practice Activity using this week's and last week's vocabulary words.

> suddenly   balance   scrambled   section
>
> 1. Can you _____ if you stand on one leg?
> 2. The sun was shining, but _____ it started to rain.
> 3. When the rain started, we _____ to get inside.
> 4. We planted flowers in one _____ of the yard.
>
> **Also online**

Day 2 Vocabulary Practice Activity

Monitor and *Differentiate*

✓ **Quick Check**

Can children read and decode words with diphthongs oi, oy?

Can children recognize and read high-frequency and vocabulary words?

Small Group Instruction

If No →	Approaching	Reteach pp. T368–371
	ELL	Develop pp. T382–389
If Yes →	On Level	Review pp. T376–377
	Beyond Level	Extend pp. T380–381

Comprehension

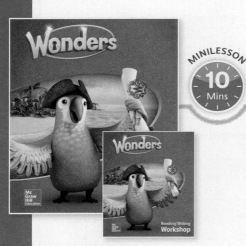

Reading/Writing Workshop Big Book and Reading/Writing Workshop

OBJECTIVES

CCSS Describe the connection between two individuals, events, ideas, or pieces of information in a text. **RI.1.3**

Understand nonfiction genre

ACADEMIC LANGUAGE
• nonfiction, key details
• Cognate: *no ficción*

SKILLS TRACE

CONNECTIONS WITHIN TEXT

Introduce Unit 3 Week 4

Review Unit 3 Week 5; Unit 4 Weeks 2, 3, 5; Unit 5 Weeks 3, 5; Unit 6 Weeks 2, 5

Assess Unit 3 Weeks 4, 5; Unit 4 Week 5; Unit 5 Weeks 3, 5

MINILESSON 10 Mins

Reread *The Joy* of a Ship

Genre: Informational Text/Nonfiction

1 Model Tell children they will now reread the nonfiction selection *The Joy of a Ship*. Explain that as they read, they will look for information in the text to help them understand the selection.

Review the characteristics of informational text. It:

• tells about real people, places, things, or events.

• gives facts and information about a topic.

• often uses text and photographs to give information.

Explain that informational text gives true information about real people, places, things, and events. The text provides facts and information. The photographs can provide additional information or can help readers better understand information explained in the text. Explain that photographs in nonfiction selections often have captions, or short sentences, that go with each photograph. Captions often give interesting facts and details about the photographs that help you understand what is shown.

Display pages 202–203. *The text on page 203 tells me cranes hoist the big parts of a ship. The caption next to the photograph explains that some cranes can lift 1,500 tons of material as high as 230 feet! This is an interesting fact that is not in the text. Facts like this tell me I am reading a nonfiction selection.*

2 Guided Practice/Practice Display pages 204–205 of *The Joy of a Ship*, and read page 205 aloud. *The text explains how workers join the sections together. The photo helps me understand what the workers have to do. The caption gives me an extra piece of information, about what tool is used for this work. This page gives important facts about building a ship.*

Go Digital

The Joy of a Ship

Genre

Cause and Effect

Skill: Connections Within Text/ Cause and Effect

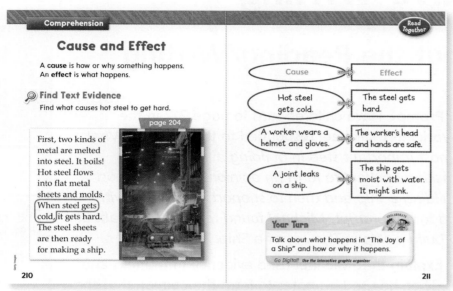

Reading/Writing Workshop, pp. 210–211

1 Model Tell children that making connections between causes and effects helps us understand what happens and why it happens. Have children look at pages 210–211 in their Reading/Writing Workshop. Read together the definitions of *cause* and *effect*. *A cause is how or why something happens. An effect is what happens.*

2 Guided Practice/Practice Read together the Find Text Evidence section and model finding causes and effects in *The Joy of a Ship*. Point out the information added to the graphic organizer. *On page 204, we found out how steel gets hard. The hot steel gets cold. Then the steel gets hard. That information is added to the Cause and Effect chart. What other cause-and-effect relationships can we find in the selection?*

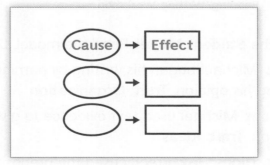

Teaching Poster

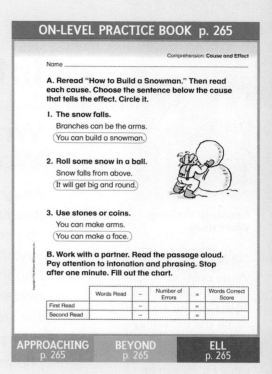
Monitor and *Differentiate*

✓ Quick Check

Can children identify causes and effects in a nonfiction selection?

Small Group Instruction

If No → **Approaching** Reteach pp. T372–373

  ELL Develop pp. T382–389

If Yes → **On Level** Review p. T377

  Beyond Level Extend p. T381

→ Language Arts

**Reading/Writing
Workshop**

OBJECTIVES

CCSS Write opinion
pieces in which they
introduce the topic or
name the book they
are writing about,
state an opinion,
supply a reason for
the opinion, and
provide some sense of
closure. **W.1.1**

CCSS Use frequently
occurring prepositions
(e.g., *during, beyond,
toward*). **L.1.1i**

**ACADEMIC
LANGUAGE**

• *opinion, topic,
reasons,
prepositional
phrases*

• Cognates: *opinión,
frase preposicional*

MINILESSON 5 Mins Interactive Writing

Write About the Reading/Writing Workshop

Analyze the Model Prompt Have children turn to page 212 in the
Reading/Writing Workshop. Michael responded to the prompt: *What
do you think is the most important step in building a ship? Why?*
Say: *The prompt is asking Michael to form an opinion about the most
important step in building a ship and then to support his opinion with
evidence. To respond to this prompt, Michael found text evidence about
the steps it takes to build a ship in* The Joy of a Ship.

Find Text Evidence Explain that Michael used evidence in the text and
photos to take notes. Then he used his notes to form the opinion that the
most important step is building a frame.

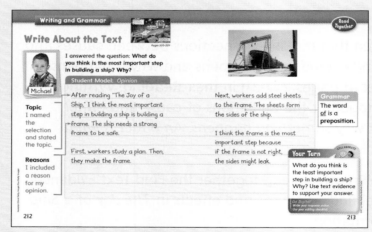

Reading/Writing Workshop

Analyze the Student Model Read the model. Discuss the callouts.

• **Topic** Michael began his writing by naming the selection and
stating his opinion. **Trait: Organization**

• **Reasons** Michael used text evidence to give reasons to support his
opinion. **Trait: Ideas**

• **Prepositions** He correctly used the prepositions *to* and *of*.
Grammar

Point out that Michael also included a concluding sentence to wrap up
his writing.

Go Digital

**Graphic
Organizer**

Writing

I see a fish.

Grammar

Your Turn: Write an Opinion Say: Now we will write to a new prompt. Have children turn to page 213 of the **Reading/Writing Workshop**. Read the Your Turn prompt together. *What do you think is the least important step in building a ship? Why?*

Find Text Evidence Say: *To respond to this prompt, we need to look back at the text and the photographs and take notes. We're looking for information about the least important step in building a ship. Look at pages 206–207. The text tells us workers check all the joints, or places where the sheets of metal meet. What might happen if a joint leaks?* (The ship might sink.) *That sounds like a very important step. On page 207, the final step is painting. Do you think painting is as important as the other steps we've read about?* (no) Remind children to make inferences about the importance of each step.

Write to a Prompt Say: *Let's use our notes to write our first sentence: The least important step in building a ship is painting it.* Guide children to give a reason to support that opinion: *Painting the ship does not help keep the ship from sinking.* Tell children you will reread the notes to help them add information about the least important step. Track the print as you reread the notes. Then guide children in forming complete sentences as you share the pen in writing them. Say: *Did we write our opinion and give reasons to support our opinion? Did we include a concluding sentence?* Read the final response as you track the print.

For additional practice with the Writing Trait, have children turn to page 270 of the **Your Turn Practice Book**.

MINILESSON 5 Mins

Grammar

Prepositions and Prepositional Phrases

1 Review Remind children that a preposition connects one part of a sentence to another. A prepositional phrase is a group of words that begins with a preposition and ends with a noun or pronoun. Write the following sentence:

> The light is above the porch.

Point out how the preposition *above* connects the words *the light is* and *the porch.*

2 Guided Practice/Practice Have children complete each sentence below with one of these prepositions: *for, in, on.*

> Snow is _____ the ground. (on)
>
> I put your mittens _____ your coat pocket. (in)
>
> There is a prize _____ building the best snowman. (for)

Talk About It Have partners work together to orally generate sentences with prepositions.

ELL ENGLISH LANGUAGE LEARNERS

Explain Read aloud the Review sentence. Ask children to circle the preposition. Then have them underline the prepositional phrase. Have them complete the sentence starter: *A preposition is a word that _____.* Clarify children's responses as needed by providing vocabulary.

Respond Display the photo of the ship on page 208 of *The Joy of a Ship.* Ask questions about the picture and provide a preposition for the child to use in responding to the promp. For example: *Where are the fireworks and smoke? above* (The fireworks and smoke are above the ship.) *Where are the people on the dock looking? toward* (The people on the dock are looking toward the ship.)

Daily Wrap Up

- Discuss the Essential Question and encourage children to use the oral vocabulary words. Ask: *What do you wish you knew how to build? Why?*

- Prompt children to discuss what they learned today by asking: *How did the skills you learned today help you read and write?*

Materials

Reading/Writing Workshop
VOLUME 4

Literature Anthology
VOLUME 4

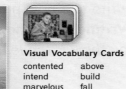

Visual Vocabulary Cards

contented · above
intend · build
marvelous · fall
project · knew
structure · money
balance · toward
section

Cause → Effect

Teaching Poster

Response Board

a b c

Word-Building Cards

joy

Spelling Word Cards

Interactive Read-Aloud Cards

→ Build the Concept

Go Digital

MINILESSON 5 Mins
Oral Language

school

Visual Glossary

The Joy of a Ship

OBJECTIVES

CCSS Identify the main topic and retell key details of a text. **RI.1.2**

CCSS Read grade-level text orally with accuracy, appropriate rate, and expression. **RF.1.4b**

Review main idea and key details

ACADEMIC LANGUAGE

• main idea, detail, exclamation mark, question mark, comma

• Cognates: *detalle, coma*

ESSENTIAL QUESTION

Remind children that this week you are talking and reading about buildings and other structures and how they are built. Remind them of how boats are built and the animals that built a house. Guide children to discuss the question using information from what they have read and discussed throughout the week.

Review Oral Vocabulary

Review the oral vocabulary words *contented, intend, marvelous, project,* and *structure* using the Define/Example/Ask routine. Prompt children to use the words as they discuss buildings.

Visual Vocabulary Cards

Comprehension/ Fluency

CLOSE READING

Main Idea and Key Details

MINILESSON
10 Mins

1 Explain Tell children they have been learning about using cause and effect to help them understand texts. Remind them they have also learned to identify the main idea and details. *As we read, we can think about the main idea, or what the selection is mostly about, and the details that give information about the main idea.*

Reading/Writing Workshop

2 Model Display page 204 of *The Joy of a Ship.* Say: *This page is mostly about steel. I read in the text that metal is melted into steel. Then it is poured into sheets and molds. When it is hard, it is ready for making a ship. These are important details. When I think about them all together, I understand that the main idea on this page is that hot steel is shaped into sheets for making ships.*

3 Guided Practice/Practice Reread *The Joy of a Ship* with children. Use text evidence to identify the main idea and key details.

Intonation and Phrasing

MINILESSON
5 Mins

1 Explain Tell children that you will change your voice to express the feelings in the words you read. Explain how you will change your voice when you read sentences with exclamation or question marks.

2 Model Read aloud a section of the Shared Read that has exclamation marks. *This sentence has an exclamation mark. I'll read it with more feeling than the other sentences.* Model reading a section with question marks. *This sentence has a question mark. I'll read it as though I am asking something.* Also point out how you pause for commas and other punctuation.

3 Guided Practice/Practice Reread the passage chorally. Remind children to show feeling and to pause slightly at commas.

Fluency Practice Children can practice using Practice Book passages.

ELL

ENGLISH LANGUAGE LEARNERS

Retell Guide children to retell by using a question prompt on each page. *What do workers use to lift the big parts?* Provide sentence starters for children to complete orally. *First, workers build a _____.*

→ # Word Work

MINILESSON 5 Mins

Phonemic Awareness

OBJECTIVES

CCSS Isolate and pronounce initial, medial vowel, and final sounds (phonemes) in spoken single-syllable words. **RF.1.2c**

CCSS Decode regularly spelled one-syllable words. **RF.1.3b**

CCSS Decode two-syllable words following basic patterns by breaking the words into syllables. **RF.1.3e**

Phoneme Categorization

1 Model Show children how to categorize phonemes. *Listen carefully as I say three words:* shirt, first, park. *Which one of these words does not belong?* Shirt *and* first *both have the /ûr/ sounds in the middle.* Park *does not. It does not belong.*

2 Guided Practice/Practice Have children practice categorizing phonemes. Do the first set together. *Now I'll say a group of words. Listen carefully, then tell me which word does not belong and why.*

verb, torn, her	barn, farm, shirt	germ, third, star
sport, corn, stir	arm, hurt, card	born, first, term

MINILESSON 5 Mins

Phonics

Blend Words with Diphthongs *oi, oy*

1 Model Display **Word-Building Cards** *b, r, oi, l.* Model how to blend the sounds. *This is the letter* b. *It stands for /b/. This is the letter* r. *It stands for /r/. These are the letters* oi. *Together they stand for /oi/. This is the letter* l. *It stands for /l/. Let's blend the sounds: /broilll/. The word is* broil. *Continue with* joy, choice, *and* cowboy.

2 Guided Practice/Practice Review the words and sentences on the Day 3 Phonics Practice Activity with children. Read each word in the first row, blending the sounds; for example: */b/ /oi/ /l/ /z/, /boilllzzz/. The word is* boils.

Have children blend each word with you. Prompt children to read the connected text, sounding out the decodable words.

Go Digital

Phonemic Awareness

Phonics

Structural Analysis

Handwriting

boils	join	point	hoist	moist	joy
joints	oil	enjoys	hoisted	joyful	soy
boy	boil	broil	mouse	moist	most
apple	candle	table	puzzle	bundle	
purple	rattle	title	gentle	sparkle	

Roy spoke in a loud voice.

That boy enjoys noisy toys.

Also online

Day 3 Phonics Practice Activity

Decodable Reader Have children read "Joy's Birdhouse" (pages 49–52) to practice decoding words in connected text.

MINILESSON 5 Mins

Structural Analysis

Final Stable Syllables

1 Model Write and read aloud *middle*. Say the word, clapping for each syllable. Have children repeat. Draw a line between the syllables: *mid/dle*. Explain when you see the consonant plus *le* spelling at the end of a word, the consonant plus *le* stay in the same syllable. The letters *le* make the sound /əl/. This is called a final stable syllable.

2 Practice/Apply Write the following words: *little, uncle, eagle, fable,* and *jungle*. Help children divide each word into syllables, identify the final stable syllable, and then read the word.

Corrective Feedback

Corrective Feedback Say: *My turn.* Model blending using the appropriate signaling procedures. Then lead children in blending the sounds. Say: *Do it with me.* You will respond with children to offer support. Then say: *Your turn. Blend.* Have children chorally blend. Return to the beginning of the word.

→ Word Work

Quick Review

High-Frequency Words: Read, Spell, and Write to review this week's high-frequency words: *above, build, fall, knew, money, toward.*

MINILESSON

5 Mins

Spelling

OBJECTIVES

CCSS Recognize and read grade-appropriate irregularly spelled words. **RF.1.3g**

CCSS Identify frequently occurring root words (e.g., *look*) and their inflectional forms (e.g., *looks, looked, looking*). **L.1.4c**

Sort Words with *oi, oy*

❶ **Model** Make index cards for *oi* and *oy* and form two columns in a pocket chart. Say the sounds with children.

Hold up the *joy* **Spelling Word Card**. Say and spell it. Pronounce each sound clearly. Blend the sounds. Repeat with *toy* and *boy*. Place the words below the *oy* card.

❷ **Guided Practice/Practice** Have children spell each word. Repeat the process with the *oi* words. Display the words *town, mouse, build,* and *fall* in a separate column. Read and spell the words together with children. Point out that these words do not contain the /oi/ sound spelled *oy* or *oi*.

Conclude by asking children to orally generate additional words that rhyme with each word. Write the additional words.

MINILESSON

5 Mins

High-Frequency Words

PHONICS/SPELLING PRACTICE BOOK p. 123

A. Read the words in the box. Say each word. Then complete each word below to make a spelling word.

spoil	coin	join	joy
toy	boy	build	fall

1. j__o__ __i__ n   2. bui__l__ __d__

3. c__o__ __i__ n   4. t__o__ __y__

5. sp__o__ __i__ l   6. f__a__ ll

7. j__o__ __y__   8. b__o__ __y__

B. Write your own sentence. Use one or two words from the box. Check that your capital and lowercase letters are clear.

9. Check letter formation.

Responses will vary.

above, build, fall, knew, money, toward

❶ **Guided Practice** Say each word and have children Read/Spell/Write it. Point out the /u/ sound spelled *o* in *money*.

• Display **Visual Vocabulary Cards** to review this week's high-frequency words.

Visual Vocabulary Cards

❷ **Practice** Repeat the activity with last week's word cards.

Go Digital

er	ir	or	ur
her			
girl curb			word

Spelling Word Sort

school

Visual Glossary

Build Fluency: Word Automaticity

Have children read the following sentences aloud together at the same pace. Repeat several times.

> She knew she needed more money.
>
> They can build a bridge above a river.
>
> He ran toward the girl when he saw her fall.

Word Bank

Review the current and previous words in the word bank. Discuss with children which words should be removed, or added back.

Vocabulary

MINILESSON · 5 Mins

balance, section

Review Use the **Visual Vocabulary Cards** to review this week's words using the Define/Example/Ask routine. Have partners generate context sentences for each vocabulary word.

Visual Vocabulary Cards

Strategy: Inflectional Endings

❶ **Model** Remind children that *-ed* and *-ing* are endings that can be added to root words. When they come to a word with an ending and they don't know what the word means, they can pick out the root word by removing the ending. Then they can use what they already know to figure out the whole word's meaning.

Think Aloud In *The Joy of a Ship* I see a word with an *-ed* ending: *melted*. The word *melted* has the root word *melt* in it. I know *melt* means "something solid becomes liquid." The *-ed* ending tells me it was something done in the past. So *melted* means something solid became a liquid in the past.

❷ **Guided Practice** Work together to find more *-ed* and *-ing* words. Help children determine the meaning of each word and use it in a sentence.

❸ **Practice** Have partners find the word *balance* in the story and discuss what it means. Then have them add *-ed* and *-ing* to *balance* and discuss the meaning of the word. Remind children that since the word *balance* ends in *e*, the letter *e* is dropped before adding *-ed* or *-ing*.

Monitor and *Differentiate*

✓ **Quick Check**

Can children read and decode words with diphthongs oi, oy?

Can children recognize and read high-frequency and vocabulary words?

Small Group Instruction

If No →	Approaching	Reteach pp. T368–371
	ELL	Develop pp. T382–389
If Yes→	On Level	Review pp. T376–377
	Beyond Level	Extend pp. T380–381

Genre Nonfiction

Essential Question
How do things get built?
Read about different kinds of bridges.

Go Digital!

Building Bridges

What kinds of bridges are there? How are they built?

1,125 feet

People **build** bridges to get from one point to another. Bridges go across water or land. They can be miles long or only a few feet.

Let's look at some of the world's most interesting bridges!

This bridge in France goes across a wide valley. It is the highest car bridge in the world.

260   261

LITERATURE ANTHOLOGY, pp. 260–261

Literature Anthology

Building Bridges

Lexile 550

Close Reading Routine

Read   DOK 1–2

• Identify key ideas and details about how bridges are built.
• Take notes and retell.
• Use **A C T** prompts as needed.

Reread   DOK 2–3

• Analyze the text, craft, and structure.
• Use *Close Reading Companion*, pp. 161–162.

Integrate   DOK 4

• Integrate knowledge and ideas
• Make text-to-text connections.
• Use the Integrate Lesson.

Read

ESSENTIAL QUESTION

Read aloud the Essential Question: *How do things get built?* Ask: *What do you predict this story will be about?* Tell children that as they read they should think about how a bridge gets built and what holds it up.

Story Words Read and spell the words *Florida, Italy, California, Scotland, London, England,* and *suspension.* Explain that they will read these words in the selection.

Note Taking: Graphic Organizer As children read the selection, guide them to fill in **Your Turn Practice Book** page 262.

The Sunshine Skyway Bridge in Florida stretches for four miles. This is a cable-stayed bridge. Sturdy wires help this bridge stay up. The wires are joined at tall towers so they don't fall.

①

This bridge is made of steel and concrete.

262

TIME FOR KIDS

This bridge is more than 2,000 years old.

An arch bridge is like an upside-down U. This bridge has two big arches for boats to go through. The arches are the same size which helps **balance** the bridge. This bridge in Italy is made of brick, so it is really sturdy.

263

LITERATURE ANTHOLOGY, pp. 262–263

① Skill: Cause and Effect

Teacher Think Aloud A cause is how or why something happens. An effect is what happens. This long bridge stays up. The text says the wires hold the bridge up. That is the cause. The effect is that the bridge does not fall down. Let's add this to our Cause and Effect chart.

Reread   *Close Reading Companion,* 161

Text Features

Reread pages 260–263. How does the author use captions to help us understand the main idea? (The author's captions tell interesting facts that help me understand different types of bridges.)

A C T   Access Complex Text

▶ **What makes this text complex?**

Genre This informational selection includes captions with each of the photos. Point out the captions on each page. Explain that the captions provide additional information that will help them understand the text.

Specific Vocabulary This selection contains vocabulary that may be difficult for children to understand. Reread difficult words as you encounter them and explain the vocabulary in simpler terms.

Build Vocabulary page 263
sturdy: strong
arch: an overhead curve

This bridge is made of steel.

The Firth of Forth Bridge in Scotland is a truss bridge. It is built **above** a river. Do you see the triangles? The roadway needs to be supported. The triangle tubes support it. The triangles join each **section** of the bridge.

264 ②

TIME FOR KIDS

Cars pay a toll, or **money**, to cross the Golden Gate Bridge in California. This suspension bridge has cables. The cables are supported by towers. Why is the bridge painted a bright color? The builders **knew** it must stand out in the fog. So they avoided colors like gray and painted it joyful orange.

The Golden Gate Bridge is a famous symbol of the United States.

265

LITERATURE ANTHOLOGY, pp. 264–265

Read

② Skill: Cause and Effect

What is the effect when triangle tubes are used to support a truss bridge? (The bridge stays up.) Let's add this information to our chart.

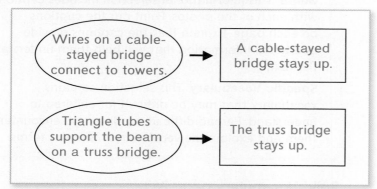

| Wires on a cable-stayed bridge connect to towers. | → | A cable-stayed bridge stays up. |
| Triangle tubes support the beam on a truss bridge. | → | The truss bridge stays up. |

Build Vocabulary page 261
supported: held up

③ Root Words

When we see a word with an ending *-ing* or *-ed*, we can look for the root of the word. What is the root word of *rolling*? (roll)

④ Maintain Skill: Main Idea and Key Details

Remember, the main idea is what the selection is mostly about. The details support the main idea. What have the details in the selection been about? (different bridges) What is a key detail on pages 266–267? (The Rolling Bridge in London curls up like a circle.) What is this selection mostly about? (how bridges are built)

The bridge is flat so that people can cross.

When a boat passes the bridge begins to move.

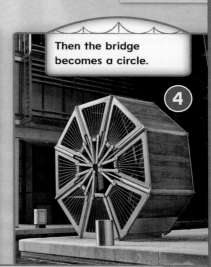

Then the bridge becomes a circle.

Some bridges are one-of-a-kind. Rolling Bridge is in London, England. What happens when a boat comes **toward** the bridge? The bridge rises up and curls into a circle. Then the boat can pass.

There are many kinds of bridges. What kind of bridge can you think up?

3

4

266

267

Respond to the Text

1. Use details from the selection to retell. SUMMARIZE

2. Which bridge do you think is the most interesting? Why? WRITE

3. What is the same about how all bridges are built? TEXT TO WORLD

LITERATURE ANTHOLOGY, pp. 266–267

Reread   *Close Reading Companion,* 162

Author's Craft: Word Choice

Reread pages 264–265. Why does the author ask and answer questions in the text? (to help me learn about what makes each bridge special)

Photographs

Reread pages 266–267. Why did the author include three photographs of the Rolling Bridge instead of just one? (The three photographs show how the bridge works and why it is such a unique bridge.)

A C T Access Complex Text

▶ **What makes this text complex?**

Prior Knowledge This selection includes challenging information about different kinds of bridges. Children may not be familiar with many of these types of structures. Ask children to share descriptions of bridges they have seen in your community, and in other places. Point out how bridges in your community may be similar to bridges in this selection.

Read

Skill: Cause and Effect

Review the information you recorded on the Cause and Effect chart.
*Let's take a last look at our Cause and Effect chart. What causes did we
record on our chart? What effects did we record? What other causes
and effects could we add to our chart?* Prompt children to discuss how
thinking about the cause-and-effect relationships in the text helps them
better understand the selection.

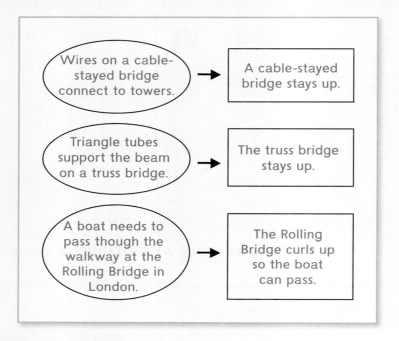

Return to Purposes

Review children's predictions. Ask children if their predictions about
the selection were correct. Guide them to use the evidence in the text
to confirm whether their predictions turned out to be accurate. Discuss
what children learned about how bridges are built. Ask children if they
learned what they wanted to know by reading the selection.

Respond to the Text

Retell

Guide children in retelling the selection. Remind them that as they read *Building Bridges*, they paid attention to causes and effects and asked and answered questions about the text. Have children use the information they recorded on their Cause and Effect chart to retell the selection.

Reread

Analyze the Text

After children read and retell the selection, have them reread *Building Bridges* to develop a deeper understanding of the text by answering the questions on pages 161–162 of the *Close Reading Companion*. For students who need support finding text evidence to support their responses, use the scaffolded instruction from the Reread prompts on pages T347B–T347D.

Write About the Text

Review the writing prompt with students. Remind them to use their responses from the *Close Reading Companion* and cite text evidence to support their answers.

For a full lesson on writing a response supported by text evidence, see pages T348–T349.

<u>Answer:</u> Opinions will vary. Possible response: The most interesting bridge is the Rolling Bridge in London, England.

<u>Evidence:</u> On page 266, the photograph shows a bridge that looks like many other bridges. Then on page 267, two photographs show what makes the bridge special. The text on page 266 explains that when a boat comes toward the bridge, the bridge rises up and curls into a circle. None of the other bridges in the text work this way.

Integrate

Make Connections
COLLABORATE

Text to World <u>Answer:</u> Bridges are built to go over water or valleys. They are all built to allow cars or people to cross them and to be safe.

<u>Evidence:</u> On page 261, we see a bridge for cars that goes over a valley. On page 262, we see a bridge for cars that goes over water. Sturdy wires hold up the bridge. On page 263, we see a bridge over water.

 CONNECT TO CONTENT
HOW ARE THINGS BUILT?

Remind children that this week they've been reading about how things get built. Ask children to think about things they see around the school. Have them think about how things such as the playground equipment are built. Ask questions such as: *What are the swing sets made of? How might they have been put together? What tool do you think the workers used to make them?*

STEM

→ # Language Arts

MINILESSON
5 Mins

Independent Writing

Literature Anthology

OBJECTIVES

CCSS Write opinion pieces in which they introduce the topic or name the book they are writing about, state an opinion, supply a reason for the opinion, and provide some sense of closure. **W.1.1**

CCSS Use frequently occurring prepositions (e.g., *during, beyond, toward*). **L.1.1i**

Use capitalization and periods in title abbreviations

ACADEMIC LANGUAGE

• *opinion, reason, topic,*
• Cognates: *opinión, razón*

Write About the Literature Anthology

Analyze the Prompt Have children turn to page 267 in the **Literature Anthology.** Read the prompt: *Which bridge do you think is most interesting? Why?* Explain that the first step in responding to the prompt is to understand what the prompt is asking. *The prompt is asking for your opinion about which bridge is most interesting in the selection* Building Bridges*. The next step is to find text evidence and form an opinion.*

Find Text Evidence Say: *To answer the prompt, we need to find evidence in the text and the photographs. What can we use from the text to help us decide which bridge is most interesting? The author gives information about different bridges around the world. Look at the photographs. Which bridge looks most interesting to you? How does the bridge work? What is special about it?* Have children take notes as they look for evidence to respond to the prompt.

Write to the Prompt Guide children as they begin their writing.

• **Prewrite** Have children review their notes and plan their writing. Guide them to decide which bridge they think is most interesting and then make a list of reasons from the text to support their opinion.

• **Draft** Have children write a response to the prompt. Remind them to end their writing with a concluding sentence. As children write their drafts, have them focus on the week's skills.

   • **Topic** Begin their writing by naming the selection and telling which bridge they think is most interesting. **Trait: Organization**

   • **Reasons** Give reasons from the text to support their opinion. **Trait: Ideas**

   • **Prepositions** Use prepositions and prepositional phrases correctly. **Grammar**

Tell children they will continue to work on their responses on Day 4.

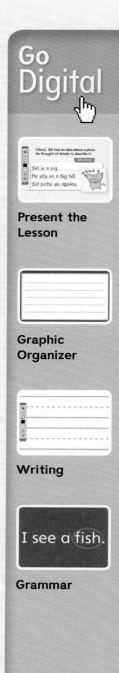

Go Digital

Present the Lesson

Graphic Organizer

Writing

I see a fish.

Grammar

Grammar

Prepositions and Prepositional Phrases

1 Review Have children look at page 213 in the **Reading/Writing Workshop.** Remind them that a preposition connects a noun or pronoun to other words in a sentence. Have children identify the prepositions in the model sentence.

Say: *Tell what preposition is in the following sentence:* The sheets form the sides of the ship. The preposition *of* connects *sides* to *ship.*

2 Guided Practice/Practice Guide children to identify other prepositions in Michael's writing. Remind them to look for words that connect a noun or pronoun to another part of a sentence. Have children work with partners to write new sentences and circle the prepositions.

Talk About It Have partners work together to orally generate sentences with prepositions.

Mechanics: Abbreviations

1 Model Display the abbreviations *Mr., Mrs., Ms.,* and *Dr.* Explain that each abbreviation is a name title people use, and explain what each abbreviation stands for. Point out that each name title begins with a capital letter and ends with a period.

2 Guided Practice Prompt children to identify the name titles in each sentence.

Dr. Powell helps me when I'm sick. (Dr.)
Mr. Brown and Ms. North teach at my school.
(Mr., Ms.)

ENGLISH LANGUAGE LEARNERS SCAFFOLD

Beginning

Demonstrate Comprehension Provide sentence frames for children as they write their opinions: ___ *is the most interesting bridge because* ___. Clarify children's responses as needed by providing vocabulary.

Intermediate

Explain Ask questions to help children support their opinions about which bridge is most interesting. Ask: *Where is it? How was is built? What makes it interesting to you?*

Advanced/High

Expand After children complete their opinions, ask: *Did you state your topic? What reasons did you use to support your opinion? What prepositions did you use?*

Daily Wrap Up

● Encourage children to discuss the Essential Question using the oral vocabulary words. Ask: *What did you learn about how things are built?*

● Prompt children to review and discuss the skills they used today. Guide them to give examples of how they used each skill.

Materials

Literature Anthology
VOLUME 4

Visual Vocabulary Cards

contented   above
intend   build
marvelous   fall
project   knew
structure   money
balance   toward
section

Teaching Poster

spoil

Spelling Word Cards

a **b** **c**

Word-Building Cards

Dinah Zike's
FOLDABLES

Dinah Zike's Foldables

→ # Extend the Concept

CLOSE READING

MINILESSON

5 Mins

Small Joy

ESSENTIAL QUESTION

Remind children that this week they have been learning about buildings and how they are built. Guide children to discuss the question using information from what they have read and discussed.

Use the Define/Example/Ask routine to review the oral vocabulary words *contented, intend, marvelous, project,* and *structure.* Then review last week's oral vocabulary words *distract, nervous, senses, squeaky,* and *volume.*

Text Feature: Captions

1 **Explain** Tell children they can use informational selections to find facts and details. Explain that informational text often has photographs with captions. Captions are short descriptions giving information about the photographs.

2 **Model** Display Teaching Poster 18. Point to the photograph of the city buildings and read the caption. *The caption gives information that the photo does not give. It explains what we see in the photo.*

3 **Guided Practice/Practice** Read together the caption *These workers use tools to fix the road.* Guide children to discuss the information in the caption. *Is this a good caption for the photo? Why do you think that? What other information could the author include in the caption?* Read another caption without pointing to the photograph and have children tell which photograph it goes with. Tell children to look for captions as they read informational text.

Close Reading

Compare Texts

Tell children to compare building a tiny house to what they learned about building bridges from *Building Bridges.*

Go Digital

school

Visual Glossary

Teaching Poster

"Small Joy"

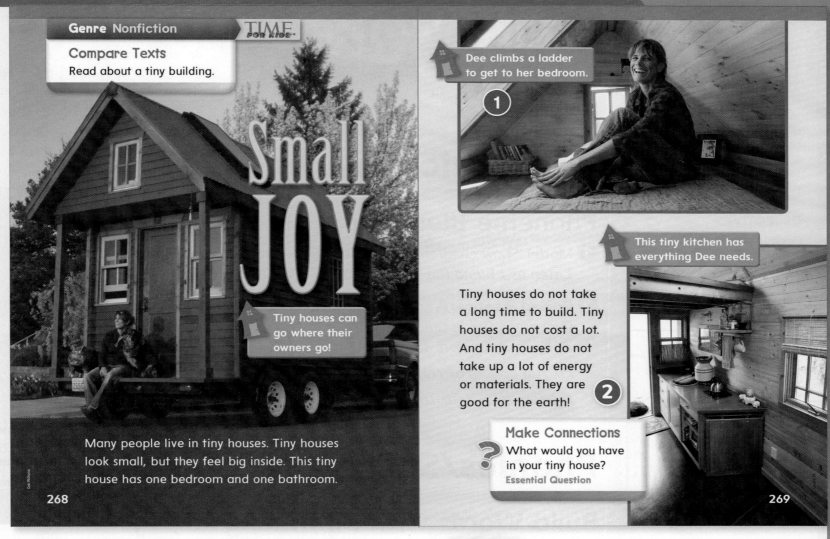

Genre Nonfiction

Compare Texts
Read about a tiny building.

Small JOY

Tiny houses can go where their owners go!

Many people live in tiny houses. Tiny houses look small, but they feel big inside. This tiny house has one bedroom and one bathroom.

268

Dee climbs a ladder to get to her bedroom.

1

This tiny kitchen has everything Dee needs.

Tiny houses do not take a long time to build. Tiny houses do not cost a lot. And tiny houses do not take up a lot of energy or materials. They are good for the earth!

2

Make Connections

? What would you have in your tiny house?
Essential Question

269

LITERATURE ANTHOLOGY, pp. 268–269

Lexile 490

Read

❶ Text Feature: Captions

Teacher Think Aloud When I look at the photograph, I wonder where Dee is. The caption explains. I can understand that she is in the bedroom in the top part of her tiny house.

❷ Skill: Key Details

What key details tell you what tiny houses are like? (They look small but feel big on the inside. They don't take a long time to build and are good for the planet.)

Retell

Guide children to use key details to retell the selection.

Reread

After children retell, have them reread to develop a deeper understanding of the text by annotating and answering the questions on pages 163–164 of the *Close Reading Companion*. For children who need support citing text evidence, use these Reread questions:

- Why does the author use photographs instead of illustrations?
- Why is "Small Joy" a good title for this selection?

Integrate

Make Connections

Essential Question Have children use text evidence to tell what they would have in a tiny house.

EXTEND THE CONCEPT/LITERATURE ANTHOLOGY **T351**

→ Word Work

Quick Review

Build Fluency: Sound-Spellings
Display the **Word-Building Cards:**
oi, oy, ar, ore, oar, er, ir, ur, ey, igh, oa, oe, ee, ea, ai, ay, e_e, u_e, o_e, dge, i_e, a_e, ch, tch, wh, ph, th, sh, ng, mp.
Have children say the sounds. Repeat, and vary the pace.

Phonemic Awareness

OBJECTIVES

CCSS Decode regularly spelled one-syllable words. **RF.1.3b**

CCSS Decode two-syllable words following basic patterns by breaking the words into syllables. **RF.1.3e**

CCSS Use conventional spelling for words with common spelling patterns and for frequently occurring irregular words. **L.1.2d**

Phoneme Blending

1 Model Show children how to blend phonemes. *Listen: /f/ /oi/ /l/. Listen as I blend the sounds: /fffoilll/. What's the word?* Foil.

2 Guided Practice/Practice Have children practice blending phonemes. Guide practice with the first word. *Listen carefully as I say some more sounds. Blend the sounds to make words.*

/t/ /oi/   /b/ /oi/   /s/ /oi/ /l/   /b/ /r/ /oi/ /l/

/v/ /oi/ /s/   /ch/ /oi/ /s/   /m/ /oi/ /s/ /t/   /s/ /p/ /oi/ /l/

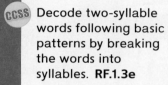

Phonics/Structural Analysis

Build Words with Diphthongs *oi, oy*

Review *The letters* oi *and* oy *can stand for the* /oi/ *sound. We'll use* **Word-Building Cards** *to build words with the* /oi/ *sound.*

Place the letters *coin. Let's blend the sounds and read the word: /koinnn/,* coin. *Now let's change the* c *to* j: /joinnn/, join. *Continue with* joy, toy, boy, boil, spoil, soil, foil, oil.

> **Decodable Reader** Have children read "Beavers Make Noise" (pages 53–56).

Final Stable Syllables

Review Write *riddle* and *cradle* on the board and divide them into syllables. Review how to determine the syllables and pronounce them when a word ends with a consonant plus *le.*

Write the following words: *apple, battle, eagle, title.* Have children work in pairs to divide the words into syllables and pronounce them using what they know about open, closed, and final stable syllables.

Go Digital

Phonemic Awareness

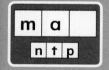

Phonics

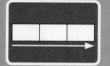

Structural Analysis

Spelling Word Sort

school

Visual Glossary

Spelling

Word Sort with *oi, oy*

Review Provide pairs of children with copies of the **Spelling Word Cards**. While one partner reads the words one at a time, the other partner should orally segment the word and then write the word. After reading all the words, partners should switch roles.

Have children correct their own papers. Then have them sort the words by /oi/ spelling pattern.

High-Frequency Words

above, build, fall, knew, money, toward

Review Display **Visual Vocabulary Cards** for high-frequency words *above, build, fall, knew, money, toward*. Have children Read/Spell/Write each word.

- Point to a word and call on a child to use it in a sentence.
- Review last week's words using the same procedure.

Expand Vocabulary

balance, section

Use the Visual Vocabulary Cards to review *balance* and *section*.

1 Explain Remind children that some words can have more than one meaning. Explain that some words can be both a noun, or naming word, and a verb, or action word. Tell children that there are different meanings for *balance* and *section*.

2 Model Write the words *balance* and *section*. Tell children *balance* can be a verb when it means "to stay in place without falling." It can be a noun when it means "a tool for weighing." Discuss both meanings. Then have children say a sentence for each meaning.

3 Guided Practice Repeat the exercise for *section*, a noun meaning "a part" and a verb meaning "to cut or separate something into parts." Have partners discuss both meanings of the word and say a sentence for each meaning. Invite them to share their sentences.

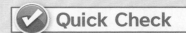

Monitor and *Differentiate*

 Quick Check

Can children read and decode words with diphthongs *oi, oy*?

Can children recognize and read high-frequency and vocabulary words?

↓

Small Group Instruction

If No → | Approaching | Reteach pp. T368–371
| ELL | Develop pp. T382–389
If Yes → | On Level | Review pp. T376–377
| Beyond Level | Extend pp. T380–381

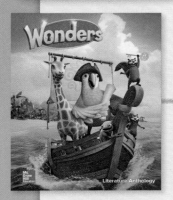

Literature Anthology

OBJECTIVES

CCSS With guidance and support from adults, focus on a topic, respond to questions and suggestions from peers, and add details to strengthen writing as needed. **W.1.5**

CCSS Use frequently occurring prepositions (*e.g., during, beyond, toward*). **L.1.1i**

CCSS Build on others' talk in conversations by responding to the comments of others through multiple exchanges. **SL.1.1b**

ACADEMIC LANGUAGE

- *revise, edit*
- Cognates: *revisar, editar*

MINILESSON 5 Mins Independent Writing

Write About the Literature Anthology

Revise

Reread the prompt about the story *Building Bridges: Which bridge do you think is most interesting? Why?* Have children read their drafts to see if they responded to the prompt. Then have them check for:

- **Topic** Did they begin their writing by naming the selection and stating which bridge is most interesting? **Trait: Organization**
- **Reasons** Did they give reasons to support their opinions? **Trait: Ideas**
- **Prepositions** Did they correctly use prepositions and prepositional phrases? **Grammar**

Peer Review Have children work in pairs to do a peer review and read their partner's draft. Ask partners to check that the response includes a topic, reasons, and prepositions. They should take notes about what they liked most about the writing, questions they have for the author, and additional ideas they think the author could include. Have partners discuss these topics by responding to each other's comments. Provide time for them to make revisions.

Proofread/Edit

Have children check for the following:

- Prepositions are used correctly.
- All sentences are complete.
- Unfamiliar words are spelled phonetically.

Peer Edit Next, have partners exchange their drafts and take turns reviewing them against the checklist. Encourage partners to discuss and fix errors together.

Go Digital

Writing

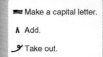
■ Make a capital letter.
Λ Add.
✐ Take out.

Proofreader's Marks

I see a fish.

Grammar

Final Draft

After children edit their writing and finish their peer edits, have them write their final draft. Tell children to write neatly so others can read their writing. Or, work with children to explore a variety of digital tools to produce and publish their writing, including collaborating with peers. Have them include details that help make their writing clear and interesting and add a drawing if needed to make their ideas clear.

Teacher Conference As children work, conference with them to provide guidance. Check to make sure they are stating their topic and opinion and giving reasons to support their opinion.

Grammar

Prepositions and Prepositional Phrases

1 Review Remind children that prepositions connect nouns to other words in a sentence. Ask: *What are some prepositions?* (Possible responses: *above, beyond, during, for, in, of, on, toward*)

2 Guided Practice Display the following sentences. Have children identify the prepositions.

> A bridge goes above water. (above)
>
> A long bridge is in Florida. (in)

3 Practice Have children use the prepositions from the Guided Practice in sentences of their own.

Talk About It Have partners work together to orally generate sentences with prepositions from the Review discussion.

Mechanics: Abbreviations

1 Review/Explain Remind children that name title abbreviations like *Mr., Mrs., Ms.,* and *Dr.* begin with a capital letter and end with a period.

2 Practice Display sentences with errors. Read each aloud. Have children work together to fix the sentences.

> Mrs Dowd had a surprise for our class. (Mrs. Dowd had a surprise for our class.)
>
> She put on a show with her funny puppet dr Short. (She put on a show with her funny puppet Dr. Short.)

Daily Wrap Up

- Have children discuss the Essential Question using the oral vocabulary words. Ask: *What marvelous structure would you like to build? Why would it be called "marvelous"?*

- Prompt children to discuss the skills they practiced and learned today by asking, *What skills did you use today?*

→ Integrate Ideas

OBJECTIVES

 CCSS Participate in shared research and writing projects (e.g., explore a number of "how-to" books on a given topic and use them to write a sequence of instructions). **W.1.7**

- Build background knowledge
- Research information using technology

ACADEMIC LANGUAGE

- *model, bridge, materials*
- Cognate: *materiales*

RESEARCH AND INQUIRY

 Make a Model

Review the steps in the research process. Tell children that today they will do a research project in small groups to learn more about how things get built. In this project, they will make a model of a bridge.

STEP 1 Choose a Topic

Review bridge types in the selection to prompt a discussion. Guide groups to choose a specific bridge or a style of bridge to research.

STEP 2 Find Resources

Discuss how to use reference materials and online sources to find information on bridges and how they are built. Have them use the Research Process Checklist online.

STEP 3 Keep Track of Ideas

Have children make a Three-Tab Foldable® to record ideas.

Dinah Zike's
FOLDABLES

Go Digital

Resources: Research and Inquiry

Collaborative Conversations

Listen Carefully Review with children that as they engage in partner, small-group, and whole-group discussions, they should:

- always look at the speaker.
- respect others by not interrupting them.
- repeat others' ideas to check understanding.

STEP 4 Create the Project: Model

Explain the characteristics of a model.

- **Copy** A model is a small copy of something large. In this project, your model will be a small copy of a large bridge.

- **Materials** A model can be made of many different materials, such as toothpicks, cardboard, blocks, craft sticks, yarn, or dried pasta. You can use glue to hold the materials together.

Have children work in small groups to use materials in the classroom or from home to create a model of a bridge. Before getting started, guide children to give and restate the directions for creating the model. Then have them follow the directions together.

- Encourage them to plan what materials they will use before they begin building.

- Display the completed bridges and give children the opportunity to ask questions and discuss each other's bridges.

STEM

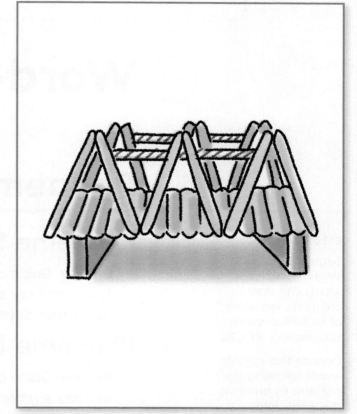

ILLUSTRATED MODEL

ENGLISH LANGUAGE LEARNERS
SCAFFOLD

Beginning	Intermediate	Advanced/High
Use Sentence Frames Use sentence frames to help children discuss their bridges. For example: *We used ____ and ____ to make our bridge.*	**Discuss** Guide children to focus on the most important details about the construction of their bridges. Ask: *How did you decide what materials to use? Was it easy or hard to build the bridge? Why?*	**Describe** Prompt children to elaborate on their bridges and how they constructed them. Ask them to tell why they chose the materials they used and how they put them together.

Materials

Reading/Writing Workshop
VOLUME 4

Literature Anthology
VOLUME 4

Visual Vocabulary Cards
above
build
fall
knew
money
toward

Teaching Poster

Word-Building Cards

spoil

Spelling Word Cards

→ Word Work/Fluency

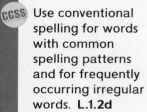

MINILESSON **5** Mins

Phonemic Awareness

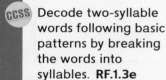
OBJECTIVES

CCSS Segment spoken single-syllable words into their complete sequence of individual sounds (phonemes). **RF.1.2d**

CCSS Decode two-syllable words following basic patterns by breaking the words into syllables. **RF.1.3e**

CCSS Use conventional spelling for words with common spelling patterns and for frequently occurring irregular words. **L.1.2d**

Phoneme Segmentation

Review Guide children to segment words into individual phonemes. *Listen as I say a word. Then say each sound in the word. Tell me how many sounds you hear: boy, join, moist, spoil, choice.*

Phoneme Blending

Review Guide children to blend phonemes to form words. *Listen as I say a group of sounds. Then blend the sounds to form a word.*
/k/ /oi/ /n/   /b/ /oi/ /l/   /j/ /oi/   /s/ /oi/ /l/   /s/ /p/ /oi/ /l/

Phonemic Awareness

MINILESSON **10** Mins

Phonics/Structural Analysis

Phonics

Blend and Build with Diphthongs *oi, oy*

Review Have children read the words *boy, noise, enjoy,* and *choice.* Then have them build the words: *spoil, soil, foil, boil, boy, joy, join, point.*

Word Automaticity Display decodable words. Test how many words children can read in one minute. Model blending.

Final Stable Syllables

Review Have children explain what a final stable syllable is. Then have them read and write: *puddle, table, apple, bottle, candle.*

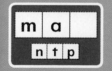

Visual Glossary

Fluency: Word Automaticity

Spelling

Word Sort with *oi, oy*

Review Have children use the **Spelling Word Cards** to sort the weekly words by diphthong spellings.

Assess Assess children on their abilities to spell words with /oi/ spelled *oi* and *oy*. Then allow them time to write down the words. To challenge children, provide an additional word with each spelling.

High-Frequency Words

above, build, fall, knew, money, toward

Review Display **Visual Vocabulary Cards** *above, build, fall, knew, money, toward.* Have children Read/Spell/Write each word. Have children write a sentence with each word.

Review Vocabulary

balance, section

Review Write *balance* and *section.* Have children use each in a sentence. Write the sentences, reinforcing word meanings as necessary. Repeat with last week's words or other previously taught words needing review.

Fluency

Intonation and Phrasing

Review Review how you change your voice when you read a sentence with an exclamation mark or question mark, and that when you come to a comma you pause slightly.

Read the first few pages of the Shared Read. Have children echo or choral read each sentence. Point out how you pause each time you come to a comma. Then have partners reread the selection, working on how they read with expression and pause for commas.

Monitor and *Differentiate*

✓ **Quick Check**

Can children read and decode words with diphthongs *oi, oy*?

Can children recognize and read high-frequency and vocabulary words?

Small Group Instruction

If No → **Approaching** Reteach pp. T368–371

ELL Develop pp. T382–389

If Yes → **On Level** Review pp. T376–377

Beyond Level Extend pp. T380–381

Literature Anthology

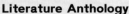

OBJECTIVES

CCSS With guidance and support from adults, use a variety of digital tools to produce and publish writing, including in collaboration with peers. **W.1.6**

CCSS Describe people, places, things, and events with relevant details, expressing ideas and feelings clearly. **SL.1.4**

CCSS Produce complete sentences when appropriate to task and situation. **SL.1.6**

ACADEMIC LANGUAGE

• *present, evaluate, magazine*

• Cognates: *presenter, evaluar*

MINILESSON
5 Mins

Independent Writing

Write About the Literature Anthology

Prepare

Tell children they will plan what they will say about their finished writing and drawing to the class. Remind children to:

• Think about how they stated their opinion at the beginning of their writing.

• Think about how they used reasons from the text to support their opinion about which bridge is most interesting.

Present

Have children take turns giving presentations of their responses to the prompt about *Building Bridges: Which bridge do you think is most interesting? Why?* If possible, record their presentations so children can self-evaluate. Tell children to:

• Describe the bridge they thought was most interesting using relevant details.

• Speak in complete sentences.

• Ask and answer questions to clear up any confusion about their topics.

Evaluate

Have children discuss their own presentations and evaluate their performance using the presentation rubric.

Use the teacher's rubric to evaluate children's writing. Have children add their writing to their Writer's Portfolio. Encourage children to look back at previous writing. Then have them discuss what they liked best about their writing. Have them share their observations with a partner.

Publish

After children finish their presentations, discuss how the class will publish a magazine about the most interesting bridges from *Building Bridges*. Display magazines so children can see the use of titles and photographs or illustrations. Have them add titles and illustrations to their articles before you assemble them into a magazine. Guide them to use digital tools to publish their articles. Display the magazine in your classroom library and allow children to read it independently.

Go Digital

Writing

Checklists

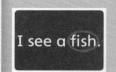

Grammar

MINILESSON 5 Mins

Grammar

Prepositions and Prepositional Phrases

1 Review Have children describe how prepositions are used in sentences. Write the following sentences and have children identify the prepositions:

> My dad is building a shelf for my room. He will hang it above my bed. He worked during the night. He surprised me in the morning. I held it for him when he hung it. Then we put stuffed animals on the shelf. (for, above, during, in, for, on)

2 Practice Ask: *How do I know which word in a sentence is a preposition?* Have children work in pairs to write sentences using *for, in, toward,* and *beyond.*

Mechanics: Abbreviations

1 Review Remind children that name title abbreviations begin with a capital letter and end with a period.

2 Practice Write the following sentences. Read each aloud. Have children fix the questions.

> **Does dr Kim work on South Street?** (Does Dr. Kim work on South Street?)

> **Does mr Dunbar drive a white car?** (Does Mr. Dunbar drive a white car?)

Daily Wrap Up

- Review the Essential Question and encourage children to discuss using the oral vocabulary words.

- Review with children that asking questions as they read and identifying causes and effects can help them better understand what they read.

- Review words with diphthongs *ou* and *ow* and final stable syllables.

- Use the Visual Vocabulary Cards to review the Words to Know.

- Remind children nonfiction text tells facts and information about a topic.

→ Integrate Ideas

Close Reading Routine

Read   DOK 1–2

- Identify key ideas and details about building things.
- Take notes and retell.
- Use **A C T** prompts as needed.

Reread   DOK 2–3

- Analyze text, craft, and structure.

Integrate   DOK 4

- Integrate knowledge and ideas and make text-to-text connections.
- Use the Integrate Lesson.
- Use *Close Reading Companion*, p. 165.

TEXT CONNECTIONS

Connect to the Essential Question

Write the essential question on the board: *How do things get built?* Read the essential question aloud. Tell children that they will think about all of the selections they have read and what they have learned about how different structures are made. Say: *We have read many selections on this topic. We will compare the information from this week's* **Leveled Readers** *and* The Joy of a Ship, **Reading/Writing Workshop** *pages 200–209.*

Evaluate Text Evidence Guide children to review the selections and their completed graphic organizers. Have children work with partners to compare information from all the week's reads.

Children can record notes using a Foldable®. Guide them to record information from the selections that helps them answer the Essential Question.

Building Things

Dinah Zike's
FOLDABLES
Study Organizer

Build It!

RESEARCH AND INQUIRY

OBJECTIVES

CCSS Participate in shared research and writing projects. **W.1.7**

Go Digital

Collaborate

Have children create a checklist and review their models:

- Does their model look like the bridge it was based on?
- Do they want to make any changes to the materials or shape of their models?
- Did they take notes about how they made their models and what they will say when presenting them to the class?

Guide children to practice sharing their models with one another. Children should practice speaking and presenting their information clearly.

Guide children to share their work. Prompt children to ask questions to clarify when something is unclear: *What steps did you take to build the bridge? Why did you choose certain materials? Where would a bridge like this one be useful?* Have children use the Presentation Checklist online.

Text to Photography

Read aloud with children the Integrate activity on page 165 of the *Close Reading Companion*. Have partners share reactions to the photograph. Then guide them to discuss how it is similar to the selections they read earlier in the week. Have partners collaborate to complete the Integrate page by following the prompts.

Present Ideas and Synthesize Information

When children finish their discussions, ask for a volunteer from each pair to share the information from their Foldable® and their Integrate pages. After each pair has presented their ideas, ask: *How does learning about the different structures help you answer the Essential Question, How do things get built?* Lead a class discussion asking students to use the information from their charts to answer the Essential Question.

OBJECTIVES

CCSS Identify basic similarities in and differences between two texts on the same topic (e.g., in illustrations, descriptions, or procedures). **RI.1.9**

SPEAKING AND LISTENING

As children work with partners in their *Close Reading Companion* or on their models, make sure that they actively participate in the conversation and, when necessary remind them to use these speaking and listening strategies:

Speaking Strategies

- Try to stay on topic and respond to the questions asked during discussions.

- Use specific words, details, and examples when describing people and things and express their ideas using complete sentences.

- Adjust their volume depending on whether they're speaking to one person, a small group, or a whole class.

Listening Strategies

- Listen to what others say without interrupting them and to think about how to build on those comments.

- Try repeating the speaker's ideas to show that they understand.

- Listen carefully to descriptions the speaker uses and think about the questions they have for the speaker.

OBJECTIVES

CCSS Build on others' talk in conversations by responding to the comments of others through multiple exchanges. **SL.1.1b**

CCSS Describe people, places, things, and events with relevant details, expressing ideas and feelings clearly. **SL.1.4**

CCSS Produce complete sentences when appropriate to task and situation. **SL.1.6**

→ Approaching Level

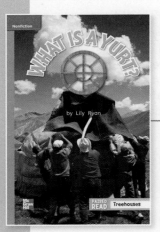

Lexile 430

CCSS **OBJECTIVES**
Describe the connection between two individuals, events, ideas, or pieces of information in a text. **RI.1.3**

Identify causes and effects

Leveled Reader:
What Is a Yurt?

Before Reading

Preview and Predict

Have children turn to the title page. Read the title and author name and have children repeat. Preview the selection's photographs. Prompt children to predict what the selection might be about.

Review Genre: Informational Text/Nonfiction

Have children recall that informational text gives facts and information about real people, places, events, and things. It presents information in logical order.

ESSENTIAL QUESTION

Remind children of the Essential Question: *How do things get built?* Set a purpose for reading: *Let's read to find out what a yurt is.*

Remind children that as they read a selection, they can ask questions about what they do not understand or want to know more about.

During Reading

Guided Comprehension

As children whisper read *What Is a Yurt?,* monitor and provide guidance, correcting blending and modeling the key strategies and skills.

Strategy: Ask and Answer Questions

Remind children that as they read, they can ask themselves questions and then read on to find the answers. Model using the strategy on pages 2–4. Say: *After reading pages 2 and 3, I still have a question: What is a yurt? I can read on to find the answer.* Read page 4. *A yurt is like a tent.*

Skill: Connections Within Text/Cause and Effect

Remind children that a cause is the reason that something happens. An effect is what happens. As you read, ask: *What caused people to add or take away mats from a yurt's structure?* Display a Cause and Effect chart for children to copy.

Go
Digital

What Is a Yurt?

Graphic Organizer

Retell

Model recording children's answers in the boxes. Have children record the answers in their own charts.

Think Aloud On page 5 I read about the mats in a yurt. Wool mats are used in winter to keep the yurts warm. It is hot in the summer, so the mats are taken out. I'll write this cause and effect in my chart.

Guide children to use the text and photographs to complete the chart.

After Reading

Respond to Reading

Have children complete the Respond to Reading on page 12.

Retell

Have children take turns retelling the selection, using the **Retelling Cards** as a guide. Help children make a personal connection by saying: *Tell about a time you built a playhouse or building from a box or fabric.*

Model Fluency

Read the sentences, one at a time. Have children chorally repeat. Point out to children how you pause when you come to a comma.

Apply Have partners practice reading. Provide feedback as needed.

PAIRED READ ...

"Treehouses"

Make Connections: Write About It *Analytical Writing*

Before reading, ask children to note that the genre of this selection is informational text. Then discuss the Compare Texts direction. After reading, ask children to make connections between the information they learned from "Treehouses" and *What Is a Yurt?* Provide a sentence frame such as: *Treehouses and yurts are both used for _____ .*

Leveled Reader

Literature Circles

Lead children in conducting a literature circle using the Thinkmark questions to guide the discussion. You may wish to discuss what children have learned about building different kinds of shelters from reading both selections in the Leveled Reader.

Level Up

Level-up lessons available online.

IF Children can read *What Is a Yurt?* Approaching Level with fluency and correctly answer the Respond to Reading questions,

THEN Tell children that they will read a more detailed version of the selection.

• Use page 5 of *What Is a Yurt?* On Level to model using Teaching Poster 32 to list causes and their effects.

• Have children read the selection, checking their comprehension by using the graphic organizer.

FOCUS ON SCIENCE

Children can extend their knowledge of camping out by completing the science activity on page 16. **STEM**

Approaching Level

Phonemic Awareness

PHONEME CATEGORIZATION

 TIER 2

OBJECTIVES
CCSS Isolate and pronounce initial, medial vowel, and final sounds (phonemes) in spoken single-syllable words. **RF.1.2c**

 I Do Explain to children that they will be categorizing phonemes. *Listen:* bird, nurse, farm. *When I say* bird *and* nurse, *I can hear /ûr/ in the middle.* Farm *has /är/ in the middle.* Farm *does not belong.*

 We Do *Listen:* store, roar, her. Store *and* roar *have /ôr/.* Her *does not.* Her *does not belong.*

Repeat this routine with the following word sets:

boy, star, joy   shirt, join, soil   dark, bird, yarn

 You Do *It's your turn. Which words go together? Which word does not belong?*

voice, barn, noise   purse, fern, moist

toy, soy, sure   march, park, first

Repeat the categorization routine with additional /oi/ words.

PHONEME BLENDING

 TIER 2

OBJECTIVES
CCSS Orally produce single-syllable words by blending sounds (phonemes), including consonant blends. **RF.1.2b**

I Do Explain to children that they will be blending phonemes. *Listen as I say a word sound by sound: /t/ /oi/. Say the sounds with me: /t/ /oi/. Now, I'll blend: /t/ /oi/, /toi/,* toy.

Listen: /s/ /oi/ /l/. Repeat the sounds: /s/ /oi/ /l/. Let's blend: /sss/ /oi/ /lll/, /sssoilll/, soil. *We made one word:* soil.

 We Do Repeat this routine with the following words:

/oi/ /l/   /b/ /oi/   /n/ /oi/ /z/   /p/ /oi/ /n/ /t/

 You Do *It's your turn. Blend the sounds to form a word.*

/j/ /oi/   /k/ /oi/ /n/   /ch/ /oi/ /s/   /s/ /oi/

Repeat the blending routine with additional /oi/ words.

PHONEME SEGMENTATION

OBJECTIVES

 Segment spoken single-syllable words into their complete sequence of individual sounds (phonemes). **RF.1.2d**

 I Do Tell children they will be segmenting words into phonemes. *Listen as I say a word:* boy. *I will say each sound in* boy *and place one marker in a box of the **Response Board** for each sound. Now I will count the markers: one, two. There are two sounds in* boy: /b//oi/.

 We Do *Let's do some together. I will say a word. Put a marker in each box for each sound you hear. Listen:* voice, /v/ /oi/ /s/. *How many sounds do you hear? Yes, three sounds.* Repeat for these words:

joy   foil   joint   spoil

 You Do *It's your turn. I'll say some words. Put a marker in each box for each sound. How many sounds do you hear?*

toy   coin   point   oil   hoist   choice

Repeat the segmentation routine for /oi/ words.

PHONEME BLENDING

OBJECTIVES

 Orally produce single-syllable words by blending sounds (phonemes), including consonant blends. **RF.1.2b**

I Do Explain to children that they will be blending phonemes to make a word. *I'm going to blend three sounds. Listen:* /j/ /oi/ /nnn/, /joinnn/, join.

 We Do *Listen:* /oi/ /lll/. *Let's blend the sounds* /oi/ *and* /lll/: /oi/ /lll/, /oilll/, oil. *We blended the word* oil. Repeat this routine with the following words:

/b/ /oi/   /k/ /oi/ /l/   /j/ /oi/ /n/ /t/   /b/ /oi/ /l/

 You Do *It's your turn. Listen to the sounds, then blend the sounds to say the word.*

/s//oi//l/   /ch//oi//s/   /m//oi//s//t/   /oi//l/   /n//oi/ /s/ /ē/

Repeat blending with additional *oi, oy* words.

ELL ENGLISH LANGUAGE LEARNERS

For the **children** who need **phonemic awareness, phonics,** and **fluency** practice, use scaffolding methods as necessary to ensure children understand the meaning of the words. Refer to the Language Transfer Handbook for phonics elements that may not transfer in children's native languages.

→ Approaching Level

Phonics

CONNECT *oi, oy* TO /oi/

OBJECTIVES

Know and apply grade-level phonics and word analysis skills in decoding words. **RF.1.3**

I Do

Display the **Word-Building Card** *oy*. *These are lowercase* o *and* y. *Together they stand for the sound /oi/. I am going to trace the letters* o *and* y *while I say /oi/.* Trace the letters *o* and *y* while saying /oi/ five times. Repeat for *oi*.

We Do

Now do it with me. Have children take turns saying /oi/ while using their fingers to trace lowercase *oy*. Then have them say /oi/ as they use their fingers to trace the letters *oy* five more times. Repeat for *oi*.

You Do

Have children connect the letters *oy* to /oi/ by saying /oi/ as they trace lowercase *oy* on paper five to ten times. Then ask them to write the letters *oy* while saying /oi/ five to ten times. Repeat for *oi*.

Repeat, connecting the letters *oy* and *oi* to /oi/ through tracing and writing the letters throughout the week.

BLEND WORDS WITH DIPHTHONGS *oi, oy*

OBJECTIVES

Decode regularly spelled one-syllable words. **RF.1.3b**

I Do

Display Word-Building Cards *j, oy*. *This is the letter* j. *It stands for /j/. Say it with me: /j/. These are the letters* o *and* y. *Together they stand for /oi/. Let's say it together: /oi/. I'll blend the sounds together: /joi/,* joy.

We Do

Guide children to blend the sounds and read: *toy, soy, oil, coin, moist, point.*

You Do

Have children blend and read: *soy, boil, joint, choice, spoil, oily, oink.*

Repeat, blending additional *oi, oy* words.

You may wish to review Phonics with **ELL** using this section.

BUILD WORDS WITH DIPHTHONGS *oi, oy*

OBJECTIVES

Decode regularly spelled one-syllable words. RF.1.3b

 I Do Display Word-Building Cards *oi, l.* *The letters* o *and* i *together stand for /oi/. The letter stands for /l/. I will blend the sounds together: /oilll/,* oil. *The word is* oil.

 We Do *Now let's do one together.* Place the letter *s* before *oil. Let's blend the new word: /s/ /oi/, /l/, /sssoilll/,* soil.

Replace *oi, l* with *oy. Let's blend and read: /s/ /oi/, /sssoi/,* soy.

 You Do Have children build and read the words *boy, toy, joy, join, coin, coil, spoil.*

BLEND WORDS WITH DIPHTHONGS *oi, oy*

OBJECTIVES

Decode regularly spelled one-syllable words. RF.1.3b

 I Do Display Word-Building Cards *c, oi, n. This is the letter c. It stands for /k/. These are the letters* o *and* i. *Together they stand for /oi/. This is the letter* n. *It stands for /n/. Listen as I blend all three sounds: /koinnn/,* coin. *The word is* coin.

 We Do Let's do some together. Blend and read the words *joy, foil, hoist,* and *enjoy* with children.

 You Do Display the words to the right. Have children blend and read the words.

Decodable Reader Have children read "Joy's Birdhouse" (pages 49–52) and "Beavers Make Noise" (53–56).

boy	spoil	noise	toy	joint	destroy
voice	soy	broil	moist	oink	choice
jay	joy	point	paint	corn	coin
oily	noisy	house	horse	torn	town

Cowboy Roy enjoys noisy toys.

Was his choice to boil or broil the meat?

The boy points to the coins in the moist soil.

BUILD FLUENCY WITH PHONICS

Sound-Spellings Fluency

Display the following Word-Building Cards: *oi, oy, ar, ore, oar, er, ir, ur, ey, igh, ao, oe, ee, ea, ai, ay, e_e, u_e, o_e, dge, i_e, a_e, ch, tch, wh, ph, th, sh, ng, mp.* Have children chorally say the sounds. Repeat and vary the pace.

Fluency in Connected Text

Have children review the **Decodable Reader** selections. Identify /oi/ words. Blend words as needed.

Have partners reread the selections for fluency.

Approaching Level

Structural Analysis

REVIEW FINAL STABLE SYLLABLES

 OBJECTIVES

Use knowledge that every syllable must have a vowel sound to determine the number of syllables in a printed word. **RF.1.3d**

I Do Remind children that a syllable is a word part that has one vowel sound. Write and read the word *apple*. Repeat the word as you clap the syllables. *I hear two vowel sounds in* apple, *so I know that* apple *has two syllables,* ap *and* ple. Draw a line between the syllables. *When a word ends with a consonant followed by* le, *like* ple *at the end of* apple, *the letters* le *make the sound /ə l/. The consonant plus* le *form a syllable.*

We Do Write and read the word *candle* and have children repeat. *How many syllables do you hear in* candle? (2) Underline *dle. Remember that a consonant plus* le *at the end of a word form a syllable. Let's break* candle *into syllables:* can/dle. Repeat with *turtle, bubble, giggle.*

You Do Have partners divide these words into syllables and then blend to read the words: *puddle, table, purple.*

Repeat Have children continue with *cradle, eagle, saddle, uncle.*

RETEACH FINAL STABLE SYLLABLES

 OBJECTIVES

Use knowledge that every syllable must have a vowel sound to determine the number of syllables in a printed word. **RF.1.3d**

I Do Remind children that a syllable is a word part that has one vowel sound. Write and read the word *jungle* and then divide it into syllables: *jun/gle. Listen to the syllables: /jun/ /gəl/. Circle* gle. *When a word ends in a consonant, such as* g, *followed by the letters* le, *the letters* le *make the sound /əl/. The consonant plus* le *form a syllable.*

We Do Write *bee/tle. Beetle has two syllables, /bē/ /təl/. Let's say each syllable: /bē/ /təl/. Now let's blend the syllables: /bē/ /təl/, /bētəl/, beetle.*

You Do *Now it's your turn. Blend these syllables to read the words.*

nee/dle   rat/tle   gig/gle   pur/ple   peb/ble

Repeat Have partners divide *apple, table, little,* and *candle* into syllables and then blend the words.

Words to Know

REVIEW HIGH-FREQUENCY WORDS

OBJECTIVES

Recognize and read grade-appropriate irregularly spelled words. **RF.1.3g**

 Use **High-Frequency Words Cards** to **Read/Spell/Write** each high-frequency word. Use each word orally in a sentence.

 Guide children to Read/Spell/Write each word on their **Response Boards**. Help them generate oral sentences for the words.

 Have partners work together to Read/Spell/Write the words *above, build, fall, knew, money,* and *toward.* Ask them to say sentences for the words.

CUMULATIVE REVIEW

OBJECTIVES

Recognize and read grade-appropriate irregularly spelled words. **RF.1.3g**

 Display the **High-Frequency Word Cards** from the previous weeks. Use the Read/Spell/Write routine to review each word.

 Have children write the words. Have children complete sentences:
I thought ____. We began early because ____. I can learn another ____.

 Have partners take turns displaying and reading the words. Ask them to use the words in sentences.

Fluency Display the High-Frequency Word Cards. Point to words in random order. Have children chorally read each word. Repeat at a faster pace.

REVIEW VOCABULARY WORDS

OBJECTIVES

Identify real-life connections between words and their use (e.g., note places that are *cozy*). **L.1.5c**

 Display **Visual Vocabulary Cards** for *balance* and *section.* Review each word using the Define/Example/Ask routine.

 Invite children to show how to *balance* on one foot and to all stand in one section of the classroom. Then work with them to complete these sentences: *(1) I can balance ____. (2) The workers build one section ____.*

 Have partners write two sentences on their own, using each of the words. Provide assistance as needed.

Approaching Level

Comprehension

READ FOR FLUENCY

TIER 2

OBJECTIVES

CCSS Read grade-level text orally with accuracy, appropriate rate, and expression. **RF.1.4b**

I Do Read the first page of the Practice Book selection aloud. Model using appropriate intonation for exclamation marks.

We Do Read the second page aloud and have children repeat after you. Point out how you pause slightly at commas.

You Do Have children read the rest of the selection aloud. Remind them to use appropriate intonation and phrasing.

IDENTIFY KEY DETAILS

TIER 2

OBJECTIVES

CCSS Ask and answer questions about key details in a text. **RI.1.1**

I Do Remind children that they read many details in an informational text. *When I read an informational text, I look for key, or important, details. I can find key details in the pictures and in the words.*

We Do Read the first page of the Practice Book selection aloud. Pause to discuss key details. *We learn two key details on this page. First we learn that there is wet, heavy snow. Then what did we learn?*

You Do Guide children as they read the rest of the Practice Book selection. Prompt them to find key details in the words and pictures.

REVIEW CONNECTIONS WITHIN TEXT: CAUSE AND EFFECT

OBJECTIVES

 Describe the connection between two individuals, events, ideas, or pieces of information in a text. **RI.1.3**

Identify cause and effect in informational text

 I Do Remind children that they can make connections when they read an informational text. *When I make connections, I think about the ideas and events I am reading. Sometimes I think about causes and effects. Causes are why something happens. Effects are what happens.*

 We Do Read the first two pages of the Practice Book selection together. Pause to discuss causes and effects. *Why can you build a snowman now? That's right. You can build a snowman because heavy, wet snow is falling. What is the effect of rolling the snow? It gets big and round.* Record the causes and effects on a Cause and Effect chart.

You Do Guide children as they continue to read the selection. Pause to have them discuss causes and effects. Record their responses on the chart.

SELF-SELECTED READING

OBJECTIVES

 With prompting and support, read informational texts appropriately complex for grade 1. **RI.1.10**

Apply the strategy and skill to read a text

Read Independently

Have children pick an informational text for sustained silent reading. Remind them to:

- think about causes and effects, or why things happen.
- ask questions about the information and then look for answers in the words and pictures.

Read Purposefully

Have children record causes and effects on a Cause and Effect chart. After reading, guide children to participate in a group discussion about the selection they read. Guide children to:

- share the information they recorded on their Cause and Effect charts.
- share questions they asked and answers they found.
- tell an interesting fact they learned and why it was interesting.
- discuss differences between selections that tell stories and those that give information.

On Level

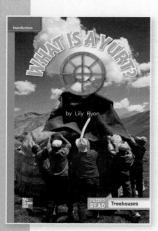

Lexile 440

CCSS **OBJECTIVES**
Describe the connection between two individuals, events, ideas, or pieces of information in a text. **RI.1.3**

Identify causes and effects

Leveled Reader:
What Is a Yurt?

Before Reading

Preview and Predict

Have children turn to the title page. Read the title and the author's name and have children repeat. Preview the selection's photographs. Prompt children to predict what the selection might be about.

Review Genre: Informational Text/Nonfiction

Have children recall that informational text gives facts and information about real people, places, events, and things. It presents information in a logical order.

ESSENTIAL QUESTION

Remind children of the Essential Question: *How do things get built?* Set a purpose for reading: *Let's read to find out what a yurt is.*

Remind children that as they read a selection, they can ask questions about what they do not understand or want to know more about.

During Reading

Guided Comprehension

As children whisper read *What Is a Yurt?*, monitor and provide guidance, correcting blending and modeling the key strategies and skills.

Strategy: Ask and Answer Questions

Remind children that as they read, they can ask themselves questions and then use the words and text to find the answers. Model using the strategy on pages 2 through 4. Say: *I read pages 2 and 3 and still wondered what a yurt is. Let's read on to page 4. What is a yurt?*

Skill: Connections Within Text/Cause and Effect

Remind children that a cause is an event that makes something happen. An effect is what happens. As you read, ask: *Why were mats removed from the yurts in the summer?* Display a Cause and Effect chart for children to copy.

Go Digital

What Is a Yurt?

Graphic Organizer

Retell

Model recording answers for children. Have children copy the answers into their own charts.

Think Aloud On page 5 I read that nomads took mats away in the summer because it made the yurt cooler. I will write that cause and effect in my chart.

Once the selection is finished, prompt children to complete the chart.

After Reading

Respond to Reading

Have children complete the Respond to Reading on page 12.

Retell

Have children take turns retelling the selection, using the **Retelling Cards** as a guide. Help children make a connection: *Have you ever gone camping or slept outdoors? If so, what do you remember most about it?*

Model Fluency

Read the sentences one at a time. Have children chorally repeat. Point out to children how you pause when you come to a comma.

Apply Have partners practice reading. Provide feedback as needed.

PAIRED READ ...

Leveled Reader

"Treehouses"

Make Connections:
Write About It *Analytical Writing*

Before reading, ask children to note that the genre of this selection is informational text. Then discuss the Compare Texts direction. After reading, ask children to make connections between the information they learned from "Treehouses" and *What Is a Yurt? How are treehouses and yurts alike? How are they different?*

 FOCUS ON SCIENCE

Children can extend their knowledge of camping out by completing the science activity on page 16. **STEM**

Literature Circles

Lead children in conducting a literature circle using the Thinkmark questions to guide the discussion. You may wish to discuss what children have learned about building different kinds of shelters from the selections in the Leveled Reader.

Level Up

Level-up lessons available online.

IF Children can read *What Is a Yurt?* On Level with fluency and correctly answer the Respond to Reading questions,

THEN Tell children that they will read a more detailed version of the selection.

• Use page 5 of *What Is a Yurt?* Beyond Level to model using Teaching Poster 32 to list a cause and its effect.

• Have children read the selection, checking their comprehension by using the graphic organizer.

On Level

Phonics

BUILD WORDS WITH DIPHTHONGS *oi, oy*

OBJECTIVES
Decode regularly spelled one-syllable words. **RF.1.3b**

 I Do
Display **Word-Building Cards** *oi, l. These are the letters* o, i, *and* l. *The* o *and* i *together stand for one sound,* /oi/. *I will blend* /oi/ *and* /l/ *together:* /oil/, oil. *The word is* oil.

 We Do
Now let's do one together. Place the letter *s* in front of the letters *o, i, l. Let's blend and read the new word:* /s/ /oi/ /l/, /sssoilll/, soil. *The new word is* soil.

 You Do
Have children build and blend: *boil, boy, toy, joy, join, joint, point.*

Repeat with additional /oi/ words.

Decodable Reader Have children read "Joy's Birdhouse" and "Beavers Make Noise," (pages 49–56).

Words to Know

REVIEW WORDS

OBJECTIVES
Recognize and read grade-appropriate irregularly spelled words. **RF.1.3g**

 I Do
Use the **Read/Spell/Write** routine to teach each high-frequency and vocabulary word. Use each word orally in a sentence.

 We Do
Guide children to Read/Spell/Write each word using their **Response Boards**. Then work with the group to generate oral sentences for the words.

 You Do
Have partners use the Read/Spell/Write routine on their own using the high-frequency words *above, build, fall, knew, money,* and *toward* and the vocabulary words *balance* and *section*. Have partners write sentences about something they have built. Tell them that each sentence should contain at least one high-frequency or vocabulary word.

Comprehension

REVIEW CONNECTIONS WITHIN TEXT: CAUSE AND EFFECT

OBJECTIVES

(CCSS) Describe the connection between two individuals, events, ideas, or pieces of information in a text. **RI.1.3**

Identify cause and effect in informational text

 I Do Remind children that they can make connections between ideas or events when they read. *When I read a selection, I make connections between causes, or why something happens, and effects, or what happens. I ask myself questions like these:* Why does this happen? What effect does this have?

 We Do Read the first two pages of the Practice Book selection aloud. Pause to discuss cause and effect. *We read about snow falling. What is the effect of the falling snow? Why does the snow get big and round?*

 You Do Guide children to read the rest of the Practice Book selection. Remind them to think about cause and effect. Then invite children to discuss how you build a snowman. Have them make connections between cause-and-effect relationships.

SELF-SELECTED READING

OBJECTIVES

(CCSS) With prompting and support, read informational texts appropriately complex for grade 1. **RI.1.10**

Apply the strategy and skill to read a text

Read Independently

Have children pick an informational text for sustained silent reading. Remind them to:

- make connections between cause-and-effect relationships in the selection.
- ask themselves questions and then look for answers in the words and pictures.
- use context to confirm or self-correct word recognition and meaning.

Read Purposefully

Have children record details on a Cause and Effect chart. After reading, guide partners to:

- share the information they recorded on their Cause and Effect chart.
- share questions they asked themselves and tell how they found the answers.
- tell something they learned from reading the selection.

→ Beyond Level

Lexile 620

OBJECTIVES

Describe the connection between two individuals, events, ideas, or pieces of information in a text. **RI.1.3**

Identify causes and effects

Leveled Reader:
What Is a Yurt?

What Is a Yurt?

Before Reading

Preview and Predict

Read the title and author name. Have children preview the title page and the photographs. Ask: *What do you think you will learn about in this text?*

Review Genre: Informational Text/Nonfiction

Have children recall that informational text gives facts and information about real people, places, events, and things. Prompt children to name key characteristics of informational nonfiction. Tell them to look for these as they read the Leveled Reader.

ESSENTIAL QUESTION

Remind children of the Essential Question: *How do things get built?* Set a purpose for reading: *Let's find out what a yurt is.*

Graphic Organizer

During Reading

Guided Comprehension

Have children whisper read *What Is a Yurt?* Have them place self-stick notes next to difficult words. Remind children that when they come to an unfamiliar word, they can look for familiar spellings. They will need to break longer words into smaller chunks and sound out each part.

Point out the glossary and index on page 15. Tell children they can use the glossary to look up an unfamiliar word in the selection.

Monitor children's reading. Stop periodically and ask open-ended questions to facilitate rich discussion, such as, *What does the author want you to know about a yurt in this part of the text?* Build on children's responses to develop deeper understanding of the text.

Strategy: Ask and Answer Questions

Remind children that as they read, they can ask themselves questions and then use the words and text to find the answers. *Asking and answering questions helps you to better understand what you read.*

Skill: Connections Within Text/Cause and Effect

Remind children a cause is an event that makes something happen. An effect is what happens As you read, ask: *What caused nomads to build yurts?* Display a Cause and Effect chart for children to copy. Model how to record the information.

Think Aloud On page 4, I connected two details that are a cause and effect. The cause is that nomads needed homes that could be taken apart and set up quickly. The effect is that nomads built and traveled with yurts. I'll write this cause and effect in my chart.

Have children fill in their charts as they read.

After Reading

Respond to Reading

Have children complete the Respond to Reading on page 11.

Retell

Have children take turns retelling the selection. Help children make a personal connection: *Describe the materials used to build your home. Draw a picture to go with your writing.*

PAIRED READ ...

"Treehouses"

Make Connections:
Write About It *Analytical Writing*

Leveled Reader

Before reading "Treehouses," have children preview the title page and prompt them to identify the genre. Discuss the Compare Texts direction. After reading, have children work with a partner to discuss the information they learned in "Treehouses" and *What Is a Yurt?* Prompt children to discuss the similarities and differences between the two types of shelter.

FOCUS ON SCIENCE

Children can extend their knowledge of camping out by completing the science activity on page 16. **STEM**

Literature Circles

Lead children in conducting a literature circle using the Thinkmark questions to guide the discussion. You may wish to discuss what children have learned about building shelters from reading the two selections in the Leveled Reader.

Gifted and Talented

SYNTHESIZE Challenge children to write about which kind of shelter they liked learning about most. Encourage them to use ideas from the selections to give the reasons for their preference.

HAVE them use facts they learned from the week or do additional research to find out more about yurts or treehouses.

Beyond Level

Vocabulary

ORAL VOCABULARY: SYNONYMS

OBJECTIVES

Use sentence-level context as a clue to the meaning of a word or phrase. **L.1.4a**

 I Do Review the meaning of the oral vocabulary word *structure*. Remind children that a synonym is a word that means almost the same thing as another word. *A synonym for* structure *is* building. *A building might be a structure that people live or work in.*

 We Do Have children take turns using the word *building* in sentences. Then help children think of synonyms for *project*. Some examples are *activity, assignment,* and *job.*

 You Do Have partners use *project* and at least one of its synonyms in sentences.

 Gifted and Talented **Extend** Have partners imagine that their project is to build a structure. Have them draw a picture of the structure. Then have them tell about it and how they would build it, using the synonyms they learned.

VOCABULARY: SYNONYMS

OBJECTIVES

Use sentence-level context as a clue to the meaning of a word or phrase. **L.1.4a**

 I Do Review the meaning of the vocabulary word *section*. Write the sentence: *I live in one section of Miami.* Read the sentence aloud and have children repeat. Discuss what *section* means. Remind children that a synonym means almost the same thing as another word. *A section is a part of something larger.* Part *is a synonym for* section: *I live in one part of Miami.*

 We Do Have partners think of other synonyms for *section*. These might include *piece, segment, region, area,* or *quarter.* Ask them to use the synonyms in sentences to show their meanings.

 You Do Ask children to draw a section of something. Have them use synonyms for *section* to tell about their pictures.

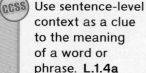

Comprehension

REVIEW CONNECTIONS WITHIN TEXT: CAUSE AND EFFECT

OBJECTIVES

Describe the connection between two individuals, events, ideas, or pieces of information in a text. **RI.1.3**

Identify cause-and-effect relationships in informational text

Discuss with children how they can make connections within a text. *How can making connections between ideas and events help you identify causes and effects in a selection?*

Ask children to read the first two pages of the Practice Book selection aloud. Pause to discuss cause and effect. *What can you do because it is snowing? Why does the snow get big and round?*

Have children read the rest of the Practice Book selection independently. Remind them to make connections between events by thinking about cause-and-effect relationships. Then ask them to discuss causes and effects in the selection.

SELF-SELECTED READING

OBJECTIVES

With prompting and support, read informational texts appropriately complex for grade 1. **RI.1.10**

Apply the strategy and skill to read a text

Read Independently

Have children choose an informational text for sustained silent reading. Tell them that they should use a Cause and Effect chart to record causes and effects.

Read Purposefully

Have children record the causes and effects in a Cause and Effect chart as they read. After reading, guide children to:

- share the information they recorded on the chart with a partner and discuss connections that they made.

- record information about the selection in a reading response journal.

Independent Study Have children write a newspaper review of the selection. Have them tell what the selection was about and whether they liked it. Remind them to include some of the cause-and-effect relationships in their review.

→ English Language Learners

Reading/Writing Workshop

Shared Read
The Joy of a Ship

The Joy of a Ship

Before Reading

Build Background

Read the Essential Question: *How do things get built?*

- Explain the meaning of the Essential Question. *Everything we use needs to be built or made: schools, houses, airplanes, boats, clothes, toys. They are made by workers using tools and machines. There is a process for building or making things.*

- **Model an answer:** *I drove my car to school today. This car was built in a factory. Workers used tools and other machines to put the parts of the car together in a special order or sequence.*

- Ask children a question that ties the Essential Question to their own background knowledge. *Have you ever put something together? What was it?* Ask partners to share their answers.

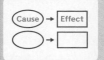

Graphic Organizer

During Reading

Interactive Question-Response

- Ask questions that help children understand the meaning of the text after each paragraph.

- Reinforce the meanings of key vocabulary by providing meanings embedded in the questions.

- Ask children questions that require them to use key vocabulary.

- Reinforce the comprehension strategies and skills of the week by modeling.

OBJECTIVES

 Ask and answer questions about key details in a text. **RI.1.1**

 Describe the connection between two individuals, events, ideas, or pieces of information in a text. **RI.1.3**

The Joy of a Ship

Pages 200–201

Point to the title. *Listen as I read the title of this selection.* Point to each word as you read it. *Let's read it together:* The Joy of a Ship.

Point to the photo of the ship. *This photo shows a ship. The ship is being built. Parts of the ship are being put together. Let's read to find out how a ship is made.*

Pages 202–203

Many people work together to make a ship. They use parts and tools. Look at the photos of the workers. What are they doing? (looking at plans, working on the ship)

Point to the section head on page 203. *Let's read the head together:* Frame It! *The first step to make a ship is to make the frame.* Point to the crane in the photo. *This is a crane. Say the word with me:* crane. *The crane moves the big parts.*

Explain and Model High-Frequency Words Point to the word *above* and have children say it with you. *Let's say the letters in this word: a, b, o, v, e.* Above *means "over." Put your hands above your head.* Give other simple directions using the word *above.*

Why must workers avoid being bumped? (Cranes are hoisting big parts in place on the ship.)

Pages 204–205

Listen as I read the section head. Then read it with me: Sheets of Steel. *Let's look at the steel in the photo. Do you think it is hot or cold?* (hot) *That's right! The steel boils and gets hot.*

Explain and Model the Skill *Information in a text is connected, or related. Some details tell about something that happens. That is an effect. Why it happens is the cause. What happens when hot steel gets cold? Yes, it gets hard. That is the effect.*

Look at the worker in the photo on page 205. The worker wears a helmet and gloves. Say those words with me: helmet, gloves. *Which one covers the worker's head? Which one covers the worker's hands?*

Why does the worker wear a helmet and gloves? (to be protected or safe)

Explain and Model Phonics Repeat the first two sentences on page 204. *Listen to these sentences. Clap when you hear a word with the /oi/ sound.* (boils) *On page 205 we read two more words with /oi/,* joins *and* joints. *Say the three /oi/ words with me.*

Pages 206–207

Let's look at the photo on page 206. The ship is almost finished. Read the first sentence with me: Workers check all the joints. *The joints are the places where the parts of the ship are joined together. Workers need to make sure that water won't leak into the boat.*

What might happen if water got in the boat? (It might sink.)

Explain and Model the Strategy *Ask yourself questions as you read. Look for the answers in the illustrations and the words. As I read page 206, I wondered how water stayed out of the ship. I read that workers check joints for leaks and fix them.*

Pages 208–209

There are many different kinds of ships. Point to the photo of the cruise ship on page 208. *This is a cruise ship. People go on this ship to see new places and have fun.* Point to the picture of the cargo ship on page 209. *This is a cargo ship. What might it carry?*

 Where would you like to go on a ship?

After Reading

Make Connections

- Review the Essential Question.

→ English Language Learners

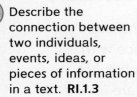

Lexile 390

OBJECTIVES

CCSS Describe the connection between two individuals, events, ideas, or pieces of information in a text. **RI.1.3**

Identify causes and effects

Leveled Reader:
What Is a Yurt?

Before Reading

Preview

Read the title. Ask: *What is the title? Say it again.* Repeat with the author's name. Preview the photographs. Have children describe the photos. Use simple language to tell about each page. Follow with questions, such as, *Why do some people like camping?*

ESSENTIAL QUESTION

Remind children of the Essential Question: *How do things get built?* Say: *Let's read to find out what a yurt is.* Encourage children to ask for help when they do not understand a word or phrase.

During Reading

Interactive Question-Response

Pages 2–3 *I still have a question about this selection. What is a yurt? What can I do to answer my question?* (keep reading) *Let's read on to find the answer to my question.*

Pages 4–5 *Let's read the words together that answer my question: A yurt is a strong tent. Tell a partner why wool mats were used in the winter but not in the summer in yurts.*

Pages 6–7 *Look at the photograph on page 6. Describe what you see. Tell about the yurt's frame. What other round things do you know about? Why do you think the frame is covered one section at a time?* (The yurt is too big to cover all at once.)

Pages 8–9 *Tell how the yurt's roof is built. Look at the pictures to help you. Now tell your partner why yurts are still used in some places.* (They are good shelters.) *Look at the picture on page 9. What do you think is most interesting about this yurt village?*

Pages 10–11 *Would you like to build or live in a yurt? Tell your partner why you would or would not.*

Go Digital

What Is a Yurt?

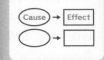

Graphic Organizer

Retell

After Reading

Respond to Reading

Revisit the Essential Question. Ask children to work with partners to fill in the graphic organizer and answer the questions on page 12. Pair children with peers of varying language abilities.

Retell

Model retelling using the **Retelling Card** prompts. Say: *Look at the photographs. Use details to help you retell the selection.* Help children make personal connections by asking: *Have you ever slept in a tent? Did you like it? Why or why not?*

Intonation and Phrasing Fluency: Commas

Read the pages in the book, one at a time. Help children echo-read the pages expressively and with appropriate phrasing. Remind them to pause when they come to a comma in their reading.

Apply Have children practice reading with partners. Pair children with peers of varying language abilities. Provide feedback as needed.

PAIRED READ ...

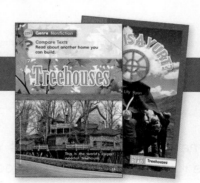

Leveled Reader

"Treehouses"

Make Connections: Write About It ✏️ *Analytical Writing*

Before reading, tell children to note that this text is informational. Then discuss the Compare Texts direction.

After reading, ask children to make connections between the information they learned from "Treehouses" and *What Is a Yurt?* Prompt children by providing a sentence frame: *A yurt is like a treehouse because _____.*

🧪 FOCUS ON SCIENCE

Children can extend their knowledge of camping by completing the science activity on page 16. **STEM**

Literature Circles

Lead children in conducting a literature circle using the Thinkmark questions to guide the discussion. You may wish to discuss what children have learned about building different shelters from reading the two selections in the Leveled Reader.

Level Up

Level-up lessons available online.

IF children can read *What Is a Yurt?* ELL Level with fluency and correctly answer the Respond to Reading questions,

THEN tell children that they will read a more detailed version of the selection.

• Use page 5 of *What Is a Yurt?* On Level to model using Teaching Poster 32 to list a cause and its effect.

• Have children read the selection, checking their comprehension by using the graphic organizer.

English Language Learners

Vocabulary

PRETEACH ORAL VOCABULARY

 OBJECTIVES
Produce complete sentences when appropriate to task and situation. **SL.1.6**

LANGUAGE OBJECTIVE
Use oral vocabulary words

 I Do Display images from the **Visual Vocabulary Cards** one at a time and follow the routine to preteach the oral vocabulary words *structure* and *project*.

 We Do Display each image again and explain how it illustrates or demonstrates the word. Model using sentences to describe the image.

 You Do Display each word again and have partners discuss how the pictures demonstrate the word. Encourage children to use each word in a sentence.

Beginning	Intermediate	Advanced/High
Have children cut out or draw pictures of a structure. Say a sentence, such as: *This structure is a house.* Have children repeat.	Have children draw or cut out pictures of structures and tell about each one. Provide a sentence frame: *This structure is ____.*	Challenge partners to tell what type of structure they would build if their project was to build a structure.

PRETEACH VOCABULARY

 OBJECTIVES
Produce complete sentences when appropriate to task and situation. **SL.1.6**

LANGUAGE OBJECTIVE
Use vocabulary words

 I Do Display images from the **ELL Visual Vocabulary Cards** one at a time and follow the routine to preteach the vocabulary words *camp* and *canvas*. Say each word and have children repeat it. Define the words in English.

 We Do Display each image again and ask children to tell how it illustrates or demonstrates the word. Model using sentences to describe the image.

 You Do Display each word again and have children say the word and then spell it. Provide opportunities for children to use the words in speaking and writing. Provide sentence starters.

Beginning	Intermediate	Advanced/High
Say a sentence about an image. Have children repeat the sentence and match it to its picture.	Say sentences about the images, leaving out the words. Have children repeat the sentences with the words.	Ask children to use the words to ask and answer questions about the images.

Words to Know

REVIEW WORDS

CCSS **OBJECTIVES**
Recognize and read grade-appropriate irregularly spelled words. **RF.1.3g**

___

LANGUAGE OBJECTIVE
Use high-frequency words *above, build, fall, knew, money, toward,* and vocabulary words *balance, section*

 Display the **High-Frequency Word** and **Vocabulary Cards** for *above, build, fall, knew, money, toward* and *balance* and *section*. Read each word. Use the **Read/Spell/Write** routine to teach each word. Have children write the words on their **Response Boards**.

 Write sentence frames on separate lines. Track the print as children read and complete the sentences: *(1) Look up. Above me, I see ____. (2) I would like to build ____. (3) Don't fall when you ____. (4) I knew ____. (5) I need money to ____. (6) Let's walk toward ____. (7) Try to keep your balance when you ____. (8) Here is a section of a ____.*

 Display the High-Frequency Word Cards from the previous weeks. Display one card at a time as children chorally read the word. Mix and repeat. Note words children need to review. Repeat with vocabulary words.

Beginning	Intermediate	Advanced/High
Use the words in sentences about photographs from a recently read selection. Have children repeat.	Have partners complete sentence frames about selection photographs: *People build ____.*	Challenge partners to use the words in sentences to tell about selections they have read.

RETEACH WORDS

CCSS **OBJECTIVES**
Recognize and read grade-appropriate irregularly spelled words. **RF.1.3g**

___

LANGUAGE OBJECTIVE
Use high-frequency words

 Display each Visual Vocabulary Card and say the word aloud. Define the word in English and, if appropriate, in Spanish. Identify any cognates.

 Point to each image again and explain how it illustrates or demonstrates the word. Ask children to repeat the word. Engage children in structured partner-talk about the image as prompted on the back of the card. Ask children to chorally say the word three times.

 Display each visual in random order, hiding the word. Have children identify the word and define it in their own words.

Beginning	Intermediate	Advanced/High
Say a word. Have children find its picture. Use the word in a sentence, and have children repeat.	Have children complete sentences frames for the words.	Have children say a sentence but leave out the word. Ask others to tell what word completes the sentence.

English Language Learners
Writing/Spelling

WRITING TRAIT: ORGANIZATION

OBJECTIVES

Write informative/explanatory texts in which they name a topic, supply some facts about the topic, and provide some sense of closure. **W.1.2**

LANGUAGE OBJECTIVE

Write steps in order

 I Do Explain that writers list steps in order. Write and read these sentences: *First, get bread. Next, put it in the toaster. Then, put on some butter. Last, eat your toast.* Have children tell the order of events.

 We Do Read aloud page 203 of *The Joy of a Ship*. Ask children what the first step is when building a ship. (build a frame) Repeat with page 206. Ask what the workers do after they build a frame. (check the joints and fix leaks)

 You Do Have children write steps to tell how they do something. Remind them to use order words (such as *first, next, then, last*) that tell the order of the steps.

Beginning	Intermediate	Advanced/High
Have children follow directions to do something, such as to draw a happy face. Say each step, and have children repeat it as they follow the direction.	Have children act out steps for making something, such as a sandwich. Ask them to tell what they do in each step. Provide sentence frames as necessary.	Have partners give each other directions for doing or making something. Remind them to use words that tell order in their steps.

WORDS WITH DIPHTHONGS *oi, oy*

OBJECTIVES

Use conventional spelling for words with common spelling patterns and for frequently occurring irregular words. **L.1.2d**

LANGUAGE OBJECTIVE

Spell words with diphthongs *oi, oy*

 I Do Read aloud the first Spelling Word, *spoil*, on page T326. Segment into sounds and attach a spelling to each sound. Point out the /oi/ sound spelled *oi*. Read aloud, segment, and spell the remaining words and have children repeat.

 We Do Say a sentence for *spoil*. Then, say *spoil* slowly and ask children to repeat. Have them write the word. Repeat the process for the remaining words.

 You Do Display the words. Have children work with partners to check their spelling lists. Have children correct misspelled words on their lists.

Beginning	Intermediate	Advanced/High
Help children say the words and copy them with the correct spelling.	After children have corrected their words, have pairs quiz each other.	Challenge children to think of other words that have the /oi/ sound.

Grammar

PREPOSITIONS AND PREPOSITIONAL PHRASES

OBJECTIVES

 Demonstrate command of the conventions of standard English grammar and usage when writing or speaking. **L.1.1**

LANGUAGE OBJECTIVE

Understand and use prepositions

Language Transfers Handbook

TRANSFER SKILLS

Speakers of Cantonese might omit prepositions. Provide extra support with prepositions by having children act out and repeat sentences like these: *I sit on a chair. I look at the clock. I walk to the door. I put my hand in my pocket.* Have them identify the preposition in each sentence.

 I Do Remind children that a preposition links a noun or pronoun to another part of the sentence. Review that a prepositional phrase begins with a preposition and ends with a noun or pronoun. Have children walk toward the window. Then write and read the sentence *You walked toward the window.* Circle *toward. Toward is a preposition. It connects the words* You walked *and the words that tell where you walked,* the window.

 We Do Write the sentences on the board. Have children read each sentence and identify the preposition.

The lights are above us. (above)

My lunch is in my desk. (in)

What is on the table? (on)

This gift is for you. (for)

 You Do Write the following sentence frames on the board:

I see _____ in the sky above us.

During the day, we _____.

Have partners complete each sentence frame. Circulate, listen in, and note each child's language use and proficiency.

Beginning	Intermediate	Advanced/High
Put things in, above, under, or on other things. Say sentences without the prepositions. Have children use the correct preposition to complete each sentence.	Have children use prepositions in sentences to tell about things they see in the classroom or classmates moving or working.	Ask partners to say as many sentences with prepositions as they can to a describe something they saw on the way to school.

PROGRESS MONITORING

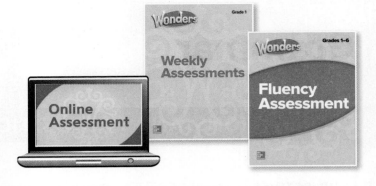

Unit 5 Week 5 Formal Assessment	Standards Covered	Component for Assessment
Comprehension Connections Within Text: Cause and Effect	RI.1.3	• *Selection Test* • *Weekly Assessment*
Vocabulary Strategy Inflectional Endings	L.1.4c	• *Selection Test* • *Weekly Assessment*
Phonics Diphthongs *oi, oy*	RF.1.3	*Weekly Assessment*
Structural Analysis Final Stable Syllables	RF.1.3d, RF.1.3e	*Weekly Assessment*
High-Frequency Words *above, build, fall, knew, money, toward*	RF.1.3g	*Weekly Assessment*
Writing Writing About Text	RI.1.3	*Weekly Assessment*
Unit 5 Week 5 Informal Assessment		
Research/Listening/Collaborating	SL.1.1c, SL.1.2, SL.1.3	• *RWW* • *Teacher's Edition*
Oral Reading Fluency (ORF) Fluency Goal: 13-33 words correct per minute (WCPM) Accuracy Rate Goal: 95% or higher	RF.1.4a. RF.1.4b, RF.1.4c	*Fluency Assessment*

Using Assessment Results

Weekly Assessment Skills	If . . .	Then . . .
COMPREHENSION	Children answer 0–3 multiple-choice items correctly . . .	. . . assign Lessons 73–75 on Cause and Effect and Lessons 88-90 on Text Connections from the *Tier 2 Comprehension Intervention online PDFs*.
VOCABULARY	Children answer 0–2 multiple-choice items correctly . . .	. . . assign Lesson 103 on Inflectional Endings *-s, -es* and Lesson 104 on Inflectional Endings *-ed, -ing* from the *Tier 2 Vocabulary Intervention online PDFs*.
PHONICS/ STRUCTURAL ANALYSIS/HFW	Children answer 0–6 multiple-choice items correctly . . .	. . . assign Lesson 94 on Diphthong /*oi*/ (*oi, oy*) and Lesson 108 on Final *e* Syllables from the *Tier 2 Phonics/Word Study Intervention online PDFs*.
WRITING	Children score less than "2" on the constructed response . . .	. . . reteach necessary skills using Section 13 on Write About Reading from the *Tier 2 Comprehension Intervention online PDFs*.
	Children have a WCPM score of 13 . . .	. . . assign a lesson from Section 1, 9, or 10 of the *Tier 2 Fluency Intervention online PDFs*.
	Children have a WCPM score of 0–12 . . .	. . . assign a lesson from Sections 2–8 of the *Tier 2 Fluency Intervention online PDFs*.

Using Weekly Data

Check your data Dashboard to verify assessment results and guide grouping decisions.

Response to Intervention

Use the children's assessment results to assist you in identifying children who will benefit from focused intervention.

Use the appropriate sections of the *Placement and Diagnostic Assessment* to designate children requiring:

Data-Driven Recommendations

TIER 2 Intervention Online PDFs

TIER 3 WonderWorks Intervention Program

The Big Idea: *How can we make sense of the world around us?*

Student Outcomes

Close Reading of Complex Text

- Cite relevant evidence from text
- Interpret information presented visually
- Navigate links
- Gather relevant information from digital sources

RI.1.5, RI.1.6, RI.1.7

Writing
Write to Sources

- Conduct research
- Select reliable sources
- Write informative text

W.1.2, W.1.7, W.1.8

Speaking and Listening

- Report on a topic
- Listen to presentations
- Ask relevant questions

SL.1.1, SL.1.3

Review and Extend

Reader's Theater

Supper with the Queen

Genre Play

Reading Digitally

TIME FOR KIDS "Great Ideas!"

Go Digital!

Level Up Accelerating Progress

FROM **APPROACHING** TO **ON LEVEL**

FROM **ON LEVEL** TO **BEYOND LEVEL**

FROM **ENGLISH LANGUAGE LEARNERS** TO **ON LEVEL**

FROM **BEYOND LEVEL** TO **SELF-SELECTED TRADE BOOK**

Advanced Level Trade Book

ASSESS

Presentations

Research and Inquiry
Project Presentations

Project Rubric

Writing
Informative Text Presentations

Writing Rubric

Unit Assessments

UNIT 5 TEST

FLUENCY

Evaluate Student Progress

Use the Wonders online assessment reports to evaluate student progress and help you make decisions about small group instruction and assignments.

Fuse/Getty Images

SUGGESTED LESSON PLAN

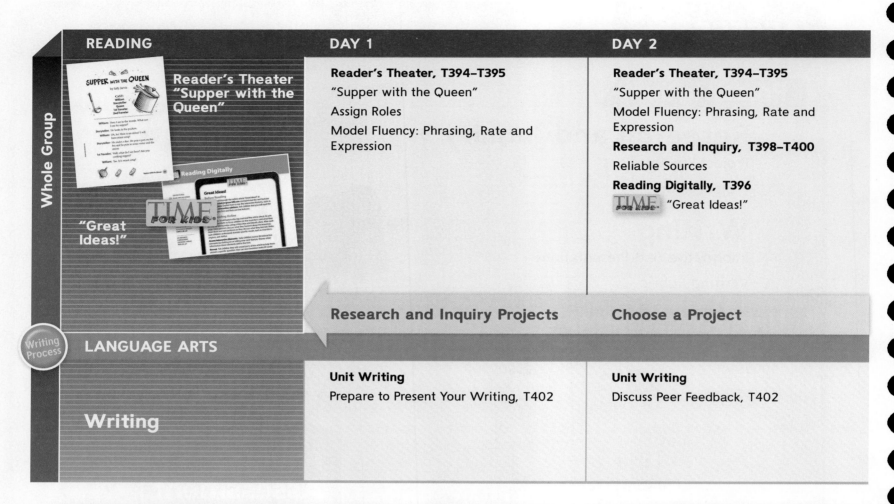

READING	DAY 1	DAY 2

Whole Group

Reader's Theater "Supper with the Queen"

"Great Ideas!"

DAY 1

Reader's Theater, T394–T395
"Supper with the Queen"
Assign Roles
Model Fluency: Phrasing, Rate and Expression

DAY 2

Reader's Theater, T394–T395
"Supper with the Queen"
Model Fluency: Phrasing, Rate and Expression
Research and Inquiry, T398–T400
Reliable Sources
Reading Digitally, T396
"Great Ideas!"

Research and Inquiry Projects — **Choose a Project**

LANGUAGE ARTS

Writing Process

Writing

Unit Writing
Prepare to Present Your Writing, T402

Unit Writing
Discuss Peer Feedback, T402

DIFFERENTIATED INSTRUCTION Level up to Accelerate

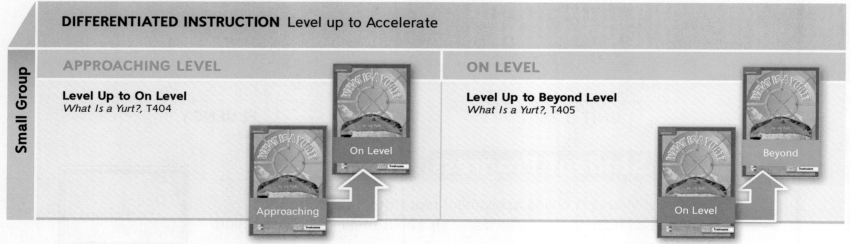

Small Group

APPROACHING LEVEL	ON LEVEL
Level Up to On Level *What Is a Yurt?*, T404	**Level Up to Beyond Level** *What Is a Yurt?*, T405

On Level

Approaching

Beyond

On Level

DAY 3	DAY 4	DAY 5
Reading Digitally, T396–T397 TIME FOR KIDS "Great Ideas!" Close Reading	**Reader's Theater, T394–T395** Performance	**Research and Inquiry, T398–T399** Presentation ✓ **Unit Assessment, T408–T409** **Wrap Up the Unit, T401**

Research and Inquiry Projects   **Choose a Project**

Unit Writing Rehearse Your Presentation, T402	**Unit Writing** Present Your Writing, T402–T403 Evaluate Your Presentation, T402–T403	**Unit Writing** Portfolio Choice, T403

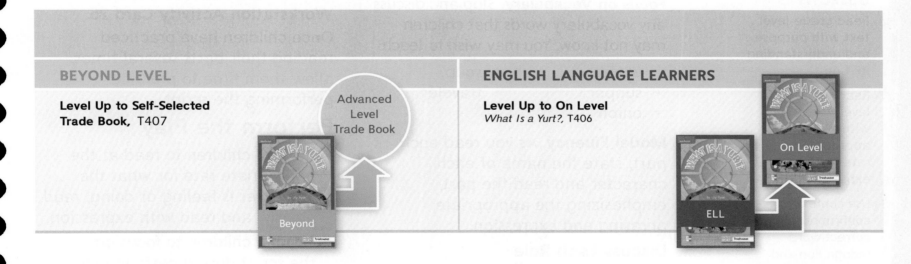

BEYOND LEVEL	**ENGLISH LANGUAGE LEARNERS**
Level Up to Self-Selected **Trade Book,** T407	**Level Up to On Level** *What Is a Yurt?*, T406

Reader's Theater

Go Digital!

Teacher's Resource PDF Online

OBJECTIVES

CCSS Read grade-level text with purpose and understanding. **RF.1.4a**

CCSS Read grade-level text orally with accuracy, appropriate rate, and expression. **RF.1.4b**

CCSS Use context to confirm or self-correct word recognition and understanding, rereading as necessary. **RF.1.4c**

Supper with the Queen

Introduce the Play

Explain that *Supper with the Queen* is a play about a man in the woods who decides to cook some soup for his supper. It tells what happens when two travelers and a queen try to help by adding other ingredients to the soup. Distribute scripts and the Elements of Drama handout from the **Teacher's Resource PDF Online**.

- Review the features of a play.
- Review the list of characters and point out that the Storyteller is the narrator. Discuss the setting. Point out that the play takes place outside in the woods, probably a time long ago.

Shared Reading

Model reading the play as children follow along in their scripts.

Focus on Vocabulary Stop and discuss any vocabulary words that children may not know. You may wish to teach:

- woods
- supper
- onion
- soup
- traveler

Model Fluency As you read each part, state the name of each character and read the part, emphasizing the appropriate phrasing and expression.

Discuss Each Role

- After reading the Storyteller part, help children to identify information he or she gives about the play.
- After reading the other parts, ask children to describe each character. Model finding character evidence.

Assign Roles

Since there are only five parts, you may wish to have more than one cast. A few casts can work on their scripts simultaneously. Another way to create additional roles is to assign the Storyteller's part to more than one child.

Practice the Play

Have children use highlighters to mark their parts in the script. Each day, allow children time to practice their parts. Pair fluent readers with less fluent readers. Pairs can echo-read or chorally read their parts. As needed, work with less fluent readers to mark pauses in their script, using one slash for a short pause and two slashes for longer pauses.

Throughout the week have children work on the Reader's Theater **Workstation Activity Card 25**.

Once children have practiced reading their parts several times, allow them time to practice performing the script.

Perform the Play

- Remind children to read at the appropriate rate for what the character is feeling or doing, read clearly, and read with expression.
- Remind children to focus on the script during performance, reading along even when they are not speaking.
- As a class, discuss how performing a play aloud is different from reading it silently. Have children tell a partner what they liked about performing and what they didn't like.

ACTIVITIES

A SPECIAL CHARACTER

In *Supper with the Queen*, one of the characters is the Storyteller. Help children focus on the Storyteller's function in the play. Discuss the idea that the Storyteller is a narrator; the Storyteller's job is to talk to the audience, filling in parts of the story that are not shown. Have children answer the following questions.

1. Where does William find an onion? How do you know?

2. What do the two travelers add to the soup? How do you know?

3. What does the Storyteller say about the Queen?

4. What does William do at the end of the play? How do you know?

PROPS AND COSTUMES

Discuss ways children can add to their performance with props and costumes. For example:

• William could use a large container, a spoon, and a crumpled paper ball as an onion.

• The travelers could carry backpacks.

• The queen could wear a paper crown.

Keep in mind that children will hold their scripts while performing. Allow time for children to practice using the props and costumes.

ELL ENGLISH LANGUAGE LEARNERS

• Review the definitions of difficult words and phrases including *pockets, fair, banana, put, good, dear me, ugh, lucky, sugar,* and *hungry.*

• Pair an ELL child with a fluent reader who is reading the same part. Have each reader take turns reading the lines.

• Work with ELLs to make sure they understand what they are reading. Ask questions to help children summarize or retell the story and clarify meanings as necessary.

Reading Digitally

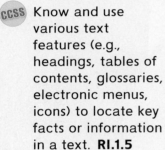

OBJECTIVES

CCSS Know and use various text features (e.g., headings, tables of contents, glossaries, electronic menus, icons) to locate key facts or information in a text. **RI.1.5**

CCSS With guidance and support from adults, recall information from experiences or gather information from provided sources to answer a question. **W.1.8**

ACADEMIC LANGUAGE
interactive, rollover, Web site, *url*

Great Ideas!

Before Reading

Preview Scroll through the online article "Great Ideas!" at **http://connected.mcgraw-hill.com** and point out the text features such as **captions**. Explain how to use the interactive features, such as **quizzes** and **interactive sidebars**. Tell children that you will read the article together first and then use the features.

Close Reading Online

Take Notes Scroll back to the top and read the article aloud. As you read, ask questions to focus children on the inventions and what they do. Model taking notes using a Main Idea and Details chart. After each page, have partners discuss what they learned about the invention. Have them use text evidence as they discuss what they learned. Make sure children understand domain-specific words, such as *inventions, engines*, and *AirPod*.

Access Interactive Elements Help children access the interactive elements by clicking on or rolling over each feature. Discuss what information these elements add to the text.

Reread Tell children they will reread parts of the article to help them answer a specific question: *How can new inventions make life easier for us?*

Navigate Links to Information Remind children that online texts may include hyperlinks. Hyperlinks help you go from the Web page you are on to another Web page that tells more about the topic.

Model how to use a hyperlink to jump to another Web page. Discuss information on the new Web page.

Before navigating back, demonstrate bookmarking the page so children can return to it at another time.

WRITE ABOUT READING Analytical Writing

Retell Review children's charts. Model using the information to retell "Great Ideas!"

Ask children to act out what the inventions they read about can do. Invite children to guess the inventions to help them retell the article.

Make Connections Have children compare what they learned about new inventions with what they learned about figuring out the world around them in other texts they read in this unit. Ask them to write a paragraph about how these new inventions might help people learn about the world.

SOCIAL STUDIES CONNECT TO CONTENT

Important Inventions

Remind children that many inventions have made a big difference in people's lives. Explain that inventions are created by inventors so inventors are important people who make important contributions to our lives.

Ask children to name facts from the article that help them understand how inventors can change our lives.

- What does a tiny aircraft do? Why do people use this invention?

- What is an AirPod? Why is it an important invention?

RESEARCH ONLINE

Reliable Sites

Explain to children that some sites are better to use than other sites. Point out that when they use the Internet, they should look for the best, or most reliable, sites. Tell children that government sites (.gov) and education sites (.edu) are usually good sites to check first. Museums and other institutions such as zoos have sites with addresses that end in .org. These are usually reliable sources too.

INDEPENDENT STUDY

Investigate

Choose a Topic Brainstorm questions related to inventions such as: *Who are some famous inventors and what did they invent? What inventions were created by kids?*

Conduct Internet Research Have children conduct an Internet search. Type in the URL for a child-friendly search engine. Enter key words. Click on a link to go to a site. Remind children to check government and education sites first.

Present Help children use their research to make a collage of famous inventions or use presentation software to share it with others.

→ Integrate Ideas

- Collaborate

- Resources: Research and Inquiry

RESEARCH AND INQUIRY

COLLABORATE

Research and Inquiry

Assign the Projects Divide students into five groups. Assign each group one of the projects or let groups self-select. Before children begin researching, present the minilesson below.

Taking Notes

- As children find information that relates to their project, explain that they will need to remember some of the information. They can take notes to keep track of important information.

- Point out that children may find articles, stories, or photos with information about the topic. Model how to ask questions that focus on information that is needed to complete the project, such as:

CHOOSE A PROJECT!

- Resources: Research and Inquiry

A Graph
Research teams will find other ways to classify and categorize objects from their Week 1 graph, such as by size, shape, material, purpose, or texture. They will create new graphs to show the information. WEEK 1

A Constellation
Research teams will find out about constellations. They will use self-sticking stars, cut-out paper with tape, or a drawing to show and label a constellation. WEEK 2

A Report
Research teams will find out about a child inventor. They will write a report about the inventor and the invention. WEEK 3

A Play
Research teams will write a short radio play to elaborate on one of the sample pages they created in Week 4. They can use more sound effects from their charts in their plays. WEEK 4

An Comparison Chart
Research teams will look at the bridges the small groups created in Week 5 to see how they stay up. Teams create a chart to compare the bridges and the way each one is supported. WEEK 5

Did I learn something new? Will I need to remember this information as we work on our project?

- Use a T-chart and write *Sources* as the left side head and *Notes* as the right side head. Then model how to write down the sources and take a simple note.

Organizing Information

- Encourage children to use a color code on their T-charts to sort information that goes together. For example, they can use blue marker for notes that are all related to one topic, pink for another topic, and so on.

- Explain that sorting their notes will help them evaluate if they have enough information for their project. If they see that they have few notes on certain topics, they can then return to their sources or find new sources in which to locate new information.

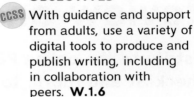

OBJECTIVES

CCSS With guidance and support from adults, use a variety of digital tools to produce and publish writing, including in collaboration with peers. **W.1.6**

CCSS Participate in shared research and writing projects (e.g., explore a number of "how-to" books on a given topic and use them to write a sequence of instructions). **W.1.7**

CONDUCT THE RESEARCH

Distribute the online Research Roadmap to children. Have them use the roadmap to complete the project.

STEP 1 **Set Research Goals** Discuss the Big Idea and the research project. Each group should develop a research plan that helps focus their research and decide how they want to present the information.

STEP 2 **Identify Sources** Have groups brainstorm where they can find the information they need. Guide children to focus on sources that will be most helpful for their particular project.

STEP 3 **Find and Record Information** Have children review the strategy for taking notes presented on page T398. Then have them do research. Guide children to find helpful web sites if necessary.

STEP 4 **Organize and Summarize** After team members have completed their research, they can review the information they collected. Help children decide what information is necessary to complete the project. Help team members summarize their findings and decide on their message. Help them to connect the key ideas of their projects to the unit theme, "Figure It Out."

STEP 5 **Complete and Present** Guide children to complete the project. Ensure children work together to create each part of the project. Encourage them to use various media in their presentations. Have teams take turns presenting their work.

Go Digital

Collaborate Manage and Assign projects online. Students can work with their team online.

INTEGRATE IDEAS **T399**

→Integrate Ideas

Review and Evaluate

Distribute the online PDF of the checklists and rubrics. Use the following Teacher Checklist and rubric to evaluate students' research and presentations.

Student Checklist

Research Process

- ☑ Did you choose a research topic?
- ☑ Did you use several sources to find information about your topic?
- ☑ Did you take notes and organize your information?

Presenting

- ☑ Did you practice your presentation?
- ☑ Did you speak clearly and loudly enough for others to hear?
- ☑ Did you give important facts and details about your topic?
- ☑ Did you answer the Essential Question?
- ☑ Did you use pictures, audio recordings, or other materials to make your presentation exciting for your audience?

Teacher Checklist

Assess the Research Process

- ☑ Selected a focus.
- ☑ Used sources to gather information.
- ☑ Used time effectively and collaborated well.

Assess the Presentation

- ☑ Presented information clearly and concisely.
- ☑ Maintained a consistent focus by staying on-topic.
- ☑ Used appropriate gestures.
- ☑ Maintained eye contact.
- ☑ Used appropriate visuals and technology.
- ☑ Spoke clearly and at an appropriate rate.

Assess the Listener

- ☑ Listened quietly and politely.
- ☑ Listened actively and asked questions to clarify understanding.

Presentation Rubric

4 Excellent	**3** Good	**2** Fair	**1** Unsatisfactory
• presents the information clearly. • includes many details. • may include many relevant observations.	• presents the information adequately. • provides adequate details. • includes relevant observations.	• attempts to present information. • may offer few or vague details. • may include few or irrelevant personal observations.	• may show little grasp of the task. • may present irrelevant information. • may reflect extreme difficulty with research or presentation.

Wrap Up the Unit

The Big Idea:
How can we make sense of the world around us?

TEXT CONNECTIONS

COLLABORATE

Connect to the Big Idea

Text to Text Write the Unit Big Idea on the board: *How can we make sense of the world around us?* Remind children that they have been reading selections about how we use our senses to understand the world and to solve problems and develop new ideas. Divide the class into small groups. Tell children that each group will compare what they learned about how we understand the world around us to answer the Big Idea question. Model how to compare this information by using examples from the **Leveled Readers** and what they have read in this unit's selections.

Collaborative Conversations Have children review their class notes, writing assignments, and completed graphic organizers before they begin their discussions. Ask children to compare information from the unit's selections and presentations. Have children work together to take notes. Explain that each group will use an Accordion

Dinah Zike's
FOLDABLES
Study Organizer

Foldable® to record their ideas. Model how to use an Accordion Foldable® to record comparisons of texts. Guide children to focus their conversations on what they learned about how we make sense of the world around us.

Present Ideas and Synthesize Information When children finish their discussions ask for volunteers from each group to share their ideas aloud. After each group has presented, ask: *What have we learned about how we make sense of the world around us?* Lead a class discussion and list children's ideas on the board.

Building Knowledge Have children continue to build knowledge about the Unit Big Idea. Display classroom or library sources and have children search for articles, books, and other resources related to the Big Idea. After each group has presented their ideas, ask: *How can we make sense of the world around us?* Lead a class discussion asking children to use information from their charts to answer the question.

OBJECTIVES

CCSS Integrate information from two texts on the same topic in order to write or speak about the subject knowledgeably. **RI.4.9**

CCSS Follow agreed-upon rules for discussions (e.g., listening to others with care, speaking one at a time about the topics and texts under discussion). **SL.1.1a**

CCSS Build on others' talk in conversations by responding to the comments of others through multiple exchanges. **SL.1.1b**

Go
Digital

**Resources:
Research and
Inquiry**

Celebrate Share Your Writing

Presentations

Giving Presentations

Now is the time for children to share one of their pieces of writing that they have worked on throughout the unit.

You may wish to invite parents or children from other classes to attend the presentations.

Preparing for Presentations

Tell children that they will prepare and present their writing to an audience. Guide children to use digital tools to prepare their work for presentation.

Allow children time to rehearse their presentation until they feel comfortable. Encourage them to read with expression and feeling.

Children should consider any visuals or props that they may want to use to accompany their presentation. Discuss different ideas.

- Do they have a map, such as one that would illustrate their directions to a place?
- Do they have photos or illustrations, such as ones to accompany their descriptions of a place?
- Do they have props, such as ones to accompany their report about a child inventor?
- Do they have examples or objects to accompany their writing, such as their how-to article?

Provide time for children to practice their presentations with a partner. Share the following Speaking Checklist to help them focus on important parts of the presentation. Discuss the points on the checklist.

Speaking Checklist

Review the Speaking Checklist with children as they practice.

- ☑ Have your notes and visuals ready.
- ☑ Speak loudly and clearly.
- ☑ Look at the audience.
- ☑ Hold your visuals so that everyone can see them.
- ☑ Adapt your voice to match what you are talking about.

Jim Craigmyle/Corbis

Listening to Presentations

Remind children that they not only will take on the role of a presenter, but they will also be part of the audience for their classmates' presentations. As a listener, children have an important role. Review with them the following Listening Checklist.

Listening Checklist

During the presentation

- ☑ Look at the speaker and listen carefully.
- ☑ Decide if you agree or disagree with the speaker's opinion.
- ☑ Make sure you understand what the speaker is talking about.
- ☑ Think of one thing you like about the speaker's presentation.

After the presentation

- ☑ Listen carefully to others and wait until it is your turn to speak.
- ☑ Comment politely on a point that you agreed with or disagreed with.
- ☑ Ask a question about something you did not understand.
- ☑ Share one positive comment about the speaker's topic.

Portfolio Choice

Ask children to select one finished piece of writing, as well as two revisions to include in their Writing Portfolio. As children consider their choices, have them use the checklist below.

Published Writing

Does your writing:

- use complete sentences?
- use describing adjectives?
- use time-order words to explain steps in order?
- have few or no spelling errors?

Sample Revisions

Did you choose a revised entry that shows:

- stronger or more interesting adjectives?
- clearer time-order words?
- added reasons to support an opinion?

Go Digital

PORTFOLIO
Children can submit their writing to be considered for inclusion in their digital portfolio. Children's portfolios can be shared with parents.

Level Up Accelerating Progress

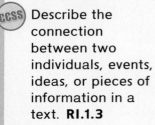

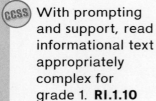

Leveled Reader

OBJECTIVES

(CCSS) Describe the connection between two individuals, events, ideas, or pieces of information in a text. **RI.1.3**

(CCSS) With prompting and support, read informational text appropriately complex for grade 1. **RI.1.10**

Approaching Level to On Level

What Is a Yurt?

Level Up Lessons also available online

Before Reading

Preview Discuss what children remember about the information they learned about a yurt. Tell them they will be reading a more detailed version of *What Is a Yurt?*

High-Frequency Words Use the **High-Frequency Word Cards** to review the high-frequency words. Use the routine on the cards.

A C T During Reading

▶ **Specific Vocabulary** Review the following social studies words that are new to this title. Model how to use the photographs and sentences to determine their meaning. *joins   shelter   Asia*

▶ **Connection of Ideas** Children may need help recognizing connections between ideas within the longer paragraphs of the higher level. Model how to paraphrase the ideas in a paragraph, then have children paraphrase to each other as they read subsequent more complex paragraphs.

▶ **Organization** The On Level text is divided into chapters, and the information within each chapter is more detailed than the information in the Approaching Level text. Help children identify the main idea of each chapter. Guide them to explain how the facts and details relate to the main idea of the chapter.

After Reading

Ask children to complete the Respond to Reading on page 12 using the new information from the On Level text. After children finish the Paired Read, have them hold Literature Circles.

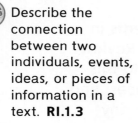

Leveled Reader

On Level
to Beyond Level

What Is a Yurt?

Level Up Lessons also available online

OBJECTIVES

CCSS Describe the connection between two individuals, events, ideas, or pieces of information in a text. **RI.1.3**

CCSS With prompting and support, read informational text appropriately complex for grade 1. **RI.1.10**

Before Reading

Preview Discuss what children remember about yurts. Tell them they will be reading a more detailed version of *What Is a Yurt?*

High-Frequency Words Use the **High-Frequency Word Cards** to review the high-frequency words. Use the routine on the cards.

A C T During Reading

▶ **Specific Vocabulary** Review the following social studies words that are new to this title. Model how to use the glossary to determine their meaning. For words that are not in the glossary, model using sentences and paragraphs to determine word meaning.
campsite textiles weather securely benefits weaved

▶ **Connection of Ideas** Children may need help recognizing connections between ideas within the longer paragraphs of the higher level. New information is presented, such as details about what people do while camping. Model how to paraphrase the ideas in a paragraph, then have children discuss how the paragraphs relate to each other.

▶ **Sentence Structure** The sentence structure at this level is more complex than in the On Level text. To help children understand the information, follow this routine when reading complex or compound sentences, such as the last sentence on page 4:

Read the sentence aloud. *When they reached their new destination, they set up the yurts once again.*

Break down the information into simpler sentences. *They reached a new destination. Then they set up the yurts again.*

Have children then read the sentence aloud.

After Reading

Ask children to complete the Respond to Reading on page 12 using the new information from the Beyond Level text. After children finish the Paired Read, have them hold Literature Circles.

Level Up Accelerating Progress

Leveled Reader

OBJECTIVES

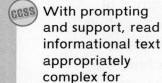

CCSS Describe the connection between two individuals, events, ideas, or pieces of information in a text. **RI.1.3**

CCSS With prompting and support, read informational text appropriately complex for grade 1. **RI.1.10**

English Language Learners to On Level

What Is a Yurt?

Level Up Lessons also available online

Before Reading

Preview Remind children informational text tells facts about real people, things, and events. Talk about what facts they remember about yurts, then tell them they will be reading a more detailed version of *What Is a Yurt?*

High-Frequency Words Use the **High-Frequency Word Cards** to review the high-frequency words. Use the routine on the cards.

A C T During Reading

▶ **Specific Vocabulary** Help children name elements in each photograph, now that there are no labels. Review the following social studies words that are new to this title. Model how to use the photographs, sentences, and paragraphs to determine their meaning. Review any cognates. *joins   shelter   Asia*

▶ **Connection of Ideas** Help children make connections between ideas within paragraphs that have much more information than the previous level. Model how to paraphrase the ideas in a paragraph, then have children paraphrase to each other as they read on.

▶ **Sentence Structure** Help children understand the information when reading complex sentences, such as the first sentence in the second paragraph on page 4:

Read the sentence aloud. *Nomads knew how to build yurts and take them apart quickly.*

Break down the information into simpler sentences. *Nomads knew how to build yurts. Nomads knew how to take them apart quickly.*

Have children then read the sentence aloud.

After Reading

Ask children to complete the Respond to Reading on page 12 using the new information from the On Level text. After children finish the Paired Read, have them hold Literature Circles.

Leveled Reader

OBJECTIVES

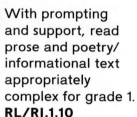 With prompting and support, read prose and poetry/ informational text appropriately complex for grade 1. **RL/RI.1.10**

Beyond Level
to Self-Selected Trade Book

Independent Reading

Level Up Lessons also available online

Before Reading

Together with children identify the particular focus of their reading based on the text they choose. Children who have chosen the same title can work together to closely read the selection.

Close Reading

Taking Notes Assign a graphic organizer for children to use to take notes as they read. Reinforce a specific comprehension focus from the unit by choosing one of the graphic organizers that best fits the book.

Examples:

Fiction
Problem and Solution
Problem and Solution chart

Informational Text
Cause and Effect
Cause and Effect chart

Ask and Answer Questions Remind children to ask questions as they read. Have them write questions on sticky notes and post them on each page as they read. As children meet, have them talk together about their questions. Encourage them to work together to find the answers to their questions before moving on to the next section.

After Reading

Write About Text

Have children use their notes, graphic organizers, and the information they shared in their discussions to write a response to the reading.

Examples:

Fiction
Do you agree with how the characters solved the problem? Why or why not?

Informational Text
Name an effect. What was its cause? How do you know?

SUMMATIVE ASSESSMENT

TESTED SKILLS

✓ COMPREHENSION:
- Point of View **RL.2.6**
- Plot: Cause/Effect **RL.1.3**
- Connections Within Text: Problem and Solution **RI.1.3**
- Plot: Problem and Solution **RL.1.3**
- Connections Within Text: Cause and Effect **RI.1.3**
- Text Feature: Use Illustrations **RI.1.6**
- Literary Element: Alliteration **RL.2.4**

✓ VOCABULARY:
- Context Clues: Multiple Meanings **L.1.4a**
- Shades of Meaning/Intensity **L.1.5d**

✓ PHONICS/STRUCTURAL ANALYSIS/HIGH-FREQUENCY WORDS:
- *r*-Controlled Vowels *ar, er, ir, oar, or, ore, ur* **RF.1.3**
- Diphthongs *ou, ow, oy, oi* **RF.1.3**
- Plurals (Irregular) **RF.1.3g**
- Comparative Inflectional Endings *-er, -est* **RF.1.3f**
- Final Stable Syllables **RF.1.3e**
- High-Frequency Words **RF.1.3g**

✓ ENGLISH LANGUAGE CONVENTIONS:
- Conjunctions **L.1.1g**
- Adjectives That Describe **L.1.1f**
- Adjectives That Compare: *-er, -est* **L.1.1f**
- Other Adjectives **L.1.1h**
- Writing Prompt: Personal Narrative **W.1.3, L.1.1, L.1.2**
- Prepositions and Prepositional Phrases **L.1.1i**

Additional Assessment Options

Conduct assessments individually using the differentiated passages in *Fluency Assessment*. Children's expected fluency goal for this Unit is **43–63 WCPM** with an accuracy rate of 95% or higher.

Use the instructional reading level determined by the Running Record calculations for regrouping decisions. Children at Level 12 or below should be provided reteaching on specific Comprehension skills.

Using Assessment Results

TESTED SKILLS	If ...	Then ...
COMPREHENSION	Children answer 0–7 items correctly ...	... reteach tested skills using the *Tier 2 Comprehension Intervention online PDFs.*
VOCABULARY	Children answer 0–3 items correctly ...	... reteach tested skills using the *Tier 2 Vocabulary online PDFs.*
PHONICS/ STRUCTURAL ANALYSIS/HFW	Children answer 0–8 items correctly ...	... reteach tested skills using the *Tier 2 Phonics/Word Study online PDFs.*
ENGLISH LANGUAGE CONVENTIONS	Children answer 0–4 items correctly ...	... reteach necessary skills using the *online Grammar Reproducibles.*
WRITING	Children score less than the benchmark score on the constructed responses ...	... reteach necessary skills using the Write About Reading lessons in the *Tier 2 Comprehension Intervention online PDFs.*
	Children who score less than the benchmark score on the writing prompt ...	... reteach necessary skills using the *online Grammar Reproducibles.*
FLUENCY	Children have a WCPM score of 0–42 ...	... reteach tested skills using the *Tier 2 Fluency Intervention online PDFs.*

Using Summative Data

Check online reports for this Unit Assessment as well as your data Dashboard. Use the data to assign small group instruction for students who are below the overall proficiency level for the tested skills.

Data-Driven Recommendations

Response to Intervention

Use children's assessment results to assist you in identifying children who will benefit from focused intervention. Use the appropriate sections of the *Placement and Diagnostic Assessment* to designate children requiring:

TIER 2 Intervention Online PDFs

TIER 3 WonderWorks Intervention Program

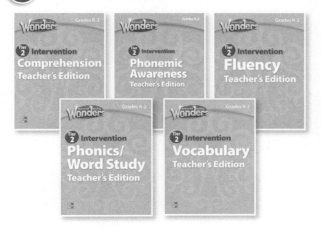

Model Lesson Reading Complex Text

Your Own Texts

Program Information

Scope and Sequence

Index

 Correlations

Reading Complex Text

Program Information

For Additional Resources

Theme Bibliography

Literature and Informational Text Charts

Word Lists

Web Sites

www.connected.mcgraw-hill.com

READING Extended Complex Text

Close Reading Routine

Read   *What does the text say?*

Select the Text

Depending on the needs of individual children, choose a book to:

- read aloud with children.
- have children read alone.

Model Note-Taking

Invite children to generate questions about aspects of the text that might be confusing for them. Model simple note-taking on the board or on chart paper. Encourage children to note:

- key ideas and details.
- difficult vocabulary words or phrases.
- details that are not clear.
- information that they do not understand.

Together, complete a graphic organizer with important information from the text.

Reread   *How does the author say it?*

Ask Text-Dependent Questions

Reread the text with children and discuss shorter passages from the text. Have children cite text evidence to answer deeper questions about craft and structure. Children should:

- talk about and identify text evidence.
- generate questions about the text.

Integrate   *What does the text mean?*

Have children draw a picture or write a short response to the text. Based on their ability, children may respond to the text by writing a short caption for a picture or two or three complete sentences that use evidence from the text to support their ideas.

Children reread to integrate knowledge and ideas and make text-to-text connections. Children should:

- work with partners to identify and discuss connections.
- draw a picture and write a short response using text evidence.

Use Your Own Text

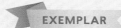 EXEMPLAR   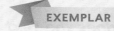 EXEMPLAR

Read-Aloud Books   **Read-Alone Books**

or Choose from your own **Trade Books**

The Top Job
Genre Fiction

Lexile 880

Snowflake Bentley
Genre Nonfiction

Lexile 830

Owl at Home
Genre Fiction

Lexile 370

A Weed Is a Flower
Genre Nonfiction

Lexile 690

Teacher's Choice

- Use this model with a text of your choice. Go online for title-specific Classroom Library book lessons.

- Select a Read-Aloud selection or a Read-Alone selection.

- Select a text that provides an opportunity to model application of the comprehension skills and strategies taught during the unit.

- Present an Essential Question. You may want to use the Unit Big Idea: *How can we make sense of the world around us?*

sync tv
Video Preview
studysync

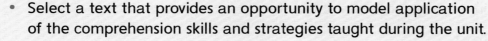
Using the Classroom Library

Selecting a Book For each unit, the classroom library includes two Read-Aloud titles for you to read with the class and two Read-Alone titles for independent reading. There is a mix of fiction and informational nonfiction.

Reading Together Use the Read-Aloud titles to model close reading. Model taking notes, and prompt children to ask and answer text-dependent questions and to participate in writing about the text. You may choose to read the selection in multiple readings.

Independent Reading If children are ready to engage in close reading independently, select a Read-Alone title. Assign the Read-Alone titles and guide children to take notes, ask and answer text-dependent questions, and to write about the text.

Use Your Own Text

Read · *What does the text say?*

Read Together

Read the text aloud. You may also invite more advanced readers to select a book to read alone and respond to independently.

Model close reading for children as well as how to take notes. Encourage children to jot down words they do not understand and any questions they have.

Ask Text-Dependent Questions

Ask children to reread a section of the text, or reread it to children, and focus on the following questions. Children should use text evidence in their answers:

Literature

- Is this a book that tells a story or that gives information? Explain your answer.
- What are the plot and setting of the story? Be sure to use the text and illustrations.
- How would you describe the main character(s)?
- What is the main message or lesson of the story?

Informational Text

- What is the main topic? What are the key details?
- What kinds of text features does the author use?
- What reasons does the author give to support points in the text?

Model how to use a graphic organizer, chosen from within the unit, to take notes on important details from the text. Together with children, use the information from the graphic organizer to retell the selection.

 Help children access the complex text features of the text. Scaffold instruction on the following features as necessary:

- Prior Knowledge
- Genre
- Organization
- Connection of Ideas
- Purpose
- Specific Vocabulary
- Sentence Structure

Reread *How does the author say it?*

Ask Text-Dependent Questions/Generate Questions

- Reread shorter passages of the text with children, focusing on how the author provides information or develops the characters, setting, and plot. Based on the selection you are reading, focus on key elements with the following questions. Remind students to use text evidence in their answers:

Literature

- Who is telling the story on this page? Is it the same person who tells the story on another page? What words did the author use to help you understand the character?

- What other story have you read with a similar character or plot? How are the two stories similar? Different?

Informational Text

- How does the author organize the information in this text?

- What reasons does the author give to support points in the text?

- Was the author's use of visuals (photos, graphs, diagrams, maps) effective? Why or why not?

Integrate *What does the text mean?*

Essential Question

Have children respond to the Essential Question as it relates to the text by drawing a picture and labeling it, writing a caption, or writing two or three complete sentences. Children can work with a partner and use their notes and graphic organizer to locate evidence from the text that can be used to answer the question.

SCOPE & SEQUENCE

FOUNDATIONAL SKILLS	K	1	2	3	4	5	6
Concepts About Print/Print Awareness							
Recognize own name							
Understand directionality (top to bottom; tracking print from left to right; return sweep, page by page)	✓						
Locate printed word on page	✓						
Develop print awareness (concept of letter, word, sentence)	✓						
Identify separate sounds in a spoken sentence	✓						
Understand that written words are represented in written language by a specific sequence of letters	✓						
Distinguish between letters, words, and sentences	✓						
Distinguish features of a sentence (first word, capitalization, ending punctuation)							
Identify and distinguish paragraphs							
Match print to speech (one-to-one correspondence)	✓						
Name uppercase and lowercase letters	✓						
Understand book handling (holding a book right-side-up, turning its pages)	✓						
Identify parts of a book (front cover, back cover, title page, table of contents); recognize that parts of a book contain information	✓						
Phonological Awareness							
Recognize and understand alliteration							
Segment sentences into correct number of words							
Identify, blend, segment syllables in words		✓					
Recognize and generate rhyming words	✓	✓					
Identify, blend, segment onset and rime	✓	✓					
Phonemic Awareness							
Count phonemes	✓	✓					
Isolate initial, medial, and final sounds	✓	✓					
Blend spoken phonemes to form words	✓	✓					
Segment spoken words into phonemes	✓	✓					
Distinguish between long- and short-vowel sounds	✓	✓					
Manipulate phonemes (addition, deletion, substitution)	✓	✓					
Phonics and Decoding/Word Recognition							
Understand the alphabetic principle	✓	✓					
Sound/letter correspondence	✓	✓	✓	✓			
Blend sounds into words, including VC, CVC, CVCe, CVVC words	✓	✓	✓	✓			
Blend common word families	✓	✓	✓	✓			

KEY	✓ = Assessed Skill
	Tinted panels show skills, strategies, and other teaching opportunities.

	K	1	2	3	4	5	6
Initial consonant blends		✔	✔	✔			
Final consonant blends		✔	✔	✔			
Initial and medial short vowels	✔	✔	✔	✔	✔	✔	✔
Decode one-syllable words in isolation and in context	✔	✔	✔	✔			
Decode multisyllabic words in isolation and in context using common syllabication patterns		✔	✔	✔	✔	✔	✔
Distinguish between similarly spelled words	✔	✔	✔	✔	✔	✔	✔
Monitor accuracy of decoding							
Identify and read common high-frequency words, irregularly spelled words	✔	✔	✔	✔			
Identify and read compound words, contractions		✔	✔	✔	✔	✔	✔
Use knowledge of spelling patterns to identify syllables		✔	✔	✔	✔	✔	✔
Regular and irregular plurals	✔	✔	✔	✔	✔	✔	✔
Distinguish long and short vowels		✔	✔				
Long vowels (silent *e*, vowel teams)	✔	✔	✔	✔	✔	✔	✔
Vowel digraphs (variant vowels)		✔	✔	✔	✔	✔	✔
r-Controlled vowels		✔	✔	✔	✔	✔	✔
Hard/soft consonants		✔	✔	✔	✔	✔	✔
Initial consonant digraphs		✔	✔	✔	✔	✔	
Medial and final consonant digraphs		✔	✔	✔	✔	✔	
Vowel diphthongs		✔	✔	✔	✔	✔	✔
Identify and distinguish letter-sounds (initial, medial, final)	✔	✔	✔				
Silent letters		✔	✔	✔	✔	✔	✔
Schwa words				✔	✔	✔	✔
Inflectional endings		✔	✔	✔	✔	✔	✔
Triple-consonant clusters		✔	✔	✔	✔	✔	
Unfamiliar and complex word families				✔	✔	✔	✔
Structural Analysis/Word Analysis							
Common spelling patterns (word families)		✔	✔	✔	✔	✔	✔
Common syllable patterns		✔	✔	✔	✔	✔	✔
Inflectional endings		✔	✔	✔	✔	✔	✔
Contractions		✔	✔	✔	✔	✔	✔
Compound words		✔	✔	✔	✔	✔	✔
Prefixes and suffixes		✔	✔	✔	✔	✔	✔
Root or base words		✔	✔	✔	✔	✔	✔
Comparatives and superlatives			✔	✔	✔	✔	✔
Greek and Latin roots			✔	✔	✔	✔	✔
Fluency							
Apply letter/sound knowledge to decode phonetically regular words accurately	✔	✔	✔	✔	✔	✔	✔
Recognize high-frequency and familiar words	✔	✔	✔	✔	✔	✔	✔
Read regularly on independent and instructional levels							
Read orally with fluency from familiar texts (choral, echo, partner, Reader's Theater)							
Use appropriate rate, expression, intonation, and phrasing		✔	✔	✔	✔	✔	✔
Read with automaticity (accurately and effortlessly)		✔	✔	✔	✔	✔	✔

	K	1	2	3	4	5	6
Use punctuation cues in reading		✓	✓	✓	✓	✓	✓
Adjust reading rate to purpose, text difficulty, form, and style							
Repeated readings							
Timed readings		✓	✓	✓	✓	✓	✓
Read with purpose and understanding		✓	✓	✓	✓	✓	✓
Read orally with accuracy		✓	✓	✓	✓	✓	✓
Use context to confirm or self-correct word recognition		✓	✓	✓	✓	✓	✓

READING LITERATURE

Comprehension Strategies and Skills

	K	1	2	3	4	5	6
Read literature from a broad range of genres, cultures, and periods		✓	✓	✓	✓	✓	✓
Access complex text		✓	✓	✓	✓	✓	✓
Build background/Activate prior knowledge							
Preview and predict							
Establish and adjust purpose for reading							
Evaluate citing evidence from the text							
Ask and answer questions	✓	✓	✓	✓	✓	✓	✓
Inferences and conclusions, citing evidence from the text	✓	✓	✓	✓	✓	✓	✓
Monitor/adjust comprehension including reread, reading rate, paraphrase							
Recount/Retell	✓	✓					
Summarize			✓	✓	✓	✓	✓
Story structure (beginning, middle, end)	✓	✓	✓	✓	✓	✓	✓
Visualize							
Make connections between and across texts		✓	✓	✓	✓	✓	✓
Point of view		✓	✓	✓	✓	✓	✓
Author's purpose							
Cause and effect	✓	✓	✓	✓	✓	✓	✓
Compare and contrast (including character, setting, plot, topics)	✓	✓	✓	✓	✓	✓	✓
Classify and categorize		✓	✓				
Literature vs informational text	✓	✓	✓				
Illustrations, using	✓	✓	✓	✓			
Theme, central message, moral, lesson		✓	✓	✓	✓	✓	✓
Predictions, making/confirming	✓	✓	✓				
Problem and solution (problem/resolution)		✓	✓	✓	✓	✓	✓
Sequence of events	✓	✓	✓	✓	✓	✓	✓

Literary Elements

	K	1	2	3	4	5	6
Character	✓	✓	✓	✓	✓	✓	✓
Plot development/Events	✓	✓	✓	✓	✓	✓	✓
Setting	✓	✓	✓	✓	✓	✓	✓
Stanza				✓	✓	✓	✓
Alliteration						✓	✓
Assonance						✓	✓
Dialogue							

KEY ✓ = Assessed Skill
Tinted panels show skills, strategies, and other teaching opportunities.

	K	1	2	3	4	5	6
Foreshadowing						✔	✔
Flashback						✔	✔
Descriptive and figurative language		✔	✔	✔	✔	✔	✔
Imagery					✔	✔	✔
Meter					✔	✔	✔
Onomatopoeia							
Repetition		✔	✔	✔	✔	✔	✔
Rhyme/rhyme schemes		✔	✔	✔	✔	✔	✔
Rhythm		✔	✔				
Sensory language							
Symbolism							

Write About Text/Literary Response Discussions

	K	1	2	3	4	5	6
Reflect and respond to text citing text evidence		✔	✔	✔	✔	✔	✔
Connect and compare text characters, events, ideas to self, to other texts, to world							
Connect literary texts to other curriculum areas							
Identify cultural and historical elements of text							
Evaluate author's techniques, craft							
Analytical writing							
Interpret text ideas through writing, discussion, media, research							
Book report or review							
Locate, use, explain information from text features		✔	✔	✔	✔	✔	✔
Organize information to show understanding of main idea through charts, mapping							
Cite text evidence	✔	✔	✔	✔	✔	✔	✔
Author's purpose/Illustrator's purpose							

READING INFORMATIONAL TEXT

Comprehension Strategies and Skills

	K	1	2	3	4	5	6
Read informational text from a broad range of topics and cultures	✔	✔	✔	✔	✔	✔	✔
Access complex text		✔	✔	✔	✔	✔	✔
Build background/Activate prior knowledge							
Preview and predict	✔	✔	✔				
Establish and adjust purpose for reading							
Evaluate citing evidence from the text							
Ask and answer questions	✔	✔	✔	✔	✔	✔	✔
Inferences and conclusions, citing evidence from the text	✔	✔	✔	✔	✔	✔	✔
Monitor and adjust comprehension including reread, adjust reading rate, paraphrase							
Recount/Retell	✔	✔					
Summarize			✔	✔	✔	✔	✔
Text structure	✔	✔	✔	✔	✔	✔	✔
Identify text features		✔	✔	✔	✔	✔	✔
Make connections between and across texts	✔	✔	✔	✔	✔	✔	✔
Author's point of view				✔	✔	✔	✔
Author's purpose		✔	✔				

	K	1	2	3	4	5	6
Cause and effect	✓	✓	✓	✓	✓	✓	✓
Compare and contrast	✓	✓	✓	✓	✓	✓	✓
Classify and categorize		✓	✓				
Illustrations and photographs, using	✓	✓	✓	✓			
Instructions/directions (written and oral)		✓	✓	✓	✓	✓	✓
Main idea and key details	✓	✓	✓	✓	✓	✓	✓
Persuasion, reasons and evidence to support points/persuasive techniques						✓	✓
Predictions, making/confirming	✓	✓					
Problem and solution		✓	✓	✓	✓	✓	✓
Sequence, chronological order of events, time order, steps in a process	✓	✓	✓	✓	✓	✓	✓

Write About Text/Write to Sources

	K	1	2	3	4	5	6
Reflect and respond to text citing text evidence		✓	✓	✓	✓	✓	✓
Connect and compare text characters, events, ideas to self, to other texts, to world							
Connect texts to other curriculum areas							
Identify cultural and historical elements of text							
Evaluate author's techniques, craft							
Analytical writing							
Read to understand and perform tasks and activities							
Interpret text ideas through writing, discussion, media, research							
Locate, use, explain information from text features		✓	✓	✓	✓	✓	✓
Organize information to show understanding of main idea through charts, mapping							
Cite text evidence		✓	✓	✓	✓	✓	✓
Author's purpose/Illustrator's purpose							

Text Features

	K	1	2	3	4	5	6
Recognize and identify text and organizational features of nonfiction texts		✓	✓	✓	✓	✓	✓
Captions and labels, headings, subheadings, endnotes, key words, bold print	✓	✓	✓	✓	✓	✓	✓
Graphics, including photographs, illustrations, maps, charts, diagrams, graphs, time lines	✓	✓	✓	✓	✓	✓	✓

Self-Selected Reading/Independent Reading

	K	1	2	3	4	5	6
Use personal criteria to choose own reading including favorite authors, genres, recommendations from others; set up a reading log							
Read a range of literature and informational text for tasks as well as for enjoyment; participate in literature circles							
Produce evidence of reading by retelling, summarizing, or paraphrasing							

Media Literacy

	K	1	2	3	4	5	6
Summarize the message or content from media message, citing text evidence							
Use graphics, illustrations to analyze and interpret information	✓	✓	✓	✓	✓	✓	✓
Identify structural features of popular media and use the features to obtain information, including digital sources				✓	✓	✓	✓
Identify reasons and evidence in visuals and media message							
Analyze media source: recognize effects of media in one's mood and emotion							
Make informed judgments about print and digital media							
Critique persuasive techniques							

KEY
✓ = Assessed Skill
Tinted panels show skills, strategies, and other teaching opportunities.

WRITING	K	1	2	3	4	5	6
Writing Process							
Plan/prewrite/identify purpose and audience							
Draft							
Revise							
Edit/proofread							
Publish and present including using technology							
Teacher and peer feedback							
Writing Traits							
Conventions		✔	✔	✔	✔	✔	✔
Ideas		✔	✔	✔	✔	✔	✔
Organization		✔	✔	✔	✔	✔	✔
Sentence fluency		✔	✔	✔	✔	✔	✔
Voice		✔	✔	✔	✔	✔	✔
Word choice		✔	✔	✔	✔	✔	✔
Writer's Craft							
Good topic, focus on and develop topic, topic sentence			✔	✔	✔	✔	✔
Paragraph(s); sentence structure			✔	✔	✔	✔	✔
Main idea and supporting key details			✔	✔	✔	✔	✔
Unimportant details							
Relevant supporting evidence			✔	✔	✔	✔	✔
Strong opening, strong conclusion			✔	✔	✔	✔	✔
Beginning, middle, end; sequence		✔	✔	✔	✔	✔	✔
Precise words, strong words, vary words			✔	✔	✔	✔	✔
Figurative and sensory language, descriptive details							
Informal/formal language							
Mood/style/tone							
Dialogue				✔	✔	✔	✔
Transition words, transitions to multiple paragraphs				✔	✔	✔	✔
Select focus and organization			✔	✔	✔	✔	✔
Points and counterpoints/Opposing claims and counterarguments							
Use reference materials (online and print dictionary, thesaurus, encyclopedia)							
Writing Applications							
Write to sources	✔	✔	✔	✔	✔	✔	✔
Personal and fictional narrative (also biographical and autobiographical)	✔	✔	✔	✔	✔	✔	✔
Variety of expressive forms including poetry	✔	✔	✔	✔	✔	✔	✔
Informative/explanatory texts	✔	✔	✔	✔	✔	✔	✔
Description	✔	✔	✔	✔			
Procedural texts		✔	✔	✔	✔	✔	✔
Opinion pieces or arguments	✔	✔	✔	✔	✔	✔	✔
Communications including technical documents		✔	✔	✔	✔	✔	✔
Research report	✔	✔	✔	✔	✔	✔	✔

	K	1	2	3	4	5	6
Responses to literature/reflection				✓	✓	✓	✓
Analytical writing							
Letters		✓	✓	✓	✓	✓	✓
Write daily and over short and extended time frames; set up writer's notebooks							

Penmanship/Handwriting

	K	1	2	3	4	5	6
Write legibly in manuscript using correct formation, directionality, and spacing							
Write legibly in cursive using correct formation, directionality, and spacing							

SPEAKING AND LISTENING

Speaking

	K	1	2	3	4	5	6
Use repetition, rhyme, and rhythm in oral texts							
Participate in classroom activities and discussions							
Collaborative conversation with peers and adults in small and large groups using formal English when appropriate							
Differentiate between formal and informal English							
Follow agreed upon rules for discussion							
Build on others' talk in conversation, adding new ideas							
Come to discussions prepared							
Describe familiar people, places, and things and add drawings as desired							
Paraphrase portions of text read alone or information presented							
Apply comprehension strategies and skills in speaking activities							
Use literal and nonliteral meanings							
Ask and answer questions about text read aloud and about media							
Stay on topic when speaking							
Use language appropriate to situation, purpose, and audience							
Use nonverbal communications such as eye contact, gestures, and props							
Use verbal communication in effective ways and improve expression in conventional language							
Retell a story, presentation, or spoken message by summarizing							
Oral presentations: focus, organizational structure, audience, purpose							
Give and follow oral directions							
Consider audience when speaking or preparing a presentation							
Recite poems, rhymes, songs							
Use complete, coherent sentences							
Organize presentations							
Deliver presentations (narrative, summaries, informative, research, opinion); add visuals							
Speak audibly (accuracy, expression, volume, pitch, rate, phrasing, modulation, enunciation)							
Create audio recordings of poems, stories, presentations							

Listening

	K	1	2	3	4	5	6
Identify musical elements in language							
Determine the purpose for listening							
Understand, follow, restate, and give oral directions							
Develop oral language and concepts							

KEY	✓ = Assessed Skill
	Tinted panels show skills, strategies, and other teaching opportunities.

	K	1	2	3	4	5	6
Listen openly, responsively, attentively, and critically							
Listen to identify the points a speaker or media source makes							
Listen responsively to oral presentations (determine main idea and key details)							
Ask and answer relevant questions (for clarification to follow-up on ideas)							
Identify reasons and evidence presented by speaker							
Recall and interpret speakers' verbal/nonverbal messages, purposes, perspectives							

LANGUAGE

Vocabulary Acquisition and Use

	K	1	2	3	4	5	6
Develop oral vocabulary and choose words for effect							
Use academic language		✔	✔	✔	✔	✔	✔
Identify persons, places, things, actions		✔	✔	✔			
Classify, sort, and categorize words	✔	✔	✔	✔	✔	✔	✔
Determine or clarify the meaning of unknown words; use word walls		✔	✔	✔	✔	✔	✔
Synonyms, antonyms, and opposites		✔	✔	✔	✔	✔	✔
Use context clues such as word, sentence, paragraph, definition, example, restatement, description, comparison, cause and effect		✔	✔	✔	✔	✔	✔
Use word identification strategies		✔	✔	✔	✔	✔	✔
Unfamiliar words		✔	✔	✔	✔	✔	✔
Multiple-meaning words		✔	✔	✔	✔	✔	✔
Use print and online dictionary to locate meanings, pronunciation, derivatives, parts of speech		✔	✔	✔	✔	✔	✔
Compound words		✔	✔	✔	✔	✔	✔
Words ending in -er and -est		✔	✔	✔	✔	✔	
Root words (base words)		✔	✔	✔	✔	✔	✔
Prefixes and suffixes		✔	✔	✔	✔	✔	✔
Greek and Latin affixes and roots			✔	✔	✔	✔	✔
Denotation and connotation					✔	✔	✔
Word families		✔	✔	✔	✔	✔	✔
Inflectional endings		✔	✔	✔	✔	✔	
Use a print and online thesaurus			✔	✔	✔	✔	✔
Use print and online reference sources for word meaning (dictionary, glossaries)		✔	✔	✔	✔	✔	✔
Homographs				✔	✔	✔	✔
Homophones			✔	✔	✔	✔	✔
Contractions		✔	✔	✔			
Figurative language such as metaphors, similes, personification			✔	✔	✔	✔	✔
Idioms, adages, proverbs, literal and nonliteral language			✔	✔	✔	✔	✔
Analogies							
Listen to, read, discuss familiar and unfamiliar challenging text							
Identify real-life connections between words and their use							
Use acquired words and phrases to convey precise ideas							
Use vocabulary to express spatial and temporal relationships							
Identify shades of meaning in related words	✔	✔	✔	✔	✔	✔	✔
Word origins				✔	✔	✔	✔
Morphology				✔	✔	✔	✔

	K	1	2	3	4	5	6
Knowledge of Language							
Choose words, phrases, and sentences for effect							
Choose punctuation effectively							
Formal and informal language for style and tone including dialects							
Conventions of Standard English/Grammar, Mechanics, and Usage							
Sentence concepts: statements, questions, exclamations, commands		✓	✓	✓	✓	✓	✓
Complete and incomplete sentences; sentence fragments; word order		✓	✓	✓	✓	✓	✓
Compound sentences, complex sentences				✓	✓	✓	✓
Combining sentences		✓	✓	✓	✓	✓	✓
Nouns including common, proper, singular, plural, irregular plurals, possessives, abstract, concrete, collective		✓	✓	✓	✓	✓	✓
Verbs including action, helping, linking, irregular		✓	✓	✓	✓	✓	✓
Verb tenses including past, present, future, perfect, and progressive		✓	✓	✓	✓	✓	✓
Pronouns including possessive, subject and object, pronoun-verb agreement, indefinite, intensive, reciprocal, interrogative, relative; correct unclear pronouns		✓	✓	✓	✓	✓	✓
Adjectives including articles, demonstrative, proper, adjectives that compare		✓	✓	✓	✓	✓	✓
Adverbs including telling how, when, where, comparative, superlative, irregular		✓	✓	✓	✓	✓	✓
Subject, predicate; subject-verb agreement		✓	✓	✓	✓	✓	✓
Contractions		✓	✓	✓	✓	✓	
Conjunctions				✓	✓	✓	✓
Commas			✓	✓	✓	✓	✓
Colons, semicolons, dashes, hyphens						✓	✓
Question words							
Quotation marks			✓	✓	✓	✓	✓
Prepositions and prepositional phrases, appositives		✓	✓	✓	✓	✓	✓
Independent and dependent clauses						✓	✓
Italics/underlining for emphasis and titles							
Negatives, correcting double negatives					✓	✓	✓
Abbreviations			✓	✓	✓	✓	✓
Use correct capitalization in sentences, proper nouns, titles, abbreviations		✓	✓	✓	✓	✓	✓
Use correct punctuation		✓	✓	✓	✓	✓	✓
Antecedents				✓	✓	✓	✓
Homophones and words often confused			✓	✓	✓	✓	✓
Apostrophes				✓	✓	✓	✓
Spelling							
Write irregular, high-frequency words	✓	✓	✓				
ABC order	✓	✓					
Write letters	✓	✓					
Words with short vowels	✓	✓	✓	✓	✓	✓	✓
Words with long vowels	✓	✓	✓	✓	✓	✓	✓
Words with digraphs, blends, consonant clusters, double consonants		✓	✓	✓	✓	✓	✓
Words with vowel digraphs and ambiguous vowels		✓	✓	✓	✓	✓	✓
Words with diphthongs		✓	✓	✓	✓	✓	✓

KEY ✓ = Assessed Skill
Tinted panels show skills, strategies, and other teaching opportunities.

BM8

	K	1	2	3	4	5	6
Words with *r*-controlled vowels		✔	✔	✔	✔	✔	✔
Use conventional spelling		✔	✔	✔	✔	✔	✔
Schwa words				✔	✔	✔	✔
Words with silent letters			✔	✔	✔	✔	✔
Words with hard and soft letters				✔	✔	✔	✔
Inflectional endings including plural, past tense, drop final *e* and double consonant when adding *-ed* and *-ing*, changing *y* to *i*		✔	✔	✔	✔	✔	✔
Compound words		✔	✔	✔	✔	✔	✔
Homonyms/homophones			✔	✔	✔	✔	✔
Prefixes and suffixes		✔	✔	✔	✔	✔	✔
Root and base words (also spell derivatives)				✔	✔	✔	✔
Syllables: patterns, rules, accented, stressed, closed, open				✔	✔	✔	✔
Words with Greek and Latin roots						✔	✔
Words from mythology						✔	✔
Words with spelling patterns, word families		✔	✔	✔	✔	✔	✔

RESEARCH AND INQUIRY

Study Skills

	K	1	2	3	4	5	6
Directions: read, write, give, follow (includes technical directions)			✔	✔	✔	✔	✔
Evaluate directions for sequence and completeness				✔	✔	✔	✔
Use library/media center							
Use parts of a book to locate information							
Interpret information from graphic aids		✔	✔	✔	✔	✔	✔
Use graphic organizers to organize information and comprehend text		✔	✔	✔	✔	✔	✔
Use functional, everyday documents				✔	✔	✔	✔
Apply study strategies: skimming and scanning, note-taking, outlining							

Research Process

	K	1	2	3	4	5	6
Generate and revise topics and questions for research				✔	✔	✔	✔
Narrow focus of research, set research goals				✔	✔	✔	✔
Find and locate information using print and digital resources		✔	✔	✔	✔	✔	✔
Record information systematically (note-taking, outlining, using technology)				✔	✔	✔	✔
Develop a systematic research plan				✔	✔	✔	✔
Evaluate reliability, credibility, usefulness of sources and information						✔	✔
Use primary sources to obtain information					✔	✔	✔
Organize, synthesize, evaluate, and draw conclusions from information							
Cite and list sources of information (record basic bibliographic data)					✔	✔	✔
Demonstrate basic keyboarding skills							
Participate in and present shared research							

Technology

	K	1	2	3	4	5	6
Use computer, Internet, and other technology resources to access information							
Use text and organizational features of electronic resources such as search engines, keywords, e-mail, hyperlinks, URLs, Web pages, databases, graphics							
Use digital tools to present and publish in a variety of media formats							

INDEX

A

Key 1 = Unit 1

H

I

M

R

W

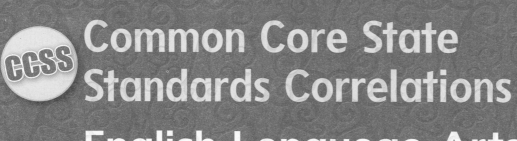

College and Career Readiness Anchor Standards for READING

The K–5 standards on the following pages define what students should understand and be able to do by the end of each grade. They correspond to the College and Career Readiness anchor standards below by number. The CCR and grade-specific standards are necessary complements—the former providing broad standards, the latter providing additional specificity—that together define the skills and understandings that all students must demonstrate.

Key Ideas and Details

1. Read closely to determine what the text says explicitly and to make logical inferences from it; cite specific textual evidence when writing or speaking to support conclusions drawn from the text.

2. Determine central ideas or themes of a text and analyze their development; summarize the key supporting details and ideas.

3. Analyze how and why individuals, events, and ideas develop and interact over the course of a text.

Craft and Structure

4. Interpret words and phrases as they are used in a text, including determining technical, connotative, and figurative meanings, and analyze how specific word choices shape meaning or tone.

5. Analyze the structure of texts, including how specific sentences, paragraphs, and larger portions of the text (e.g., a section, chapter, scene, or stanza) relate to each other and the whole.

6. Assess how point of view or purpose shapes the content and style of a text.

Integration of Knowledge and Ideas

7. Integrate and evaluate content presented in diverse media and formats, including visually and quantitatively as well as in words.

8. Delineate and evaluate the argument and specific claims in a text, including the validity of the reasoning as well as the relevance and sufficiency of the evidence.

9. Analyze how two or more texts address similar themes or topics in order to build knowledge or to compare the approaches the authors take.

Range of Reading and Level of Text Complexity

10. Read and comprehend complex literary and informational texts independently and proficiently.

Common Core State Standards

English Language Arts

Grade 1

Each standard is coded in the following manner:

Strand	Grade Level	Standard
RL	1	1

Reading Standards for Literature

Key Ideas and Details	McGraw-Hill *Wonders*
RL.1.1	Ask and answer questions about key details in a text.	**READING/WRITING WORKSHOP: Unit 1:** 24, 25, 44, 45, 64, 65 **Unit 2:** 44, 45, 84, 85 **Unit 3:** 24, 25, 64, 65 **Unit 4:** 88, 89 **Unit 5:** 130, 131, 190, 191 **Unit 6:** 232, 233, 272, 273 **LITERATURE ANTHOLOGY: Unit 1:** 19, 41, 63 **Unit 2:** 21, 43, 81 **Unit 3:** 23, 45, 67, 73 **Unit 4:** 29, 89, 125 **Unit 5:** 155, 195, 225, 255 **Unit 6:** 295, 325, 357, 393 **LEVELED READERS: Unit 1, Week 1:** *We Like to Share* (O), *Class Party* (B) **Unit 1, Week 2:** *A Trip to the City* (O), *Harvest Time* (B) **Unit 1, Week 3:** *Mouse's Moon Party* (A), *Pet Show* (O) **Unit 2, Week 1:** *Pick Up Day* (A), *Ben Brings the Mail* (O), *At Work with Mom* (B) **Unit 2, Week 2:** *What a Nest!* (A), *Staying Afloat* (O) **Unit 2, Week 4:** *The Sick Tree* (A), *Squirrels Help* (O), *Wow, Kitty!* (B) **Unit 3, Week 1:** *Busy's Watch* (A), *Kate Saves the Date!* (O) **Unit 3, Week 2:** *Corn Fun* (A), *Yum, Strawberries!* (O) **Unit 3, Week 3:** *The Magic Paintbrush* (O) **Unit 4, Week 1:** *Fly to the Rescue!* (O) **Unit 4, Week 4:** *The Hat* (O) **Unit 5, Week 1:** *Nuts for Winter* (A), *Dog Bones* (O), *Spark's Toys* (B) **Unit 5, Week 2:** *Hide and Seek* (O) **Unit 5, Week 4:** *Thump, Jangle, Crash* (A), *Down on the Farm* (O) **Unit 6, Week 1:** *Two Hungry Elephants* (A), *What a Feast!* (O) **Unit 6, Week 3:** *Snow Day* (A), *Heat Wave* (O), *Rainy Day Fun* (B) **Unit 6, Week 4:** *The Quilt* (A), *Latkes for Sam* (O) **CLOSE READING COMPANION:** 1-3, 8-10, 15-17, 34-36, 41-43, 55-57, 67-69, 74-76, 81-83, 100-103, 121-123, 133-135, 140-142, 154-156, 166-168, 180-182, 187-189 **YOUR TURN PRACTICE BOOK:** 7, 17, 42, 44, 117, 127, 147, 162, 193, 205, 217, 229, 241, 246, 253, 258, 277, 282, 301, 306, 313, 318 **READING WORKSTATION ACTIVITY CARDS:** 1, 3, 8, 14, 16, 23, 26, 28 **WRITING WORKSTATION ACTIVITY CARDS:** 9 **INTERACTIVE READ-ALOUD CARDS: Unit 1, Week 5:** 2, 4 **Unit 2, Week 2:** 3, 4 **Unit 3, Week 2:** 4 **Unit 3, Week 3:** 4 **Unit 3, Week 5:** 4 **Unit 4, Week 1:** 3, 4 **Unit 4, Week 5:** 4 **Unit 5, Week 1:** 4 **Unit 5, Week 2:** 4 **Unit 5, Week 4:** 2, 4 **Unit 5, Week 5:** 3, 4 **Unit 6, Week 1:** 4 **Unit 6, Week 2:** 2, 4 **Unit 6, Week 3:** 3, 4 **TEACHER'S EDITION: Unit 1:** T105, T113B, T113C, T113D, T113E, T113F, T113G, T183, T191B, T191C, T191D, T191E, T191G, T217, T221, T225 **Unit 2:** T269A-T269J, T412-T413, T415 **Unit 3:** T191A-T191J, T412-T413, T415 **Unit 4:** T11, T21, T35C, T35H, T167, T177, T191A-T191P, T269A-T269R, T407, T412-T413, T415 **Unit 5:** T269A-T269P, T245, T255, T261, T269D, T269E, T300, T322, T333, T407, T412-T413, T415 **Unit 6:** T35C, T191A-T191F, T191G-T191L, T191M-T191R, T269A-T269H, T269I-T269R, T407, T412-T413, T415 www.connected.mcgraw-hill.com: **RESOURCES: Units 1–6: Student Practice:** Genre Study, Approaching Reproducibles, Beyond Reproducibles, ELL Reproducibles, **Graphic Organizers:** Graphic Organizers, **Cards:** Retelling Cards

Reading Standards for Literature

Key Ideas and Details		McGraw-Hill *Wonders*
RL.1.2	Retell stories, including key details, and demonstrate understanding of their central message or lesson.	**READING/WRITING WORKSHOP:** Unit I: 24, 25, 44, 45, 64, 65 **Unit 4:** 28, 29 **Unit 5:** I50, I5I **Unit 6:** 232, 233, 272, 273, 292, 293 **LITERATURE ANTHOLOGY:** Unit I: I9, 40, 63 **Unit 2:** 2I, 42, 8I **Unit 3:** 23, 45, 67 **Unit 4:** 29, I25 **Unit 5:** I55, I95, 255 **Unit 6:** 295, 357, 393 **LEVELED READERS: Unit I, Week 3:** *Pet Show* (O) **Unit 2, Week I:** *Pick Up Day* (A), *Ben Brings the Mail* (O), *Atē Work with Mom* (B) **Unit 3, Week 3:** *The Magic Paintbrush* (O) **Unit 4, Week I:** *Fly to the Rescue!* (O), *The Hat* (O) **Unit 5, Week 2:** *Little Blue's Dream* (A), *Hide and Seek* (O) **Unit 5, Week 4:** *Down on the Farm* (O), *Going on a Bird Walk* (B) **Unit 6, Week 4:** *The Quilt* (A), *Latkes for Sam* (O), *Patty Jumps!* (B) **CLOSE READING COMPANION:** I64, I69, I89 **YOUR TURN PRACTICE BOOK:** I38, 274, 277, 282, 3I3 **READING WORKSTATION ACTIVITY CARDS:** 2, 6, I4, I6, 23 **WRITING WORKSTATION ACTIVITY CARDS:** 9 **INTERACTIVE READ-ALOUD CARDS: Unit I, Week 2:** 4 **Unit I, Week 5:** 4 **Unit 2, Week 2:** 3, 4 **Unit 3, Week 2:** 4 **Unit 3, Week 3:** 4 **Unit 3, Week 5:** 4 **Unit 4, Week I:** 3, 4 **Unit 4, Week 5:** 4 **Unit 5, Week I:** 4 **Unit 5, Week 2:** 4 **Unit 5, Week 4:** 4 **Unit 5, Week 5:** 3, 4 **Unit 6, Week I:** 4 **Unit 6, Week 2:** 4 **Unit 6, Week 3:** 4 **TEACHER'S EDITION: Unit I:** S32, TII, T3I, TI09, TTII3I-TII3J, TI87, TI9IF, T269A-T269J, T4I4-T4I5 **Unit 2:** T35I-T35J, T345 **Unit 3:** TII, T3I, TII3J, TI87, TI9II-TI9IJ, T269I **Unit 4:** TII, T35K-T35L, T269R **Unit 5:** TII, T35I, T89, TII3R, T245, T269P, T297, T4I4-T4I5 **Unit 6:** TII, T27, T35B, T35D, T35E, T35N, T89, TI9IQ, TI9IR, T269B, T269C, T269M, T300-T30I www.connected.mcgraw-hill.com: **RESOURCES: Units I–6: Cards:** Retelling Cards **Media:** Fluency Passages **Graphic Organizers:** Graphic Organizers, Think Aloud Clouds **Student Practice:** Approaching Reproducibles, Beyond Reproducibles, ELL Reproducibles
RL.1.3	Describe characters, settings, and major events in a story, using key details.	**READING/WRITING WORKSHOP: Unit 2:** 24, 25, 44, 45, 84, 85 **Unit 3:** 24, 25, 44, 45, 64, 65 **Unit 4:** 28, 29 **Unit 5:** I50, I5I, I90, I9I **Unit 6:** 272, 273 **LITERATURE ANTHOLOGY:** Unit I: I9, 4I, 63 **Unit 2:** 2I, 43, 8I **Unit 3:** 23, 45, 67 **Unit 4:** 29, I25 **Unit 5:** I55, I95, 255 **LEVELED READERS: Unit I, Week I:** *We Like to Share* (O) **Unit I, Week 3:** *Pet Show* (O) **Unit 2, Week I:** *Ben Brings the Mail* (O) **Unit 2, Week 2:** *Staying Afloat* (O) **Unit 2, Week 4:** *The Sick Tree* (A), *Squirrels Help* (O) **Unit 3, Week I:** *Busy's Watch* (A), *Kate Saves the Date!* (O) **Unit 5, Week I:** *Dog Bones* (O) **Unit 6, Week I:** *What a Feast!* (O) **YOUR TURN PRACTICE BOOK:** 42, 44, 50, I04, I07, II4, II7, I24, I27, I44, I47, I54, I57, I90, I93, I98, 202, 205, 2I4, 2I7, 222, 226, 229, 234, 238, 24I, 246, 258, 277, 298, 30I, 306, 3I3, 3I8 **READING WORKSTATION ACTIVITY CARDS:** I, 2, 3, 4, 6, 7, 8, I2, I3, I6, 23, 28 **WRITING WORKSTATION ACTIVITY CARDS:** 9, 23 **INTERACTIVE READ-ALOUD CARDS: Unit 2, Week 2:** 4 **Unit 3, Week 3:** 2 **Unit 3, Week 5:** 2, 4 **Unit 4, Week I:** 4 **Unit 4, Week 5:** 4 **Unit 5, Week I:** 4 **Unit 5, Week 2:** 3, 4 **Unit 5, Week 4:** 2, 4 **Unit 5, Week 5:** 3, 4 **Unit 6, Week I:** 4 **Unit 6, Week 2:** 4 **Unit 6, Week 3:** 3, 4 **TEACHER'S EDITION: Unit I:** T27, T35D-T35F, T35H, TI05, TII3D, TI83 **Unit 2:** T27, T35B, T35E-T35G, T35I, T35J, T5I, T69, T70-T7I, T72-T73, TI05, TII3E-TII3F, TI38, TI39, TI40, TI4I, T27IB-27ID, T296, T297 **Unit 3:** T27, T35B-T35H, T35J, T52-T53, T69, T70-T7I, T72-T73, TII3B-TII3C, TII3G-TII3H, TII3J, TI47, TI48-TI49, TI50 **Unit 4:** T27, T3I, T35E, T35G, T35I, T35L, T52-T53, T60-T6I, T62-T63, T65, T66-T67 **Unit 5:** T27, T3I, T35C-T35D, T35F, T60, T65, TI04-TI05, TI38-TI39, T269C, T269F-T269H, T305, T204, T307, T407, T4I5 **Unit 6:** T35D-T35F, T35I, T35K, TI82-TI83, T2I6 www.connected.mcgraw-hill.com: **RESOURCES: Units I–6: Graphic Organizers:** Graphic Organizers **Cards:** Retelling Cards **Student Practice:** Approaching Reproducibles, Beyond Reproducibles, ELL Reproducibles

Craft and Structure		McGraw-Hill *Wonders*
RL.1.4	Identify words and phrases in stories or poems that suggest feelings or appeal to the senses.	**READING/WRITING WORKSHOP:** Unit I: 7 **Unit 2:** 7 **Unit 3:** 7 **Unit 4:** II **Unit 5:** II3 **Unit 6:** 2I5 **LITERATURE ANTHOLOGY:** Unit I: 84, 85 **Unit 2:** 62, 63 **Unit 3:** 68, 69, 70, 7I, 72, 73 **Unit 4:** 90, 9I **Unit 5:** 222, 223, 224, 225 **Unit 6:** 324, 325 **CLOSE READING COMPANION:** 86, I50, I52, I78 **READING WORKSTATION ACTIVITY CARDS:** 2I **WRITING WORKSTATION ACTIVITY CARDS:** I3, I5 **INTERACTIVE READ-ALOUD CARDS: Unit 3, Week 3:** I **TEACHER'S EDITION: Unit I:** T272-T273 **Unit 2:** TI94-TI95 **Unit 3:** TI8, T35E-T35F, T35I, T76, TI94, TI95A-TI95B **Unit 4:** TI94-TI95 **Unit 5:** T35H, TI95, TI95A-TI95B **Unit 6:** TII6-TII7, T269D www.connected.mcgraw-hill.com: **RESOURCES: Media:** Images

Reading Standards for Literature

RL.1.5	Explain major differences between books that tell stories and books that give information, drawing on a wide reading of a range of text types.	**LITERATURE ANTHOLOGY: Unit I:** 47, 67, 83, 93 **Unit 2:** 21, 25, 43, 47, 61, 81, 93 **Unit 3:** 23, 27, 45, 66, 89, 101 **Unit 4:** 29, 55, 89, 125, 137 **Unit 5:** 155, 195, 221, 255, 267 **Unit 6:** 295, 323, 357, 393, 405 **LEVELED READERS: Unit I, Week I:** *We Like to Share* (O), *Class Party* (B) **Unit I, Week 2:** *What Can We See?* (A), *A ēTrip to the City* (O), *Where I Live*, pp. 13–16 (O), *Harvest Time* (B) **Unit I, Week 3:** *Mouse's Moon Party* (A), *Pet Show* (O), *Polly the Circus Star* (B) **Unit I, Week 4:** *Friends Are Fun* (A, O, B) **Unit I, Week 5:** *We Can Move!* (A, O, B) **Unit 2 Week I:** *Pick Up Day* (A), *Ben Brings the Mail* (O), *At Work with Mom* (B) **Unit 2, Week 2:** *What a Nest!* (A), *Stone Castles*, pp. 13–16 (A), *Staying Afloat* (O), *City Armadillo, Country Armadillo* (B) **Unit 2, Week 3:** *Meerkat Family* (A, O, B) **Unit 2, Week 4:** *The Sick Tree* (A), *Squirrels Help* (O), *Sharing Skills*, pp. 13–16 (B) **Unit 2, Week 5:** *How Maps Help* (A, O, B) **Unit 3, Week I:** *Busy's Watch* (A), *Kate Saves the Date!* (O), *Uncle George Is Coming!* (B) **Unit 3, Week 3:** *How Coquí Got Her Voice* (A), *The Magic Paintbrush* (O), *The Storytelling Stone* (B) **Unit 4, Week I:** *The King of the Animals* (A), *Lions and Elephants*, pp. 13–16 (A), *Fly to the Rescue!* (O), *Animal Traits*, pp. 13–16 (O), *Hummingbird's Wings* (B) **Unit 4, Week 2:** *Penguins All Around* (A, O, B) **Unit 4, Week 4:** *Come One, Come All* (B) **Unit 5, Week I:** *Nuts for Winter* (A), *Dog Bones* (O), *Spark's Toys* (B) **Unit 5, Week 5:** *What Is a Yurt?* (A, O, B) **Unit 6, Week I:** *Two Hungry Elephants* (A), *What a Feast!* (O), *Beware of the Lion!* (B) **Unit 6, Week 4:** *The Quilt* (A), *Latkes for Sam* (O) **TEACHER'S EDITION: Unit I:** S14, S32, S56, S62, S92, T113F, T269F **Unit 2:** T26, T113G, T191H, T260, T269E, T338 **Unit 3:** T35E, T269D **Unit 4:** T26, T35H, T113H, T191I, T269D, T347D **Unit 5:** T35C, T35J, T113K, T182, T191L, T269J, T338, T347F **Unit 6:** T26, T35J, T113L, T191R, T269J, T347F www.connected.mcgraw-hill.com: **RESOURCES: Units I–6: Teacher Resources:** Theme Bibliography, Literature/Informational Text Chart, Book Talk, Reader Response **Graphic Organizers:** Graphic Organizers
RL.1.6	Identify who is telling the story at various points in a text.	**READING/WRITING WORKSHOP: Unit 2:** 24, 25, 44, 45, 84, 85 **Unit 3:** 24, 25 **Unit 4:** 88, 89 **Unit 5:** 130, 131, 190, 191 **Unit 6:** 272, 273 **LITERATURE ANTHOLOGY: Unit 4:** 125 **Unit 5:** 155 **TEACHER'S EDITION: Unit 3:** T26, T113B, T113I **Unit 4:** T261, T269E-T269F, T269H, T269K, T269O, T269R, T295, T299, T415 **Unit5:** T26-T27, T35B-T35E, T35G, T35I-T35J, T395 www.connected.mcgraw-hill.com: **RESOURCES: Graphic Organizers:** Graphic Organizers

Reading Standards for Literature

Integration of Knowledge and Ideas		McGraw-Hill *Wonders*
RL.1.7	Use illustrations and details in a story to describe its characters, setting, or events.	**READING/WRITING WORKSHOP: Unit 4:** 88, 89 **Unit 5:** 130, 131 **LITERATURE ANTHOLOGY: Unit 1:** 63 **Unit 2:** 21, 42, 81 **Unit 3:** 23 **LEVELED READERS: Unit 1, Week 1:** *A Fun Day* (A) **Unit 2, Week 1:** *Pick Up Day* (A), *Ben Brings the Mail* (O), **Unit 6, Week 3:** *Heat Wave* (O) **CLOSE READING COMPANION:** 41, 55, 102, 167, 181 **YOUR TURN PRACTICE BOOK:** 44, 144, 147, 154, 193, 198, 202, 205, 210, 214, 246, 258, 277, 298 **READING WORKSTATION ACTIVITY CARDS:** 2, 4, 28 **INTERACTIVE READ-ALOUD CARDS: Unit 6, Week 1:** 4 **Unit 6, Week 2:** 2, 4 **TEACHER'S EDITION: Unit 1:** T35B-T35D, T38-T39, T104-T105, T113H-T113I, T216 T261 **Unit 2:** T27, T35B-T35E, T113B-T113I T261, T269D, T269G, T269J, T308 **Unit 3:** T35B, T35D, T113D, T141, T167, T191D, T208, T298 **Unit 4:** T11, T35B, T35J, T71, T269G **Unit 5:** T35C, T269D, T269N, T269P, T305, T306-T307, T323 **Unit 6:** T183, T191C, T191E, T191H, T191P, T227, T269G, T269P, T306-T307 www.connected.mcgraw-hill.com: **RESOURCES: Graphic Organizers:** Graphic Organizers; **Media:** Images; Cards: Retelling Cards; Student Practice Approaching Reproducibles 44, 144, 147, 150, 154, 190, 193, 198, 202, 205, 210, 214, 246, 250, 258, 277, 298; Beyond Reproducibles 44, 144, 147, 150, 154, 190, 193, 198, 202, 205, 210, 214, 246, 250, 258, 277, 29, ELL Reproducibles 44, 144, 147, 150, 154, 190, 193, 198, 202, 205, 210, 214, 246, 250, 258, 277, 298
RL.1.8	(Not applicable to Literature)	
RL.1.9	Compare and contrast the adventures and experiences of characters in stories.	**READING/WRITING WORKSHOP: Unit 2:** 24, 25, 44, 45, 84, 85 **Unit 3:** 64, 65 **Unit 4:** 88, 89 **Unit 5:** 130, 131, 150, 151 **Unit 6:** 272, 273 **LEVELED READERS: Unit 3, Week 3:** *How Coquí Got Her Voice* (A), *The Magic Paintbrush* (O) **CLOSE READING COMPANION:** 11-13, 15, 43, 76, 168 **READING WORKSTATION ACTIVITY CARDS:** 23 **INTERACTIVE READ-ALOUD CARDS: Unit 6, Week 1:** 3 **TEACHER'S EDITION: Unit 1:** T128, T206 **Unit 2:** T128 **Unit 3:** T128, T191I, T206 **Unit 4:** T50 **Unit 5:** T50, T128, T284 **Unit 6:** T50, T206 www.connected.mcgraw-hill.com: **RESOURCES: Units 1-6: Graphic Organizers:** Graphic Organizers

Range of Reading and Level of Text Complexity		McGraw-Hill *Wonders*
RL.1.10	With prompting and support, read prose and poetry of appropriate complexity for grade 1.	**WRITING WORKSHOP: Unit 1:** 7, 14-23, 34-43, 54-63 **Unit 2:** 7, 14-23, 34-43, 74-83 **Unit 3:** 7, 14-23, 34-43, 54-63 **Unit 4:** 11, 18-27, 78-87 **Unit 5:** 113, 120-129, 140-149, 180-189 **Unit 6:** 215, 222-231, 262-271, 282-291 **LITERATURE ANTHOLOGY: Unit 3, Week 2:** *The Big Yuca Plant*, 28 **Unit 3, Week 3:** *The Gingerbread Man*, 50 **Unit 3, Week 4:** *Mother Goose Rhymes*, 68 **Unit 4, Week 1:** *How Bat Got Its Wings*, 10 **Unit 4, Week 4:** *When It's Snowing*, 90 **Unit 5, Week 1:** *A Lost Button*, 140 **Unit 5, Week 2:** *Kitten's First Full Moon*, 162 **Unit 5, Week 3:** *Windshield Wipers*, 222 **Unit 6, Week 2:** *Abuelita's Lap*, 324 **Unit 6, Week 3:** *Rain School*, 236 **LEVELED READERS: Unit 1, Week 1:** *I Like to Play*, pp. 13-16 (A, O, B) **Unit 2, Week 3:** *I Live in a House!* (A, O, B) **Unit 4, Week 3:** *Ducklings*, pp. 12-16 (B) **Unit 5, Week 3:** *Fly Away, Butterfly*, pp. 13-16 (A, O) **Unit 6, Week 2:** *Fire!* pp. 13-16 (A, O); pp. 12-16 (B) **YOUR TURN PRACTICE BOOK:** 5, 6, 15, 16, 25, 26, 35, 36, 42, 45, 46, 55, 56, 65, 66, 75, 76, 85, 86, 105, 106, 115, 116, 125, 126, 145, 146, 155, 156, 191, 192, 203, 204, 215, 216, 227, 228, 239, 251, 252, 275, 276, 299, 311, 312 **READING WORKSTATION ACTIVITY CARDS:** 1, 2, 3, 4, 6, 7, 8, 12, 14, 16, 20, 23, 25, 26, 28 **TEACHER'S EDITION: Unit 1:** T16-T17, T52-T53, T140-T141, T142-T143, T144 **Unit 2:** T16-T17, T35A, T61, T62-T63, T297, T298-T299, T305, T306-T307 **Unit 3:** T65, T66-T67, T94-T95, T113A, T130-T131, T172-T173, T191B, T191C, T195, T195A-T195B, T225 **Unit 4:** T16-T17, T191B, T219, T299, T303, T304-T305, T306-T307 **Unit 5:** T16-T17, T35D, T69, T70-T71, T72-T73, T143, T144-T145, T260-T261, T295, T296, T306-T307 **Unit 6:** T35B, T35H, T61, T62-T63, T151, T217, T303, T407 **LITERATURE BIG BOOKS: Unit 1, Week 1:** *This School Year Will be the Best* **Unit 1, Week 2:** *Alicia's Happy Day* **Unit 1, Week 3:** *Cool Dog, School Dog* **Unit 2, Week 1:** *Millie Waits for the Mail* **Unit 2, Week 2:** *The 3 Little Dassies* **Unit 2, Week 3:** *Babies in the Bayou* **Unit 3, Week 1:** *A Second is a Hiccup* **Unit 3, Week 2:** *Mystery Vine* **Unit 3, Week 3:** *Interrupting Chicken* **Unit 3, Week 4:** *The Last Train* www.connected.mcgraw-hill.com: **RESOURCES: Units 1-6: Teacher Resources:** Theme Bibliography, Literature/Informational Texts Chart **Student Practice:** Approaching Reproducibles, Beyond Reproducibles, ELL Reproducibles

Reading Standards for Informational Text

Key Ideas and Details	McGraw-Hill *Wonders*
RI.1.1	Ask and answer questions about key details in a text.	**READING/WRITING WORKSHOP: Unit I:** 84–85, 104–105 **Unit 2:** 64–65, 104–105 **Unit 3:** 84–85, 104–105 **Unit 4:** 48–49, 68–69 **LITERATURE ANTHOLOGY: Unit I:** 83, 93, 94, 95 **Unit 2:** 61, 88, 89, 91, 93 **Unit 3:** 26, 49, 75, 89, 101, 103 **Unit 4:** 35, 55, 89, 137 **Unit 5:** 221, 267 **Unit 6:** 301, 323, 405 **LEVELED READERS: Unit I, Week 4:** *Friends Are Fun* (A, O, B) **Unit 2, Week 3:** *Meerkat Family* (A, O, B) **Unit 2, Week 5:** *How Maps Help* (A, O, B) **Unit 3, Week 4:** *Schools Then and Now* (A, O, B) **Unit 3, Week 5:** *Apples from Farm to Table* (A, O, B) **Unit 4, Week 2:** *Penguins All Around* (A, O, B) **Unit 4, Week 3:** *Go, Gator!* (A, O, B) **Unit 5, Week 3:** *The Wright Brothers* (A, O, B) **Unit 5, Week 5:** *What Is a Yurt?* (A, O, B) **Unit 6, Week 2:** *Helping Me, Helping You!* (A, O, B) **Unit 6, Week 5:** *It's Labor Day!* (A, O, B) **CLOSE READING COMPANION:** 22-24, 29, 43-45, 62-63, 88-90, 95-96, 107-109, 114-116, 147-149, 154-156, 173-175, 194-196 **YOUR TURN PRACTICE BOOK:** 94, 97, 100, 137, 161, 169, 181, 221, 257, 265, 270, 286, 289, 294, 305, 317, 322, 325, 330 **READING WORKSTATION ACTIVITY CARDS:** 5, 9, 11, 13, 15, 27 **WRITING WORKSTATION ACTIVITY CARDS:** 27, 29, 30 **INTERACTIVE READ-ALOUD CARDS: Unit I, Week 3:** 4 **Unit 2, Week I:** 3, 4 **Unit 2, Week 3:** 1, 4 **Unit 2, Week 4:** 3, 4 **Unit 2, Week 5:** 1, 3, 4 **Unit 3, Week I:** 4 **Unit 3, Week 4:** 4 **Unit 4, Week 2:** 2, 4 **Unit 4, Week 3:** 1, 4 **Unit 4, Week 4:** 3, 4 **Unit 5, Week 3:** 4 **Unit 5, Week 4:** 4 **Unit 6, Week 5:** 3, 4 **TEACHER'S EDITION: Unit I:** T244-T245, T255, T261, T269A-T269J, T322-T323, T332-T333, T338-T339, T343, T347A-T347F, T362, T374-T375, T404, T412-T413 **Unit 2:** T191A-T191H, T218, T347A-T347F, T374, T394-T395, T407, T412-T413, T415 **Unit 3:** T255, T261, T265, T260-T261, T269A-269J, T269I-T269J, T294, T362, T372, T389, T394-T395, T407, T412-T413, T415 **Unit 4:** T89, T99, T105, T113B-T113I, T117B, T130, T140, T144, T148-T149, T167, T183, T191C, T191F, T191H, T208, T216, T218, T222, T227, T228, T347A-T347D **Unit 5:** T167, T191A-T191L, T208, T218, T222, T284, T338-T339, T364, T374, T379, T382-T383 **Unit 6:** T113F-T113J, T113L, T128, T372, T394-T395, T407, T412 www.connected.mcgraw-hill.com: **RESOURCES: Units I-6: Graphic Organizers:** Graphic Organizers, Think Aloud Clouds **Tier 2 Intervention:** Comprehension **Student Practice:** Approaching Reproducibles, Beyond Reproducibles, ELL Reproducibles

Reading Standards for Informational Text

RI.1.2	Identify the main topic and retell key details of a text.	**READING/WRITING WORKSHOP: Unit 2:** 64, 65, 104, 105 **Unit 4:** 48, 49, 68, 69 **LITERATURE ANTHOLOGY: Unit 1:** 83, 93 **Unit 2:** 61, 93 **Unit 3:** 89 **Unit 4:** 55, 89 **Unit 5:** 221 **Unit 6:** 323 **LEVELED READERS: Unit 2, Week 3:** *Meerkat Family* (A, O, B) **Unit 2, Week 5:** *How Maps Help* (A, O, B) **Unit 4, Week 2:** *Penguins All Around* (A, O, B) **Unit 4, Week 3:** *Go, Gator!* (A, O, B) **CLOSE READING COMPANION:** 50, 62, 109 **YOUR TURN PRACTICE BOOK:** 10, 20, 30, 40, 50, 60, 70, 80 90, 100, 110, 120, 138, 150, 186, 198, 210, 274, 277, 282, 310, 313 **READING WORKSTATION ACTIVITY CARDS:** 5, 10, 11, 27 **WRITING WORKSTATION ACTIVITY CARDS:** 24, 27 **INTERACTIVE READ-ALOUD CARDS: Unit 1, Week 3:** 4 **Unit 2, Week 1:** 4 **Unit 2, Week 3:** 2, 4 **Unit 2, Week 4:** 3, 4 **Unit 2, Week 5:** 1, 3, 4 **Unit 3, Week 1:** 4 **Unit 3, Week 4:** 4 **Unit 4, Week 2:** 4 **Unit 4, Week 3:** 1, 4 **Unit 4, Week 4:** 4 **Unit 5, Week 3:** 4 **Unit 6, Week 4:** 4 **Unit 6, Week 5:** 4 **TEACHER'S EDITION: Unit 1:** T261, T265, T269D-T269J, T342 **Unit 2:** T167, T182-T183, T191B-T191H, T218-T219, T220-T221, T227, T228-T229, T230-T231, T323, T339, T347E-T347F, T383, T384-T385, T396-T387, T397, T405 **Unit 3:** T269I-T269J, T307, T338-T339, T347C-T347F, T375 **Unit 4:** T89, T105, T113G, T113K, T128-T129, T151, T245, T347B-T347C, T347E-T347F, T379 **Unit 5:** T167, T191H, T191K, T191L, T223, T385, T414-T415 **Unit 6:** T109, T131, T245, T347F, T363 **www.connected.mcgraw-hill.com: RESOURCES: Units 1–6: Graphic Organizers:** Graphic Organizers, Think Aloud Clouds **Tier 2 Intervention:** Comprehension **Student Practice:** Approaching Reproducibles, Beyond Reproducibles, ELL Reproducibles **Cards:** Retelling Cards
Key Ideas and Details		**McGraw-Hill** *Wonders*
RI.1.3	Describe the connection between two individuals, events, ideas, or pieces of information in a text.	**READING/WRITING WORKSHOP: Unit 3:** 84, 85, 104, 105 **Unit 4:** 38–47, 108, 109 **Unit 5:** 170, 171, 210, 211 **LITERATURE ANTHOLOGY: Unit 1:** 94, 95 **Unit 2:** 61, 93 **Unit 3:** 49, 89, 101 **Unit 4:** 35, 37–53, 55, 89, 137 **Unit 5:** 221, 267 **Unit 6:** 323 **LEVELED READERS: Unit 2, Week 5:** *How Maps Help* (A, O, B) **Unit 3, Week 5:** *Apples from Farm to Table* (A, O, B) **Unit 4, Week 4:** *Wings*, pp. 13-16 (A) **Unit 4, Week 5:** *Teach a Dog!* (A, O, B) **Unit 5, Week 5:** *What Is a Yurt?* (A, O, B) **Unit 6, Week 5:** *It's Labor Day!* (A, O, B) **CLOSE READING COMPANION:** 90, 93, 140 **YOUR TURN PRACTICE BOOK:** 134, 137, 257, 262, 265, 317 **READING WORKSTATION ACTIVITY CARDS:** 9, 13, 15, 17 **INTERACTIVE READ-ALOUD CARDS: Unit 6, Week 4:** 4 **Unit 6, Week 5:** 3 **TEACHER'S EDITION: Unit 1:** T285, T347B, T347E-T347F, T404-T405, T406 **Unit 2:** T183, T206, T404-T405, T406 **Unit 3:** T261, T269B-T269G, T285, T286-T287, T295, T296-T297, T299, T300-T301, T303, T304-T305, T306-T307, T339, T347B-T347E, T365, T373, T375, T377, T379, T381, T385, T404-T405 **Unit 4:** T105, T109, T113D, T113F, T113H, T339, T347B, T404-T405, T406 **Unit 5:** T183, T187, T191B, T191E, T191H, T191I, T208-T209, T216-T217, T218-T219, T223-T225, T226-T227, T228-T229, T339, T347C, T347E-T347F, T339, T364-T365, T373, T375, T377, T379, T384-T385 **Unit 6:** T95, T113D-T113E, T129, T404-T405, T406 **www.connected.mcgraw-hill.com: RESOURCES: Units 1–6: Student Practice:** Approaching Reproducibles, Beyond Reproducibles, ELL Reproducibles **Graphic Organizers:** Graphic Organizers **Interactive Games & Activities:** Comprehension
Craft and Structure		**McGraw-Hill** *Wonders*
RI.1.4	Ask and answer questions to help determine or clarify the meaning of words and phrases in a text.	**CLOSE READING COMPANION:** 31, 44, 124-125, 158 **TEACHER'S EDITION: Unit 2:** T176, T273A, T396 **Unit 3:** T269F **Unit 4:** T113, T113F, T146, T191G, T269, T269G, T347 **Unit 5:** T35, T113C, T269, T269K, T347 **Unit 6:** T40, T113G, T191J **www.connected.mcgraw-hill.com: RESOURCES: Units 1–6: Media:** Visual Glossary **Tier 2 Intervention:** Vocabulary **Interactive Games & Activities:** Vocabulary

Reading Standards for Informational Text

RI.1.5	Know and use various text structures features (e.g., headings, tables of contents, glossaries, electronic menus, icons) to locate key facts or information in a text.	**READING/WRITING WORKSHOP: Unit 2:** 61, 94–103 **Unit 3:** 74–83, 96, 98, 103 **Unit 4:** 43, 45, 47, 98–107 **Unit 5:** 162, 164, 166, 200–209 **Unit 6:** 302–311 **LITERATURE ANTHOLOGY: Unit 1:** 94, 95 **Unit 2:** 59 **LEVELED READERS: Unit 2, Week 5:** *How Maps Help* (B) **Unit 3, Week 4:** *Schools Then and Now* (B) **Unit 4, Week 2:** *Penguins All Around* (B) **Unit 6, Week 5:** *It's Labor Day!* (O,B) **CLOSE READING COMPANION:** 65, 128, 129, 131 **YOUR TURN PRACTCE BOOK:** 19, 29, 49, 59, 69, 99, 109, 119, 139, 149, 161, 173, 197, 209, 221, 233, 269, 281, 305, 329 **READING WORKSTATION ACTIVITY CARDS:** 18, 19, 20 **TEACHER'S EDITION: Unit 1:** T38, T39A-T39B, T338, T347C, T347F, T350-T351, T396, T415 **Unit 2:** T117, T117B, T274-T275, T275B, T338, T347A, T350-T351, T385, T396, T415 **Unit 3:** T260, T273, T273A, T322, T338, T339, T347B-T347C, T347E, T350-T351, T396, T415 **Unit 4:** T38, T39A-T39B, T104, T273, T273B, T284, T338, T339, 347B, 347C, 347E, T396, T415 **Unit 5:** T38-T39, T116, T117A, T396, T415 **Unit 6:** T195, T195A-T195B, T273A, T338, T350, T396, T415 www.connected.mcgraw-hill.com: **RESOURCES: Media:** Images; Time for Kids Online Articles; **Collaborate:** Projects; **Student Practice:** Approaching Reproducibles 19, 29, 49, 59, 69, 99, 109, 119, 139, 149, 161, 173, 197, 209, 221, 233, 269, 281, 305, 329, Beyond Reproducibles 19, 29, 49, 59, 69, 99, 109, 119, 139, 149, 161, 173, 197, 209, 221, 233, 269, 281, 305, 329; ELL Reproducibles 19, 29, 49, 59, 69, 99, 109, 119, 139, 149, 161, 173, 197, 209, 221, 233, 269, 281, 305, 329
RI.1.6	Distinguish between information provided by pictures or other illustrations and information provided by the words in a text.	**READING/WRITING WORKSHOP: Unit 1:** 84, 85, 104, 105 **Unit 2:** 104, 105 **Unit 5:** 210, 211 **CLOSE READING COMPANION:** 23, 48-50, 161, 164 **YOUR TURN PRACTICE BOOK:** 173, 181, 209, 233, 269, 281 **READING WORKSTATION ACTIVITY CARDS:** 20 **INTERACTIVE READ-ALOUD CARDS: Unit 1, Week 1:** 4 **Unit 1, Week 3:** 4 **Unit 1, Week 4:** 4 **Unit 2, Week 1:** 4 **Unit 2, Week 3:** 4 **Unit 2, Week 4:** 4 **Unit 2, Week 5:** 3, 4 **Unit 3, Week 1:** 4 **Unit 3, Week 4:** 4 **Unit 4, Week 2:** 4 **Unit 4, Week 3:** 3, 4 **Unit 4, Week 4:** 2, 4 **Unit 5, Week 3:** 4 **Unit 6, Week 4:** 3, 4 **Unit 6, Week 5:** 4 **TEACHER'S EDITION: Unit 1:** T38-T39, T39B, T269B, T269C, T269E-T269F, T347B-T347C **Unit 2:** T35C, T39A, T191B, T191C, T347D, T350, T351 **Unit 3:** T269D **Unit 4:** T182 **Unit 5:** T182, T273, T338, T347B, T347D, T350-T351 **Unit 6:** T113E-T113F, T113H, T338 www.connected.mcgraw-hill.com: **RESOURCES: Media:** Images; Graphic Organizers; **Student Practice:** Approaching Reproducibles 173, 181, 209, 233, 269, 281, Beyond Reproducibles 173, 181, 209, 233, 269, 281, ELL Reproducibles 173, 181, 209, 233, 269, 281 **Interactive Games & Activities:** Comprehension

Integration of Knowledge and Ideas — McGraw-Hill *Wonders*

RI.1.7	Use the illustrations and details in a text to describe its key ideas.	**READING/WRITING WORKSHOP: Unit 1:** 104, 105 **Unit 2:** 104, 105 **LITERATURE ANTHOLOGY: Unit 1:** 83, 93, 95 **Unit 2:** 59, 61 **Unit 3:** 49, 89, 103 **LEVELED READERS: Unit 1, Week 1:** *A Fun Day* (A), *Our Classroom Rules*, pp. 13-16 (B) **Unit 3, Week 1:** *Make a Clock*, pp. 13-16 (A) **Unit 3, Week 4:** *Schools Then and Now* (A, O, B) **Unit 4, Week 3:** *Go, Gator!* (A, O, B) **Unit 4, Week 4:** *Wings*, pp. 13-16 (A) **Unit 5, Week 1:** *Sort by Color*, pp. 13-16 (A) **CLOSE READING COMPANION:** 22, 23, 24, 29, 30, 31, 48 **YOUR TURN PRACTICE BOOK:** 99, 137, 166, 169, 174, 181, 186, 221, 233, 269, 281, 294, 305, 317 **READING WORKSTATION ACTIVITY CARDS:** 20 **INTERACTIVE READ-ALOUD CARDS: Unit 1, Week 1:** 1, 2, 4 **Unit 1, Week 3:** 4 **Unit 1, Week 4:** 4 **Unit 2, Week 1:** 4 **Unit 2, Week 3:** 4 **Unit 2, Week 4:** 2, 4 **Unit 2, Week 5:** 3, 4 **Unit 3, Week 1:** 4 **Unit 3, Week 4:** 4 **Unit 4, Week 2:** 4 **Unit 4, Week 3:** 3, 4 **Unit 4, Week 4:** 2, 4 **Unit 5, Week 3:** 4 **Unit 6, Week 4:** 3, 4 **Unit 6, Week 5:** 4 **TEACHER'S EDITION: Unit 1:** T38, T261, T269B-T269G, T304-T305, T306-T307, T347C, T347F, T372-T373, T374-T375 **Unit 2:** T39, T117, T191B-T191D, T191G-191H, T274-T275, T349B-T349F, T385, T386, T387 **Unit 3:** T39, T117, T117A-T117B, T269D, T269I-T269J, T273, T273A, T273B, T287, T307, T350, T351, T365, T372, T383, T384-T385 **Unit 4:** T38, T149, T150, T167, T191G, T191II, T191O, T229, T245, T339, T365, T374-T375, T384-T385 **Unit 5:** T38-T39, T39A-T39B, T191B, T191D, T228, T347F, T372 **Unit 6:** T31, T38, T39A, T113D-T113I, T113K-T113L, T148-T149, T150-T151, T273, T273A, T338-T339, T347B-T347D, T350-T351, T365, T383 www.connected.mcgraw-hill.com: **RESOURCES: Media:** Images; **Student Practice:** Approaching Reproducibles 99, 100, 137, 166, 169, 174, 181, 186, 221, 233, 269, 270, 281, 294, 305, 317, 330, Beyond Reproducibles 99, 100, 137, 166, 169, 174, 181, 186, 221, 233, 269, 270, 281, 294, 305, 317, 330, ELL Reproducibles 99, 100, 137, 166, 169, 174, 181, 186, 221, 233, 269, 270, 281, 294, 305, 317, 330

Reading Standards for Informational Text

RI.1.8	Identify the reasons an author gives to support points in a text.	**READING/WRITING WORKSHOP:** Unit 6: 252, 253, 312, 313 **LITERATURE ANTHOLOGY:** Unit 6: 323, 405 **LEVELED READERS:** Unit 6, Week 2: *Helping Me, Helping You!* (A, O, B) Unit 6, Week 5: *It's Labor Day!* (A, O, B) **CLOSE READING COMPANION:** 108, 174 **WRITING WORKSTATION ACTIVITY CARDS:** 26 **TEACHER'S EDITION: Unit 1:** T260-T261, T269D-T269F, T285, T363 **Unit 2:** T183, T191G, T207, T363 **Unit 3:** T261, T280, T347D, T330, T363 **Unit 4:** T105, T113F, 113H, 113J, T129, T363 **Unit 5:** T183, T207, T339, T363 **Unit 6:** T104, T105, T113B-T113K, T129, T339, T347B-T347E, T363 www.connected.mcgraw-hill.com: **RESOURCES: Units 1–6: Cards:** Retelling Cards, **Graphic Organizers:** Graphic Organizers
RI.1.9	Identify basic similarities in and differences between two texts on the same topic (e.g., in illustrations, descriptions, or procedures).	**LITERATURE ANTHOLOGY: Unit 1:** 84, 94 **Unit 2:** 22, 44, 61, 62, 82, 94 **Unit 3:** 24, 46, 90, 102 **Unit 4:** 30, 56, 59, 90, 126, 138, 139 **Unit 5:** 156, 201, 222, 256, 268 **Unit 6:** 296, 301, 324, 394, 406 **LEVELED READERS: Unit 1, Week 5:** *What's Under Your Skin?* pp. 13–16 (A, O, B) **Unit 2, Week 5:** *On the Map,* pp. 13–16 (A, O); pp. 12–16 (B) **Unit 3, Week 4:** *School Days,* pp. 13–16 (A, O, B) **Unit 4, Week 1:** *Lions and Elephants,* pp. 13–16 (A, O); pp. 12–16 (B) **Unit 4, Week 2:** *Penguins All Around* (A, O, B), *Animals Work Together,* pp. 13–16 (A, O), pp. 12–16 (B) **Unit 4, Week 5:** *Teach a Dog!* (A, O, B), *Working with Dolphins,* pp. 13–16 (A, O), pp. 12–16 (B) **CLOSE READING COMPANION:** 54, 73, 99, 153 **READING WORKSTATION ACTIVITY CARDS:** 22 **TEACHER'S EDITION: Unit 1:** S32, S62, S92, T39B, T50, T128, T206-T207, T284-T285, T351, T362-T363, T379, T385 **Unit 2:** T50-T51, T39B, T117B, T191H, T194, T206-T207, T275B, T284-T285, T350, T353, T358, T359, T362-T363, T367, T381, T387 **Unit 3:** T117B, T273B, T284-T285, T286, T287, T297, T307, T362, T363, T379 **Unit 4:** T39B, T117A, T128, T131, T141, T145, T151, T206, T209, T219, T273B, T284-T285, T287, T297, T301, T307, T350, T351, T362-T363, T365, T375, T379, T385 **Unit 5:** T39B, T117B, T195A, T206-T207, T209, T219, T223, T273B, T284-T285, T297, T301, T350, T362, T365, T375, T385 **Unit 6:** T195B, T206-T207, T273B, T284-T285, T287, T297, T301, T307, T351, T362, T365, T375, T379, T385 www.connected.mcgraw-hill.com: **RESOURCES: Units 1–6: Graphic Organizers:** Graphic Organizers **Cards:** Retelling Cards

Range of Reading and Level of Text Complexity		**McGraw-Hill *Wonders***
RI.1.10	With prompting and support, read informational texts appropriately complex for grade 1.	**READING/WRITING WORKSHOP: Unit 1:** 94-103 **Unit 2:** 54-63, 94-103 **Unit 3:** 74-83, 94-103 **Unit 4:** 38-47, 58-67, 98-107 **Unit 5:** 160-169, 200-209 **Unit 6:** 242-251, 302-311 **LITERATURE ANTHOLOGY:** These Units reflect the range of text complexity found throughout the book. **Unit 1, Week 4:** *Friends,* 68 **Unit 2, Week 5:** *Fun with Maps,* 86 **Unit 3, Week 4:** *Long Ago and Now,* 74 **Unit 4, Week 2:** *Animal Teams,* 36 **Unit 4, Week 5:** *Koko and Penny,* 130 **Unit 5, Week 3:** *Thomas Edison, Inventor,* 202 **Unit 6, Week 5:** *Happy Birthday, U.S.A.!,* 398 **LEVELED READERS: Unit 1, Week 1:** *We Share,* pp. 13–16 (O) **Unit 2, Week 2:** *What a Nest!,* pp. 13–16 (A), *Staying Afloat,* pp. 13–16 (O), *City, Armadillo, Country Armadillo,* pp. 13–16 (B) **Unit 3, Week 4:** *Schools Then and Now* (A, O, B) **Unit 4, Week 3:** *Go, Gator!* (A, O, B) **Unit 5, Week 1:** *Dog Bones,* pp. 13–16 (O) **Unit 6, Week 4:** *Latkes for Sam,* pp. 13–16 (O) **TEACHER'S EDITION: Unit 1:** T39A, T117, T195A, T250-T251, T269A, T328-T329, T347A, T373, T374-T375, T404-T405, T406-T407 **Unit 2:** T39A, T117A, T172A, T173, T191A, T328-T329, T340-T341, T383, T384-T385, T386-T387, T412-T413, T414 **Unit 3:** T39A, T117A, T250-T251, T269A, T286-T287, T304-T305, T306-T307, T328-T329, T347A, T377, T378-T379 **Unit 4:** T39, T94-T95, T113A, T140-T141, T226-T227, T328-T329, T382-T383 **Unit 5:** T117, T172-T173, T191A, T208-T209, T221, T222-T223, T338-T339, T381, T382-T383, T384-T385 **Unit 6:** T94-T95, T113A, T195A, T273A, T328-T329, T347A **LITERATURE BIG BOOKS: Unit 1, Week 4:** *Friends All Around* **Unit 1, Week 5:** *Move!* **Unit 2, Week 4:** *The Story of Martin Luther King, Jr.* **Unit 2, Week 5:** *Me on the Map* **Unit 3, Week 5:** *Where Does Food Come From?* www.connected.mcgraw-hill.com: **RESOURCES: Unit 1: Teacher Resources:** Theme Bibliography, Literature/Informational Text Chart **Student Practice:** Approaching Reproducibles, Beyond Reproducibles, ELL Reproducibles

Reading Standards: Foundational Skills

Print Concepts — McGraw-Hill *Wonders*

RF.1.1	Demonstrate understanding of the organization and basic features of print.	
RF.1.1a	Recognize the distinguishing features of a sentence (e.g., first word, capitalization, ending punctuation).	**TEACHER'S EDITION: Unit 1:** S34, S64, T28-T29, T185, T205, T349 **Unit 2:** T88, T166, T331, T341, T349, T361 **Unit 3:** T19, T29, T49 **Unit 4:** T107, T115, T121 **Unit 5:** T97, T107, T115, T127 www.connected.mcgraw-hill.com: **RESOURCES: Units 1-5: Student Practice:** Grammar Practice **Interactive Games & Activities:** Writing & Grammar

Phonological Awareness — McGraw-Hill *Wonders*

RF.1.2	Demonstrate understanding of spoken words, syllables, and sounds (phonemes).	
RF.1.2a	Distinguish long from short vowel sounds in spoken single-syllable words.	**TEACHER'S EDITION: Unit 1:** T168, T196 **Unit 4:** T22, T168, T196, T246 www.connected.mcgraw-hill.com: **RESOURCES: Unit 3: Interactive Games & Activities:** Phonemic Awareness **Cards:** Word-Building Cards **Tier 2 Intervention:** Phonemic Awareness **Unit 4: Interactive Games & Activities:** Phonemic Awareness **Cards:** Word-Building Cards **Tier 2 Intervention:** Phonemic Awareness
RF.1.2b	Orally produce single-syllable words by blending sounds (phonemes) including consonant blends.	**YOUR TURN PRACTICE BOOK:** SS1, SS2, SS6, SS7, SS11, SS13, SS14, SS18, SS19, SS23, SS25, SS26, SS31, SS35, 1, 41, 121, 171 **PHONICS WORKSTATION ACTIVITY CARDS:** 5, 15, 16, 20, 23, 28, 29 **TEACHER'S EDITION: Unit 1:** S53, S65, S71, T32, T55, T91, T110, T132, T168, T178, T210, T280, T289 **Unit 2:** T12, T46, T110, T124, T178 **Unit 3:** T124, T188, T280, T334, T358 **Unit 4:** T32, T46, T178, T202, T280, T344 **Unit 5:** T32, T110, T124, T188, T266, T280, T288, T324-T325, T352, T366-T367 **Unit 6:** T110, T266, T280, T334 www.connected.mcgraw-hill.com: **RESOURCES: Units 1-6: Interactive Games & Activities:** Phonemic Awareness **Student Practice:** Phonics/Spelling Practice, Approaching Reproducibles, Beyond Reproducibles, ELL Reproducibles **Cards:** Word-Building Cards
RF.1.2c	Isolate and pronounce initial, medial vowel, and final sounds (phonemes) in spoken single-syllable words.	**YOUR TURN PRACTICE BOOK:** SS1, SS2, SS6, SS7, SS11, SS13, SS14, SS18, SS19, SS23, SS25, SS26, SS31, SS35, 31, 39, 129, 245 **TEACHER'S EDITION: Unit 1:** S5, S11, S41, T22, T40, T100, T188, T324 **Unit 2:** T22, T40, T54-T55, T100, T118, T132, T168, T188, T198, T212-T213, T246, T258, T276, T290-T291, T369 **Unit 3:** T12, T40, T256, T274 **Unit 4:** T22-T23, T54, T90, T110, T118, T132-T133, T168, T188, T196, T210-T211, T246, T288-T289, T324, T352, T366-T367 **Unit 5:** T12, T22, T40, T168, T256, T274, T288-T289, T334, T366 **Unit 6:** T12, T90, T118, T132-T133, T168, T196, T210-T211, T289, T366-T367 www.connected.mcgraw-hill.com: **RESOURCES: Units 1-6: Interactive Games & Activities:** Phonemic Awareness **Student Practice:** Phonics/Spelling Practice, Approaching Reproducibles, Beyond Reproducibles, ELL Reproducibles **Cards:** Word-Building Cards
RF.1.2d	Segment spoken single-syllable words into their complete sequence of individual sounds (phonemes).	**TEACHER'S EDITION: Unit 1:** S77, S83, T46, T202, T256, T266, T280, T334, T358 **Unit 2:** T46, T124, T202, T280, T324, T358 **Unit 3:** T46, T110, T124, T178, T196, T246, T288, T358, T367 **Unit 4:** T46, T100, T124, T266, T280 **Unit 5:** T46, T202, T334, T358 **Unit 6:** T22, T46, T124, T178, T202, T210, T256, T274, T288, T367 www.connected.mcgraw-hill.com: **RESOURCES: Units 1-6: Interactive Games & Activities:** Phonemic Awareness **Student Practice:** Phonics/Spelling Practice **Tier 2 Intervention:** Phonemic Awareness **Cards:** Word-Building Cards

Phonics and Word Recognition — McGraw-Hill *Wonders*

RF.1.3	Know and apply grade-level phonics and word analysis skills in decoding words.	
RF.1.3a	Know the spelling-sound correspondences for common consonant digraphs (two letters that represent one sound).	**READING/WRITING WORKSHOP: Unit 2:** 72, 73, 92, 93 **PHONICS WORKSTATION ACTIVITY CARDS:** 9, 10 **TEACHER'S EDITION: Unit 2:** T246-T247, T250-T251, T256-T257, T266-T267, T324-T325, T328-T329 **Unit 6:** T168-T169, T172-T173, T179, T188-T189 **YOUR TURN PRACTICE BOOK:** SS25, 13, 18, 23, 25, 26, 28, 29, 31, 33, 49, 91, 93, 103 www.connected.mcgraw-hill.com: **RESOURCES: Unit 2: Tier 2 Intervention:** Phonics **Cards:** Sound-Spelling Cards **Teacher Resources:** Sound-Spelling Songs **Interactive Games & Activities:** Phonics **Student Practice:** Phonics/Spelling Practice, Approaching Reproducibles, Beyond Reproducibles, ELL Reproducibles **Unit 6: Tier 2 Intervention:** Phonics **Cards:** Sound-Spelling Cards **Teacher Resources:** Sound-Spelling Songs **Interactive Games & Activities:** Phonics **Student Practice:** Phonics/Spelling Practice, Approaching Reproducibles, Beyond Reproducibles, ELL Reproducibles

Reading Standards: Foundational Skills

Phonics and Word Recognition		McGraw-Hill *Wonders*
RF.1.3b	Decode regularly spelled one-syllable words.	**READING/WRITING WORKSHOP: Unit 1:** 12, 13, 32, 33, 52, 53, 72, 73, 92, 93 **Unit 2:** 12, 13, 32, 33, 52, 53, 72, 73, 92, 93 **Unit 3:** 12, 13, 32, 33, 52, 72, 73, 92, 93 **Unit 4:** 16, 17, 56, 57, 76, 77, 96, 97 **Unit 5:** 118, 119, 138, 139, 158, 159, 178, 179, 198, 199 **Unit 6:** 220, 221, 240, 241, 260, 261, 280, 281, 300, 301 **YOUR TURN PRACTICE BOOK:** SS3, SS4, SS9, SS15, SS16, SS21, SS22, SS27, SS28, SS33, SS34, 1, 3, 5, 6, 8, 11, 13, 15, 16, 18, 19, 21, 23, 25, 26, 28, 29, 31, 33, 35, 36, 39, 41, 43, 45, 46, 49, 51, 53, 55, 56, 59, 61, 62, 63, 65, 66, 69, 71, 73, 75, 76, 79, 81, 82, 83, 85, 86, 91, 92, 93, 95, 96, 101, 102, 103, 105, 106, 111, 112, 113, 115, 116, 119, 121, 122, 123, 125, 126, 129, 133, 135, 136, 138, 141, 142, 143, 145, 146, 151, 152, 155, 156, 159, 163, 164, 167, 168, 171, 175, 176, 179, 183, 187, 188, 191, 192, 195, 199, 203, 204, 207, 211, 212, 215, 216, 219, 223, 224, 227, 228, 231, 235, 236, 239, 243, 245, 247, 248, 251, 252, 253, 255, 257, 259, 260, 263, 264, 267, 271, 272, 275, 276, 279, 283, 284, 287, 288, 291, 295, 296, 299, 303, 307, 308, 311, 312, 315, 319, 323, 324, 327 **PHONICS WORKSTATION ACTIVITY CARDS:** 3, 6, 7, 8, 9, 10, 11, 12, 13, 14, 15, 16, 17, 18, 19, 20, 21, 22, 23, 24, 25, 26, 27, 28, 29, 30 **TEACHER'S EDITION: Unit 1:** S30, S31, S48-S49, T32-T33, T110-T111, T196, T266-T267, T368-T369 **Unit 2:** T32-T33, T118-T119, T188-T189, T215, T252-T253, T336-T337 **Unit 3:** T16-T17, T168-T169, T266-T267, T324-T325 **Unit 4:** T17, T22-T23, T32-T33, T40-T41, T64, T95, T101, T134-T135, T173, T188-T189, T212-T213, T250-T251, T290-T291, T324-T325, T328-T329, T346 **Unit 5:** T12-T13, T124-T125, T212-T213, T324-T325, T344-T345, T368-T369 **Unit 6:** T16-T17, T22-T23, T32-T33, T40, T46, T56-T57, T64, T90-T91, T94-T95, T100-T101, T134-T135, T142, T168-T169, T172-T173, T188-T189, T196-T197, T202-T203, T212-T213, T246-T247, T250-T251, T256-T257, T266-T267, T274-T275, T290-T291, T298, T324-T325, T328-T329, T334-T335, T344-T345, T352-T353, T368-T369, T376 **www.connected.mcgraw-hill.com: RESOURCES: Units 1-6: Tier 2 Intervention:** Phonics **Cards:** Word-Building Cards, Spelling Word Cards **Interactive Games & Activities:** Phonics **Student Practice:** Approaching Reproducibles, Beyond Reproducibles, ELL Reproducibles
RF.1.3c	Know final -*e* and common vowel team conventions for representing long vowel sounds.	**READING/WRITING WORKSHOP: Unit 3:** 12-13, 32-33, 72-73 **Unit 4:** 16, 17, 36, 37, 56, 57, 76, 77, 96, 97 **Unit 6:** 220, 221 **YOUR TURN PRACTICE BOOK:** 101, 103, 111, 113, 131, 133, 138, 151, 159, 163, 171, 175, 183, 187, 195, 199, 207, 271, 279, 292 **PHONICS WORKSTATION ACTIVITY CARDS:** 3, 11, 12, 13, 14, 16, 17, 18, 19, 20 **TEACHER'S EDITION: Unit 3:** T12-T13, T16, T17, T22-T23, T32, T33, T40, T46, T56-T57, T64, T90-T91, T100-T101, T110-T111, T118, T124, T134-T135, T142, T210, T246-T247, T256-T257, T266, T267, T274, T290-T291 **Unit 4:** T12-T13, T22-T23, T24, T32-T33, T40, T46, T56-T57, T64, T76, T90-T91, T101, T110-T111, T118-T119, T124-T125, T134, T142, T168-T169, T213, T220, T246-T247, T256-T257, T266-T267, T280, T290-T291, T334, T335, T352-T353, T358-T359, T368-T369, T376, T388 **www.connected.mcgraw-hill.com: RESOURCES: Unit 3: Tier 2 Intervention:** Phonics **Cards:** Word-Building Cards, Spelling Word Cards **Interactive Games & Activities:** Phonics **Student Practice:** Approaching Reproducibles, Beyond Reproducibles, ELL Reproducibles **Unit 4: Tier 2 Intervention:** Phonics **Cards:** Word-Building Cards, Spelling Word Cards **Interactive Games & Activities:** Phonics **Student Practice:** Approaching Reproducibles, Beyond Reproducibles, ELL Reproducibles
RF.1.3d	Use knowledge that every syllable must have a vowel sound to determine the number of syllables in a printed word.	**YOUR TURN PRACTICE BOOK:** 138, 328 **TEACHER'S EDITION: Unit 2:** T179, T257 T267, T275 **Unit 3:** T257 **Unit 4:** T179, T189, T196, T214 **Unit 5:** T335, T370 **Unit 6:** T101, T335, T345, T352, T370 **www.connected.mcgraw-hill.com: RESOURCES: Cards:** Word-Building Cards **Interactive Games & Activities:** Phonics
RF.1.3e	Decode two-syllable words following basic patterns by breaking the words into syllables.	**READING/WRITING WORKSHOP: Unit 2:** 73, 93 **Unit 4:** 56, 57, 76, 77, 94, 95, 96, 97 **Unit 5:** 116, 117, 118, 119, 139, 156, 157, 158, 159, 176, 177, 178, 179, 196, 197, 198, 199 **Unit 6:** 220, 221, 240, 241, 260, 261, 280, 281, 298-301 **YOUR TURN PRACTICE BOOK:** 138, 184, 208, 268, 304, 314, 328 **PHONICS WORKSTATION ACTIVITY CARDS:** 8, 28 **TEACHER'S EDITION: Unit 2:** T257, T267, T275, T281 **Unit 3:** T257, T267, T275, T281 **Unit 4:** T179, T189, T196, T202 **Unit 5:** T335, T345, T352, T358 **Unit 6:** T101, T111, T118, T124, T179, T335, T345, T358 **www.connected.mcgraw-hill.com: RESOURCES: Cards:** Word-Building Cards, Student Practice Approaching Reproducibles 138, 184, 208, 268, 304, 314, 328, Beyond Reproducibles 138, 184, 208, 268, 304, 314, 328, ELL Reproducibles 138, 184, 208, 268, 304, 314, 328

Reading Standards: Foundational Skills

RF.1.3f	Read words with inflectional endings.	**READING/WRITING WORKSHOP:** Unit 1: 52, 53, 72, 73, 92, 93 **Unit 2:** 32, 33, 73 **Unit 3:** 32, 33, 72, 92, 93 **Unit 4:** 16, 17, 36, 37, 56, 57, 76, 77 **Unit 5:** 118, 139, 178, 179, 198 **Unit 6:** 240, 260, 261, 280, 281 **YOUR TURN PRACTICE BOOK:** 8, 28, 58, 78, 98, 118, 128, 148, 196, 225, 232, 249, 256, 266, 316 **PHONICS WORKSTATION ACTIVITY CARDS:** 8, 13, 15 **TEACHER'S EDITION:** Unit 1: T23, T33, T179, T189, T197, T203 **Unit 2:** T23, T33, T41, T47, T179, T189, T199, T204, T216, T337, T347, T354, T360 **Unit 3:** T101, T111, T119, T125, T179, T189, T203, T214, T335, T345, T352, T358, T370 **Unit 4:** T257, T267, T274, T280, T353 **Unit 5:** T101, T111, T118, T124, T136, T257, T267, T274, T280, T392 **Unit 6:** T40, T257, T267, T274, T280 www.connected.mcgraw-hill.com: **RESOURCES: Units 1–6: Cards:** Word-Building Cards **Student Practice:** Phonics/Spelling Practice, Approaching Reproducibles, Beyond Reproducibles, ELL Reproducibles
RF.1.3g	Recognize and read grade-appropriate irregularly spelled words.	**READING/WRITING WORKSHOP:** Unit 1: 10, 11, 30, 31, 50, 51, 70, 71, 90, 91 **Unit 2:** 10, 11, 30, 31, 50, 51, 70, 71, 90, 91 **Unit 3:** 10, 11, 30, 31, 50, 51, 70, 71, 90, 91 **Unit 4:** 14, 74, 94 **Unit 5:** 116, 156, 176, 177, 196 **Unit 6:** 218, 238, 258, 298, 299 **YOUR TURN PRACTICE BOOK:** 188, 296 **PHONICS WORKSTATION ACTIVITY CARDS:** 28 **TEACHER'S EDITION:** Unit 1: T15, T16-T17, T92-T93, T94-T95, T171, T172-T173, T327, T328-T329 **Unit 2:** T15, T16-T17, T92-T93, T94-T95, T103, T171, T172-T173, T249, T250-T251, T327, T328-T329, T337 **Unit 3:** T15, T16-T17, T25, T93, T94-T95, T249, T250-T251 **Unit 4:** T14-T15, T16-T17, T47, T112-T113, T180-T181, T258-T259, T326-T327 **Unit 5:** T14, T25, T26, T17, T92-T93, T94-T95, T170-T171, T172-T173, T248-T249, T250-T251, T346-T347 **Unit 6:** T24-T25, T102-T103, T248-T249, T250, T252, T326-T327, T328-T329 www.connected.mcgraw-hill.com: **RESOURCES: Units 1–6: Cards:** High-Frequency Word Cards, Spelling Word Cards, Word-Building Cards **Student Practice:** Approaching Reproducibles, Beyond Reproducibles, ELL Reproducibles

Fluency		**McGraw-Hill** *Wonders*
RF.1.4	Read with sufficient accuracy and fluency to support comprehension.	
RF.1.4a	Read grade-level text with purpose and understanding.	**YOUR TURN PRACTICE BOOK:** SS3, SS4, SS9, SS15, SS16, SS21, SS22, SS27, SS28, SS33, SS34, 5, 6, 11, 12, 13, 15, 16, 18, 21, 22, 23, 25, 26, 28, 31, 32, 33, 35, 36, 42, 43, 45, 46, 47, 55, 56, 65, 66, 75, 76, 82, 85, 86, 95, 96, 99, 101, 103, 105, 106, 109, 111, 113, 115, 116, 121, 123, 125, 126, 131, 132, 133, 135, 136, 138, 139, 141, 143, 145, 146, 149, 151, 155, 156, 157, 159, 161, 163, 167, 168, 169, 171, 173, 175, 179, 181, 183, 185, 187, 191, 192, 193, 195, 197, 199, 203, 204, 205, 207, 209, 211, 215, 216, 219, 221, 223, 227, 228, 231, 233, 235, 239, 241, 243, 247, 251, 252, 255, 257, 259, 263, 264, 265, 267, 269, 271, 275, 276, 277, 279, 281, 283, 287, 288, 289, 291, 293, 295, 299, 301, 303, 305, 307, 311, 312, 313, 315, 317, 319, 323, 324, 325, 327, 329 **READING WORKSTATION ACTIVITY CARDS:** 1, 2, 3, 4, 5, 6, 7, 8, 9, 10, 11, 12, 13, 14, 15, 16, 17, 19, 21, 22, 23, 24, 25, 26, 27, 28 **TEACHER'S EDITION:** Unit 1: T16-T17, T104-T105, T250-T251, T328-T329 **Unit 2:** T94-T95, T182-T183 **Unit 3:** T94-T95, T284-T285, T394-T395 **Unit 4:** T104-T105, T172-T173, T394-T395 **Unit 5:** T16-T17, T260-T261, T328-T329, T343, T394-T395 **Unit 6:** T94-T95, T182-T183, T328-T329, T343, T344, T395 www.connected.mcgraw-hill.com: **RESOURCES: Units 1–6: Student Practice:** Reader's Theater, Approaching Reproducibles, Beyond Reproducibles, ELL Reproducibles
RF.1.4b	Read grade-level text orally with accuracy, appropriate rate, and expression.	**YOUR TURN PRACTICE BOOK:** 157, 169, 181, 193, 205, 241, 265, 277, 289, 301, 313, 325 **READING WORKSTATION ACTIVITY CARDS:** 24, 25 **TEACHER'S EDITION:** Unit 1: T31, T113, T125, T191, T265, T394-T395 **Unit 2:** T31, T63, T109, T141, T151, T187, T221, T267, T299, T394-T395 **Unit 3:** T31, T63, T141, T187, T219, T265, T294, T343, T375, T394-T395 **Unit 4:** T31, T47, T109, T187, T203, T219, T265, T297, T343, T359, T375, T394-T395 **Unit 5:** T31, T47, T63, T109, T125, T141, T187, T203, T265, T281, T297, T343, T359, T375, T394-T395 **Unit 6:** T31, T47, T63, T109, T125, T141, T187, T203, T219, T281, T297, T343, T359, T375, T394-T395 www.connected.mcgraw-hill.com: **RESOURCES: Units 1–6: Media:** Fluency Passages **Student Practice:** Reader's Theater, Approaching Reproducibles, Beyond Reproducibles, ELL Reproducibles **Tier 2 Intervention:** Comprehension **Interactive Games & Activities:** Fluency
RF.1.4c	Use context to confirm or self-correct word recognition and understanding, rereading as necessary.	**YOUR TURN PRACTICE BOOK:** 53, 73, 83, 103, 112, 123, 132, 133, 142, 152, 164, 175, 176, 183, 187, 188, 201, 207, 212, 219, 223, 231, 236, 237, 243, 259, 272, 284, 295, 296, 303, 308, 319 **TEACHER'S EDITION:** Unit 1: T39, T394-T395 **Unit 2:** T394-T395 **Unit 3:** T269F, T394-T395 **Unit 4:** T113, T113F, T269, T269G, T394-T395 **Unit 5:** T35 **Unit 6:** T113G www.connected.mcgraw-hill.com: **RESOURCES: Units 1–6: Student Practice:** Reader's Theater, Approaching Reproducibles, Beyond Reproducibles, ELL Reproducibles **Media:** Fluency Passages **Interactive Games & Activities:** Fluency

College and Career Readiness Anchor Standards for WRITING

The K–5 standards on the following pages define what students should understand and be able to do by the end of each grade. They correspond to the College and Career Readiness anchor standards below by number. The CCR and grade-specific standards are necessary complements—the former providing broad standards, the latter providing additional specificity—that together define the skills and understandings that all students must demonstrate.

Text Types and Purposes

1. Write arguments to support claims in an analysis of substantive topics or texts, using valid reasoning and relevant and sufficient evidence.

2. Write informative/explanatory texts to examine and convey complex ideas and information clearly and accurately through the effective selection, organization, and analysis of content.

3. Write narratives to develop real or imagined experiences or events using effective technique, well-chosen details, and well-structured event sequences.

Production and Distribution of Writing

4. Produce clear and coherent writing in which the development, organization, and style are appropriate to task, purpose, and audience.

5. Develop and strengthen writing as needed by planning, revising, editing, rewritings, or trying a new approach.

6. Use technology, including the Internet, to produce and publish writing and to interact and collaborate with others.

Research to Build and Present Knowledge

7. Conduct short as well as more sustained research projects based on focused questions, demonstrating understanding of the subject under investigation.

8. Gather relevant information from multiple print and digital sources, assess the credibility and accuracy of each source, and integrate the information while avoiding plagiarism.

9. Draw evidence from literary or informational texts to support analysis, reflection, and research.

Range of Writing

10. Write routinely over extended time frames (time for research, reflection, and revision) and shorter time frames (a single sitting or a day or two) for a range of tasks, purposes, and audiences.

CCSS Common Core State Standards
English Language Arts
Grade 1

Writing Standards

Text Types and Purposes		McGraw-Hill *Wonders*
W.1.1	Write opinion pieces in which they introduce the topic or name the book they are writing about, state an opinion, supply a reason for the opinion, and provide some sense of closure.	**CLOSE READING COMPANION:** 36, 90, 109, 135, 162, 195 **YOUR TURN PRACTICE BOOK:** 60, 140, 150, 222 **READING/WRITING WORKSHOP: Unit 2:** 26-27, **Unit 3:** 86-87, 106-107 **Unit 4:** 50-51 **Unit 5:** 132-133, 212-213 **Unit 6:** 315-316 **READING WORKSTATION ACTIVITY CARDS:** 14 **WRITING WORKSTATION ACTIVITY CARDS:** 4, 11, 26, 30 **TEACHER'S EDITION: Unit 2:** T18, T28-T29, T36, T42 **Unit 3:** T252, T262-T263, T270, T276, T340-T341, T348, T354 **Unit 4:** T96, T106-T107, T114, T120 **Unit 5:** T18, T28-T29, T36, T42, T330, T340-T341, T348, T354 **Unit 6:** T330, T340-T341, T348, T354 www.connected.mcgraw-hill.com: **RESOURCES: Units 1-6: Teacher Resources:** Writer's Checklists/ Proofreading Marks
W.1.2	Write informative/explanatory texts in which they name a topic, supply some facts about the topic, and provide some sense of closure.	**CLOSE READING COMPANION:** 24, 50, 57, 83, 90, 96 **YOUR TURN PRACTICE BOOK:** 10, 20, 40, 50, 70, 80, 100, 162, 174, 186, 198, 210, 234, 246, 294, 306 **READING/WRITING WORKSHOP: Unit 1:** 26-27, 46-47, 86-87, 106-107 **Unit 2:** 26-27, 46-47, 66-67, 106-107 **Unit 4:** 70-71, 91-92, 110-111 **Unit 5:** 151-152, 173-174 **Unit 6:** 192-193 **LITERATURE ANTHOLOGY: Unit 2:** 60, 80 **Unit 3:** 44, 88 **Unit 4:** 54 **LEVELED READERS: Unit 4, Week 3:** *Go, Gator!* p. 16 (B) **Unit 5, Week 3:** *The Wright Brothers,* p. 16 (B) **Unit 6, Week 5:** *It's Labor Day!* p. 16 (O, B) **READING WORKSTATION ACTIVITY CARDS:** 10 **SCIENCE & SOCIAL STUDIES WORKSTATION ACTIVITY CARDS:** 9, 19, 27 **READING WORKSTATION ACTIVITY CARDS:** 5, 6, 9, 10, 27, 28, 29 **TEACHER'S EDITION: Unit 1:** T18, T28-T29, T36, T42, T96, T106-T107, T114, T120, T252, T262-T263, T270, T330, T340-T341, T348 **Unit 2:** T18, T96, T106-T107, T114, T120-T121, T126, T174, T184-T185, T192, T252, T262, T270, T330, T340-T341, T348 **Unit 3:** T330 **Unit 4:** T96, T174, T184-T185, T198, T252, T262-T263, T270, T330, T340-T341, T348 **Unit 5:** T18, T96, T106-T107, T114, T174, T184-T185, T192, T330 **Unit 6:** T18, T96, T106-T107, T114, T174, T184-T185, T192, T330 www.connected.mcgraw-hill.com: **RESOURCES: Units 1-6: Teacher Resources:** Writer's Checklists/ Proofreading Marks
W.1.3	Write narratives in which they recount two or more appropriately sequenced events, include some details regarding what happened, use temporal words to signal event order, and provide some sense of closure.	**READING/WRITING WORKSHOP: Unit 1:** 66-67 **Unit 2:** 86-87 **Unit 3:** 26-27, 46-47, 66-67 **Unit 4:** 30-31 **Unit 5:** 132-133 **Unit 6:** 234-235, 294-295 **LITERATURE ANTHOLOGY: Unit 3:** 22, 66 **Unit 4:** 124 **Unit 5:** 154, 254 **Unit 6:** 322 **LEVELED READERS: Unit 2, Week 1:** *Ben Brings the Mail,* p. 16 (O,B) **Unit 3, Week 3:** *The Storytelling Stone,* p. 16 (B) **Unit 4, Week 1:** *Fly to the Rescue!* p. 16 (O), *Hummingbird's Wings,* p. 16 (B) **Unit 5, Week 1:** *Spark's Toys* (B) **Unit 6, Week 1:** *Beware of the Lion!* p. 16 (B) **Unit 6, Week 4:** *Patty Jumps!* (B) **CLOSE READING COMPANION:** 17, 57, 69, 76, 83, 102, 156, 168, 189 **YOUR TURN PRACTICE BOOK:** 30, 90, 110, 120, 130, 258, 272, 318, 330 **READING WORKSTATION ACTIVITY CARDS:** 10, 16 **WRITING WORKSTATION ACTIVITY CARDS:** 21, 23 **TEACHER'S EDITION: Unit 1:** T174, T184-T185, T192 **Unit 2:** T252, T262-T263, T270 **Unit 3:** T18, T28-T29, T36, T96, T106-T107, T114, T174, T184-T185, T192 **Unit 4:** T18, T28-T29, T36 **Unit 5:** T252, T262-T263, T270 **Unit 6:** T18, T28-T29, T36, T252, T262-T263, T270 www.connected.mcgraw-hill.com: **RESOURCES: Units 1-6: Teacher Resources:** Writer's Checklists/ Proofreading Marks

Writing Standards

Production and Distribution of Writing		McGraw-Hill *Wonders*
W.1.4	(Begins in grade 3)	
W.1.5	With guidance and support from adults, focus on a topic, respond to questions and suggestions from peers, and add details to strengthen writing as needed.	**YOUR TURN PRACTICE BOOK:** 20, 30, 40, 100, 110, 120, 150, 234, 282, 294 **WRITING WORKSTATION ACTIVITY CARDS:** 1, 2, 3, 4, 5, 6, 7, 8, 9, 10, 11, 12, 13, 14, 15, 16, 17, 18, 19, 20, 21, 22, 23, 24, 25, 26, 27, 28, 29, 30 **TEACHER'S EDITION: Unit 1:** T42-T43, T120-T121, T174, T198-T199, T252, T276-T277, T330, T354-T355 **Unit 2:** T42-T43, T120-T121, T174, T198-T199, T252, T276-T277, T330, T354-T355 **Unit 3:** T42-T43, T120-T121, T174, T198-T199, T252, T276-T277, T330, T354-T355 **Unit 4:** T42-T43, T120-T121, T174, T198-T199, T252, T276-T277, T330, T354-T355 **Unit 5:** T42-T43, T120-T121, T174, T198-T199, T252, T276-T277, T330, T354-T355 **Unit 6:** T42-T43, T120-T121, T174, T198-T199, T252, T276-T277, T330, T354-T355 **www.connected.mcgraw-hill.com: RESOURCES: Units 1-6: Graphic Organizers:** Graphic Organizers **Teacher Resources:** Writer's Checklists/Proofreading Marks
W.1.6	With guidance and support from adults, use a variety of digital tools to produce and publish writing, including in collaboration with peers.	**TEACHER'S EDITION: Unit 1:** T36, T48, T114, T122, T126, T192, T204, T270, T282, T348, T360, T397, T398-T399, T400-T401, T402 **Unit 2:** T36, T48, T114, T126, T192, T204, T270, T282, T348, T360, T397, T398-T399, T400-T401, T402 **Unit 3:** T36, T48, T114, T126, T192, T204, T270, T282, T348, T360, T397, T398-T399, T400-T401, T402 **Unit 4:** T36, T48, T114, T126, T192, T204, T270, T282, T348, T360, T397, T398-T399, T400-T401, T402 **Unit 5:** T36, T48, T114, T126, T192, T204, T270, T282, T348, T360, T397, T398-T399, T400-T401, T402 **Unit 6:** T36, T48, T114, T126, T192, T204, T270, T282, T348, T360, T397, T398-T399, T400-T401, T402 **www.connected.mcgraw-hill.com: RESOURCES: Units 1-6: Time for Kids Online Articles, Research & Inquiry:** Weekly Lessons **Teacher Resources:** Writer's Checklists/Proofreading Marks; **Digital Resources and Tools:** Writer's Workspace; Graphic Organizers; My Binder (My Work, My Portfolio); Collaborate (Projects)

Research to Build and Present Knowledge		McGraw-Hill *Wonders*
W.1.7	Participate in shared research and writing projects (e.g., explore a number of "how-to" books on a given topic and use them to write a sequence of instructions).	**TEACHER'S EDITION: Unit 1:** T44-T45, T51, T122-T123, T207, T278-T279, T285, T356-T357, T363, T379, T397, T398-T399, T400-T401 **Unit 2:** T44-T45, T51, T122-T123, T129, T207, T202-T203, T285, T362-T363, T359, T397, T398-T399, T400-T401 **Unit 3:** T44-T45, T51, T122-T123, T129, T200-T201, T207, T278-T279, T285, T356-T357, T363, T397, T398-T399, T400-T401 **Unit 4:** T44-T45, T51, T122-T123, T129, T200-T201, T207, T278-T279, T285, T356-T357, T363, T397, T398-T399, T400-T401 **Unit 5:** T44-T45, T51, T122-T123, T129, T200-T201, T278-T279, T285, T356-T357, T363, T397, T398-T399, T400-T401 **Unit 6:** T44-T45, T51, T122-T123, T129, T200-T201, T207, T278-T279, T285, T356-T357, T363, T397, T398-T399, T400-T401 **www.connected.mcgraw-hill.com: RESOURCES: Units 1-6: Research & Inquiry:** Weekly Lessons **Teacher Resources:** Writer's Checklists/Proofreading Marks **Graphic Organizers:** Foldables
W.1.8	With guidance and support from adults, recall information from experiences or gather information from provided sources to answer a question.	**LEVELED READERS: Unit 1, Week 3:** *A Mouse in the House*, pp. 13–16 (A), *Love That Llama!* pp. 13–16 (O), *Birds That Talk*, pp. 13–16 (B) **Unit 1, Week 4:** *I Like to Play*, pp. 13–16 (A, O, B) **Unit 2, Week 3:** *I Live in a House!* (A, O, B) **Unit 4, Week 2:** *Animals Work Together!* pp. 13–16 (A, O); pp. 12–16 (B) **Unit 4, Week 3:** *Ducklings* (A) **Unit 4, Week 4:** *Let's Look at Insects!* pp. 13–16 (O), *Compare Insects*, pp. 13–16 (B) **Unit 5, Week 2:** *Hello, Little Dipper!* pp. 13–16 (A), *Our Sun Is a Star!* pp. 13–16 (O), *Sunrise and Sunset*, pp. 13–16 (B) **Unit 5, Week 3:** *Fly Away, Butterfly*, pp. 13–16 (A, O); pp. 12–16 (B) **Unit 6, Week 5:** *Four Voyages*, pp. 13–16 (A, O); pp. 12–16 (B) **SCIENCE & SOCIAL STUDIES WORKSTATION ACTIVITY CARDS:** 4, 5, 6, 7, 8, 9, 10, 11, 12, 13, 14, 15, 16, 17, 18, 19, 20, 22, 23, 24, 25, 26, 27, 28, 29, 30 **WRITING WORKSTATION ACTIVITY CARDS:** 1, 2, 3, 4, 5, 6, 7, 8, 9, 10, 11, 12, 13, 14, 15, 16, 17, 18, 19, 20, 21, 22, 23, 24, 25, 26, 27, 29, 30 **INTERACTIVE READ-ALOUD CARDS: Unit 1, Week 3:** 1 **Unit 3, Week 1:** 1, 3 **Unit 5, Week 1:** 3 **Unit 5, Week 2:** 1 **Unit 5, Week 4:** 1 **Unit 6, Week 2:** 1 **Unit 6, Week 5:** 2 **TEACHER'S EDITION: Unit 1:** T200, T398-T399, T400 **Unit 2:** T398-T399, T400 **Unit 3:** T200-T201, T398-T399, T400-T401 **Unit 4:** T122, T398-T399, T400 **Unit 5:** T44, T122, T200-T201, T278, T398-T399, T400 **Unit 6:** T44, T129, T278, T398-T399, T400 **www.connected.mcgraw-hill.com: RESOURCES: Units 1-6: Research & Inquiry:** Weekly Lessons, Note-taking Tools **Graphic Organizers:** Graphic Organizers
W.1.9	(Begins in grade 4)	

Range of Writing		McGraw-Hill *Wonders*
W.1.10	(Begins in grade 3)	

College and Career Readiness Anchor Standards for SPEAKING AND LISTENING

The K–5 standards on the following pages define what students should understand and be able to do by the end of each grade. They correspond to the College and Career Readiness anchor standards below by number. The CCR and grade-specific standards are necessary complements—the former providing broad standards, the latter providing additional specificity—that together define the skills and understandings that all students must demonstrate.

Comprehension and Collaboration

1. Prepare for and participate effectively in a range of conversations and collaborations with diverse partners, building on others' ideas and expressing their own clearly and persuasively.

2. Integrate and evaluate information presented in diverse media and formats, including visually, quantitatively, and orally.

3. Evaluate a speaker's point of view, reasoning, and use of evidence and rhetoric.

Presentation of Knowledge and Ideas

4. Present information, findings, and supporting evidence such that listeners can follow the line of reasoning and the organization, development, and style are appropriate to task, purpose, and audience.

5. Make strategic use of digital media and visual displays of data to express information and enhance understanding of presentations.

6. Adapt speech to a variety of contexts and communicative tasks, demonstrating command of formal English when indicated or appropriate.

CCSS Common Core State Standards

English Language Arts

Grade 1

Speaking and Listening Standards

Comprehension and Collaboration		McGraw-Hill *Wonders*
SL.1.1	Participate in collaborative conversations with diverse partners about *grade 1 topics and texts* with peers and adults in small and larger groups.	
SL.1.1a	Follow agreed-upon rules for discussions (e.g., listening to others with care, speaking one at a time about the topics and texts under discussion).	**CLOSE READING COMPANION:** 5, 44, 65, 124 **PHONICS WORKSTATION ACTIVITY CARDS:** 3, 10, 11, 12, 17, 18, 19, 20, 22, 23, 24, 30 **READING WORKSTATION ACTIVITY CARDS:** 1, 2, 3, 4, 5, 6, 7, 8, 9, 10, 11, 12, 13, 14, 15, 16, 17, 19, 20, 21, 22, 23, 24, 25, 26, 27, 28 **TEACHER'S EDITION: Unit 1:** T9, T48, T50-51, T87, T128-T129, T165, T282, T284-T285, T360 **Unit 2:** T48, T87, T122, T126, T128-T129, T165, T200, T204, T276-T277, T284-T285, T321, T356, T360, T362-T363, T403 **Unit 3:** T9, T165, T200, T204, T206-T207, T243, T278, T321, T356, T360, T362-T363, T403 **Unit 4:** T48, T87, T122, T126, T165, T200, T243, T278, T284-T285, T356, T403 **Unit 5:** T44, T48, T50-T51, T87, T122, T165, T200, T282, T284-T285, T321, T403 **Unit 6:** T48, T87, T122, T126, T165, T200, T206-T207, T282, T321, T356, T403 **www.connected.mcgraw-hill.com: RESOURCES: Units 1–6: Media:** Images, Videos **Collaborative Conversations Videos Teacher Resources:** Speaking and Listening Checklists
SL.1.1b	Build on others' talk in conversations by responding to the comments of others through multiple exchanges.	**READING WORKSTATION ACTIVITY CARDS:** 2, 5, 10, 13, 16 **TEACHER'S EDITION: Unit 1:** T42-T43, T128-T129, T276-T277, T320, T321, T354-T355, T356, T403 **Unit 2:** T9, T42-T43, T44, T49, T50-T51, T206-T207, T354-T355, T362-T363, T403 **Unit 3:** T42-T43, T87, T122, T198-T199, T206-T207, T276-T277, T354-T355, T403 **Unit 4:** T50-T51, T120-T121, T128, T276-T277, T354-T355, T362-T363, T401, T403 **Unit 5:** T120-T121, T128-T129, T354-T355, T362-T363, T403 **Unit 6:** T42-T43, T198, T278, T284-T285, T403 **www.connected.mcgraw-hill.com: RESOURCES: Units 1–6: Media:** Images, Videos **Teacher Resources:** Speaking and Listening Checklists
SL.1.1c	Ask questions to clear up any confusion about the topics and texts under discussion.	**TEACHER'S EDITION: Unit 1:** T20, T98, T164 **Unit 2:** T128-T129, T204, T242, T282, T284-T285, T403 **Unit 3:** T120-T121, T282, T284-T285, T321, T356, T403 **Unit 4:** T9, T44, T50-T51, T96, T106-T107, T122, T206-T207, T276-T277, T282, T403 **Unit 5:** T9, T198-T199, T206-T207, T243, T278, T403 **Unit 6:** T9, T44, T120-T121, T128-T129, T321, T354-T355, T362-T363, T403 **www.connected.mcgraw-hill.com: RESOURCES: Units 1–6: Graphic Organizers:** Graphic Organizers, Think Aloud Clouds **Teacher Resources:** Speaking and Listening Checklists
SL.1.2	Ask and answer questions about key details in a text read aloud or information presented orally or through other media.	**CLOSE READING COMPANION:** 1-3, 11-13, 33, 44-46, 66, 74-76, 97-98, 114-116, 163-164, 187-189 **READING WORKSTATION ACTIVITY CARDS:** 2, 6, 11, 13, 14 **INTERACTIVE READ-ALOUD CARDS: Unit 1, Week 1:** 1, 2, 4 **Unit 1, Week 2:** 1, 3, 4 **Unit 1, Week 3:** 4 **Unit 1, Week 4:** 4 **Unit 2, Week 3:** 4 **Unit 2, Week 4:** 2 **Unit 3, Week 1:** 4 **Unit 3, Week 2:** 4 **Unit 3, Week 3:** 2, 4 **Unit 3, Week 4:** 1, 3, 4 **Unit 3, Week 5:** 4 **Unit 4, Week 1:** 3 **Unit 4, Week 2:** 4 **Unit 4, Week 3:** 1, 3, 4 **Unit 4, Week 4:** 2 **Unit 5, Week 1:** 4 **Unit 5, Week 2:** 4 **Unit 5, Week 3:** 4 **Unit 5, Week 4:** 4 **Unit 5, Week 5:** 4 **Unit 6, Week 1:** 4 **Unit 6, Week 2:** 4 **Unit 6, Week 3:** 4 **Unit 6, Week 4:** 4 **TEACHER'S EDITION: Unit 1:** S8, S14, S26, S38, S44, S50, S56, S68, S74, S80, S86, T48, T50-T51, T198-T199, T206-T207, T245, T255, T284, T403 **Unit 2:** T20, T99, T120-T121, T126, T177, T198-T199, T255, T403 **Unit 3:** T11, T21, T31, T89, T99, T109, T126, T128-T129, T167, T177, T245, T255, T282, T333, T360, T403 **Unit 4:** T11, T21, T89, T99, T126, T167, T177, T255, T282, T284-T285, T333, T403 **Unit 5:** T21, T50-T51, T99, T245, T255, T282, T333, T403 **Unit 6:** T21, T28-T29, T48, T99, T206-T207, T284-T285, T333, T360, T403 **www.connected.mcgraw-hill.com: RESOURCES: Units 1–6: Graphic Organizers:** Think Aloud Clouds **Teacher Resources:** Speaking and Listening Checklists

Speaking and Listening Standards

SL.1.3	Ask and answer questions about what a speaker says in order to gather additional information or clarify something that is not understood.	**TEACHER'S EDITION: Unit I:** TI26, TI65, T206-T207, T243, T282, T284-T285, T360, T403 **Unit 2:** T48, T206-T207, T243, T360, T403 **Unit 3:** T9, T50-T5I, TI26, TI28-TI29, T32I, T360, T403 **Unit 4:** T9, T48, T87, TI28-TI29, T204, T282, T32I, T362-T363, T403 **Unit 5:** T9, TI28-TI29, TI65, T243, T282, T284-T285, T360, T403 **Unit 6:** T9, T48, T50-T5I, T204, T32I, T362-T363, T403 www.connected.mcgraw-hill.com: **RESOURCES: Units I-6: Research & Inquiry:** Note-taking tools **Graphic Organizers:** Graphic Organizers **Teacher Resources:** Speaking and Listening Checklists

Presentation of Knowledge and Ideas		**McGraw-Hill** *Wonders*
SL.1.4	Describe people, places, things, and events with relevant details, expressing ideas and feelings clearly.	**LITERATURE ANTHOLOGY: Unit I:** 47, 63, 85, 86, 94, 95 **Unit 2:** 25, 43, 47 **Unit 5:** I95, 259 **Unit 6:** 392 **LEVELED READERS: Unit I, Week 2:** *My Home,* pp. I3-I6 (A), *Where I Live,* pp. I3-I6 (O), *Where We Live,* pp. I3-I6 (B) **Unit 2, Week 3:** *I Live in a House!* pp. I3-I6 (A, O, B) **Unit 2, Week 4:** *The Sick Tree* (A), *Squirrels Help* (O) **Unit 3, Week 4:** *School Days,* pp. I3-I6 (A, O); pp. I2-I6 (B) **Unit 4, Week I:** *Animal Traits,* pp. I3-I6 (O) **Unit 4, Week 5:** *Working with Dolphins,* pp. I3-I6 (A, O); pp. I2-I6 (B) **Unit 5, Week I:** *Nuts for Winter* (A), *Spark's Toys* (B) **Unit 5, Week 2:** *Hello, Little Dipper!* pp. I3-I6 (A), *Our Sun Is a Star!* pp. I3-I6 (O), *Sunrise and Sunset,* pp. I3-I6 (B) **Unit 6, Week 4:** *The Quilt* (A), *Latkes for Sam* (O) **Unit 6, Week 5:** *Four Voyages,* pp. I3-I6 (A, O); pp. I2-I6 (B) **READING WORKSTATION ACTIVITY CARDS:** I, 2, 3, 4, 7, 8, 9, I0, I3, I5 **SCIENCE & SOCIAL STUDIES WORKSTATION ACTIVITY CARDS:** 2, 3, 4, 5, 6, 7, 8, 9, I0, I2, I3, I4, I5, I6, I7, I8, I9, 20-30 **WRITING WORKSTATION ACTIVITY CARDS:** I-I0, II, I2, I3, I4, I5, I6, I7, I9, 20, 2I, 22, 23, 24, 25, 26, 27, 28, 29 **INTERACTIVE READ-ALOUD CARDS: Unit I, Week I:** 2 **Unit I, Week 2:** 3 **Unit I, Week 3:** 3 **Unit 3, Week I:** 2, 3 **Unit 3, Week 2:** I **Unit 3, Week 4:** I **Unit 6, Week 4:** 3 **TEACHER'S EDITION: Unit I:** S26, S50, S74, T9, T50-T5I, T87, T98, TI26, TI28, T204, T282, T284, T32I, T360, T362-T363 **Unit 2:** T9, T50-T5I, T87, T206-T207, T245, T32I, T360, T362-T363 **Unit 3:** T9, T48, T87, T89, TII3J, TI26, TI28-TI29, TI65, T206-T207, T243, T284-T285, T32I **Unit 4:** T9, T48, T50-T5I, T87, TI65, T206-T207, T243, T269R, T282, T360, T362-T363 **Unit 5:** T9, T48, T50-T5I, T87, TII3R, TI26, TI65, T204, T243, T273, T284-T285, T32I, T360, T362-T363 **Unit 6:** T48, T87, TI26, TI77, T243, T282, T360, T362-T363 www.connected.mcgraw-hill.com: **RESOURCES: Unit I: Graphic Organizers:** Graphic Organizers
SL.1.5	Add drawings or other visual displays to descriptions when appropriate to clarify ideas, thoughts, and feelings.	**LITERATURE ANTHOLOGY: Unit I:** I8, 40, 62, 82 **Unit 2:** 20, 42, 80 **Unit 3:** 22, 44, 66, 88 **Unit 4:** 28, 88, I24 **Unit 5:** I94 **Unit 6:** 356, 392 **LEVELED READERS: Unit I, Week 2:** *Where I Live,* pp. I3-I6 (O) **Unit 2, Week 3:** *I Live in a House!* pp. I3-I6 (A, O, B) **Unit 3, Week 4:** *School Days,* pp. I3-I6 (A, O); pp. I2-I6 (B) **Unit 4, Week 3:** *Ducklings,* pp. I3-I6 (A, O); pp. I2-I6 (B) **Unit 5, Week 3:** *Fly Away, Butterfly,* pp. I3-I6 (A, O); pp. I2-I6 (B) **Unit 6, Week I:** *What a Feast* (O) **YOUR TURN PRACTICE BOOK:** I65, I89, 225, 249, 26I, 285 **READING WORKSTATION ACTIVITY CARDS:** I, 2, 3, 4, 5, 6, 7, 8, 9, I0, II, I2, I3, I5, I7, I9, 20, 23, 26, 27, 28 **SCIENCE & SOCIAL STUDIES WORKSTATION ACTIVITY CARDS:** 2, 3, 4, 5, 6, 7, 8, 9, I0, I2, I3, I4, I5, I6, I7, I8, I9, 20, 2I, 22, 23, 24, 25, 26, 27, 28, 29, 30 **WRITING WORKSTATION ACTIVITY CARDS:** I, 2, 3, 4, 5, 6, 7, 9, I0, I3, I4, I7, 20, 2I, 22, 23, 24, 25, 26, 27, 28, 29 **TEACHER'S EDITION: Unit I:** T43, T45, T48, T5I, T48, TI2I, TI23, TI26, TI28-TI29, TI9IJ, T204, T279, T284-T285, T355, T360, T398-T399 **Unit 2:** T43, T48, T50-T5I, TI2I, T282, T284-T285 **Unit 3:** T48, TI2I, TI26, TI98, TI99, T204, T277, T279, T282, T284-T285, T360, T362-T363 **Unit 4:** T42-T43, T48, TI2I, TI23, TI26, TI28-TI29, TI99, T204, T282, T354-T355, T357, T360 **Unit 5:** T43, TI2I, TI23, TI26, TI28-TI29, TI99, T204, T206-T207, T276-T277, T282, T360 **Unit 6:** T43, T48, TI2I, TI23, TI26, TI28-TI29, T204, T276-T277, T282, T360
SL.1.6	Produce complete sentences when appropriate to task and situation.	**LEVELED READERS: Unit 3, Week I:** *Busy's Watch* (A), *Kate Saves the Date!* (O), *Uncle George Is Coming!* (B) **Unit 5, Week 2:** *Sunrise and Sunset,* pp. I3-I6 (B) **Unit 6, Week I:** *Two Hungry Elephants* (A) **Unit 6, Week 2:** *Fire!* pp. I3-I6 (A, O); pp. I2-I6 (B) **YOUR TURN PRACTICE BOOK:** 2, I2, I7, 22, 32, 5I, 52, 58, 6I, 62, 7I, 72, 8I, 9I, 92, 93, I0I, III, I5I, I65, I89, 2II, 22I, 225, 249 **SCIENCE & SOCIAL STUDIES WORKSTATION ACTIVITY CARDS:** 2, 4, 5, 6, 7, 8, 9, I2, I4, I5, I7, I8, I9, 20, 23, 24, 25, 26, 27 **WRITING WORKSTATION ACTIVITY CARDS:** I, 2, 3, 4, 5, 6, 7, 8, 9, I0, II, I2, I3, I4, I5, I6, I7, I8, I9, 20-30 **INTERACTIVE READ-ALOUD CARDS: Unit I, Week 4:** 3 **Unit I, Week 5:** I **Unit 2, Week I:** I **Unit 2, Week 3:** 3 **Unit 3, Week 4:** 2 **Unit 4, Week I:** 2 **Unit 4, Week 4:** I **Unit 5, Week 5:** 2 **Unit 6, Week 3:** I **TEACHER'S EDITION: Unit I:** S5, SI4, TI9, T37, T43, T48, TI75, TI85, TI93, T206-T207, T34I, T355, T362-T363 **Unit 2:** T9, TI9, T29, TI28-TI29, TI75, TI93, T354 **Unit 3:** T37, T43, T48, T87, TI65, T204, T253, T27I, T362-T363 **Unit 4:** T9, TI07, TI9I, T253, T263, T282, T284-T285, T32I, T360 **Unit 5:** TI9, T29, T42-T43, T48, TI26, TI85, TI99, T204, T206-T207, T277, T362-T363 **Unit 6:** T9, TI9, T29, T42-T43, TI28-TI29, TI65, TI98-TI99, T206-T207, T243, T253, T360, T263

College and Career Readiness Anchor Standards for
LANGUAGE

The K–5 standards on the following pages define what students should understand and be able to do by the end of each grade. They correspond to the College and Career Readiness anchor standards below by number. The CCR and grade-specific standards are necessary complements—the former providing broad standards, the latter providing additional specificity—that together define the skills and understandings that all students must demonstrate.

Conventions of Standard English

1. Demonstrate command of the conventions of standard English grammar and usage when writing or speaking.

2. Demonstrate command of the conventions of standard English capitalization, punctuation, and spelling when writing.

Knowledge of Language

3. Apply knowledge of language to understand how language functions in different contexts, to make effective choices for meaning or style, and to comprehend more fully when reading or listening.

Vocabulary Acquisition and Use

4. Determine or clarify the meaning of unknown and multiple-meaning words and phrases by using context clues, analyzing meaningful word parts, and consulting general and specialized reference materials, as appropriate.

5. Demonstrate understanding of word relationships and nuances in word meanings.

6. Acquire and use accurately a range of general academic and domain-specific words and phrases sufficient for reading, writing, speaking, and listening at the college and career readiness level; demonstrate independence in gathering vocabulary knowledge when encountering an unknown term important to comprehension or expression.

CORRELATIONS

Language Standards

Conventions of Standard English	McGraw-Hill *Wonders*
L.1.1	Demonstrate command of the conventions of standard English grammar and usage when writing or speaking.
L.1.1a Print all upper- and lowercase letters.	**YOUR TURN PRACTICE BOOK:** SS5, SS8, SS12, SS17, SS20, SS24, SS29, SS32, SS36 **TEACHER'S EDITION: Unit 1:** T13, T91, T169, T247 **Unit 2:** T13, T91, T120, T169, T247, T325 **Unit 3:** T13, T91, T169, T247, T276 **Unit 4:** T13, T42, T91, T169, T247, T325 **Unit 5:** T13, T91, T169, T247 **Unit 6:** T13, T91, T169, T247 **www.connected.mcgraw-hill.com: RESOURCES: Unit 1: Student Practice:** Grammar Practice, Approaching Reproducibles, Beyond Reproducibles, ELL Reproducibles **Interactive Games & Activities:** Writing & Grammar
L.1.1b Use common, proper, and possessive nouns.	**READING/WRITING WORKSHOP: Unit 2:** 27, 47, 67, 87, 107 **YOUR TURN PRACTICE BOOK:** 2, 32, 49, 59, 92, 102, 112, 132, 152, 165, 176, 213, 237, 248, 261, 272, 273, 284, 296, 297, 321 **PHONICS WORKSTATION ACTIVITY CARDS:** 5 **TEACHER'S EDITION: Unit 2:** T19, T28-T29, T37, T43, T97, T107, T115, T175, T184-T185, T193, T199, T205, T253, T262-T263, T271-T272, T276-T277, T281 **Unit 3:** T42 **Unit 4:** T199, T276 **Unit 5:** T36, T42, T121, T114, T198 **Unit 6:** T120 **www.connected.mcgraw-hill.com: RESOURCES: Unit 2: Student Practice:** Grammar Practice, Approaching Reproducibles, Beyond Reproducibles, ELL Reproducibles **Interactive Games & Activities:** Writing & Grammar **Unit 4: Student Practice:** Grammar Practice, Approaching Reproducibles, Beyond Reproducibles, ELL Reproducibles **Interactive Games & Activities:** Writing & Grammar **Unit 5: Student Practice:** Grammar Practice, Approaching Reproducibles, Beyond Reproducibles, ELL Reproducibles **Interactive Games & Activities:** Writing & Grammar
L.1.1c Use singular and plural nouns with matching verbs in basic sentences (e.g., *He hops; We hop*).	**READING/WRITING WORKSHOP: Unit 3:** 47, 87 **Unit 4:** 31, 51 **YOUR TURN PRACTICE BOOK:** 2, 8 **PHONICS WORKSTATION ACTIVITY CARDS:** 5 **TEACHER'S EDITION: Unit 2:** T106, T017 **Unit 3:** T97, T106, T107, T252-T253, T262-T263, T270-T271, T276-T277, T283-T284 **Unit 4:** T18-T19, T28-T29, T36-T37, T42-T43, T48-T49, T114 **Unit 5:** T42 **www.connected.mcgraw-hill.com: RESOURCES: Units 3: Student Practice:** Grammar Practice, Approaching Reproducibles, Beyond Reproducibles, ELL Reproducibles **Interactive Games & Activities:** Writing & Grammar **Unit 4:** Approaching Reproducibles, Beyond Reproducibles, ELL Reproducibles, Grammar Practice, Interactive Games & Activities (Writing & Grammar)
L.1.1d Use personal, possessive, and indefinite pronouns (e.g., *I, me, my; they, them, their; anyone, everything*).	**READING/WRITING WORKSHOP: Unit 6:** 235, 254, 255, 275, 295 **YOUR TURN PRACTICE BOOK:** SS3, SS4, SS9, SS15, SS16, SS21, SS22, SS27, SS28, SS33, SS34, 32, 152, 296, 308, 309 **WRITING WORKSTATION ACTIVITY CARDS:** 21 **TEACHER'S EDITION: Unit 6:** T18, T19, T28-T29, T36-T37, T42-T43, T48-T49, T96-T97, T106-T107, T114-T115, T121, T127, T175, T185, T193, T198, T199, T205, T252-T253, T262-T263, T270-T271, T276, T277, T283 **www.connected.mcgraw-hill.com: RESOURCES: Unit 6: Student Practice:** Grammar Practice, Approaching Reproducibles, Beyond Reproducibles, ELL Reproducibles **Interactive Games & Activities:** Writing & Grammar

Language Standards

Conventions of Standard English		McGraw-Hill *Wonders*
L.1.1e	Use verbs to convey a sense of past, present, and future (e.g., *Yesterday I walked home; Today I walk home; Tomorrow I will walk home*).	**READING/WRITING WORKSHOP: Unit 3:** 27, 47, 67 **Unit 4:** 71, 91 **YOUR TURN PRACTICE BOOK:** 58, 78, 225 **PHONICS WORKSTATION ACTIVITY CARDS:** 5 **TEACHER'S EDITION: Unit 3:** T96-T97, T106-T107, T114-T115, T120-T121, T127-T128, T175, T185, T193, T198, T199, T205, T252-T253, T263, T271, T276, T277, T283 **Unit 4:** T19, T29, T42, T43, T49, T175, T185, T193, T198, T199, T205, T252-T253, T262-T263, T271, T276-T277, T282-T283 **Unit 5:** T198 www.connected.mcgraw-hill.com: **RESOURCES: Unit 3: Student Practice:** Grammar Practice, Approaching Reproducibles, Beyond Reproducibles, ELL Reproducibles **Interactive Games & Activities:** Writing & Grammar **Unit 4: Student Practice:** Grammar Practice, Approaching Reproducibles, Beyond Reproducibles, ELL Reproducibles **Interactive Games & Activities:** Writing & Grammar
L.1.1f	Use frequently occurring adjectives.	**READING/WRITING WORKSHOP: Unit 5:** 152-153, 173 **YOUR TURN PRACTICE BOOK:** SS15, SS16, SS33, SS34, 22, 42, 52, 62, 92, 102, 112, 122, 132, 142, 152, 153, 164, 165, 176, 185, 189, 201, 212, 213, 236, 237, 248, 256, 272, 293, 309 **WRITING WORKSTATION ACTIVITY CARDS:** 17, 22, 25 **TEACHER'S EDITION: Unit 5:** T96-T97, T106-T107, T114-T115, T120-T121, T126-T127, T174-T175, T184-T185, T192-T193, T198-T199, T204-T205 **Unit 6:** T276 www.connected.mcgraw-hill.com: **RESOURCES: Unit 5: Student Practice:** Grammar Practice, Approaching Reproducibles, Beyond Reproducibles, ELL Reproducibles **Interactive Games & Activities:** Writing & Grammar
L.1.1g	Use frequently occurring conjunctions (e.g., *and, but, or, so, because*).	**READING/WRITING WORKSHOP: Unit 5:** 133 **YOUR TURN PRACTICE BOOK:** SS15, SS16, SS21, SS22, 164 **TEACHER'S EDITION: Unit 5:** T18-T19, T28-T29, T36-T37, T42-T43, T48-T49 **Unit 6:** T120 www.connected.mcgraw-hill.com: **RESOURCES: Unit 5: Student Practice:** Grammar Practice, Approaching Reproducibles, Beyond Reproducibles, ELL Reproducibles **Interactive Games & Activities:** Writing & Grammar
L.1.1h	Use determiners (e.g., articles, demonstratives).	**READING/WRITING WORKSHOP: Unit 5:** 193 **YOUR TURN PRACTICE BOOK:** SS3, SS4, SS9, SS15, SS16, SS21, SS22, SS27, SS28, SS33, SS34 **TEACHER'S EDITION: Unit 5:** T252-T253, T262-T263, T270-T271, T276-T277, T282-T283 **Unit 6:** T42 www.connected.mcgraw-hill.com: **RESOURCES: Unit 5: Student Practice:** Grammar Practice, Approaching Reproducibles, Beyond Reproducibles, ELL Reproducibles **Interactive Games & Activities:** Writing & Grammar
L.1.1i	Use frequently occurring prepositions (e.g., *during, beyond, toward*).	**READING/WRITING WORKSHOP: Unit 5:** 213 **YOUR TURN PRACTICE BOOK:** SS9, SS33, SS34, 72, 92, 122, 142, 152, 164, 176, 308 **TEACHER'S EDITION: Unit 5:** T330-T331, T340-T341, T348-T349, T354-T355, T360-T361 **Unit 6:** T198 www.connected.mcgraw-hill.com: **RESOURCES: Unit 5: Student Practice:** Grammar Practice, Approaching Reproducibles, Beyond Reproducibles, ELL Reproducibles **Interactive Games & Activities:** Writing & Grammar
L.1.1j	Produce and expand complete simple and compound declarative, interrogative, imperative, and exclamatory sentences in response to prompts.	**READING/WRITING WORKSHOP: Unit 1:** 107 **Unit 5:** 132-133 **Unit 6:** 294-295 **YOUR TURN PRACTICE BOOK:** 2, 12, 17, 22, 51, 52, 58, 61, 62, 70-71, 72, 80-81, 90-91, 92, 93, 100-101, 110-111, 120, 130, 140, 148, 150-151, 162, 165, 174, 186, 189, 198, 210-211, 221, 222, 225, 234, 246, 249, 258, 261, 270, 282, 285, 294, 306, 314, 318, 330 **PHONICS WORKSTATION ACTIVITY CARDS:** 1, 2, 4, 9, 10, 11, 12, 15, 17, 18, 19, 22, 23, 29, 30 **SCIENCE & SOCIAL STUDIES WORKSTATION ACTIVITY CARDS:** 2, 4, 5, 6, 7, 8, 9, 12, 14, 15, 17, 18, 19, 20, 23, 24, 25, 26, 27, 28, 30 **WRITING WORKSTATION ACTIVITY CARDS:** 1, 2, 3, 4, 5, 6, 7, 8, 9, 10, 11, 12, 13, 14, 15, 16, 17, 18, 19, 20, 21, 22, 23, 24, 25, 26, 27, 28, 29, 30 **TEACHER'S EDITION: Unit 1:** T19, T28-T29, T37, T43, T49, T51, T120, T175, T185, T193, T198-T199, T205, T253, T263, T271, T276-T277, T283, T354, T361 **Unit 2:** T42, T198 **Unit 3:** T42 **Unit 4:** T276, T354 **Unit 5:** T19, T29, T37, T43, T49, T120, T276, T354 **Unit 6:** T42, T198, T354 www.connected.mcgraw-hill.com: **RESOURCES: Unit 1: Student Practice:** Grammar Practice, Approaching Reproducibles, Beyond Reproducibles, ELL Reproducibles **Interactive Games & Activities:** Writing & Grammar **Graphic Organizers:** Graphic Organizers **Teacher's Resources:** Writer's Checklists/Proofreading Marks
L.1.2	Demonstrate command of the conventions of standard English capitalization, punctuation, and spelling when writing.	**YOUR TURN PRACTICE BOOK:** 10, 20, 30, 40, 50, 60, 70, 80, 90, 100, 110, 120, 130, 140, 150, 162, 174, 186, 198, 210, 222, 234, 246, 258, 270, 282, 294, 306, 318, 330 **TEACHER'S EDITION: Unit 1:** T37 **Unit 3:** T330, T340, T348, T354-T355, T360

Language Standards

L.1.2a	Capitalize dates and names of people.	READING/WRITING WORKSHOP: Unit 2: 86–87 TEACHER'S EDITION: Unit I: T42 Unit 2: T253, T263, T271, T277, T283 Unit 3: T120 Unit 4: T97, T175, T185, T192, T205 Unit 5: T42, T175, T185, T193, T199, T205, T276 Unit 6: T97, T107, T120, T114–T115, T120–T121, T126–T127, T354 www.connected.mcgraw-hill.com: RESOURCES: Units I–6: Student Practice: Grammar Practice, Interactive Games & Activities: Writing & Grammar Teacher Resources: Writer's Checklists/Proofreading Marks
L.1.2b	Use end punctuation for sentences.	READING/WRITING WORKSHOP: Unit I: 47, 87, 107 TEACHER'S EDITION: Unit I: T97, T107, T115, T121, T127, T175, T185, T193, T205, T253, T263, T271, T277, T283, T285, T331, T341, T349, T355, T361, T366 Unit 2: T198, T331, T341, T349, T355, T361 Unit 3: T198, T276, T354 Unit 4: T97, T107, T114, T115, T120–T121, T127–T128 Unit 5: T97, T107, T115, T120–T121, T127, T276 Unit 6: T120, T198, T270 www.connected.mcgraw-hill.com: RESOURCES: Units I–5: Student Practice: Grammar Practice, Interactive Games & Activities: Writing & Grammar Teacher Resources: Writer's Checklists/Proofreading Marks
L.1.2c	Use commas in dates and to separate single words in a series.	READING/WRITING WORKSHOP: Unit 3: 27 TEACHER'S EDITION: Unit 2: T19, T28, T29, T37, T43, T49 Unit 3: T19, T28, T29, T36–T37, T42–T43, T49, T175, T185, T192, T198–T199, T204–T205, T253, T262–T263, T271, T276, T277, T283 Unit 4: T331, T341, T348–T349, T354–T355, T360–T361 Unit 6: T175, T185, T193, T198, T199, T205, T253, T263, T263, T270–T271, T276–T277, T282–T283 www.connected.mcgraw-hill.com: RESOURCES: Units I–6: Student Practice: Grammar Practice, Interactive Games & Activities: Writing & Grammar Teacher Resources: Writer's Checklists/Proofreading Marks
L.1.2d	Use conventional spelling for words with common spelling patterns and for frequently occurring irregular words.	YOUR TURN PRACTICE BOOK: 196, 232, 256 PHONICS WORKSTATION ACTIVITY CARDS: 1, 2, 3, 4, 5, 6, 7, 8, 9, 10, 11, 12, 13, 14, 15, 16, 17, 18, 19, 20, 21, 22, 23, 24, 25, 26, 27, 28, 29, 30 TEACHER'S EDITION: Unit I: T14, T24, T34, T41, T47, T92, T170, T196, T274 Unit 2: T25, T92, T93, T112, T113, T120, T190, T191 Unit 3: T34, T35, T103, T120, T180, T181, T258, T259, T326, T327 Unit 4: T92, T93, T170, T171, T268, T269, T336, T337, T346, T347, T354 Unit 5: T14, T47, T119, T180, T353 Unit 6: T41, T125, T248, T276, T281, T326, T327, T359 www.connected.mcgraw-hill.com: RESOURCES: Units I–6: Student Practice: Phonics/Spelling Practice, Approaching Reproducibles, Beyond Reproducibles, ELL Reproducibles Interactive Games & Activities: Phonics Cards: Spelling Word Cards, Sound-Spelling Cards Teacher Resources: Sound-Spelling Songs
L.1.2e	Spell untaught words phonetically, drawing on phonemic awareness and spelling conventions.	PHONICS WORKSTATION ACTIVITY CARDS: 1, 2, 3, 4, 5, 6, 7, 8, 9, 10, 11, 12, 13, 14, 15, 16, 17, 18, 19, 20, 21, 22, 23, 24, 25, 26, 27, 28, 29, 30 TEACHER'S EDITION: Unit I: T14, T92, T170, T248, T326 Unit 2: T14, T92, T170, T248, T276, T326 Unit 3: T15, T92, T170, T248, T326 Unit 4: T15, T42, T170, T248, T326 Unit 5: T14, T92, T170, T248, T326, T354 Unit 6: T14, T92, T170, T248, T326 www.connected.mcgraw-hill.com: RESOURCES: Units I–6: Student Practice: Phonics/Spelling Practice, Approaching Reproducibles, Beyond Reproducibles, ELL Reproducibles Interactive Games & Activities: Phonemic Awareness Cards: Spelling Word Cards, Sound-Spelling Cards Teacher Resources: Sound-Spelling Songs

Knowledge of Language	McGraw-Hill *Wonders*
L.1.3	(Begins in grade 2)

Vocabulary Acquisition and Use	McGraw-Hill *Wonders*
L.1.4	Determine or clarify the meaning of unknown and multiple-meaning words and phrases based on *grade 1 reading and content,* choosing flexibly from an array of strategies.
L.1.4a	Use sentence-level context as a clue to the meaning of a word or phrase.

READING/WRITING WORKSHOP: Unit 4: 15, 35, 55, 75, 95 Unit 5: 117, 137, 157, 177, 197 Unit 6: 218, 239, 259, 279, 299
YOUR TURN PRACTICE BOOK: 194
INTERACTIVE READ-ALOUD CARDS: Unit I, Week I: 3 Unit 4, Week 2: 3 Unit 5, Week 3: 3 Unit 6, Week 3: 2
TEACHER'S EDITION: Unit I: T195A Unit 2: T39A, T113C, T224, T269G, T273A Unit 3: T39A, T113F, T269F, T273A Unit 4: T113, T113F, T117A, T191J, T269, T269H Unit 5: T35, T39, T117, T224, T273A Unit 6: T39, T113G, T146, T195A, T273A, T302

www.connected.mcgraw-hill.com: RESOURCES: Units I–6: Student Practice: Approaching Reproducibles, Beyond Reproducibles, ELL Reproducibles Interactive Games & Activities: Vocabulary Cards: Visual Vocabulary Cards

Language Standards

Vocabulary Acquisition and Use		McGraw-Hill *Wonders*
L.1.4b	Use frequently occurring affixes as a clue to the meaning of a word.	**YOUR TURN PRACTICE BOOK:** 172, 206, 218, 242, 254 **PHONICS WORKSTATION ACTIVITY CARDS:** 17 **TEACHER'S EDITION: Unit 4:** T101, T111, T118, T124, T136 **Unit 5:** T146, T191, T269, T269K **Unit 6:** T23, T33, T58, T191J www.connected.mcgraw-hill.com: **RESOURCES: Units 3–6: Student Practice:** Approaching Reproducibles, Beyond Reproducibles, ELL Reproducibles **Interactive Games & Activities:** Vocabulary **Cards:** Visual Vocabulary Cards
L.1.4c	Identify frequently occurring root words (e.g., *look*) and their inflectional forms (e.g., *looks, looked, looking*).	**YOUR TURN PRACTICE BOOK:** 118, 128, 148, 196, 266, 316 **TEACHER'S EDITION: Unit 4:** T146, T347, T347D **Unit 5:** T113C, T269K, T347 **Unit 6:** T41, T119, T191J, T197 www.connected.mcgraw-hill.com: **RESOURCES: Units 3–6: Student Practice:** Approaching Reproducibles, Beyond Reproducibles, ELL Reproducibles **Interactive Games & Activities:** Vocabulary **Cards:** Visual Vocabulary Cards
L.1.5		With guidance and support from adults, demonstrate understanding of figurative language, word relationships and nuances in word meaning.
L.1.5a	Sort words into categories (e.g., colors, clothing) to gain a sense of the concepts the categories represent.	**TEACHER'S EDITION: Unit 4:** T191G, T191H **Unit 6:** T35K, T191M www.connected.mcgraw-hill.com: **RESOURCES: Units 1–6: Cards:** High-Frequency Word Cards, Visual Vocabulary Cards **Teacher Resources:** Word Games and Activities, Word Lists **Interactive Games & Activities:** Vocabulary
L.1.5b	Define words by category and by one or more key attributes (e.g., a duck is a bird that swims; a *tiger* is a large cat with stripes).	**TEACHER'S EDITION: Unit 4:** T191G, T191H **Unit 6:** T35K, T191M www.connected.mcgraw-hill.com: **RESOURCES: Units 1–6: Cards:** High-Frequency Word Cards, Visual Vocabulary Cards **Teacher Resources:** Word Games and Activities, Word Lists **Interactive Games & Activities:** Vocabulary
L.1.5c	Identify real-life connections between words and their use (e.g., note places at home that are *cozy*).	**TEACHER'S EDITION: Unit 1:** T20, T30, T194 **Unit 2:** T38, T39A, T116 **Unit 3:** T30, T38, T116 **Unit 4:** T186, T332 **Unit 5:** T186, T194, T264, T272 **Unit 6:** T30, T264 www.connected.mcgraw-hill.com: **RESOURCES: Units 1–6: Cards:** High-Frequency Word Cards, Visual Vocabulary Cards **Teacher Resources:** Word Games and Activities, Word Lists **Interactive Games & Activities:** Vocabulary
L.1.5d	Distinguish shades of meaning among verbs differing in manner (e.g., *look, peek, glance, stare, glare, scowl*) and adjectives differing in intensity (e.g., *large, gigantic*) by defining or choosing them or by acting out the meanings.	**YOUR TURN PRACTICE BOOK:** 177, 189, 230 **TEACHER'S EDITION: Unit 4:** T191D, T191G, T302 **Unit 5:** T113 **Unit 6:** T191K www.connected.mcgraw-hill.com: **RESOURCES: Units 1–6: Cards:** High-Frequency Word Cards, Visual Vocabulary Cards **Teacher Resources:** Word Games and Activities, Word Lists **Interactive Games & Activities:** Vocabulary
L.1.6	Use words and phrases acquired through conversations, reading and being read to, and responding to texts, including using frequently occurring conjunctions to signal simple relationships (e.g., *because*).	**WRITING WORKSTATION ACTIVITY CARDS:** 26 **INTERACTIVE READ ALOUD CARDS: Unit 1:** Weeks 1-4 **Unit 2:** Weeks 1-4 **Unit 3:** Weeks 1-4 **Unit 4:** Weeks 1-4 **Unit 5:** Weeks 1-4 **Unit 6:** Weeks 1-4 **TEACHER'S EDITION: Unit 1:** T30, T38, T66, T108, T116, T194, T254, T255, T264, T332, T342 **Unit 2:** T20, T30, T38, T98, T108, T116, T176, T186, T194, T264, T272, T332 **Unit 3:** T20, T30, T38, T108, T116, T176, T186, T194, T254, T264, T272, T332, T342, T397 **Unit 4:** T20, T30, T98, T108, T116, T176, T186, T194, T254, T264, T272, T332 **Unit 5:** T20, T30, T38, T98, T108, T116, T176, T186, T194, T254, T264, T272, T332, T342 **Unit 6:** T20, T30, T38, T98, T108, T116, T176, T186, T194, T254, T264, T272, T332, T342 www.connected.mcgraw-hill.com: **RESOURCES: Units 1–6: Student Practice:** Grammar Practice **Interactive Games & Activities:** (Writing & Grammar) **Cards:** Retelling Cards, Visual Vocabulary Cards

Solr Books
3415 Madison St.
Skokie, IL 60076

$14.80
$ 4.99 (shipping)